The Flute in Jazz

Also by Peter Westbrook:

Divine Harmony: The Life and Teachings of Pythagoras
(with John Strohmeier)

See: ***www.pythagoras-divineharmony.com***

For more information on ***The Flute in Jazz: Window on World Music***, including
discography, updates, links, etc. see:

www.fluteinjazz.com

The Flute in Jazz:
Window on World Music

by

Peter Westbrook

Harmonia Books
Second edition - 2011

Harmonia Books
13012 Magellan Avenue
Rockville, MD 20853

Publisher's Cataloging-In-Publication Data
(Prepared by The Donohue Group, Inc.)

Westbrook, Peter, 1944-
   The flute in jazz : window on world music / by Peter Westbrook. -- 2nd ed.

   p. ; cm.

   A supplementary documentary film, The flute in jazz, is available separately.
   Includes index.
   ISBN: 978-0-615-31087-9

   1. Flute music--History. 2. Flute music (Jazz) 3. Flute players--Interviews. 4. Jazz
musicians--Interviews. 5. Flute music (Jazz)--Discography. I. Title.

ML937 .W47 2011
788.32/09   2011911192

Credits:

Cover photo of James Moody by Ned Radinsky,
courtesy of Rocky Mountain Jazz, *www.rockymountainjazz.com*

Photo of Peter Westbrook courtesy of Edward O. Savwoir, *www.savwoirphotography.com*

Cover design by Ira Simson

Layout and formatting by Imagic Digital Imaging,
Albuquerque, NM. *www.imagic-usa.com*

To Carol

Acknowledgments

I am indebted to a number of people who have assisted in the preparation of this book. I would like to thank James Newton for his constant support and his eloquent foreword. When it came to preparing the manuscript I could not have even begun without Fiona Carson's tireless work in transcribing the interviews. Fran Clark and Laurie Yelle were enormously helpful in proofreading and correcting my own error-filled typing, while Mary Beth Miller, Barbara M. Smith and Kathy Van Der Kamp were indispensable in negotiating some of Microsoft Word's more esoteric features. Michael and Myriah at *Imagic* in Albuquerque went above and beyond the call of duty in formatting the manuscript for printing.

Several people have read and commented on sections of the manuscript, including Prof. Eugene Helm, Dr Saïs Kamalidiin, Howard Motteler and Tony Ellis, for which I am most grateful. I would also like to thank Ned Radinsky for the beautiful image of James Moody that he generously provided for the cover, and to Ira Simson for the cover design itself. Thank you also to Russell Turner for providing arrangements for the *Flutin' Jazz* jazz flute choir, and the workshops we will be conducting around the country to promote the flute in jazz.

I would also like to mention the musicians themselves. I have been deeply touched by the graciousness of these artists who have given so generously of their time and support to assist in completing the work. They reviewed their sections for accuracy and made numerous suggestions. I am particularly grateful to those who assisted me in developing the profiles of flutists who have passed away, frequently friends, family and/or former colleagues of theirs. Their unselfish devotion to honoring these artists revealed something very special about the jazz community. I should also mention the help I have received from so many people to locate film clips of these artists for the film that will accompany this book. The memory I have, for example, of Steve Turré rummaging in his basement to find rare footage of Rahsaan Roland Kirk is symbolic of these efforts.

Many thanks to Ali Ryerson and Holly Hofmann for their support, and for their efforts to promote jazz within the National Flute Association, particularly to Ali for the countless hours she has put into developing the Jazz Flute Big Band, whose second performance will accompany the first release of this book at the NFA convention in New York City, August 13-16, 2009, and whose third appearance, in Charlotte North Carolina, coincides with the completion of this second edition.

Finally, as always, I must thank my wife Gina for putting up with all the rigors involved in living with a writer. As if it isn't hard enough being married to a musician, he had to be a writer too!

Table of Contents

Foreword
by James Newton

The art form of jazz, when at its best, always demands new approaches to accessing its essential roots. In the development of jazz, each of the different instruments has played an important role in defining this great art form's unique way of expressing the human condition. The flute has added a distinctive voice to the jazz tradition because it can speak in the language of jazz and also readily and facilely embrace other world music traditions.

The first great jazz composer, Jelly Roll Morton, molded for all time the cast of jazz into a world music; his compositions fused elements from the African, European and American continents. To realize his artistic aspirations, Morton amalgamated the Catholic-based Creole, and the Protestant-dominated African-American cultures, sacred and profane music, French and Italian romantic opera, Afro-Cuban rhythmical structures and melodic contours, African-American and European dance forms, along with African and American folk polyphonic practices, microtonality and the Western tempered scale.

One might ask, what does this have to do with the role of the flute in jazz? In each of the aforementioned cultures, the flute has held a prominent place in the evolution of its music. In fact, in the great majority of the cultures on our planet, one will find some form of flute playing that expresses the aspiration of its people.

The flute did not have a prominence in New Orleans jazz of the early twentieth century. Even though Sidney Bechet played the instrument, he never actually recorded as a flutist. Had he done so, the path that the instrument would have taken in jazz history might have been radically different. While some consider the instrument to be on the fringes of jazz, a sort of second-class instrument that lacks the pedigree of the trumpet or tenor saxophone, when reviewing jazz history I have often extrapolated that women and men choose to play the flute because it has the capability of expressing something entirely different than the traditional front-line instruments. As you will discover in this insightful book, this desire for a different manner of expression results in a unique view of the jazz canon, one that reflects a broad path that easily connects with the various world music traditions.

One of the most important points related to the history of the flute in jazz is that many of the artists that have played the instrument were inspired by other musics. Consider the groundbreaking career of Hubert Laws, whom I refer to as the Jackie Robinson of the flute. His visionary approach to the instrument, rigorous work ethic, and studies with the master classical flutist Julius Baker helped him to perform with both the New York Philharmonic and the Metropolitan Opera Orchestra. Mr. Laws also worked with the most distinguished conductors of the time including Pierre Boulez, Herbert Von Karajan, Leonard Bernstein, James Levine and Zubin Mehta. To my knowledge, he is the first African-American flutist to have performed in these major orchestras. While enjoying this substantive classical career during a period of lingering segregation and intense racial upheaval in American society, he also performed with master artists in the Latin jazz and jazz fields including The Crusaders, Herbie Hancock, Mongo Santamaria, Chick Corea, Ron Carter, McCoy Tyner and many others. This hybridist approach created a new paradigm for the flute in jazz, and led to some of the most exquisitely constructed flute solos in its history. Most notable were his solo performances on Sonny Rollins' composition *Airegin* and John Coltrane's *Moment's Notice*. Like Jelly Roll Morton, Hubert Laws envisioned a new art by building on the foundations of jazz while deftly incorporating the influences of John Coltrane's *Giant Steps* period with gospel, rhythm and blues, Latin jazz and European classical music.

The malleability of the Western concert flute enables jazz players to look to the performance techniques of other cultures that play non-Western, indigenous flutes, and to adapt aspects of these performance practices to the Western instrument. When I use *glissandi* on the flute, my inspiration may come from Billie Holiday, Johnny Hodges or the *shakuhachi* artistry of Watazumi Doso. The blending of all three of these influences in one musical phrase results in a hybrid expression that is truly new.

When examining these non-Western approaches, the jazz flutist can also comprehend the immense inspiration that nature provides for the flute. Flutists have the capability of using birdsong more than any other instrument, certainly much more than a saxophone, trumpet or trombone. Whether we are referring to the Chinese *dizi,* the Malian *peul flute* or the Japanese *shakuhachi*, one can find a diverse canon of birdsong music. An illuminating fact that the great genius of Afro-Cuban music, Rolando Lozano, revealed many years ago, is that he developed his style and language by listening to the sounds of the birds. It is the same with Danilo Lozano, his son, who is equally a genius in this and many other styles of music. And we can look to Eric Dolphy, who was highly inspired by birdsong. For example *You Don't Know What Love Is* from the *Last Date* recording and *Ode to Charlie Parker* from the *Far Cry* recording with Booker Little, are very obvious examples of inspirations from bird calls. Buddy Collette informed me that Dolphy listened to birdsong all the time, partly because of the amazing variety of birds in southern California. When speaking with Freddie Hubbard at the Mt. Fuji Jazz Festival in 1986, I learned that when he and Dolphy were roommates in New York, Dolphy often went to the roof of their apartment building to play his flute and dialogue with the birds. Dolphy also found inspiration from the music of the *Twa* people of Africa, whose use of both birdsong and octave displacement were employed in his highly evolved, seamless cultural multiplicity. When examining Dolphy's octave displacement use, one must also attribute it to his love and respect for the music of Thelonious Monk and Arnold Schoenberg. Eric Dolphy was also very much aware of the music of Olivier Messaien, who examined birdsong more carefully and longer than any other Western composer.

I believe that some of the essential elements that a great majority of the flutists in *The Flute in Jazz: Window on World Music* share are their profound experiences with blues, spirituals and/or gospel music, and also the standard jazz repertoire, whether it is the compositions of our great composers, or the American popular song. Some flutists in this book have pushed the instrument and its language to extremes, conquering new territory with a dedication to innovation that an art form constantly needs to sustain itself. Many have also examined the flute's ability, in the hands of its masters, to move people very deeply, in part because of its close proximity to the human voice. The instrument has been an oasis for many saxophone players because it provides another avenue of expression different than their main instrument. I am reminded of how some painters feel the need to embrace sculpture, video, or mixed media to reveal another side of their aesthetic. I think there was something compelling for all of these saxophonists, something about the alluring sound of the instrument that is really profound and ancient. Flutists have the ability to access flute traditions that are thousands of years old.

The much younger saxophone, in turn, has provided a conduit for the flute to the front line of the jazz ensemble. Flutists and doublers have learned much from each other, and have enriched jazz in the process. Many of the doublers have given flutists great insights into the translation of articulations and inflections used by traditional front line jazz instruments. Flutists who have focused solely on their instrument have provided a great degree of timbral sophistication and variation. Peter Westbrook has wisely chosen to focus on the uniqueness that both groups add to the body of jazz flutists. If one examines the role of articulation in jazz, we have to look at the powerful contributions of James Moody, Eric Dolphy, Frank Wess, Yusef Lateef, Joe Farrell, Wayman Carver, Henry Threadgill, Pedro Eustache, Maurico Smith, Herbie Mann, Rashsaan Roland Kirk and many other doublers. In this current era, one can also observe the progress the instrument has made in jazz by observing that many more performers choose to focus solely on the flute, including Nicole Mitchell, Jamie Baum, Danilo Lozano, Dave Valentin, Kent Jordan, Holly Hofmann and many others.

Tracing the history of the flute in jazz gives us a unique perspective, not only on the instrument, but also on this noble music that is only slightly more than a century old. The innovative research in PeterWestbrook's *The Flute in Jazz: Window on World Music*, coupled with his ability to speak with great authority on both jazz and world music, sheds much new light on a field that is sorely under-researched. This book will also give inspiration to the next generations of jazz musicians and scholars who are drawn to the unique expressive capabilities of the flute.

James Newton
Professor of Ethnomusicology,
University of California, Los Angeles
Down Beat magazine poll winner for flute performance, 1982-2004, 2008

Part One

The Beginning

Introduction

The story of the flute in jazz has a lot to tell us, both about the flute and about jazz. It provides a fresh perspective on the past, present and future of one of the most potent musical genres to emerge in recent history, and certainly the most compelling that America has given to the world. We can also learn a great deal about the expressive potential of one of mankind's most ancient instruments.

For the most part, this story is told, in their own words, by the musicians who have lived it. Having interviewed many of the major contributors to this genre I was convinced that my insights into this subject should take a back seat to theirs. As a result, it is these conversations that form the majority of the narrative. This is as it should be; the history of jazz is essentially the history of the musicians who have created it.

More so than other aspects of jazz history, the story of the flute in jazz is a relatively recent one. As a result many great jazz flutists are still active, some of them recognized jazz masters such as Frank Wess and Hubert Laws. There are also, of course, a number who have passed away, some of them quite recently. In these cases I have had a great deal of help from colleagues of theirs who have given generously of their time to help me tell their stories. In five instances, the interviewees have passed away since our conversation, a fact that has lent some urgency to my efforts to bring this volume before the public.

Aside from this interview material here, readers will find that I have indulged my instincts as a musicologist to supply some analysis and commentary, primarily in the Introduction, Chapter One and the Conclusion. If there appear to be any omissions in the narrative it is due to lack of space. As the work progressed, more and more flutists came out of the woodwork, from many parts of the world. They in turn introduced me to others. "Have you not heard of so-and-so?" they would say. So it became clear that my original intention of giving a comprehensive picture of my subject was going to be impossible unless I produced a prohibitively expensive, 1,000 page book.

It is here that the Internet comes to my aid. Whatever I could not find space for in these pages will appear on the accompanying website at: **www.fluteinjazz.com**, including some complete interviews which will be available for downloading, along with news, analysis and other material of interest to both flutists and jazz lovers. In addition, it was intended to include a discographical section in each chapter, with discussion of some of the artists' main recordings. Space considerations would not allow for this either, so all of these sections have been collected into a booklet which can also be downloaded from the **www.fluteinjazz.com** website. I was surprised to find that this was not a more common practice; it seems an obvious enhancement to printed books in the Internet age. I trust that it will catch on. In the meantime, however, I hope readers will find this arrangement convenient.

* * * * * *

It was largely by accident that I wrote this book, at least to begin with. The idea was born one day in Berkeley, California. I was speaking with the publisher of an earlier book of mine, *Divine Harmony: The Life and Teachings of Pythagoras.* He had published a number of volumes on jazz, and, knowing my background as a musician and musicologist, he was asking my opinion about a proposed book on the jazz trombone. "I don't know about that," I told him, "but you should definitely do one on the flute in jazz." His response took me by surprise. "You mean you can play jazz on the flute?"

I was stunned, "gobsmacked" as they say in England! I could not understand his question. Growing up in London in the 1960s I had heard several fine musicians, both foreign and domestic, play jazz on the flute: Tubby Hayes, Harold McNair, Bobby Jaspar and--in concert with John Coltrane--Eric Dolphy. I loved the instrument and what it could do in jazz. Later, with the government grant money intended for my upkeep at a British university I acquired a Selmer alto saxophone and an Armstrong flute. (Saxophones have come and gone, but that flute stayed with me over four decades, on three continents.) Many examples of the jazz repertoire seemed--still seem--to work well on it: *Sugar, Alice in Wonderland, Nardis, The Duke, In Your Own Sweet Way, How My Heart Sings...*

I arrived in the US in the early 1970s, only to learn that I knew more about jazz than the music majors at the university I was attending in Caliornia. Later I taught Western music history at Bombay University, studied the *bansuri* with the great master Hariprasad Chaurasia, wrote a Ph.D. dissertation about the Music of the Spheres and a book about Pythagoras. Throughout, I continued to play jazz on my flute, and, until that moment in Berkeley, it never occurred to me that there was anything unusual about that whatsoever.

But then I began to look into it. I quickly learned that the flute still faces a battle for acceptance in jazz. I came across a best-selling reference work that referred to the flute as "... a distinctly marginal jazz instrument." At this, my musicological instincts kicked in. Is this true? If so, why should this be? The flute is the most ubiquitous of instruments, so why should it not play as prominent a role in jazz, America's classical music, as it does in European art music?

In essence the simplest of wind instruments, the flute is found in one or another of its forms in virtually every culture, in every historical period from antiquity to the present. An ancient bone flute segment, the oldest known musical instrument, estimated to be from 43,000 to 82,000 years old, was found recently at a Neanderthal campsite. More complete flutes dating back 7,000 to 9,000 years, also made from bone, have been excavated in central China; others have been found at the site of Mahenjo-Dara in the ancient Indus valley. References to the flute abound in literature and legend from the earliest times. A Chinese legend, for example, recounts that the emperor Huang-Ti, desiring to systematize all the sciences around a theory of music, sent his minister Ling Lun to the "Western mountains" to cut acoustically perfect lengths of bamboo. These were used to define the correct musical scale, but also to form the basis for standards of measurement, calendrical calculations, and other scientific applications. These proto-flutes also developed into a variety of performance instruments, the *dizi* and the *xiao* that play a major role in Chinese classical music, the *bansuri* in India, the *shakuhachi* in Japan, and similar instruments throughout South-East Asia.

In the modern world, the flute continues to play a major role in virtually all folk and classical traditions. In Western music it is sometimes considered to be a minor instrument, but only relative to the piano and the violin; it has contributed to every period of this tradition while evolving through various forms. Indeed, it was the most popular wind instrument in Europe for long stretches of the seventeenth and eighteenth century, before being challenged by the clarinet. With the development of a sophisticated key mechanism for the flute by Theobald Boehm (1794-1881), and more recent adjustments to its scale to perfect its intonation in all registers, the modern flute has become an instrument of great flexibility and agility, and, when constructed from metals such as silver, gold, or platinum, has a voice of brilliance and warmth. It is, of course, a significant member of the symphony orchestra, but it also has a rich and extensive solo literature, as well as several superstar soloists. The proliferation of flute societies on different continents attests to its ongoing popularity.

Similar developments have occurred in other parts of the world. In India, for example, through the efforts of Pannalal Ghosh in the 1950s, the flute has been re-established as part of the classical tradition, having, for centuries, been given the reduced status of a folk instrument. In the hands of artists such as Hariprasad Chaurasia, Raghunath Seth, and Ronu Majumdar in the north, and Dr. N. Ramani and the young prodigy Shashank in south India, the flute has developed into a major voice in that tradition. Similarly, the flute has been lifted to high technical and expressive levels in Irish folk music in the hands of Paddy Carty and Matt Molloy, and has seen something of a Renaissance in Chinese classical music. The Bulgarian pan flutes have found a champion in Zamfir, the Native American instrument in R. Carlos Nikai, and even the humble recorder in Michala Petri.

The flute is a major voice in many of the multiple musical genres found in South America, both in the form of the indigenous pan-pipe, and of the transverse flute initially introduced by the Spanish. The pan flutes, known as *zampoñas*, are most evident in the *huayno*, the traditional music of the Andes, land of the *Inca* and the *Aymara*, lending it the ancient, mystical quality which has become something of a cliché in movie soundtracks but which remains very real in its original context. The *kena*, or *quena* which originated in southern Peru and Bolivia, is among the most popular instruments in the broad mixture of Native, Spanish, and African styles that are found in these regions, which also feature the *siku, charango*, guitar, and *bombo*.

Brazil also has some wonderful instrumental music. Indeed, Paquito D'Rivera, Cuban clarinetist and saxophonist, has written that "Brazilian music is the most balanced formula of rhythm-melody-harmony in the world." The most common instrumental music in Brazil is the *samba*, its derivation the *bossa nova*, and the *choro* with its ragtime-like feeling. The instrumentation for these often features the flute or clarinet, along with mandolin and/or the ukelele-like *cavaquinho*, the seven-string guitar and the tambourine-like *pandeiro*. Brazil's southern neighbor Venezuela, like Colombia, also finds a place for the flute in its *musica llanera,* along with the *arpa llanera,* a small harp, the *cuatro venezolano*, a small four-stringed guitar, and often a mandolin. The flute is also found in the *tango* of Argentina, and plays a prominent role as the lead instrument in the *charanga* ensemble of Cuba.

The continent of Africa has a wide variety of flute traditions. Regarding the flute and flutists in Africa, Dr. Saïs Kamalidiin, writes:

> Historically, flutes (both indigenous and foreign) have always been major voices in the music of the African continent. From the Egyptian *ney*; the *xegovia* [chigovia] of Mozambique; the *tambin* of Guinea; the "lela" flutes of Cameroon; the *atenteben* of Ghana; the *seyse* of Niger and the *endere* of Uganda; in contemporary times, flute sounds of many kinds continue to be a

major part of African music in most areas of the continent. Great flutists in various African music traditions include: Yacouba Alzouma Moumouni (Niger), Zim Ngqawana (South Africa), Bailo Bah (Guinea), Abdouleye Fofana (Mali), Sipho "Hotstix" Mabuse (South Africa), Samite Mulondo (Uganda), Francis Bebey (Cameroon) and Habib Koite (Mali) as well as many others. Music from traditional African societies such as the Fula flute tradition of the Fulani people of Guinea and the *lote (ndewhoo)* flute music of the Mbuti (Efe, Asua, Aka, Babanzele,) people of the Ituri rainforest in Central/East Africa continues unabated within both ritual and non-ritual contexts. Flute-related traditions such as the tin whistle (kwela) music of urban South Africa (featuring performers such as Spokes Mashiyane, Lemmy "Special" Mabaso, Duzi Magwaza, Elias Lerole and Sydney Banda) while less popular today than when at its zenith in the 1950s and 60s, continue to attract enthusiastic practitioners and audiences.

* * * * * *

Against this background, it would seem reasonable to expect the flute to play a major role in jazz. Certainly it plays a role, but, so far, not a major one. With one or two exceptions, it was completely absent from the first fifty years of the music's development, and today flutists in the jazz realm continue to fight for equality with more traditional instruments. It is true that the flute is widely accepted as the primary doubling instrument for saxophone players, having largely replaced the clarinet; it is in fact a required double under performance standards established by the International Association for Jazz Education. But the number of jazz artists involved solely with flute performance is minimal compared with the standard wind instruments: trumpet, trombone and saxophone.

For confirmation of this fact we need merely to turn to the Critics and Readers Polls of *Down Beat* magazine. These are by no means a perfect guide to jazz history, but they can be a useful barometer. The flute was not given an independent category in these polls until 1956 for the readers and 1960 for the critics; prior to that it was included as a "Miscellaneous Instrument." The first time a flutist made it into this category was in 1956, when Frank Wess was included for his flute work with Count Basie. Now the category is well established, and most of the significant performers on the instrument are represented, although it must be said that many of these players are primarily saxophonists. Yet one can read many issues of *Down Beat* and other jazz journals without finding a single mention of any flutist. James Newton has won the Critics' poll for over ten years but has never been featured on the magazine's cover. Most tellingly, perhaps, only two flutists have ever been inducted into the *Down Beat* "Hall of Fame," and both of them were multi-instrumentalists.

As I set out to understand the reasons for all this, I realized that I needed to look at the instrument's history in a broader context.

No Need For Flutes!

"The flute is not an instrument that has a good moral effect--it is too exciting"

Aristotle, Poetics

"I think the flute is a stupid instrument to be playing jazz music on."

Bud Shank, ex jazz flutist

Aside from its antiquity and universality, the flute and its music have other connotations; it has evolved a reputation as the instrument of distraction and sensuality. Consider, for example, the following from T.S. Eliot:

Blown hair is sweet, brown hair over the mouth blown,
Lilac and brown hair,
Distraction, music of the flute...

Such associations of the flute appear to spring from deep levels of the collective unconscious, in contrast with stringed instruments which are found in folklore representing spirituality and the intellect. This distinction hinges upon fundamental mythic influences. Friedrich Nietzsche, in the *Birth of Tragedy*, identifies these forces in terms of the Greek gods Apollo, representing reason, order, logic, music and the contemplative life, and Dionysius, the god of wine, sensuality, raw power, and the life of action. These archetypes are polar opposites; holding them in balance, in Nietzsche's view, is the key to the highest achievements of civilization. Interestingly, Apollo, like his follower Orpheus, is usually shown playing the lyre, a stringed instrument, while Dionysius is associated with a wind instrument, the aulos. From the Dionysion tradition spring his alter-ego Pan, also known as Syrinx, described by Professor Kamalidiin as "a woodland deity that is depicted as half man, half goat who is usually shown as playing either pan-pipes (*syrinx*), the *aulos*, or a transverse flute. In Greek myth," he writes, "the flute music from this creature produces sexual ecstasy in any person who hears it." This image is echoed by a variety of other flute-playing figures in mythology such as the prehistoric deity Kokopelli who has been a sacred figure to Native Americans of the southwestern United States for thousands of years. Seen primarily as a fertility symbol, Kokopelli, who was thought to bring about the end of winter by warming the earth with the music of his flute, was one of the sources of phallic images associated with the instrument, adding to its disreputable connotations. One writer, Daniel Clemence Fawcett, in his *Mobius Music: The European and Afro-American Flute Traditions*, has even gone so far as to develop the thesis that "flute music was originally the aural incarnation of a pre-conscious state of mind, and flute playing continues to conjure vestiges of pre-conscious awareness."

This tension between Apollo and Dionysius, as expressed in the contrast between wind and stringed instruments, is a recurring motif in many cultural settings. In ancient India, for example, the flute is seen in the hands of the divine incarnation Lord *Krishna*, who is also known as *Muralidhara,* "flute holder," and who appears in the immensely popular stories of his mischievous dalliances with the *gopis*, or milkmaids. *Krishna* and his music thus evoke poetic and romantic sensibilities, subtly blended with devotional impulses. As the *Bhagavata-Purana* recounts, "When Krishna plays the flute the whole world is filled with love. Rivers stop, stones are illumined, lotus flowers tremble; gazelles, cows and birds are entranced; demons and ascetics enchanted." By contrast, the *vina*, a stringed instrument, is seen in the hands of the goddess *Saraswati*, presiding deity of more serious areas, central to the Vedic world-- sound, speech and knowledge. In ancient China, the *Ch'in*, a table-harp, was taken to be the appropriate instrument for the cultured Confucian gentleman, to the exclusion of the flute, while in Celtic tradition, the finest music was to be played on the harp rather than on wind instruments, which were kept for more coarse amusements, or for the battlefield.

The flute carries a similar symbolism in African culture. As Dr. Kamalidiin notes:

> Across the continent, flutes are part of the vast array of African musical instruments that are carriers of cultural significance beyond their use as contributors to the musical milieu of a given society. In some areas of Africa, the flute and flute playing are thought to represent or symbolize notions of masculinity and virility, partly because of its phallic shape, material (bamboo, horn or wood, etc.) and the results achieved through the various methods of ceremonial and ritual usage. Often, flutes and their music are used ceremonially in fertility rites because of their purported power to sexually arouse women (and men) and to enable those who are barren to conceive. In earlier times, women were often forbidden to come in contact with ceremonial flutes because of the flute's societally-derived importance and power to incite both lust and inappropriately masculine behavior. Within these cultural contexts, for a woman to touch a man's ceremonial flute was tantamount to her touching his "manhood."

Similar associations are found in the European tradition. One need only consider Debussy's choice of solo instrument for the *Prélude à l'après-midi d'un faune*, with its pervading sense of sensuality and distraction, and the seemingly inevitable, almost clichéd, linking of the flute with birdsong (witness *Peter and the Wolf* and *Carnival of the Animals*) which brings a further association--that of freedom, perhaps to a point beyond respectability. Debussy goes so far as to invoke *Syrinx* directly in his famous composition for solo flute. It is clear then that this view of the flute persists well into the modern world; should not such an instrument be well-suited for the emerging sensibilities of jazz music?

* * * * * *

When jazz emerged at the beginning of the twentieth century, it was part of an upsurge of Dionysian values into an overly Apollonian European culture sorely in need of balance. To some extent such a reaction was already occurring internally, with so-called "primitive" elements erupting from the collective unconscious of European artists, as in works by Stravinsky, Picasso, Gaugin, James Joyce, T.S. Eliot and others. In America, this impulse was to flow directly through the heart of popular culture, bringing a new infusion of energy into music. Initially short on refinement, but long on spirit, jazz represented the first cultural product of the American mixing bowl, initially in New Orleans, the thriving seaport where the cultural mix was at its most intense, with enslaved Africans interacting with immigrants from every kind of European background. The resulting blending of tonal and rhythmic elements from Africa with harmonic and formal elements from Europe was the foundation first for ragtime, then for jazz, and subsequently for the whole spectrum of American popular music. There were Dionysian excesses, perhaps, in some later developments, such as Heavy Metal and other forms of rock music. At the same time, in the area of "serious music," a reaction against these energetic forms eventually led to a dry obscurity, with many European and American composers resorting to slide rules and computers. Along the way, however, a moment of cultural balance resulted, as it always seems to do, in the emergence of a new genre of great potential, in this case jazz. There may have been foreign components, but it was assembled in America.

But here is the irony. At a moment in history when Dionysius and Pan exerted a new and powerful influence, their instrument of choice was nowhere to be found! In spite of the fact that jazz was a mixture of several traditions, each of which had a place for the flute, the flute itself was missing from the hybrid, at least initially.

There are a number of reasons for this. Primarily, the wave of energy that drove jazz music forward was too intense even for the instrument of Syrinx, both acoustically and emotionally. "When jazz came into fashion," writes the Sufi teacher Hazrat Inayat Khan, "everyone said, 'Something crazy has come into society.'" This view was quite widely held. As John F. Szwed writes in his book *Jazz 101:*

> Jazz was perhaps the first art to challenge the definition of high European culture as *the* culture, the first to challenge the cultural canon, the idea of the classics as "time-honored' and "serious." This challenge did not pass unnoticed. In 1917, the year the Original Dixieland Jazz Band of New Orleans made the first jazz recording, an article in the *New Orleans Picayune* disavowed the music, asserting that any music strong in rhythm and weak in harmonic and melodic content could only appeal to lower sensibilities. Eleven years later the *New York Times*, in assessing the state of American civilization, would list the "jazz mode of thought and action" along with lawlessness, boasting, intolerance, and jealousy on the deficit side of the ledger. Even jazz's defenders among the high arts found it vaguely threatening. When it first reached Paris during World War I, the response of the cognoscenti to jazz registered as shock--it was physical, visual, social, and emotional as well. And everyone noticed that this was a black music, even if it was sometimes played by whites.

Twenty years later, in Germany, this association did not escape the attention of the Nazi propaganda machine, which produced the infamous poster entitled *Entartete Musik* (Degenerate Music), that depicted a jazz musician of African origin, wearing a Jewish star and an earring. Significantly, this black-Jewish-gypsy degenerate is blowing a saxophone, indicating that, with all its primitive and sensual expressiveness, it has taken over from the flute as the Dionysian instrument *par excellence*. This suggestion also surfaced in Hermann Hesse's 1929 novel *Steppenwolf*, wherein Apollonian values are represented by the immortal Mozart, and the Dionysian by Pablo, a "swarthy" saxophone player. Whatever the symbolism of these various instruments, the inrush of raw energy represented by early jazz music found the flute's voice becoming lost in the mix, a situation that was reinforced by the emergence of the saxophone as a strong front-line voice, along with the trumpet, the trombone, and the clarinet.

And so, in the many wonderful photographs of early jazz orchestras, with all the instruments arranged in the front, there is hardly a flute to be seen until 1934, when Harry Carney crops up in a picture of the Ellington orchestra holding an alto sax and a flute. There is no evidence that he ever played the instrument.

The most commonly cited explanation for this phenomenon concerns the dynamics of the early jazz bands. It is true that the primary source for this music was the marching band, predominantly made up of brass instruments, augmented with percussion. The fife and the piccolo have a role to play in such bands, mainly in reinforcing the upper registers of cornets and trumpets. But by the time Buddy Bolden was making his horn heard clear across the bay in New Orleans, no one thought to match his sound with a flute. The trombone was the ideal partner on the low end, and adding a commentary in a higher register was ideal work for a second cornet or for the upper register of the clarinet. Many different combinations of front line were tried until the standard ones were established--trumpet, trombone and clarinet for the early New Orleans ensemble, evolving into the swing orchestra with trumpet, trombone and saxophone sections. The sax section was the doorway through which the flute was eventually to appear, but this would take a while. When the big bands slimmed down during the bebop era the quintet became the norm, with trumpet and saxophone the most common horns, perhaps augmented with a trombone or second saxophone, with even the clarinet disappearing for the most part. Without proper amplification the flute simply could not compete. In addition, as Leonard Bernstein has suggested, the sound, or coloration, of the African-American singing voice is one of the essential elements of jazz, along with its melodic, harmonic, and rhythmic elements. When Bernstein lists the instrumental sounds that best echo that sound he includes the muted trumpet, the trombone, and definitely the saxophone. But not the flute

Then there is percussion. The African influence, brought to the New World by the influx of slaves, essentially brought drums back to the forefront of Western music after two thousand years of neglect. While percussion is an important feature of most ancient and Eastern music traditions, it was largely missing from Western music. Initially banned from Christian worship in an attempt to avoid similarities with other religious traditions of the first-century Mediterranean world, percussion instruments never regained a prominent place in European performance traditions. Instruments themselves were peripheral for several centuries, medieval church music being exclusively vocal. It is in medieval times, specifically the eighth century, that European music finally differentiated itself from other traditions. As Richard Crocker writes in his *History of Musical Style*, "The history of Western music properly begins not with the Greeks or Romans but with the Franks." Under the influence of the leader of the Franks, the Holy Roman Emperor Charlemagne, other Eastern elements had been wrung out of Christian music to produce the tradition that exists to this day in the church, the unaccompanied vocal music known as plainchant, sometimes called Gregorian chant. For the next few centuries, chant was used as the basis of sacred and secular musical forms that were primarily vocal, with instruments, when they were used, acting as support to the vocal line.

Eventually instrumental music rose to equal prominence, beginning in fifteenth-century Venice and culminating in the great symphony orchestras of the nineteenth and early twentieth centuries. But even then, in the Western tradition, the use of percussion has been limited. Since the *vingt-quatre violins du Roi,* at the court of Louis XIV, the heart of the orchestra has been the strings. These could be augmented, initially by military horns and kettle drums, later with brass and woodwinds, but percussion writing for the symphony orchestra has continued to be used largely for color and emphasis, with the timpani still playing a central role. And certainly, with a few exceptions in contemporary music, percussion is completely absent from chamber music groups, string quartets, piano trios and so forth, all of which are acoustically well-balanced ensembles.

Suddenly this situation changed. The African and later Afro-Cuban influences coming into America brought percussion into the center of the jazz ensemble where it remains to this day. The result is that such ensembles are dynamically out of balance. A string bass, played pizzicato, cannot easily be heard over drums and piano; it requires amplification. Even a trumpet or saxophone can be drowned out by a loud drummer, as anyone who has heard Miles Davis with Philly Joe Jones can attest. What to say of a flute? After many years of experimenting with microphones and pickups for live performance, and with recording techniques in the studio, flutists can finally compete acoustically within the modern jazz ensemble. For many years, however, it simply did not work.

There is more to this than pure dynamics, however, even if that is the most significant factor. A famous picture of the King Oliver band shows the standard ensemble of cornet, trombone, clarinet, saxophone and rhythm, but a violinist is also to be seen. Now the violin can probably do better than a flute in cutting through a brass ensemble, but not by much. There are other factors at work, sociological factors. One of these has to do with gender.

Even today, the flute carries an association as a woman's instrument. In my experience, having conducted dozens of middle and high-school bands and orchestras, I still find that the majority of flutists at that age are girls. Perhaps this has grown out of practical considerations--the flute suits smaller hands better than some other instruments in the early years--but it has grown into a subtle prejudice. Consider the following:

> In a study conducted by musicologists Susan Yank Porter and Harold F. Abeles in 1978, musicians and non-musicians were asked to rate various musical instruments in terms of masculinity and femininity. The results were instructive, if hardly surprising. For both groups of participants the flute took the highest marks as the most feminine instrument followed by the violin and clarinet; the drums were perceived as most masculine, followed by the trombone and trumpet. In another study, Porter and Abeles measured parents' views about the instruments they would choose for their children. Given a choice of eight instruments they preferred the clarinet, flute and violin for their daughters, and the drums, trombone and trumpet for their sons. A test of attitudes among the public in general toward the "propriety" of various instruments for girls and boys reflected the same biases.

This is from Linda Dahl's book *Stormy Weather: The Music and Lives of a Century of Jazzwomen.* She reports that these attitudes towards instruments extend to children as well as to their parents:

> Perhaps the most interesting study conducted by Porter and Abeles was their survey of attitudes among children themselves. Though very young children showed little difference in their selections of instruments, by the third grade "the girls' selections consistently moved toward traditionally 'feminine' instruments, with the difference between the sexes maximizing around third and fourth grade."

Such prejudice has very real effects; several of the people I interviewed for this book were directly influenced by it. Lew Tabackin reports that he did not want to be seen walking through South Philadelphia carrying a flute when he was in school back in the fifties, while Bud Shank had no interest in learning flute early on, as "the flute was always a girl's instrument, and I wouldn't have anything to do with it." Dave Valentin, on the other hand, started playing the flute initially so that he could sit next to a girl he liked! Jamie Baum's parents "... pushed me to do the flute because it was a more 'female' instrument in those days." Pianist Horace Tapscott, writing in *Central Avenue Sounds: Jazz in Los Angeles* (University of California Press, 1998), confirms that this view extended to the violin, and even the piano. He first took up the trombone:

> We already had the piano in the house, but I wanted a horn. Growing up in those days, if you'd play the piano and the violin, you'd go outside and the cats would want to beat up on you. That was just for girls, playing the piano. If you're going to play an instrument, you're going to play a horn or something.

And it appears that the flute did not qualify as a "horn." True, this prejudice disappears when the first orchestral chairs and recording contracts for soloists are being handed out, but this is true of many women's issues. Suffice it to say that the flute has developed a reputation as a girl's instrument, and in the early decades jazz was decidedly a man's game. Women did make a contribution to be sure, but primarily as vocalists and pianists. New York flutist Jan Leder, author of *Women in Jazz: A Discography of Instrumentalists 1913-1968,* reports that fully half of all the women she documents were, or are, pianists, and she does not include vocalists, although the role of singer was even more acceptable for women in the first half of the twentieth century. Even in 2004, when I reviewed the *Mary Lou Williams Women in Jazz Festival* at the Kennedy Center in Washington, DC, I noted that of the fifteen women featured, four were vocalists and four pianists, so the situation has not changed that much. I can remember that in England, in the 1950s, the first time I saw a woman--Kathleen Stobart with the Hymphrey Littleton band (herself an occasional flutist)--playing jazz on the saxophone, it seemed a distinct novelty. Eventually this was to change, both in Europe and the United States, and women instrumentalists are now commonplace, although, ironically, the first flutists to make their mark in jazz were men.

Today, as we shall see, there are several leading women flutists in jazz, but this has taken several decades. In the early days the flute simply had too many strikes against it: it was too soft; it was a girl's instrument; it was altogether too refined. The following are the lyrics to Stuff Smith's vocal on the 1937 recording *Onyx Club Spree:*

Now first you call, call the pi-a-nist
Then you call the drummer man
Boy pick up that old guitar And swing,
'cause swing's so grand!

Then you add a little classy trumpet
Pull out all your mutes
I'm sorry to disappoint you
but There isn't any need for flutes!

 Now all you need is one more man
To give a demonstration of the thing called jam
What's wrong with the fiddle
Hi diddle diddle
The cow jumped over the moon!

Put your horns where they belong
Come on folks, join in this song
Pat your hands and shout with glee
Cause this is the Onyx Spree!!

And so, for almost half a century of jazz, there "wasn't any need" for flutes! This is not to say that no one played the flute during these years, but on the whole, the instrument tended to turn up away from the music's mainstream. A flute and piccolo specialist named 'Flutes' Morton reportedly appeared at Chicago's Sunset Café in the mid 1920s, in what context it is not clear. Most flute practitioners, however, were confined to the woodwind sections of larger ensembles. Not surprisingly, for example, given its partly light-classical repertoire, the Paul Whiteman orchestra saw several flutists pass through its ranks. Some, such as Jack Bell, Bernard Daly, Vincent Capone and George Ford were flute specialists. Others like Rube Crozier or Red Mayer also played clarinet, all the saxophones, and the double reed instruments--oboe, English horn, and bassoon. One of Whiteman's 1939 "specialty" groups, the Sax Octette, featured four saxes, three flutes, and an oboe.

Cab Calloway's repertoire was earthier than Whiteman's, but even here, as composer and jazz historian Gunther Schuller reports (*The Swing Era: The Development of Jazz 1930-1945*), "... in the reed section there was considerable diversity and skill. Walter "Foots" Thomas played all the saxophones plus flute, Andrew Brown all the saxes plus bass clarinet, and William Thornton Blue lead alto and all the clarinet solos." Schuller cites other examples where the flute is featured in the context of the reed section: Glenn Miller's arrangements for Benny Goodman, for example, whose "... instrumental coloring includes Larry Binyon's flute lead in the first chorus of *Walkin' (My Baby Back Home)*..."; Artie Shaw, who, reforming his orchestra in1939-40, wanted 65 pieces but "settled for thirty-two players--a fifteen-piece jazz compliment plus thirteen strings and a wind quartet of flute, oboe, bass clarinet and horn." For Tommy Dorsey, Schuller reports, "The emphasis instrumentationally (*sic*) was primarily on clarinets, including almost always a bass clarinet, occasionally a flute, all set in a pleasant danceable two-beat dance tempo," while another white swing band, the Casa Loma orchestra, found room for the flute in some of what Schuller calls their "more unusual pieces," such as *Sophisticated Lady* (featuring soft flute and woodwind colors, and a muted violin stating Ellington's theme)..." or *Sunrise Serenade*, probably arranged by Larry Wagner, which presented Glenn Miller's clarinet-lead reed sound plus "a most astonishing quasi-atonal intro and coda, set in woodwind colors dominated by flute and bass clarinet." On the other hand, Jimmie Lunceford, although a flutist himself, failed to give the instrument much, if any, prominence, even in his novelty features. Referring to Lunceford's *I'm Nuts About Screwy Music,* Schuller writes, "One is surprised to find... that the mention of flute and cello in the lyrics did not elicit a bit of word-echoing flute music from Lunceford himself (one of the instruments he played)."

As for out-and-out jazz solos on the instrument, some pioneers managed to introduce the occasional flute solo into their repertoire, but again, strictly as a novelty. It is intriguing that the first of these was to come from a Cuban artist. Latin music plays a significant role in the development of the flute in jazz, as we will see, and Cuban music, particularly the *charanga,* is a genre in which the flute is prominently featured, usually played by men. One such Cuban musician was clarinetist and flutist Alberto Socarras, who came to the U.S. in the 1920s where he became a pioneer of Afro-Cuban music. He went on to lead his own ensembles, featuring sidemen such as Cab Calloway and Mongo Santamaria, and securing a residence at the Cotton Club in the late 1930s. He was also a pioneer of jazz flute; he is credited with recording the earliest known flute work on a jazz recording, essentially fashioning an obligato to the vocal on *Shootin' The Pistol* with the Clarence Williams band, in July of 1927. His other recordings include *You're Such a Cruel Papa To Me*, with vocalist Lizzie Miles in 1928, two sides with Eva Taylor--alongside Buster Bailey on clarinet, Clarence Williams on piano and cellist David Martin-- further sides with Clarence Williams' Jazz Kings, and *You Can't Be Mine and Somebody Else's Too* in 1930, with Bennett's Swamplanders.

While acknowledging the contributions made by Socarras, however, jazz historians generally credit Wayman Carver as being the first true jazz flutist. Primarily a saxophonist, Carver performed with a number of bands during the thirties. Now and then he managed to sneak a little flute into their recordings, such as on *Loveless Love* with Dave Nelson in 1931, *How Come You Do Me Like You Do?* and *Sweet Sue, Just You,* with Spike Hughes and his Negro Orchestra, and *Devils Holiday* with Benny Carter, all in 1933. From 1933 to 1941, Carver worked with the big band of drummer Chick Webb. This was a very popular and influential outfit, best remembered for featuring vocalist Ella Fitzgerald, who actually took over leadership of the band after Webb's premature death in 1939. While with this band, Carver recorded a number of flute solos with a small group called the Little Chicks; Webb created this ensemble out of the big band personnel, just as Benny Goodman created a trio and a quartet out of his orchestra. Built around Carver's flute, along with the clarinet of Chauncey Haughton and a rhythm section of Tommy Fulford on piano, bassist Beverly Peer, and Webb on drums, the Little Chicks recorded four sides in November of 1937, *In A Little Spanish Town*, *I Got Rhythm*, and *I Ain't Got Nobody, plus* another version of *Sweet Sue-Just You.*

Gunther Schuller has harsh words for Carver's contributions to Webb's band generally, and for these performances in particular, placing them in the context of other excesses from this era:

> ...a similar foreign element--apart from the encroaching commercialism of Ella's puerile songs--was beginning to infiltrate Webb's orchestra in the form of Wayman Carver's flute solos and arrangements. The first of these was an arrangement of Wilbur Sweatman's 1911 *Down Home Rag. Down Home* begins with a "classical" woodwind trio of flute and two clarinets, straightfacedly rendering Sweatman's jerky dotted rhythms.

More of this type of novelty arrangement was on the way. Not only Chick Webb and his Little Chicks, with their childish flute-clarinet versions of *I Got Rhythm* and *Sweet Sue*...but other swing bands succumbed to a growing trend to "upgrade" jazz with pseudo-classical models.

Jazz Times writer Doug Ramsey has a similar evaluation:

Carver may have been a trailblazer, but his solos on Webb recordings like *Down Home Rag* (1934) and *I Got Rhythm* (1937) suggest that the flute had a long way to go as a fully expressive improvisational instrument. Indeed, tenor saxophonist Carver rarely soloed: his doubling ability was called upon mainly for novelty ensembles passages like that in *Down Home Rag*. His four-bar solo on *Rhythm* was a rarity.

Schuller and Ramsey are correct up to a point, but their evaluations seem unduly harsh. These are bright, interesting performances, with the flute/clarinet front line providing a unique sonority. Haughton's clarinet gets the bulk of the solo time, taking two full choruses on *I Got Rhythm*, for example, while Carver gets eight measures on the bridge (not four as Ramsey suggests). But the flute holds its own. It may have been a novel sound for its time, but the instrument, at least to this writer's ears, is not being presented purely as a novelty, and Carver handles it adroitly, adopting phrasing that both swings and lends itself well to the sound of the flute.

These were the only flute solos Wayman Carver was to record. After World War II he moved to Atlanta and took up a teaching position at Clark College, where he remained until his death in 1967. (Among his students were two who were to become prominent saxophonists, George Adams and Marion Brown.)

* * * * * *

It was a promising beginning, but just a beginning. Apart from Carver, the only other vaguely jazz-oriented performance in the early 40s was to come from a Hollywood studio player, Harry Klee, who recorded a quasi-jazz version of *Caravan* with Ray Linn, and, as Doug Ramsey notes, "made a mild splash playing with Phil Moore and later with the iconoclastic Boyd Raeburn Orchestra." Any further development of the flute had to wait for another generation, and some new developments in jazz. The turning point came about a decade later, in the late 1940s and early 1950s, a time when the music was passing into a new phase, following what Dan Morgenstern, in his *Jazz People* (Da Capo Press, 1993) has described as a golden age:

No matter what one's predilections, given a more than nodding acquaintance with the music's history, the period roughly from 1935 to 1945 must be recognized as the golden age of jazz. As this period began, the music's growing pains had ended and a mature, perfectly poised style had evolved. In the words of the French critic and musician André Hodier, a man who certainly can't be accused of bias against modernism: "Never before or since have so many great musicians existed side by side, uniting their efforts to found a marvelously rich and diversified school of jazz--and all the more rich and diversified for being both classical and romantic at the same time."

The school of jazz to which Morgenstern and Hodier refer is known as "swing," a style that emerged from the "territory" bands of the 1920s and '30s that burst out of New Orleans and spread to Chicago and St. Louis and Kansas City. It was the period when jazz was truly the popular music of America, when the big bands reigned supreme--Count Basie, Duke Ellington, Benny Goodman, Tommy and Jimmy Dorsey, Jimmy Lunceford, Glenn Miller and hundreds of others. Being larger and more formalized into sections--trumpet, trombones, reeds, rhythm--these bands were built on the arrangements of Ellington and Billy Strayhorn, Fletcher Henderson, Miller, Bill Challis, Don Redman, Mel Powell and others, but they also fostered some of jazz' greatest soloists, one of whom--tenor sax player Lester Young--was laying the seeds for the next development of the music. Compared to the style that had been forged earlier by Coleman Hawkins, and that had become the standard for tenor saxophonists, Young's playing was lighter, more detached, laid-back, with less vibrato and more flowing melodic lines. It was the beginning of bebop--as Charlie Parker was to build directly on Lester's approach--and also of the "cool" school that was primarily associated with the West Coast. Lester was not the first jazz player to work in this vein; we can point to saxophonist Frank Teschmaker and cornetist Bix Beiderbeck, among others. But it was Lester who brought this kind of playing to a new level, and to a greater degree of popularity through his work with Count Basie, who was also responsible for promoting one of the first jazz flute soloists a decade or so later.

Whether or not this period was jazz' finest is open to debate. Certainly, it did not last long; with the war years the big bands that had been so important to swing went into a sudden decline. The effects of this were far-reaching. In his book *A Jazz Retrospect*, about composer/arranger Gil Evans, British jazz critic Max Harrison writes:

> Despite their undoubted--if somewhat overrated--contribution to jazz, the swing bands, once established, stood in the way of further orchestral developments. These could only resume when the bands came off the road and orchestral jazz was created by *ad hoc* groups assembled mainly, if not exclusively, for recording purposes. Such conditions allowed far more varied instrumentation than hitherto... So did improved recording techniques. If you wanted to put classical guitar in front of a jazz orchestra, you could do it. These improved techniques permitted the use in jazz, even with big bands, of the flute. Gil abandoned the standard jazz instrumentation of trumpets-trombones-saxes-and-rhythm section, using instead flutes, oboes, English horns, French horns, tuba, and a few of the conventional jazz instruments. He enormously expanded the vocabulary of the jazz orchestra.

Gil Evans' work in developing orchestration began with the Claude Thornhill orchestra in 1947. It continued through his collaborations with Miles Davis, beginning in 1949 with the *Birth of The Cool*, and in a series of ground-breaking recordings thereafter--*Miles Ahead, Porgy and Bess, Sketches of Spain*. It was this kind of writing that helped to establish the flute as a part of the palette of tonal colors for jazz, and made the instrument a required double for reed players. But Miles and Gil Evans were not the only performers forging into new musical territory. Robert Gordon reports, in his *Jazz West Coast*:

Another batch of recordings, cut at the same time, may have had more to do with the development of cool jazz than the Miles Davis sides. These were the recordings of pianist Lennie Tristano and a coterie of followers that included saxophonists Lee Konitz and Warne Marsh and guitarist Billy Bauer. Although he came to prominence at the height of the bebop era, Tristano steadfastly followed his own path, influenced at least as much by his own studies in European concert forms as by the jazz tradition as reinterpreted by Gillespie and Parker.

Such interests make Tristano typical of a trend that, while not new, began to assert itself more during this period, leading other performers and arrangers to experiment more freely with European forms and, consequently, with instrumentation. As Gordon reports, Tristano himself was known to perform Bach two-part inventions during his (not surprisingly infrequent) jazz club dates in New York, and his 1949 sessions for Capitol were filled with complex and abstract improvisations. Just as Lester Young's tenor solos fed into both cool jazz and bebop, so Tristano's work was seized on by certain musicians in the forties and others of quite another generation, the free jazz practitioners of the 1960s. Robert Gordon emphasizes the similarities of the 1949 developments:

> It would seem a remarkable coincidence that two unrelated groups of musicians (that Lee Konitz appeared in both groups was happenstance), working independently, would record the definitive statements of a new style of jazz almost simultaneously. Actually, it's now apparent that the cool approach to jazz was one of those ideas 'in the air' as the forties drew to a close.

Gordon cites further manifestations of this style that emerged at the time: Stan Getz' famous 1948 solo on Woody Herman's recording of *Early Autumn* that inspired a whole generation of tenor saxophonists to follow him in emulating Lester Young; Tadd Dameron's composition *Lady Bird*, also from 1948, that moved bebop into more legato, melodic territory; and "a host of young arrangers [who] attempted, with varying degrees of success, to apply their knowledge of twentieth-century classical music theory to their jazz writing." For the most part, these were white musicians with more formal training than their black counterparts, many of whom made their way to Los Angeles looking for work in the movie studios after the breakup of the bands that had formerly provided them with employment.

This is not to suggest that all the writing that emerged from the so-called "cool" school included the flute, nor that all the flutists who emerged at this time were part of this school. For the most part, arrangers were simply expanding the general range and scope of jazz writing while the flutists were engaged in adapting bebop to the instrument. But the elements of cool jazz emerged from the bebop revolution, while the emergence of the flute both reflected and added to that process.

Other musical developments were the result of social and technological changes. For example, new tax laws were enacted that penalized bands with singers and dancers by classifying them as entertainment rather than purely music. This contributed to the decline of the big bands which often depended on featured vocalists, such as Frank Sinatra, Ella Fitzgerald, or Sarah Vaughan, to maintain their popularity. As bebop developed, bands adjusted, became smaller, and started to play for listeners, rather than for dancers. The music took a new turn away from the dance halls and toward night clubs and, eventually, the concert stage. Added to this, amplification technology was advancing. The modern era of the microphone, for example, is said to have begun in 1945 with the introduction of the Neumann/Telefunken multi-directional mike, the TeleU47 also known as the 'Telly'. (It is reported that

Frank Sinatra would not sing without his 'Telly'.) The time was ripe for flutists to step forward and exploit these new technologies, just as Charlie Christian exploited the newly developed guitar pickup to bring the electric guitar to the level of a distinct solo voice. Finally, the war had shifted the gender equation in music; as Rosie the Riveter filled in for male workers in the factories who had been drafted, so more and more women musicians and even all-female bands began to appear, allowing women to gain acceptance by performing on a wider range of instruments. The first generation of flute soloists were still male, but the women, as we shall see, were not far behind.

With all of this, as a new generation of saxophone players emerged, it became apparent that the demands of the musical environment had changed. Doubling on other woodwind instruments always increases the employment possibilities for a reed player. During the swing era the standard double for saxophone players was the clarinet, but suddenly, as bebop gained ascendancy in the mid-1940s, the clarinet virtually disappeared as a major solo instrument. This has always seemed something of a mystery, especially as it reached such heights of popularity in the hands of Benny Goodman and Artie Shaw. "Face it:" wrote Leonard Feather in a 1961 *Down Beat* piece, "the instrument that for the better part of a decade, from 1935, was the worldwide symbol of jazz, has suffered a severe and inexplicable decline and fall." He continues:

> The history of the clarinet goes back almost to the beginning of jazz. A shrill and exuberant voice in the early marching bands, an exciting element in the sword-crossing improvisations of the early Dixieland and New Orleans ensembles, it ranked for years with cornet (or trumpet) and trombone as one of the three principal horns, reaching its zenith with the glorification bestowed on it by Benny Goodman.
>
> Perhaps it was the extraordinary impact of Goodman, and the high level of musicianship set by him and his contemporaries, that made further progress a challenge almost impossible to meet. As jazz evolved and placed ever greater technical demands on the performer, the role of the clarinet moved on an inverse ratio.
>
> It seems to me (and having struggled with it for quite a while as an exasperating student of Jimmy Hamilton, I can speak from experience) that the technical problems confronting the clarinetist are terrifyingly hard to surmount, in these far-more-demanding times than they were back when 16th notes were only occasionally played.

The maestro himself, Benny Goodman, seems to agree with this assessment. He is quoted by Philip Elwood, (in the 1979 sleeve notes to *Jimmy Knepper in L.A.*). "Benny Goodman explained the decline in the use of the clarinet in jazz, from 1945 on, by saying that 'it's too difficult an instrument for these modern bopsters to learn: you can play bebop on a saxophone with less training and practice.'"

The person who has done more than any other to revive the clarinet in recent years is Eddie Daniels. I asked him if he had an opinion about why the clarinet had fallen out of favor in the first place. His view was the same as Goodman's. "Because it's hard!" he told me:

> The clarinet has always been difficult, but the music changed. The music became more chromatic. The vocabulary became different. We started listening more to bebop, Charlie Parker, Coltrane--post-swing music. Swing music fits right on the clarinet, up and down, up and

down the arpeggios--it works great. Then suddenly when the music changes to something more subtle... being able to make the clarinet more contemporary started to make more demands on it. It seemed to fit very well in the swing era because it was a more up and down arpeggiated kind of music, but as soon as it became more chromatic, more linear, more harmonic, suddenly the clarinet became much more difficult. The flute has a more cool sound and it fits the modern idiom more comfortably.

Sam Most, flute pioneer and himself a fine clarinetist, agrees with this assessment. When he first became aware of bebop in the late forties, he explained to me, he found himself applying it to the flute rather than to the clarinet. And for most other reed players involved in the new idiom the saxophone was the primary horn. So it was that, until Daniels' emergence in the eighties, with the exception of a handful of players such as Buddy de Franco, Alvin Batiste and John Carter, clarinet specialists were few and far between, with only one or two saxophonists focusing on the clarinet as a double for solo work-- apart from Sam Most, Art Pepper and Phil Woods come to mind. Again, however, this was within the sphere of bebop and the genres that followed. As with swing, there was a core of major soloists during this period who concentrated on one instrument; apart for a couple of dates where he was required to play tenor, for example, Charlie Parker played the alto saxophone exclusively. Others, such as Sonny Rollins or Dexter Gordon, stayed strictly with the tenor. But for wind players who wanted to work in other areas, the pressure to expand their capabilities by doubling became more intense. I asked Eddie Daniels if that was his motivation for taking up several instruments:

> Well that was it--being able to play a Broadway show. The first show I ever did was *Mame*, with Angela Landsbury. I sat in the pit for *Mame* and for the third chair that I did you had to play the bass clarinet, the saxophone, and clarinet and piccolo. Then I moved to first chair and I needed alto [sax], flute, piccolo, clarinet and possibly bass clarinet.

Saxophonist Joe Lovano has a similar perspective:

> If you stay on one horn then your total focus is there. But I have to double in order to play in some working bands. As a saxophone player I have to play some clarinet and I have to play some flute. So as a young player my father really hipped me to that. He said when that phone rings you've go to be able to do the gig. And before I knew it, as I was studying those horns, I was able to take solos on the flute and be confident about that. So I was able to play in a lot of different situations that I would not have been able to do. Later, when I joined the Woody Herman band, there were some important flute parts--introductions to tunes, solos here and there--and there were times playing behind Tony Bennett or Mel Torme, or Sarah Vaughan or Billy Eckstine, where you had to play some clarinet or flute. Those things factor in also--having things you can deal with from your arsenal of instruments. From an early age, I had to be able to execute certain things on these instruments so that I could sit in a saxophone section and take a gig. As you developed, you would focus more on one horn or the other. The tenor for me is my voice, but all these other instruments that I have played and studied all give me a lot of ideas. Now I try to write music and do things that are specific for different horns, you know. It's the

passion you have, and the ideas.

Steve Kujala, a fine flutist, is also a first-call artist for major productions in Los Angeles. He recalls the setup for a recent production of Mel Brooks' *The Producers*:

> I played the second book, which means second alto sax, second flute, second clarinet and bass clarinet. The first book, including first flute, went to a guy, Dick Mitchell, who is an excellent lead alto sax and woodwind player, though I am known more as a flutist than he is. It is quite common, unless the orchestrator is writing for specific players, that your book will include an instrument that you'd rather not play, as was the case with me. But most of these guys are so good they have no "weak" doubles. They're all strong! In L.A., we don't even call them "doublers" anymore--they're called "woodwind players."

These procedures have become standardized in recent years, but the trend toward woodwind doubling has been accelerating since the early years of the recording industry. As well as arrangers, many instrumentalists were in search of work after the breakup of the big bands. The answer for many of them was to be found in the studios serving the movie and recording industries in Los Angeles, New York and Toronto. And to work steadily in this setting, for wind players, doubling gave a very definite competitive edge. This was especially true for black musicians; being an African-American studio musician in the forties was impossible without being able to play at least two instruments. With the clarinet less in demand for jazz work (although it is still needed in the studio and the theater) the flute became the standard double for many saxophone players. Several of them were to become the first generation of major jazz flutists.

Part Two

The Pioneers

The First Wave

As the twentieth century approached its halfway mark, and the bebop revolution gained in strength and breadth, the flute began to appear with greater frequency in the hands of jazz woodwind players. It was the beginning of a process that was to culminate in a statement by Leonard Feather, in the sleeve notes to the 1973 recording *The Many Faces of Yusef Lateef*: "In sum," he wrote, "the flute today occupies a position comparable in importance to the clarinet during the swing era."

There are those who would dispute Feather's view. The flute may have replaced the clarinet as the primary double for saxophonists, but not as the central voice of the era, as the clarinet had been in the hands of Benny Goodman and Jimmy Dorsey. It cannot be denied, however, that the flute enjoyed a substantial change in status during these years, and we can attribute this development to two factors that have been significant throughout the development of the flute in jazz. First, each generation of flutists has gained greater command of the instrument and found more ways to adapt it to jazz performance. Second, the music itself has changed--broadening, evolving, incorporating elements from external sources: European, Latin and non-Western. As a result, while it has proved possible to present a history of jazz with hardly a mention of any flutist--remember: just two flutists in the *Down Beat* Hall of Fame-- the flute has been very active at the periphery of the music. This has been interpreted in some quarters as irrelevance--"Really, people play jazz on the flute?" But we ignore this trend at our peril. Like a living cell, the music takes in nourishment, and communicates with the external environment, through its outer wall, not through its inner core.

This is not to say that the artists who have developed the flute as a jazz instrument have been at the periphery of jazz music. On the contrary, four of them--Yusef Lateef, Hubert Laws, James Moody, Frank Wess--are National Endowment of the Arts Jazz Masters. Other members of that august group have, at one time or another, featured flutists prominently in their ensembles, or on their recordings; we can cite: Toshiko Akiyoshi, Kenny Barron, Count Basie, Ray Brown, Kenny Burrell, Ron Carter, Chick Corea, Gil Evans, Dizzy Gillespie, Chico Hamilton, Herbie Hancock, Freddie Hubbard, Milt Jackson, J.J. Johnson, Elvin Jones, Hank Jones, Quincy Jomes, McCoy Tyner, Sun Ra and Phil Woods, as well as jazz icons Duke Ellington, John Coltrane, Cannonball Adderley, Charles Mingus and Buddy Rich.

If there is a contradiction here, we can see it in the life and work of the generation of flute artists who emerged in jazz in the late 1040's and through the 1950s. Without exception, they were multi-instrumentalists. Some were reluctant flutists, but all of them would have made a significant contribution to the music without ever playing the flute. But play the flute they did, and the instrument grew in stature through their work.

There is no better example of the new breed of multi-dimensional performers that was emerging at this time than **Jerome Richardson.** In the course of his long career, Richardson rose to the top of his profession as a studio musician. Fluent on the entire saxophone family as well as all the flutes, and, on occasion, the clarinet (unwillingly, it seems--as he told his manager Suzi Reynolds, he wanted to take the darn thing and make a lamp out of it!). Richardson worked in both Hollywood and New York, and was recognized by Leonard Feather as "a first-class soloist on every instrument he has played," while Jack Meher called him "... one of the ablest multi-instrument men in the business. He's a prime choice for record dates, pit bands and big band work." His reputation led him eventually to become the first-call reed player for a wide range of artists, from Peggy Lee to Frank Sinatra, Quincy Jones to Woody Allen, and he was still in demand when he passed away in 2000. Unlike many session players, however, he was also a fine jazz artist, and along the way he stepped forward to record what many believe to be the first jazz flute solo after Wayman Carver's efforts in the 1930s.

Born in Texas in 1920, but raised in Oakland, California by adoptive parents, Richardson took up the alto saxophone at the age of eight. He received classical training from the beginning, but he was also eager to emulate the great jazz players on the instrument: Johnny Hodges, Benny Carter, and Willie Smith. By age fourteen he was working professionally when his reading ability got him a brief job with Lionel Hampton's orchestra. In need of a lead alto saxophone player while passing through the Bay Area, Hampton heard of Richardson's abilities and contacted him. Richardson related the story during an interview with Bob Bernotas that appeared in Bernotas' excellent *Reed All About It* (New York, Boptism Music Publishing, 2002):

> Hamp found out that I was the only one in the area that could read. He came to my house and asked my father if I could play with the band. So Dad took me there and brought me back. I was scared to death, but I played the music anyway. And then after that Hamp wanted me to go out with the band, but Dad said, "No, no. You go to school."

Disappointing at the time perhaps, but excellent advice as it turned out. Jerome stayed in town to complete a degree at San Francisco State University. And being in the Bay Area afforded Richardson the chance to work with another famous band--the Jimmie Lunceford orchestra. Richardson speaking to Bernotas again:

> Yeah. [Lead alto] Willie Smith left the band in Oakland, and I was always a great admirer of that band. I was like the mascot. Whenever they came, I was the first one in the door and the last one out, and I stood behind the saxophones all the time. During the time that they were there and playing, Lunceford used to let me hold that big flute he had. I didn't know what it was. Of course, it was an alto flute.

Lunceford was an occasional and not very proficient flutist, and the instrument was more for show than anything else. But it was enough to inspire the young Richardson who took it up in earnest shortly thereafter. He goes on:

> I loved the band so much, I had memorized everything they played. So when Willie left I got an audition, and the first thing that Lunceford asked me, he said, "Can you play loud?" I said, "Yeah." He said, "Do you like Willie Smith?" I said, "Yeah." He said, "Well, come join us at the Oakland Auditorium.

Unfortunately, this was 1940 and Richardson was with Lunceford for only two weeks before he was drafted into the navy. As it happened, however, he was able to get into one of the two navy jazz bands, the one led by altoist Marshall Royal. (The second navy band was led by another pioneer flutist, Buddy Collette.)

After his discharge, Richardson returned to San Francisco. By 1949 he had hooked up with Lionel Hampton again, this time for a two or three year stint as second altoist. It was with Hampton that he recorded his first flute solo. He explained how it came about to Bob Bernotas:

> Now there was a gentleman by the name of Wayman Carver who was with Chick Webb's band way before, in the '30s, who actually was the first real flutist. But according to what I can figure, I was the first one to record a flute solo in my era. Maybe there were other people playing flute then. I'm sure Frank Wess was, but I think I put out the first jazz flute solo of the era. (I understand Herbie Mann claims that he did, but I don't think he put anything out in 1949 or '50 even.)
>
> How did it come about? It was because of Quincy Jones, really. Quincy was a good, young trumpet player who was also an arranger and composer. He had written a piece called *Kingfish*. We were rehearsing it and I was playing the alto part. [Lead altoist] Bobby Plater was standing and listening.
>
> About that time I got a phone call from my wife. So I said, "Bobby, go ahead and play my part, I gotta answer the phone." When I came back I picked up the flute and transposed the trumpet part and played that on top. And Quincy said, "That's it!" and he decided that I would play a flute solo on it. And for a long time, he used the sound of the flute blending with the trumpet. But that's how it came about, really by accident.

This was by no means the last happy accident in the history of jazz flute, but it is an historic moment. It is just twelve measures, but the flute sounds quite at home, no more out of place emerging from the ensemble than the trumpet, the trombone, the tenor saxophone, or Hampton's vibraphone. For Richardson, it was just one of over 4,000 recordings and the beginning of a career during which he worked with, among others, Earl Hines, Oscar Pettiford, Cootie Williams, Hank Jones, Chico Hamilton, Kenny Burrell, Johnny Richards, Manny Albam, Dizzy Gillespie, Cannonball and Nat Adderley, Gerald Wilson, Ray Brown, Gerry Mulligan, Charles Mingus, Steely Dan, Quincy Jones, Ella Fitzgerald, Frank Sinatra, Peggy Lee and Sarah Vaughan. By 1965, he was so well thought of that he became a founding member of the Thad Jones/Mel Lewis big band--what amounted to an all-star ensemble of musicians' musicians--where he led the saxophone section for ten years. He not only helped to develop the flute in jazz, he was also one of the earliest bebop players to master the soprano saxophone. And the education that he had gained at his father's insistence had a good deal to do with his success. The elder Richardson was a firm believer in the value of education and of the cultivation of excellence in general as the African-American's antidote to prejudice. Richardson was a highly thoughtful and cultivated man, highly skilled at his craft, and so trusted by both musicians and producers that he found himself as the contractor for many of the sessions he worked on, hiring the other musicians for the date. I spoke with percussionist Emil Richards, who worked with him on many sessions in Los Angeles. Like all of his colleagues he remembers Jerome very fondly. "He was always nice to be around," he told me, "very co-operative with the music and everything to do with camaraderie."

He was an asset to every session that we had. He certainly had a lot to say. If he was on the session and there was a solo to be played, he was the one who was always given the solo. Not only on tenor but on flute, of course--he did that shouting into the flute.

Did you not have to be both respected and well-liked to do that?

That's right. He used to contract some things for Quincy. What happened was, in order to make the kind of bread some guys were demanding, they would put them in as contractors so they would get a better taste. So that was how that came about. But he was so well liked... when he came here from New York he went right to work, I mean there was no hesitation at all, he came to town and went right to work. Everybody loved him and we all enjoyed listening to him play.

I received the same picture of Jerome from everyone who knew him. It is an irony of the literature on jazz that such a musician gets less attention than those who kill themselves with self-destructive behavior. "Exceptional artistic talent, a colorful yet somewhat shrouded personal life, and a premature, tragic death seem to be the essential ingredients that go into the making of a jazz legend," writes Chris Albertson in his notes to *Charlie Parker: The Verve Years*. This may have worked for Bird, Chet Baker and some others, but it has not the formula for fame when it comes to the many artists, several of them featured in this book, whose careers are based simply on commitment and professionalism. In Jerome Richardson's case it also didn't help that literally hundreds of his sessions were done anonymously, without fanfare, reviews, or written credits.

Being so much in demand on other people's recordings, Richardson did not find time to make many of his own, but he did make three or four fine albums. His first, *Midnight Oil*, was recorded in 1958, and he chose to feature his flute on four of the five tracks. These are spirited performances, with Richardson finding a remarkably well-developed voice on flute, blending well with Jimmy Cleveland's trombone on a suitably exotic-sounding *Caravan,* and with the right hand of pianist Hank Jones on the fleet line of Artie Shaw's *Lyric.* 1958 recording techniques make the flute tone a little thin, and there are moments of uncertain articulation, but, on the whole, it is an impressive outing. Yet Richardson was not satisfied. He spoke about this to critic Nat Hentoff who writes in the sleeve notes to *This Is Ray Brown,* an album on which Richardson appears:

> Richardson has been trying to make a jazz instrument of the flute since around 1940-41. He believes his flute solo in Quincy Jones' *Kingfish* with Lionel Hampton's band sometime between 1949 and 1951 was the first jazz flute solo on record after Wayman Carver with Chick Webb. Since he came to New York in 1954, he's been studying the instrument seriously with Victor Just, formerly on the ABC staff.
> Richardson doesn't think anyone now playing jazz flute has yet "arrived" on the instrument. "Very few have been able to combine a good, swinging beat with the correct inflection and a non-classical tone. Many tongue the flute on nearly every note and you don't get a good swinging bow with it that way. By 'bow' I mean the way the cats bow when they're swinging. Frank Wess, I think, is the best of the jazz flutists."

These are thoughtful comments. Richardson was one of the first flutists to realize that articulation is the key to making the flute work in jazz. He understood that the way both sound production and articulation--the use of the tongue in forming and stopping notes--are taught during traditional flute training are not entirely appropriate for jazz playing. As a case in point, some years later flutist Jamie

Baum found that she could not keep up both jazz and classical performance because of the very different technical demands involved. She also spoke to Bob Bernotas in *Reed All About It*:

> ... I find when I play classical music my vibrato is going to be different. Usually I'm going to use a lot more of it, and it's probably going to be faster. I find that my articulation is going to be different, where I place my tongue when I articulate. My tongue will be much more forward. Not to say that I won't use these things in jazz, maybe for a certain effect or a certain expressive manner. However, when I'm playing classical, generally it's more forward, you get a more pure attack and a crisper attack, and also I use more vibrato because that's the style of that music... And of course the [rhythmic] feel, which is a big thing, is different--how the eighth notes feel. I mean the thing about classical music is you tend to want all notes to have the same sound, the same quality, whereas in jazz certain notes are more prominent. Certain notes in the line carry more value. The approach is very different.

Baum, from whom we will hear in a later chapter, goes on to comment that, in her opinion, it is possible to master both styles of playing, but doing so is very demanding and time consuming. We will come across this again with reference to Hubert Laws, James Newton and others. For Richardson and his generation of jazz flute pioneers, these were problems that took some time to solve. Wayman Carver and Alberto Socarras were well trained flutists, but playing in a swing context encouraged a jerkier style of playing that would not work for bebop as that style requires a unique balance between legato flow and rhythmic punctuation, and it took some time for flutists to develop this. Jerome Richardson was most perceptive in singling out Frank Wess as the model for his generation, but as Leonard Feather concludes in his notes: "Richardson is working on his own approach that he thinks can result in making the flute fully a jazz instrument. On the evidence here and in other recent work of his, he's already one of the most convincing of the jazz flutists."

In spite of this, it is evident that Richardson did not think of himself primarily as a flutist. In a 1987 interview with *Cadence* magazine (vol xiii, No. 12) we find the following exchange:

> **Jerome Richardson:** First place, I'm a saxophone player and that's all I am, whatever else you heard me play is something else, flute or anything else, I'm a saxophone player.
> **Cadence:** That will surprise many who admire your flute work.
> **JR:** Okay they like my flute playing, fine. But I'm a saxophone player, and I think I understand the various saxes...
> **CAD:** ...doubling on the reeds and flute--doesn't that present a conflicting embrochure (sic)
> **JR:** Yes. I had to learn it, study to play the flute. The difference is between pursing your lips very hard or blowing out. On flute I wanted to play jazz so that's what I tried to do. I tried to simulate playing tenor or trumpet on it sometimes to get a swinging kind of sound and not an esoteric flutist sound for jazz. But I find if you play a lot on the sax it's hard to pick up the flute and get a good sound; the muscles are set in a certain way from the saxophone that you have to then revert to another set of muscles to play flute. When I go from a woodwind instrument to the flute I blow out (my lips).

CAD: Do you have a favorite flutist?
JR: Hubert Laws.
CAD: As an improvisor though?
JR: I hear a lot of people say that. Maybe I'm enamored of his technical ability but I like it very much. There are other people that I like too."

We will hear from Hubert Laws in due course. To conclude the interview, however, Jerome was asked about his most exhilarating musical experiences. His response: "As for as I am concerned the most exhilarating two people I played with were Quincy Jones and Thad Jones. Their bands and their music." It is very revealing that he did not cite the recordings he made under his own name. There are only a handful of these. There is *Midnight Oil, Going to the Movies*, on which he plays very little flute, the commercial recording *Groove Merchant* and an album for New Jazz, *Roamin' with Jerome*. He is also featured prominently on some recordings by other jazz artists, such as *This is Ray Brown* from the prominent bassist, *Ritmo Caliente* by vibraphonist Cal Tjader, and Oscar Pettiford's classic *Bohemia After Dark*, all from 1955, all of which feature Jerome's flute playing exclusively. The following year he participated in a jam session for Prestige with Donald Byrd, Kenny Burrell, Hank Mobley and Mal Waldron that was issued under Burrell's name with the title *All Night Long*. Again, Jerome features the flute extensively.

There are many more recordings of this quality in Richardson's discography, but when it comes to his own albums, while he may have been satisfied with their musical content, it was always a source of disappointment to him that they were never properly promoted or distributed by the record companies. Even when he was asked for copies, he recounts, by radio stations particularly, he could not get hold of any to give to them. *Groove Merchant*, in particular, seemed to disappear without a trace. "I had a radio hit with it in four states," he recalls, "but the record company just didn't promote it. I was badly hurt and disillusioned by that."

Disgusted with the recording industry, he gave up on trying to make his own albums, until he finally found someone who could help him. Suzi Reynolds is a well-known and well-respected manager and producer in New York City. Learning of Jerome's situation she became his manager for the last few years of his career. Determined to see Jerome record his own music at its best, she took the project in hand, and with her help--and against all odds--he finally put together one album that represents his musical vision. Still available, it is called *Jazz Station Runaway*. Reynolds explained to me that Jerome had had bad luck with his previous releases, such as *Midnight Oil*:

At that time, Verve was in the process of being taken over by Polygram and the whole Polygram distribution chain, and it was not a smooth transition. Jerome's record came out right at that time and, it kind of fell through the cracks; it was never widely distributed to wholesalers. So, even though they sent him on a whole promotional tour, and people were lining up to buy the record, there were no records to be found in the bins. It was very frustrating for him, and he never got over it. It was a never-ending source of heartbreak to him because he poured his heart and soul into the record and people really wanted it and it just wasn't available. And it was a tumultuous time in the industry; jazz was being swept aside by the Beatles and Rock and Roll and Jerome just didn't have a chance.

To prevent this from recurring, Suzi decided to take charge of *Jazz Station Runaway*. She told Jerome:

> I am going to make this record and this is how we are going to do it. If you can bankroll the first session for five tunes, I know I can take this and get you a deal. And that's what we did. It still didn't get the distribution we wanted, but it got great reviews and Jerome sold it on the road; it sold very well in Europe. And from a musical point of view, he felt he accomplished what he had always wanted to accomplish, made the statement he had always wanted to make.

Reynolds acted as producer on the recording, from suggesting the sidemen to supervising the sessions from the control booth, and guiding him through the post-production process. Jerome wrote all the arrangements, creating the ideal settings for each of his horns, including a flute feature on *Nouveau You Know*. From the evidence of these performances, the work that Jerome had put in since the late fifties had paid off. When I spoke to Eddie Daniels, who sat next to him in the Thad Jones/ Mel Lewis saxophone section, he expressed the opinion that Jerome had spent some time studying with Harold Bennett, based on the sound quality he drew from the instrument:

> Jerome had a little more focused sound--he was a good flute player. You know, back at that time, as a doubler, he was probably one of the better flute doublers; he played the flute very well--very nice sound... I didn't hear Jerome play a lot of jazz flute, he was more of a doubler studio guy. But he sat next to me and I heard him play a lot of flute parts, focused–he played an old Powell, around a 2000 series. It's possible Jerome studied with Harold Bennet for some time, his tone is in that realm, very clear, very focused.

Eddie concluded by comparing Jerome with Frank Wess. It would be hard to think of a greater compliment. Another of those unassuming professionals, Wess achieved prominence as a flutist after devoting considerable formal study to the instrument. As far as we know, Jerome Richardson was largely self-taught as a flutist, but this did nor prevent him, among many other accomplishments, from making a great contribution to the jazz flute tradition.

Before examining Frank Wess' work there are some other figures who made important contributions in the late forties and early fifties. One of these is a musician whose career parallels Jerome Richardson's in many ways. **Seldon Powell** is another example of the all-round woodwind players who emerged in the 1950s, and who can be found playing the flute, along with all the saxophones, on hundreds of sessions with major artists in both jazz and popular music.

There is not a great deal of biographical information available about Powell, as his few jazz recordings were insufficient to earn him a mention in the various jazz guides. His interest in the flute probably came from his early training, which was in a classical context, albeit as a clarinet major, beginning at the Brooklyn Academy of Music and continuing at the Juilliard School in New York, from where he eventually graduated in 1957. His earliest employment was with Tab Smith, following which he joined Lucky Millinder, with whom he recorded in 1950. After a brief stint in the military, Powell returned to New York to settle into a career as a studio musician, rising to the demands of that role by adapting his playing to every style that came along over forty-plus years. "He's not a great soloist, ambitious composer or spectacular arranger;" writes Ron Wynn, in the *All Music Guide*, "he's simply a good, consistent player who's survived many changes and trends to remain active from the late '40s until the '90s."

Powell's adaptability and musicianship can be seen from the list of people with whom he worked and recorded, which included Pearl Bailey, Louie Bellson, Neal Hefti, Friedrich Gulda, Johnny Richards, Sy Oliver and Erskine Hawkins, Clark Terry, Nat Adderley and Ahmed Abdul-Malik. He worked in the bands of Benny Goodman, Woody Herman, Buddy Rich, and Gerry Mulligan, for whom he was a principal soloist. Powell was a staff player for ABC television in the 1960s, and in the 1970s he expanded his range still further, working soul jazz and pop dates with artists such as Richard 'Groove' Holmes, big band dates with Gato Barbieri, Dizzy Gillespie and Anthony Braxton.

Powell recordings are hard to come by; he recorded as a leader for Roost, and Epic, primarily featuring his tenor playing. The only track featuring the flute on his own recordings is *Afro-Jazz*, on the 1973 session *Messin' With Seldon Powell*. His flute can be heard to good effect, however, on a couple of other sessions. One is a 1964 recording by Latin percussionist Willie Rodriguez. Highly in demand by bandleaders from Paul Whiteman to Herbie Mann, Rodriguez made only one session under his own name, *Flatjackets,* a quartet setting featuring guitarist Barry Galbraith, bassist George Duvivier, and Powell on alto, tenor, clarinet and flute. On five of the twelve tracks he demonstrates considerable command of the latter instrument, with a full rich tone and well controlled phrasing. He can also be heard on the multi-flute session *Flutin' The Bird*, where he trades flute solos with Frank Wess and Bobby Jaspar. From the way he holds his own with these emerging masters, it appears quite unfortunate that Seldon Powell did not record more on the flute, as he clearly had the technique to make a considerable contribution to the instrument's future in jazz.

* * * * * *

Of the other flutists to emerge in this generation, it is interesting that several of them were associated with trumpeter Dizzy Gillespie. Apart from being one of the most important trumpeters in jazz, and one of the founders of bebop, Dizzy was also, like Miles Davis after him, a great recruiter and developer of new talent. The list of prominent jazz artists that passed through his big band and small groups reads like a who's-who of modern jazz, and begins with Charlie Parker who first came to prominence in Dizzy's quintet. Several of his subsequent sidemen were flutists, probably due to Dizzy's interest in Latin music. One of the earliest of these was an unusual figure in that he undertook the unique double of flute and guitar.

Les Spann was from Arkansas, born in 1932. He was initially attracted to the guitar and taught himself to play during high school. He then decided to become a music major at Tennessee State University, only to find that he was expected to select a secondary instrument. He made the rather unusual choice, for a guitarist, of selecting the flute. By the time he graduated he was already in demand, primarily as a guitarist, working with such artists as Phineas Newborn, Ben Webster and Nat Adderley. But for one year, in 1958-59, he worked with Dizzy Gillespie who called upon him to play the flute as well as the guitar, both in concert and on two albums *The Ebullient Mr. Gillespie* and *Have Trumpet*

Will Excite. Later, Duke Ellington thought enough of Spann's ability as a flutist to hire him when recording the score for the movie *Paris Blues.* And Ellington altoist Johnny Hodges hired Spann to play on his *Blue Hodge* album. Even Jerome Richardson decided to feature him on his 1962 album, *Going to the Movies,* showcasing Spann's flute on *No Problem.*

Eventually, Spann was able to make a record under his own name on which he divided his time between the two instruments. Perhaps because of this, the album was called *Gemini.* As producer Orrin Keepnews writes in the album notes:

> Gemini, the constellation that forms the third sign of the zodiac, is pictorially represented as having the shape of a set of twins, sitting side by side. Not that we intend to get too deeply into the astrology of the situation, but the fact is that Les Spann, who is the focal point of this unusual-sounding album, was born under this sign. ... Les is one of those extreme rarities in jazz, an artist equally worth listening to on two quite dissimilar instruments.

Adding to the unusual sound of the session was Spann's choice of Julius Watkins to play what is still regarded as a miscellaneous instrument, the French horn. Working with a fine rhythm section of Tommy Flanagan, piano, Sam Jones, bass and Albert Heath or Louis Hayes, drums, Spann divides his time equally between flute and guitar. The date is 1960, and Spann's flute work is typical of that time-- he is still looking for solutions to some of the problems Jerome Richardson had described earlier. His lines are interesting but the tone is rather thin and his articulation is far from perfect when executing boppish lines. The recording is still well worth hearing, however. Spann's flute contrasts nicely with his guitar work and blends pleasantly with the burry sound of Watkins' French horn to create an interesting sonority, especially on a tune like *Afterthought.* He is suitably lyrical on the ballad *It Might As Well Be Spring*, while digging into a blues vein on *Blues For Gemini.*

This was to be Spann's only recording under his own name. After leaving Gillespie in 1959, and working with Ellington in 1961, his career took a downward turn and he succumbed to various forms of addiction. Alyn Shipton, in his *Groovin' High: The Life of Dizzy Gillespie* recounts an interview between pianist Junior Mance, who worked with Spann in Dizzy's group, and Gene Lees.
[Quite recently] Les died... he ended up on skid row, at rock bottom. Somebody rescued him and checked him into the hospital to dry him out. Cats were taking him music paper, because he loved to write. They gave him every encouragement. One day, he checked himself out of the hospital and back to skid row. He died in the Bowery.

This was in 1989. Another talent wasted. Les Spann had something to say, both on flute and on guitar. Perhaps Shipton sums him up best as "wayward but original." Spann's flute work is not on the level of Frank Wess' or Jerome Richardson's, but he holds his own and his sole recording is always interesting, as is his work with Gillespie, which helped to establish the flute as part of Dizzy's small group sound. So much so, that when Spann left the group, Dizzy sought out another flutist to replace him.

Leo Wright was primarily an alto saxophonist, learning the instrument at an early age from his father who played alto professionally, working with rhythm & blues bands in the Texas area. Leo also studied with saxophonist John Hardee of Dallas, and played in his high school band. Precocious and mature, and set on a career in music, Leo won a scholarship to Huston-Tillotson College in Austin and later transferred to San Francisco State College. Trumpeter Bobby Bradford knew Wright in Austin. "Leo Wright and I were roommates in college. Leo was very precocious. This guy was smokin' man. As a freshman in college, Leo was killing. The rest of us were scared to death of him. He was so mature at that point as a player." He was disappointed, however, to find that he could not major in saxophone at that time. He was already playing the flute, so he decided to focus his studies on this instrument, but he was frustrated, and his frustrations did not end there. Drafted into the army, he found he was forced into playing the flute there also. The following is from *Down Beat,* February 1st, 1962:

> Wright said he had been playing flute for more than five years, but not always of his own volition. "The instrument was put upon me" he said. "I had a flute, messed around on it, but I was devoted to the alto saxophone. When I registered at San Francisco State College I found I couldn't major on saxophone. I didn't have a clarinet so I took a flute class."

That was in 1956. Later, when Wright found himself in the army, he had the same problem. Reporting to the army band as a saxophone player the response was "We have too many saxes--don't you play anything else?" So again, he was forced to play the flute. He did manage to play some jazz while he was in the service. This is clear from a radio interview tenor player Eddie Harris gave in New York, on June 29, 1994: "...Cedar Walton and I were outside of Stuttgart, at Vahingen, and we had a Jazz band out of the orchestra that had formed. It was quite a jazz band. Leo Wright was head of the jazz band, people like Lanny Morgan, Don Menza were in the band...It was a very good band..." For the most part, however, Wright's military band work was on flute and even after the service, he continued to be a reluctant flutist. *Down Beat* again:

> When he was released and returned to San Francisco State he again was thwarted in his desire to study sax. "I began to resent flute," he said. "When am I going to learn sax? I asked myself." He left college and went to New York and Charlie Mingus in 1959. Then he joined Gillespie. "Back on flute again," he said wryly. "I decided to get down and study it."

He was only twenty-six when he joined Gillespie. Alyn Shipton writes:

> Wright had been playing in Charles Mingus' band at the Five Spot in New York when a telegram arrived from Dizzy asking him to join the group in one week's time at the Regal in Chicago. Mingus let Wright go without holding him to his notice, and Wright arrived at the South Side's main theater to find he was expected to play in the pit orchestra supporting the other headline act, singer Dinah Washington, and then join the Gillespie band on stage.

Thrown in at the deep end, Wright decided to swim rather than sink. As quickly as possible he put in the time and work to learn the parts and the special skills required to work with Dizzy. Shipton quotes a passage from Wright's memoires:

> I put in a lot of time trying to get the arrangements down to perfection. [But] Dizzy didn't want

them that way... he wanted the front line to be a bit looser, more flexible. So I got into the habit of watching his breathing and fingers at the same time. That way I could spot which micro-second Birks would be using to lead into the next riff. Through that we got to be a helluva front-line team.

Shipton's conclusion:

> Wright's gutsy, bluesy Texan alto, with his simultaneous debts to Charlie Parker and the broad ballad playing of Johnny Hodges, made him a far more robust counterfoil to Dizzy than Spann had been. The nod in the direction of Miles and cool jazz was over for good, and even Wright's flute playing managed to convey heat rather than an impression of cool.

Now, at last, Wright was studying both sax and flute at the post-graduate school of Dizzy Gillespie. And he went on to do some of his best work with the group, his flute playing remaining a vital component. With the arrival of Argentinian pianist/composer/arranger Lalo Schiffrin, this became one of Gillespie's classic ensembles, with which he was to record several fine albums. It was this group that I heard live in London in 1960, and this group that was at the heart of one of Dizzy's most important projects, a large-scale work written by Schiffrin called *Gillespiana.*

Completed in less than a month, recorded by Verve and finally performed at Carnegie Hall in March of 1961, *Gillespiana* is conceived as a suite, each section of which is designed to display one facet of Gillespie's talent. The format of the piece is a kind of *Concerto Grosso*, a Baroque form in which a group of soloists is set off against an orchestra. In this case, the soloists consist of Dizzy's quintet, and the orchestra of a brass ensemble. Along with Dizzy, and Schiffrin himself on piano, the work gives Wright a good deal of solo space, his flute being featured on the second movement *Blues*, his alto elsewhere in the work. "The suite was an unqualified success with the public," writes Alyn Shipton, "and continues to be performed... It was also a success with some critics. *Down Beat*'s John Tyson voted it five stars..." It also served to bring attention to Wright's work, as did the several albums he recorded with Dizzy, and the extensive tours--including two of Europe and one to South America--that he undertook with the quintet.

Wright benefitted considerably from these excursions. By accompanying Dizzy to South America he participated in the first contact between American jazz performers and Brazilian musicians. Shipton quotes bassist Bob Cunningham: "It was that particular group that was responsible for bringing back from that trip the now-popular *bossa nova*. We came back with these songs *Desafinado, Chega De Saudade,* and quite a number of others." Dizzy was to feature this material in performances, such as at the Monterey Jazz Festival, upon his return. The trips to Europe brought Wright into contact with European musicians with whom he would work extensively later, and with Eric Dolphy who was also on the tour as part of John Coltrane's group. Furthermore, it was on one of these visits that he met Sigrid Vogt whom he married in 1960, and with whom he was to have twin daughters, Susanne and Gisela.

In 1962, after three years with Dizzy, Leo left the group, to be replaced by James Moody. Some writers have suggested that he made this move in order to form his own group. Shilton has a different view.

To some extent this had to do with the band's still playing clubs and theatres that expected entertainment as well as good music. Wright was never much of a comic foil for Dizzy... Moody's witty stage presence and his formidable musicianship, let alone his friendship with Dizzy, made him a natural front-line partner for Gillespie.

Also, Dizzy was not overly keen on sharing the limelight with another soloist in his own quintet, and Wright made up for any lack of stage presence with ever more blistering and crowd-pleasing solos.

Dizzy was also aware, according to Shipton, that Wright was developing a solo career. This would not have been enough for Dizzy to fire him but, "Wright believed he was given notice [because] he had incurred the displeasure of Lorraine Gillespie, who was still Dizzy's manager."

Out on his own, Wright remained in demand, working with a wide variety of artists including Tadd Dameron, Antonio Carlos Jobim, Dave Pike, Blue Mitchell, Gildo Mahones and Jean-Luc Ponty. By 1964, he was married and settled in Europe where he worked steadily with many of the musicians he had met during his tours with Dizzy, including Francy Boland, George Gruntz and Lee Konitz's *Alto Summit*. Wright's last concert was with Jimmy Witherspoon in 1990; he died four days into 1991.

Wright's recordings are quite extensive from this period, but the most significant legacy he has left is two albums under his own name while he was still with Dizzy. His 1960 debut album *Blues Shout* was recorded for Atlantic and received considerable critical acclaim. The record has two distinct sections. With the excellent rhythm section of Junior Mance, piano, Art Davis, bass and Charlie Persip, drums featured throughout, Wright plays several tracks on alto alongside trumpeter Richard Williams. These are strong, assured performances in the post-bop idiom that were to be echoed a few months later when Leo played on Richard Williams' debut album, *New Horn In Town*, for Candid, (with pianist Richard Wyands, bassist Reggie Workman and drummer Bobby Thomas.) But for four tracks, the first four of the album, Wright plays flute, working on three of them (*Autumn Leaves* is a pure flute feature) with a very different front-line partner, violinist Harry Lookofsky. (This album was re-issued in 1999, together with Hank Crawford's *The Soul Clinic*, on one CD for Atlantic/Collectables Records.)

These are remarkable performances, a milestone for jazz flute. Wright shows the same level of invention he displays on the alto, with the bluesy phrasing tempered by the smaller sound of the flute. His tone is more centered than that of Les Spann, but still not as full and centered as the next generation of flutists was to display. The vibrato is less measured, but the articulation is clean and fast. Wright is still, perhaps, the reluctant flutist, but in spite of this he makes the instrument swing, and makes it perfectly viable for his brand of bebop. And Wright's choice of partner for the flute tracks is inspired. Harry Lookofsky's name appears on many jazz recordings, but usually as concert master leading a string section; he rarely receives solo space. Like Spann's choice of French horn on the Gemini recording, Wright decides to feature another "miscellaneous instrument" to offset the flute. The unison passages between violin and flute provide an attractive, bright sonority. And by giving Lookofsky his head on three tracks, Wright adds another dimension that almost overshadows his own work as the violinist turns in exuberant, masterful solos, whether these are improvised or written out as in some of his other recordings.

With this project under his belt, Wright waited two years, until April 1962, to record his second album *Suddenly The Blues* (Atlantic) with Ron Carter on bass, Rudy Collins on drums and a close friend, guitarist Kenny Burrell. This is a sparser sound than the first album, which appears to have been a conscious aim. In the notes to the album, Wright states that his goal in both his playing and his writing, is "to express myself with simplicity and directness, minus clutter and pretense. From studying the records of Charlie Parker and from working with Dizzy Gillespie, I have learned that simplicity, clarity and economic organization of musical materials are the marks of really great jazz performance, and not just being able to play very difficult music." Wright alternates between flute and alto sax, playing flute on *Greensleeves, The Wiggler, Dionysos*, and *Willow Weep for Me*, and both on *Tali*. "His flute sound," wrote one reviewer, "supported by a superb technique, is airy and resonant." The album is, in many ways, typical of the early 60s, and was to be surpassed by later players, and *Greensleeves* is a mistake--a bit too coy for a jazz record. But *Willow* is a fine ballad performance, and Wright is suitably articulate on the other selections. Overall, these are two fine albums.

James Newton remembers an encounter with Leo Wright in Vienna, "... a great man and a very nice person," he recalls. "He wrote out some things for me, different patterns and different things, and we talked a lot about articulation as a matter of fact." And Atlantic Records has remembered him by keeping his albums in print. Others have largely forgotten him. Major reference works such as the *Rough Guide to Jazz* make no mention of him. Perhaps he was not a major artist, but his contribution to jazz flute was considerable and he was a fine alto saxophonist. But, "Out of sight, out of mind." Having settled in Europe, Wright enjoyed a quarter-century of music and camaraderie with European musicians and American ex-patriots while dropping into obscurity as far as American critics and audiences were concerned. It was their loss.

But Leo Wright was not the only flutist who moved to Europe in search of greener pastures; several others took a similar path, one of whom was another early contributor to the flute in jazz.

Edmond Gregory was born on June 23, 1925, in Savannah, Georgia. In 1947, he was one of the first jazz musicians to accept the Muslim faith, at which time he took the name under which he is better known--**Sahib Shihab**. Like Jerome Richardson and others of his generation, Shihab began playing the alto saxophone but then added several reed instruments, and like Richardson he was working professionally from a very early age, joining the Luther Henderson band at the tender age of 13. At 16, after some initial study with Elmer Snowden, he attended the Boston Conservatory. By age 19, he was working as lead alto with Fletcher Henderson, and also played with Roy Eldridge's big band. But he was attracted by the bebop revolution, and soon he was working with Thelonious Monk, being featured on his early Blue Note records in 1947 and 1951, including the original recording of the classic *'Round Midnight*. He also worked with Art Blakey, Tadd Dameron, Miles Davis, Kenny Dorham, Benny Golson, and John Coltrane, appearing on Coltrane's first full session as leader for Prestige, *First Trane*. For a while, Shihab was forced to take odd jobs in order to survive, but by 1951 he was working with Dizzy Gillespie, and later, from 1952 to 1955, with Illinois Jacquet. He was with the Oscar Pettiford big band in 1957, and with singer Dakota Staton toward the end of the decade.

Shihab's work with the Gillespie big band was a turning point in his career, not only for the exposure this gave him, but also because Dizzy asked him to switch to baritone saxophone. It is his work on the big horn for which he is probably best known; he was able to find a unique voice on the instrument, his work often being referred to as "quirky." And it was he and Leo Parker who were initially credited with adapting the baritone to bebop.

By the late fifties, after several more years of working intermittently, Shihab was tired of combating discrimination and indifference in the United States. "I was getting tired of the atmosphere around New York," he informed *Down Beat* in 1963. "... and I wanted to get away from some of the prejudice. I don't have time for this racial bit. It depletes my energies." Along with Jerome Richardson, he left for Europe with the band Quincy Jones assembled for *Free and Easy*. After Quincy's musical failed, Shihab decided to stay in Europe. He settled in Copenhagen, working, like Leo Wright, with local musicians and visiting Americans, but also writing scores for television, cinema and the theater, and teaching at the Copenhagen Polytechnic. In 1963 he landed the baritone saxophone chair with the big band founded by Belgian pianist Francy Boland and another American ex-patriot, Kenny Clarke. He stayed with the band for nearly ten years before returning for an extended visit to Los Angeles between 1972 and 1975. He worked as a session man for rock and pop artists and did some copy writing for local musicians. He returned to Europe and married a Danish woman, but could not stay away from the United States, in spite of the revulsion he still felt over racial discrimination. He worked with Art Farmer in New York, and recorded with Charlie Rouse, escaping back to Scandinavia from time to time. Eventually, Sahib Shihab returned to the U.S. for good, until he died in Tennessee in 1989.

Overall, Shihab is probably best known for his work on baritone, but, along the way, Shihab also took up the flute, which he also played with the Boland/Clarke band. An example of his work can be heard on the track *Om Mane Padme Om* from the *Handle With Care* Album. He solos over a Latin groove, displaying a strong, full sound which he supplements with the range of vocal effects associated with Sam Most, Roland Kirk, Yusef Lateef and others, humming and singing into the instrument. Shihab has his share of solos with the big band, but his work on the instrument is displayed to best advantage in a small group, a sextet, that was drawn from the band and which made a number of recordings, the best known being *Calypso Blues*. The sextet consists of Shihab playing flute exclusively, Fats Sadi, vibes and bongos, Boland on piano, and Americans Jimmy Woode Jr, bass and occasional vocal, Clarke drums, and Joe Harris on percussion. Again, Shihab's flute playing is very strong, and works very well with the Latin flavor of many of the selections, such as *Calypso Blues* itself. Shihab solos on virtually every song, alternating fleet lines executed with the same full, well developed sound with the sprinkling of vocal effects. When not soaring over a Latin accompaniment he is playing delicate obbligati to Woode's vocals, or blending with Boland's right hand bebop lines. These recordings were made in 1964 and '65, so some of the groundwork for jazz flute had been laid; Frank Wess had been recording for ten years. But it is still a remarkable outing, demonstrating, again what we have lost in some of the more overlooked artists in jazz. Quite apart from his work on soprano, alto and baritone saxophone, Sahib Shihab should definitely be remembered for furthering the role of the flute in jazz.

If both Leo Wright and Sahib Shihab earned a degree of obscurity through lengthy sojourns in Europe, it is worth noting that one of the finest flutists of the 1950s was himself European and possibly even less well-known. **Robert "Bobby" Jaspar** overcame very difficult circumstances to become a fine tenor saxophonist and perhaps even more impressive flutist. Moving to the United States, he worked with some of jazz' leading lights before his very promising career was cut short by his premature death at age thirty-seven.

Jaspar was born in Liège, Belgium on February 20th, 1926. He began playing the piano at the age of eleven and subsequently took up the clarinet. Then, somehow, he managed to acquaint himself with jazz under about the most difficult possible circumstances, as this was during the occupation of Belgium by the Nazis, who, to put it mildly, discouraged such activities. Things changed dramatically, however, when liberating American G.I.s arrived, bringing jazz recordings with them, and setting up military clubs where Jaspar was able to perform with a Belgium group, the "Bob Shots" and the vibraphonist Sadi. Real live American artists followed soon, particularly Don Byas and Lucky Thompson who made a profound impression on Jaspar who, by this time, had taken up the tenor saxophone.

By 1950 Jaspar was ready to move to Paris and work with some of France's leading jazz players, such as Henri Renaud, Bernard Peiffer, René Utreger and Sacha Distel, as well as visiting Americans. Jaspar did more than hold his own in this context, he became the center of jazz in Paris, leading his own quintet at the Club St. Germain from 1954 to 1956, the year that he married singer/pianist Blossom Dearie. By this time, he had also taken up the flute, and it is evident from the first side he recorded on the instrument, *I'll Remember April*, made in Paris in 1955, that he was going to be a force to be reckoned with. The rest of the session, initially released under the title *Modern Jazz Au Club Saint Germain,* and now available on CD from Emarcy under the title *Memory of Dick,* features Jaspar on tenor saxophone, and reflects his early influences, Don Byas and Lester Young. If not entirely original, his playing is both fluent and inventive. One testament to his tenor work came from guitarist Jimmy Raney, who spotlighted Jaspar's tenor on his 1954 album, *Jimmy Raney Visits Paris*. As Peter S. Friedman wrote in *Coda* magazine, "According to writer Alun Morgan, there is a story behind that record. Raney heard Jaspar playing at a club in Paris and was so favorably impressed that he canceled his boat ticket back to New York so he would be able to record with Jaspar."

In the spring of 1956, Jaspar took a bold step: he moved to New York to see if he could make it at the center of jazz activity. Within two months he was hired by the great bebop trombonist J. J. Johnson for his quintet which also included pianist Tommy Flanagan and drummer Elvin Jones. "Bobby," wrote Johnson on their 1959 Columbia recording *Really Livin'*, "is a perfect courier of the fine new jazz that is coming out of Europe." By the end of the year he appeared in the *Down Beat* poll as a new star on tenor, and completed a recording for French Columbia with Flanagan, Jones, guitarist Barry Galbraith, and bassist Milt Hinton (*Bobby Jaspar With Friends*) and a session for Riverside with Jones, George Wallington and Idrees Sulieman (*Tenor and Flute).*

These are confident performances. Jaspar's tenor style had moved ahead after first-hand contact with players such as Sonny Rollins and Hank Mobley. He shows considerable mastery of the clarinet on *Clarinescapade* on the French Columbia recording, and it is on this record that he also demonstrates, on *In A Little Provincial Town* and *Tutti Flutti* (one of the first in a series of bad flute puns to emerge over the next thirty years!), that his flute work is among the best of his time. This impression is reinforced by his appearance on record with Herbie Mann the following year, 1957, in which he more than keeps up with--some would say he outshines--his more celebrated American colleague, on both flute and tenor. On this Columbia session he also becomes one of the first jazz artists to record on the alto flute which he uses to good effect on *Spring Is Here.*

Jaspar stayed with J. J. Johnson for over a year, after which he reached what some would regard as the pinnacle of achievement for a jazz musician, a stint with the Miles Davis group. It was a brief stay, however. Sonny Rollins had just left the group and John Coltrane had not yet joined. As Ira Gitler writes in the notes to *Relaxin' with the Miles Davis Quintet*:

In the fall Miles reorganized once more. Bobby Jaspar, on tenor and flute, replaced Rollins, Tommy Flanagan was at the piano bench instead of [Red] Garland and Philly Joe returned in place of [Arthur] Taylor. Again there were better than good performances, but not *the* Miles Davis Quintet. Jaspar, a more than capable tenorman, did not fit with the spirit of the group. *The flute furthered this difference* (italics mine).

It is not clear if this is Gitler's opinion, or reflects Miles' view. I learned from Sonny Fortune that Miles had no aversion to the flute when Sonny worked with him fifteen years later. But it is revealing that the flute was not seen as workable during the height of the hard bop era. At a time when Blue Note and Prestige were cranking out blowing sessions by the dozen, featuring artists such Art Blakey and the Jazz Messengers, the Horace Silver quintet, John Coltrane, Jackie McClean, Lee Morgan, Cannonball Adderley, etc., the flute was still a rare and fragile voice.

After Miles, Jaspar continued to perform with top flight musicians in New York, including Donald Byrd, Jimmy Raney and the young Bill Evans, as well as singers Chris Connor and Blossom Dearie, with whom he continued to work even after they divorced in 1959. He also undertook some tours of Europe where he was given a warm welcome, working with another brilliant Belgian musician, guitarist René Thomas, along with Belgian bassist Benoit Quersin and Swiss drummer Daniel Humair. They recorded with Chet Baker and John Lewis in Italy and also made a live album during an engagement at Ronnie Scott's Club in London in January of 1962. The resulting album is very close to my heart, as I was in attendance during the session. The quartet is in excellent form. Jaspar's tenor sounds stronger than ever and his flute work on two ballads, *It Could Happen To You* and *Darn That Dream*, compares favorably with any other flutist of the time. Both ballads kick into a fast-tempo workout, showing off Jaspar's technical command and unfailing inventiveness. In his notes to Jaspar's 1956 New York recording, Dan Morgenstern writes: "On the flute, there were of course fewer role models, and when it comes to this instrument, Jaspar must be ranked at the very top, with a more virile and venturesome approach than customary in the pre-Eric Dolphy phase of jazz flute playing."

Whatever the quality of these recordings, there is one other, recorded in Paris in December of 1958, which is perhaps Jaspar's finest legacy to the jazz flute tradition. Originally issued on the Barclay label and simply called *Bobby Jaspar*, it has been reissued on CD by Emarcy as *Phenil Isopropil Amine*. Jaspar plays the flute exclusively on this recording, blending his sound with the vibraphone, played on some tracks by Michel Hausser and on the others by Sadi Lallemand. Paul Rovère and a visiting Jimmy Merritt play bass, and the drums are in the capable hands of Kenny Clarke. Adroitly exploiting the bright flute/vibraphone sonority--one that had already been exploited by Sahib Shihab with Francy Boland and would be echoed some years later by Milt Jackson and Frank Wess--Jaspar works through a program of his own originals, along with some standards, and jazz classics by Charlie Parker and Thelonius Monk. Each track is relatively short, and the solos are succinct and uniformly eloquent. Jaspar does not put a foot wrong, his sound is excellent, his ideas fluent, and the two vibraphonists are equally sure-footed. The addition of percussionist Humberto Canto on nine of the twelve tracks adds the touch of Latin that is always welcome to a flutist. Whatever the day-to-day output of Blue Note and Prestige at this time, this recording belongs as much in the jazz mainstream as any of them. Indeed, it belongs among the finest in the history of jazz flute.

Not long after returning to New York in 1962, Bobby Jaspar suffered a heart attack. Six months later, his doctors attempted a bypass operation, considering this to be his only chance of recovery. Unfortunately, four days later, he passed away.

Who knows what Bobby Jaspar could have accomplished had he lived beyond his thirty-seventh year? As it is, he should be better known. Daniel Humair summed up the situation, writing about his experience working with him in 1962. "One of my first real emotions playing with a jazz group was certainly with Bobby Jaspar and René Thomas. They both possessed an incredible jazz technique, sensitivity and knowledge of the music. I always felt that *they were both underestimated, surely because they were European*." (Italics mine.) At the same time, according to Scott Yanow (*Jazz On Record: The First Sixty Years*), "Jaspar served as one of many pieces of evidence that jazz in Europe was catching up to the United States very quickly in the 1950s." Additional evidence of this was a pair of fine saxophonists in England who also became significant jazz flutists. While one is now something of a cult hero, the second has almost been forgotten. Both, like Jaspar, passed away before they could realize their full potential.

Tubby Hayes was more than just the better known of these two musicians, he has been called "... arguably the most prodigiously talented jazz multi-instrumentalist the British Isles has ever produced." British trumpeter and jazz writer Ian Carr clearly agrees with this assessment when he calls Hayes "...one of the most robust talents Britain has ever produced, and one of her most famous musicians." Tubby's story is remarkable for the amount he accomplished in such a short lifetime. Particularly striking was the speed with which his prodigious talent emerged.

Hayes was born into a musical family in London in 1935, the son of a violinist who worked regularly for the BBC. Inspired by his father he took up the violin, but, as he told English jazz journalist Les Tomkins in a 1966 interview, "As a little boy of five or six I can remember wanting to own a saxophone. I tried to talk my father into buying me one, but he told me: 'You'll never be able to blow that--it's much too big for you.' So I had a few years on violin and piano--which I don't regret, because it was a good grounding." By the age of eleven he had the saxophone he wanted, however, and by the age of fifteen he was working professionally with some of the notable British bandleaders of the period: Kenny Baker, Vic Lewis, Ambrose and Jack Parnell. It was to be the briefest of apprenticeships as he immediately began to make an impression as a solo artist. Tomkins recalls:

> In telling the Tubby Hayes story, it must be said that he was a remarkably impressive musician at 14--his age when I first met him. Listening to his present--day demonstrations of tenor saxophone mastery, I tend to do a mental flashback to March, 1950, when I was running a jazz club in a little hut near Raynes Park, S.W. (Tubby's place of birth in London). One evening, a curly--haired, rather corpulent lad walked in, and asked if he could sit in with the resident group, which included Lennie Hastings on drums. Somebody loaned him a baritone, as he didn't have his tenor with him, and--as you've guessed--he proceeded to astound everybody.

Five years later a similar encounter was to give a big boost to his career. This time Tubby sat in with another tenor player, Ronnie Scott, who was already a star of British jazz, and soon to open the famous club that bears his name. Scott was so impressed that, some time later, the two of them teamed up to form a quintet named the *Jazz Couriers* that may well be the most successful small group in the history of British jazz--certainly one that helped to solidify the hard bop style in that country. Their popularity peaked when they opened for Dave Brubeck on a British concert tour. "They sound more like an American jazz group than we do," Brubeck is quoted as saying. The Jazz Couriers lasted for two and a half years, and Tomkins reports, "Tubby looks back on it as a period that was a happy one, but bound to come to an end." He quotes Hayes:

> I've always admired Ronnie's playing a lot, and Ronnie I like very much as a person. We had a very good time. I did practically all the arrangements for that group. But two tenors is a limited sound.
> Towards the end, of course, Ronnie had ideas for opening a club, and I felt I wanted to be completely free and work on my own with a rhythm section. I didn't want to be bothered with having to prepare arrangements all the time.

It was now 1959. Tubby's tenure with the *Jazz Couriers* was enough to secure his position on the London jazz scene, and for the rest of his career he was to lead his own groups, while recording prolifically. But his time with the *Couriers* had also added further dimensions to his work. He developed his writing and arranging skills, and he took up other instruments. First it was the vibraphone. To some extent he was seeking some variation to the two tenor sound of the *Jazz Couriers,* but he was also inspired by another British prodigy. Simon Spillett, whose biography of Hayes is in preparation, writes:

> In 1957, Tubby had taken up the vibes after Vic Feldman had bequeathed his instrument to him before his return to the United States. With typical precocity, less than six months later Tubby was recording on them and sounding for all the world like Milt Jackson (on "Reunion" from the *Jazz Couriers* first LP). The vibraphone increasingly became Tubby's ballad instrument of choice.

"I haven't got the technique on vibraphone to do half the things I can do on the saxophone," he told Les Tomkins. "But I like playing mainly ballads and pretty tunes with nice changes, using the four hammers and things like that."

Hayes work on vibes is well documented throughout his recordings, interspersed with his tenor. But his restless spirit was not content with mastering these highly disparate instruments; a couple of years later Tubby took up the flute. There are differing accounts of why he did this. According to Spillett: "In 1959 he took up the flute, again in quintessential Tubbs style; he had gone to a music shop to purchase a new alto saxophone for a session date but emerged with a flute instead and was playing the instrument on a gig within days."

Tubby's own version of the story was a little more playful. In a fascinating conversation with tenor player Sal Nistico Tubby explains that he finds playing different horns keeps his thinking fresh:

> **Hayes**: ...everything you play is in a different key, so that makes you think more. When you've got used to playing a certain tune in B flat on the tenor for years and years--well, you can't always be fresh.

Nistico: I agree completely, man.
Hayes: That's why I enjoy playing the flute, because, although the embouchure is difficult--it's in concert pitch, and all that--the fingering's not so different, except up the top.
Nistico:: That's a wild double, though!
Hayes: Another thing with that was--I started getting calls for studio work. But it wasn't just playing the vibes. They said. "Right, will you bring a xylophone, a marimba, a glockenspiel."
Nistico: Jeezus--you gotta hire a truck!
Hayes: I thought: 'Well I think I'll take up the flute'!

Whatever his motivation, Tubby approached the flute with the same easy virtuosity that he demonstrated with his other instruments. Indeed, the instrument quickly became an extension of his tenor playing. "As a flautist," writes Spillett, "Hayes claimed to play 'like a trumpet player,'"

> ... although, once again, familiar patented saxophone phrases occurred regularly enough for his work on the instrument to remain recognizably his own. Flute features are scattered throughout Tubby's albums and include the impressive lyricism of "In The Night," the driving pyrotechnics of "A Night In Tunisia" and his adaptation of Roland Kirk's eccentric style on "Raga."

These sides confirm Hayes approach to the instrument. As much, if not more so, than any other player, Tubby's phrasing on the flute closely mirrored his saxophone work, his trademark high-energy, helter-skelter outpouring. Stylistically, like other British musicians, Hayes took a 'home-grown' approach to begin with, absorbing the music from recordings for the most part. It was only later that he could learn from visiting American musicians, as these had been noticeably absent during a musician's union ban in the late fifties. Once the ban was lifted, and Ronnie Scott had opened his club, he began by bringing over a string of tenor players: Dexter Gordon, Al Cohn/Zoot Sims, Johnny Griffin, Sonny Stitt, Sonny Rollins. Bobby Jaspar visited the club in 1962. Both Scott and Hayes reflected the influence of these players. Later, Tubby visited the United States where he performed with such jazz stars as Roland Kirk, Clark Terry, James Moody and Charles Mingus, appearing in New York at Birdland and the Blue Note, and in L.A. at Shelly Manne's Manne Hole, with the likes of Horace Parlan, Clark Terry, George Duvivier, Reggie Workman, and Albert Heath. He was also a member of Friedrich Gulda's Euro-Jazz Orchestra where he interacted with the best European players as well as some American ex-patriots.

All of these experiences and influences resulted in a style described by another British jazz writer, Dave Gelly, as "Cockney tenor--garrulous, pugnacious, never at a loss for a word and completely unstoppable." Some writers were less complimentary, accusing Tubby of playing too many notes, a criticism about which he was a little sensitive:

> There are times when I will not use those fast runs and things--and there are times when I will. Sometimes I do it out of sheer exuberance--and get carried away with myself and get things going. But I read these things where people say "too many notes" and so on, and, quite honestly, I couldn't give a damn. I play as I want to play. And I can play a ballad. I love playing ballads.

If this was the background to Tubby's tenor work, it worked its way through to his flute playing also. There is no indication that he was able to hear many American jazz flutists, although both Roland Kirk and James Moody were on one of his U.S. recording sessions. Basically, however, the flute was an extension of his tenor work, and his contribution to the instrument was in helping to bring it to the fore, rather than any particularly original approach.

One person who knew Tubby very well was Pete King who, until his recent retirement, ran Ronnie Scott's Club for over forty years. I met with him at the club during a visit to London, asking him first of all if he knew how Tubby came to take up the flute. King responded:

I'm not sure if it was a natural progression for Tubby to take up the flute or not. When he was with Jack Parnell, Jack could ask the arranger to put something in, or the individual could speak to the arranger and say, "look could you put something in for the flute," for example. Or he could play something on the flute instead--it was the instrumentalist's choice.

Like Frank Wess with Count Basie--he had that freedom to play flute or tenor on a solo?

That's right, yeah. If you had a chorus to play you could play it on the flute or whatever... But I'm not quite sure what jogged Tubby into playing the flute. I know what jogged him into playing the vibes and that was Victor Feldman. Victor Feldman was over here; of course he was a British boy, and he went to America and joined Woody's band. Than he came back and played for us at the club in Gerrard Street, and that's where Tubby got into playing the vibes. But the actual playing of the flute, I'm not quite sure what the progression was. I know Roland Kirk, Rahsaan, came in and he was very much a flute player. Whether that gave Tubby ideas... But like anything else that Tubby turned his hand to he was a complete and utter natural.

Do you know much about Tubby's background?

I know his father was a violinist; he played in the BBC orchestra. What I do remember is Ronnie [Scott] being booked as a guest star, I think it was at the White Hart in Acton, which was a jazz-oriented pub--I'm not sure if it still is, but it was very prominent in those days. And Ronnie was playing and this young boy came up and asked if he could sit in. And Ronnie said okay, and then he said this boy just played and played and played--and he was phenomenal. And of course the outcome of that, years and years later, was that Tubby and Ronnie got together and formed the Jazz Couriers. But in between times, Ronnie had this nine-piece band that I was happy to be a member of, with Derek Humble, Jimmy Deuchar, Tony Crombie, and Lenny Bush. And Victor joined it, and Phil Seaman the drummer joined also--there were a few changes. This must have been about '56 or '57. We opened in 1959 in Gerrard Street and this was prior to that. And Tubby and I got together and we had an arrangement where I withdrew slightly from playing and I managed Tubby. And I remember vividly that we went out to dinner, with his wife and my wife, and we sat down on the floor of his flat over in Notting Hill, and we worked out a schedule for the way forward for Tubby. At that stage I was just getting out of negotiating a reciprocal deal with America that we eventually set up. And there was a plan for Tubby to go to America and get a record deal and, hopefully, a television series. And all three clicked. The going to America came after a short while, when I had arranged with the unions for Americans to be allowed to come into the country.

I think the more protective of the two unions was the British musicians union, because they didn't want the place swamped with American performers, which is perfectly understandable, so there had been a ban on American musicians coming into the country. The outcome of it was we got both unions to agree to a reciprocal arrangement. The only thing was, to send a British jazz musician to America was like sending coals to Newcastle. But there were a few around who could adequately, more than likely, hold their own and startle a few situations over there, and of course the biggest choice was Tubby.

That was when he made that recording with Clark Terry and Eddie Costa?

Yes, it must have been between '57 and '59.

So before all this, you don't know how he got to the level he had as a player, how he was trained, whether he had any schooling. That type of thing...?

No, well the most amazing thing to me was that in my managerial capacity, I went out looking for anything that Tubby could possibly get into, and one of the things was a BBC series where he fronted a large orchestra, and I mean a large orchestra, not just trumpets and trombones but French horns and strings. And I said to Tubby well, you know, who's going to do all the writing? And he said "I am." So I said "that's fantastic--I hadn't thought that you would undertake such a thing." And he got a book out of the library or bought it, or something; it was about the ranges of all the instruments...

Orchestration.

Right. And he wrote. And it was incredible. I remember at one stage that a very big classical American lead violinist who was over here came over and introduced himself to Tubby and said that he was available to do anything that was required, 'cause he'd be around for a couple of months or something; I can't remember his name. And he led the string section. And the band was phenomenal. And, funnily enough, a long while after that Benny Golson came over, after we got the exchanges going. And he asked for the same orchestra because he wanted to record with it, which he did. But Tubby was a complete and utter natural.

So do you agree with me that if he had been born in New York, for example, he would have been up there with the greatest...

Well when he went to New York he just took them by storm. He was just a giant, a giant. Tubby was a natural master. When Americans came over here some of them were a little bit, "Well, here I am." But then when they heard Tubby they were completely flabbergasted.

I remember Sonny Stitt coming over and sitting in with British guys and calling blues in C#, and trading threes and stuff... just sort of showing off and trying to throw them.

That's right, yes, that was one of his tricks, always taking it up a semitone all the time.

Tell me about the time Tubby sat in with Duke Ellington.

One day I was in the office where I worked with Ronnie and Tubby--the Jazz Couriers--and somebody called me and said, "Is Tubby or Ronnie around?" And I said, "Well Tubby is around but Ronnie isn't around at the moment. What's the problem?" And they said "Well, Duke's band is at the [Royal] Festival Hall tonight and Paul Gonsalves has gone missing. They need a tenor player. I couldn't find either Ronnie or Tubby for a while but them by a stroke of luck I found Tubby and he said "Yes, I'd love to go down."

He wasn't fazed by it, nervous or anything?

No. I went down with him and he just sat in the section and played his ass off. He knew most of the writing, and what Gonsalves was playing anyway.

Did they give him any solos?

Oh, yeah. Oh yeah. It was incredible. It was just a very, very moving thing. Here was an opportunity of hearing Duke's band with Tubby. It was phenomenal, just phenomenal.

Undoubtedly, this was one of the highlights of Tubby Hayes' career; there were many others. He appeared in the movie *All Night Long* with Charles Mingus and on TV with George Shearing and Mel Torme. In 1968, his record *100% Proof* was voted best LP for the year. He had a burgeoning career as a session musician, for which he played the whole range of single reed woodwinds and tuned percussion instruments, until he gave up the vibes in 1966. Woody Herman, repeatedly offered Tubby a place in his big band, but Hayes preferred to stay in London, where he consistently topped all the polls and worked with the cream of British musicians, such as John Dankworth and Cleo Laine. The peak of his career was probably in 1965, when the following appeared in the annual Reader's Poll edition of *Melody Maker* magazine, under the headline: "Tubby Hayes Does it Again."

"Tubby Hayes bestrides the British jazz scene like a colossus. Once again his name dominates the British section of the annual *Melody Maker* Readers' Jazz Poll. He is musician of the year, top combo leader, top tenorist, number one on flute and our best vibist. If winning five sections outright was not enough, he also came second among big bands, composer and arranger."

Throughout Hayes' career, the moments which stood out in his mind came during his U.S. visits. "I had to follow John Coltrane into the Half Note," he recalled. "Then there's Stan Getz and Zoot [Sims] and Al [Cohn] sitting there listening to you--it does certainly gee you up a bit." He remembered working in Los Angeles with Victor Feldman, playing flute with Feldman on vibes.

> We had a whole load of Hollywood studio musicians, especially the flautists and woodwind players, who came in to hear me play. I met the guy from England who's regarded as one of the greatest classical flautists in the world--Arthur Cleghorn. He's working out there. Bob Burns, Frank Reidy and people like that know him pretty well. I'd never met him before, but he's a wonderful guy. He came in about three or four times and listened. I felt a bit of a twit, standing up there blowing my 12 bar blues in F, you know. But he told me he really dug what I was doing.

It was an exciting career while it lasted, but in 1969 it came to a screeching halt. A heart condition aggravated no doubt by his lifestyle, finally caught up with him. Spillett reports:

> He had always drunk heavily with no apparent effect on his performance, but by the mid-1960s he was using serious narcotics with appalling regularity. Such stimulants may have ensured that solos of twenty-five choruses rolled off the fingers seemingly without effort, but these were now false achievements made by a body that was close to breaking point.

By the time I met Tubby it was very evident that he was sick. There was one occasion when I went to his flat in London to collect him for a gig. I had to get him out of bed with the help of a bottle of whiskey; it was heartbreaking. I asked Pete King what he knew about Tubby's health.

In those days a heart problem was a very delicate, serious thing. Today, well last year, I had a triple bypass operation. It's almost like having a tooth pulled; it doesn't seem to register the importance in any shape or form. But Tubby had a defective heart valve and it was altered. Then it started playing up again. He said to me "They want me to go back in and I know if I go back in I'm not going to see it through." I said, "But you've got to go and do it, Tubby." And he died on the operating table.

It is hard to articulate how keenly his loss was felt among British musicians. Even today, Tubby Hayes is still remembered with great fondness. Spillett again:

Figures celebrated in their own lifetime, such as the drummer Phil Seamen or the saxophonist Harold McNair (both of whom also died young in the early 1970s), have achieved a kind of posthumous apocryphal value, but their music is now all but forgotten. The music of Hayes, however, still possesses a charisma and vitality that ensures it is remembered both by fans and fellow musicians.

Harold McNair was another artist of great promise whose career was cut tragically short. As a flutist, he was at least as accomplished as--some would say superior to--any of the pioneers we have discussed so far Yet he is one of those artists who have disappeared from the radar screen of jazz history. Even the *Rough Guide to Jazz* and *Jazz On CD*, both produced in the UK, and both by British writers, fail to include an entry for McNair, so details about his life are sketchy.

One British writer, David H. Taylor, has suggested a reason for this. When I wrote to him to question McNair's absence from his website about leading British jazz musicians, he sent me the following response:

Harold was never more than a very minor figure on the British jazz scene. He did not arrive in London until the early 1960s when British jazz was running out of steam a bit, and musicians were looking for new avenues, and fusion and free style jazz were all the rage. As you know he came to London from Jamaica and followed in the footsteps of other West Indians, Joe Harriott and Dizzy Reece. These two had a lot of success in the mid 1950s but Dizzy Reece left for America in 1959 due to lack of work, and Joe Harriott, although making records, found work hard to come by. I was a jazz club goer in London in the 1950s and 1960s, and by 1961 the scene was pretty bleak. Jazz work was hard to come by and I believe Harold went into the commercial "pop" studio scene and did record a number of commercial albums on his own and with others in the mid 1960s and 1970s.

The other thing that may have held him back was that, although he was a fine sax player, he wanted to play the flute which was not a popular instrument in the London clubs! I saw Tubby Hayes on many club dates but he never played the flute when I saw him--just tenor, baritone and vibes, although there are a few jazz flute solos on record. British jazz fans of that period were very anti-flute.

So I do not think Harold was ever really on the "radar screen" as far as British jazz was concerned. Unfortunately, he arrived at the wrong time when the London scene was in decline, and he played the wrong instrument.

What we do know about Harold McNair is that he was born in Kingston, Jamaica, where, according to his nephew, Reggae artist Dave Bryson, "he learned music from Victor Tulloch who taught at the Alpha Boys, and Harold played with, amongst others, Gaynair and the Babba Motta band." He moved to London in the late 1950s or early 1960s, where he established himself as both a jazz and a session player on both saxophone and flute. At one time or another he worked with most of the British jazz musicians, including Ronnie Scott and Tubby Hayes. He did sessions for Quincy Jones and Philly Joe Jones, and appeared with Tubby Hayes in the Mingus movie *All Night Long*. He crossed over into the blues field with Alexis Korner and Ginger Baker's Airforce, and perhaps the most high-profile artist he worked with was the folk rock singer Donovan, with whom he recorded several albums, although frequently anonymously.

I was fortunate enough to meet Harold in London on a couple of occasions during the sixties. He was very willing to discuss the flute and the saxophone, explaining that he had switched from alto sax to tenor, as this provided less interference to his flute embouchure. After his passing, I started to get more calls for sessions, as there were few flutists who could go into the studio and improvise a part.

Nevertheless, the picture we have of Harold McNair is very incomplete. But he has left us some recordings which rank among the finest examples of jazz flute performance, and which have achieved cult status. I have used these sides to introduce McNair's work to some American jazz artists, and they have been astonished by the power and quality of his playing. Carol Sudhalter, leader of the Astoria Big Band in New York, and herself a fine flutist and saxophonist, was deeply impressed by McNair's recording *The Fence.* She contributed the following appreciation:

I have so many things I'd like to say about Harold McNair. He was, to me, the quintessential jazz flutist. His sound was quite correct, right smack in the middle of the pitch, with a nice roundness to it. It sounds to me as though he was classically trained. So that's the first thing, the correct sound--not pinched, not the "doubler" sound--and his vibrato stays within the boundaries of the note, whereas some jazz players' vibratos wave around outside the upper and lower limits of the note, which annoys me.

Next, he plays every note with his whole heart and soul. There is no holding back. When he plays with joy, as on *The Night Has a Thousand Eyes,* it is pure joy, it is very apparent, it is an energy that would be felt even by the last person in the last row of the concert hall. As with classical music, this is one of the goals I was taught to go after. When he plays a ballad, such as *You Are Too Beautiful*, he tells a whole story. It's not just one note or chorus after another, it's more like a novel or short story, with a beginning, middle and end. I get the feeling that he is telling me his whole life.

Lastly, I guess I've come to discover that I have a preference for visceral players: musicians who get into the guts of the instrument. Buzzing, singing along, not holding back, using the whole rainbow of colors, dynamics, various speeds of vibrato or using no vibrato...whatever it takes..just giving all the instrument has to give. I feel that Harold fits into this category.

Bobby Jaspar, Tubby Hayes and Harold McNair were not the only European musicians to reach a high level of accomplishment in jazz, or to be underrated. And we will encounter several more who have made significant contributions to the flute in jazz. There have also been some significant contributions from Canadian and Australian artists.

There has been a thriving jazz scene in Australia for many years, and some very fine musicians have emerged from it. Few, if any, of them have gained any long-term recognition with American audiences, however, even when they have gained the respect of American musicians. There is also some irony in the fact that one of the earliest Australian groups, known as the **Australian Jazz Quartet**, worked and recorded largely in the United States, although this has not prevented them from sinking into obscurity. One member of this group is of interest to our story, however, as he was an early jazz flutist. Dick Healey was actually an American who resided in Australia for many years, who played flute, clarinet, alto sax, and, occasionally, bass. This tendency toward multi-instrumentalism extended to other key members of the group, including drummer and vibraphonist Jack Brokenshaw, and Errol Buddle who played tenor saxophone and bassoon. The fourth member of the quartet was pianist Bryce Rohde, although the group augmented its numbers with bassists Jimmy Gannon, John Fawcett, and Jack Lander and drummers Nick Stabulas, Osie Johnson.and Frankie Capp, becoming, at different times, a quintet, a sextet or a quintet + 1.

Between 1954 and 1959, the group achieved some popularity, touring with the Dave Brubeck quartet, and appearing opposite artists such as Miles Davis, Stan Getz, Oscar Peterson, Gerry Mulligan, Chico Hamilton, Count Basie and Woody Herman. They also made five interesting and enjoyable albums for Bethlehem records, who billed them, at one point, as "the only combo in jazz history to feature a bassoon lead," (a fact that remained true until the early sixties when Wilton Felder featured the instrument alongside Hubert Laws' flute with The Crusaders). This was not the only factor that made the group unusual. In the liner notes to their Bethlehem album *The Australian Jazz Quartet* we find:

> By whatever means the AJQ became internationally famous, the key to their continued success is the extraordinary musicianship which these men have displayed from the start. The novelty of a foreign aggregation blowing characteristically American jazz has given way to the realization that jazz has no geographical boundaries, which makes it available to some and unavailable to others.
>
> Each member of the AJQ is a thoroughly schooled musician. Collectively they represent many years of intensive study and their use of several instruments within the group is proof of their desire to broaden the scope of jazz through experimentation.
>
> By now it must be common knowledge that eleven instruments are featured in the quartet. Blending the sounds of these horns to create a mood for a particular tune over the basic rhythm structure is the true skill of the Australian Jazz Quartet.

Of most interest to our study is the flute work of Dick Healey. Playing the instrument a good percentage of the time through these recordings, he demonstrates a good command of the instrument, with a sound that compares favorably with his contemporaries. The group sound reflects the interest in contrapuntal interplay typified by Brubeck and the Modern Jazz Quartet, and their experiments with instrumental color pre-date by several years similar explorations by jazz artists, especially on the West Coast.

The group could perhaps have achieved greater popularity had it stayed together. But three of the members wished to return to Australia, including Healey, even though he was American. And so the group broke up. As its recordings became unavailable, the group faded to the status of an interesting footnote to jazz history. Healey's flute work, ahead of its time as it was, deserves to be slightly more than a footnote in the history of the flute in jazz.

If Dick Healey is little known in Australia, there is another musician, also a flutist, who is a household name there. It is said that there are few Australians who haven't heard of **Don Burrows**. This talented multi-instrumentalist has received just about every honor bestowed by his native land, including honorary Doctor of Music degrees from the Universities of Sydney and Perth, the Order of Australia, an MBE--twice, once in 1988 and again in 1998, culminating in his being officially named a "Living National Treasure" by the government of Australia. Now in his eighties, Burrows has been at the forefront of the jazz world for over 60 years, and respected in many parts of the world, both as a result of his numerous international tours--South and North America, Europe, the Middle East and Asia--and through his work with the prominent musicians who have visited Australia, a list that includes Oscar Peterson, Dizzy Gillespie, Nat King Cole, Mel Tormé, Stephane Grappelli, Tony Bennett, James Morrison, Cleo Laine, and Frank Sinatra.

In his lengthy career, Burrows has seen many firsts: he was the first Australian jazz artist to win a gold record; the first to play at the Montreaux and Newport festivals; the first to play in China; the first awarded a Creative Arts Fellowship; the first inducted into the ARIA (Australian Recording Industry Association) Hall of Fame; the first director of a jazz studies course in Australia. He hosted his own television show, *The Burrows Collection*, for six years on ABC TV, has released over forty albums, and worked with a wide range of groups, from his own quartet, often featuring guitarist George Golla, to the Sydney Symphony Orchestra. Burrows plays flute, clarinet and all the saxophones, from alto to baritone. He is also well known as a composer and arranger. "A Don Burrows concert," states a publicity piece,"is a journey from classic swing and the gentle sway of Brazilian *bossa nova* to exciting modern jazz."

Beginning on what is known as the Bb school flute in Australia, then progressing to the clarinet and the tenor saxophone, Burrows finally took up the concert flute around 1958. As he recounts it, he was inspired by two things--one was hearing Herbie Mann, the other was his great love for Brazilian music, and the realization of how well the flute worked in that context. So from the late '50s until very recently, Burrows has been finding his own solution to making the flute work in a jazz setting.

During a (very!) long-distance conversation, Don confided in me, "I'm mainly a clarinet player, but I do play, and have for years, a lot of flute and alto flute." He compared himself to Sam Most in this respect. As a kid, growing up in Sydney, he heard many bands playing American-style music, and then, with the arrival of World War II, many musicians left on military duty, leaving gaps for younger musicians like him to fill. He thus got an early start on working and never looked back. It was a very practical, hands-on education.

Tell me about your early education. Did you have a teacher when you were starting out?
Not for some time. I actually was a pro before I realized I needed to study some bits and pieces.

Many of my generation were self-taught because of the circumstances with war time, you see. But the point was I was very quickly playing professionally--very quickly. Because I mucked around with jazz sitting in front of the wireless until the age of three, which meant I was taking it all in, not knowing what to call it, but just loving it, and building anything I could hit to play drums with the wireless, and then the kazoo playing along with the wireless. Then I got a B flat school flute--six holes and five keys, like a fife--and I played that in the school band when I was eight-and-a-half. So, as I started playing professionally, my mind and my ear and my pitching, were all there; I'd been doing it for years in other ways. I did my first professional gig on the clarinet three weeks after I had it. After that stage, I just put everything I taught myself on other instruments, and just followed where my fingers went. And away I went.

Following this self-teaching method, the flute seemed to come just as easily for Burrows. And he seems to have been a good teacher--his flute work exhibits the same firm tone and fluid phrasing as his work on other instruments. And he does turn to the flute for both Latin music and for ballad performance. He continued:

Once I got the flute, the big thing was that I was fighting such an affinity and love of the music of Brazil that we were starting to hear out here, on records and radio and stuff, and the flute ... It was a better instrument for me to be on for that sort of love, you know.

So many people have found that it works better for Latin music one way or another.
Yes, that's true. I found the same.

In fact, Herbie said he'd never felt comfortable playing straight bebop on the flute. He started to feel more comfortable when he added a congo player and started the African-Cuban thing.
Exactly! I felt the same. And also the more ballad type of tunes, which I love playing on the alto flute.

Were there any other flute players from the U.S. that you heard as you went along?
Mmm. No too many actually. There weren't any that sort of stood out. I can't think of anyone much. I guess Sam Most later on...

So you've been playing flute or all these years, and you've been doing a lot of Brazilian things ...
I've played in Brazil quite a bit, and in Venezuela, Argentina and Mexico.

So it's like a story of many many many hundreds of performances...
Thousands...

Thousands of performances... What percentage of time do you play the flute do you think, with all of that?
Half.

Really! And you don't only play Brazilian music, you do play some straight-ahead things?
Oh Yeah--all sorts of things. In fact, when we played in Carnegie Hall during the Newport Jazz Festival in 1972, the review by John S. Wilson the next day said, "This Australian quartet offers an amazing variety." But Australia is not a country of specialization. It's a country with a huge area and a very small population, comparatively--particularly in those days. So, musically, as well as in many other ways, the demand is that you change hats constantly. One minute I'm a jazz player and the next minute I'm a bebop alto player, then a funky bozo saxophone player, and so on. That's how it is. And we never

think about it, because that's how we all play. So we when we go over to play on Newport we just come out playing the thing we usually do, which means there's no two tunes in the set that sound similar.

Yeah, I noticed on that one Tasmanian recording, there was a sort of Herb Albert thing there as well.

That was the period when that was the thing to do. The guitar player and I flew over on a Saturday morning. We recorded that on the afternoon with the guys, finished it on Sunday morning, and were home in Sydney Australia for tea! No rehearsal or anything. We had studio guys as well who were well used to doing that sort of thing.

Paul Horn was talking about touring Russia and having to just do something at a moment's notice with Russian musicians. He just said, "Thank God for jazz musicians."

That's right. Because I had to do that in all those countries I told you about--South American countries, and in the Asian countries. I've done India, China, Iraq, and Egypt, and all over the place. That's the beauty of being a jazz musician.

Working with local musicians?

Oh, all the time. Yeah. My word, that's part of the fun. I have been lucky enough to have met and played with several of those great artists on your list. For example, Bud Shank and I were the two alto sax/clarinet/flute players in the section behind one of Frank Sinatra's tours of Australia. The conductor was Don Costa. James Newton and I played together in Germany's Freiberg Festival some years ago, along with the fine Dutch jazz flute-player, Chris Hinze. On this marvelous occasion, the three of us teamed up with three truly great classical players--William Bennett from England, Aurele Nicolet, from France, and Philippe Racine of Switzerland--in an experimental improvisational performance, using a mixture of bass flute, alto flute, concert flutes, E-flat flute and piccolo--a meeting of the classical minds and the jazz minds. No rehearsal, strictly off the cuff!!!

So, all those different kinds of music must work their way back into your playing.

Yes, and composing.

Do you have any advice for flutists wanting to explore jazz?

There's no escape from the fact that music being a language, and jazz being a dialect of that language, it's like any other language, if want to learn how to speak it, you must listen--especially to people who speak it fluently. Put the headphones on and listen. And then in the beginning, not using the eye, only the ear, try and feel out what they're hearing. If it's a flute or a trombone it doesn't matter. It's just to learn the feel from those who speak eloquently. The best--listen to the best people. It doesn't have to be the same instrument. You cannot try to do it off paper. Don't rely on notes. It's only ink.

I started jazz education in this country and it was the only thing of its kind in the southern hemisphere. And the only reason that I moved to do that was that my *alma mater*--dance halls, nightclubs, jazz joints and so on--they were disappearing at a rate of knots, because everyone was sitting around watching television and not going out. They couldn't go out as easily as I could as a child to go and hear the good players playing. So I had to go somewhere, and eventually school was the answer.

And so one day, at a Board of Studies meeting, they were all sitting round this big table, and I was the only jazz guy in the room, the others were all from opera and strings and God knows what. And one of them tried to sort of, I guess, find something to criticize out of my very successful department. He was looking through the handbook at all the courses, and he said, "Mr. Burrows, I can't help noticing you've got no books." I said, "I'm a book, that's how you learn jazz. Not out of a book. It's through people!"

You know how sophisticated the music is in India, and nothing comes out of a book there.

Not a note. And that's some of the greatest experiences I've ever had over there, just listening to Hariprasad Chaurasia and so on.

Did you ever meet him?

Oh yes. I was instrumental in getting him out to Australia. The people were spellbound. They couldn't believe what they were hearing. He's the best flute player I've ever heard.

Yeah. I sat at his feet in Bombay for several months.

It was the first time I heard him play. I was kind of distressed somehow. I couldn't go backstage and meet him. I couldn't go. I wouldn't have known what to say, and it just knocked me out so much. I didn't meet him until a week later by chance. And he said, "Weren't you the one who was supposed to come?" And I said, "Yes, I wouldn't have known what to say." I don't think I could've spoken. I was just overwhelmed. And it took me a long while to sort of realize just what an impact he had on me as a player of anything. It wouldn't have mattered if I had been an accordianist. He's the finest I've ever heard. Full stop. This was in India, around 1980, then later in Australia. I still have not recovered! He gave me one of these flutes that he'd made himself. And I've still got it. I used to play it. But I have pretty bad osteoarthritis in my fingers. In fact the thing that I did last Sunday at the conservatory with the symphony, I had to play the first movement on flute. I just made it and I think that'll be the last time I'll try. I think my flute playing days are over. I might be able to play the alto flute for a while yet, but the C flute--forget it. I ended up with corks in the holes, and heaps of corks build up on the keys and I just can't reach them. I can't bend the index fingers, and it's hard enough to play the clarinet now, but I'll keep playing the baritone and alto and tenor saxophones, and I've taken up the trombone because I don't have to use my fingers on it. I'm in a plain brass band--it's beautiful. I'm going back to the beginning on trombone. Only because of my fingers--they're pretty bad.

One of the most common expressions in Australia is "no worries," and it was amazing to me how easily Don Burrows was accepting the fact that his playing career, at least on the flute, was coming to an end. But his enthusiasm for the trombone and the brass band made his love and devotion toward music absolutely clear. He may not be able to play the flute any longer, but his accomplishments from the other side of the world have added immeasurably to the jazz flute tradition throughout the world. In that sense, he is truly a Living International Treasure.

Don Burrows was not the only musician to contribute to our story from beyond U.S. shores. Indeed, it was a Canadian, **Moe Koffman**, who was to introduce the sound of the jazz flute into popular consciousness by producing a hit record. The tune, *Swingin' Shepherd Blues*, has become something of a standard (or perhaps a cliché) for jazz flutists since it first appeared in 1958. Koffman, along with the legendary pianist Oscar Peterson, was to become one of Canada's few jazz icons, eventually receiving the Order of Canada in 1992 in recognition of his contribution to music. Koffman passed away in 2001 after an 18-month battle with cancer. While he is not well known among jazz fans, he is remembered very fondly by musicians in Canada and he can still be heard regularly on C.B.C.--the Canadian Broadcasting Company.

Morris Koffman was born in Toronto in 1928. By age nine he had already begun music studies, beginning with the violin. But later, by age thirteen, he switched to woodwinds, taking up clarinet, alto saxophone, and flute. There does not seem to have been much doubt in his mind about his future profession by this time; he soon enrolled at the Toronto Conservatory of Music, where he studied clarinet and theory. By his mid-teens he was playing in dance bands, working with some of Canada's best known bandleaders including Horace Lapp, Leo Romanelli, and Benny Louis. He later moved to New York to pursue further study and to seek work experience as a sideman. It did not take him long to make an impression, and recognition came quickly in both Canada and the U.S. He won a C.B.C. "Jazz Unlimited" poll as best alto saxophonist, and a jazz poll in *Metronome* magazine, both in 1948. The result was a record deal with Mainstream Records in New York who released his first recordings in the form of two 78 rpm records.

To establish himself in New York, Koffman worked as a sideman with a series of big bands--Sonny Durham, Buddy Morrow, Jimmy Dorsey, Ralph Flannagan, Charlie Barnet, Tex Beneke, and Doc Severinsen--and toured with several Latin ensembles. And he continued his education at the highest level, studying flute with Harold Bennett, and clarinet with Leon Russianoff, principal of the New York Philharmonic Orchestra. In all, Koffman spent about six years serving his New York apprenticeship. When the time came for him to form his own group, however, he decided to do so back in Toronto. Working with a quartet or quintet, Koffman quickly built a reputation that led to another record deal, this time with Jubilee Records. The first album he made for them included an original that he originally called *Blues A La Canadiana.* At the suggestion of the producer, however, the name was changed to *Swingin' Shepherd Blues*. Released as a single, it was a smash hit, climbing as high as 23rd in the *Billboard* chart. The effect on Koffman's career can hardly be overstated. It was not only immediate it was remarkably long-lasting. Koffman was to record the tune again several more times, but so did about 300 others; there are versions by Count Basie, Herbie Mann, Oscar Peterson, Jimmy Smith, Woody Herman, Mantovani, Henry Mancini, Ella Fitzgerald, and more recently by Natalie Cole. In 1977 it appeared as an encore (played on a bamboo flute) in a program given by the Shanghai Ballet on its Canadian tour. There was even a flute ensemble led by Buddy Collette called the *Swinging Shepherds* that issued two albums in the late 50s. Koffman eventually received a BMI award for the millionth performance of the tune.

Koffman continued to use *Swingin' Shepherd Blue*s as his signature tune, essentially for the rest of his career, until 2000. I joked with Kieron Overs, his bassist for several years, that Koffman's group must have played the tune as often as Dave Brubeck played *Take Five*. "It was exactly that," he responded. "He always held it as long as he could. It was usually the last tune."

If this tune helped put the flute on the map, it certainly boosted Moe's name recognition, but it was his high level of musicianship that brought him his bread and butter, as the main thrust of his career was in session and studio work. It was a long career, in spite of the ups and downs of the Canadian music business. I asked Kieron Overs:

He was active in the Toronto scene for what--four decades?
Yes, I reckon so, about that.
How big a scene was there in Toronto in those days? Was there a lot of competition
There were some fantastic reed players in Toronto, but they stayed more in the studios and the pit bands. In the '70s especially there was a core group there which included Moe, [trombonist] Rob

McConnell and [trumpeter] Guido Basso, and just about all the guys in [McConnell's] Boss Brass. The studio scene was booming. There was a motherlode of work in the seventies. But all those studios are gone now. It's all changed.

He must have been an awfully accomplished musician to have been in demand that long.

Well, he practiced like crazy. He was always practicing. Flute mainly--classical exercises. But his clarinet playing was gorgeous. He rarely brought it to the gig but when he did... And he could really play the alto--beautiful sound. He leaned toward the [David] Sanborn sound on some of the commercial work, but when we were just playing he had his own sound. But he was most known as a flute player with *Swingin' Shepherd Blues* and all the classical stuff.

With the security provided by his craft, Koffman was also able to pursue his art. Gathering some of Canada's finest musicians--guitarist Ed Bickert, Bernie Senensky, Don Thompson or Doug Riley on keyboards, bassist Kieron Overs and trumpeter Guido Basso among them--he fronted his own ensemble that performed regularly, particularly at George's Spaghetti House in Toronto where Koffman was music director for over twenty years. The group appeared at Expo '67, performed in 1975 at the Shaw Festival in a Mozart program with the ensemble Camerata, and was featured at the 1979 Monterey Jazz Festival. Koffman also appeared with several orchestras, including the Toronto Symphony (with which he was a soloist in Lucio Agostini's Flute Concerto in 1975), the Hamilton Philharmonic, the Sudbury Symphony Orchestra, Orchestra London Canada, the Kitchener-Waterloo, Calgary, and Edmonton symphony orchestras. The Koffman quintet toured Australia in 1980, South America in 1985, Germany in 1990, and made several appearances at U.S. universities during the decade. Koffman was also an integral part of Rob McConnell's Boss Brass from 1972 to 2000.

While Koffman was essentially the first Canadian jazzman to adopt the new bebop style in the 1940s, he was still experimenting in the 1960s, playing two saxophones at once, working with electronics and with rock and popular genres. All of this brought him unusually wide exposure for a Canadian jazz musician, culminating with appearances on the *Tonight Show* in the mid sixties, and an opportunity to lead his own big band in 1974 for Global TV's *Everything Goes.* In 1982, after a performance together in Stratford, Ontario, Koffman began an association with trumpeter Dizzy Gillespie that resulted in a series of concerts--on a Canadian tour in 1987 and at the Budapest Spring Festival in 1989--and several appearances with Gillespie's United Nations Big Band.

Koffman's flute also became a regular on Canadian radio. In 1968 C.B.C. began a news show called *As It Happens* that continues to this day. (It can be heard on many NPR stations in the U.S.) The following year Koffman released an album called *Moe's Curried Soul*, and the show's producer, Mark Starowicz, promptly adopted the title tune as the show's theme. As reported on the show's website:

> *As It Happens* has always had a special bond with Moe Koffman. He's always felt like a part of the show, probably because for years and years his theme has opened the programme. Originally we played Moe's version of *Curried Soul,* and later we used a version of his tune performed by Parachute Club. Then we went back to the original. When CBC Toronto held a big open house in November of 1996 we invited Moe and his quintet along to be part of the fun and play the theme live.

So, if anyone wants to hear what Moe sounded like, they need only tune in to the nightly broadcast of *As It Happens* on National Public Radio.

The diversity of genres Koffman explored is reflected in his recorded output. During his career he released more than thirty albums, which included some fine jazz work sandwiched in between more commercial work. He was particularly successful with a series of LPs in the 1970s devoted to music by classical composers: Bach, Berlioz, Debussy, Gluck, Grieg, Mozart, and Vivaldi, the Bach and Vivaldi albums reaching gold record status in Canada.

Koffman's recordings are hard to get hold of now; he is best remembered for the series of honors he received during his professional career: PRO Canada's William Harold Moon Award in 1981, the Toronto Arts Award for music in 1991, induction into the Order of Canada in 1993 and the Canadian Music Hall of Fame in 1997. He was named Flutist of the Year by the Annual Jazz Report Awards for 1993 and 1994, and was honored by SOCAN in 1993 for jazz songwriting.

Perhaps the best indication of the quality of the Moe Koffman quintet is the number of guest appearances Dizzy Gillespie made with the group. I put it to Kieron Overs:

If Dizzy chose to play with him that says a lot about his jazz playing.
Yes, well he had a lot of fun playing with the band. We would play Moe's material basically for the first half of the show, and he would play flute the whole time. Then we would play *Swingin' Shepherd Blues* and we would take a break. In the second half Dizzy would come out and play a bunch of tunes and then Dizzy would bring out Moe and we'd play *Night in Tunisia* and *Salt Peanuts* or something. And that was the gig. We did that for about five years or maybe longer.

Koffman's pianist and music director during these years was Bernie Senensky--a Moe Koffman tribute band, led by Senensky, tours Canada to this day. I asked him how long he worked with Moe:

I worked with Moe for twenty years plus. I joined the band in January 1980, but I had toured with him in '79.
You did quite a few concerts with Dizzy didn't you?
Yes. Dizzy was a special guest with the Moe Koffman Quintet for about seven years. We did several tours, mostly in Canada, but some in the States. And we also went to Budapest, Hungary.
Moe recorded in a variety of different genres, including a lot of commercial work. But if he was free to play, or record, whatever music he liked best, would it be straight-ahead bebop?
Oh definitely. That was closest to his heart. That's the music he grew up with. His major influence was originally Charlie Parker, and later Cannonball Adderley.
I also hear some of the West Coast players, like Lenny Neihaus. But it is his flute work we are most interested in. He kind of put the flute on the map with **Swingin' Shepherd Blues.**
Yes, that happened in the fifties. '56 I think--somewhere around there. And within a year it became really big. That was his claim to fame, his signature tune, and we played it at every concert.
Every concert? You must have played it as many times as Brubeck played **Take Five?**
Well, almost.
I understand Moe was a real workaholic. Rob McConnell was telling me that whenever the rest of the band was taking a break, Moe would be in a corner someplace practicing, particularly the

flute. Was that your recollection?

Yes. He was always practicing. He was very conscientious. He was very business-like about his career and the group, very fastidious about starting on time and so forth, at concerts but especially in clubs. We used to play George's Spaghetti House [in Toronto] for one week every month, and the sets were pre-determined, and we used to end each set to the second just about. He would time it to the second. He was very concerned about details, let's say.

How many horns did he bring with him when he played that kind of gig? Alto and flute?

Alto [sax], flute and soprano.

And how many items did he play on flute?

About half, I guess.

So it wasn't just an occasional double for him, for extra color, or something exotic.

Oh, no, no. He was a real flutist. He played classical music, a lot of Bach. He was really schooled in the classics. That was his training.

So during the heyday of that group, was he the best known jazz musician in Canada, given that Oscar Peterson was pretty much part of the U.S. scene?

Yes, I would say so. Let's say, next to Oscar, he was always the most famous Canadian jazz musician. Moe, for many years, was considered the top jazz musician, and the top jazz group.

Of course there weren't too many top quality flutists in jazz at that time.

Not really. Not that specialized in the instrument, and had such high visibility, and had so many hits. Moe specialized on the flute.

Tell me about the tribute band.

The idea originally came from the radio station *91.1 Jazz FM* in Toronto. For many years they had a series called "Live at the Ontario Science Center" They had an auditorium there. It took place once a month during spring and fall seasons and they would record them for airplay. And this went on for many, many years. So after Moe passed away, they had a tape of a concert from, I think, 1985 that they decided they wanted to release. They had just instigated their own record company and their first release was going to be *Moe Koffman Live at the Toronto Science Center, 1985*. I think they included a couple of interviews that Moe did on the air. And to correspond with the release of this they decided to put on a concert, a tribute to Moe Koffman at the Science Center. They called me to be the musical director, and we decided to use some of the people that played in Moe's group along with me. Ed Bickert was not playing guitar any more so we used Lorne Lofsky who used to sub for Ed, he was a fantastic guitar player on his own. Bill McBirnie was in the group also, he was chosen to play the flute.

So they decided to represent Moe purely with a flute player?

Yes, to begin with. But then we decided Moe was more than a flute player. That was only half of it. So we would have to get someone to play the alto and soprano sax. So we decided on Kirk McDonald. So we had a six-piece group, with Kieron Overs on bass, and Terry Clarke was the drummer. Moe also did some pop-fusion stuff, theme albums. That was another side of him. And he used some studio players for those recordings. A lot of the material was originals that I wrote, and I enjoyed playing that music so much that I got hold of the original charts from Moe's widow, and made that the music we played with this group. So we are re-creating Moe Koffman concerts. All the music is arrangements played exactly the way Moe played them.

Will you make a recording of this?

I don't know. We have done a few concerts since then, but I can't say whether we will actually record the group. For all of Moe Koffman's fans, to hear all the original charts the way Moe played them is quite a kick. It is kind of nostalgic, but the music sounds as great as ever. And the *Swingin' Shepherd Blues* has had a lot of versions made of it.

In his final decade, Koffman continued to compose, and to perform, both as a soloist and with his quintet, at clubs and festivals. Beginning in 1989, and through the following decade, he booked orchestral musicians for shows such as *Phantom of the Opera, Showboat*, and *Ragtime*. He made his last recording, *The Moe Koffman Project*, in the summer of 1999. His last public performance was in June 2000 for the Downtown Jazz Festival, in Toronto. At the time of his death, he was inducted (as an inaugural member) into Canada's Jazz and Blues Hall of Fame.

Like the other members of this group of pioneers, whatever the final assessment may be of his place in the history of jazz, his contribution to the establishment of the flute in this music is inestimable.

It is perhaps ironic that every member of this first wave of jazz flutists was male, given that, as we have seen, the flute's association with women was a major barrier to its adoption by the earliest generations of jazz musicians. It was a change of both attitudes and performance styles that allowed these multi-instrumentalists to pick up the flute at a time when women instrumentalists were still struggling to break into jazz. Both of these barriers were broken in the early 1970s with the emergence of **Barbara Anne "Bobbi" Humphrey**, the first woman ever signed by Blue Note Records, who also happened to be a flutist.

While studying at Southern Methodist University in Dallas, Texas, Humphrey performed at a talent contest which included Dizzy Gillespie among the judges. Dizzy encouraged Bobbi to move to New York and pursue a career in jazz. It tuned out to be excellent advice--that career continues to this day. It received a major boost after a successful appearance at the Apollo Theater's. She subsequently worked with major jazz artists from Duke Ellington to Lee Morgan, and R&B stars such as Stevie Wonder. Her recordings have included a number of commercial successes and Humphrey has received numerous awards as both flutist and vocalist. Since 1994 she has recorded for her own label, Paradise Sounds Records. She heads up her own publishing and management companies, Bobbi Humphrey Music and Innovative Artist Management. She is a record producer, composer of commercial jingles and TV theme music, businesswoman and political activist. She has organized fundraising concerts for the United Negro College Fund and spoken before the General Assembly of the United Nations about the Ehiopian famine in the 1980s. According to former New York City Mayor David N. Dinkins, "Bobbi Humphrey's dedication to artistic excellence is matched only by her social activism and concern for those in need."

Throughout it all she has continued to perform and record as a flutist, primarily in the crossover realm between jazz and R&B. Before she came on the scene the flute in jazz and women in jazz were both novelties. It is no accident that the list of flute specialists in jazz discussed in Part Five below contains more female than male performers. They all owe a dept to Bobbi Humphrey.

The Next Wave

It is difficult to place an exact chronological sequence on the emergence of the first flutists in jazz; as we have seen, several came out of the starting gate together. The same is true of the next wave of jazz flutists. The way they are presented here is slightly artificial, however, as I have chosen to begin with those who are no longer with us. Another group of pioneers were also emerging at this time who were available for me to interview, however; they will speak for themselves in the next section. Taken together, their work reveals some basic trends in the development of the flute in jazz.

One thing that stands out is that jazz flutists do not fall easily into schools; these performers do not have a great deal in common. This is in contrast to the history of the tenor saxophone in jazz, for example, with followers of Coleman Hawkins, Lester Young and John Coltrane forming distinct schools, or lines of influence. Nevertheless, the work of these artists exhibits two basic approaches to making the flute work as a jazz instrument.

We find one group of players, such as Jerome Richardson, Moe Koffman, Bobby Jaspar and Tubby Hayes, working to develop a jazz technique on the flute, to bring it up to the same expressive level they were able to achieve on the saxophone. These players were not necessarily able to pursue a thorough conservatory training on the instrument; that path was being followed by Frank Wess. The members of this group who took college flute classes were saxophonist Leo Wright, who did it against his will, and guitarist Les Spann, who was required to elect a minor. Regarding their efforts, it was Richardson who made the most cogent assessment, and he was still unsatisfied.

At the same time as we see these players attempting to bring the flute into jazz, we can see Sahib Shihab and Harold McNair making early attempts to bring jazz into the flute, introducing vocalizations and other techniques to enable the flute to express "them dirty blues," a process that would be taken up later by Sam Most, Yusef Lateef and, above all, by Rahsaan Roland Kirk. If these do indeed form two performance schools, then the first group was to be followed by artists such as Frank Wess, Bud Shank, and Hubert Laws, while the second has attracted Nicole Mitchell and James Newton, among others.

Of the next group, five have passed away since I interviewed them for this book, but four are still active and continue to perform on the instrument.

As we have said, it is hard to say exactly who was the first to pick up the flute, or the first to work with it seriously in a jazz ensemble. Apart from Wayman Carver and Harry Klee, Jerome Richardson is said to be the earliest to record on the instrument with his 1949 date for Lionel Hampton. Bud Shank was recording around the same time with Stan Kenton. But another fine flutist was actually making recordings as early as 1946. It is with him that we will begin.

Buddy Collette: Jackie Robinson of the Networks

"…an inspiration to everyone who meets him and a [jazz] historian's dream"
R.J. Smith

"The thing about Buddy was that when he got his foot in the door, he kept opening it up for other musicians. That's the kind of person he was." *John Clayton*

"Musicians should be judged on how they play, not the color of their skin"
Buddy Collette

William "Buddy" Collette was born on August 6th, 1921 in the Watts district of Los Angeles. Beginning on the piano at a very early age, and then taking up the saxophone, and later the clarinet, Collette had formed his first group by the time he was twelve. He had already settled on the idea of a career in jazz after attending a Louis Armstrong concert with his parents. His motivation was reinforced by the company he kept as an adolescent, as he met and befriended several future jazz luminaries, including saxophonist Dexter Gordon, drummer Chico Hamilton, trombonist Britt Woodman, and bassist Charles Mingus. Mingus was his classmate in high school and a member of that early ensemble, and Collette would remain a close friend of the bassist until Mingus' death in 1979, appearing on several of his recordings. But while Mingus' life and career in music was stormy and volatile, Collette was the model of courtesy and responsibility. He has not shied away from controversy, having been in the forefront of the battle for racial integration in the music business. But he has conducted this battle without rancor, and in the context of a long career characterized by professional excellence. Sadly, Buddy suffered a stroke in 1998, rendering him unable to perform until his passing in 2010. Overall, however, he has made a very significant contribution to the flute in jazz.

Buddy's life and career have been well documented in an autobiography, written with Steven Isoardi, *Jazz Generations: A Life in American Music*, as well as a recorded memoir issued on two CDs as *Buddy Collette: A Jazz Audio Biography* (Lawndale, CA: Issues Records, 1994). His story provides a very different perspective on the "jazz life" than the lurid stories found in many musicians' autobiographies.

Buddy's early development as a musician was fostered by several devoted teachers at Jordan High School, and by 1942, at age 21, he was already working steadily in music. He played initially with Les Hite's band, a well-known Los Angeles-based outfit that, at one time or another, included Lionel Hampton, Dizzy Gillespie, T-Bone Walker, Marshall Royal, Joe Wilder, Al Morgan, Woodman and Lawrence Brown. Another alumnus of this band was Lloyd Reese, who went on to build quite a reputation as a music teacher in Los Angeles. Seeing the results of Reese's teaching on some of his own students, Collette began to study with him, joining an elite group that was eventually to include Mingus, Ben Webster, tenor saxophonist and oboist Bob Cooper, and Eric Dolphy. Reese's training was very rigorous, grounded in theory and keyboard skills, and his students were exceptionally well prepared. It certainly paid off for Buddy, who quickly found himself in demand, working with popular bands and participating in radio broadcasts and movie soundtracks. He was beginning to make good money, but rather than letting this go to his head, as some of his contemporaries tended to do, Collette chose a different direction, one that was to characterize the rest of his career. He bought a new suit and a new car, but decided against many of the other temptations that have led many young musicians astray. As he recalls:

> I'm 19 or 20 and the chorus girls start to notice me. Five or six of the most beautiful women in the world want to ride with me. And they were into all kinds of good stuff--drinking, smoking a little bit. But I knew I couldn't go the party route because I wanted to be a good musician and take care of my health. Two or three of these girls would ask me over for a late dinner but I had to get up early and practice for my lessons with Lloyd. It was beautiful to have something to keep you strong, and study did that for me at the time.
>
> We all drank a little. But I stayed away from it because when you're studying and you wake up with a heavy head, it's pretty hard when Lloyd Reese asks you to "play that a tone higher." You've got a fight on your hands!

It is with this attitude that Collette went on to pursue his career, becoming a mentor to many younger musicians, and a leader of the music community in the Los Angeles area.

With the advent of World War II, Collette joined the service, where he led one of the two navy jazz bands. (The other, directed by altoist Marshall Royal, included Jerome Richardson.) Once released from the military, he utilized the GI Bill to further his education, attending the California Academy of Music and the American Operatic Laboratory, working with private teachers on both clarinet and saxophone, and developing his arranging skills by studying with one of Stan Kenton's staff arrangers, Franklyn Marks.

It was at this time that Buddy picked up the flute and began to study it in earnest. "I played the flute because I liked the sound of it," he reports. Writing in *Jazz Generations,* he recalls hearing a recording of some modern woodwind pieces by Alec Wilder, in particular one that featured flutist Julius Baker and that included sixteenth-note phrases with wide intervals. "Wow!" he said to himself, "This is the first time I've heard the flute with that kind of exposure."

> I could hear some possibilities with this instrument. There were things that hadn't been done that I wanted to try. That was why I started playing flute. About this time Lee Young made a record called *Route de Flute*, and Harry Klee, first flutist at Columbia Studios, played a jazz solo on flute. That also inspired me.

By chance, Buddy ran into a friend who had pawned his flute and couldn't afford to get it out. Buddy went down and bought it for forty dollars. It was not a very good instrument, and his first teacher insisted that he buy a better one. But it got him started. And he worked hard at mastering the instrument with private instruction from Marty Rudiman and then with Henry Woephner, whom he describes as "the top flutist at MGM." At the same time, Collette was freelancing in the L.A. area with such bands as the Stars of Swing, a co-operative band with Collette, Mingus, Woodman and Lucky Thompson, with which he first began to feature the flute, as well as with Edgar Hayes, Louis Jordan, Benny Carter, and

Gerald Wilson, with whom he made his first, ground-breaking, but, unfortunately unissued, flute recordings. As he reports in *Jazz Generations:*

> It wasn't until about 1948, '49, '50 that the flute began to generate some interest. Even with the Stars of Swing at the Down Beat in 1946, I might play it on only one number and people would ask, "What was that you played?" It was never an instrument that had a foreground role, playing the lead by itself and soloing. So it was very rare before the late 1940s.

Adding the flute to his range of instrumental capabilities opened new doors for Buddy. In particular, he joined, and helped develop, an inter-racial symphony orchestra, creating an opportunity for himself and other black musicians from a primarily jazz background to gain greater exposure to classical literature. (A fortunate by-product was the amalgamation of the formerly segregated musicians unions in the Los Angeles area, locals 767 and 47, a process in which Buddy played a central role.) This activity, plus Buddy's facility on a range of woodwind instruments, brought him to the attention of Jerry Fielding, the contractor for the band on the Groucho Marx show *You Bet Your Life.*

Fielding happened to hear Buddy play a flute solo from Bizet's *Carmen* with the symphony orchestra and was greatly impressed, particularly when he learned that Buddy had only been playing flute for two years. Fielding was actually trying to get in touch with Marshall Royal to fill a vacancy in the *You Bet Your Life* band, only to learn that Royal had left town with Count Basie. "It's a shame you don't play clarinet and sax too," he told Buddy, assuming he was a symphony player. When he learned of Buddy's full capabilities on all these instruments he hired him on the spot. Buddy was to stay with the show from 1950 to 1959, becoming the first black musician to get a permanent spot in a West Coast studio band, making him, as he titles a chapter of his autobiography, *The Jackie Robinson of the Networks.* It was a great time for Buddy, as he built a solid reputation for his musicianship and professionalism. It didn't hurt that he won the *Down Beat* poll on clarinet in 1956, and that Groucho took every opportunity to promote his "jazz guy" both on and off the air. But it was his next project that was to bring Buddy Collette to national prominence.

The person who played a major role in Buddy's musical life at this juncture has actually helped launch the careers of several jazz flutists, including Buddy, Paul Horn, Eric Dolphy and Charles Lloyd, and continues to do so today, fifty years later, featuring Eric Person, Erik Lawrence, and Karolina Strassmeyer in his more recent ensembles. Drummer Chico Hamilton, 2004 recipient of the National Endowment for the Arts Jazz Master's award, had known Buddy since high school days and had worked with him, Charles Mingus, and others on the Central Avenue jazz scene in Los Angeles. He had figured prominently as the drummer in Gerry Mulligan's first quartet, and then gone on to work with Lena Horne. Buddy joined him with Horne for a week in 1955, at which time Chico mentioned that he was ready to leave the singer and form a group of his own:

> Chico and I always talked about doing something together, but now he was planning on leaving Lena Horne. Before that Chico had met Fred Katz, a pianist and cellist, who was playing piano with Lena, just before Gerry [Mulligan] started. Chico and Fred had also talked about getting a group together. Chico wanted to use Fred on piano and then have him play cello as a soloist between sets, when the band was off the stand. When they had both left Lena, they decided to

form a band, and called me.

They brought in bassist Carson Smith who had been Chico's rhythm section partner with Mulligan and then, by some stroke of fate, found the then unknown guitarist Jim Hall working in a bookstore. Thus the original Chico Hamilton Quintet was born. They started working in a bar called Strollers close to Hermosa in Long Beach, home of the popular Lighthouse jazz club, and were quickly picked up by DJ Sleepy Stein on KFOX who broadcast them live from the club. They quickly became something of a sensation, packing Strollers almost immediately as a result of the broadcasts. Soon they were on the road, touring extensively and recording several albums for Dick Bock at World Pacific Records. The reason for their success was the unique sound that emerged from the ensemble. George T. Simon, in the sleeve notes to their first album, had this to say about it:

> No chamber-music style group to come along during the past few years swings as much as the Chico Hamilton Quintet. Its exciting drive, light, delicate, yet assured, and its highly original sound, made it the highlight of last year's Newport Jazz Festival and subsequently the most talked-of new jazz group of 1956.
>
> This is jazz that is modern not because of any self-conscious desire to sound different, but rather because it has intelligently and with feeling broadened the tonal basis of jazz to capture some daringly different sounds. As such, it is modern jazz with a purpose, as well as modern jazz with exquisite taste and imagination, and through it all a definite jazz beat.
>
> The instrumentation of these groups accounts in part for their unique and refreshing sounds. One features an instrument hardly ever heard in jazz before, the cello, used not only as a solo vehicle but also in combinations with the guitar, with the clarinet, and with *another rather unorthodox jazz instrument, the flute* (italics mine).

How this particular instrumentation came about was, according to Buddy, another one of those happy accidents that have been so much a part of the jazz flute story. He told me about this during one of our conversations:

Tell me about your time with Chico Hamilton. You made a lot of records?
Yes, five or six. There's a whole boxed set of the things we did with Chico. Paul Horn told me about that.
Now how did that come about–that instrumentation you had with Chico. Was it something he dreamed up? Was it accidental? or do you...
Chico was very close to Fred Katz who was in that first group; they were working together with Lena Horne. Fred was a piano player but he also played cello. When we first had the group in Long Beach, Fred played piano. Jim Hall was there too but nobody learned how great Jim was because with Fred playing all the chords, Jim was just staying out of the way. They didn't know about his talent before that. This guy was working in a book store; Chico went and found him. But when they started their rehearsal--I didn't start with the band, for the first week or so there was a guy named Bob Hardaway--Fred was an aggressive player and he would play all the chords. Jim was waiting for a

chance to play a chord. So they played in Long Beach for the first week and nobody heard Jim Hall except for his solos. Then I came up with a bunch of music that I had written. Fred's job at that time was to play piano with the band and then at intermission to get his 'cello and go out and play a couple of concertos. Nobody wrote for the cello at that time, it was just the piano and the horn and guitar, so that was the sound. Except that the stand was very small with railings on the side and the piano was at the back. And so Fred would start playing the cello right in front and then he's the kind of guy who would play for half an hour even if he was supposed to play for 15 minutes. But one night the club owner said "Let's get back on the stand guys." So we got back up there, but he couldn't get back to the piano when we were all in our places. He was caught out front with the cello, so he had to try and play what he played on the piano, you know, the same lines. And then, when we heard the sound, we heard Jim for the first time playing those nice chords in the right place, not just where they were written, but right where you need them. It just kind of happened.

Apart from the cello's role with that group, were you also focusing on flute for that kind of sound? Because it starts to make more sense with that kind of instrumentation, cello, guitar and flute.

Well the sound of the group began to happen at that point with instruments that worked well together. When Fred wasn't playing the piano, you see, the flute and guitar was a lovely sound and there were times when we would have flute and cello. There would be more changes of color.

But before that, with the more traditional instrumentation, you were playing more tenor?

No, I was playing a lot of flute. We were getting those colors you see, but the instruments attract each other. When you have the flute and the cello you've got a sound--flute and cello, you've got a real sound. Then there's the tenor also, and the clarinet. But you have a lot of space, a lot open spaces, you see. We had more sounds when he wasn't playing the piano, because when you have the piano playing chords, and the guitar playing chords, you don't have a sound, you have a whole lot of chords, and it's too heavy.

I have some idea of what you are talking about. I had a trio with flute, guitar, and cello. We could do classical pieces and jazz.

Well that's what we had--we did a lot of classical stuff. We had a traditional jazz group, but Chico would play sticks, or he also had the brushes, so we could play a chamber style. People couldn't figure out what we were doing. Each tune was different You can catch a whole album of that group and you had eight different tracks, and they were all different. They could be from a different group but still we were the same because of the personality of the guys.

Is that where they coined the term Chamber Jazz?

Possibly, yes. But, as I said, it was just a thing where we had other colors. And Jim developed more and more when he had the room to put the colors in. He knew what to do. And he still has that talent--that's why he keeps going like that. He left us and went with Jimmy Giuffre. And Giuffre had his own trio with country-type clarinet (sings, de-de-de-de-de-de-da). I went and heard him at the same place where we used to play. Jim was a different guitar player when he went with Giuffre. I told him this and he said "you have to play what fits the occasion," and that's the way he was with us--he's really flexible. We enjoyed playing together. He's probably the only guitar player I ever met who would click on every little groove. I'd change the groove and he'd change right with me. He calls all the time now just to say hello to me. But that was the basis of the group--we had a lot of talented people.

When I spoke with Chico Hamilton in New York, he was very clear about Buddy's importance to that first group. "The reason I got started," he told me, "is because of Buddy Collette. Buddy played flute, clarinet, and alto, and tenor, so we utilized all the instruments."

You knew Buddy back in those days, so it was natural for you to invite him in?
Buddy and I grew up together out in Los Angeles. Buddy Collette, Charlie Mingus, Jack Kelson, and all those fellows. We all grew up together.

Now he told me a story about the cello in the lineup, originally being a little bit of an accident.
Exactly. Originally the group was going to have French horn, but the first day of rehearsal John Graas, who was a very popular French horn player in L.A., had a heart attack and at that particular time I was doing a thing with Fred Katz, with a singer, and I told them what happened. So Fred said, "Why don't I come over with the cello?" So I thought, "dynamite," and that's how it all got started. Fred was playing cello when I was with Lena Horne. When Lena was carrying a big group he would double on cello as well as piano. The bottom line to it man, is the fact we just happened to be five guys in the right place at the right time.

Buddy mentioned that it really worked with the cello because Jim Hall could play a lot more and it really brought him out.
Yeah, well, everybody's got a concept!

You're credited with inventing this thing called "chamber jazz." Do you laugh when you hear these terms, or is that a reasonable description? You know how writers like to put categories on things.
Well, that's the writer's thing. I didn't call it chamber jazz.

But it was very different from what was going on. What year did you first put this together?
It was in 1955.

So what was coming out in 1955, at least from the East Coast, was hard bop really. It couldn't be further away from what you were doing!
Exactly.

Without a doubt, the Hamilton quintet was a phenomenon. Collette remembers, "It was a fabulous period for us. We had a new, exciting group and all of us were very enthusiastic. We all wrote and we had plenty of music. We loved to rehearse and were very successful. Our sound came as we worked together and spent so much time rehearsing and performing."

Listening to the group's recordings, the range of sonorities available to this instrumentation is certainly striking, but so are the care of the arrangements and the freshness of the improvisations. What is not so well known is that, during live performance, the group engaged in a lot of free improvisation. As Buddy recalls:

> ... although we all wrote, we did more improvisation. We didn't even need music, although we did have a lot of things written down. Fred Katz liked to write everything out. Jim Hall sometimes would write pieces out. But 50 percent of the time we'd just play--improvise, not even discussing what we would play. Somebody would start a line and the line would continue

with answers, fugue statements, recapitulations, and those kinds of things. It might have begun with just a look, and before we knew it all our minds would be locked into one. We'd frequently get requests for certain pieces but couldn't play them again for any amount of money!

It was in the spirit of the times, with similar experiments going on within the Dave Brubeck quartet on the West Coast, and the Teddy Charles group in New York, among others. One song in particular, a composition of Buddy's called *Blue Sands*, typified this approach within the Hamilton group. It was built around an exercise to develop high notes and wide leaps on the flute. It was a very quiet piece but, to the surprise of the group, it had an electrifying effect on audiences.

They first tried it in a club where the audience had been very noisy. They had tried playing louder to overcome this, without success. The next night Buddy suggested they tried the opposite approach. "I took the flute and played the line, and it took about fifteen seconds before the house got so quiet I couldn't believe it. People stopped talking and started looking as if to say, 'What's going on?' They hadn't heard this kind of approach." Subsequently, the piece became a regular flute feature for Buddy, constantly evolving, and lasting longer and longer with each performance, and seeming always to calm down and quiet audiences. "It seemed to have a hypnotic kind of control over the public...You could see it. Whatever it meant to you, whatever it meant to me, it always made people kind of quiet." Finally, they played it as the final piece in their set at the 1956 Newport Jazz Festival, causing a sensation by getting quieter and quieter!

> We finally ended the piece with a triple *piano*, the softest we'd ever done. Chico was on mallets and I was trilling on the flute, walking away from the mike. For about ten seconds we just stood there with our hearts pounding. No one moved. No applause Nothing. Then, suddenly, the crowd leapt out of the trance. They screamed and shouted... that was the biggest ovation anyone had received up to this point in the festival.

The final act of the evening, right after the Hamilton quintet's set, was the Duke Ellington orchestra. As Buddy was coming down from the stage he walked right into Ellington. "Wow!" said Duke, "You all made it hot for me, didn't you?" Ellington responded with the famous *Diminuendo and Crescendo in Blue* with twenty seven choruses from tenor player Paul Gonsalves. It was the only response he could think of; no one else in jazz was exploring the quiet end of the sound spectrum.

Later that year, after Buddy had been replaced by Paul Horn, the Hamilton group recorded a TV special. George Lane, in the liner notes for the resulting album, records the following interchange.

> "I hope," the announcer for the television station said nervously, "that I'm not saying the wrong thing, but I couldn't help thinking that your music sounds almost classical at times. It's so soft."
> "Jazz," Chico Hamilton told the announcer and the thousands who were viewing the program on a Los Angeles video channel, "doesn't have to be loud. It can swing and be soft too."

Ellington agreed with him, apparently. Some time later he called Buddy up and invited him to join his band, citing his admiration for Buddy's flute playing. Buddy could not get away from his professional and family commitments in Los Angeles, however, and had to turn him down, although he did work with him about ten years later on a movie score, along with another flute pioneer, Bud Shank.

After some time with Hamilton, Buddy decided to move on. Chico remembers: "Buddy had a family. Buddy was a single parent. He had a family to raise, and that's why he didn't come out on the road." Buddy's recollection is very similar:

How long did that last with Chico?
Oh, I would say about a year. It was a great group, the music was great but the people didn't know how great it was. We were doing all right, but there was a lot of traveling. I was doing a lot of studio work then and I was losing money with being on the road, flying back and forth two or three times a week to do jobs. It wasn't a money thing, but my family was getting big. And how far can you go? I sent Charles Lloyd to Chico, I sent Eric to him, Paul Horn also, so he had players who worked out well with him, so I shouldn't have stayed too long. I had stayed long enough. I had shown what I could do. But for Chico, now he's got the sound, where's he going to go? I didn't feel I had to keep going in that direction. I got my own group and we did *Man of Many Parts, Nice Day*, I did about 12 or 15 albums. You do what you've got to do, that's what makes you the person you are. Later I did the *Flute Talk* album with James Newton.

Buddy is referring to the spate of recordings that he made after leaving the Hamilton group. In fact, his time was now divided between studio work, including more time with Groucho's show, and jazz performance. The flute played a vital role in both. There was still a limited numbers of players on call who could play the instrument, Buddy recalls: "I also had an advantage with the flute. It began to get popular around 1950, 1951, 1952. Before then most saxophone players just played clarinets and saxophones. When it became in demand for saxophone players to have clarinet and flute also, I was ready... I also played a lot of piccolo, alto flute and bass flute." This was in the studio. But doubling remained an essential element of Buddy's jazz work also.

> In my working band I always had four instruments on the stand with me. I was playing alto and tenor, flute and clarinet. Later on I began to play more tenor. I liked both saxes, but in the context of a small group, I felt I got more contrast between the flute, clarinet, and tenor. With the tenor it was a bigger contrast than with the alto. One night recently, I just had my flute and tenor on the stand and it didn't seem complete. I like to look at the clarinet, and in the course of the evening I'll figure out one tune or so to play on it. But three is enough! One is plenty, two is a headache, and three... You wonder about the person who wants to do that!

Yet Buddy did do it, and he did it at a very high level for a very long period of time. As Nat Hentoff writes in the notes to one of Buddy's later recordings, "Versatility has been the downfall of many jazzmen, but Collette seems able to make the switch from one instrument to another with the utmost ease, and without the tone of any one suffering. Always graceful, he has a flair for melody." Ian Carr and Digby Fairweather, in *A Rough Guide to Jazz*, refer to Collette as "a brilliant clarinetist and flautist (sic) who has made a better case than many post-swing players for the use of these instruments in jazz."

Such plaudits could act as a summary of Buddy's body of recorded work, but his music was also quite advanced for its time. Indeed, Buddy ran into some initial resistance to his first recording, *Man of Many Parts.* Lester Koenig of Contemporary Records had given Buddy the date based on the reputation he had been developing with Chico Hamilton, but Koenig didn't know much about jazz, and Buddy's music was not what he was used to. As Buddy recalls in *Jazz Generations*:

> When I told him who was on the date... he didn't recognize any of the names. In addition, I had different music that wasn't like what he had been getting from the lighthouse guys. "Jungle Pipe," for example, had a twelve-tone structure.
> Poor Les. When he came into the recording session, he just couldn't get his beat going, and as the day went by his face got longer and longer. At the end of the day, he said, "I thought you were going to bring me a jazz album."
> I looked at him and said, "I thought I did."
> "But I didn't know any of the people, and I didn't know any of the music that you played."
> "Well, let's just forget it."
> I knew I had some sounds there, but I was tired and just disgusted. I left and didn't call him back. After eight, ten days, Les called me. I didn't even want to hear him.
> "What is it, you found something else wrong?"
> "Buddy, you can record for me anytime you want."
> "What are you saying?"
> "I've had a chance to sit with this record, with Shelly [Manne] and André [Previn]. They all said the guy's got something."

They were right; *Man Of Many Parts* is a fine recording, and Buddy went on to record several more jazz albums of similar quality over the next few years, each of which featured his flute playing on several tracks. With the arrival of the late sixties and early seventies, however, came tough times for jazz. As with many artists, there was a lull in Buddy's recording activity, at least as far as jazz albums under his own name were concerned. He focused more and more on studio work, recording numerous sessions as a sideman with popular artists such as Frank Sinatra, Nat Cole, Percy Faith, Helen Reddy, Quincy Jones, Carole King and Ella Fitzgerald, and working on TV shows with Danny Kaye and Carol Burnett, while finding time to continue his teaching and mentoring activities. Later, he was in demand as an organizer and contractor for big bands, particularly at the Monterey Jazz Festival, where he put together outfits for Mingus and Monk (both in 1964), Dizzy Gillespie (1965) and Gil Evans (1966).
It is a career that in many ways mirrors that of Jerome Richardson, both in its scope and in its emphasis on excellence and continued growth and study. And like Richardson, he found his way back into the recording studio to make jazz albums in more recent years. Unlike Richardson, however, he has received recognition on a national level, being invited to the Library of Congress in Washington DC in 1996, to perform with his own big band, and to be honored for his contributions to music over half a century. Sadly, it was not long after this that Buddy's career as a performer was cut short by a stroke. In his eighties, and confined to a wheelchair, he remained mentally vibrant and unfailingly gracious as I learned during my visits to his home. I asked him how things were when he first started learning the flute. He recalled:

We didn't hear too many flutists in the early days. The only ones we heard were Wayman Carver with Chick Webb--just little fills. I did something with Gerald Wilson in 1946, but they never released it. It was with a big band. The full band was playing and they miked the flute the best they could, but they didn't know how to record it. It wasn't till... I did some things with Spud Murphy, Abe Most and then, of course, with Chico Hamilton. Red Norvo would play vibes. I know Frank Wess was recording then, but we got to the point where we could get a sound out of them. The flute has to be isolated you know, and you have to put mutes in the trumpets.

Jerome Richardson, back in the fifties, commented that it was not obvious how to make the flute work for jazz, finding the right articulations and phrasing. Does that make sense to you?

It does make sense, but it depends who you are listening to, the different approaches that people have. I think some of the doublers--I doubled myself, and Jerome was a doubler, and Frank Wess of course, playing a lot of jazz on the saxophone. It just depends whether you want to maintain a good sound on the flute like a classical guy would play it, without getting too jazzy.

Well you certainly have to approach it differently from the saxophone.

Of course. The sound and everything is different. And you can growl on the flute. But if you can swing on the saxophone, you swing on the flute, you swing on the oboe, and everything. But a whole lot of guys, like Frank Wess and James Newton, approach it like they want to get a good sound as a voice, not so much playing fast, or high, but it's a question of presenting the instrument and your story in that context. Because when you're doubling, the way I always thought about it--you've got your clarinet and that's one approach, you know?--the sound of the clarinet and the way you play that. There's a sound you have to get, and then playing in a register that's not so much appealing to me. It's not so much that I would copy Benny Goodman or Artie Shaw, although I liked those guys. I would play in the middle register or low register, for example, but I still wouldn't sound like [Barney] Bigard who I loved. And with the flute, approaching it with my voice, what did I think a flute player should sound like? And that was the way I would approach it. It was almost like comparing the classical flute with the jazz guys. I liked the jazz guys, but the only ones I heard in person in the early years was Harry Klee who was with me on my album called *The Swinging Shepherds*. We also had Bud [Shank] and Paul [Horn].

Which instrument did you start out on?

I started on piano first, then the saxophone--from 12 to about 15--then clarinet, then flute. I was very sound conscious with the saxophone. I got a good sound and really studied the saxophone, so when I did play flute I was a pretty good player. I had been through the service--I didn't pick up flute there but Jerome Richardson was already playing flute and we went through the service together. When I did pick it up I was playing a lot with a symphony rehearsal group. I played with string quartets where I was playing the first string part, so I had a chance to play with people who had a good sound. I wouldn't have been there if I hadn't had a good sound, and I could read everything because I had played for about twenty years before that. So I kind of agree with what Jerome was saying, but I think there were a lot of guys playing the flute quite well. They weren't great players, they just had a nice sound. When I heard Hubert Laws for example--he came to California with the *Jazz Crusaders*--he had such a big nice sound. His technique was good, he had studied with a good teacher, and it was lyrical--the main thing was the great sound and intonation. He could certainly play and tongue fast, but I wasn't only impressed with that, his main thing was playing that beautiful instrument. My teacher once said to me--I was playing an etude or something and I had connected everything together--he said, "don't ever play it better than that." He meant, this is what you need--you are a pro. Not stumbling around but being relaxed. I first started playing flute with a group we had called the *Stars of Swing*, with Britt Woodman and Charles Mingus. There were two or three things I played flute on--we were in a club, the *Down Beat* in Los Angeles in 1946. We recorded it but it was never issued.

What made you pick it up?

I think the sound of it. I heard--not a jazz flute, a classical thing--it featured all the instruments, on a recording with an oboe, a bassoon, a flute. Who would that be? The composer I don't remember--but it was Julius Baker on flute. I didn't know him then but he was one of the finest players; Hubert studied with him. He stood out to me. I said, "man that's the sound." That instrument was speaking to me. Before then, when I started with Chico and some of the early stuff we did, there was Harry Klee--he did a thing with Lee Young, he had a little group and they did *How High The Moon* or something like that, and there was a flute solo on those changes. Harry used to be at Columbia studios as a studio musician and also a jazz saxophone player, and of course he just heard the changes and took a nice flute solo. There was no one else doing anything at that point that I heard in person. It was a little like saxophone, but not really. He did a lot of classical stuff but he also liked Lester Young so he put in some of those things (sings) But I knew there were a lot of other approaches, you know, from hearing Harry. Then we did the four flute thing for Mercury Records.

Do you think that changed people's perception of the flute?

Well it changed people's perception here in L.A. Especially the one with movie themes.

And Bud Shank was out here too in the studios?

Right. We did some things together with Duke Ellington, on the movie *Assault On The Queen.*

Bud doesn't play the flute any more.

No, he doesn't like it.

Did he like it then?

Well you know, Bud's got a kind of robust personality. He's kind of a tough guy, so he plays the alto like he's blowing the bell off of it, you know? He needs the sax to handle his power and energy. But Bud certainly was a good flutist when he played the instrument.

James Newton was telling me that some of the younger players are putting so much air into the instrument that some people are saying "are you a flute player or a trumpet player," you know. They sure get a big sound that way.

Well a lot of them approach it like that. Marshall Royal, once the lead alto player with Count Basie. He had a flute too but he always hated it. "It's too soft, I can't play it." He's a loud, really strong player, if you ever heard that sax section. A lot of people say "that's the way I like to hear lead," but it's almost like too much lead! If you have that strong a lead you miss some of the other parts. But Marshall would say, "I can't hear it," so he didn't like it. No matter how hard he tried to play it, it didn't get any louder--it was frustrating for him. But I heard good players. I liked Frank [Wess] and Jerome [Richardson] and Harry [Klee] and Paul [Horn]. They all played loud enough.

That was like one whole generation of flute players right there. Of course Herbie Mann did a lot for the flute. You knew Herbie right?

Yes, we did a record together, *Flute Fraternity*. He contacted me out here and I knew who he was because of his playing. And he said "I want to do a record with you." So we went into the studio for a whole day and did about ten sides you know--good record. I played everything--on the *Swinging*

Shepherds you've got everything, piccolo, alto, bass flute.

Who played bass flute on that?

Well, Harry Klee, but I played a lot of it also. Harry even played the E flat flute--we had all kinds of things going on. I wrote some, Paul Horn wrote some, Bud Shank wrote some.

Chico Hamilton has done a lot for the flute also, with the people he has brought into his group. After you there was Paul Horn, and then Eric Dolphy, whom you knew right?

Yes, he was a student of mine.

How did you like his playing?

Great player. He was a good musician. He was a jazz saxophone player but he really played the flute. He studied with Lloyd Reese. He learned all the tunes so by the time he came to me he was doubling, playing flute and bass clarinet and saxophone. That doubling is hard, I was keeping it all up for the studio work.

Now, after Eric with Chico, was Charles Lloyd. Now there's another person who doesn't play the flute much any more.

Well--it's the doubling thing. It's difficult. It's double work. Charles and I used to get together and practice and he would always say "I just don't get the flute." But he played well. But it's difficult, especially when you're traveling like Charles, when do you have time to practice the flute?

You need to play all those things to get the studio work?

Yes. And there would be so many things. There would be symphony things. And the guy would say, "You need to play clarinet on this, do you want to look at the part?" And I would say "okay." You go in the corner for five or ten minutes and try to get yourself together. It's a very nervous kind of thing because you don't ever want to be embarrassed. Then they may say, "Okay, the last one's a flute thing." So it's a concerto, or a little Latin jazz solo. You have to be on top of everything. You get some surprises. There's a hot tenor solo and you have to sound like Lester Young and then like Ben Webster. You've got to do all that--they expect that. Eric [Dolphy] didn't get a lot of studio work but he could do it. He could read--we used to go through clarinet books, duos and stuff. He was a marvelous clarinet player and bass clarinet also. Eric had come from a good family and he liked all the music. He liked Ellington, and he was only 20 years old.

There a few people now who concentrate on the flute and play it exclusively. Was Herbie Mann the first one to do that? Of course, he dabbled a bit on tenor.

But he stopped that. There are some people who can do all of them and take it to a good level, but for me it was hard. Playing the flute right after the saxophone, you would lose the sound sometimes.

There are books of exercises for doublers these days.

It's not just the sound. It's picking it up and remembering where everything is, you know. You have been playing the saxophone for half an hour and now you've got a flute solo.

Harold McNair was a fine saxophonist and flutist in London. He told me he switched from alto to tenor to preserve his flute embouchure. You played both, right?

Yes, at one time or another.

Then there's Jane Bunnett who plays flute and soprano, that's going in the exact opposite direction!

Well, like I said, I don't think there's any set way. Some people play with a very tight embouchure even on baritone! Some people would say "I just can't do it." I could do it and keep my sound, and just relax everything. And I would say, "Well, what is the flute supposed to sound like?" Then I would move everything until I found it. Not so much to do with what I read in a book, more like what I wanted it to sound like. There are just some basic things you have to do: relax, drop the jaw, open the throat--you know. I got a lot of credit from writers where they would say "you play flute on this track and then saxophone on this one and they both sound like just a straight flute player or a saxophone player rather than sounding like a doubler," you know. Well that's a talent too. Some have that and some don't.

Which of your recordings would you like me to list? Do you have some favorites?

Well, none of them are purely flute records, but *Jazz for Thousand Oaks* has both Sam Most and myself on it. Then my first album, after Chico's group--1956 I think--called *Man of Many Parts.* I did the writing and the playing, flute, clarinet, and saxophone. Then we had the big band thing in 1996 that's called the *Music of Buddy Collette.*

The last of these was the recording of a 1996 tribute concert to Buddy at the Library of Congress in Washington DC, a fitting climax to a long career. As we concluded our conversation, I reminded Buddy of one of his earlier compositions, *Blue Sands.* I had been playing the tune myself for years and asked him if I could play it for him. I ran out to my car and got my flute, and he was good enough to listen to me play it, and to give me a few suggestions. It was a very special moment with a very gracious man.

Frank Wess: Making The Blues Turn Green

"He was the first and the best of the jazz flute players."

Marshall Royal

"…the first jazz star to record extensively and with complete success as a flute soloist."

Leonard Feather

"I think Frank Wess is a quintessential jazz flute player."

Lew Tabackin

The polls that appear annually in *Down Beat* magazine, while they are not perfect reflections of developments in the world of jazz, do give us a broad indication of major trends over the last fifty years. One such trend is the widening acceptance of the flute as a jazz instrument. Prior to 1959 the flute simply did not appear in the magazine's Critics Poll, but in that year first place in the Miscellaneous Instrument category went to a flutist--**Frank Wess** (with fourth place going to another flutist--Herbie Mann). The magazine's readers seem to have been a step ahead of the critics in this area, as the flute appears in its own category in that year's Readers Poll. The winners: Herbie Mann and Frank Wess. By 1960 however, enough flutists had emerged in jazz to warrant a separate category for the critics. The first winner--Frank Wess. Forty years later Wess is still active, performing and recording regularly, representing the jazz flute tradition at the highest level.

Universally admired as flutist, alto and tenor saxophonist, composer, and arranger, Frank Wess has truly carried the baton of jazz flute from its very beginning to the present, passing it on to two or three generations of performers while, magically, still retaining it himself. When he first started there was virtually no one for him to model himself on as a jazz flutist, even though he knew both Alberto Socarras and Wayman Carver personally. But, like Herbie Mann, his first major influence was tenor saxophonist Lester Young, and Young's approach turned out to be strong enough not only to inform Wess' tenor style, but also to give him the whole cloth out of which he could construct a style of jazz flute playing, one of the very first that did not treat the instrument simply as a novelty. Later, given a popular platform in Count Basie's reed section, he was one of the first to bring the sound to a wide public. That he is still doing this in his 89th year is one of life's small miracles.

Frank Wess was born January 4th, 1922 in Kansas City, Missouri, but grew up in Sapulpa, Oklahoma. This is a small mining town, with a population around 20,000 at that time, but it was a curiously fertile ground for musicians; guitarist Barney Kessel, trumpeter Howard McGee, altoist Marshall Royal and bassist Oscar Pettiford all grew up in the area.. Whatever it is in the water in Sapulpa got to Wess by the time he was ten years old when he took up the alto saxophone and began taking lessons from a Mr. Ted Rice. Three years later, in 1935, the family moved to Washington DC, where Wess attended Dunbar High School and later Howard University's Conservatory of Music.

Outside of his formal training, Wess wasted no time in gaining practical experience, performing in dance, theater and club bands in the area. At the same time, he was exposed to a number of formative influences. Neither of his parents were musicians, they were both schoolteachers, but Frank heard various territory bands on the radio and at local dances; he particularly remembers Andy Kirk and his Clouds of Joy. His interest in jazz was also stimulated by one his schoolteachers, an alto sax player. As he told *Jazz Times* in 1983, "He used to have a little group that rehearsed in his house for different gigs. I used to hear them all the time, and they were always playing jazz. That's what caught my ear. That's what made me want to play." Once he began playing he found plenty of role models: Ben Webster and Chu Berry, Don Byas whom he met in 1932, Eddie Barefield with Cab Calloway, Joe Thomas with Jimmy Lunceford, and Dick Wilson with Andy Kirk.

While at Howard University, Wess continued to perform regularly. He worked with the house band at the Howard Theater, for example, and by 1940 he was a sideman with Cab Calloway's elder sister, singer and bandleader Blanche Calloway. In the meantime, however, two events occurred that were to help shape Wess' musical direction. "My high school teacher, Henry Grant, gave me a flute when I was 14 years old. But I didn't have the money to get a teacher and I couldn't do it by myself. So I just waited until I could do it." The next year, he heard Lester Young, the "president," or "Prez" of the tenor saxophone.

"When I heard Lester Young, that was that," he recalled in a recent *Down Beat* interview (March 2003):

> Basie came through town for a dance at the Lincoln Collonades... Prez was staying at a three-story rooming house, and a friend of ours brought us there. Prez came out in his pajamas, with his horn in his arm and a little powder-box full of joints. He offered everybody a joint! We asked him how he made all those funny sounds, and he showed us.

Lester's influence was profound.

> His playing was different. Before then, most tenor saxophonists were influenced in some way by Coleman Hawkins. Prez' sound was totally different from the Hawkins sound. His concept was different, and his rhythm was so good. I was very influenced by him as a kid. I used to try to play all the things he played.

Wess switched from alto to tenor to get closer to the Young sound. And later, he and Don Byas would jam with Lester when Young was in town. But at this point World War II intervened and, like so many musicians of his generation, Wess found himself in the army. He was assigned to an army band where he honed his skills on both tenor and clarinet, and gained experience as an assistant bandleader with an outfit that toured Africa with singer Josephine Baker. Undoubtedly, he was not the only Lester Young follower in the service at this time; there was at least one other in the person of Herbie Mann. Both Wess and Mann were to become major jazz flutists, although their involvement with the flute was to come later. Mann was to take it up to get a gig. Wess was a little more methodical. He possessed a flute and had had a long-standing desire to take it up. When he got out of the army, the opportunity presented itself. He had gone on the road with the Billy Eckstine orchestra, (along with Gene Ammons, Fats Navarro and Art Blakey), and worked some with Eddie Heywood, Bull Moose Jackson and Lucky Millinder. But Wess was tired of all the traveling; he wanted to stay in

Washington with his young family. So, in 1949, as he was eligible for the G.I. Bill, Wess finally took out his flute and enrolled as a flute major at a Washington conservatory. As he recounted it to me:

When I came back to Washington, I had a chance to study flute on the G.I. Bill. I studied with Wallace Mann. That was in 1949. Then I got a degree in flute from the Modern School of Music.

That was right here in Washington?

Right. That school no longer exists. But I got a degree from there in flute.

Was that because it was easier to get a legit degree on flute than on saxophone?

No, I had always wanted to study the flute.

Wallace Mann was principal flute with the National Symphony Orchestra. Later, Wess was to study with Harold Bennett of the Metropolitan Opera Orchestra. Working with these teachers, Wess obtained a solid grounding in classical flute technique, unlike the other flutists emerging in jazz at this time, as Herbie Mann, Sam Most, Bud Shank et. al. were largely self-taught. But their paths were running parallel; Mann was developing his flute work with Mat Matthews in 1953 when Wess graduated from the Modern School of Music with a bachelor's degree in flute performance.

Wess did not delay in putting his flute skills to use; while he pursued his formal training in school, he started playing the instrument on his jazz gigs. And he seemed to have no difficulty in gaining acceptance for the instrument. In his typical, matter-of-fact way, he explained it to Mark Roman at *Jazz Times*, "People like anything if it's done correctly, you know." In fact, it seems he had been doing a lot of things correctly, as he was now admitted to graduate school--the Count Basie Orchestra.

It was an extensive education; he stayed with the Count until 1964. He had a lot to contribute, and in fact he was largely responsible for the renewed success of the band in the mid 1950s. He teamed up with Frank Foster to form the duo of tenor soloists that had become a hallmark of the band following the partnership of Herschel Evans and Lester Young. Later, when Basie needed a lead alto, Wess took on that role. He exploited his writing skills to become one of the principal composer-arrangers for the band, and was also involved in helping Basie identify and recruit key players, including trumpeters Al Aarons, Snooky Young and Thad Jones, trombonist Bill Hughes, flutist and tenor player Eric Dixon, bassist Eddie Jones and drummer Sonny Cohn. Most important of all, from our perspective, Basie started to feature Wess' flute:

Later on, when Count Basie heard you could play flute--what was that story?

Well Don Redmond asked Basie if he had heard me play flute. Basie said no, so Redmond said you should hear him. Basie said okay, and told me to play whatever solos I wanted on flute.

Did you feature it a lot?

Oh, I can't remember. It varied. If I felt like playing it I played it. If I didn't I didn't. It depended on how I felt that night.

And Basie liked it?

Yeah.

Basie liked it well enough, as did his arrangers, mainly Neal Hefti, who began to incorporate the flute sound in the reed section. Frequently he voiced the flute with a muted trumpet, to produce a lighter sound, in contrast to the hard-driving swing audiences had come to associate with the band.

This new sonority made its recorded debut, along with Wess' first flute solo, on *Perdido*, in 1954, and from this point on the instrument gained extensive exposure during Basie's popular radio broadcasts. This was to continue after Wess left the band, as Basie had brought in another flutist in Eric Dixon, who can be heard with Wess in Basie's small group, the Kansas City Seven.

Through the mid-fifties the Basie band flourished, providing a perfect framework for Wess' development both as soloist and arranger. By 1964 the situation had changed, however. Some of the better players had left, the standard had started to slip, and Wess felt it was time to move on. But his legacy was secure. Eddie "Lockjaw" Davis came in to replace his tenor sound, with Eric Dixon taking up the flute chores.

Emerging from the Basie band and beginning to freelance around New York, Wess found a musical climate very amenable to his style. The flute was making substantial inroads into jazz: Bud Shank was taking flute solos with the Stan Kenton orchestra; Sam Most was recording with Buddy Rich; Herbie Mann was two years away from his first major hit; Moe Koffman had already had his-- with *Swinging Shepherd Blues;* and Wess himself had just won the *Down Beat* Critics Poll for the sixth successive year. In short, he found himself very much in demand. "A lot of people knew me from playing flute, especially with Basie. That was one thing that was good about being in the band. Because of Basie I got the exposure that I hadn't gotten in all the years prior to that when I had been on the road." As he told *Down Beat*, his transition from Basie into another paying gig, in the pit band for a Broadway show, was almost seamless: "I came home and I got everything straightened out for doing *Golden Boy* with Sammy Davis. I went out and got paid with Basie one Thursday; the next Thursday I got paid for *Golden Boy.* I never missed a payment."

For the next twenty years, Wess made his living, and put his kids through school, doing commercial work. He played for numerous Broadway shows, did television and studio work, and was also in demand as a composer and arranger, with several movie scores to his credit. He interspersed this activity with the more purely jazz-oriented gigs that came his way. He worked with Clark Terry's occasional big band from 1969, and in 1974 joined the New York Jazz Quartet, an interesting but underrated group founded by pianist Roland Hanna, initially with flutist Hubert Laws, bassist Ron Carter, and drummer Billy Cobham, later with Wess, bassist George Mraz, and drummer Ben Riley.

Frank worked with Philly Joe Jones' *Dameronia* band from 1981 to 1985, and co-led a quintet with fellow Basie alumnus Frank Foster from 1984 to 1986. He played in Toshiko's big band, Woody Herman's Herd, and the Frank Wess/Harry Edison Orchestra (including a Concord recording, *Dear Mr. Basie*), played on numerous sessions as a sideman, and led recording sessions for the Commodore, Savoy, Prestige, Moodsville, Pablo, Progressive, Uptown, Concord, and Town Crier record labels.

It has been a long and illustrious career, one that is more active than ever at this writing. Modest to a fault, Wess attributes much of his success to luck!

What are the work opportunities like at the moment?
It's just like it's always been--feast or famine. Either you've got more work than you can handle or you can't buy a job. Right now it's feast. I've been lucky. I've been lucky all my life. I've never done anything else.

Well it may not be just luck. You are a professional.
There are a lot of professionals--a lot of good ones. But many have not been as lucky as I have. You've got to be qualified but you still have to be lucky!

For the last twenty years, Wess has been lucky enough to concentrate almost exclusively on performing and recording jazz, as his most recent CD title puts it, *Making My Blues Turn Green!* And the flute has continued to play a major role. Most of Wess' albums primarily feature his tenor playing, but there are almost always one or two features for flute. And he has appeared on a number of recordings playing flute exclusively. He has also been active as a teacher. Overall, however, he remains something of a musician's musician. He is still better known among his peers than among the public. Remarkably little has been written about Wess, for example, or about the New York Jazz Quartet which deserved to be far better known. Wess' bibliography in The Grove Dictionary of Jazz contains just four items, although he has added one *Down Beat* interview since that edition. This is not much to show for a fifty-year career. (By contrast, James Newton--thirty years his junior--has twenty articles listed.) A major reason for this is that Wess is suspicious of journalists and does not like to give interviews. It's hard to blame him as there is a good deal of inaccurate information about him in print, as I found out when we talked during the summer of 2003:

I have read that you studied with Wayman Carver. Is that correct?
No. I knew him. I never studied with him. But I knew him, and when I lived in Atlanta, we used to have lunch, and we would play duets together. He was my earliest influence. Do you know about Socarras?
Alberto Socarras, the Cuban gentleman? Did you know him?
Yes, he lived close to me, right on 53rd street. I'm on 55th. I knew him a long time.
He worked with Clarence Williams, back in the late twenties. Do you know who else he worked with?
He had his own group.
He is referred to as the first jazz flutist, at least on record. But I understand he was best known as a clarinetist?
I don't know. I only knew him as a flute player, although he probably played clarinet, saxophone and everything. But primarily he was a flutist. He was a hell of a flutist too.
You didn't start on flute did you?
No, I started on saxophone.
At what point did the flute come into the picture?
That was after the army, after the war.
There was more work on saxophone in those days I imagine?
Mmmmm.
Eric Dixon played flute too with Basie. There's that great recording with both of you in the Kansas City Seven.
Yeah. Well I got him in the band. But he passed away.
*It must have been while you were with Basie that the **Down Beat** poll came out, the very first one for flute? You were the first winner.*
That's right. Before that it was a miscellaneous instrument.

Do you know how many records you have put out?

Not really.

Do you have any favorites though? If you had to pick just a few for readers to get hold of.

Well there was this session with Gene Harris. We did it out in Pittsburgh. It is called *The Real Soul.*

There are a few where you just play flute, one with Milt Jackson, one with John Lewis, the one with the four trombones, and my personal favorite, the one with (harpist) Dorothy Ashby. Do you remember that one?

Yes, I had heard her out in Detroit, so we got together. I let her pick the tunes because it is difficult to play jazz on the harp, you've got all these pedals to deal with. So she picked what she liked, and that's what we recorded. I did a concert with her at the Shakespeare Library in Washington too.

How about the flute solos with Basie. Do you recall any specific recordings?

I like *Flute Juice* and *Midgets* with Joe Newman.

That's with muted trumpet and flute?

Right.

Now, what year did you leave Basie?

1964.

So from '64 till the present you were basically freelancing.

I was doing Broadway shows. I worked with Sammy Davis for a while. Then I played with some of the repertory orchestras. I played with Toshiko's band for a while.

Then there was the New York Jazz Quartet.

Yes, we worked a lot, from '75. I had some nice recordings with them too. My latest octet recording is *Trying to Make My Blues Turn Green*. And I just recorded with three flutes: Ali Ryerson, Holly Hofmann and myself.

These days the flute is an almost automatic double for saxophone players.

Yes, they're all over the place now.

But when you were first coming up was there anyone else for you to listen to, to model your approach on?

Not really.

It was the other way around. Everyone else was listening to you.

Yeah.

When you first started playing jazz on the flute did it work immediately for you?

Oh, I knew it worked before I started doing it. I just had to get command of the flute.

It just came naturally to you? Jerome Richardson talked about the problems he had finding the right articulations for playing jazz on the flute. Did you have to think about that?

I had an ear for that so it wasn't a problem.

I think there were some people playing jazz back in the 50s and 60s who were great jazz players but not very good flutists.

It's the same thing today.

Although I think most players are better schooled today.

It's all a question of the right concept. There are a lot of people playing all the instruments today but who don't have the right concept. It's a different thing altogether

How would you advise students to formulate the right concept?

You have to learn the language. You have to listen to jazz. You can't just listen to European music and think that because you know that and have some technique you can play jazz. It's not that way. It's two different heads altogether.

Clark Terry has this thing about learning jazz: first emulate, then assimilate, then innovate. You think some kids start innovating before they've emulated and assimilated?

(Laughs) Well they think they're innovating.

Have you done much teaching?

Yes.

For technique, or improvisation?

Both.

How do you approach teaching improvisation?

The first thing I have them do is have them sing, to see if they have any concept to start with. If you can't sing, you know... That way you don't have to worry about flute technique or anything else. Either you got it or you ain't. You have to teach them how to phrase the lines and everything.

So phrasing is the first thing. Just like Jerome Richardson found working with the flute?

On a whole lot of instruments!

Well, Bud Shank told me he basically played sax lines on flute to begin with. Other people say this is the worst thing you can do, playing sax on flute. Herbie Mann told me he listened to trumpet players. You have to find the right approach for the instrument.

Every instrument has its own voice, even among the saxophones. I mean, you can't approach the alto like the tenor. Every instrument has its own voice and you have to honor that.

And what is the flute's voice, in your opinion?

Well it has a voice of its own, and some people have a solo voice and some people don't You take someone like Julie Baker. He doesn't have a solo voice. But the Irish flute player...

Sir James Galway?

Yes. Now he has a solo voice. Most classical players do not have a solo voice. The instrument has a sound of its own and that's what you have to try to understand, along with the jazz concept. It's just like speaking a language. You can't speak English using Russian vowels. Well it's the same thing with jazz. You can't play jazz using a foreign concept.

What do you think of smooth jazz? The kind of thing you hear from most jazz radio stations these days?

Well everyone takes the flute and tries to make it their own. What jazz is, is black folk music. Like gospel and the other things, you know. Like rock and roll and rap and the whole thing. It has influenced the whole scene. There is very little folk music or popular music that hasn't been influenced by jazz. And what jazz is--black folk music. That's what it is. And that's what it has been and that's what it will continue to be.

Although I read recently that there is concern because the black audience is turning away from jazz.

They're not turning away from jazz. They are just responding to what they hear. The media does that. They're not turning away from jazz. You read all that kind of bullsh--t. And just what it is.

Because I've had black kids come up to me and ask me what I am doing playing white folks music.

Really?

Sure; because that's what they hear on the TV and the radio.

Because they water it down?

No, they hear bands like Benny Goodman and Tommy Dorsey. They hear them playing all the music. But they don't stop to realize that all those bands had black arrangers. Benny Goodman would not have done anything without Jimmy Mundy and Fletcher Henderson and all those arrangers he had.

I meant the radio stations today water it down.

Well, they try to categorize. You've got soft jazz, you've got hard jazz. It's a bunch of bullsh–t. You put a name on it so you can sell it.

Actually, Yusef Lateef won't talk to anyone who is writing about jazz.

I don't blame him. Most people talking about jazz aren't even qualified to be talking about it.

It's not that. He says what he is doing is not jazz anymore. He doesn't want to be associated with the word, the concept jazz at all.

I can understand that too because they have tried to make it different from what it is.

What do you think of the job Wynton Marsalis and his associates have done in presenting jazz to the public?

He's doing a good job because he's making more people aware. But still, you know, he makes his mistakes but I'm not going to shoot him down for that because he's doing a hell of a job. Anytime you can get money for jazz you're doing all right. There's no one putting money into jazz right now. But if they find out that jazz makes money everybody wants to get in on it.

I'm not sure it makes money right now.

It's been making money. If it didn't people wouldn't be involved in it.

Do you do most of your work in the U.S. or do you do work much overseas?

Well, I've been moving around too much. I just came back from Chicago. Then I have to go out Thursday to Vienna. That's moving more than I want to.

How are the audiences in Europe?

They're good. They're good for me wherever I go.

I'm from London myself. But what I found when I came over here in 1972 was that I knew more about jazz than the kids here did--the music majors.

That's the way it is all over. The people out of this country know more about jazz than they do here. It's just like anything else. If you walk in a room and you see a chair, that ain't no big thing. A chair is supposed to be in a room. That's like jazz here. It's always been here so they don't pay it no mind. They never really paid any attention to it until people in Europe started to want it. And jazz musicians found audiences in Europe. Then they started paying attention to it. And as soon as they found they could make some money out of it then everyone started to jump on that wagon.

So you don't agree that the flute is a "marginal" jazz instrument?

No. No more than any other instrument. I tell you it's a matter of concept.

So what would be your advice to someone who is a flute player who would like to play some jazz?

Listen to jazz, the good jazz players, on every instrument.

In January of 2003, Frank Wess appeared as the guest artist with the Flutes of Howard University, at their 3rd annual *Flute Fête*. In the program notes, the event's organizer, Dr. Saïs Kamalidiin wrote: "Frank Wess is the woodwind artist who, more than any other single person, permanently established the flute's place, and widespread popularity, in contemporary, improvised, American music." Emphatic about this, and knowing that I was writing this chapter, Dr. Kamalidiin sent me the following in which he goes even further:

> I think that Frank Wess, because of the uniform excellence of his recorded output on the instrument, is the pivotal figure in the history of the flute in jazz. None of the other early pioneers of the genre--Collette, Lateef, Moody, Most, Richardson, etc.--had the combination of favorable factors that are present in the life, music and career of Frank Wess. His emergence on flute in 1954 with the Count Basie Orchestra resulted in unparalleled exposure of both his playing style and the flute sound in an improvisational context. There were no other nationally renowned jazz flutists performing and recording as extensively at the time. The consistent quality of his jazz playing; his repertoire, and the level of musicians with which he has surrounded himself; the diversity of musical contexts in which Mr. Wess has performed--from John Coltrane's music, to Basie, to his *Memphis Sound* recordings; the longevity and vibrancy of Frank Wess' recording career--over 50 years--and the fact that his life spans the entire history of the flute in recorded jazz; all combine to make him perhaps the most influential flutist in the history of the music.

We could say something similar about Herbie Mann. We may say something similar about Hubert Laws and James Newton, as they carry the tradition forward. But there is no contradiction. Each of these artists has played a major role in the development of jazz flute. Herbie Mann brought the instrument to a mass audience through a variety of often exotic genres. Hubert and James have greatly developed the technical side of the instrument in a jazz context. But Frank Wess developed the flute's voice at the very heart of mainstream jazz itself.

If there is one thing that characterizes Frank Wess it is consistency; it is virtually impossible to hear a bad performance or recording by him, either as leader or sideman. In addition, his style has remained remarkably consistent over a long career. Emerging in the late 40s and early 50s, from the cusp between swing and bebop--Lester Young and Don Byas were major influences--his first recordings on flute, with Count Basie in 1954, find his style virtually fully formed. From this point his playing gradually matures, adapting to each setting in which he works, with the more harmonically complex bebop elements coming to the fore over time, particularly with the New York Jazz Quartet in the early 70s, until, by 2000, with *Flutology* he sounds as contemporary as the other two flutists who are thirty years younger than him.

For the school of jazz playing that retains the pure flute tone, often developed through classical training, and applies it to a harmonically sophisticated and rhythmically driving melodic line--the style of Hubert Laws, James Moody, Holly Hofmann et.al.--its fountainhead is Frank Wess, the "quintessential jazz flute player." Hubert, James and the other artists are indebted to him.

Sam Most: Father of Jazz Flute

"The order of jazz flutists is Wayman Carver with the Chick Webb band, Harry Klee with Phil Moore, and Sam Most. Then the rest of us followed."

Herbie Mann

Sam Most has been referred to as a "vital but often overlooked virtuoso." There could be no more apt description. Still performing today, at age 80, mainly in the Los Angeles area, Sam has been honing his craft for a half century, without really receiving the recognition he deserves. To a large extent, this is due simply to his personality--he is a very unassuming man--but the very passage of time also has a lot to do with it. Better known in the fifties, after stints with Tommy Dorsey, Boyd Raeburn, and Don Redman, Sam made a number of recordings for Prestige, Debut, Vanguard, and Bethlehem, between 1953 and 1958, that did a great deal to put the flute on the jazz map. Along the way, he carried on a rivalry with Herbie Mann that briefly caught the public's attention. Later, he worked with Chris Connor, Paul Quinichette, Teddy Wilson, and, from 1959 to 1961, with Buddy Rich's Orchestra, after which he moved to Los Angeles where he made another batch of recordings for Xanadu in the mid to late seventies. For several years after that, however, Sam did not appear on record, while many of his earlier recordings became unavailable. And so, gradually, over the years, his star has been eclipsed by bigger names such as Herbie Mann, Hubert Laws and James Newton.

For all of this, Sam Most remains a seminal figure in the history of the flute in jazz. Charles Mingus, who grew up with Buddy Collette and worked with Eric Dolphy stated, quite simply, "He is the world's greatest jazz flute player." Others think of him as the first major artist in this field. Critic and jazz historian Leonard Feather referred to him as the "father of jazz flute," writing that "Justice should demand that the history books document Most's role as the first truly creative jazz flutist." Herbie Mann agrees, according to writer Doug Ramsey:

> As Herbie Mann has pointed out it was Sam Most who found a way to use the flute as a full-fledged solo instrument and, in Mann's words, "the rest of us followed." "The rest of us," in the late forties and early fifties, included Mann, Bud Shank, Frank Wess, and very few others of national reputation. It was years before James Moody, Yusef Lateef, Hubert Laws, Jeremy Steig, Paul Horn and Joe Farrell took up the horn.

Yet, while he is still active, Sam Most's name is conspicuous by its absence, both in the various polls and in the jazz bins of the major record stores. Universally admired and liked by his peers, especially in Los Angeles, where he is best known, the "father of jazz flute" has largely been forgotten in the larger jazz world, with one exception; he is the subject of a documentary film, *Sam Most, Jazz Flutist*, made by Argentinian flutist and producer Fernando Gelbard in 2001, in which he documents his life and his music, while performing several live selections on the flute.

I caught up with Sam in Los Angeles. We met at his local supermarket and talked while he selected some groceries. The next day I caught him playing in a small club--a bar really--in Los Angeles, with guitarist Al Viola. He played flute, clarinet and tenor saxophone, each of them beautifully, as well as some piano during Viola's guitar solos. To find such talent laboring in obscurity seemed criminal to me, especially considering his role in developing the flute as a jazz instrument. He is certainly well aware of the role he has played, as I discovered in several subsequent conversations:

Wasn't it Leonard Feather who referred to you as the father of jazz flute?
Yes, I guess, because I was one of the early people, especially to do bebop.
Well, there certainly weren't many others. And some, like Herbie Mann, were certainly influenced by you.
Yes, in fact, he says he was listening. Like it says in one of my books, he listened to me, and then he tried to copy me.
Well, tell me how you got started on flute. Of all the other people I've spoken to, none of them really set out to be a jazz flutist, it kind of just happened.
When I set out, I idolized my brother [Abe Most]. He was on the road, was ten years older. He was playing with, I guess, Les Brown and different people, and he had his own group. It was like the Joe Mooney group, with accordion, clarinet and rhythm. My brother had the same instrumentation, with Chuck Wayne on guitar.
Was he playing flute? I thought he was a clarinetist.
Yes, he was a clarinetist. He also played flute and alto, but his primary thing was the clarinet. So he sent me his clarinet and I started to learn it, and my father took me for lessons when I was 11. Then of course I started to play saxophone or flute after that. I just took to it sort of naturally and I tried to, I guess, emulate some of the saxophonists. It seemed to come easy to me.
Do you remember your first professional gig? I understand you had a group up in the Catskills.
I'm not sure about my first job, but that was one of the summer jobs in the Catskills. I had a little bebop band. I played alto and flute, I guess. Then there was another job where I was singing and playing piano. As a rough guess, I would say this was the early 50s or late 40s. That was in the summers when I was in the Catskills. The rest of the time I was in New York.
What was the first name band you worked with?
I worked about eight months with Shep Fields. They played society music, for dances and so forth. Although I don't think I played much flute with them. I was in my 20s.
So when did you actually take up the flute?
I think I was about 18--so 1948.
What motivated you to start?
Well I got my brother's flute just like I got his clarinet. It was becoming necessary. If you were going after a big band gig they would ask: "Do you play flute too?" So I think I might have started when I was 18. And I took to it easily. I started to play some of the things you might play on the saxophone on the flute. And I also started humming into it.
So you needed the flute to play with the big bands? It wasn't so much during the Swing era.
Well it was just becoming more common, but sax players did need to play flute very often.
So, as the Swing era was winding down, when many bands stopped touring, the ones that kept going did experiment more.
So they would start including the flute. That makes sense to me. Yes it was just changing. Remember Eddie Sauter and Bill Finnagan? They were experimenting with flutes and different things. But after Fields, I had a stint with Tommy Dorsey. I was 22. My brother helped me get that job. I was

about 22 and just learning to read and to play with a big band.

Was there any call for flute with Dorsey?

No. But He let me play clarinet solos. He'd say, "Take another one kid!"

Then you went with Buddy Rich?

Yes. I am not sure of the dates, but I stayed with the small group for two or three years and toured all over the place, with the big band in Vegas, and then we went to Reno and Tahoe. We also toured abroad--Afghanistan, Indonesia, Nepal. They disbanded around 1960. And there was definitely flute with that group.

Oh yes. And also you were with Teddy Wilson?

Yes, around 1969. We did a little jazz tour.

And Red Norvo?

Yes. And with Norvo I played almost exclusively flute--perhaps just a little alto. It was a quintet. That's when Frank Sinatra came in. And he gave me a flute, a Rudell Carte wooden instrument. People want to buy it but I'm not ready to sell it any time soon. His teacher had suggested it to improve his breath control, but he felt he didn't need it any more.

This is the same story that I hear from the others, that you needed to have as many horns as possible to get the gigs, and flute was a natural thing. And at that time the clarinet was dying out in jazz as the natural double for a saxophone player. The clarinet went through some hard times and the flute kind of took over.

Whatever it is, I guess I had a few opportunities and I recorded on the flute--I guess it was 1952 or 1954. I did a recording, *Undercurrent Blues*, and that was one of the earliest things. I guess I was just at the right time as far as history, to be one of the first to start playing jazz on the flute.

That was the one Herbie tried to copy, or at least to learn from.

That's right. Herbie said he had listened to *Undercurrent Blues* when he was learning. He copied me. It came out on a 45 and then it was on a little album called *Introducing A New Star*, on Prestige.

Do you remember the lineup on that record?

I believe it was Clyde Lombardi on bass, Jackie Moppet on drums, Chuck Wayne, he had a good name. And if I'm not mistaken I might have had Dick Hyman on piano.

I've worked with Chuck Wayne! It was at a college where I was teaching. What a great guy, and a wonderful guitarist. But it's hard to know who the first flutist was to record a true bebop solo. If that was 1952, that's at least a year before Frank Wess went with Count Basie, and before anything appeared from Herbie Mann

Well I thought I was one of the first. And I was the first to hum into it, but I never really get credit for that. But Herbie and Frank did a lot to popularize it. And so it got started.

Well you were certainly one of the first, but you all kind of came out of the starting gate together! But on that recording, it was a regular rhythm section with piano, bass, drums, guitar right? You're playing straight ahead standards or jazz originals--there was no question of trying to introduce anything exotic, to pander to the flute, as it were?

No. At that time I think I had some help from a friend who kind of pushed me along because I wasn't so good at promoting myself. So somehow I got that thing out, and of course the next thing was he helped me to do some other things, I think you have the record: Louis Bellson, Percy Heath, Bob Dorough...

Well, I can't seem to get a copy but they have one in the British Library. I heard it there.

Might be. Where Bob Dorough wrote some arrangements and Charlie Mingus picked it up for his Debut label. That was my first, before I got with Bethlehem I believe, playing clarinet and flute.

Did you find that you approached these instruments differently? You talk about how you were exposed to bebop when you were getting started in music, and how you adapted it to the flute. But did you also try to adapt it to the clarinet at that time?

Well, you know, the clarinet doesn't seem to fit bebop that well. Not too many people were playing the clarinet at that time because it is easier to play bebop on the saxophone. I might have tried with the clarinet, but I guess it seemed easier on the flute and the saxophone.

So you agree with Eddie Daniels? He was telling me that the clarinet dropped out of favor because it was so hard to play bebop on it.

Yes. Of course, Eddie came up a little later and you grow up with the influences that were around you at the time--like learning to speak a language. Eddie grew up in the Coltrane era, where I grew up in the Charlie Parker era, so the music had become more advanced harmonically and so on. Eddie seemed to be able to translate a lot of those idioms to the clarinet. Someone has to be chosen to do it, and he seems to be the one. I just felt whatever limitations I had on the clarinet I would work within those. And it still doesn't seem to be in vogue. I used to bring it out but I have too many instruments, so primarily I have been concentrating on flute and alto and tenor.

But I like your clarinet work. And when you do play the clarinet you don't revert to some older style; essentially you are playing bebop just like with everything else. And there's that record, Sam Most Plays Bird. You play clarinet throughout that don't you?

Well, yes, and of course the more I practice the more fluent I am. But I still wouldn't try to emulate Benny Goodman.

It's still a bitch! The clarinet, that is!

Well it's a beautiful sound, but I still emulated my brother and he was more on the swing style.

There are some other records, if I'm not mistaken, where you play only flute, the one with Tal Farlow for example. And with the guy who does that whistling thing, Rob McCroby. Then, more recently there are the duos the Stefano Benini.

That's right. Yes, I think they are only flute.

At this point, did you consider flute your primary instrument, or was it just appropriate for those recordings?

No, I guess flute is still my primary instrument; it's probably the instrument that I feel like probably I'm most capable on. I like the other ones because it does give you a different color, so I continue to play all the saxes, baritone alto and tenor, and clarinet. It seems to be best. I spoke to Hubert Laws once and he said, "That's why I play flute: I don't have to worry about reeds."

Of all the gigs you've played, have there been many where you've just taken the flute, or are you always packing all the horns?

Seems like I'm always packing the other ones, but strangely enough there are musicians recently who said, "Why don't you just bring your flute?"

What if they said, "Just bring whatever instrument you want," would it be flute? Is that your first love at this point?

It would be flute.

Did you encounter any technical difficulties trying to make the flute work as a jazz instrument? There are critics who claim that it's not really a jazz instrument, that it doesn't work too well for jazz.

Maybe I didn't think about it at the time. It just seemed to be natural to play the articulations of saxophone. It was much easier for me at the time than on the clarinet. I was listening to people like Charlie Parker, Lee Konitz, Stan Getz, at the time, maybe some others too, and it seemed like I could do some of the things on flute without thinking that it was difficult.

And there were no flute players for you to listen to, to speak of.

No, I was listening to sax players.

Is there any classical training in your background?

I had just very little, maybe some exposure to records, but very little classical training.

Often sax players have trouble forming the embouchure correctly when they first pick up the flute. Did anyone help you with that?

I went to a teacher named Victor Goldring and took a few lessons, not even months or years. And then I was on my own, but it seems like I took to it easily.

One thing about the flute is that bending notes and some of the "dirtier" sounds are harder than on sax. But that's not your style on the saxophone very much, is it?

Dirty things, I don't mess with too much. I get, as I've been told, a sort of airier sound.

But you did start with this humming thing.

Yeah, and I think that's a story that's been told a few times. I couldn't make noise in my apartment, so I started to play at home so they couldn't hear me practicing and annoy anybody. I would sing along with the notes, and of course you can get a little breat into the flute sound, and humming, like... (Demonstrates).

It's surprising how a flute carries in an apartment building...

Yeah, people might say, "Hey, would you stop it, giving us a headache!"

So your approach to the flute was very straightforward: I can get a good sound out of the instrument, and it lends itself to those same lines--as Charlie Parker used to say, "going through the changes, looking for the pretty notes,"--that you can play on the saxophone or the clarinet. So what's the big deal? Some people have written reams about how the flute should be approached, and it seems your approach was "Hey, I just play it the same way as I do my other instruments."

That's it, fundamentally.

And the strength of your playing, in my view, is the lines that you come up with.

I guess I became conscious that it's important to make a good line. And after listening to saxophone players' lines, they were so good so I guess it's unconscious emulation.

Herbie Mann told me he listened to trumpet players, when he was formulating his flute style.

Ah, I didn't know that. I listened to saxophone players, Lee Konitz, Stan Getz, Charlie Parker.

All people who play clean, interesting, melodic lines.

Beautiful lines and emotions and all that stuff.

Now a lot of people who play flute have been drawn to different genres with exotic rhythms and stuff, Afro-Cuban, bossa nova, because the flute works well in those kinds of settings.

When the bossa nova came in I just loved it. I did go to Brazil with Buddy Rich and heard that stuff there, beautiful stuff.

But you didn't jump on the bossa nova bandwagon, or make a bossa nova record any time?

Not as far as recording, but I love to play 'em. That friend I had, who had been helping promote me, stayed in New York, and was no longer available, so I just did what I could on my own. But I didn't have the push to maybe continue the career, and I myself wasn't really much of a pusher.

Not too aggressive at promoting yourself?

That's right--unfortunately.

How many years have you been gigging and recording on the flute?

I started in 1954, so it's over 50 years.

Wow! And how many recordings have you made under your own name?

I would just say, roughly, 12 or 15. And a few more as a side man. Then there's a thing I did in Japan with Hank Jones and Ray Brown. That's out only in Japan, I think. But I think most of the others are listed. Except for some things I did with Stefano Benini in Italy.

That would be two flutes plus rhythm section? And then that record with Joe Farrell is also excellent--Flute Talk. Do you have any advice at this point for people who want to continue to perform jazz on the flute, or maybe classical players who are interested in jazz?

The standard advice: you have to love the instrument or the music, jazz. Do a lot of listening, and hopefully find ways to play with other musicians so that you can express yourself on it. For instance, there were opportunities in New York. I used to get together every Saturday with a few black musicians in Harlem. We would go play some tunes in all the keys. We used to find little spots where we'd play with other musicians, and practice. They were things like sessions. Probably they have things like that today.

Not as much as needed. Are there any flutists today that you admire in jazz?

Strangely enough, it seems like I was influenced mostly by saxophone players, but I do like what other people do. Hubert Laws is excellent, Lew Tabackin. All these people are fine flutists. I think they've done some wonderful work. I was influenced mostly by the saxophone players but I certainly like a lot of the guys. I liked Joe Farrell, and then the Belgian guy, Bobby Jaspar, more like a bebop type thing. Then there are most of the people you mentioned, like Buddy Collette. Who did I leave out? James Newton gets a beautiful sound. And there's Frank Wess of course. Yeah, all these guys, I admire their expertise, but I just thought that perhaps my influences were mostly on saxophone.

Sometime in the late '50s, Sam was questioned about his future plans. His response: "I'm going to continue studying flute, clarinet, and the various reeds, and eventually attain virtuosity on one of them." Today, almost fifty years later, he continues with this quest, and many who have heard him feel that he has achieved his goal, on several instruments but particularly on the flute. There are many performers who are a lot better known than Sam Most, but very few who are better, a fact that demonstrates the eternal verity that promotion is more important than talent in the music business.

Author's Note

The next four sections of my narrative, and one earlier one, hold a special poignance for me. As the reader will have noticed thus far, I have constructed biographical profiles of those artists who are no longer with us, but, wherever possible, conducted interviews with those who are still living. In the case of Bud Shank, Herbie Mann, David Newman Buddy Collette and James Moody, however, I was able to hold several conversations with them in order to write these chapters, but all of them have subsequently passed away.

These were all distinct originals both as people and as artists, but what they shared in common was that they were all warm, gracious individuals who gave unsparingly of their time. This is not to say that others did not; I have been deeply touched and impressed by the generosity of all the musicians I spoke to in the course of preparing this book. But the extent to which these three artists shared their thoughts and feelings with me--and their opinions; these were not shy people!--has made their passing all the more personal for me.

In the case of Herbie, I believe mine was the last interview he gave. He knew that he did not have much time and, as a result, during the several conversations I had with him, he was totally honest in assessing the pros and cons of his career. I deeply appreciated his openness and have reproduced his comments in their entirety. Herbie did not enjoy much support from critics, his name is not found prominently in histories of jazz, and he was well aware of his own limitations. However, from the comments of his fellow musicians it is clear that his contribution to the music was significant, especially in opening jazz to the influence of other world music traditions. I am happy that a study of the flute in jazz can help put Herbie Mann's life and music into a better perspective.

David was a friend and colleague of Herbie's. I met him and his wife Karen at the Cape May Jazz Festival, on the New Jersey shore, where he was part of a tribute to Herbie that also featured Hubert Laws, Dave Valentin, Andrea Brachfeld and Larry Coryell, among others. We also met when David appeared at the University of Maryland, and at the East Coast Jazz Festival. He appeared to me as a perfect southern gentleman--gentle, polite, unassuming, deeply spiritual.

Speaking of perfect gentlemen, you could not hope to meet a more gracious individual than Buddy Collette. I was fortunate enough to visit him at his Los Angeles home on two or three occasions and always received a warm welcome. Perhaps if Buddy had accepted Duke Ellington's offer to join his orchestra, or perhaps if Buddy had moved to New York rather than staying on the West Coast he might have become more of a household name in jazz. As it was, he seemed to have no regrets about the choices he had made, but well aware of the contribution he had made to the music, not only through his own performances but also through the students he had mentored, among them Eric Dolphy and James Newton.

As for Bud Shank, after our extensive telephone interviews, we met when he came to Washington DC to play at Blues Alley. I joked with him that I would bring my flute if he would like to play it on one number. Inevitably, he declined. His statement at the beginning of this book gives a suggestion of his forthrightness; all his convictions about music were deeply held, but always expressed without criticism of others. And I was struck at the fecundity of his memory. He would have been a wonderful subject for a biography, the kind that illuminates the history of the music. It is fortunate that he did share much of his recollections on camera for a fine documentary film, *Bud Shank: Against the Tide* from Jazzed

Media. The film is billed as a "Portrait Of a Jazz Legend."

Bud Shank was certainly a legend. But what can one say about James Moody. He was, without a doubt, one of the greatest legends of his generation. Until his passing in December of 2010 he was one of the last musicians whose roots could be traced back to the founding fathers of bebop, especially Dizzy Gillespie, with whom Moody enjoyed an association that lasted for over 50 years. The Who's Who of jazz masters who showed up at New York's Blue Note to celebrate his 80th birthday is a tribute to his music, but also to his personality--no-one was more loved than Moody. And he was always learning. "I wish I had gone to school for music," he once told Gillespie. Dizzy looked at him: "Well, you ain't dead!"

All of these gentlemen were legends. It was a privilege to know them. In addition, I was privileged to speak with another legend of the music business, record produced Joel Dorn. His extensive background working with major jazz artists at Atlantic records brought him into contact with several major jazz flutists, and he was happy to discuss their work. Unfortunately, Joel passed away suddenly in 2007. It is a great loss to American music. Unfortunately we never met. We conducted our interview by telephone while he soaked in his bathtub smoking a cigar. It is one image that has remained with me most vividly from the time I spent working on this book!

Bud Shank: Retiring Jazz Flute Master

"…one of the most graceful and adept exponents of bebop flute."

John Fordham--Jazz on CD

In the history of the flute in jazz, **Bud Shank** presents us with an enigma. Gene Lees sums it up in his essay "Escape to Freedom: Bud Shank," in *Waiting for Dizzy* (New York: Oxford University Press, 1991):

> It is not yet generally known that a man who was considered one of the premier flutists in jazz has given the instrument up entirely. Nor is it known that Shank's standards for the instrument were so high that he despised his own playing. He hasn't played the instrument at all in several years. Bud has put aside the flute forever to concentrate on the saxophone, and only one of the saxophones at that. He no longer plays baritone. He plays only alto. And he is opposed to doubling.

This would not be so significant if it was not for the huge contribution Shank made to the flute in jazz. John Fordham is right; before he turned his back on the instrument Shank was one of its foremost exponents. He was also one of the finest alto saxophonists in jazz, particularly of the rather ill-defined "West Coast" school. Writing in the *Rough Guide to Jazz*, Ian Carr and Digby Fairweather extend the irony with one of their typically pithy assessments (complete with British spellings!):

> Shank's early alto work reflected a polite blend of Charlie Parker and Benny Carter influences, with a touch of the early Art Pepper for flavoring. This was later roughened up considerably in terms of tone quality and rhythmic emphasis. It is perhaps, however, his flute-playing which is his most important achievement, as the instrument had been hard to take seriously in a bebop context. Yet Bud's phrasing and articulation, and even more so his pliant tone, make the listener aware not of the flute's limitations in jazz but of its real communicative power.

The authors seem unaware that Bud had not touched the flute in fifteen years. They are very accurate in their assessment of Bud's flute playing, however. He was one of the first flutists I ever heard in jazz, and his work remains impressive exactly for the reasons the authors describe. So why did he quit? Gene Lees puts his finger on it: his standards were so high that he simply could not live up to them on more than one instrument. And the saxophone was his first love. (He was still carrying on that love affair until the day before his passing, in April 2009.)

Clifford Everett "Bud" Shank, Jr. was born May 27th, 1926, in Dayton, Ohio, and there is a lot to learn from his musical journey of almost seventy years, as well as from his strong views on the challenges in mastering one instrument, never mind more than one. He outlined this journey to me during several conversations, and even though he was no longer playing the flute, he was still very willing and able to discuss it. I began by mentioning that I had just spoken with Buddy Collette, Sam

Most and Herbie Mann, which made him the missing link! I mentioned their stories about how they got started on flute and asked him what his experience had been.

I know you don't play flute any more. Is this a question of going back to your first love?

Well I started out on clarinet when I was ten, which is typical for a saxophone player. And my first saxophone was at twelve. Around about nineteen, the band I was playing with at the University of North Carolina, Chapel Hill, which was a marvelous band---this was around 1946--the whole band quit college together to go on the road; the big bands were doing very well at that time. We made it through six weeks and there were no more jobs, and I didn't want to go back to school. I was in my third year of college and was not too blown away by what I was being taught. I had already given up my music major and was majoring in business administration. My only reason for being there was to play with this band.

Anyway, my father had been in the army, that's how I got to North Carolina in the first place, my home is in Ohio. He had retired and the family had gone back to the family farm in Ohio. So rather than go back to school, I went back to Ohio. I had been in New York several times from North Carolina to take saxophone lessons. I liked it but I wanted to see what L.A. was all about, and, lo and behold, I got a call from a friend who was driving somebody else's car from New York to Los Angeles, and he said, "Meet me in Nashville at the train station in something like a week or two," or something like that. And I said, "Okay, I'm going to L.A." But let me back up a little bit.

When I was at the University of North Carolina music department, there was one guy on the faculty who I really bonded with. He was the head of the marching band of all things, but he was a flute player and this broke the ice for me. Up until this time the flute was always a girl's instrument, and I wouldn't have anything to do with it. And so I said, "Wait a minute, this is a macho mother f----r, man, what's wrong with this?" So that opened the door--if I wanted to be a flute player it was okay to do it.

So then--this is now a few years later--I'm back in Dayton, not going to school. I conned my father into thinking I was going to school, and was going to register at USC, which I didn't do, but I didn't tell him that! But, I did borrow a hundred dollars from him and went down to the local music store and bought a flute. Now that was really a stretch. I really had no reason to do it other than I was fascinated by the instrument. As I said, it had been proved to me that it was enough of a macho instrument that it was okayfor a guy to do it. So I bought the thing. I couldn't play a note on it, but I bought it, and it was in my baggage when I got in the car at Nashville to go to L.A.

What was your motivation? Was it a question of trying to expand into studio work and needing to play more than saxophone?

I didn't know from studio work. I didn't know from jazz. I didn't know what I was going to do. I just knew I was going to be some kind of a professional musician. I had known that since I was twelve years old. I did not know what a studio musician meant, or what it required, or anything. I found out when I got there but, naturally, I was broke by then. Then another friend of mine from North Carolina who had been in the service as a naval officer had a pretty good pension coming from the navy, and we were roommates along with two other guys. And so he had enough money to take flute lessons. So he would go to the studio, take the lessons, come back to the pad, and tell me everything the flute teacher told him. And that's how I got started with the flute. And then later on I was able to take my own lessons with him--quite a bit later on.

You were playing alto sax at this time?

I still had my clarinet. I wasn't really through with it. But actually, I was playing tenor at that time. Alto didn't come 'till later. I started out as a tenor saxophone player. I played all the time during college and then after as a tenor player. But that's how I got started with the flute thing. Then, in 1946, beginning of '47, I got a job with Charlie Barnet's band, playing his solos every time he was off the bandstand, which was most of the time. Then, we go to New York and the lead alto player quit. So I said, "Charlie, can I play lead alto in your band?" And he said, "Sure!" So I went down on 48th Street, where all the music stores were at that time, and bought an alto saxophone. Okay, the first thing I encountered was playing a show backing Mel Tormé, and the first thing I see is a flute part. And I said, "Oy, I got a flute but I don't know how to play it real well." We were in Mel's library at the time, and I had been messing around with it enough where I could get through the part. It didn't bother Charlie at all, I mean he didn't like clarinet, let alone flute! So when we got back to New York I started... I said, "I gotta study this thing." So I studied with a guy named Victor Goldring. He was an old-time flute player, flute teacher, again down on 48th Street. I took quite a few lessons from him while we were in New York. And that gave me a good start, a good foundation. That was the first formal lessons that I had ever had, and it gave me enough courage, enough interest, to keep on practicing.

When I got back to Los Angeles with Charlie Barnet at the end of 1948 he broke up the band, and by coincidence, Stan Kenton broke up his band at that same time. In the meantime, I was playing a lot of jam sessions on alto saxophone, and I met all those Kenton guys. Stan was in the process of forming what he called The *Innovationist Modern Music Orchestra,* which was a jazz band with a full string section, French horns, tuba, double percussion, and woodwind players that had to double. The first alto player was going to double the flute, the second alto player played clarinet, and the first tenor player was Bob Cooper, who played oboe. The fourth tenor chair was the bassoon player, and the baritone guy's double was being the band manager! So when the time came at the end of '49 to put that band together, Stan started looking for a jazz alto saxophone player that played flute. But he couldn't find any, because there weren't any! And the guys that I had met--Shelly Manne, Bob Cooper, Art Pepper, and Buddy Childers--well all of them recommended me! They knew I owned a flute, but I don't think they ever heard me play it!

I was performing at the Million Dollar Theater in L.A. for a week with what was called The Charlie Barnet All Star Band, which I had a lot of saxophone solos in. So they took Stan down there. He heard a couple of shows we did and liked what he heard with the saxophone. He says, "Okay, you have to audition." I'd never auditioned for anything in my life but we had to see about the flute playing thing. I had two weeks lead time, so I did nothing but practice the damn flute and I got the job, to shorten the story.

This was a breakthrough for me, a chance to put flute in the proper perspective in a jazz band that was using flute. I didn't play any jazz flute solos with the band--I think there was one Latin record somebody dug up a few years ago, when we did a thing written by Neal Hefti that I played a short jazz solo on, but that was the only thing I played that was a jazz solo--I was hired as a legit type flute player. And it really helped prepare me for a lot of things, because this was the first time I had to play in unison with a string section. It didn't take long at the rehearsals for the concert master to come across the band behind Stan, right in front of me, and say "Look, I determine where the pitch is, you don't." And that was a hell of a lesson--a strong lesson! And I said "Okay baby, you got it!" And I learned to play with other people, to play in unison; lots of guys wrote the flute at different times in unison with strings.

Neal Hefti was fond of those voicings, I think, with the flute?

Neal Hefti, Pete Rugolo... A lot of those guys were great writers. But, anyway, being on the road all the time, I didn't have the chance to do any more studies with an organized teacher, but I was playing hard flute parts every night. I have gone back and listened a couple of times to the records that we made during that time, and I don't believe that I could play the thing, because I'd hardly spent any time at all with it. But anyway, it was a beginning.

Now, where did the jazz come from? Okay, occasionally Bob Cooper and I, while we were with Stan's band, would be backstage during warm-up periods, and we'd start playing jazz licks on flute and oboe, trading fours with each other. Everybody was laughing, but we were doing it. And we did that and enjoyed it.

Now, moving forward a few years, I left the band--almost everybody in the band quit in 1952--and stayed in Los Angeles. Several of them, Shelly Manne, Bob Cooper, Frank Rossolino, Conte Candoli, all got jobs at the Lighthouse in Hermosa Beach, which was great for jazz music. But I did not. I was working with a rhythm-and-blues band for the next year or so. But, somebody left--I forget who--and the job opened up, and once again I was recommended for that job, probably by Bob Cooper. So I went to work at The Lighthouse. Now we're into 1953, I guess. And again here are Cooper and I up in the dressing room playing jazz things on flute and oboe, but when we went down to the bandstand we just had our saxophones. Finally somebody said, "Why don't you bring those things down on the bandstand and play them? We'll just play something easy, some blues things or something like that." So we did, and it broke everybody up. And that was the beginning of that Lighthouse *Flute n' Oboe* album.

Although the album didn't come out until later?

Oh no, the original album was '54, '53, it was a ten inch. That was how long ago it was. It was Bob and myself and the Lighthouse rhythm section, which was [pianist] Claude Williamson, I think, and [bassist] Howard Rumsey, and Max Roach, of all people, on the drums. That was made in 1954 probably. And then it was expanded to a twelve inch in '56 after I had left, with Buddy Collette playing the last four tracks. So that's where all that started, from, '53 and '54.

This was still a novelty for most people, when Down Beat was still calling the flute a "Miscellaneous Instrument."

Oh yeah, of course.

It was around this time that Jerome Richardson was quoted as saying that he didn't think anyone had really figured out how to play jazz properly on the flute.

And he was right!

There were a lot of early jazz flutists who were great jazz players but not very good flute players.

That's the thing. They could get away with it.

The articulations were wrong, and it didn't swing, etc. Did it seem awkward to you, or did it seem...

Until I started applying saxophone principles to it, it felt that way too. But then, all of a sudden, I figured out how to make the thing work, with use of the tongue and things like that. Rather than slur every note, or tongue every note, I did what I call a doodle tongue thing. (Demonstrates, singing). And I discovered that way back in those days. To tell you the truth, when I first started it I'd listened more closely to piano players and vibraphone players because they couldn't bend notes. Technically, nobody had been bending notes on the flute yet. So I said, "Okay, they can swing without bending notes, what do they do?" That's what I learned first. And then, all of a sudden, I kept getting stronger chops.

By that time I was starting to study more with good teachers. I got better control, I was able to do the bending of the notes, and those kinds of inflections which helped tremendously, you know, with that kind of tonguing. There are still flute players around that tongue every note. I hate 'em; they sound terrible. And the ones that slur every note--they're even worse! You know who I'm talking about! That's not what is done. I applied what I had learned from the saxophone, but it took me a while to get strong enough to do that.

Several people have told me that they figured it out by applying saxophone techniques to the instrument. Others have said, like Herbie, that they listened to trumpet players. No one listened to flute players because there weren't any to listen to.

That's right.

Others have emphasized that you can't try to play the flute like a saxophone.

I tried! But you can't do it. I put as much balls into it as you possibly could, probably more so than some other people.

Then Herbie found that Latin rhythms helped the flute swing.

Well that's going in the back door. But now he's left true jazz music. That's taking the easy way out. Herbie's a businessman; he wanted to make a success out of the thing. I wanted to incorporate the instrument into the world of jazz as much as I could. Was I successful? I don't know.

So, okay, at this point you were thinking equally about saxophone and flute, like a 50/50 thing?

...and again, when I was studying, I was studying with legit teachers. And just toward the end of the fifties, jazz music was starting to be accepted in the studios. It had been blackballed before then, jazz musicians and jazz composers, both. And jazz scores. Hank Mancini came along and did *Peter Gunn*, a television show, and a couple of other little things...

*Then Ellington did a score for, what was it--***Anatomy of a Murder?***

And there was another one which actually I did with him. But let's also remember, since I was there, that all Duke did was write a bunch of music and the film editors cut it in. You can't just bring in a jazz composer and say "Write me a film score," it's a highly technical business. John Mandel, Michel Legrand, Shorty Rogers, they all had to study a lot in order to learn how to write film scores. Anyway, what I was leading up to was that I became very busy in the film world.

Which instruments were you playing through all this?

I had all the instruments.

Showing up for sessions with sixteen horns?

Oh, I had all that crap. I've still got a lot of it. I'm trying to sell it off! (Laughs.) You want to buy any of it?

Sure! If the price is right! You were playing alto, baritone, clarinet...

Actually, most of the work that I was doing was on flute. It was my entire life from the late '50s, I guess, early '60s, up until '73 or 74, until I walked away from the studios.

The low flutes also?   That became a bit of a cliché in film scores.

Oh, had all the flutes, a couple of bass flutes, alto... But I was successful at it; I was hired quite frequently. The basis for a film score is a symphony orchestra, right? And the departures come from that. Okay, the orchestra usually has three flutes in it. I was frequently hired as the second or third flute player in those orchestras, which meant, number one, I got to sit right at the end of the section with some fabulous flute players. Arthur Kleghorn was one. Louise Di Tullio, Sheridan Stokes--those kind of people. And I learned so much from that. But then, after the film score was over, they'd say, "Everybody leave except Bud Shank and the rhythm section." And then I'd do source music for them, which were little jazz flute things, or a George Shearing type thing with the flute in it instead of vibes. That kind of stuff.

So the flute got you in the door, and then the other stuff came along because you could do more than other flute players could do.

Well, yes. Those guys could do that kind of source music, but it gave me a chance. My whole point was to play with some marvelous conductors and some marvelous flute players. That's an education you can't buy! And I still approached the instrument from a classical standpoint. Any jazz thing that I did, well, it was like when I did play jazz on flute I forgot that I was a legit flute player--I was a whole different person. It's a mindset thing. I had to do it that way or otherwise the chops would get in the way, you know? I had long since forgotten about transferring saxophone things over to the flute and jazz music. I was strong enough now on the instrument where I could do it by itself.

I did that for years. I did a trip to Europe in 1963 and I went a couple of times to do some jazz festivals--I went to Rio and Buenos Aires in the mid 60s to do some festivals down there. But other than that, I hardly did any jazz things at all, there were not that many to do in the 60s. Jazz music had really left us. The Beatles were strong, the Rolling Stones were strong. People were confused by the avant-garde. General audiences as well as musicians were confused by Coltrane, he'd gone too far, too fast. It took a lot of years for all of us to catch up. So as a result, jazz music was in the toilet all through that period and didn't resurface again, for me, until the middle '70s.

So you weren't making any small group recordings, or anything that you remember?

No. I made some commercial records.

You did something with Ravi Shankar.

Oh yes, I did that kind of stuff. I did Ravi Shankar, and I did a thing with a guy named Kimio Eto. [A player of the *koto*, a Japanese table harp.] There was no improvisation in it. The reason why they got me to do that job is that Kimio Eto was blind and he spoke no English whatsoever. The phrasing was important, but all he could do, when we came to a passage, would be to play on the *koto* the phrasing he wanted me, the flute player, to play, and I had to interpret it. Now most classical flute players can't do that. Or won't do it is probably a better word. But for a jazz guy, that's easy--that's all we do! So that's why they got me to do that job. They said "Here is a jazz guy with a little bit of classical training, he will be able to do it." Again, there was no improv in it; the piece of music that he gave me was written in Japanese characters on one side, and you turn it over and it was written in regular notation. So the music was there. But the phrasing was important.

It may not be jazz but you had to have a jazz musician to get it done.

Exactly. It was the same thing working with Ravi Shankar. I did the record with him. I did a film score with him, which was the same kind of thing. He wrote the music for his group, but he had a classical oboe player, me, some strings which he had an orchestrator write parts for. But again, Ravi had to play the music to show the phrasing he wanted, and we had to adapt it. I had to show the oboe player how to do it--I had to show him. He was an excellent oboist who I had worked with a lot, but the music Ravi wanted was very loose.

It shows some of the shortcomings of our music education system.

Yes, "This is the way you have to go and you can't deviate from that." The academic world still believes that everybody has to start with a legit education in music, which is good, and this works on all instruments except saxophone. "Legitimate" (I hate to use that word but I can't come up with another one!) saxophone performance and jazz performance on the saxophone are totally different. They're almost like two different instruments. Clarinet is closer, and the stringed instruments are closer, but still there is a huge difference. And there are very few places where you can get a degree in jazz saxophone. I guess some of the newer schools will do that, Berkeley and Boston and North Texas College and places like that, but it's been a recent thing. I guess the reason is that jazz music, improvisation, is very difficult to teach. There are very few people who are qualified to do it. There are many who try. And so they say,"Okay, we'll give you a good foundation and then go do what you wanna do."

So the college jazz bands have great ensemble work but the solos can be very poor.

That's typical. I have a workshop that I do in Port Townsend for a week every year, and we do our best to take those kids and teach them about improvisation as much as we can. We let them be exposed to it, and stand up and do it, with critiques coming from the faculty members who are all professional performing musicians. And that's done for a reason...

At some point you did start making jazz recordings again? Was that the LA4? [The LA4 comprised Bud, guitarist Laurendo Almeida, Ray Brown on bass and Shelly Manne on drums.]

I made a couple of things. A guy named Carl Jefferson has a record company up in Oakland, around '73, or '74. I guess we made the LA4 thing for him first, and the first LA4 record which was probably made in '75, I guess. Then, shortly after that, I started making jazz records on saxophone with him. The LA4 things were extremely successful, but it was a chamber jazz group. Laurindo was a classical musician; he could not improvise. He played solos which sounded like they were improvised, but he had written them out!

Those solos were not improvised?

No, he wrote them out, at home. Then he played the same solo every time because he had to read it. So, we had three jazz musicians and a classical guitarist, and theoretically that should not have worked. Laurindo, Ray Brown and I, and Shelly Manne--later on Jeff Hamilton--the three of us made it work. Here again is the looseness, the ability, the resilience of jazz musicians being able to put themselves in another person's music and make it work. So here's three of us making Laurindo's music work. Because Laurindo wouldn't change. He couldn't do what we did, but we could do what he did!

Now performers such as Keith Jarrett, Fred Hersch, Wynton and Branford Marsalis, Hubert Laws, are doing the same thing, recording classical pieces as well as jazz and saying "I can do what you do, can you do what I do?"

This is what I got into in the late '70s, early '80s. I was really getting into classical music. And I made several records that way. I was going to the flute conventions and doing what I do, but doing what they did too. I got a terrible cold shoulder! With the exception of a few people--again I mentioned two of their names a while ago, Sheridan Stokes and Louise Di Tullio--most of the people in the flute convention, they didn't like this. You know. Because they're the ones that are always saying, "Oh, if I only had the time, I could do this." But they can't do what we do. There's one flute player who was with the L.A. Philharmonic, Jimmy Walker, but there's a different situation. Jimmy Walker could improvise. He discovered it by accident, but he couldn't stop playing too many notes because he was too good a player. That was his biggest fault. I was coaching him, like, "Slow down, Jimmy! Hey! Play one fifth that many notes!" But he is a true improviser. He does more improvising on the later records.

He's certainly a fine flutist.

I had a piano player, Bill Mays, write a suite for me. It's called *Explorations.* It's a five movement suite on one side and on the other side are adaptations I did, an unaccompanied Bach thing, except I wrote the changes out and put chords on a Fender-Rhodes behind it and then improvised on the chord changes. It was recorded in 1979, and we had the music printed and all my solos were written out. I know a lot of Sheridan Stokes' students at UCLA have been performing the thing, because he always assigns it to them.

And I do like that other record, **Crystal Comments.**

Yeah, that was fun to do. It was done at exactly the same time as *Explorations.* The record company owner, Carl Jefferson, knew I was doing *Explorations.* But while I was there I said, "Let's do this other thing too." So we brought in the other piano player, Alan Broadbent, and recorded it, and did the whole damn thing in two hours without telling him [Jefferson].

You do sound like a schooled player on those recordings. And also you recorded something I saw in the Library of Congress, classical pieces with Laurindo. How many albums did you do with the LA4?

Oh gosh, I don't know. Ten or twelve albums.

And at what point did you walk away from it?

When we got to around 1983 or so, Ray Brown and I looked at each other and said, "Hey, look, we've been at this for seven years, and it was theoretically impossible in the beginning. But why keep pushing it and trying to make something out of it, we've done everything we can do." So we broke it up.

You were doing what--50/50 on alto and flute throughout most of those recordings?

Oh probably more flute than saxophone. The original records I made with Laurindo in the early fifties which started all that was all saxophone. So the roots of that sound were saxophone and classical guitar. But then we had to expand it somehow, and the flute fit in perfectly because Laurindo wanted to play classical music. It was what he did the best, and he liked to write adaptations. He transcribed *Concerto de Aranjuez* for four people and he did a damn good job of it. But... we broke it up.

And the flute went with it?

Well, not quite yet. By now I was living in the North West, I'd already left L.A. and I was living in a little town called Port Townsend. Now I'm through with the studios, I'm through with LA4, and I was back to the beginning. I wanted to be a jazz saxophone player, and I had to go back and start working hundred dollar jobs again round the North West. I mean I literally had to go back because it now had been twenty something years since I'd been a "jazz" musician, disregarding anything I did with the LA4--that was really not a jazz group.

In our conversation, Bud was not quite as emphatic about the break he made both with studio work and the flute as he was when speaking to Gene Lees in *Waiting For Dizzy*. It is helpful to include a section from that interview here:

> Giving up the flute came after a great deal of thought, when I decided to make a break for it out of the studios. It was a long drawn-out decision. I had really concentrated on the flute, and I really practiced. I used to go over on my boat to Catalina Island for two weeks at a time just to

practice the flute. I was really getting more and more into the classical thing and learning how to play it, realizing that I was bugged with my jazz on the flute because I really couldn't play the damn instrument.

I knew I could not play the flute as well as I play the saxophone, so it was a matter of finding out how I'd feel really learning the instrument. I spent a couple of years doing a really concentrated thing. I did some recitals. Bill Mays wrote a suite for me for flute and piano. We made an album in 1980.

All the stuff I did with the LA4 was mainly based around the flute instead of the saxophone. Finally I reached the point around 1984 or 1985 when I said, "This is not what I want to do. I want to be a saxophone player and I always wanted to be a saxophone player." I was not getting very far either. Even though I was becoming better and better and better on the flute, it was still, as far as playing jazz music is concerned, not making any sense to me. It was still not what I could do on the saxophone...So I saw that the problem with the saxophone was really the flute, because the flute was taking all the practice time.

From this insight, Bud came to the conclusion that doubling--playing more than one instrument and doing it well--was simply asking too much, at least for him. As he told Gene Lees:

Flute will not bother the saxophone playing, but a lot of saxophone playing can bother the flute, at least until you get to the point where you are so strong that nothing is going to bother you...

I could play saxophone all night and still pick up the flute and play one of those little classical things. I had gotten myself to that point... but I could not master two instruments. It's physically impossible. Nobody's done it yet. Most... people who are trying to play both are... insulting the instrument.

Doublers ain't going to make it. There isn't enough time. You can be a master of doublers but you're not going to be a master of anything else.

This is something of a controversy among woodwind players, and everyone has their opinion. In the case of Bud Shank, the irony is that he performed at such a high level on two instruments for so many years before deciding that it wasn't achievable! I felt that, perhaps, in his case, it was just a question of returning to his roots and simplifying his life. It certainly coincided with his move out of Los Angeles to a less hectic atmosphere, first in Washington State, and later in Arizona. And, as I suggested to him, the alto saxophone was simply his first love:

The French have an expression--On retour toujours a son premier amour! One always returns to one's first love.
Yes, and so while doing this I was economically okay. I had done some good things where I was making money in the studios, and it was an insult to have to go back to work $100 jobs, but I did it because I wanted to, and because I wanted to get my feet wet again doing nothing but straight-ahead jazz music. After about 1985 or '86 I decided to take a good look at myself and what it was that I wanted to do, what I'd always wanted to do, and what was standing in the way of me becoming better at what I wanted to do. All those hours of practicing the flute were standing in the way of me becoming a better

saxophone player, and I really said all I wanted to be in the beginning was be a jazz alto player. And so that's when the decision was made. Still, even at that time, I was not convinced, and am not convinced now, that flute is that great of a jazz instrument. When you get down to it, the traditional jazz instruments--tenor saxophone, alto saxophone, trumpet, trombone--are still the best to interpret jazz music. I don't want to knock anybody who's doing jazz flute things, because I think it's got a future, but it wasn't there for me, and I don't have that much time to waste--I wanted to do what I wanted to.

Well, I have found that flutists have very broad interests, beyond jazz, Latin music and so forth.
Well, that was what I was doing in the 60s, although no one cared back then.

Well you did some bossa nova things, **Brasamba** *and those things.*
Yeah, well, *Brasamba* was an extension from what I had done with Laurindo back in the early fifties. So after the Stan Getz/Charlie Byrd record came out, and it was so big, I started getting calls. "You want to do something like this?" I don't remember if I did anything with Laurindo, but I got involved with Clare Fischer who was very, very knowledgeable about sambas and spoke perfect Portugese, and Spanish for that matter...

You don't have to step very far out of jazz playing to play that music, though, surely?
No, but again being able to adapt yourself in that kind of... have you every heard what Cannonball Adderley did to the *bossa nova*? The *bossa nova* craze just irritated the s--t out of a whole lot of New York black musicians. They were not able to do it right--to start with. Being able to adapt yourself, being able to put yourself in someone else's surroundings, is the thing that most jazz musicians can do. But not all jazz musicians can do this. So that's why it was easy for me to do that, to make the very first records I made with Laurindo, and then to make all those things I did in the early '60s. Like I mentioned before, jazz music was down the tube in the '60s. But in the very early part, '60 and '61, at least we had *bossa nova*, and I jumped on that-- well I didn't jump on it, it was comfortable for me.

So now you're doing alto saxophone exclusively, quartets, straightforward rhythm section, excellent players, richharmonic things--what mainstream jazz is all about, if I can use that word. But along the way you did a lot to help establish the jazz flute.
I hope I did. Most of what I did rubbed off on Holly Hofmann. And I am sure it rubbed off on some other people.

I think there is a whole generation of jazz flutists that have solved the problems of playing jazz on the flute and are doing some very interesting things. They owe you a lot.

It is clear that jazz flutists do owe Bud Shank a great deal. It is also evident that he still cares, at least a little, about the instrument. As he told Gene Lees:

> I don't know what it is going to take to produce jazz on the flute at the level I want to hear it. Maybe there is some kid out there somewhere who has dedicated his life to the flute and done nothing but play the flute. That's what is going to take to make the breakthrough and make it make sense... Hubert [Laws] is close to doing it. Dave Valentine is close, but the closest is Steve Kujala.

All three of the people Bud mentions are fine flutists, and now there is quite a crop of jazz flutists who concentrate exclusively on the instrument. All of them owe a huge debt to Bud Shank.

Herbie Mann: World Music Pioneer

"What Herbie.Mann managed to do, throughout his life, is to put many cultures in conversation, moderated by a flute."

From a tribute on National Public Radio

"Because of what he did, the kind of music he presented, he made jazz fans out of many people who would not otherwise have been jazz fans."

Larry Coryell

Without **Herbie Mann** this book may never have been written, for it was he, more than anyone else, who put jazz flute on the map. This is not to underestimate the contributions of the others in this book, particularly as Herbie himself would have been the first to acknowledge many of them as better flutists. But he was the first jazz artist to become primarily identified with the flute, and one of the first to explore different aspects of world music. He was also one of the very few purely instrumental jazz performers to achieve popular success. Critical success was another matter, however; Herbie was never really liked by the jazz writers. He himself was not proud of all his recordings (he made over a hundred). But he has left us a great deal of interesting music, he worked with a multitude of fine musicians, and he accomplished something few musicians can lay claim to: he created the style, or styles, of music within which he worked; according to producer Marty Ashby, "Herbie had his own unique voice from the beginning." With his passing, jazz was robbed of one of its most interesting and articulate figures, and jazz flute of a major trailblazer. Fortunately, I was able to interview him just a few weeks earlier-- probably the last person to do so. Intriguingly, I learned that his love affair with the flute came about by accident.

It was no accident that Herbie--born Herbert Jay Solomon, in 1930--became a musician; he was fascinated by music at an early age, and enjoyed banging on pots and pans in his family's kitchen. But, living in a small apartment in Brooklyn, this created a problem with the neighbors and his family was not keen on his pursuing a career as a percussionist! As he explained to me: "I wanted to be a drummer but my cousin convinced my mother that the neighbors wouldn't really appreciate a beginner drummer!" Then, in 1939, his mother took him to see Benny Goodman at the Paramount Theater in New York.

The experience made a huge impression on the nine year old: "... the band came up from the pit playing *Let's Dance* and it was like the Beatles, it really was that way. The electricity in the theater was so dramatic that I was completely blown away." Fortunately, he was blown away by Goodman rather than Gene Krupa! His mother saw to that: "Two weeks later I was home with a cold and my mother bought me a $45 metal clarinet, and before I had any lessons I started playing myself and seeing how to play it." Early studies on the clarinet led to Herbie taking up the tenor saxophone, and this, in turn, led him to his first major influence. As he recalled: "So I wanted to be a clarinet player. But then my music teacher said if I was going to be a successful studio musician I had to play the saxophone. So I picked the tenor sax--I went from wanting to be Benny Goodman to wanting to be Coleman Hawkins, to Illinois Jacquet, to finally wanting to be Lester Young."

Did you hear Lester play live?

Oh many many times. The first time was at Jazz At The Philharmonic, at Carnegie Hall but I wasn't really impressed.

It wasn't the best setting!

Well yes, but I was more impressed by Illinois Jacquet and Flip Phillips, more by squeaking and honking, you know, it was that kind of energy. Of course, once I converted into a Youngite then that was it.

So Herbie's course was set; he wanted to become a jazz tenor player. At this point, however, military service intervened and Herbie found himself in an army band, first in New York and later in Trieste, Italy. It was three years before Herbie returned to New York, his desire undiminished for a career as a tenor saxophonist. Initially, until fate intervened, this turned out to be a lot harder than he had anticipated. He recalls:

I just wanted to be a jazz tenor player. But when I got back out of the army I found that there were a lot of great Youngites out there, you know, Stan Getz, Al Cohn, Zoot Sims. So I might have been a second level, talented, Lester Young disciple. But then a friend of mine was trying to get me work, he was a drummer. He was playing at a club in Brooklyn and right next door there was a Dutch accordionist named Mat Mathews. And my friend said to me that this man was looking to hire Sam Most for his band. Sam Most was established at that time; he was the only man I was aware of who improvised on the flute. But my friend told Mat Matthews that Sam was out of town. He lied to him. And he told me the whole story, that Matt was looking for a jazz flute player. He said "Do you play jazz on flute?" I said "I do now!"

What was Matthews' motivation? He was looking for something that didn't exist? Or had he heard Sam Most?

No. He wanted to emulate George Shearing's sound, with tight chords. But instead of using vibes and piano, he wanted to use accordion and flute.

How did that work?

Oh, the sound was beautiful.

Mann convinced Matthews to take him on, even though, initially, he arrived for rehearsals without a flute. The instrument was being repaired, he explained, but meanwhile he could learn the arrangements on the saxophone. He was playing for time; he had taken some lessons on flute, but he had no idea how to play jazz on the instrument. As he freely admitted:

To get the gig, I lied. I told him I could play flute. Now Sam Most had one song that he had made where he played flute and I listened to it as much as I could to see what it could do for me.

You mean one recording?

Yes, Benny Goodman's *Undercurrent Blues.* I wanted to see if it could give me any more insight about what I could do with the instrument.

Mann was breaking almost completely new ground. Apart from Sam Most's solitary flute recording, and some flute players he had heard in various Latin genres, there was not much to go on. But Herbie needed to develop a playing style in a hurry. So he turned to a different source for inspiration:

I thought I should listen to trumpet players. So Miles, and Clifford Brown and Art Farmer were my main flute influences.

It's a cleaner sound, isn't it, the flute. It doesn't have those noise elements that you have with the saxophone. So trumpet players might be a better model.

Yes, and of course, with the saxophone you've got the reed, but with the flute or the trumpet, or the trombone, you just have the open hole to blow into, or across. But I think you will find that my sound was always more percussive, because I didn't say I am going to play flute jazz, based on the limitations of the flute. I thought I had a great opportunity because at the time you didn't have many people playing jazz on the instrument.

What year are we talking about?

1952.

So there were some players coming along then, or a little later...

Right. I think Bud Shank had started playing flute with the Stan Kenton band, out on the West coast. And I think both Jerome Richardson and Frank Wess had started.

There is this statement by Jerome Richardson on the liner notes of one of his albums. He says that, in his opinion, no one had quite solved the problem of how to play jazz on the flute, particularly with articulation, making the instrument swing, and that he was trying to find a solution to that. I know what he was getting at. You can hear this in a lot of early jazz flute, a bit too percussive--too staccato to the point of being jerky.

Yes. But remember--all these guys were doublers. They were applying what they knew from their other instruments.

Well that doesn't always work. I remember when I first played flute--trying to play it like a saxophone.

Right. But when I found this ethnic opening it made it much easier.

Herbie is referring to his earliest forays into Latin music. Up to this time, after two years with Matthews, and several more as a sideman with various groups around New York, his main focus had been in developing a flute style that centered on bebop--straight-ahead improvisations over chord sequences, mostly in 4/4 time. He was only moderately successful, however, encountering the same difficulty that Jerome Richardson described. This is evident from his earliest recordings. They work reasonably well but at times the flute seems out of context, like a thin-voiced saxophone perhaps. Lester Young's influence is evident in Mann's phrasing and harmonic sense, and the flute comes close to Young's lighter tenor sound. But Herbie was never really comfortable in this musical context. Suddenly, however, he discovered that changing the rhythmic structure created a context where the flute seemed more at home. I asked him how this happened:

When did you start to get into these other genres? Were you looking for something different or did you just come across Latin music?

Well, growing up in New York I heard a lot of Latin bands. And there was a DJ in New York whose name was Symphony Sid. [Note: Sid Torin 1909-1984, immortalized by the Lester Young tune *Jumpin' with Symphony Sid.*] He was a big Latin fan. I had played once at Birdland with a straight ahead band, but he suggested to my manager Monty Kay that if I added some Latin percussion it would work better. So I did and it did.

It does feel very natural for flute; I have found that myself. You are drawn towards the bossa nova and other kinds of rhythm.

Yes, but what I learned--with other instruments you can dictate the rhythmic energy, but with flute you can float on top of the waves rather than row the boat. And so Latin, Brazilian, Jamaican… that has been my approach all along.

So it's not an oversimplification to say that over the years you went looking for different contexts, one after another?

Oh yes, totally. Totally, because each door that I went through, there was another door. And also, at the same time, I really didn't think I wanted to be a straight-ahead player. So when I added these other genres I attracted audiences that weren't just straight ahead fans. You know I got fringe Latin, Brazilian, Reggae, pop fans who wanted to hear more than the melody of the music they liked.

The first door that Mann went through was labeled Afro-Cuban and, as well as helping him to carve a niche for the flute in jazz, it also opened the door to commercial success, for the public quickly took to the emotional intensity and rhythmic excitement of this form. And exciting it was. Mann's ensembles featured at least two, often up to four drummers, drummers such as Candido, Willie Bobo, Carlos 'Patato' Valdes, Ray Barreto and the great Nigerian Michael "Babatunde" Olatunji. Sometimes he worked with a trombone section, and he featured exciting soloists, guitarists Larry Coryell and Sonny Sharrock, pianist Pat Rebillot and David 'Fathead' Newman on tenor sax and flute, to name just a few.

It was very different from the jazz of the time. For the first decades of its existence, from its origins in New Orleans to the Swing era of the 1930s and 40s, jazz was popular music, frequently played for dancing. By the late 40s, however, a combination of musical and extra-musical developments--the innovations of Charlie Parker, Dizzy Gillespie, et. al. on the one hand, and on the other, new tax laws that penalized bands with singers and dancers--resulted in jazz taking on the aura of art rather then entertainment. Much of bebop was cerebral, played for, hopefully, attentive listeners. This was followed by the 'cool' school, led by artists such as Miles Davis and Gil Evans, as well as Stan Getz and other followers of Lester Young. The balance between African and European elements, always critical in jazz, was shifting toward the European, toward 'legit' music. This was to be a very significant development for the flute in jazz, one that Herbie exploited for a while. Suddenly, however, the musician most associated with jazz flute went in the opposite direction. In 1949, while Miles, a leading black musician, was making his *Birth of the Cool* recordings, Herbie, a New York Jew, was touring Africa where he received the stimulus for a new direction in his music. Dramatically shifting the balance toward Afro-Cuban elements, he re-introduced gut-level excitement into the music. As he told a *New York Times* interviewer in 1973, "The audience I developed wasn't listening intellectually; they were listening emotionally."

Mann also changed his recording contract at this time. Having recorded several albums for Verve Records, Mann signed with Atlantic, a much larger label, for whom he was to record fifty-two albums over twenty years, in a variety of genres. His initial success was within the Afro-Cuban groove, his live album *Herbie Mann at the Village Gate* selling over half a million copies with one track, *Comin' Home Baby*, making it into the Top 30 of the pop charts. He went on to become a seminal figure in the American jazz scene of the 1960s and '70s. He won the flute category in Down Beat Magazine's poll for several consecutive years, and had 25 more recordings reach the Top 200 pop charts.

After his Afro-Cuban period, Herbie went on to explore many other genres, going through the many doors that opened themselves to him while continuing to achieve popular success. He told National Public Radio, "Straight-ahead music is in a box--1,2,3,4. Ethnic music is a circle. It bubbles more for me." As Afro-Cuban forms began to lose their appeal to him, owing to their harmonic simplicity, he discovered the music of Brazil, initially by seeing the movie *Black Orpheus*, but following this up with a tour of Brazil in the early 60s, inspiring recordings with Antonia Carlos Jobim and a young Sergio Mendes. Next he turned to R&B, and to disco. Later he returned to Brazilian forms, and to straight-ahead playing. In between he found time to record with a symphony orchestra. But whatever the genre, the formula was the same: find the best musicians in the field, interact with them, try to record the best work. The same formula worked for Miles Davis throughout his career. And like Miles, Herbie helped to discover and promote many good young musicians. Unlike Miles, he had a difficult time gaining critical acceptance:

At what point did you lose touch with the jazz critics?
Almost immediately.
Really? Did you care?
No. I did not think that somebody who did not understand where I was coming from should dictate, based on their taste, how I should play.
Well, I have never been much for putting down other people's music. I know what I like. What I don't like I try to keep to myself.
I totally agree with you. But you know, Ira Gitler, who was a friend of mine, early on, once I started playing Latin music, he said "Well I thought you wanted to be the Charlie Parker of the flute." I said "Ira, I want to be the Herbie Mann of the flute!"
Has anyone been the Charlie Parker of the flute?
How can you be? Charlie Parker was a special individual with a unique way of playing his instrument. For a reviewer to always compare, or to have a particular hook to explain his taste, misses the entire point. That for every player, and every listener, their criteria is only their own taste. Everyone is an individual and to compare them, like saying someone is the Charlie Parker of the flute, is like saying Pavarotti is the Sinatra of opera. For want of a better word, it's silly.

Mann's endeavor, to become the Herbie Mann of the flute, took him on a journey through Africa, Brazil, the Middle East, Japan, Hungary... through Reggae, Country, Disco, Samba, Gagaku, the Blues... a road with many twists and turns, some rough, some smooth. One thing for sure, it was never boring. And as he went through one door after another, he carved a path that other flutists have followed and continue to follow to this day.

It has been interesting talking to jazz flutists. They tend to look beyond the boundaries of what most people call jazz.

Yes, well my feeling really is that flute players' jazz is different than other instrumentalists' because there was no tradition of jazz history on the flute, you know, where all the other instruments were classical instruments that were adapted to New Orleans and jazz music. I think that flute players... I know with me, I realized when I started improvising, it was such a novelty that people could not comprehend it. And it didn't really feel right for me just playing bebop.

Playing straight ahead in 4/4 with a regular rhythm section?

Right, but I realized that if you think jazz means improvising on a melodic and rhythmic concept, and don't think that it only means 4/4, there are many examples of flute improvising in other traditions. Rather than being a novelty it was an accepted part of the music.

One of the most ubiquitous instruments there is, apart from percussion, maybe.

Yeah, well if you go back in history, obviously just banging on something and getting a sound is probably the simplest. But getting a hollow tube of some kind of wood or stone or something also is simplistic. I have flutes from Russia that have the same four notes as flutes from South America.

You have a collection of flutes? I'd sure like to see that.

A lot of them are manufactured, but I have a very old Mayan or Inca flute and it's the same scale. Maybe they just got on the Internet and said well here are the flutes and the spaces are this kind of way! Or I am sure that people traveling over continents took their instruments with them. But it's pretty bizarre.

Indeed, there are ancient bone flutes from China and some that were dug up at Mohenjo-daro the ancient Indian city, that's now in Pakistan. One of my teachers in Calcutta, Mr. Debu Banarjee, was petitioning the government to allow us to go and examine them to see if that had the same scale. Because these are possibly some of the oldest flutes anywhere. He never overcame the bureaucracy, but I understand your point very well. Tell me about other flute players though. Hubert Laws started winning the polls on flute after you had been doing so for what, twenty years?

Yes. Hubert is the most well-rounded flutist there is, for me. He organizes incredible melodies. I'm funkier than he is but his sound is better. Another one that plays like Hubert is Toshiko's husband.

Lew Tabackin.

He's an excellent player.

When was the last time you played anything other than the flute?

I did an album with Jay McShann--with him, Doc Cheatham, and Gus Johnson. That was probably, fifteen years ago. I played all tenor on that. We did things like *Lester Leaps In.* I had my dream of being Lester Young!

But now you are essentially a pure flute player?

Yes. You can tell the doublers. There are very few doublers who have as good a flute sound as Frank Wess. David Newman, James Moody. Usually you can tell that they are doublers.

Chris Vadala, at the University of Maryland, has published has a book for doublers, with exercises to develop the different embouchures.

You know, there was a studio woodwind player in New York named Romeo Penque. And what he used to do was to carry around a tuba mouthpiece. And in between switches he would just take it blow through it like... (Makes raspberry sound)

To sort of free up the embouchure?

Right. Guys like Romeo Penque would switch from oboe to baritone to piccolo to bass flute to bass clarinet...

Paul Horn used to do that kind of work.

You know Paul got his job with Chico Hamilton because I didn't want it.

Really. That's a whole other thing. Chico approached you about that?

Chico approached me to replace Buddy Collette. But listening to the music for a couple of days I decided that I really didn't want to play it. So I was in the union hall in New York, and Paul came in. I had met him a couple of years before when he was still in the army. I suggested that he go and see Chico. He did and he got the job.

And he was followed by Eric Dolphy? Did you like his work?

Not particularly, or Rahsaan Roland Kirk. There was, for me, too much energy in their playing.

Too much energy? You mean not enough control?

They probably had enough control for what they wanted to do but it was a little bit more than I wanted to hear from the instrument. I like the sound of the instrument enough that I don't want to change it.

Ah, well I can see why you like Hubert Laws and Lew Tabackin! And there are others now with that kind of sound, like Ali Ryerson. She also plays a lot of alto flute. But you play alto a good deal too don't you?

It truly is my main personality, the alto flute.

Really? It's not on the majority of your tracks.

Well, ultimately I am not too comfortable playing rhythmic tunes on it.

And do you play bass flute at all?

On the *Peace Pieces* album I play bass flute on the two flute choir tracks. But again, that's pretty cumbersome.

And you have made some flute duet recordings. One with Sam Most...

...and one with Buddy Collette. Actually, we were going to do a tour with Jimmy Galway and Ian Anderson. Jimmy always used to come by the Blue Note, and called me all the time. But the road block was with Anderson; he makes too much money.

There have been some good players now, recently, who really have developed classic bebop on the flute. At the same time, there have been others who have gone even further into non-Western genres; the flute leads you there.

Then there are guys like James Newton.

That's right. He has developed techniques from other genres. But then you finish up with all the problems of categorization. Which bin do you put the record in? It's the same with books. My last book was on Pythagoras. We marked it metaphysics but the bookstores put it in mathematics, or classics. But, anyway, did the critics ever jump back onto your band wagon?

What I think happens is when you're growing up and all your friends are listening to the Rolling Stones and you are championing what you love, you develop defenses about what you're going to accept and what you're not, and you put up all these walls. You know, fans who become reviewers. And you go out of your way to say, truthfully, if it sells too many records that shows that the music can't be good because there are not many people out there who really know what good jazz is. So if somebody sells half a million copies they must be bad. So what I think happened is that I became the Kenny G of the sixties.

Well, that works both ways. I'm no fan of Kenny G. I've nothing against him but I just hate to see people think that's jazz.

Well the stores should not put him in jazz.

He could be in R&B.

Or in pop instrumental.

Yeah, even better. Then there would be different criteria.

Same with David Sanborn.

Although he's an excellent player.

So is Kenny. He's just found his genre. One thing you have to say about Kenny--the first note you hear, you know it's him--which you can't really say about the sound-alikes.

Which is not a small thing. I can remember when I was an undergraduate I could tell every musician on the old Blue Note recordings, down to the bass player and the drummer.

Oh sure, sure.

People used to bring records to my house just to try and stump me. Then I was away from jazz for some years, and when I got back into it, two things hit me immediately. Wow! These players are a lot better schooled than they used to be. And number two--they all sounded the same!

Oh yes.

It's the result of schooling I suppose. There was only one Thelonius Monk but now there are a hundred Bill Evans out there! Well, not that many, but you know what I mean.

I think you're right. But you know, you start with who your favorite is and you listen to their hooks. There's a pop record out that they've used on a car commercial where there's a loop that sounds like Charlie Parker. (Sings bebop-like phrase) Da da da da da da da da dada. And they just do it over and over again. But you've got to remember too that the market has become better defined as far as making money, so everybody wants to have a SpyroGyra sound, every record label wants to have a squeeze alto player, not a tenor player, you know what I mean, a squeeze alto player. And they all sound alike. I mean, my wife and I, we lived in Brewster New York, and we used to drive into the city. And we used to listen to CD 101. We would always try and guess who the players were--and you couldn't tell. But you know, that is what this time is--everything is generic. And the buyers of the music, the people who are buying CD 101, don't seem to care. There is no time, or room for individuality.

Yes, I agree with that. But now, going back to the different stages you went through, is there any one genre that you explored as you went along that you found more satisfying than the others? Any that you think resulted in more satisfying music?

Well I would say, if I had to choose one, it would be Brazil.

Bossa nova?

Well *bossa nova* is only one of the genres of Brazil. But I went to Brazil because I was bored to death of playing two chord tunes, like Latin music...

The Afro-Cuban things?

Sure, but then going to Brazil... being a romantic and being able to play basically Ravel with a *samba* beat took care of all my needs. Because here were these gorgeous melodies, where with Latin music, the harmonies were rhythmic, and with African music the harmonies were rhythmic. But with

Brazil, it was equal between this sensual pulsating rhythm and these melodies that would knock you over. That combination I would say, really turned me on.

I have read that after you discovered Brazilian music you had a parting of the ways with Atlantic. What was the reason for that?

Well they wanted me to move on and do other things.

And you wanted to explore the Brazilian groove some more.

Right. But then I made some disco records.

Did you like those?

No. No, I didn't like them.

I'm glad to hear you say that because I didn't like those records very much. There was some pressure from Atlantic to do them? With that kind of music...there's nothing feeding anything into you... no stimulation or inspiration.

Oh not at all... it's like... overdubbing.

Well one of the defining elements of jazz, it seems to me, is that it is performed in real time, so that the musicians are playing off of each other. I've done a good deal of that kind of studio work and it's hard to be inventive when you're playing that way.

Yeah, well it's like playing in a morgue. You know, I made a couple of Reggae records. One I did live in London with the Jimmy Cliff band and the next one I did in Jamaica. We went into the studio--it was the studio where they did *I Shot the Sheriff?* You know, Eric Clapton. And everyone came in by themselves. And I said "What is this?" We couldn't record live, we had to have the separation. Of course it depends on the genre. If it's layered we're talking more pop. Mostly it's uninteresting, although lately I have done some Brazilian records where the band already had the tracks down. That's easy.

At least you're hearing something with some ideas in it. But disco must be so hard, so square-- thud, thud, thud... You can't play anything subtle.

No, no. But finally they [Atlantic] wanted to restructure my contract. Truthfully, I should have left them five years before. Because by the time I finished I had been with them twenty years. And it does get old.

What would be a short list of your recordings you would like people to hear? I know you have made many.

Over a hundred.

But if you had to choose five or six.

I would probably say *Live at the Village Gate, Memphis Underground, Push Push* and the album I did of Bill Evans' music, *Peace Pieces.*

There was also the album Nirvana, that you made with Bill Evans. Did you like that?

No I didn't. I didn't like my playing on that. At all!

Was there not a meeting of minds on that session?

I was so totally intimidated! It was like playing a basketball game with Michael Jordan. I worshiped his playing and I felt so insecure. It took me years to realize that I just couldn't do it by ear alone. I really had to study the harmonies. Basically, your ear only takes you as far as the roots. So what I do now, whenever I play anything, I have the pianist, or the guitarist, write out the hot notes, the notes you can't just automatically hear. This gives me some cues, something to grab onto. That's why with the *Peace Pieces* album--I spent a lot of time on that record.

You're referring to the higher parts of the chord, beyond the triad?

Yes, the easiest is always the root. That you always hear. But the sevenths, the extensions, like the ninths, these are not so obvious. So these are the ones I have written out. Then what happens is, if you have those notes in your arsenal, it opens up the rest of the chord, then you hear other things. You know, I was never a guy who could look at a chord symbol and automatically know everything that it meant. But it's never too late to learn. It frees you up.

So it's useful to go through a chart and arpeggiate the chords?

Oh totally, totally. But then, look--the ear is king. But if you combine the two ways of playing together it makes it easier. But, you know, I marvel at... when I listen to Herbie Hancock... God how do they find those notes?

The voicings?

Yes, it's just like learning how to walk. Or... the more you learn the more creative you can be.

So, I'm sorry. I interrupted you. You were giving me a list of albums...

Yes, so, *Live At The Village Gate, Memphis Underground, Push Push, Peace Pieces,* and the last one I did, *Sona Terra*

Yes I have that. I like that record.

Thank you. And there's a company called Collections Inc. They have put out every record I made for Atlantic. I made 52 records for them. Also, there is an album that Frank Wess, Jerome Richardson and I did with Billy Taylor.

Boy I would like to hear that! Have you seen the record called Heavy Flute? There are several players on there, a couple tracks of yours, Fathead Newman, Yusef Lateef, Charles Lloyd, etc. But it could almost be a Herbie Mann album. The genre is basically, almost, one you created.

Well it's funky flute. It's Joel Dorn's favorite genre--soul. That's what he looks for.

So, you seem to be always interested in hearing new things!

Oh always. The only thing I don't buy is jazz. I am always interested in what Herbie Hancock is doing but I'm not really interested in Wayne Shorter for instance. For me it doesn't do anything. I'd rather wait for an Ivan Lins record. I buy every one of his records because of the songs he writes.

And now you are interested in Hungarian music. Tell me a little bit about this recording. These Eastern European genres are very rich. Actually, once in a bit of a flippant mood, I suggested to my doctoral committee that I should do a dissertation on great Yiddish jazz musicians. But it's not far from the truth. There have been some great ones, especially woodwind players. Artie Shaw, Paul Desmond, Stan Getz... and yourself, of course. Is your family Hungarian?

No, they were Romanian and Russian. But the whole catalyst for the music was when I was diagnosed with prostate cancer. All of a sudden your time is limited. And was I happy with what music I had played? And what would be my legacy? And I realized that I'm not Brazilian, I'm not black, I'm not Jamaican. I'm a second generation, East European Jew. So let me look into this music. I started writing the music and it came so easily, it just flowed out. Some of it I had written earlier but I had put it away, thinking it couldn't really make it, even to my fans who are very broad. But I started looking into the music again, and writing the music and I was ready to record. And my wife said "I don't think you're ready to record. You have to get into the crease itself." So we went to Hungary, met a lot of musicians and actually recorded one or two Hungarian bands.

Was it your original intention to use Hungarian musicians?

No.

Just to create the charts and use...

...Jewish musicians. But it was a good thing we went because it changed my concept. First of all, to hear these guys, they reminded me of the bebop musicians of the '40s and '50s because all they wanted to do was play their music. They didn't even think about the marketplace. And even under Communism they were listening to Coltrane, and Charlie Parker, and Miles and Dizzy. So now they're comfortable enough playing that way. To make a living, they have to play many different styles. They even developed a unique brand of jazz. In fact, I just finished a whole album just with the Hungarian musicians.

Great! And that will come out on you own label?

I'm not quite sure. I'm speaking to two different people to see if they are interested in putting the record out. And I came up with a funny title for the band. I call it the Carpathian Basin Street Band. Because Hungary is like the New Orleans of Eastern Europe--because of the geography; everybody from Bulgaria, Croatia, Transylvania came through Hungary. And it already had a built-in art area there due to the Austrian-Hungarian Empire. It was fertile. And so these musicians would get together, and meet together, and play all these styles together.

Were there any flute players in these ensembles?

I haven't seen any! There may be some vertical flute players. Saxophonist Mikhail Borbeli co-produced and organized the music, and plays all these instruments. But, you know, they have to. They play traditional dance music, they play jazz, they play pop. They do recordings. They have been influenced by gypsies, gypsies are influenced by them. But really, the genre is the most interesting music I've heard since I went to Brazil.

So there is a synthesis going on there from all these streams of influences flowing in, just as in New Orleans in the early days of jazz.

That's right.

And there is an East meets West aspect there also?

The West part is basically in the foundation to their jazz approach, but what they do with the spirit of jazz is completely original because they are basing their playing on their music, on their folk music, on their harmonies, a different scale and a different harmonic structure.

Was it a lot of work to assimilate that?

No, not for me, because they are all great players. This Borbeli, he's the musicologist, so he knows all the genres. He wrote a piece called *Balkan Caravan* that's like a journey through the whole area. And I've got a cymbalum player, a gypsy percussionist, two different guitarists, a saxophone player from Transylvania, trumpet, accordion, me, my son playing drums... it was quite a production.

And are there soloists? Apart from yourself?

Oh yes, all of them.

Is soloing something that you imposed on top of that or was it a part of the structure?

Oh it's all part of the structure.

And odd time signatures?

No. Well it's funny, they came up with the idea of doing some things in seven but it didn't work. So it seems that if you are just imposing that from outside... if you can't find the Down Beat, which can be tough in seven, then don't do it. To a Western ear it's uncomfortable. My son also wrote a piece for the hurdy-gurdy. And so we have two different singers, one from Budapest. *Sona Tera* is a free Carpathian introduction. It takes you to a totally different place.

So your thinking is always on the future?
Oh yes. People always say to me "which is your favorite record?" I always say "the next one!"

Sadly, there was not to be a next recording. Just a few weeks after our conversation, Herbie Mann passed away. As he mentioned, he had been fighting cancer for over six years. At the time he was diagnosed he could easily have rested on his laurels; he had nothing to prove to anyone. But this was not the nature of his spirit. The diagnosis of his cancer became the stimulus for him to open one more door, a very special one for him that directed him to a final area of world music, the one where he would find his own personal and musical roots.

With his passing, jazz historians are beginning to evaluate Herbie Mann's work. The purists among them are ready to dismiss him. He himself was the first to recognize that his recorded output was inconsistent, but with such breadth, this was almost inevitable, and even the greatest jazz artists have made poor records from time to time. For me, above all, Mann should be remembered as a pioneer; without his efforts, a great deal of wonderful music would never have been possible. The flute may never have become established in jazz, and the baton never passed to a generation of young players. As National Public Radio put it during their recent tribute, "Thanks in part to Herbie Mann, North American music now includes Afro-Cuban and Brazilian jazz, Jazz-Rock Fusion, and what we think of as world music." It would be very difficult to ask more than this from one artist.

An Appreciation from Larry Coryell

Guitarist Larry Coryell has had a distinguished career in jazz, rock, and classical contexts, extending more than thirty years. He has worked with artists as diverse as Chico Hamilton, Gary Burton, John McLaughlin, Chick Corea, Charles Mingus, John Scofield, Stephan Grappelli, Paco de Lucia, Hariprasad Chaurasia and Dr. L. Subramaniam. More importantly, he worked with Herbie Mann from 1968-1974 I talked with Larry not long after Herbie's passing:

The critics never seemed to like Herbie. Some critics believe he played down to people to make a buck. I asked him how soon he lost touch with the jazz critics. He said, "Almost immediately."
(Laughing) Well, one thing--Herbie was not Hubert Laws.
No, right. He would have been the first to admit this.
But there are a lot of lessons to be learned in here, which I can share with you if you like.
Please!
Well, there's a saying, I think it comes from Chinese lore or literature. You can have a lot of generals, but to win you have to have one general, a general of generals, who can marshal the direction of all the people, you know, the highly motivated leader types, having them create something they otherwise wouldn't be able to. Herbie did this because of his great ability to interact with people and his total understanding of the music. He also cared very much about... was very aware of what the audience

liked. He put together bands that were always doing something different. Even in the beginning, before I even met him, his bands were doing something different. Very early on he brought in the Afro-Cuban stuff, then, when I was on the scene, he had a band with guys like Miraslov Vitous, Roy Ayers, Bruno Carr... they made a record called *Windows Open,* and that record was fantastic. Herbie was really well-versed in the blues--and the blues sound good on flute. He was good with the blues, he was good with melodies, and he left all the really complicated stuff to be played by the others--and when you have those kind of players...

You could say something similar about Miles Davis. Much of his greatness had to do with the players he surrounded himself with.

Yeah--the same kind of thing. It was never a straightforward bebop blowing session when Miles appeared, or when Herbie Mann appeared, and the audiences really were attracted to that. And it was still strong music. He was a general among generals! And he never played down to an audience. If you think having the balls to bring in beautiful Brazilian Jobim things for a hard-core jazz audience... that's not playing down. That's giving them a different set of changes and a new melody. I'll never forget hearing Herbie and Roy Ayers play one time. It was that Jobim tune, *Wave.* He played the melody and then Roy Ayers took a solo you wouldn't believe. I thought about that solo, that song, that series of performances...

You know *Wave* is really a blues. It's twelve measures--well there is that little vamp (sings). You have D-major, Bb diminished, A minor seven, D seventh, A minor, then D, G on the fifth, G minor on the sixth, C sharp suspended, C altered, C ninth, sharp eleventh... and so on. It's really like a blues. By bringing in a Jobim song that was like a blues, the audience didn't even know it, but they were getting another form of the blues, with all those nice changes and a Brazilian sensibility. That's not playing down to anyone; they don't know what they are talking about.

Look, I can sit and listen to Albert Ayler all night, or today Kurt Rosenwingle, because I'm a jazz musician--I love that stuff. Hey you listen to Kurt Rosenwingle and his new stuff with Mark Turner, you play that stuff for an ordinary person, they are going to say, "What is that? Take that off!" But if it hadn't been for Herbie...

I left the Gary Burton quartet and switched over to playing with Herbie on the George Wein tour in 1967 or '68. With Gary Burton we would be playing along and then we would drop out and there would be a five minute bass solo. The audience was lost. All of a sudden I'm with Herbie and we're doing *Hold On I'm Coming* as the last tune, finishing the last chorus with a big flourish. And the people would be on their feet screaming for more. Herbie knew how to do that. You can't just play like you're in your living room, although a lot of jazz comes out of that. No, to me, Herbie struck the right balance. And he was always sincere in what he was doing. He was a general among generals. And you know, he did everything he wanted to do with his life in his life, and even when he had problems he turned that into something good. Like when he got prostate cancer, he turned that into a campaign to help other men in our age bracket take better care of their health.

Not only that, he also decided to explore his musical roots, and started working with those Hungarian musicians.

Yes, that was beautiful. I have that record. You know, I've told this story before, but legend has it that Herbie was walking at night in a questionable neighborhood in New York. All of a sudden he was confronted by a bunch of black toughs. And they said, "Let's get Whitey!" But then one of them said,

"That's not Whitey--it's Herbie Mann.!" Herbie had integrated bands. He had diverse cultures. He was a pioneer in that.

Tell me about his group when you were with him.

Well, one touring group we had--we broke up into small groups as part of an extravaganza-- there was Miraslov Vitous, Jack DeJohnette, Steve Marcus, myself--it was the *crème de la crème* of the young guys.

He helped launch a few careers!

He helped launch mine! You know, when I auditioned for Herbie the first time I didn't make it.

What was the problem? Were you nervous?

I have no idea. Sure I was nervous, I was just a kid.

Maybe he was looking for something different. So who got it?

Sonny Sharrock. Then later I did join and, depending on the economics of the gigs, sometimes he used me, sometimes he used Sonny, and sometimes he used both of us. Sonny was a great guy, and a fresh voice. And you know I played Herbie's last concert, in New Orleans. He was on oxygen. His wife was there by his side to help him because he needed oxygen in order to complete his performance. He had slowed down a little but he could still play, the ideas were still there. Herbie taught me the value of a melody. And he made jazz accessible for a huge number of people. As hokey as it may seem, when we made that *Memphis Underground* album, and Herbie put in that soul version of *Battle Hymn of the Republic*, that was my mother's favorite tune on that whole album, because it had a melody. Because of what he did, the kind of music he presented, he made jazz fans out of many people who would not otherwise have been jazz fans.

David 'Fathead' Newman: Texas Flute

"David has got that magnificent sound and that whole Texas thing, and he came
out of Ray Charles."

Joel Dorn

In 1960, the flute found another entry point into jazz, again under rather unusual circumstances. Tenor saxophonist **David Newman** was walking by a pawn shop...

> I was playing with the Ray Charles big band, and I had had a little inkling to pick up the flute and start playing it as it was a mellow sounding instrument and I really liked the sound of it. I was in Orlando, Florida and I happened to pass by this pawn shop, and they had these two beautiful Haynes wooden flutes there, ebony flutes, one alto and one C. Some guy from the symphony had left them there and never came back for them. So I purchased the C flute. It was very reasonable--the guy only wanted 25 bucks for it--he didn't realize its value. And when I got back to the band and showed it to the guys they said, "Do you know what you have there?" I said, "Well yes, it's a wooden flute." And they said, "That's not just a wooden flute, it's a Haynes. That's a very expensive instrument."

I asked David if he still had the instrument: "No, it was stolen from me. At the time it was probably worth $5,000--it's probably worth $25,000 today." An unfortunate loss! But it was enough to get Newman going on the instrument.

> So I started on it. I never took lessons, I taught myself how to play it--I am pretty much self-taught on the flute. And then I started recording on it. I was recording with Atlantic Records and so I started doing flute tunes on some of my LPs on that label, and since the late 70s and early 80s I started featuring the flute more and more. Now it's on most of my recordings.

David Newman, who passed away in 2009, occupied a rather unique position in the music world, adding another dimension to our difficulty with categories. As one of the featured performers on Joel Dorn's *Heavy Flute* album, Newman would seem to belong in the top echelon of jazz flutists, yet he never appeared in the *Down Beat* polls for that instrument. As a young performer he worked with altoist Buster Smith, a major influence on Charlie Parker. (He portrayed Smith in the motion picture *Kansas City*, some thirty years later.) He has been a major soloist with a big band, but rather than Basie or Ellington, he worked with popular blues singer Ray Charles. And while he has gigged with Lee Morgan, Kenny Dorham, Billy Higgins, Kenny Drew Sr. and many other jazz musicians in New York and elsewhere, he has also worked, and recorded, with Aretha Franklin, Natalie Cole, T-Bone Walker, B.B. King, Little Jimmy Scott, Donnie Hathaway, Freddie King, and Ben E. King. In his notes to Newman's *Davey Blue* album, Geoffrey Hines writes: "A musician's reputation doesn't always reflect the music he or she actually makes. A case in point is David Newman, who has devoted much of his 50-year career to mainstream jazz and yet is still mostly known for his early R&B playing." This is true in part, but also misses the point. Newman's style was remarkable to the degree that he was able to integrate these influences. In recent recordings under his own name, Newman definitely works in the jazz idiom, but with a direct, bluesy approach that reflects his lifelong association with R&B artists. If there is one category that might describe Newman he might be called, like Booker Ervin, Dewey Redman, King Curtis and his friend James Clay, a "Texas Tenor" (although he also played alto and soprano.) This background resulted in a unique and refreshing approach to the flute.

David Newman was born in Corsicana, Texas on February 24, 1933. His family later settled in Dallas where David attended Lincoln High. David had taken up the saxophone in seventh grade, after hearing R&B artist Louis Jordan who helped to popularize the alto saxophone. He does not speak much about his music education, other than to mention the high school band teacher who gave him his nickname. "I played an arpeggio wrong in a Sousa march and my music was upside down on the stand. The band director saw this so he hit me on the head and called me Fathead." Like many other self-taught jazz players he was soon working with local bands, and it was during this time that he worked with James Clay and (the then unknown) Ornette Coleman.

After graduating from high school, Newman was set on a career in music and would like to have studied music in college. This did not prove to be possible: "In the late 40s you had to have a scholarship if you wanted to attend college. I wanted to go to North Texas State as it was a very good music school, but it was out of the question."

Through his church, however, it was possible for Newman to go spend some time in college cultivating other areas of interest: "I did get a scholarship to get to Jarvis Christian College. And there I got interested in different religions. I wasn't so interested until I got started but then I was intrigued with the different religions and seeing how Christianity related to all these."

Comparative religion was a pretty progressive subject in the 1940s. I asked him if this was still an interest. "To a degree--it can be an interesting thing to get into discussions of different religions, but some people don't understand this, or some don't want to understand how these are connected. They are all saying the same things. Most of the religions come together and say the same things."

In spite of these interests, a career in music was still Newman's primary goal. After two years of college, David decided to go on the road full time with Buster Smith. There followed the usual series of one-nighters through Texas, Arkansas, Oklahoma and California. On one of these tours David met Ray Charles, who was working as a sideman with another group. It was immediately obvious that they shared similar musical goals, and when Charles started his own band Newman was one of the first people he called. This was in 1954, and Newman stayed with the Ray Charles band for ten years. He began as the group's baritone saxophonist, but when a tenor chair opened up Newman made the switch, going on to become the featured tenor soloist. He was beginning to qualify as a "Texas Tenor."

In 1959, with Ray Charles support, Newman recorded his first album as a leader. In spite of the fact that Charles did not like to call him "Fathead"--he called him "Brains"--the album was called "Ray Charles Introduces Fathead Newman" and included his famous rendition of *Hard Times*--although this was before he started playing the flute.

Newman continued with the Ray Charles band until 1964, at which time he decided it was time to move on and form his own band. His style on tenor and alto was well developed, and he was now creating an original voice on the flute, which he had been featuring with the band: "I didn't record on flute but he [Charles] did have an arrangement of *Georgia on My Mind* that we did on appearances where I accompanied Ray on flute. That was really my first outing on the flute. From that point on I started playing it more and more and that's when I decided to use it on my recordings."

Newman returned to Dallas where he began leading his own bands and continued to develop his Texas Tenor sound. Sooner or later, however, if he wanted more national exposure, Newman knew he would have to move to New York. He finally made the leap in 1980 and it turned out to be a good move. He began to gig around the East Coast with his own quartet, to work as a studio musician, and to make albums under his own name for Atlantic, Warner Brothers, Prestige and Muse, working with such sideman as Cedar Walton, Larry Willis, Jimmy Cobb, Louis Hayes, Buster Williams, Walter Booker, Hank Crawford, Howard Johnson and Marcus Belgrave, and later, with Stanley Turrentine and Hank Crawford. David's own band toured extensively, going beyond the East Coast to the rest of the country, as well as to Europe and Japan.

It was during this time that Newman met Herbie Mann in the studio and began an association that lasted until Herbie's passing in June 2003. He joined the "Family of Mann" group which included such musicians as Cal Tjader, Roy Ayers, Larry Coryell, Sonny Sharrock, Pat Rebillot, Steve Gadd and a host of other great rhythm players. This dynamic group recorded several albums for Atlantic records. I asked him about this period in his musical life:

How many albums did you make with Herbie?
Four or five.
Playing mainly tenor? Or some flute.
On the records I play mainly tenor--I can only think of one flute track. But in concerts we did play flute duets.
Is it easy to tell you apart on your flute duets?
I think so. We had very different conceptions on flute--very different sounds.
There are still some critics, even some musicians, who claim that the flute is a marginal instrument for jazz.
I don't agree with that. I think it is just as important as any of the other instruments. The flute is a beautiful instrument with a beautiful sound. Not every flutist is able to get into jazz; it all depends on the person playing it whether it is a good jazz instrument or not. Everyone has a different approach to the flute, but the flute is a beautiful jazz voice in my opinion. I think it is a wonderful instrument.
I think it took a while for the earlier players to find the right approach to the instrument, though.
Yes, I think that's true. But it doesn't hold these days. I have heard some great flutists out there: Paul Horn, Dave Valentin, Frank Wess, James Moody, Hubert Laws. There are a lot of artists out there who can really play the instrument. Not a lot of saxophonists, not a lot of reed players get into it so much, but I really do like the flute, and I am including it more and more in my repertoire these days. I'm going into the studio to record again next month with some new material and there will be at least a couple of tunes on flute.
How did you develop your style on the flute? Herbie Mann told me he listened to Miles Davis and other trumpet players as there were few flutists around. How did you approach it? Did you simply adapt your tenor lines to the flute?

Well I started by playing basic things--scales and chord changes. But most of all I concentrated on getting a good sound on the flute. Believe it or not, I had kind of a self-made technique on the instrument; I would take a soda pop bottle and blow across it. I did that for a long time--I still do it from time to time to get my embouchure up to par. I found that really helped me to get a full sound, the sound I really wanted on the flute.

We still do that with kids when they first start on the instrument.

Nobody told me about this, though. I just started doing it on my own. Well it's something you do anyway when you're a kid.

Then we get them started on the head joint.

That's right.

But it's very easy to have a wrong embouchure when you come to the flute from the saxophone.

Very much so.

So it's all about sound then? If you get a good sound on the flute, and you know how to play good jazz lines from the saxophone, then you can transfer that and away you go.

Yes, absolutely. A lot of times classical flutists have to make an adjustment as it is a big transition from playing classical to jazz.

Would you have any advice for classical players trying to make that transition?

It has to do with the thinking. You have to think in a different mode. You have to be thinking about improvisation and apply it to the instrument. When I do clinics and so forth I stress that to the students. Most students are interested in that. They want to know how to approach improvisation, how to do that.

What do you tell them?

Well, some of the same things I am telling you now. Improvisation is such an important part of jazz as you complete playing the melody the next thing you have to do is solo. I don't know what the technique is, but improvisation is so much to do with what you are thinking as long as it is in the chord structure of the melody.

But then you have to know some theory and a lot of students try to slide by theory.

That's right. But mainly you have to know what not to play.

Do you think playing transcriptions is a good way to learn jazz lines and phrasing?

That's a good start, because it gives the student a way to play and execute on the instrument. I did that--we played Charlie Parker solos. We would listen to records and play the solos note for note, by ear mainly, and then we could write what we heard.

So playing along with records is not a bad way of practicing?

Not at all. In fact, I think it's a good way.

That's the approach in India--copying the teacher note for note until you assimilate the style.

Nowadays they have programs for the computer. I know Phil Woods has a system for example. You can adjust the key and the tempo and so forth, sort the notes out, and get it into memory.

Are there any flute solos of yours you would direct students to?

I've had some compositions that students and fans have said were useful. There's one called *Thirteenth Floor*.

That's the one on the **Heavy Flute** *album.*

That's right. That was one of the better recordings I did. It was with a large group--orchestrated. And I had another one more recently called *Cousin Esau* that worked out very well. I like to play in the minor. The flute seems to fit so well with the minor situations.

It also seems to fit well with bossa nova and Afro-Cuban rhythms, as Herbie found. Often the flute seems to fit better with Latin rhythms than with straight-ahead bebop.

Yes. And Herbie was able to pick up a lot with his experience of playing with Latin musicians, especially Brazilian players.

Have you done any of that?

We worked with one musician on the tribute, Romero Lubambo. He has a trio called Trio da Paz. They work together regularly and it was a great experience working with them. But going back to solos, I also like *A Child is Born* on the *Davey Blue* Album, and *The Gift* on my new CD which is also called *The Gift*. All on High Note.

So what are you working on now?

I am working on a new recording with [trombonist] Curtis Fuller as guest artist, mostly featuring tenor as tenor and trombone blend well. But I will feature a couple of flute tunes, so we will see how that works with the trombone.

That's an unusual combination, although the flute often blends well with muted brass.

That's a great idea. I think Curtis will take some solos on those tracks.

Are you still touring a lot? You're not a teenager any more!

This is true. I tour about five or six months a year. Not so much in clubs but more festivals and so forth. In particular I won't play where people are smoking! But I have reached my three score years and ten and I am grateful for that.

David Newman showed no sign of slowing down even as he approached his seventy-first birthday. He continued to perform regularly and to put out interesting, high-quality recordings. He received a Grammy nomination in 1990 for *Bluesiana Triangle* with Dr. John and Art Blakey, and an INDIE for best traditional jazz record, also in 1990 for *Return To The Wide Open Spaces*. In 2004 Newman was portrayed in the biographical film about Ray Charles, *Ray.* It was not a particularly flattering portrayal, although it dealt with an early stage in his life, and David was a very different person by the time I met him.

As it turned out, his time on Earth was to extend to close to three score years and sixteen. Whatever else he accomplished in that span of time, he certainly made his own unique contribution to the flute in jazz. There are many who will miss him.

James Moody: Flute 'N The Blues

"... a presence unmatched by any other flutist in jazz."

Ira Gitler

During the course of his long and illustrious career, Dizzy Gillespie employed a number of flutists, both in his small groups and his big bands. Les Spann, Leo Wright, Sahib Shihab, Roger Glenn--all of them play a role in our story, and all of them have made significant contributions to the flute in jazz. James Moody, on the other hand, was with Gillespie, on and off, for longer than any other of his sidemen, during which time he has become a jazz icon. He is probably best known as a saxophonist, but he has also accomplished much as a jazz flutist.

As one of the few surviving musicians to come straight out of the original bebop school, Moody is one of the very few who performers who brought this genre directly to the flute. Of course, there have been several flutists who, lacking other models, developed a jazz style by adapting the work of other instrumentalists: Frank Wess with Lester Young, Sam Most with Lee Konitz and Stan Getz, Herbie Mann with Miles Davis. What James Moody did was simpler and more direct. He picked up the flute and did exactly the same thing that he was doing on the saxophone. And it worked. He has never looked back, nor given the matter a great deal of thought. His unique talent does not require him to be overly analytical.

Moody's career as a flutist began in 1956. At this point he had already established his reputation as a saxophonist. It had been ten years since his first appearance with Gillespie, and eight since his first recording under his own name. And then, out of the blue, he issued a recording, *Flute 'n The Blues,* with two flute performances: *Boo's Tune* and *Flute 'n the Blues.* Seemingly out of nowhere, he arrived as a mature, inventive flute improviser who found a way to translate the bluesy elegance of his bebop style to an instrument that at that time was thought by some to be sonically insubstantial, and too limited in emotional range for jazz performance. What is truly remarkable is that he had only taken up the flute a matter of weeks before making this recording.

Several writers have asked Moody how and why he began playing the flute. In an interview with Bob Bernotas in *Saxophone Journal,* Moody responded:

> Yusef Lateef said to me one time, "Moody, why don't you play flute?" I picked up his flute and I really didn't enjoy it. I didn't dig it. Then somehow or other a couple of years later I acquired a flute in Chicago. I wasn't particular about the instrument and it wasn't that good a flute. I would go to the hotel room and fool around with it. I did that for about a month and then I made a record on it.

In a 1972 *Down Beat* interview with Charles Suber, Moody elaborated on this story:

> Well, I had a problem with alcohol. After I was with Dizzy, I went to Europe and I became an alcoholic. I became a wino. And (long pause) I was in Chicago, juicing as usual. Eddie Jefferson and I were standing outside the club, the Crown Propeller, I think it was and a guy

came by and wanted to sell me a flute. And I bought it for 25 or 30 bucks. After I bought it, you know me, a couple of nights later, I played me a solo on it. Sounded like hell, but I played a solo. Very shortly after that I recorded *Flute 'n the Blues!* Sounds like it, too, doesn't it? I began playing the flute because it was available. I was never particular about it. I mean, you know, I heard other people play it--Sam Most, Yusef Lateef, Herbie Mann--but I never thought I was going to play a flute. It was one of those events, you know. Circumstances did it, I guess.

Moody went on to discuss his method for developing as a flutist. It did not involve systematic instruction at any conservatory.

I never really studied the flute; although I had help from many beautiful people. Anybody that played flute, I'd ask them to help me--Hubert Laws, Joe Farrell, Herbie Mann, Brother Yusef (Lateef). (And) I still don't have the sound like flute players have, but the more I play, my sound becomes a little bigger and better. (So) I just got a flute and started "spittin'" into it, not knowing what I was doing. The fingerings, some of them, seemed similar to (the) saxophone, I just blew like that and that's how I started.

Moody's early view of his ability on the flute is drastically different from the way his work is seen today by musicians and music writers. Preston Love, in his book *A Thousand Honey Creeks Later: My Life in Music from Basie to Motown*, for example, assesses Moody's musical creativity and technical mastery on flute by comparing them to Hubert Laws' widely acknowledged virtuoso technique. Love writes:

Probably the only "schooled" musician whom I regard as one of the important forces in jazz is Hubert Laws. Laws reflects an equal degree of formal training and natural ability on his instrument, but the flute is that kind of instrument. It probably requires more formal study than most other instruments used extensively in jazz. I would still rate Moody as a greater pure jazz player than even Hubert Laws, however. Moody doesn't have as much "legitimate" technique as Laws, but he is a greater source of inventive jazz ideas, and he plays with more of the jazz feeling and the jazz beat. Both Laws and Moody are rather phenomenal flute players, and one might say that comparing them is like comparing apples and oranges. But I think the comparison is relevant, because I want to stress that a naturally gifted jazz genius like James Moody accomplished his tremendous jazz virtuosity through innate ability and his own personal devices, whereas Laws accomplished his virtuosity largely through concerted formal studies on the instrument.

While this statement may reveal more about Preston Love than it does about Moody or Laws, it does state a very widely held view about Moody's work; he is one of the most respected and influential flute artists in the history of jazz. Discuss influences with flutists today and he is on everyone's list. The reason is deceptively simple. As Ira Gitler writes, "On flute, (Moody) displays a great facility and a sound all his own that is so big you would swear he is playing an alto flute." Other critics seem to agree.

Moody was selected "Best Flutist" in the *Down Beat* Critics Poll from 1967 until his withdrawal from the jazz circuit in 1974. He has held second place in the *Jazz Times* poll from 1993 through the present.

James Moody was born on March 26, 1925, in Savannah, Georgia. He was actually raised in Reading, Pennsylvania, and later in Newark, New Jersey, but at the time of his birth, his mother, Mrs. Ruby Waters, was visiting Savannah to find Moody's father, a freelance trumpet player who had performed with Tiny Bradshaw, but who was at the time performing in a circus band. "My mother was living in Reading, Pennsylvania," Moody told Ira Gitler ("James Moody: Surviving The Tough Clouts" *Jazz Times,* April 16th, 1987). "She went to Savannah looking for my father. After I was born, she recuperated and went back to Reading. I wasn't in Savannah three months."

Moody had a few obstacles to overcome during his early years, particularly his poor hearing. In grade school this was initially mis-diagnosed as mental retardation, causing Moody's mother to take him out of the school, leave Reading, and move to Newark, New Jersey. As he told Ira Gitler:

> We went to Newark because of my being hard of hearing. They had me in a school for retarded children because they thought something was wrong with me. What it was, was that I couldn't hear... When we came to Newark, my mother told the teacher and the teacher sat me up front. I skipped a couple of grades and everything was going fine and, finally, a doctor came by and examined me and said, "The kid's going to go deaf, so he's going to have to go to school for the deaf."

When Gitler asks Moody how he overcame his deafness, his response is simple; "I didn't overcome it." But it was only a partial deafness, predominately in one ear. "That he makes the miraculous music which people with two good ears cannot hope to create," Gitler concludes, "is testimony not only to his talent but to his determination."

Deaf or no, it was certainly not enough to prevent him developing a love of music, particularly jazz. Moody's mother was a jazz fan; she was particularly fond of Maxine Sullivan, Chick Webb, Benny Goodman, Jimmie Lunceford, Charlie Barnet, and the Dorsey brothers, and she played their records incessantly around the home. During his youth, Moody would reserve many Saturday afternoons for listening to Martin Block's *The Make-Believe Ballroom* from WNEW, a radio program out of New York City that featured the music of the most popular big bands at that time. When he was old enough, he started frequenting the Adams Theater in Newark, where he had an opportunity to see the Count Basie Orchestra with tenor saxophone soloists Buddy Tate and Don Byas. Moody was profoundly affected by that experience and it helped clarify his life's ambition--to be a musician, preferably a saxophonist. He remembers staring in the window of a music store. "They had rows of saxophones in the window and I used to put my nose up against the glass, just look at them and say, 'One day I'll have one, hopefully.'"

That day came by age 16 when his uncle Louis had given him a second-hand silver alto saxophone, and Moody began to study the instrument seriously, first the alto and then the tenor. His early models were Ben Webster, George Auld, Jimmy Dorsey, Charlie Barnet, and Coleman Hawkins. Then he heard Lester Young. As he told Steve Voce in an interview for *Jazz Journal International* in 1983:

When I heard Lester Young there wasn't any more Charlie Barnet! Coleman Hawkins, Chu Berry, Ben Webster, I loved them, but Lester had something else, that swing feel that he had. Then later on I came to find out that Coleman Hawkins and Chu Berry were more into the changes and the chordal structure than Prez, but he had that marvelous feeling. Of course I tried to take it into my own playing.

It wasn't long before another revelation appeared, and the young Moody's playing changed direction again. "I heard Charlie Parker and Dizzy Gillespie," he recalls, "and that was it!" It was more than an inspiration in Gillespie's case, it was soon to become a lifetime association. Within a few short years, through a fortunate series of events, Moody found himself working with the trumpeter, and Gillespie would remain a constant musical and personal inspiration for Moody throughout the remainder of Gillespie's life; it is said that Moody was with Dizzy as he lay on his death bed saying his last words.

The path from relative obscurity to working with one of the leading jazz orchestras began while Moody was in the U.S. Air Force, where he served from 1943 to 1946. While working with an unauthorized, segregated, military band, Moody got an opportunity to meet Dizzy Gillespie when his orchestra gave a performance in Greensboro, North Carolina. Dizzy told the young saxophonist to contact him following his discharge, and he did just that, joining Gillespie's outfit, playing tenor. This was truly an all-star ensemble, featuring bebop pioneers such as Milt Jackson, Kenny Clark, Ray Brown, and Thelonius Monk. It was not long before Moody made his mark, gaining attention with a solo on an early recording of Gillespie's composition *Emanon.* While only sixteen bars, it helped to establish Moody's reputation as a top quality, bop-oriented tenor soloist. "Moody's time with Dizzy established his name," writes Ira Gitler, "and jazz fans knew, even then, that here was an individual, recognizable sound and style."

Moody's first stint with Dizzy was fated to be quite short. Having traveled to Europe with Gillespie's band, Moody was so attracted by Paris that he decided to move there. "Those were nice days," he told Voce, "I came to Europe with Dizzy's big band in 1947 and liked it so much that when we got back to the States I left and came right back to Europe." He stayed in Europe for several years, touring and recording in France, Switzerland and Sweden, and taking up the alto saxophone again after having focused exclusively on the tenor for some time. He played in the quintet of Miles Davis and Tadd Dameron at the 1949 Paris Jazz Fair, substituted for Charlie Parker at a Max Roach led recording session, and worked with Kenny Clarke's band at clubs in Paris and Tunis, joining Clarke for a tour of Europe in a band accompanying Coleman Hawkins, from November 1949 to January 1950. He also led sessions in Zurich, Paris and Stockholm.

By 1951 home beckoned and Moody returned to the United States, to learn that one of his songs had become a hit! *I'm in the Mood for Love* was recorded as an afterthought on a date in Stockholm, Sweden, using an alto saxophone borrowed from Swedish baritone player Lars Gullin. The recording caught the attention of vocalist Eddie Jefferson, who wrote lyrics to Moody's improvisation and titled it *Moody's Mood for Love*. Later, when King Pleasure (Clarence Beeks), another master of "vocalese," recorded it, the composition reached the top of the R&B and jazz charts. This composition has been James Moody's signature song since that time, and he has recorded the song numerous times over the years. In the short term, it enabled Moody to work steadily for the next five years, touring and recording for the Argo and Prestige record labels, initially with a septet with a strong rhythm and blues influence, later with Kenny Barron and Tom McIntosh, along with a succession of fine vocalists: Babs Gonzales, Brook Benton, Dinah Washington, and, of course, Eddie Jefferson, whom Moody met in 1951 in Cleveland. It was during this period that Moody began performing and recording on the flute.

By 1963 he was tired of leading his own groups. He worked briefly with Sonny Stitt and Gene Ammons, but then he was ready to rejoin Gillespie. He performed in the trumpeter's quintet on and off for the remainder of the decade, fitting his flute into the Gillespie sound as Les Spann and Leo Wright had before him, along with his robust tenor. It was, however, at this time that James Moody's health and career were devastated by alcoholism. The combination of a very difficult touring schedule and Moody's unassuming personality caused him to seek solace in alcohol. As Eddie Jefferson reports, "He was to the point where he needed alcohol to face people." He voluntarily entered the Overbrook Sanitarium in New Jersey in order to dry out and recover his health. Once he had done this, he decided that a more settled existence might help him maintain it. He had a daughter living in Las Vegas whom he wanted to raise, so, in 1973, Moody secured an engagement with the Las Vegas Hilton Orchestra. During his seven year stint with the orchestra he accompanied a wide range of artists including Bill Cosby, Ann-Margaret, John Davidson, Glen Campbell, Liberace, Elvis Presley, The Osmonds, Milton Berle, Redd Foxx, Charlie Rich, Lou Rawls and many others. It was not jazz, but these were lean years for the music and Moody was taking care of his health and his family.

Eventually, however, musical taste changed again and jazz began to re-emerge, tempting expatriates such as Dexter Gordon, for example, to return from exile in Paris and Stockholm. His family obligations satisfied, Moody returned to New York and put together his own band again. It did not take long for his work to get attention. In 1985, Moody received a Grammy Award Nomination for Best Jazz Instrumental Performance for his playing on Manhattan Transfer's *Vocalese* album. With his name recognition re-established, he put an end to his decade-long recording drought and put out a series of albums: *Something Special,* in 1986, followed by *Moving Forward,* which showcased his vocals on *What Do You Do?* and his woodwind virtuosity on jazz standards such as *Giant Steps* and *Autumn Leaves.* Since then he has continued to tour and to record, fronting his own groups or working with ensembles such as the United Nations Orchestra and the Dizzy Gillespie Alumni Orchestra, the group I saw him with trading flute choruses with Frank Wess at a concert at Washington DC's Kennedy Center. Shortly thereafter, he celebrated his eightieth birthday over five nights at the *Blue Note* in New York, followed by a jazz cruise in the Carribean!

Moody is a wonderfully warm human being, but when it comes to his music he is a man of few words, not overly given to analysis of his music. I began our conversation by asking him how he got started:

You started on saxophone, right?
That's right.
Your uncle gave you an alto when you were a kid but you took up tenor when you heard Don Byas with Count Basie.
That's right.
Did you take music in college?
No. I learned in the Air Force.

I understand many other players got their start that way. And after the Air Force, in 1946, you went straight into Dizzy's big band?

That's right. And I was with him on and off for 47 years.

Dizzy liked flutists didn't he? Like Leo Wright. Did he encourage that?

Well I had the flute, and there were parts for flute. He had certain things he wanted flute played on. When I joined his band I took over from Leo Wright. So I played the parts that Leo played.

This was in Dizzy's quintet?

That's right--the quintet.

And there were some Latin things?

And Then She Stopped was one of them.

I understand you have some hearing impairment.

Yes. I'm partially deaf. I was born that way.

How has that affected your playing?

Well I don't go too high on flute. Perhaps I go up to a high G.

I understand you stopped touring for a while and went to work in Las Vegas.

I was in Las Vegas for seven and a half years, in a show band at the Hilton. I wanted to be with my daughter. I wanted to raise her, so I didn't want to be on the road while she was growing up. So I stayed in Las Vegas. Eventually I got a divorce. I went back on the road and was living in New York.

Did you find the music scene had changed much during that time you were away from it?

Well music changes every minute. For me it was just a matter of getting back into it that's all.

Were you leading your own groups at this point?

Yes, a quartet mainly.

As you went on from there, were you playing all your horns on every gig?

Yes I was playing tenor, alto, soprano, flute.

Do you have a particular approach to playing the flute? Did it come naturally to you to play jazz on the instrument? It has been referred to as a marginal jazz instrument by some critics.

Well to me it's the person who's playing the instrument. If they think it's a jazz instrument then that's what it is. Look at Moe Koffman for instance (sings)... what he played on the instrument. Everybody's an individual.

But do you approach it very differently from the saxophone in terms of...

Oh, of course, yes. They have some similar fingerings, but everything else about them is quite different. But I'm having a problem with my sound. I've had it for years.

Did you take any lessons at all?

Yes I did, in New York. I took about 10 lessons. But I can't remember the guy's name.

Concentrating on the sound?

Well yes, but my sound has never been quite right. I mean I'm working on it now. Because it's never too late!

Is it the doubling that makes it more difficult?

No. It's not the doubling. It's the flute. It's so demanding!

Are there any particular recordings people should listen to for your flute playing?

(Silence.) You know...not really. I don't know. When I make a recording, I really don't like to look back.

Right. I understand. Which flute players do you like? Who else was playing flute when you started?

Well Frank was playing, Herbie Mann, Sam Most, Buddy Collette. Everybody has something to say.

And Hubert is a great player.

Fantastic. Oh and the Latin players--Dave Valentin. We've played together. Not on flute, but I've played on gigs with Dave.

So what would you like me to put in there about your flute work?

Well, just that I'm still trying, still trying. But evidently I'm not trying hard enough because I'm not getting what I want.

Well that's not the way it sounds on the recordings. One CD I have here, **Something Special,** *you play flute on one track --Nubian Fantasies. Do you find that you pick the flute for things that have a little more exotic flavor to them? The way Herbie used to do for example?*

No. You can play flute on whatever you want. Ballads. Anything.

And Moody has done exactly that. He can be heard playing flute on up-tempo numbers, ballads and bossas, with the same fluency and inventiveness that he displays on all of his horns. Yet, unless he is guilty of false modesty, he does not consider his flute work to be on the same level as his performances on the soprano, alto and tenor saxophones. Clearly, like Jerome Richardson, he thinks of himself primarily as a saxophonist; certainly he has never said that he is not getting what he wants on tenor! As he told Bob Bernotas "I don't consider myself a flute player. Man, I'm a flute holder. I am a saxophone player who also plays the flute. I play flute, but I don't play flute, I'll put it that way. That's the way I feel about it."

Listening to his flute work, however, one can only be profoundly impressed, not so much for his command of the details of flute playing--he continues to insist that he is no Hubert Laws in this respect–but for the same qualities admired by Preston Love, his "inventive jazz ideas... jazz feeling and jazz beat." In that sense, Moody is a throwback to some of the early jazz flutists who may not have been great flutists but were great jazz players. In Moody's case, he is such a great jazz player that we can overlook any shortcomings he may have had, or thought he had, as a flutist. We have seen plenty of great flutists emerge in jazz since the emergence of Hubert, but Moody has been as much of, maybe more of, an inspiration to later jazz flutists. As such, he has made, and continues to make, an enormous contribution to the flute in jazz.

Mike Longo on James Moody: An Appreciation

Pianist Mike Longo has worked with James Moody, on and off, for over thirty years, initially when they were both in Dizzy Gillespie's group, later on some of Moody's own projects. I met Mike at the New York Bahá'í Center, where he presides over a Tuesday night jazz series in the John Birks Gillespie Auditorium. I was there to hear Jamie Baum, but later we spoke about James Moody.

What is it about Moody that makes him so special?

Two things. Number one, he has the gift of the blues--he's the master of it. It's like on a level of genius-almost like a savant kind of thing. He was just born with that gift. If you think about the fact that he played a solo off the top of his head and the solo became a hit... His sense of melody is such that he is able to play melodies, spontaneously, that sound like a composer sat down and pondered over them for hours at a time.

This is a gift. He is not overly analytical about what he does?

He used to be not analytical at all until 'Trane and all those guys started studying, and then he began studying harmony with me and Tom McIntosh over the years. Then back when he had a drinking problem, he told me that he was winning all these jazz polls and he didn't know anything!

Because it is an innate gift for him--he may have done all that studying but now he is not all that analytical about what he does.

Not at all. No one is analytical while they are playing. But he knows he has that innate gift, and he knows that he has this connection that probably he is aware of in an entirely different way than how it manifests itself to other people. Because I've seen times when I have shared things with him that I have found, or figured out, and Moody will take it right away and start to convert it from that place he plays from, and start putting his own slant on it. And if it agrees with that then he knows it's valid.

And he's been remarkably consistent as a player for a remarkably long period of time!

Right. The other thing, the second thing, is that the bebop thing is something he mastered, in the sense of the rhythmic innovation that is one of its components. Moody is one of the leading exponents of that, having mastered it from a technical standpoint. One of the byproducts of that, as it can appear from the outside, is an amazing technical facility.

Again, is that something he had to work at or did it come almost automatically for him?

It was communicated to him through Dizzy and the people he worked with as a player--especially Dizzy. There is a unique thing there. What Dizzy did was to organically change musical time. Moody was exposed to that and digested it. And so one of the by-products of that time conception is, again, what can appear to be from the outside a dazzling technique. Moody has digested all of that.

Now this book is about jazz flute. So speaking about his flute work, are you aware that Moody made a recording **Flute 'N The Blues** *a very short time--just a couple of weeks--after he first started playing the flute?*

Well there again, that would be a by-product of his digestion of the bebop breakthrough and the time breakthrough. Once somebody has invested himself with that concept they could pick up a kazoo and sound good on it. You see Moody's not really playing the flute--he's playing James Moody.

I think you've really put your finger on it!

Yes. Moody is going to sound like that no matter what he plays.

Right. He improved his flute technique as he went along, or he is still doing that actually is how he put it. He claims he is still unhappy with it.

Well that's Moody, man. He's never been... he's a very self-deprecating kind of person. Everyone says "Are you kidding? That sounds gorgeous." And he'll say "No man, I'm still trying." I remember when I first joined Dizzy's group we were in San Diego down in a place--I think it was called Jazzland or something like that. Anyway, the band rooms were down in the basement. And Moody and I became best friends on the road so--he used to call me Mikel because his daughter couldn't say Michael, so he's called me that ever since. So we'd go down there and he'd say "Mikel man, show me something about the scales." And I'd say "What are you talking about? You know that." And he'd say "No, there's something I don't understand about the scales!" So I'd say "Well, play me an F sharp harmonic minor scale." And he'd go *dgdgdgdgdgdg*. It just sounded great and I'd say "Moody, get out of here man!" And he'd start chasing me down the hall: "No man I'm serious--I need to know more about it." He's like that man. He called me up a few years ago. He was at Lincoln Center doing a clinic and called me up and he said "Man, can you tell me the changes for *Con Alma*?" I said "What are you talking about? Are you crazy? You've been playing *Con Alma* for thirty or forty years? He said "Yeah, I've been playing it but I want to be able to call the changes out so I can be intellectual!" (Laughs) He has a little eccentricity about that stuff but he knows it, and what he thinks he doesn't know is usually a slant on it that he didn't get. So if you tell him that slant then he figures he understands it.

So you worked with him for a long time! Was he the horn player with Dizzy the whole time you were with that group?

Not the whole time, but a good deal of the time. And then we worked together on several occasions after that, with his groups, and he recorded with me on some of my records, and I recorded with him on his, and we became... We actually refer to each other as brothers. I remember when Moody got married his wife said "Mike is your best friend?" and Moody said, "No, he's more than that." He's like family to me.

I understand. Well, there are some critics who say the flute is not really a jazz instrument. I guess they haven't heard Moody play it!

Well that borders on idiocy. A jazz musician like Dizzy could pick up a pot and a pan and a tablespoon and make jazz out of it. So to say something like that about an instrument sounds like someone who doesn't know what jazz is.

I think that sums it up pretty well! That could be it. Tell me, are there any recordings you liked where Moody played flute that you would like me to mention? Ones that you play on?

Well there was one of Moody's called *Heritage Hum*. I think it was Moody, myself, Sam Jones and Freddy Waits on drums. He's also on one of my records called *The Awakening* which he plays flute on.

Do you have anything else you wanted to add?

Well, I told you that story about when Moody was in Atlanta one time and he invited a guy from the Atlanta Symphony over to the hotel to practice duets. I had the room right next door so I could hear them practicing. They were playing some classical literature. So, afterwards, Moody called me up and said "Mikel, did you hear that? What did you think?" I said, "Well, it sounded like the guy from the symphony was playing the flute, but it sounded like you were playing James Moody!" Because Moody's sound on the flute--it's his voice. He's playing his voice, you know?

Yusef Lateef: "Gentle Giant" of World Music

"If jazz musicians were graded on seriousness of purpose, as are school children, Yusef would be at the head of the class."

Joel Dorn

As the first group of artists began to find ways to integrate the flute into the jazz idiom, a number of trends began to emerge that would gain in importance with subsequent generations of flutists: the application of formal, conservatory training to the mastery of the instrument, of which Frank Wess was a pioneer at the end of World War II; the integration of the flute into a multi-woodwind armamentarium for musicians in search of a broad expressive pallette, following the example of Buddy Collette; and the interest in the music traditions of cultures beyond American shores, which was to become a hallmark of a number of flutists. While these trends emerged as important to the jazz idiom in the sixties, all of them were embodied in the work of one performer who set them in motion in the mid-fifties and is still pursuing them to this day. It is therefore impossible to trace the history of the flute in jazz without considering the contribution of the great multi-instrumentalist **Yusef Lateef**. Doing so presents a problem, however.

Whenever possible, I prefer to portray the work of a musician in his/her own words. When I approached Dr. Lateef to request an interview, however, he turned me down flat, going so far as to request that I leave him out of the book altogether. Quite simply, he does not like the term jazz and does not wish to be associated with it. For some time, I did not know what to do; I did not want to disregard his wishes, or to offend him in any way. Yet I knew that the story of jazz flute would be incomplete without him. Then I came across the following from famed jazz writer Ira Gitler, in his notes to the 2004 CD *Yusef Lateef: Autophysiopsychic*.

In gathering information for the *Encyclopedia of Jazz in the Seventies*, I ran into numerous blocks, wrong address, no address, no response. When a questionnaire did not come back, from neither musician nor post office, I would reach for the telephone. When I spoke to Yusef Lateef, he told me that he didn't care to be part of the book. Although I respected his feelings I had to use my own judgment. The entry that I wrote is self-explanatory. "Lateef did not want to be included in this book," it begins, "because it is an encyclopedia of jazz and not an encyclopedia of music. This points up two things: that American society has not given the jazz writers and performers the respect and recognition commensurate with their art; and that many of these artists, especially among the black composers and players, are strongly affected by this attitude despite their high degree of artistic achievement. Lateef's music is wide-ranging, encompassing areas long identified with jazz and those associated with "serious" music (an inadequate terminology that further underlines the dichotomy), and "pop" points in between. In whatever directions his many talents are manifest, his exclusion from this volume would be conspicuous.

Given that Lateef's first recording on the flute was made in 1950, and that he continued to issue influential recordings utilizing the flute through the 1970s, his exclusion from this volume would be even more conspicuous. In addition, I realized that Lateef's name had already come up in several of the other artist's interviews, especially when they were discussing their influences. The cat was out of the bag. I decided to press ahead.

There is a good deal of biographical information for Yusef Lateef, from various sources, some of it contradictory. Many of his bios agree, for example, that he was born in 1920 in Chattanooga Tennessee, although some state his year of birth as 1921. Moreover, while most published biographies, including liner notes to some of his own albums, report that he was born William Evans, others, including his own web site and a recent National Public Radio interview, give his name as William Huddleston. Whichever it was, he was destined to change it some years later, to something more 'exotic.' But it would have been hard to predict this from his early years.

From Chattanooga, Evans (or Huddleston) moved with his family to Detroit in 1925. This was to prove a fertile environment for a burgeoning jazz musician, considering that it was there that he was eventually to meet and befriend Milt Jackson, Tommy Flanagan, Barry Harris, Paul Chambers, Donald Byrd, Hank, Thad, and Elvin Jones, Kenny Burrell, and Lucky Thompson. By 1938, at age eighteen, he had taken up the saxophone, his first instrument being an $80 Martin alto, although by the following year he had switched to tenor. He was fortunate to have the early guidance of trumpeter Teddy Buckner at Miller High School, and by the time he graduated from high school he was proficient enough on the instrument to work professionally, initially with the Thirteen Spirits of Swing, whose arrangements were written by Buckner's older brother, organist/pianist Milt. He went on to tour with a series of touring swing bands, among them the groups of Hot Lips Page, Roy Eldridge, Ernie Fields, Teddy Buckner and, in 1946, Lucky Millinder. The last of these gigs, which came about through the recommendation of his friend from Detroit, Lucky Thompson, took him to New York where he heard cutting edge musicians such as Coleman Hawkins, Charlie Parker and Dizzy Gillespie.

By 1948 the young saxophonist was in Chicago working with the Ernie Fields orchestra, and with Eugene Wright and his Kings of Swing, a group that included pianist Sonny Blount, later known as Sun Ra. Also at this time he befriended saxophonist Sonny Stitt with whom he practiced regularly.

It was at this point that both his life and his career took a dramatic change in direction. In his personal life he became one of the earliest African-American musicians to embrace Islam, as a result of which he changed his name to Yusef Abdul Lateef. Professionally, he reached the culmination of this first phase of his career, when, in 1949, he joined the Dizzy Gillespie Orchestra, replacing the Europe-bound James Moody. He stayed with the band for ten months, and participated on recordings for Spotlite and RCA records, cementing his reputation at the highest levels of the jazz community, while stylistically graduating from swing to bebop.

The economics of the music business in 1950 would not support a large jazz orchestra and Dizzy was forced to disband. Lateef returned to Detroit where he continued to perform, both with Kenny Burrell and with his own groups, although at one point he found it necessary to work on an assembly line at a Chrysler plant. It was while he was back in Detroit, however, that he embarked on an educational process that he was to pursue for several decades. He began by enrolling at Wayne State University where he studied flute and composition. Lacking an interview, we have no way of knowing if he was attracted to the flute in and of itself, inspired to take it up by Kenny Burrell as many articles state, or whether, as was common in 1950, he was simply unable to major in saxophone at a state university music department. One clue, however, is the fact that eight years later he picked up the oboe and began to take instruction from Ronald Odemark of the Detroit Symphony. Whatever contributed to his decision, Lateef was clearly interested in moving beyond the sound of fifties hard-bop, and extending his capabilites beyond the saxophone. The flute had a major role to play in this effort.

As he explored a broadening musical palette, he put it to use in his first working group, a quintet featuring such Detroit stalwarts as trombonist Curtis Fuller, pianists Hugh Lawson and Barry Harris, bassists Doug Watkins and Ernie Farrow, and drummer Louis Hayes. From 1955 to 1959 he produced a series of recordings in which his robust, hard-bop based tenor is offset by outings on flute, oboe and *argol* [or *arghul*, a traditional single-reed instrument found in Egypt and other parts of the Middle East]. This direction was set for him very early in this process. As he explained to his NPR interviewer: "After I made the first recording for Savoy records, I said if I should to continue to record I would have to enhance the canvas of my presentations, and one way of doing that sent me helter-skelter to the libraries searching out music, instruments and scales of other cultures, and then I tried meld what I had learned in a different fashion."

The first fruits of these labors can be heard in albums such as 1957's *Jazz and the Sounds of Nature,* which contain classic jazz material such as Ellington's *I Got It Bad And That Ain't Good* juxtaposed with more exotic items such as *Song of Delilah* and *Sounds of Nature.* In the same year, Lateef recorded *Prayer To The East*, on which the title track is placed alongside Gillespie's *Night In Tunisia,* the standard *Lover Man* along with *Gypsy Arab.* It is in the pursuit of such exotica that Lateef tends to use the flute in these sides, although he does not restrict his flute work to this kind of material, as he also employs it on jazz standards such as *Take The A Train*, for example, on a 1957 Prestige session. Along with Yusef's own aesthetic impulses, some writers have suggested that it was part of his contractual agreement with Prestige that he should the study music of other cultures and incorporate it into these recordings. Without being able to confirm this, it is very clear that this period saw the beginning of a lifetime of such study for the young Yusef, a pursuit that also led him to begin collecting and constructing flutes, many of which he was to feature on later recordings. And it is clear that these interests began at a very early stage in Lateef's career. Some bios state that he took up flute in 1956 at the suggestion of guitarist Kenny Burrell. Clearly this was not the case if he had begun taking college courses on flute as early as 1950. Lateef gave his recollection of this period in an interview with Fred Jung of *Jazz News* in 2000:

FRED JUNG: When did you begin to include the flute into your repertoire?

YUSEF LATEEF: I started to study the flute in 1951. The flute has been utilized by African-American musicians as far back as the early twenties. If you take a look at some of the old pictures of Chick Webb, then you will see the flute right there on the bandstand among the woodwinds.

F.J.: You also presented the oboe and the bassoon, not traditionally considered in improvised music, in performances.

Y.L.: Well, in high school, my teacher tried to get me to play the oboe and later on, I reflected on that and then I took him up on it. After I started to record, I didn't want to reinvent the wheel with each album, so then I studied the bassoon and included it as well as some miscellaneous instruments like Japanese flute, and then I began to make flutes to enhance the canvas of my expression.

F.J.: That kind of dedication and sacrifice to your art seems like something of another era these days.

Y.L.: Well, oboists make their reeds so it is nothing new in a sense. It is just another part of musical expression.

As the fifties drew to a close, Lateef's career took another step forward. Although he had been making regular visits to New York (often Rudy Van Gelder's Hackensack, NJ studio), for recording sessions, Lateef had resisted the urge to make a permanent move there. But, by 1959 it was finally time to take the plunge. Ten years would seem a long time for a bourgeoning musician to spend in Detroit, but the talent pool was so fecund in the Motor City that no musical compromises were necessary on his part in order to pursue his performance career there, and his ongoing studies were of great importance to him. Eventually, however, both his career as a performer and his academic interests led him to the center of jazz activity. His reputation preceded him, it seems, creating a pent-up demand for his services, especially as a multi-instrumentalist. His discography for 1959-1960 shows him in sessions with the likes of Ernie Wilkins, Louis Hayes, Doug Watkins, Paul Chambers, Nat Adderley, Curtis Fuller, Clark Terry, Grant Green, Art Blakey, Ray Brown and Ernestine Anderson. He also cut sides with his own quintet--with Ron Carter playing cello. By May of 1960 he was working with Charles Mingus, sitting in the reed section with Eric Dolphy and Joe Farrell on Mingus' landmark *Pre Bird* recording. At the same time, Lateef continued his formal flute studies with Harold Jones and John Wummer at the Manhattan School of Music, from which he was to receive a Bachelor's Degree in Music in 1969, followed by a Master's Degree in Music Education in 1970.

The decade of the sixties was to be an exciting time in jazz history, with many new developments, including experimentation with new instruments and the importation of melodic and rhythmic ideas from non-Western music traditions. None of these were new ideas for Yusef Lateef, however. He had been investigating these areas since the early fifties, and was well into the process of incorporating them into his work as the decade drew to a close. This is evident both from his session work at the time--playing tenor sax, flute, oboe and English horn with the Randy Western Orchestra on *Uhuru Africa,* or on *Color Changes* with Clark Terry and his Orchestra–on his own 1960 recording *Centaur And The Phoenix,* or on Olatunji's *Afro Percussion* in 1961. Then there was a new development, one which gave Lateef's career a significant boost.

By 1961, altoist Cannonball Adderley's quintet had become, according to producer Orrin Keepnews, "... one of the most dazzling success stories in modern jazz history." With his brother Nat on cornet and Junior Mance, then Bobby Timmons and later Victor Feldman on piano, the quintet had issued several highly successful albums--particularly 1960's *Them Dirty Blues*--and had major hits with *Work Song,* and *Mercy, Mercy, Mercy.* Sensitive to criticism that his group was lightweight, Adderley decided to add gravitas in the form of another horn player. His choice was Yusef Lateef, who was with the group from Christmas of 1961 to 1964, touring extensively and appearing on several of their recordings.

Cannonball Adderley was, without a doubt, one of the finest saxophonists in jazz history, and he had recently spent a year holding his own alongside John Coltrane in Miles Davis' sextet, participating on the best-selling jazz album of all time, Miles' *Kind of Blue.* For him to select Lateef as his front-line partner in his own group was a great compliment to Yusef's ability as a saxophonist. It is evident from the sides recorded with his new sextet that Adderley valued Lateef primarily for his robust tenor style, with a few select features for his other instruments--primarily his bluesey oboe--with just one or two special flute features. In some cases, such as *Gemini,* on the *Live In New York* album, the flute is used just for the theme statement, with Lateef switching to tenor for his solo, an approach followed by Nat Adderley on his 1960 recording *That's Right*, that finds Lateef stating the theme of *The Old Country* on the flute. Lateef's flute is heard throughout on *New Delhi*, introduced by Cannonball as featuring "our flutist, brother Yusef Lateef." The solo itself is of interest for its juxtaposition of the strong, full tone that resulted from Lateef's formal training on the instrument, with the vocalizing into the instrument that was to become the stock-in-trade of several leading jazz flutists. Similar elements are found on another flute feature with Adderley, *Jive Samba.*

It is on Lateef's own recordings, however, such as *Eastern Sounds,* made a few weeks before joining Adderley, or *Into Something,* made just four days after joining the sextet, that he displays his preference in allotting time between his different instruments. On *Into Something*, for example, the presence of Elvin Jones on drums prompts him to feature several strong tenor outings, but he still includes one of his patented blues compositions for oboe, and applies his flute to a standard, *I Remember April.* "What I'm always striving for is contrast," he told Nat Hentoff, as reported in the liner notes, "as wide a range of moods, forms, and textures as I can create. But always, I try to remember that craftsmanship is not enough. You've got to have depth of feeling. Effect for its own sake is hollow. You've got to believe in what you're doing."

By 1964, for unknown reasons, Lateef decided to leave the Cannonball Adderley group, to be replaced by another up and coming flutist, Charles Lloyd. For Yusef, however, it is clear that his time with the sextet had given him great exposure, which afforded him a degree of freedom to pursue his own musical goals. This would result in a series of recordings exploring the range of moods, forms and textures with which he was occupied. Throughout all of these, the flute had a major role to play. Indeed, critic Gary Giddins, writing in the liner notes to his 1974 Prestige recording *Blues For The Orient.*

> On tenor, he is a persuasive and powerful player, a master of the modern style... a confidently swinging style that identifies him in the tradition of Dexter and Stitt... His most significant work, however, is on flute. He stands, I think, with Eric Dolphy, Rahsaan Roland Kirk, and James Moody, among the most consistently satisfying flutists in jazz. His authoritative, full sonority combines with unflagging inventiveness on the instrument. The flute demands a firm embouchure and lungs of leather or it will sound weak and pasty. Lateef's flute is as comforting as an electric blanket.

In the 1970s, a new dimension was added to Lateef's work as he began to explore the possibilities of more formal composition, often for larger ensembles. In 1969, musician's agent Michael Daniel, after hearing Lateef's second Atlantic Album *Blue Yusef,* which includes backup singers and a string quartet, had picked up the phone and called the composer with an intriguing suggestion. "No one has ever written a blues suite for orchestra. Why don't you write one--I think I can get it played." Lateef's response was immediate, "Okay, I'll get started." The result was the *Symphonic Blues Suite,* also known as *Suite 16*, which was indeed performed: it was premiered in 1969 by the Augusta, GA Symphony Orchestra, performed in 1970 with his hometown Detroit Symphony Orchestra at the Meadowbrook Music Festival, and finally recorded by the Cologne Radio Orchestra. The piece features orchestral forces, plus rhythm section, with the composer playing C flute, pneumatic flute, bamboo flute, tambourine and bells. In 1974 the NDR Radio Orchestra of Hamburg commissioned him to compose and perform the tone poem *Lalit*, named for an early morning *raga* of Hindustani music. The Hamburg ensemble also premiered and recorded his Symphony No.1 (*Tahira*). Since that time an extensive catalogue of works has flowed from his pen, from the originals he writes for his quartets and quintets, to works for symphony and chamber orchestras, stage bands, small ensembles, vocalists, choruses and solo pianists. Many of the works, such as the *Symphonic Blues Suite,* include a part for the composer himself, executing both written and improvised material. One of these, *Yusef Lateef's Little Symphony*, from 1987, found him performing all the parts on multiple wind instruments as well as a synthesizer. Lateef was probably startled to receive a Grammy for the recording, mainly because it was in the "New Age" category, the first album to be honored in this category.

Lateef's most ambitious work to date is *The African American Epic Suite*, which was commissioned by the WDR Orchestra producer Ulrich Kurtz in 1993. A four-movement work written for quintet and orchestra, it depicts the plight of African Americans under 400 years of slavery. Premiered and recording by the WDR Orchestra, the suite was also been performed by the Atlanta Symphony Orchestra under Yoel Levi as a centerpiece of the National Black Arts Festival in 1998, and by the Detroit Symphony Orchestra under Thomas Wilkins in 2001.

If the 1970s found Lateef preoccupied with composition, it was also a time for further educational pursuits, as he somehow found the time to earn a Ph.D. in Education in 1975, an accomplishment that was celebrated with his 1976 album *The Doctor Is In... And Out*. His doctoral dissertation was entitled "An Overview of Western and Islamic Education." He followed this, in the early eighties, with a research trip to Africa. From 1981 until 1985, he was a senior research Fellow at the Center for Nigerian Cultural Studies at Ahmadu Bello University in Zaria, Nigeria, where he did research into the *Sarewa,* or Fulani flute.

As Lateef's work over the last two decades has expanded into a variety of genres--classical, New Age, or whatever--this is paralleled by his increasing dissatisfaction with the word jazz as a description of his music. He began his 2000 interview with *Jazz News'* Fred Jung with the statement "First of all, Fred, in this interview, I request that you don't refer to me as a jazz musician. My music is jazz." That same year he told Chris M. Slawecki "Well, I've never played jazz, so, and, please, if you write an article about me, please don't write that I play jazz. Please." "I don't call myself a jazz musician," he recently told NPR, "I am just a musician, a teacher, a composer... trying to blend the music of many different traditions, a goal [I have] achieved only in the last few years." He concluded, somewhat enigmatically, "Jazz is where modern music begins."

Lateef prefers to refer to his work as "autophysiopsychic music," a term which first appeared on his 1977 CTI album entitled simply *Autophysiopsychic,* and which he defines as "that which comes from one's spiritual, physical and emotional self." It is this subject that he taught at the University of Massachusetts at Amherst, and Smith College, until his retirement. It is this that, for him, describes the music he has been producing since that time, as well as the books he has published such as the *Repository of Scales and Melodic Patterns,* and *Method on How to Perform Autophysiopsychic Music,* (available, ironically, from www.playjazz.com). He is not the first musician to reject the labeling of art; he will not be the last. Whatever he calls his music, however, it is fair to say that anyone who enjoys jazz will find his work of great interest. And there can be no doubt that his work has been of enormous influence on those who play the flute in the jazz idiom.

James Spaulding: Sideman Extraordinaire

"Music has been the life force by which I have been able to express my emotions and culture. Through music, I have gained a pride and sense of contribution to the world's societies. Music has enabled me to recreate meaningful, human and emotional experiences and to express life in all its utterance, through the medium of sound."

James Spaulding

If it has been hard to find flutists in the mainstream of jazz there have always been exceptions that proved the rule. A prime example is **James Spaulding,** who for many years was the almost the sole exponent of jazz flute in that most mainstream of jazz settings, the Blue Note record catalog. Growing up in Indianapolis, Spaulding was a friend of trumpeter Freddie Hubbard from an early age, and when James arrived in New York in 1962, Freddie provided him with both work and, for a while, a roof over his head. An appearance on Hubbard's recording *Hub Tones* brought James well-deserved attention, and he went on to record several more albums with Hubbard, as well as with Bobby Hutcherson, Wayne Shorter and other major Blue Note artists..

James Spaulding was from a musical family; his father was a professional musician who played the guitar and led his own big band. James' musical training began with him playing the bugle in grade school, later taking up the trumpet. After hearing Charlie Parker, however, he took up the also saxophone, and the flute quickly followed. He made his professional debut playing around Indianapolis with a rhythm & blues group.

From 1954 to 1957, Spaulding was in the army playing in service bands. When he was discharged, he settled in Chicago where he led his own group, and worked with the Sun Ra Orchestra. He furthered his flute studies at the Chicago Cosmopolitan School of Music before moving to New York City, In 1975, he received a bachelor's degree in music from Livingston College in New Jersey where he taught flute as an adjunct professor.

As of this writing in his 74th year, Spaulding has been a working musician for over half a century, with a career of great variety and breadth. He has received support from the National Endowment for the Arts to produce and perform original music--a suite entitled "A Song of Courage." He has worked with artists as diverse as Louis Armstrong, Duke Ellington, Max Roach, Sun Ra, David Murray, Abbey Lincoln, Art Blakey, McCoy Tyner and the World Saxophone Quartet. He has appeared on well over 100 recordings, including several fine sessions as a leader, but many more as a sideman. In many ways, in fact, Spaulding remains an overlooked jazz master. This was the first thing I brought to his attention:

The 1995 edition of Tom Lord's Jazz Discography shows you as having nine sessions as a leader, but 103 sessions as a sideman.

Gee Whiz! 103 sessions as a sideman! My pockets should be having the mumps, right? (Laughs.) Have you ever heard that expression?

No, that's a new one on me! Apparently the most recorded sidemen were Jerome Richardson and Milt Hinton. Jerome had over 4000 sessions.

Jerome was really a fantastic musician!

The **Rough Guide to Jazz** *refers to you as "James Spaulding--Sideman Extraordinaire." Does that bother you?*

It's fine. I used to be called the "utility man."

That's another way of saying the same thing. But tell me how you got started. I understand you grew up in Indianapolis and then you were in Chicago for awhile.

Yes, I joined the U.S. Army. I was in the Army before then, in 1954, when I was 17. I finished basic training and I went to band camp training in Fort Ord, California.

So, you were already playing before you went into the Army?

Yes, I had already taught myself to play the flute.

Was the flute your first instrument?

No, I started on a bugle that my father gave me. My father was a great jazz guitarist. I learned to play the bugle at five years of age. In grade school, I switched to trumpet. When I went into high school, after I heard Charlie Parker on the records that my father brought home, I told my dad that I wanted to learn to play the alto saxophone. He said "Okay, get yourself an alto saxophone from the school and get someone to show you the fingerings." They also had a flute there at the high school, so I checked it out and brought it home. I taught myself how to play the flute and the saxophone. I was about ten years old when I became serious.

Charlie Parker inspired your interest in the saxophone. Had you heard anyone play jazz on the flute?

No, not at all. There were probably some flute players, but my father was a guitarist, so he brought home music that mostly featured the guitar, the Nat King Cole trio, for example. Then he brought home the "new wave" in jazz. That was Charlie Parker and Dizzy Gillespie, Max Roach and Charlie Mingus. And that was my whole awakening to this music as a kid. The music saved my life. When I first heard it I said, "This music sounds like it is from another planet!" I wanted to learn how to play this music from that age, so this music has been keeping me together all those years. I have a wonderful wife who is helping me to do that. I have a wonderful family, my two daughters. All of that is ingrained in there too. I think family is so important. My family helped me out; they stayed together. My father tried to be a musician, tried to play this music. It was rough. He had to stop playing in order to feed us; there were seven of us in the whole family.

Have you worked steadily through the years?

Mostly, yeah! Ever since I joined the army. Before then I was playing with a little group, a little teenaged group in high school before I dropped out in my first year. I only stayed there long enough so that I could hang out in the band room and rent instruments. Music and art were my friends.

Have you ever had to take a day job along the way?

Oh, of course. My father made me work. As a child I had to get jobs shining shoes and emptying garbage in the neighborhood. In those days people had little garbage pits.

But once you started as a professional musician?

I was able to read, so my first gig was with older musicians my father's age, at my father's suggestion. He brought me in and had me play a gig with them. I was the only kid in the band. I got the job because I was able to read arrangements like [Glenn Miller's] *In the Mood*. That was one of my first arrangements that I ever tried to read with a big band.

Was this on saxophone?

Yes. I played alto.

Do you remember the first time you heard jazz played on the flute?

I still can't remember. I finally began to hear some jazz flute with Frank Wess on one of his recordings with a rhythm section. I also remember Yusef Lateef performing on some recordings.

I notice that the first recordings listed for you are with Sun Ra. Tell me a little bit about that experience, working with Sun Ra. That must have been extraordinary.

It was marvelous. I didn't know how fantastic the man was when I joined the band. In fact, Pat Patrick and John Gilmore were responsible for pulling me into the band. I met these guys down at a jam session at a place called the Pershing Lounge in Chicago, during the time I was living there, going to school. That's the place where pianist Ahmad Jamal did that famous recording *Live at the Pershing Lounge.* This session was down in the basement. They'd have breakfast parties and musicians would come down there and jam until ten or eleven o'clock the next morning and have breakfast--it was great. Sun Ra was down there one night, and he heard me play with the guys. John Gilmore and Pat came over and introduced themselves and asked me if I would like to rehearse with Sun Ra. I said, "Sure, of course! What time? Who is he?" I didn't know him. It didn't make any difference. I was out there trying to communicate with musicians.

Well, I see that the first recording was Sun Ra Visits Planet Earth, *in late 1957 or early 1958. It looks like he visited long enough for you to climb on board!*

Actually there was an earlier recording. That was with Jerry Butler, on the Chess label, only I wasn't listed on it. I took a flute solo as a matter of fact. But anyway, I was working with Sun Ra. Yeah! That was really great. I was going to school at night and I had a little day job that my cousin had gotten for me so that I could live in Chicago during this period, so that I could go on my G.I. bill. I was attending the Cosmopolitan School of Music which is now closed. It was a great school. They taught everything on jazz and improvisation, orchestration and everything. But anyway, I made the rehearsal and Sun Ra heard me play and liked it. He wrote some stuff out at the piano and it was great. I was very in tune with the music he wrote. He said, "Okay, you've got the gig." Sun Ra had so many things going on that you had to always be thinking musically. It was great!

In Sun Ra's Arkestra, didn't all of the saxophone players play flute?

I know that Marshall Allen was a flutist. Marshall is still with us. He is in his eighties, almost eighty five.

Do you remember being featured on flute with Sun Ra?

I just played a little flute here and there. I just did whatever Sun Ra asked me to do.

After Sun Ra, you recorded with Larry "Wild" Rice.

That was on the Pacific Jazz Label.

And then you recorded with the trumpeter Bobby Bryant.

Bobby Bryant was one of my first teachers in improvisation. I met him when I was in Chicago.

But then 1962 was a milestone. You recorded the album Hub-Tones *with Freddie Hubbard for Blue Note Records.*

I went to New York in 1961 to live and to try to get involved with the music scene. The only people I knew were Freddie Hubbard and Slide Hampton. Freddie helped me out and let me stay at his home for a while.

Had you known him in Indianapolis?

Yes, we met at a jam session. *Hub-Tones* was my first recording with Freddie.

***You have a lovely flute solo on* Lament for Booker.**

That was a beautiful piece that Freddie wrote for Booker Little--a lovely ballad.

And then* Prophet Jennings *also.

I met the guy. He was an artist. He had a wonderful conception of painting African Art. There were very few flute players back then that I can remember. There was Eric Dolphy, Yusef Lateef and Rahsaan [Roland Kirk] of course.

Did you ever adopt any of the techniques that Rahsaan used with the flute?

Rahsaan liked to use those effects. I experiment with those, if I feel like it.

So once you got your foot in the door through your recordings with Freddie Hubbard, then you did a lot of sessions for Blue Note.

Yeah, I did a lot of recordings. Duke Pearson called me. He was a producer there.

I just got hold of a recording of his that features your flute work,* Sweet Honey Bee. *It's a really nice session that was only recently reissued. Another big favorite of mine is* Components *with Bobby Hutcherson.

That was my first recording with Bobby. He frequently calls me out to California to work with him.

You missed the Blue Note Records 40th Anniversary Concert held at Town Hall in New York City, but James Newton performed on* Little B's Poem, *your flute feature from the* Components *album. You performed on a large number of sessions for Blue Note during those days. That was really jazz right down the middle, wasn't it?

I was blessed to come to New York at that time, to have the hook up with Freddie. After I did *Hub-Tones* my phone continued to ring. I had just gotten married in 1963 to my wife Jean.Gigs continued to come in. I was quite busy during the sixties.

Yes, so I see. Freddie Hubbard, Wayne Shorter. . . And many of your sessions were done in Rudy Van Gelder's studios in Englewood Cliffs, New Jersey. I was talking to Jerry Dodgion earlier and he said that was a wonderful studio for flute.

Jerry Dodgion and I did a recording together with Duke Pearson called *The Right Touch* in September of 1967.

Things started to get a little leaner for you as you got into the 70's?

Yes, I went out to New Jersey to go to school on my G.I. bill. I went out there with Larry Ridley in 1975 to teach at Livingston College as a professor of flute. It was the alternative school to Rutgers University, out in New Brunswick. I taught there and attended classes at the same time. I was there starting in 1971and I graduated with my B.A. in 1975.

Were there fewer gigs during this period?

During this period, Larry [Ridley] helped me get a gig with the Duke Ellington Band. This was after Duke died, in 1975. I worked a few gigs with that band under the direction of Mercer Ellington. I left that group to go back to school and finish my B.A. in 1975. My father passed away during that same year, right before I graduated. He was supposed to come up for my graduation.

You began a Master's degree later, didn't you?

I tried for a Master's degree at Rutgers University, but because of numerous difficulties, I didn't finish it. My wife completed her Bachelor's degree in 1980 and we moved back to New York.

You had a session in 1980 with Louis Armstrong,* What a Wonderful World. *Tell me about that.

That session was the highlight of my career--shaking the hand of Louis Armstrong and being at his 71st birthday party. On that session there was a string orchestra. Oliver Nelson was the arranger and I was given a flute solo on *What a Wonderful World*. Oliver Nelson transcribed my solo from the Leon Thomas album *Spirits Known and Unknown* from October of 1969, and orchestrated it with strings for the Louis Armstrong session.

So here you are working with people like Archie Shepp and Pharoah Sanders, who were moving into more experimental types of music, and the next thing you know you are with Louis.

I was working with the Flying Dutchman label at the time. Bob Theile who was the producer of the Armstrong session called me for recording session dates.

What was the first recording you made under your own name?

The first recording I made was *James Spaulding plays the Legacy of Duke Ellington*.

You also made a recording titled **Brilliant Corners** *that features the music of Thelonius Monk. I don't hear flutists perform Monk tunes very often.*

[Spaulding sings *Little Rootie Tootie*.] That's a rough piece. That is not an easy piece to play.

Yes, but with Ron Carter, Mulgrew Miller and Kenny Washington, you can't go wrong. Do you have any thoughts on the subject of doubling?

I went from bugle to trumpet. I have played clarinet, soprano sax, baritone sax--in the army-- flute and tenor sax. The alto saxophone is my first love. I think one instrument is enough.

James Spaulding is a very modest man. Whatever he says, the record is clear; he has distinguished himself as a soloist on both alto saxophone and flute. He is probably best known for his work on saxophone--this is not unusual in among doublers in jazz. But he has always found time and space for the flute, and his assertive, clean-toned playing has kept the flag flying for the flute in jazz for many years.

Part Three

New Sounds

The 1960s

If the use of the flute in jazz began in earnest with the emergence of bebop in the mid 1940s and the subsequent cool jazz movements of the 1950s, it was during the 1960s that the jazz flute truly came of age. This was but one of many new developments during this decade. As Michael J. Budds writes in his *Jazz In The Sixties: The Expansion of Musical Resources and Techniques*:

> The decade of the sixties was like no other in the history of jazz: the mighty river that had represented the mainstream of the jazz tradition up to that time was diverted into countless streams. Some of these spilled wildly across the flood plains: some were strengthened by contact with other bodies of water: others meandered: others dried up. The musicians themselves, acting as an army of self-indulgent engineers, forced the river beyond its banks according to their own individual interests. . . Some of these developments might have been predicted on musical terms: several of them had been initiated in the late fifties. Others appear to have been timely responses to the distinctive cultural profile of the sixties.

The cultural profile in question was one of political upheaval, social change, and, in the arts, experimentation, rapid diversification, and the testing and breaking of boundaries. In jazz, in Budds' view, this new approach manifest itself in ". . . an awakening of interest in 'world music,' a new attempt to synthesize jazz and the music of the European fine-art tradition into a 'Third-Stream' of music, the revitalization of the big band, and the continued incorporation of popular music into the jazz tradition." These developments, according to Budds, "created a stylistic diversity unprecedented in the history of jazz."

None of these developments were entirely new, but the earliest jazz flutists were involved with almost all of them. The incorporation of Latin music into jazz had already made a big impact on the career of Herbie Mann; others such as Yusef Lateef were beginning to experiment with Middle-Eastern forms; flutists such as Frank Wess, Paul Horn and Hubert Laws were working with classical teachers to master instrumental techniques they would later apply to jazz; composers and arrangers such as Gil Evans and Henry Mancini were writing for the flute along with other new colors and textures, in both the jazz big band and the movie score. And providing the context for these trends were experiments began in the late 1950s, with Miles Davis, John Coltrane and others expanding the harmonic and tonal frameworks for jazz improvisation.

With all of this, 1960 was a watershed for jazz in general and for jazz flutists in particular: It was in 1960 that *Down Beat* introduced a separate flute category in its Critics Poll. The first winner was Frank Wess, while a future winner, Hubert Laws, won a scholarship to the Juilliard School of Music in New York in 1960, the same year that Joe Farrell arrived in New York to begin his career in earnest, and David "Fathead" Newman found a flute in a pawn shop.

As this remarkable decade unfolded, a new generation of flutists emerged that brought the instrument to a new level of development within jazz, while several of the earlier group continued to grow and flourish. 1964 was a particularly fertile year which saw a quite extraordinary collection of seminal jazz flute recordings. These included *I Talk With The Spirits* by Rahsaan Roland Kirk, *Out To Lunch* and, sadly, *Last Date* by Eric Dolphy, *The Laws of Jazz* by Hubert Laws, *Discovery!* by Charles

Lloyd, Paul Horn's *Jazz Suite on the Mass Texts* and *Live at Pep's* by Yusef Lateef and his quintet. Meanwhile, Frank Wess--after recording *It Might As Well Be Spring* with Frank Sinatra and the Count Basie Orchestra--left Basie to strike out on his own, Leo Wright left the U.S. for good and settled in Europe, while Sahib Shihab, already in France, recorded an all-flute album--*Calypso Blues*. Seldon Powell stepped out of the studios to make one of his rare Latin jazz recordings with percussionist Willie Rodriguez, and Buddy Collette made an album called *Warm Winds,* which features his flute work throughout. It is possible to get a decent snapshot of the flute in jazz simply from recordings made in 1964.

While the 1960s saw the birth of several important jazz flutists' careers, three of the most important of these artists are, unfortunately, no longer with us. We will look at these first.

Eric Dolphy: Outward Bound

"Eric Dolphy was a saint--in every way, not just his playing."

Charles Mingus

"I can only say my life was made much better by knowing him. He was one of the greatest people I have ever known, as a man, a friend and as a musician."

John Coltrane

"Best damn flute player I ever had."

Chico Hamilton

So far, only two flutists have been inducted into the *Down Beat* Hall of Fame. One is Rahsaan Roland Kirk, voted in by the critics in 1978. In 1964, a matter of weeks after his tragically premature death, **Eric Dolphy** was also afforded this honor by the magazine's readers. It had been barely four years since he had burst onto the scene with his first recording as a leader. With the possible exception of Clifford Brown or Booker Little, both close friends of Dolphy's, it is hard to think of anyone in the history of jazz who has contributed more to the music in such a short period of time.

I only saw Dolphy play live once, but the memory is still vivid. I was still in high school in November 1961 when he toured England with the John Coltrane group which was opening for Dizzy Gillespie's quintet. I was already in possession of Dolphy's debut album, *Outward Bound,* as well as Coltrane's breakthrough recording *My Favorite Things,* but still starved of live performance by top-flight American jazz artists, so the anticipation was intense. There was only one London date, at the Walthamstow Odeon, and I set off to drive across the city with four or five friends including Evan Parker, now well known tenor and soprano saxophonist. Half way there our ancient automobile gave up the ghost. Scrambling to get across town on public transportation we arrived at the venue just in time to hear the final few bars of Coltrane's set, the climactic "My Favorite Things.*"* Dizzy's set--with Leo Wright on alto and flute--was excellent, but it was hard to enjoy it so great was our disappointment. Fortunately, a sympathetic usher allowed us to creep back into the back of the hall for the second set, and we sat transfixed by the hypnotic power of Coltrane's music, to which Dolphy contributed a unique voice on all three of his instruments. When the set was over we walked around the theater for half an hour trying to find a stage door where we could meet the musicians, but everything was locked up tight and eventually we wandered back toward the tube [subway] station. The next day Evan set out in search of a soprano saxophone--a rare commodity in 1961. For my part, I had to wait until I went to college three years later to acquire my first flute, but the first thing I played was "Glad To Be Unhappy," from *Outward Bound.*

It is hard to put into words the impact that Dolphy's music had, and even harder to express the sense of shock that was engendered by his death. A decade earlier, jazz fans, shocked by the death of Charlie Parker, comforted themselves with the slogan "Bird lives." But in some ways Dolphy's passing was even harder to bear. The Hollywood stereotype of the self-destructive jazz musician has been fed by dozens of real-life examples, from Bix Beiderbeck to Bird to Chet Baker. Even the saintly John Coltrane was brought low by the damage wrought on his system by his earlier lifestyle. But Eric Dolphy, by all accounts, was addicted to one thing only: music. From the time he took up the clarinet in second grade, to his death from diabetic shock in Berlin, at age 36, he was entirely one-pointed--music: practicing music, studying music, performing music, living music. But by the greatest irony, it was, in a sense, music that killed him. His death was not caused by drug or alcohol abuse. An obituary in the Los Angeles sentinel, written by a friend of his family, stated: "Those of us who knew Eric believe that it was his driving determination, his zest and preoccupation with his work, which eventually caught up with Eric and led to his fatal attack." There were secondary effects: poverty--his access to health care was, to say the least, limited; his quest for purity--he was attempting a purifying honey fast when he went into diabetic shock; and his race--doctors in Berlin failed to save him because they assumed that, being a black jazz musician, he must be suffering from a drug overdose.

So ended one of the most intensely creative lives in music, but in the short time he had, Eric Dolphy made a wildly disproportionate endowment to the music he loved: he moved forward very substantially the development of the alto saxophone; he virtually single-handedly introduced the bass clarinet to jazz; and he made an enormous contribution to the flute in jazz, one that, to this day, has not been fully comprehended or absorbed by contemporary performers.

The details of Dolphy's life do not take long to summarize; they are available in a thoughtful and highly recommended biography by Vladimir Simosko and Barry Tepperman which also contains a thorough discography. There is also an excellent article by John Kruth that will be part of a forthcoming anthology. We only need to touch on the highlights here. It has been forty years since Dolphy's passing and, sadly, many of his closest associates have also passed away, so details are hard to come by. One thing is clear: as Eric Dolphy's was a life dedicated to music, a life defined by music.

It appears that Dolphy awoke to his avocation at an early age. His parents, Eric Sr. and Sadie, who were immigrants of West Indian origin, were keen music lovers who passed on their enthusiasm to their son. Sadie sang in a church choir and Eric Jr. followed in her footsteps when he was old enough. His attraction to woodwinds began even earlier. By age seven or eight he was playing the clarinet, which was followed by the alto saxophone by around age sixteen. His parents encouraged this trend, with thoughts of Eric becoming a symphonic musician, perhaps on oboe, which Eric also loved. Events were to lead him on a different path, however. The musicians and teachers with whom he came in contact included more jazz players than classical performers, largely through the good offices of his first teacher, Lloyd Reese, a brilliant saxophonist in his own right, whose other students included Harry Carney, Ben Webster, Charles Mingus and, as we have seen, Buddy Collette. Eric was also close with pianist Hampton Hawes whose father was the pastor at a church where Eric taught Sunday school. By 1954 he had met both Ornette Coleman and John Coltrane. He was to record later with Mingus, Coltrane and Coleman.

As well as providing music teachers for their son, Eric's parents built a small studio behind their house so that he would have a place to practice and rehearse. Alan Saul, a Dolphy enthusiast who maintains a website devoted to his music, conducted an with interview with Eric's parents some years ago that John Kruth draws upon for his article. Sadie Dolphy describes her son's practice routine when he was a teenager:

> He would get up in the morning before he went to school, say about 4:30 or 5. He practiced until it was almost time to get his breakfast and leave for school. And he'd hurry home to start practicing again, until late in the evening. And he [meaning Eric Sr.] had a little studio built outside for him. So, afterwards, he could be out there without...

. . . presumably, without disturbing them. She continues: "Sometimes we'd be asleep, and we'd hear plunking on the piano, and we'd say 'Hey, what're you doing?' He said, 'I just got an idea.' And he'd [say] he'd been writing, you know. And we'd tell him his daddy had to go to work. He had to get up and go too, but he'd stop and do all that."

Apart from providing Eric with a refuge, his little studio was also an attraction for other musicians, both local and from out of town. A newly issued CD, *Clifford Brown + Eric Dolphy: Together 1954*, contains home recordings of Dolphy jamming with Clifford and Max Roach who were frequent visitors to Eric's studio. On this occasion they used the place to audition tenor saxophonists for their group after Teddy Edwards left. The tenorman they selected, Harold Land, was a another close friend of Eric's who also appears on the recording. It was a dream environment for a young musician to grow up in.

Exactly where the flute enters the picture is uncertain. On the 1954 sessions Dolphy is heard on the alto saxophone exclusively, as he is on his earliest recordings, in 1948-1949, with Roy Porter and his Orchestra, otherwise known as Roy Porter's 17 Beboppers. Porter was a Los Angeles-based drummer who led a group that also included Art Farmer and Jimmy Knepper, and Dolphy played lead alto for a period. Gerald Wilson also remembers Eric playing alto with his big band, and photos of Dolphy taken during his stint with the US Army from 1950 to 1953, which was spent at Fort Lewis, Washington, and later the U.S. Naval School of Music, show him with a clarinet. It appears that while in Washington state he appeared with the Tacoma Symphony, but again, whether he played flute or clarinet, we do not know.

Upon his return to Los Angeles, Eric went back to Buddy Collette for more instruction. When I asked Buddy about this, he told me that Eric was definitely playing flute by this time; they used to play duets together on flutes and clarinets. But being too busy with studio work to do much teaching, Buddy recommended Eric to various other teachers. He mentioned a clarinet teacher, Dominique Fera, and for flute, Elise Baxter Moennig. Elise, a prominent teacher and performer in Los Angeles, was the daughter of Harry Baxter, the proprietor of Baxter-Northup, a firm involved with manufacturing and repairing woodwind instruments. According to Chico Hamilton, Dolphy also studied with William Kincaid at one time, although exactly when is unclear, especially as Kincaid taught in Philadelphia. Whoever the teachers were, they were happy to work with Eric, according to Buddy Collette. "He was such a fine student, one in a million really, he studied so hard, and had such good technique. He was a pleasure to work with." This was evident just from my conversation with Collette. I called casually just to ask a quick question, but Buddy spoke eloquently for some time about Eric's qualities, both as a musician and a human being. Simosko and Tepperman's biography contains equally enthusiastic endorsements of Eric's personality from associates and personal friends.

Another woodwind teacher, Merle Johnston, was very influential in Eric's development during these years. A very well-known teacher in the L.A. area, Johnson was quoted as saying that "the three greatest musicians I turned out were Buddy Collette, Eric Dolphy, and Frank Morgan." Johnston was instrumental in Dolphy's decision to take up the bass clarinet. They went together to find an instrument in a pawn shop, and once Eric had purchased it, Johnston helped him set up the right mouthpiece and reed combination and work to develop his sound on the instrument. Dolphy went on to establish the instrument in jazz performance, for some the most significant achievement of his short career. To do this involved a great deal of work during these years, however, and with the alto saxophone his predominant voice in his early work, the flute had to be his third instrument. Indeed, Buddy Collette confirmed to me that, during this period, Eric was unable to devote the same amount of time to developing his flute technique as he did to the other two instruments. Bassist Reggie Workman, who worked with Dolphy in John Coltrane's quintet, also told me that he felt Eric's flute technique was less developed than his chops on the two reed instruments. Rather than minimizing his contribution to the instrument, however, it makes it all the more remarkable.

The years following Dolphy's military service were filled with work, study and the development of a musical vision. He appeared with groups led by Gerald Wilson, George Brown, Buddy Collette and Eddie Beal, the latter an extended stay through 1956 and '57. He also led his own groups with some success; local newspapers in May 1956 record a 14-week engagement at the *Oasis* club for Eric Dolphy and his Men of Modern Jazz. It was still too early for Eric to have developed an independent voice. As the 1954 recordings with Clifford Brown confirm, Eric's style was still very much under the shadow of Charlie Parker. But according to eye-witness accounts, he was thrilled to have the opportunity to work professionally. He was restricted to the Los Angeles area, until, in 1958, his first big break finally arrived. And it arrived in the person of a figure who pops up several times during the story of the flute in jazz--Chico Hamilton.

While he had been instrumental in the formation of the New Chico Hamilton Quintet, Buddy Collette was reluctant to continue touring with the group, in spite of the pressure exerted by Hamilton. So Buddy recommended Eric. Whatever his initial hesitation, Hamilton did not regret hiring him. When I spoke with Chico, I mentioned that the flute seemed to play an important role in the sound of that quintet:

The thing that strikes me, reading about the original quintet, is that the writers keep referring to Paul Horn and Buddy Collette and Eric as flutists, ignoring the fact that they were playing clarinet and saxophone also. The flute seems to have really stuck in their minds as an important part of that sound.

Yeah, well I'll tell you, as far as I'm concerned, Eric Dolphy was the best flutist out of all of them.
Wow. I'm glad you told me that.

He first started recording with me. The album was called *Strings Attached*. Fred Katz did all the arrangements, and I used the full string section, fifteen, sixteen, strings, something like that, with the quintet. The quintet at that time consisted of Eric Dolphy, [guitarist] Dennis Budimir, [bassist] Wyatt Ruther, [cellist] Nate Gershman, and myself.

Then there was the recording of Duke Ellington pieces... a session with Eric. How long was he with you?

He was with me I guess two or three years. I took him from L.A. I brought him to the East Coast.
Right. So this was the first time that he got some recognition.

I'm telling you, as far as I was concerned, Eric Dolphy was the best of the flutists, you know, his sound, his concept, and his swinging ability.

And I understand he was a real gentleman also.

A perfect gentleman--one of the nicest people you could possibly ever meet.

Record producer George Avakian worked with the Hamilton group at that time. He adds his voice to the chorus of appreciation for Eric Dolphy: "At the first session we ever did together, the Hamilton Quintet doing Ellington in April 1958, he was a splendid musician to work with: consistent, thoroughly professional, brilliantly capable." In the recordings that he made with Chico's group, Eric was beginning to find his own voice. Only two years away from the ground-breaking recordings he was to issue under his own name, he is no longer merely a Charlie Parker clone on alto, and his flute and clarinet are much more in evidence in the context of the multi-colored vignettes that comprised Hamilton's repertoire. Eric is heard to good effect on three Hamilton recordings, _Gongs East, With Strings Attached_ and the recently discovered _Original Ellington Suite._ At times, such as on "In A Sentimental Mood" the Parker overtones are still very much in evidence. But at the same time, it is clear that he has been hanging out with Ornette Coleman--the voice that is emerging is balanced nicely between the two extremes. As for his flute, while thin-toned at times, it swings as hard as his saxophone. Overall, for Eric and Chico it was a good marriage--Eric complimented the Hamilton sound perfectly. He clearly benefited from the discipline of the group and, even more so, from the exposure it provided him, as it criss-crossed the country, appearing at major venues on both coasts, including the 1958 Newport Jazz Festival. Here they were captured on film for what was to become the full-length movie _Jazz On A Summer's Day,_ with fleeting glimpses of Eric playing the flute on Buddy Collette's composition "Blue Sands."

Eventually it was time for Eric to go out on his own. In late 1959 Hamilton disbanded the quintet, leaving Eric free to move to New York. The fact that he landed on his feet was no accident, his reputation as a consummate professional and a great human being preceded him. He also found friends there waiting for him; he joined Charles Mingus' group in late December and stayed with him, on and off, through 1960. This was the beginning of a period of intense activity, and it is documented by one of the richest bodies of recordings ever assembled by a single artist in a four year period. From _Outward Bound_ in April of 1960 until _Out To Lunch_ in February of 1964 and _Last Date_ a few weeks later, Dolphy issued a series of fine recordings under his own name, while also appearing and recording with Mingus, Oliver Nelson, Ken McIntyre, John Lewis, Gunther Schuller, Orchestra USA, Ornette Coleman, Abbey Lincoln, Max Roach, Booker Little, Ted Curson, George Russell, Ron Carter, Mal Waldron, Freddie Hubbard, Gil Evans, Andrew Hill, and, most famously, John Coltrane.

It is a list that defines the New York jazz avant-garde. "Eric Dolphy arrived in Manhattan," writes John Kruth, "at a time when the revolutionary concepts of Ornette Coleman and Cecil Taylor had turned jazz on its ear. The term avant-garde no longer belonged exclusively to painters, sculptors and experimental musicians with classical backgrounds." Eric clearly found himself at the center of this movement. He added his horns to a wide range of cutting-edge musical contexts. Indeed, to gain a perspective of the avant-garde during the early '60s, Eric Dolphy's discography would give a pretty comprehensive overview. One can only imagine how stimulating it must have been for a musical mind as inquisitive as Dolphy's. He went from exploring Indian scales with Coltrane to the _Lydian Chromatic Concept of Tonal Organization_ with George Russell, to Coleman's harmelodics.

On one day, December 21st, 1960, Eric took part in two record sessions. First, he joined Ornette Coleman for the historic *Free Jazz* recording, on which he added the darker color of his bass clarinet to the sonorities of Ornette's double quartet in its collective improvisations. Later that day he went over to Rudy Van Gelder's studio in Englewood Cliffs, New Jersey where he recorded an album under his own name--*Far Cry*, with Booker Little, Jaki Byard, Ron Carter, and Roy Haynes. One of Eric's most successful sessions, it reveals the essence of his own concept. While there is a lot of freedom in his phrasing on all of his instruments, it is far more rooted in harmonic forms than Coleman's, extending, rather than breaking with, the traditions of jazz improvisation. "As I play more and more," he told Leonard Feather, "I hear more notes to play against the common chord progressions. A lot of people say they're wrong. Well, I can't say they're right, and I can't say they're wrong. To my hearing, they [these notes] are exactly correct."

Similarly, Eric's compositions are essentially boppish, although extended with more jagged lines, while he continues to draw on popular song forms with *Left Alone, Tenderly* and *It's Magic*. Moreover, he uses all three of his horns, including two particularly fine flute features. His lines on all his horns are full of rapid runs, wide leaps, and unusual intervals. On the reed instruments he adds smears and speech-like inflections. On the flute, where these are less possible, he incorporates what sound like bird calls; indeed, he recounts in an early interview that he liked to play outside in California, and would stop from time to time and play along with the birds. "He'd copy the birds singing," recalls Eric Dolphy Sr., during his interview with Alan Saul. "He'd copy the birds and play his instrument. And I guess those birds knew he was copying them, because they'd whistle back at him." (His interest in contemporary composition would probably have also brought him into contact with Olivier Messiaen and his experiments with birdsong in such pieces as *Catalogue d'oiseaux* and *Réveil des Oiseaux.*) Eric's own perspective: "There's so much to learn and so much to try and get out. I keep hearing something else beyond what I have done. There's always been something else to strive for. The more possibilities of new things I hear, it's like I'll never stop finding sounds I hadn't thought existed until just now."

Some writers have suggested that Eric was under some constraints at Prestige, and that his playing would have been more "outside" if he had more freedom, without accompanists who were more conservative than he was. But on the basis of his live performances, such as those recorded at New York's Five Spot in July 1961, this appears to be the balance that Dolphy favored. And it is somehow significant that *Far Cry* includes two tributes to Charlie Parker, both by Jaki Byard, *Mrs. Parker of K.C. (Bird's Mother),* and *Ode To Charlie Parker,* the latter another feature for Eric's flute. (This is, perhaps, a significant moment--when a tribute to Parker can feature the flute rather than the saxophone!)

Of course, every writer has a different perspective. In Kruth's opinion, "For whatever reason, many of Eric's best solos were recorded as a sideman. Free from the pressures of leading his own band, Dolphy may have been able to express himself on a deeper level..." Certainly, he did some of his best work with Mingus, Russell, et. al., and probably the greatest interest in his work came during his time with Coltrane. Pianist McCoy Tyner, quoted by Kruth, recalls:

> He was the first guy to come on as a guest with the band. At the time he came along he was doing his own thing and made a tremendous impression... John was the leader and he was the one that made the final decisions. He decided that maybe if I do this, this will cause something else to happen. And it did! They played so differently. Eric added another dimension to the

sound. John never rested on his laurels. He was like a scientist in the laboratory, always searching for something new or different. By adding Eric he was expanding the music. John and Eric had a very different type of life experience. Eric had a very academic approach. He studied a lot. John, coming from the South, had that real gutsy approach.

It was for a few short weeks, during the winter of 1961-1962, that Dolphy added his voice to the now legendary Coltrane quartet, touring Europe--where I caught them in November--and participating in several of their key recordings. Like his work with Mingus and Russell, it predominately featured his saxophone and bass clarinet--there are no recordings of Dolphy playing flute with Mingus, for example. With Coltrane, however, Eric was featured on flute on the centerpiece of many of their sets, *My Favorite Things.* Recently issued live recordings from the group's European tour give us an example of one such performance. Less disciplined, perhaps, in the purely modal context than on other more harmonically based compositions, with more than the usual share of bird-like cadences, Dolphy's flute still sounds fresh after almost a half-century.

At the time, this music was the center of considerable controversy, particularly after it was labeled "anti-jazz" in a *Down Beat* article by John Tynan. The discussion of the pros and cons of their music raged on for months in the magazine, with many readers writing in with their opinions, culminating in an interview with both Coltrane and Dolphy in which the former tried to sum up the esthetic that was producing their music. "I think the main thing a musician would like to do is to give a picture to the listener of the many wonderful things that he knows of and senses in the universe," was Coltrane's contribution, while Dolphy weighed in with "Music is a reflection of everything. And it's universal."

Having worked with Dolphy in his Third Stream *Jazz Abstractions* sessions, composer Gunther Schuller was one of the people I contacted to gain a better perspective on Eric's work. His first response focused on Eric's relationship with John Coltrane. As he told me:

I am shocked and horrified by how much Eric Dolphy is now forgotten and neglected, particularly in comparison to John Coltrane. It's almost as if the only two musicians worth talking about any more are Miles Davis and John Coltrane. I worked so much with Eric and I know how much at that time--we're talking about the '60s I guess--Coltrane and Eric Dolphy were considered very much equal. And by the way, they were very good friends, and really admired each other. They were both in the forefront of activities in different ways.

Eric, along with Ornette Coleman, was one of the absolute major innovators in jazz, and his recordings are also forgotten. Those he made with Mingus, for example, are never talked about, and I find that very alarming. So I have been spending a lot of time and effort reminding people about the importance of Eric. He was somewhat controversial because he was very wide-ranging, particularly in his harmonic language, which could go all the way from more or less modern harmonic language, as in bebop, all the way out into regions of atonality, and there were people who couldn't follow him that far. But everybody knows Coltrane was controversial with many people but now he is being deified as the god of the saxophone. Now there are 10,000 Coltrane clones in the world.

But how many Dolphy clones are there?

That's right, I know. And nobody even listens to his recordings to be reminded about how great he was. If you listen to *Stormy Weather,* which he recorded with Mingus, that's one of the most amazing improvisations in the history of jazz--a wide-ranging approach with incredible invention, both technically and musically. Those two guys, on top of that, they made classically perfect counterpoint together while they were improvising. It's unbelievable. So with all of that, I'm very unhappy with the situation. We live in a world where selling something, and promoting something through the media, has taken over in really frightening ways. So if the jazz media have decided that Coltrane is the greatest that ever was, forgetting even Ellington and Hodges, Coleman Hawkins, Lester Young and many others, well then this gets to be the conventional wisdom.

Anyway, as far as the flute goes I would put it this way. He worked for years perfecting his work on the bass clarinet. I know how much he would practice in those days, 8 or 9 or10 hours--he wouldn't even eat or go to the bathroom. Once he had conquered the bass clarinet, then next he tackled the flute. I like to thing that he worked out things on the flute to the extent that he did on the bass clarinet. One might quibble with that, because there are some who would say that his tone on the flute was a little bit rough compared to say, classical flute playing which is very, very pure. But as jazz violinists--say someone like Stuff Smith--played with a rough tone that would never be permitted in a Tchaikovsky violin concerto, so Eric went for this more expressive, gutsy, way of playing the flute. And of course, it was technically amazing. He could get around on that instrument in ways that were really remarkable.

I understand that he applied himself to twentieth-century literature and had a chance to play **Density 21.5** *for Edgar Varèse at one point.*

Well yes, that's true; I was the one who instigated that. I organized a tour of concerts in various universities--I think it was 1962--a little tour. And in that tour I programed a variety of jazz and classical pieces, including, by the way, some of Eric's compositions and some of my own. I remember, for example, a piece by Ives, in which he uses ragtime elements--a piece that he wrote as early as 1903. Eric played the clarinet in those pieces because he could translate those written ragtime passages into something more authentic, in terms of the feel--as real ragtime, not as some classical player might play it. And then because I wanted to feature him in a solo capacity I said to him "Why don't you present Varèse's *Density 21.5*?" He knew about it, and I coached him for a period of two weeks prior to this tour. And he played the Varèse in probably every one of those concerts. And then I think, after that, when we got back I told him "Let's go visit Varèse"--I was very close to Varèse myself–"let's play it for him." It's all so long ago, and my memory isn't perfect on all of this. But that's what I recall.

Then, on top of that, in Mozart's *Don Giovanni,* in the last act, there is this scene with three little orchestras that play on the stage as entertainment and dance music, for the Don. And it's an amazing invention by Mozart because these three orchestras finally play together, simultaneously, but in different meters and different tempos. It's the first simultaneous use of different musics that I know of.

Anyway, I programmed that, and Eric played the clarinet in one of those three little orchestras. So he was very deeply interested in classical music, particularly modern music, and he spent a lot of time listening--through recordings--to all kinds of music, from the *Rite of Spring* to Schöenberg and God knows what. So I was his partner in all of that and, in all modesty, I think I helped him to become even more deeply acquainted with all that literature. Not just listening to it, but learning how to perform it.

During that period, I remember that, even though I was married, I lived for a whole week with Eric in his apartment in Brooklyn, because we were so close and we were working together on various projects--he also stayed in my house for a week. And I remember, when I did stay with him, I did my work in his little apartment. And by the way, there was no furniture there, he was so poor--there was maybe one chair there.

Another flutist, Lloyd McNeil, studied with Eric for a while, and he told me Eric was quite confused when Lloyd asked him what he should pay for the lessons. He hadn't really considered it.

That wasn't in his thinking at all. He was so modest and so humble and so dedicated to his art that he just felt that this was just his obligation and commitment. And it never occurred to him to ask for help. As I say, I remember his practicing 10, 12 even 15 hours a day on his various instruments. He was almost obsessive. That's how I differentiate Eric from John Coltrane, because Eric did all of his practicing at home and then when he went out and played on gigs one heard the result of that development, or that practicing. But Coltrane practiced in public, and when he would play down at the Vanguard, he would play these 25 minute improvisations which were his way of practicing, but doing it in public. And often his practicing would not solve the problems that he was working on, whether it was musical or technical, harmonic or whatever. Eric did all of that at home. I am witness to that, and I am writing about that in my autobiography. But Eric was an amazing person; he was so dedicated, with a deep love for music, every kind of music.

Well, I have shocked some people by pruning my Coltrane collection, just retaining those sides where the music seemed to be working. This is not entirely acceptable these days.

No, it's almost dangerous to say these things. I don't know. I'm not happy about all of that. But anyway, I would say that the flute became an equally important instrument for Eric, because I think it is true of Eric, more than almost anyone I can think of, that he did play all of those instruments equally well, except the clarinet; he didn't really devote that much time to the clarinet. But the flute and the bass clarinet--and, of course, the alto saxophone--on those he was a giant.

So you would disagree with those who say that his least significant contribution was on the flute?

Well, I suppose you could say that. But if I were to join in on that view, I would have to qualify that by saying that that "least" was very little different from what he did on the bass clarinet. Perhaps not all of those instruments were absolutely equal. But that is irrelevant. The point is that he played the flute remarkably well. Certainly he was one of the early experimenters in getting into the really modern and open free jazz flute playing.

You would be equally impatient with those who claim that the flute is a marginal instrument in jazz.

No I don't agree with that. There really is no such thing. Look, I played the French horn, and I grew up at a time when the horn was not considered a jazz instrument. But, of course, that's a long time ago, and now the horn is one of the family of jazz instruments. It depends on who is playing it, of course, and how well. But no there is no such thing as an instrument that shouldn't, or cannot belong to jazz. It's just that for 50, 60, 70 years the main jazz instruments were the saxophone, the trumpet and trombone, and the rhythm instruments, and all those others--the violin, the flute, the bassoon--were not considered part of the jazz family. But that has all changed. That doesn't pertain any more. For heaven's sake, there are now five or six jazz bassoonists in the country and they play everything as well as any trumpet player, sometimes better. So, all this prejudice against certain instruments is just baloney.

There are all kinds of people saying this is jazz, or this is not jazz. But it is all a matter of personal taste, or lack of knowledge. I went through all those wars 40 or 50 years ago. I remember some very great jazz musicians, some good friends of mine, saying, "Well, if it doesn't swing it isn't jazz." Well, there are pieces that don't swing, and aren't intended to swing, but they are jazz. I mean, who says jazz has to swing? It's wonderful when it does, and the swing era is one of the great periods on the history of jazz. But to go so far as to say that it is not jazz, or because the harmonic language in a certain piece is atonal, it is, by definition, not jazz. That's just stupidity. You don't have to play blue notes. It's wonderful if you do, but it's not written in the constitution!

Schuller's comments about Eric Dolphy were echoed by a number of artists. One who was anxious to record his impressions of Dolphy's work was saxophonist Joe Lovano:

Well I never had the pleasure of hearing Eric live, but I loved his music. I think listening to him through the years gave me a lot of confidence to try new things, to try to discover the music and the possibilities of improvising. His flute playing in particular was so expansive and amazing. I started playing flute as a teenager after hearing James Moody when he came through Cleveland--also Rahsaan Roland Kirk. I had a chance to hear them live when I was still in high school. They played in some clubs where my dad was playing around Cleveland. I would be able to get in there. Moody and Rahsaan were the first real giants that I was able to sit in a room with, listen to, and watch play. They both inspired me to go out and get a flute and try to study that instrument. I was playing the saxophone by then. I started on alto and moved onto tenor. Flute and clarinet came a little later.

Do you use them much these days?
I do when playing my music. I play a lot of alto clarinet, as a soloist and within the ensembles. I play alto clarinet on my next recording, *Streams Of Expression,* on Blue Note records, and on *Birth Of The Cool Suite,* for which Gunther Schuller did the orchestrations. The flute I've recorded some, the last time on a recording with Greg Osby called *Friendly Fire.* We played the Dolphy piece *Serene.* Eric played it on bass clarinet but I played it on flute on that session.

In general, is it possible to put into words how important he was to the jazz tradition and what he brought to it?
For me, standing toe to toe with John Coltrane during that incredible period in the early sixties, and playing with such confidence and personality, taught us all about how you could be yourself in the midst of such powerful music all around you.

Without being overshadowed by it.
Yes, and standing on your own two feet, taking charge, and being an equal voice. I think that's why he was in that band. Coltrane loved his playing because it inspired him to be himself in the same way that Coltrane inspired Dolphy. That was a big thing for me growing up, knowing those records, and realizing the power of the two of them within that incredible band, with McCoy Tyner and Elvin Jones and Reggie Workman.

Some people say the flute was the least important of Eric's instruments, the least influential for later jazz.
As a musician, his flute playing to me was so expansive and amazing. He incorporated a lot of sounds from nature. He did things on the flute that were so musical. But he wasn't just playing on chord changes and scales. He created a lot of different atmospheric qualities on the flute that I thought were so

beautiful and expansive--in the upper register, but all over the instrument. He had such a rich command of all of his horns that I think they all fed each other. Like the way he played bass clarinet--the expansive range of the bass clarinet especially--filtered into his alto playing and his flute playing. I think each instrument influenced the other. He had an amazing personality on each instrument, and he had a command over all of them that gives you a lot to reach for.

Can you explain why there are hundreds of Coltrane clones but very few altoists, or flutists, who sound like Eric?

Well, for one thing, Eric had a shorter recording career. If it wasn't for a few dates he did with, say, Oliver Nelson, and other projects that he was on other than his own, not as many people heard him. Coltrane's recording career wasn't that long either, but he played with Dizzy's big band and played a lot of standard tunes--he recorded a lot of songs.

And, of course, he is on the best-selling jazz record, **Kind Of Blue.**

And before that, all the Miles Davis quintet things. Then *A Love Supreme.* He created quite a few records that everybody focused on. I think Eric didn't quite have the recording career that Coltrane had. That influences a lot of people. Also, the tenor emerged at that time in a different kind of way. He and Sonny Rollins really made a big impact after Bird. Of course, Eric and Cannonball Adderley also made a very big impact.

But it was kind of the tenor's time in the spotlight?

It's hard to explain why these things happen. For me, though, Eric stood on his own, and he was always a giant among all those cats. Especially the way he played with Coltrane. And with all these new releases coming out you can really hear that.

This is a question I ask everyone, but how would you respond to the critic who wrote that the flute is a marginal jazz instrument at best?

I don't agree with that. I think that every personality, whatever instrument you play--if you're a creative improviser, if you have something to say--then it comes through no matter what the instrument. We wouldn't have [harmonica player] Toots Thielmans make the beautiful impact he has made if we thought like that. He is one of the most poetic musicians of all time--it doesn't matter what he is playing. I think the flute, throughout the whole history of jazz, when it did emerge, especially through the bebop period and through to today, there have been some really strong and beautiful improvisers on the flute. And Eric was one of the most creative.

Lovano's views about the pros and cons of doubling can be found in the first chapter, above. I asked him how Eric fit into this picture. His response:

There have been some amazing musicians in jazz who have doubled on different horns and have said a lot. Dolphy was one of the key musicians who did that, and not many cats have come up to his level of execution and ideas on of the three horns that he focused on. And as a composer, his tunes were developed around his technique and his ideas. His tunes are totally himself. He didn't just write a melody and chord changes. He wrote things that he was really hearing and executing in his solos, and also pieces that were giving him a foundation and structure to vibrate on and contribute through, to give interpretations to. His pieces were amazing. To play any of his music is a real challenge. And the things he did with Ornette Coleman and some of those things where Gunther put those two together were really beautiful. I am so happy that we have that in the library of recorded music.

Dolphy left the Coltrane group in March 1962. In May he traveled to California to take part in the Ojai Festival where he performed a number of experimental compositions, including Edgar Varese's *Density 25.1* for flute, and Gunther Schuller's *Variante on a Theme By Thelonius Monk (Criss Cross)*. In October he was back with Charles Mingus for his infamous Town Hall concert. By April 1963 he was appearing at Carnegie Hall with his own quartet and a string section. In February of 1964 he recorded what many feel is his masterpiece album, *Out To Lunch,* for the Blue Note label. In April he joined Mingus again on a tour of Europe, after which he stayed on to fulfill some individual engagements.

Despite of all the historical, ground-breaking performances and recordings Dolphy had been involved in, however, he was still unable to make a living in music. When he learned he had been voted *Down Beat*'s new star on alto, flute and miscellaneous instrument (bass clarinet), his response was "Great. Does this mean I am going to get some work?" So, having enjoyed his previous visit to Europe in the summer of 1961, Dolphy decided to see if there was a way to fulfill his musical potential outside of the United States.

On June 2nd, Eric was recorded in concert in Hilversum, Holland, the session that has been released as *Last Date* and that includes the flute performance that many, including James Newton, include among his finest, *You Don't Know What Love Is*. It was very well received. It could have been a new beginning. But it was not to be. By June 29th Eric Dolphy was dead.

An Appreciation from Evan Parker

Soprano and tenor saxophonist Evan Parker is recognized as one of the leading figures in the development of European free jazz. He is described by critic Ron Wynn as "among Europe's most innovative and intriguing saxophonists." Eric Dolphy was an early influence on Parker who has provided the following appreciation:

I was fortunate enough as a teenager to be able to fly to America; my father had worked for the airline all his life and it was a perk of the job. As a consequence, I was able to visit New York for two weeks in the summer of 1962. I heard Dolphy play at Birdland. The band was Edward Armour on trumpet and flugelhorn, Herbie Hancock on piano, Richard Davis on bass and J.C. Moses on drums. The other band on the bill was the Charles Persip All Stars.

The sheer presence of Dolphy was already an electrifying experience, and his sound in the room was amazing. I had never heard of Herbie Hancock--this was clearly before he played with Miles Davis -- and Edward Armour I have only since seen on posthumously released Dolphy recordings. The specifics of what tunes they played and so on has disappeared into the mists of time, but I would think it was somewhere between the Five Spot repertoire and the *Out to Lunch* book.

Apart from the presence and sound of the man, the great enthusiasm of the audience generated a context in which the music went to another level. It became something like aural vitamins. I had heard Dolphy with Coltrane in London the year before--also a live-for-ever memory--but here, with his own band playing his own compositions, it was an experience that was at the highest point. The full implications of his music are still being absorbed to this day. His language is so highly developed and personal that any trace of his influence is instantly identifiable, but so technically demanding that few attempts to copy it are ever made. Dolphy lives!

Rahsaan Roland Kirk: Talking With The Spirits

"There couldn't possibly be another like him. He is all music. There is music emanating from his every pore."

Michael Zwerin

As we have noted, both flutists who now occupy the *Down Beat* Hall of Fame produced seminal jazz flute recordings in 1964. With *I Talk With The Spirits,* **Rahsaan Roland Kirk** established an approach to the flute that was as unique as everything else he did in the course of a remarkable, tumultuous, twenty year career.

To say that Rahsaan was unique is, to say the least, an understatement. He absorbed the whole history of jazz, along with a great deal of popular, classical and world music, but his style, although rooted in hard bop, never fell into any easily definable school or fad. He was one of the most accomplished instrumentalists in jazz history, and could have become a major figure on any one of his instruments, the flute as well as the tenor saxophone. But he preferred to experiment with all kinds of horns, frequently modifying or even inventing them, and to indulge in all kinds of unconventional performance practices, most notably playing three saxophones at once. Whatever he did, he made it entirely his own. "He should not be looked at as a multi-instrumentalist," wrote Michael Zwerin, "but as a Kirkophone player." As a flutist, he developed a way of playing that was, remarkably, both completely idiosyncratic and extremely influential--his own solution to making the flute viable as a true jazz instrument.

On top of all this Roland Kirk was, supposedly, handicapped--blinded soon after his birth when a nurse put incorrect medication in his eyes. Yet Kirk turned this to his advantage. Cut off from what, for sighted people, is the dominant mode of interacting with the outside world, he developed a rich interior world that he both nourished and expressed primarily through sound. It is the inner life that is of greatest importance to any artist, and, perhaps surprisingly, it is the sense of hearing that connects us most directly to that domain. As musicologist Victor Zuckerkandl writes, "We attain the inwardness of life by hearing and its outwardness by seeing." He points out that for the ancients, "it was not the motion of the spheres but their *harmony*, their sounding together, of which men talked when they thought of the universe as alive. It seemed to them that the universal life must reveal itself as something audible rather than visible." He continues:

> We are led to similar considerations if we observe certain differences in the behavior of blind and deaf people. The quietness, the equanimity, the trust, one might almost say the piety, so often found in the blind are in strange contrast to the irritability and suspicion encountered among so many of the deaf... it is not the blind man who shows the typical reaction of the prisoner... who must always be upon his guard; it is the deaf man, whose most [supposedly] important organ of connection with the outside world has remained unimpaired.

For Roland Kirk, or Rahsaan as he later became known, that sense of equanimity, while glimpsed by those who got to know him well, existed alongside a volatile personality, a major part of which was a social conscience, a sensitivity to injustice, that imbued much of his work with great emotional intensity. "'Rahsaan created a universe of his own, musically, spiritually, and aesthetically and that was just too heavy for most people," declared Kirk's friend Todd Barkan.

Barkan's statement is cited by John Kruth in his *Bright Moments: The Life and Legacy of Rahsaan Roland Kirk.* Kruth's brilliant biography makes compelling reading. Filled with anecdotes from friends and fellow musicians, it paints a vivid picture of this extraordinary musician. Suffice it for me to touch on the high points of Rahsaan's story before examining his contribution to the flute in jazz.

The muse that was to drive Roland Kirk throughout his life made an early appearance. At age five, in 1941, he was playing the garden hose in his Columbus, Ohio back yard. "I didn't ask my mother to buy me a trumpet or a violin," he recalled some years later, in the liner notes to *Dog Years in the Fourth Ring,* "I started right on the water hose. My uncle used to come over to the house and play on the piano, and I'd get a water hose and play the melody with him." From this he graduated to a bugle, and then to trumpet, but his doctors advised against exposing his facial muscles to excess pressure because of his damaged eyes. He finally found the vehicle he needed while he was attending the Ohio State School for the Blind, where, by the age of twelve, he was playing clarinet and saxophone in the school band. "The school had a good music program," a friend remembers. "At lunchtime he'd always be in the band room practicing. Then he started playing gigs at night and he would come to school in the daytime." He was only a teenager but he was already competent enough to lead his own group, playing for dances in the Columbus area which was home to a small but thriving jazz and R&B scene. As he was to do throughout his life, Kirk learned by osmosis, soaking up everything he heard, on the bandstand, at the local Baptist church, on records. He was particularly thrilled when friends introduced him to Bird and Dizzy, Sonny Stitt, Dexter Gordon et. al. via recordings. Kirk could not get enough of this music; wherever his ear and his imagination might lead him, this was to form backbone of his style. He had settled on the tenor saxophone and was steadily mastering it. With work and dedication he could have risen to challenge Rollins and Coltrane. His muse had other ideas.

With some other career we might have said that, at this point, Fate intervened. But Fate comes from the outside world. With Rahsaan, it was an inner voice that sent him in a new direction. In a dream he "saw" himself playing three instruments at once. The next day he went to a music shop in search of the instruments in question. None of the standard reed instruments seemed to be what he was looking for, so the store owner took Rahsaan to the basement and showed him some bits and pieces of old, obsolete, saxophone-like instruments of the kind used by turn-of-the-century European military bands. One was like a straight alto sax, the other was somewhere between an alto and a soprano. Kirk was to dub them the stritch and the manzello, respectively. Today there is something of an emergent interest in instruments of this type, a case in point being Joe Lovano's use of a straight alto sax. In the early 1950s, however, ten years before John Coltrane took up the instrument, even the soprano saxophone was neglected outside of Dixieland bands. It took an extraordinary imagination and a great deal of ingenuity to find a use for these strange instruments. But once the store owner had put them into some semblance of working order, Rahsaan found ways to hold and finger them simultaneously with the tenor saxophone to produce lines and riffs, sometimes in three-part harmony, sometimes with a technique that sounded like a horn soloist backed by a riffing sax section. It was a tour-de-force of both music and engineering.

It also got him noticed. For the most part critics had a hard time with it, accusing Kirk of gimmickry, of being an entertainer rather than a serious musician. He was able to issue his first album, *Triple*

Threat, in 1956, but a combination of critical indifference and poor distribution ensured that it went virtually unnoticed. Gradually, however, musicians were becoming aware of Kirk and his unusual talents, especially when he struck out from the Columbus area to pick up one-nighters wherever he could find them. Multi-instrumentalist Ira Sullivan told me about an encounter with Kirk in Louisville, Kentucky which led to his appearing on Kirk's next recording:

I wanted to ask you about Rahsaan. You were on his first record, right?

Well I helped to set up that first record date for him. I saw him in a little magazine. Do you remember the early *Jet* magazine? It could fit in the palm of your hand, it was about 2/12 inches across, and about 4 inches long, and it had articles about the soul brothers and soul sisters and so on. And in there at one time there was this picture of a young man with a big basket hat--the kind that Thelonius Monk would wear--with three saxophones coming out of his mouth at once. And it said "Roland Kirk, touring with Dinah Washington's entourage. A wonderful musician who plays three instruments at once." It looked like a magic trick or something. So I said, "That must be something!"

All of a sudden--I will never forget, it was 1957 or '58 maybe--I was playing in Louisville Kentucky and we were in the tap room. The stage was suspended in a loft and you could look down and see the whole length of the bar. You had to walk up these stairs like the galley of a ship. Now I had heard about this guy Roland Kirk, "Oh you gotta hear this guy Roland Kirk. He plays three saxophones at once. He's playing at a little joint in town." I said "Really? Wait a minute. I think that's the guy I read about in *Jet* magazine." So all of a sudden--we were in the middle of a set, I think the last set at night, because it was late--all of a sudden I see this guy coming up the stairs, and he's got one saxophone around his shoulder and he's carrying another one, and there's another one hanging on his neck. It was the guy I saw in the picture. And he says "Ira? Ira Sullivan?" I said "Yeah. Who is that?" He says "Roland Kirk. I'm coming up to play with you." And so there he was. He came up on the stand and I think the owner locked the door and let us play for an extra hour that night, because it was sensational to see this guy.

So then he says "Ira, look we're going to Chicago. How do I go about getting a record date?" I said, "Roland, you call Joe Segal." So Joe Segel set up the date with Argo Records or Chess or whichever it was--Chess or Argo. And so Roland called me after he got the business done and said "Ira, I want you to be on my record." So it was called *Introducing Roland Kirk Featuring Ira Sullivan,* I think that was the name of it. So that's how that came about.

He didn't play any flute on that record.

No, no, he didn't. He got into the flute with that little voice thing. But that was later.

What did you think of that?

Oh I can do that. Jeremy Steig does it. I've heard guys do it. But Roland really had it together. He gave me the idea of doing that when I heard him doing it one night.

Introducing Roland Kirk, which appeared in 1960, received considerably more attention than his earlier album, but it was a mixed response. There was a growing appreciation of Kirk's unique abilities from many critics and musicians, but continued accusations of gimmickry from some. Never shy or lost for words, Kirk defended himself tirelessly. Everything he did was for a purpose, he told whoever would listen as he tried to realize sounds that he heard in his head. These included whistles and sirens along with the all-spare-parts reed instruments, and at some point the flute entered the picture. His unique approach to that instrument was unleashed on the world on his third recording. First, however, a major jazz artist added his voice to the chorus of Rahsaan suporters. Charles Mingus hired Kirk for a four-month tour of California and featured him on his recording *Oh Yeah!* Mingus and Rahsaan were kindred spirits. "Kirk's contribution to Mingus' *Oh Yeah* was unmistakable," writes John Kruth. "His raucus horns honk, growl, and wail on *Ecclusiastics, Hog Callin' Blues,* and *Eat That Chicken.* Like a pair of muscle-bound musical tag-team wrestlers, Mingus and Kirk pinned crowds to the walls with their performances at the Five Spot Café and Birdland." "This man is what jazz is all about," declared Mingus. "He's real." It took one to know one; no one was more real than Charles Mingus!

One item missing from Kirk's sound in these earliest outings was the flute. All this changed with the appearance of his next recording. The very first track of *We Free Kings* finds Rahsaan bursting out of the starting gate with his trademark three-saxophone riffing. After this however, instead of manzello or tenor, it is Kirk's flute that is heard. Exactly when he had added this instrument to his arsenal is not documented but it is clear that he has developed--what other word can we use?--a unique voice on the instrument. While players such as Paul Horn and Joe Farrell--and later, of course, Hubert Laws--brought the flute to jazz, Rahsaan brought jazz to the flute, in the form of what Cannonball Adderley, in his 1960 album, called "Them Dirty Blues." Rather than merging a classical flute sound with jazz phraseology, Rahsaan brought a vocalized African sensibility to the flute sound. If it is striking on *Three For The Festival* it is astounding on *You Did It, You Did It!* In less then three minutes, Kirk sets a new standard for blues-drenched flute playing, augmenting the basic flute sound with humming, singing, cries, and shouts, and bringing into being .a new school of jazz flute playing that has found adherents from Harold McNair and Ian Anderson in England, to Jeremy Steig, Dave Valentin, Jane Bunnett and a hundred others.

John Kruth reports the reactions of several writers to Kirk's flute playing. One of them was British critic Steve Voce who wrote:

> I have always had doubts about the role of the flute in jazz. The snorting, bucketing instrument that Kirk handles so easily is a long way from the fairies-at-the-bottom-of-the-garden trench into which most modern flautists (Wess and Shahib excluded) seem to have dragged its fellows. He has now perfected the ability to play flute and sing a vocal at the same time. Indeed, I believe if you put a piece of bread under his beret while he does it, he makes very good toast.

Noted jazz author, critic and radio host Neil Tesser, conceding that Kirk could only play one flute at a time, writes (in the liner notes to *I Talk With The Spirits)* that "Kirk needed no more than that to profoundly influence the art of jazz flute, an often (and often justly) maligned musical category." He continues: "More than any previous jazzman except Eric Dolphy, Kirk gave the flute guts and grit--a virility that placed it in the same league as saxophones when it came to swinging and testifying. In both man's hands, the instrument gained a depth of expressivity in jazz that it previously lacked." He described an "unnamed technique," wherein Kirk "sang or hummed into the instrument while playing it, which created new sounds ranging from the percussive to the general."

The German musicologist Joachim-Ernst Berendt commented on the technique itself: "Ever since the sixties this technique has been employed by a growing number of flutists, most intensely, 'most hot' by Rahsaan Roland Kirk. He seemed to explode in a dozen different directions with the many different sounds he created simultaneously while blowing the flute (and at the same time, blown through the nose, his so-called nose flute)." "Even without singing into the instrument," according to Neil Tesser, "Kirk sounded different from the other jazz flutists. He avoided the rounded, classically oriented tone favored by Yusef Lateef and Herbie Mann, instead achieving a rougher and indeed 'heavier' timbre."

Rahsaan unveiled his flute work, plus his range of other special techniques, to a broader public at the Newport Jazz Festival in the Summer of 1962, repeating the material from *We Free Kings,* "kicking off the show," writes Kruth, "with a smouldering version of *Three For The Festival*, which featured the three-horn onslaught followed by a stop-time, turbocharged buzzing flute solo." By all accounts, the audience was astounded by the full range of his extraordinary virtuosity. "Thrilled as the audience was," concludes Kruth, "the critics sadly had little to say. Kirk's performance was all but ignored by the press." Ignoring the critics, Rahsaan began a series of regular tours abroad with his own quartet, including the first of several residencies at London's Ronnie Scott's club where I first saw him. For the rest of the 1960s and into the 1970s he led his group the *Vibration Society* in clubs, concerts and major festivals throughout the USA, Canada, Europe, Australia and New Zealand, while turning out a series of recordings for several labels, each more remarkable than the last, among them *I Talk With The Spirits.*

It was a wild ride, colorfully and sympathetically documented by John Kruth. The period from 1965 to 1975 was perhaps Kirk's most productive. He recorded a series of albums for Atlantic Records in partnership with producer Joel Dorn. Both on record and in live performance his playing continued to draw on his encyclopedic knowledge of jazz history, incorporating everything from ragtime to Swing and free jazz, with forays into classical, blues, soul and popular genres, and street music. At the same time, his instrumental arsenal continued to expand as he experimented with the harmonica, the English horn, the piccolo, recorders, sirens, whistles and nose whistles, as well as hybrid instruments of his own design, including the trumpophone and the slidesophone, brass instruments fitted with saxophone mouthpieces. (He played the trumpet well enough to record a solo on *Bye Bye Blackbird* that was a pastiche of Miles Davis.) An appendix in *Bright Moments* called "Kirk's Confectionary" lists all the instruments he played: there are almost fifty entries. He also mastered the technique of circular breathing which enabled him to sustain a note for over an hour. As his instrumental techniques developed, his modes of expression expanded along with them, from his surreal sense of humor to his involvement with social activism. His 1969 album *Volunteered Slavery* highlighted his involvement with the "Jazz and People's Movement," for example. Sometimes his activism verged on violence, as on his 1970 appearance on the Dick Cavett Show and other planned incursions into television shows to protest their lack of black staff musicians.

All of this frenetic activity was virtually halted in 1975 when Kirk suffered a stroke. He came out of it partially paralyzed. For most saxophonists, or flutists, such a handicap would have ended their career, but even with the use of only one arm Kirk continued to perform. For another year and a half he managed to tour internationally, play some festivals and appear on TV. In 1977 a second stroke resulted in his death.

The many lives Rahsaan Roland Kirk touched during his mercurial career included many fine musicians. One of these was trombonist Steve Turré who accompanied Kirk for a good portion of his musical journey. Like most of Kirk's sidemen, Turré was only too happy to recall his time with Rahsaan:

You were with Rahsaan in1976?

Well that's when I joined his touring band. But the first time I played with Rahsaan was in the Fall of '66. It was in San Francisco at the Jazz Workshop. Then I played with him many times after that. Whenever he came through the Bay Area again he'd hire me--give me a little something, you know. He'd call me up if I wasn't working and give me a New Years Eve gig. Then I joined the band regularly for the last two years I guess, from 1975 until he passed in December of '77.

And at some point in between he had that stroke?

Yes.

But he was still able to perform?

Sure was. He played with one hand.

Still playing with three horns? That's pretty amazing.

Two horns actually.

Did he still play flute?

Yes, but he bent the head joint like an L and he played it with one hand. He only had half the range but he had some little blues things that he could do.

Everyone states that Rahsaan was utterly unique. I don't need to repeat that, but I want to get your perspective. Were you able to get close to him?

Oh sure, and to say he was unique is an understatement. (Laughs)

They say he was like a volcano in a bottle.

Oh, and many, many more things too. He covered the whole gamut of life. Rahsaan was never one-dimensional. He was profound. He covered all kinds of stuff. He was blind, you know, so his world was a world of sound. He had the most ridiculous record collection that I had ever seen in my life. At that time it was LPs. In his house it was literally walls and walls of racks with LPs in them, floor to ceiling. And he knew where everything was. He would play all kinds of stuff if I went over to his house. Not just jazz music--classical music, indigenous music from different countries. He had records of animals, birds singing, whales singing, insects and frogs. All this was music to him.

So he had very acute hearing.

Oh forget it. He could hear around the corner!

Bela Bartok was an insect expert--the same kind of thing.

I can believe it.

So he was like a sponge, just absorbing everything.

Oh, totally. And he was up to date on all kinds of politics. In those days it was Nixon and Vietnam and all that stuff. It was a time not unlike now (laughs). But Rahsaan, he was so outspoken--he would speak out politically against the injustices and the hypocrisy, and of course that didn't endear him to the media or to the powers-that-be. And he would really speak out against racism. At the same time he had friends from all different colors and all different nations.

So he was never into the bitter "I don't want to talk to any white folks" sort of thing.

No. It was you as an individual and your vibration; if your heart was cool he could feel that. He was a beautiful cat.

He used to bait Herbie Mann a bit, because Herbie was so popular.

Well Herbie wasn't a real flute player. And he changed his name--his real name was Herbert Solomon. He was an unsuccessful tenor player and he changed to flute and had a hit record and got promoted, so he got over. And I guess, somewhere along the line they had some kind of incident--I don't know what it was. What was that hit he had, *Comin' Home Baby*?

Yes, but Herbie was the first to admit his limitations as a flute player. Do you have any idea what Rahsaan's training was? Was he self taught on everything?

Well, for the most part. He would ask me this and that about different things. I know he went to a school for the blind when he was younger. I don't know to what degree music was involved in that.

The thing about Rahsaan that I've always felt is that all the different things he did were great, the multiple horns and all that. But had he decided just to play tenor, for example, he would have been up there in the top four or five tenor players. Don't you agree?

Oh sure. Forget about it, without question.

As for his flute playing, obviously there was that distinct sound that he used.

Well to me, he had two or three different sounds. Since he played all the saxophones and played them all at once, his embouchure was incredible--very flexible. But at the same time, if you play three saxophones at the same time, then the flute, that requires quite an adjustment.

It's an adjustment to switch from one saxophone to flute, never mind three!

Yeah, well I have many videotapes of his live performances, besides having played with him for many, many performances. And sometimes, if he had to make that switch, it might take him sixteen bars to find the center. It could be a little bit ragged, but the feeling would always be there. So the music and the musical intention was more than with most of us anyway. But then he'd find the center, and sometimes he could get the most beautiful pure tone out of the flute when he wanted to--orchestral.

Like a Hubert Laws, a classical kind of tone?

Almost. I don't know anybody who... nobody has a tone like Hubert. nobody. What a tone he has, golly. I haven't worked with him, but I know him quite well. Anyway. Rahsaan would get that real pure sound. He'd get a real airy sound and then he'd do that talking in the flute thing. So he had three tones that gave him three different emotional voices so to speak.

That's a perspective I've never had better before, because everyone associates him with the last of these--the talking and humming.

I have a video of him of him playing *My Ship*. It's from a concert in Europe during the sixties. And he doesn't do any of the talking on the flute. He did do the circular breathing on the flute. He also had this thing attached to his flute made out of tape.

Yes, you can see that very clearly in all the pictures. Did he ever tell you what that was for?

Yes. Two things. It reflected the sound up to his ears so that he could hear himself better. And also he felt that he liked the sound better on the mike when it reflected off of that thing that he made. And then the mike was off to the side rather than putting the mike right in front. Because the way he did the talking in the flute, sometimes it was kind of forceful, and if he put the mike right in front of him there was too much air on it. (Blows.) You know what I mean?

I do.

So he put this thing on the flute, and it sounded good. That was unique. I've never seen anyone else do that.

There have been a lot of people after him who have used that humming technique. Do you think any of them come close? Like Dave Valentin on your CD, The Spirits Up Above?

Yeah, he sounded real good. He was influenced by Rahsaan but he does his own thing. He's not just copying his licks.

Do you think any of the others come close to Rahsaan with that?

Hell no! For the talking in the flute thing Rahsaan wrote the book. For the flute, man he could play the blues, with the talking and the whole emotional thing. It was uncanny, man. Nobody could play the blues like Rahsaan on the flute. Unbelievable. And then he had another thing he did. It was almost like the Pied Piper or something. I don't know. It was magical and it was child-like at the same time. Mature musically and emotionally, intellectually too, but it had this simplicity that was so direct it would communicate with you on a basic level. Not just with the flute, but with music generally. Rahsaan Roland Kirk! I never saw him play where he didn't touch his audience.

He didn't have off days?

Not emotionally.

He never mailed it in?

No. It always came from his heart. He played from his soul. It was always that kind of sincerity of expression.

What kind of emotions drove him? Was he an angry person?

He was many things. Sometimes he could be angry. Sometimes he was a lot of fun.

Was he ever bitter? He was black, he was blind...

Well sometimes he would get pissed off about stuff, but the bitterness never overwhelmed him. It didn't drive his life. He had an insatiable curiosity about so many things. He lived a twenty hour day, every day. He didn't sleep much. He'd go to bed late and get up early. And go all day every day. It's like he just burned himself out. He burned out young. He was young to have a stroke and all that.

Did he take care of himself?

Nah, not really. Has going too hard, and he didn't rest, and he didn't eat a good diet.

Did he smoke?

He smoked a pipe. But no, I think what did it was in his family they had high blood pressure, and then when he ate all that greasy food... You know, it didn't work out.

So there was this multi-faceted emotional thing going on the whole time.

You know, my father was a doctor, and he would come over and have dinner sometimes when I was playing with Rahsaan in the Bay Area. My dad lived out in the country in the East Bay, and he would come out for the day and hang out and listen to the birds singing. And he and Rahsaan would talk for an hour--they'd talk about pipe tobacco or different kinds of pipes and all different kinds of things, not just music and not just politics, you know. He was a very worldly kind of person. He could talk with all kinds of people on all different levels.

Where did he get his information? Did he listen to the radio a lot, or read Braille newspapers?

Everything, he was a total sponge. He would keep his ears open on the street or from there to the television, and the radio. Speaking of the radio, this is a little crazy, but at one time he had this little transistor radio and on the gig, he'd get a mike and he'd put it on the radio. And he'd dial whatever station came on and he would play the music along with the radio. And he could just hear things immediately. After he heard 20 seconds or 30 seconds then he'd change the station and play along with that, whatever style of music it was. Any kind of music, he would play along with it and it would sound good.

Without a doubt, Rahsaan's catholic taste in music was part of his uniqueness. But he found a kindred spirit in producer Joel Dorn, who also moved effortlessly between genres in his professional life. The two of them worked closely together for several years while Kirk was recording for Atlantic records. Rahsaan came up early in our conversation:

So this was not a typical guy!
Not a typical guy on any planet!
Which recordings did you make with Rahsaan? Did you make a lot of those?
All of his Atlantic records plus the three Warner Bros. records, plus the five that I put out since his death. I would say I'm Rahsaan's principal producer.
I don't even know what questions to ask about him except to say tell me about...
It's like trying to describe a typhoon in a bottle or something. There's no way to describe him. He's a guy like, if you had never heard him, but you had read something about him, right, and then you met me and you said, "You're his producer could you describe him to me?" Well, you know, I can't. You have to listen to the records. If you were lucky enough ever to have seen him even once, then you understand that he was "other." He had no precedent, he had no contemporary who was his equal. The closest person to having the scope and variety and uniqueness and chops and originality of Rahsaan was Yusef, who in his own way is just as unique, it's just a much subtler, quieter uniqueness. Rahsaan was like the Fourth of July every time he woke up.
I'm guessing with Rahsaan that whether it was jazz or not jazz, or commercial or not, he didn't care, he didn't give a flying...
… s--t about any of it. He cared passionately about what he called "Black Classical Music," all of the music that came out of the American Black experience. He didn't call it jazz either. He called whatever anybody else called jazz, Black Classical Music. When you have as much passion, and when you are as driven and committed as Rahsaan was, the social graces really don't come into play. He was an over-the-top guy. And for all the over-the-top good he was, there was over-the-top stuff that wasn't so good and I believe held him back.
You've put it very elegantly I think.
But he was completely... he had no precedent. None of his contemporaries were even close to him. And since he started, no one even came within a thousand yards. He's like any other one-of- a-kind person in history.
One thing about Rahsaan I feel--I saw him only two or three times in London-- when he put down all those other things and just played tenor for a whole tune, or just played flute for a whole thing, he was awesome just playing one instrument.
I always said that if Rahsaan didn't do anything but play the tenor he would've been right up where he is. He's right up at the top at tenor playing. With anybody who plays the tenor. He's in that league.
In one sense, the other stuff detracted from it, but in a sense it didn't because that's who he was.
Right, but that's who he was, you know, so it really added to who he was as opposed to like, well, if you'd like him to be a tenor player too bad! Because he's a lot of things. And the same thing for the flute. If he had never played any instrument other than the flute, he's right up top.
He made one record of just flute. **I Talk With The Spirits.** *Was that one of yours?*
That was his flute record. It was great. That was on Limelight. I think that was Jack Tracy.

That's the record of choice for people who want to hear what he does with flute.

Well, once again, I could put together a record of nothing but Rahsaan on flute on Atlantic, and I think it would stun you. And I might do that. Because if I put together a Rahsaan flute record and a Yusef flute record, you would be stunned, number one, at the scope of what they did on flute, and number two, of the uniqueness of their approaches. So you can't look at Rahsaan other than a category of his own. Same with Yusef, because Yusef started out playing, you know, in Lucky Milliner's band, way back. He was in Dizzy's '48 band. Rahsaan was a force of nature--one of a kind. One of the things he did was flute, and so uniquely and so distinctively. And so unto himself that once you saw him do that, it wasn't so much about flute being a jazz instrument or not, it was like--you should've heard a solo he took.

Bassist Steve Novasel worked with Rahsaan for many years. His recollections of the multi-instrumentalist phenomenon reinforced many of Turré's and Dorn's. I asked him about Kirk's unique approach to the flute:

Was he doing that when you were with him, singing into the flute?

Well, it was really part of his whole persona. Each instrument had a different voice. He had the saxophone, the stritch... The flute was another extension, another voice.

According to Steve Turré, he had another approach to the flute. Apart from the humming thing he had a very pure, almost classical sound that he used from time to time. Do you remember that?

Oh yes. Roland was the consummate musician. He could pretty much do anything he wanted to do. If there is such a thing as a sixth sense that they say blind people have, he certainly had it. He heard it before he played it. Whatever he was trying to play he heard it through the instrument. That's pretty much the way I understood the way he played. Of course it was always spontaneous, you know. You never knew what he was going to do from one moment to another.

It really caught on though. Jeremy Steig, Yusef Lateef, Sam Most...

Who knows who originated that? It is more of an effect that flute players found in the instrument as they played it and Roland added it to his way of playing on the flute. I think it was a natural transition from what was going on in the music, when he got to the flute. The flute came after a saxophone solo. He played two choruses on saxophone then two choruses on manzello, another chorus on the stritch, and then go to the flute. The sequence may have been different but...

Did you ever find yourself wishing he would play tenor, for example, or flute, for a whole set? That something interesting would come out of that?

Well, he used to do that. Not necessarily on our jobs, but he liked to go out after we finished playing and sit in in clubs. I remember going out with him after a night working at the [Village] Vanguard, and he would just take his tenor.

Ira Sullivan remembers him showing up to sit in with all his horns, but other times he would just take his tenor? He didn't get recorded that way. But he was right up there with the best players.

Oh sure. But you have to remember, in those days Roland didn't get the respect he deserved. A lot of times the critics panned him for... well they had different names for someone who played like that. He was a clown, or just trying to be different. But it was not that way at all--he heard those instruments. I think he was far ahead of his time, but they didn't pick up on him, or they refused to pick up on it.

Did that bother him at all?

Well a lot of things bothered him. Which may have been expressed through his music, or he would vocalize about it. Something may have happened at any given time, and if it pissed him off he would get on the microphone and tell you about it.

One on one, though, he was a very sweet person, if he thought you were cool.

Oh, yeah. Well, he had a way of checking you out, I guess through your voice, because he didn't see as we see. I remember one instance. We were on the bandstand at the Vanguard, and Dewey Redman came into the club and was standing in the doorway at the bottom of the steps. And Roland finished a tune and grabbed the mike and said "Thank you very much ladies and gentlemen. Now I would like to acknowledge the presence of Dewey Redman." Whenever I see Dewy he says "How did he do that?" I remember riding in a cab with him in England, coming from the airport. We're driving down the street and he says "Cabbie, you missed a turn back there." I'm sure he had been there before. And he was right--the cabbie had missed a turn.

You did many gigs with him. Was he very consistent from night to night, or was it an adventure every time?

Well, he was the consummate jazz musician--he was spontaneous. In those days, if you played a club you worked five or six nights. But you never knew what he was going to do. It was always at the whim of what he felt at that particular time.

Did he have rehearsals?

(Pauses.) Hmmm. I don't remember too many rehearsals. When I joined the band I didn't rehearse. I came on the job not knowing what was going to happen. And the first night [pianist] Ron Burton was late. It was just myself and Jimmy and Roland. And he pulled out his clarinet and started playing some Dixieland. You never knew what he was going to play.

Were there any complex pieces where you couldn't pick up the changes right away?

There were tunes that would come to him at that moment; that he would just compose on the bandstand. You would have to get it with your ears, because there was nothing written down. Ron [Burton] had been with him for years but it would be the same with him. Roland was always composing, hearing new tunes. And when he brought them in was when we rehearsed them, on the plane or on a bus or whatever. We would supply the harmonies and that's how we learned them. There was never anything written down.

Well, that sounds like an education right there. Did he play flute on most sets?

He played it when the spirit moved him. But he always came out with something different, triangles, a derringer...

A derringer? Was that musical or for self-defense?

Well he was upset because someone had a tape recorder and was recording the session.

How was his aim?

Well, he never did release a bullet, but he sure did scare a lot of people!! But I think he scared a lot of people playing the saxophone! At least a lot of saxophone players!

Like Turré, Novasel has vivid memories of Kirk's enormous record collection, his interest in any and all kinds of music. Indeed, Rahsaan Roland Kirk lived in a musical world without boundaries. He was once invited to sit in with Frank Zappa and the Mothers of Invention. This was by no means unprecedented; he had jammed regularly with rock stars such as Eric Clapton and Steven Stills. He told Zappa he wasn't sure if he would fit in. Zappa told him to listen to his group for a while and just jump in if he felt comfortable. "So we played for about five or ten minutes and he came wheeling out there with horns hanging all over him and blew his brains out." *Down Beat* critic Alan Heineman found the resulting set "quite literally indescribable." I felt the same about trying to write a conclusion to this chapter--to sum up Rahsaan Roland Kirk. I was saved by the following contribution from Saïs Kamalidiin, another flutist who knew Kirk well:

That Rahsaan Roland Kirk was a musical genius is unquestioned by those who knew and worked with him. His boundless creativity, musical virtuosity, and flair for the theatrical combined to make a presentation by Kirk much more than a purely musical event. At the height of his career, before the stroke that would have completely ended live performances by a lesser musician, club or concert appearances by Rahsaan were whirlwinds of sound, color and movement, always performed with humor and an extraordinary cast of supportive musicians. These seminal performances were experiences that have become legendary for their variety of musical material. Rahsaan could and often did perform the entire history of African American music: early New Orleans music, pop, avant-garde, country blues, ballads, bebop, gospel and everything in-between, while employing 10-15 different instruments alone and in combination over the course of a two hour performance. Rahsaan's sometimes frenetic stage atmosphere, as well as his running serio-comic commentary on anything and everything from politics to male-female relationships, were also integral parts of his musical feast.

Like so many of the world's great musical artists, the full scope of Rahsaan's live performance persona[e] did not transfer well to recorded media. Sound recordings and even video were unable to adequately capture Rahsaan's energy and spontaneity. For that reason, much of Rahsaan's importance as an artistic innovator is sometimes undervalued by those who did not see his live presentation, and who therefore must rely solely on his recordings, or anecdotal accounts, for evidence of the richness of his art. For those of us who knew Rahsaan and who frequently experienced him in performance, his later recordings--many of them on Atlantic--serve often as uneven, imperfect reminders, grainy, often blurred snapshots if you will, of unforgettable live concert experiences that were unlike anything in music short of a full onslaught by Sun Ra and his Arkestra. So much so that record producers such as Joel Dorn got into the habit of including some live tracks on several of Rahsaan's studio albums just to demonstrate that Rahsaan could produce these extraordinary sounds in real time rather than through overdubbing or some other studio technology.

Rahsaan's flute playing was a part of this musical smorgasbord and was never less than compelling. The funky, bluesy, raucous hum-speak-sing-scream aspect of his flute style was one of the most liberating and influential developments for flutists in and out of jazz during the 1970s. Many fine flutists tried incorporating this style feature into their playing at some point during that period. Upon Rahsaan's death, however, the widespread use of this technique seemed to all but disappear from the flutists' lexicon just as quickly as it had appeared. Of course, there are major flute artists who still use these techniques regularly--James Newton, Dave Valentin and Robert Dick are all notable examples--but it is not as popular as it once was.

Times and musical tastes have changed. What remains with us however, are Rahsaan's recordings and our cherished memories of this master practitioner of the improviser's art. What also remains for us is the difficult task of convincing younger musicians that the seemingly impossible musical accomplishments of Rahsaan Roland Kirk that they hear on those influential recordings are not only possible for one man to do, but could be done, and were done--live, on any given evening, two shows: at 8:00 PM and 11:00 PM.

Joe Farrell: Flexibility and Artistry

"Joe Farrell was the most complete horn player I ever met. He was the only one who could play tenor, soprano and flute with such perfection. Plus I loved his sense of humor!"

Airto Moreira

"He [Joe] was the best reed doubler probably that ever lived."

Joe Beck

"Jazz is the purest form of music because it comes from within. It's not my impression of the world... it's not political. It's music for music's sake."

Joe Farrell

If the 1960s ushered in a new era in jazz history, then **Joe Farrell** was on its cutting edge--in the most literal sense. It was January 1st, 1960 when Farrell drove into New York City "... with my luggage, my horns and $500 I had managed to save on the road." He had not been in the city for very long before he found himself at an audition for the Maynard Ferguson orchestra. Ferguson hired him on the spot and a vital jazz career entered its major phase. Farrell was a year out of college and only twenty-three. Sadly, his life was to be cut short by leukemia at age forty-eight. By then, however, he had made a huge contribution to the flute in jazz, indeed to woodwind performance in general. Loved, admired, and, after his death, sorely missed by musicians, his life and work passed largely unnoticed by writers and critics. A 1980 press release from Contemporary Records refers to Farrell as "one of the most recognizable names in jazz." I doubt that a survey of jazz fans would bear that out, but students of jazz flute cannot afford to ignore him.

Joe Farrell was born Joseph Carl Firrantello near Chicago on December 16th, 1937. His future never seems to have been in doubt; both his father and his brother were keen amateur musicians, as was his brother-in-law Carmine. "He played tenor saxophone and clarinet," Farrell recalls, "and it was through his inspiration that I got interested in playing tenor, though he started me on clarinet." This was at age eleven. By age sixteen he finally took up the tenor saxophone, inspired now by other Chicago-area musicians: Gene Ammons, Johnny Griffin and, in particular, Ira Sullivan, with whom he struck up a friendship. Sullivan recalls:

I lived in a community called Park Forest, about an hour outside Chicago. I was twenty-four years old and I got a job in this clothing store--Maurice Rothschild Clothing Store I think it was. And one day this young man walks in. I'm behind the counter, and he says "I'd like to look at a couple of ties." So he looks at some ties and then he says "You're Ira Sullivan aren't you?" I said, "Why yes, how did you know that?" "Well my name's Joe Farrell and I play the saxophone. I heard about you." He was eighteen years old. That started our friendship. We would get together with a drummer named Dick Borden, who I understand has just passed away, and we would go to a grocery store Joe's father owned just a few miles from Park Forest. While the family slept, we would go to the grocery store and play all night in the basement. This was when Joe was still eighteen.

It was with Sullivan that Farrell began attending the many jam sessions that were available in Chicago, frequently traveling from session to session from Sunday afternoon until Tuesday night, the kind of apprenticeship that has produced so many great jazz performers but which is sorely lacking on today's scene. I asked Ira Sullivan about this:

The stories that I hear are that you and he used to go all weekend, from one jam session to another.
Yes. Joe was part of that scene. We lived in the suburbs, but we would get together Friday night and go into Chicago, and our families wouldn't see us until Monday or Tuesday morning.
These days there aren't that many places where you can do that.
Well there are in Chicago, When I go back to Chicago I have places where I can go. Little places where I still have friends who are sixty-five and seventy-five years old, and they are still going to these little clubs. I remember when I was at the Jazz Showcase. I'm usually out of there by one, so they would take me to the Bop Shop where you can jam until 2:30. Then when that closed we would go to the Green Mill where we could jam until four o'clock in the morning. So in Chicago it's still alive and well, and probably in New York too.

It was in clubs such as these in Chicago that Farrell served his early apprenticeship. When it was time for him to attend college it was in the music program at the University of Illinois. "Later, Joe told me he had gone to Champaign," recalls Ira Sullivan, "and by then he played tenor and alto and baritone and clarinet--all the horns." It was here that Farrell laid the foundation for his later mastery of the flute, for he majored in that instrument. The reason for this is not recorded anywhere, but whatever options were available to him, Farrell opted for a formal training on the flute while continuing to develop his skills as a saxophonist and clarinetist on the local jazz circuit. He played baritone in Ralph Marterie's band, and tenor with Tommy Flanagan, Art Farmer and Philly Joe Jones. Having graduated from college he ventured into New York only to rejoin Marterie who took him on the road for several months. The last date was in Chicago on New Year's Eve of 1960. The next day Joe Farrell set off back to New York. Ira Sullivan again:

After he had been around Chicago for several years, Joe got married and moved to New York, and he told me he was trying to get work in the studios. And Al McKibbon the bass player told him, "Joe, if you want to get some work, learn to play the oboe." And he says, "The oboe?" But he did. It took him about a year to nail it down but the next thing you know he was getting studio work.

The rapidity with which he became established on the New York scene was characteristic of his whole career. By 1968, in eight short years, he was to win the *Down Beat* Critics Poll on tenor. A year later he won for flute. Over that period, he performed with a virtual who's-who of jazz musicians. His tenure with Maynard Ferguson, along with his regular participation at the Monday night jam sessions at Birdland, brought him in contact with Charles Mingus, Eric Dolphy, Yusef Lateef and other influential artists. By March 1960 he had made his first record date with Ferguson. In May he was sitting beside Yusef Lateef on Charles Mingus' *Pre Bird* recording, and before the year was out he had appeared at Birdland. He left Ferguson in 1961, worked briefly with Tito Rodrigues, recorded with Hank Jones, Ron carter and Dizzy Reece. In 1962 he joined Slide Hampton and continued to build his reputation in the studios, recording with Kenny Durham, Wynton Kelly, Charles Mingus, Andrew Hill, Pat Martino... the list goes on and on.

In spite of these successes, Farrell still had a couple of years of scuffling to go through, but 1964 was a definite turning point in his career. First he was invited by George Russell to join him on a tour of Europe. Upon his return he worked with Charles Mingus, Horace Silver, Jaki Byard and Slide Hampton. At the same time, he was getting more and more calls for record dates. Farrell was doing what few musicians have managed to accomplish--simultaneously building successful careers as a studio musician and a jazz performer. "The studio dates keep coming," wrote Ira Gitler in a 1968 *Down Beat* article, "because Farrell has mastered all the saxophones, clarinets and flutes, and has added oboe and English horn to his bag of instruments with the same perseverance and dedication that has made him a fine jazzman."

It is a measure of the regard in which Farrell's jazz playing was held that, in 1965, he was invited to be a charter member of one of jazz' elite ensembles, the Thad Jones-Mel Lewis big band. Jones explained why: "Joe knows what the horn is all about technically," he told Ira Gitler, "but how does he use the technique? Joe's put his to work between his brain and his fingers. He's so fluid. Seems like the instance he thinks of something, he's played it. He has a fantastic chord knowledge." "Jones paused significantly," writes Gitler, "and continued: 'Attitude is very important. You've got to have that spark that comes from within. *This cat's got a gang of that.*'" (Italics mine.) "The truth is," concludes Gitler, "that Joe Farrell is a *real* jazz player. How he got there is a story of honest inspiration and unadulterated love of playing."

Farrell's career continued to gain strength. In the late 60s he joined the Elvin Jones trio, which also included ex-Coltrane bassist Jimmy Garrison. It must have been a daunting prospect for a tenor saxophonist to replace John Coltrane in front of the former Coltrane rhythm section! Farrell considered it "the most important job I ever had because I had to play rhythmically and to learn to improvise more freely and more often." As he told Ira Gitler: "Originally I wanted to play jazz without frills, agents, or wanting to be a star. Then you run the gamut. Now I've reached the point of 'let's just play.' The basis of my playing is melodic construction. Elvin has taught me about the right tempo and rhythmic placement."

Farrell stayed with Elvin until 1969, but in the meantime he still found time for a hectic performance and recording schedule, with artists as varied as Roy Eldridge, Al Cohn, Zoot Sims, Peggy Lee, Johnny Hodges, Laura Nyro, Harry Belafonte, Antonio Carlos Jobim and Mose Allison. In 1970 he began to record under his own name with CTI records.

1972 saw the formation of another historic ensemble, Chick Corea's *Return To Forever.* Again, Joe Farrell was invited to be a charter member. And while his work with Elvin Jones had focused on the saxophone, Corea's writing brought Joe's flute work to the forefront. Corea sent me the following reminiscence:

Early on, I really thought that flute was a great instrument to help render my music, and I started gravitating towards flute players. Hubert Laws was the first great flute player that I worked with and he really sold me on the instrument. Of course, not too long after that I understood that it's really not the instrument, it's the player. When I formed *Return to Forever* I had already known Joe's work, we had played together. In fact, he was a great friend to me in introducing me to New York City when I moved there in 1960--he was working with Maynard Ferguson's orchestra on the saxophone. Anyway, when I put *Return to Forever* together Joe was definitely a first choice, and he had all the instruments together plus flute. Actually I didn't start having him use the flute at first because tenor was his main instrument. But for my music the flute really worked well, also the soprano saxophone--the higher pitched instruments. Joe really, really delivered on all of them.

I'm actually not sure how Joe came up and how he learned music; he was a fully formed musician in 1960 when I met him. He was always just very competent and professional, and very free with his music--a great improviser too; he had it all together. He had a way of playing the flute that I really loved, because flute is very often associated with classical music, not so much with jazz at that time, and Joe had a beautiful sound, played very much in tune technically. But as an improviser he was very free with his improvisations and he played the instrument in a really spontaneous way. I thought that it fit the music of that first *Return to Forever* band really beautifully.

Later on, when we recorded *The Leprechaun* together, I think in 1975, Joe really came through as well on the oboe. It turns out that he could play a lot of the woodwinds. He told me that he developed it to be a really needed studio player--I think he made some of his best money working in the studios in New York at that time. He was just the consummate musician.

The memorable thing about Joe, to me, is that he was a really fun guy to be with--he never took life that seriously. He enjoyed playing music, he wasn't pedantic or authoritative about it--he just loved to play. And somehow we connected--he connected with my music and really helped me create some memorable stuff in the seventies. So I owe him a lot. I and many other musicians loved him dearly.

The recordings Farrell made with Chick Corea, including *Return to Forever* and later Corea projects, were to include some classic examples of jazz flute performance. After leaving Chick, however, Joe stepped up his own recording career as a leader, particularly for CTI. Many of these sessions paired Farrell with guitarist Joe Beck. I spoke with Beck about the late reed player:

You worked with him rather extensively?
Oh yes.
In what context?
A quartet.
And you are on several of his recordings?
Yes, almost all of them, after he left Chick. He was playing with Elvin Jones in that trio for a long time, and it was during that time that he and I got together. We did three or four or five albums together,

Penny Arcade, Canned Funk, Upon This Rock--the last few albums that he did. I also used him extensively as a sideman when I was writing for films or commercials, because he was the best reed doubler probably that ever lived.

Wow! That's saying something! Do you know anything about his background or training.

He came up out of Chicago as far as I know. I don't know if he graduated from a music school, but he was the most natural doubler that I ever saw. He could play the double reeds, the saxophones, of course, and he played flute like a 'legit' flute player. The only flute player around that played anything like as well as him, as far as I am concerned, was Hubert Laws. When you start talking about Frank Wess and Eric Dolphy and Yusef Lateef and all those guys, they couldn't play the flute like Joe. Joe could pick up a trumpet and play it. It didn't matter--if you blew through it he could play it.

Many flutists say they can spot a doubler any time...

Not with Joe Farrell they wouldn't! Unfortunately, there's nothing that you would have access to that could prove that point, but he could play anywhere, in legitimate situations, in orchestra situations... When he was playing jazz flute it would be apparent that he's a doubler as he had the kind of facility that only saxophone players have anyway. He had so much technique that [flutists] would instantly say he was a doubler, because of that. Most flute players don't show off that kind of technique. But if they heard him in an orchestral context they could never tell. Also, he was a really good oboe player. I used to write oboe parts for him all the time.

There aren't many musicians with such a breadth of skill. He sounds almost like a Romeo Penque.

Well, he was like Romeo, or any of those guys, except that he was an infinitely better player.

Those guys didn't have the jazz chops.

Exactly. None of the doublers that worked in the New York studios that I ever knew--granted I didn't know the guys from the 50's, just from the 60's onward--none of them could sit in the same chair with Joe.

What happened to him toward the end of his life?

I don't know exactly. He died of cancer eventually.

Was he a family guy?

He had a wife and kids and he lived in a brownstone in New York that he bought, years and years ago when they were cheap.

He must have been working steadily in the studios then.

Oh yes, he was a busy, successful, studio guy, and a great jazz player. And the work did not disappear in his lifetime--that came later. He was trying to become a fusion artist from, oh, I don't know, we started working together in 1974. He was trying very hard to break into this kind of fusion music, but it really wasn't his *metier* you know. He was good at it, but his best performing was done with Elvin, I think. He played great with Chick because he had such a grasp of harmony. He heard chords better than anybody. He was a very serious musician. All of us who knew him considered him the unsung master of all the doublers there ever were. He definitely is the guy.

And yet there is so little written about him. He didn't really grab the spotlight I guess, or behave extravagantly.

I don't know why that would be. When he was really busy--there was so much work going on--he was overlooked. If he were alive today there would be no overlooking him. If you look at the tenor players that are around today--Joe was worth ten of any of them. He was just spectacular.

How old was he when he passed away?

In his forties. It was a great tragedy. I was so sorry to see him go. We had a long relationship and we did a lot of work together all over the world. And when we had our quartet, Steve Gadd joined our band before anybody--we were the first band that he played with before he became the "world's greatest drummer." Tony Levin was the bass player. It was an extraordinary band. That's the band that is on *Penny Arcade. Penny Arcade* was a tune that I wrote that became the title tune of that record. Herbie Hancock played on it. It was a good record. The next two were more blatant attempts at funk and were less successful, I think, although people liked them.

And did he play much flute in that context?

Yeah. Maybe thirty percent.

And there are many studio recordings with him on that nobody knows about?

Absolutely. That's the way it goes.

Indeed, the Tom Lord Jazz Discography lists 217 sessions for Joe Farrell, but there were probably hundreds more--it is estimated that Jerome Richardson did over 4,000 sessions, but he is listed on only 597. The comparison does not end there. Like Richardson, Farrell was a consummate professional, fluent on a range of woodwind instruments, and widely admired by his colleagues. And like Richardson, his studio work went largely unnoticed by jazz writers. Unlike Richardson, however, Farrell achieved considerable success as a jazz soloist. Disillusioned by the record business, Richardson withdrew into the studios until the last years of his life. Farrell, by contrast, was hired by several high-profile performers--Maynard Ferguson, Slide Hampton, Charles Mingus, Elvin Jones, Chick Corea--and did not need to make recordings under his own name in order to establish his reputation, although he did indeed make several. At the time of his passing, his recorded output was already impressive. Who knows what he could have accomplished if he had been given another twenty years?

His last recording was made with his close friends the Brazilian percussionist Airto Moreira, and his wife, vocalist Flora Purim. When I asked Flora to talk to me about her friend she was only too happy to share some reminiscences. I asked her how she and Airto came to know Joe Farrell. She recalled:

He recorded for CTI and so did we. And then later with Chick Corea, when we formed the group *Return To Forever*. To me Joe was one of the most underrated musicians that passed through my lifetime. Because I never met anyone who could play the piccolo flute the way he did, or the flute, or even the saxophone. He was unique, he had his own voice, and I learned a whole lot from him.

He was certainly underrated. Yet as a flute player he had such a great sound. Sometimes playing the saxophone spoils the flute tone, but not with Joe.

No! Never, never. In fact two of my favorite flute players are Dave Valentin and Joe, and I always opted for Joe when I had recordings with my group because he was older, and more experienced. If you told him what you were looking for he knew immediately what you wanted. He was a first-rate professional, and a very humorous person, he made fun of everything. He was always happy, he was never upset with anything. It was my first big loss in America. The first friend who was real close to me that I lost--and I lost so early--was Joe Farrell. Because we were together every single day. Later on I lost

Jaco [Pastorius], and I lost other musicians, some because they were very old. But Joe was not that old, you know. It caused an impression in me that is very strange. In fact, every time I sing music from Chick Corea, I can't help it but I feel the presence of Joe Farrell. It's like he's next to me telling me "watch the vibrato--don't lean on the phrase" because we were supposed to play in unison with each other. And we worked on it--we kept the vibrato until the end of the phrase so that his vibrato and mine would not be out of sync.

Was this when he was playing flute?

Flute or soprano. I am a soprano/contralto but I also have a six octave range, so I also could sing with the flute. With many, many songs there were no lyrics, so my voice had to come in very close to the range of the flute. And I learned from him, everything. He was a great friend. Not just like a co-worker, but someone you could hang out with, and have a drink, and travel with. He always had a joke to tell you. And he is so missed, you know. I did an album last year and I sang *Crystal Silence*, and it was for him that I did that song.

Do you know anything about his background?

I know he was Italian--not born in Italy but he came from an Italian background. His real name was Fiorentello, his last name. He liked to be Italian, he appreciated it. They are a very close community, you know. He was the one who introduced John Pattitucci to the music scene. John is also from an Italian background. They were both excellent musicians.

I have this album of yours, **Three Way Mirror,** *with some lovely work by Joe Farrell.*

Oh yes, I love that record! It's beautiful. He recorded with so many people. He recorded with Jimmy Garrison, with Elvin. If you go into the CTI catalog you will find Joe Farrell on so many people's records--doing his best. I think he did a magnificent job on Airto's record called *I Am Fine, How Are You?* And he did one or two of his own records with CTI. He had a couple of classics in there. For the blues there was nobody like him. He did most of the saxophone work for the Manhattan Transfer when he was alive. And he also worked with [drummer] Elvin Jones very much. They were very close friends. And the band, since John Coltrane died, was the trio, Jimmy Garrison, Joe and Elvin, with no keyboard player.

Did he ever talk about his background?

No, I never talked to him about these things. Every time we got together we just played and played, and when we were exhausted of playing we would go for some coffee, or hang out on the street, and then go into another jazz club and sit in and jam with the other guys. Our lives were based all around music, nothing else. We never asked "What is your religion?" or "What color is your skin?" or anything like that. It was irrelevant because we felt good with each other and that is what it is all about. When musicians find... they meet, they group, and they stay together for a long, long time.

I understand he was not in good shape at the end of his life?

Well the thing started when he found out he had leukemia. And then we went looking for a bone marrow [transplant]. You cannot find a match unless you find someone from the family, but he had been separated from his wife for a long time, and his sister could have donated but she chose not to. He stayed three or four or maybe five months in the hospital. We used to go there almost every day. Sometimes when we would go on the road when we got back we would go straight there. Between Airto and Keakagi and myself we spent most of the time with him--at the end. And a lot of musicians came to pay their respects to him and to say goodbye. And he called many of them. In fact I was there when he called

Elvin and thanked him and apologized to him if he ever did anything wrong. Some people he would call and ask for their forgiveness. He knew he was going. The doctor gave him one day to go out and get his business together. And he chose to come to Santa Barbara and spend it in my house. And he spent the whole day walking on the beach with us. And he seemed normal--he wasn't very sick or anything like that. And the next day he started... it took three or four days before it was over.

One of the biographies, in a jazz encyclopedia, says he was homeless at the end of his life.

No, he was not homeless. I don't like people to think of him like this. He was the type of person who didn't like to stay in the same place for a long time. So every two or three months, or maybe six months, he would move, to the East Coast or to San Francisco. He would just move. If he was not committed with a band he would keep moving. He liked the thrill of living like a gypsy. His family was living in Florida. He had no attachments. To him music was the first thing. His life was music. A gig is always a gig. He had a woman that he loved at the time, and we were always together and it was nice. He was never homeless--we wouldn't let that happen to him.

These comments from Flora Purim are absolutely typical of the respect and affection that musicians had for Joe Farrell. And even though he remains something of an unsung hero, it is hard to overestimate Joe Farrell's contribution to the flute in jazz. All his work, on all of his instruments, was characterized by a wonderful balance between technique and imagination. As a soprano saxophonist, for example, it is striking how perfectly he controls that tricky instrument, his tone and intonation never less than perfect, no matter where his improvisations take him. This applies equally to his flute work, with the additional advantage in sound production and fluency of execution that his early formal training provided him. His work is always uncompromising; he approaches the flute with the same sinewy strength that characterizes his saxophone work. In addition, he was at home in a broad stylistic range. As Ira Gitler writes, in his 1968 *Down Beat* article: "The word 'Freedom' reminds that Farrell is one of the players who can go 'outside' and still retain the 'burning' jazz essence so vital to him." In short, Joe appeared to have a tremendous, inborn, natural talent. I asked Ira Sullivan if everything seemed to come easily for him:

Well he had to work. When he was eighteen he had a real natural talent. Like a lot of guys--Wynton, Wallace Rooney, Scott LaFaro--I heard them all when they were eighteen. But you have to wait until they're forty or so for them to really have it together. But Joe...that's why I used to take him with me, back in Chicago. There were a lot of guys I heard play, but Joe was one of those guys, I knew he was really after it when he made all those sessions.

Those who say you can't get a good flute sound if you play the saxophone--it always foxes them when I play one of Joe's records. He sounds like a real flute player.

I know. He was a real flute player. Well, he got that scholarship, as a flute major. And it showed.

Dr. Billy Taylor sums up Farrell's talents nicely in his liner notes to the Elvin Jones Trio recording *Putting It Together*: "A gifted improviser with both big band and small combo credits which mark him as a musician of distinction," writes Taylor, "Joe is a tower of strength on tenor saxophone, a highly sophisticated swinger on soprano saxophone, a lyrical melodist on flute, and an irrepressible humorist on piccolo. Because of his flexibility and musicianship Joe is in great demand with groups of many different persuasions--far in--far out--you name it and he can play it."

Had Joe Farrell been spared, there is every reason to suppose that today, in his seventies, he would still be in great demand. Sadly, all we have is Farrell's body of recordings, but these contain some of the most important examples of the flute in jazz.

Paul Horn: Inside

"Music creates positive bonds among peoples and nations and cultures... Music is the universal language precisely because it touches us at that deep essential, universal level. It has a unifying and healing power."

Paul Horn

There are very few musicians who do not share these sentiments, but no one exemplifies them more than the man who uttered them--**Paul Horn**. Paul has had a remarkable career spanning fifty years, every populated continent on the planet, and three or four different genres, two of which he practically invented. While he has always been a multi-instrumentalist, the flute has played a central role in all his work, and is probably the instrument with which he is still most closely identified. Furthermore, he is one of the first musicians who has taken a thorough classical training and applied it to jazz performance. He went on to apply his skills to the development of what has come to be called New Age Music, and he has also conducted some of the first experiments in blending jazz with the music of Africa, India, China, Brazil, and other non-Western traditions. His life and career have been well documented in a 1990 autobiography, written with Lee Underwood, *Inside Paul Horn: The Spiritual Odyssey of a Universal Traveler* (Harper Collins, 1990). We need only touch on the high points here.

Paul Horn's interest in music started early. Inspired by his mother, who had her own radio show in New York in the 1920s, singing and playing the piano, Paul began piano studies at the age of four. But it was the woodwinds that beckoned. By age twelve, after hearing Benny Goodman, he took up the clarinet. A couple of years later, around 1944, he was playing third alto saxophone in a dance band. When he enrolled at the Oberlin Conservatory of Music in Ohio, it was as a clarinet major, but it was not long before he also picked up the flute. "I knew that someday I wanted to travel to Hollywood and do studio work, so I took up the flute at age nineteen in my second year at Oberlin." From Oberlin, Horn went on to the Manhattan School of Music where he took a Master's degree. Paul recalls his time there in his autobiography:

> Simeon Bellison, one of the greatest clarinet players alive at the time, taught me clarinet, and Fred Wilkins, principal flutist with the New York City Opera and Ballet, and with the Firestone Symphony, taught me flute. Neither bothered with basics, which we were supposed to know already. Instead, they spent their time discussing interpretation, musicianship and phrasing. It was a great opportunity to be able to study with them.

Paul was not the first jazz musician who based his career on a sound classical training, but certainly it was not yet a trend. There were no jazz studies programs at this time, but Horn was not interested in learning jazz in school. As he told Pete Welding (in the liner notes to his album *Plenty of Horn)*:

> You know, it's funny to find there are still people around who think if a musician has schooling, it automatically makes him a lesser jazz player. But you don't learn jazz in school. You don't *learn* it; you have to do it. You have to go out and learn jazz by playing. Jazz is a

way of life, and you have to learn about it on the street, so to speak. But the training comes in by giving you the tools to work with.

After graduation, Paul set out to put these principles into practice. Once he had completed a stint in the army, he landed a gig with the Sauter-Finegan big band in New York. It was an ideal setting for his burgeoning skills. Welding reports:

> While not strictly speaking a jazz band, this unit, a great favorite of musicians, was widely hailed for the adventurous, imaginative approach to orchestration developed by its leaders and chief arrangers, Edie Sauter and Bill Finegan.... In this generally stimulating atmosphere Horn thrived, finding ample outlets for his growing command of saxophone, clarinet, flutes and piccolo, all of which were variously used in the band's repertoire.

For all the Sauter-Finegan band had to offer him, however, it was Horn's next gig that was to put his career into high gear, and, not for the last time, fate seemed to play a hand. Paul recalls: "I had fantasized to myself the same way I had fantasized about Sauter-Finegan. 'Of all the jazz groups in the country, which one would I like to be in?' Answer: The Chico Hamilton Quintet." His fantasy was soon to become reality. The time was right--Buddy Collette was leaving Hamilton--and with his skills on clarinet, flute and saxophone, Paul was an obvious choice to replace him. Initially he was not aware that there was an opening, but then, quite by accident, Paul ran into Herbie Mann who told him of the opportunity and put him in touch with Hamilton. After a brief audition, Horn was hired. He toured with Hamilton between 1956 and 1958, and appeared on four recordings with the quintet: *The Chico Hamilton Quartet, The Sweet Smell of Success, South Pacific,* and *Ellington Suite.*

Working with Chico Hamilton opened many doors for Horn, as the Quintet had already achieved national prominence. But this had never been his motivation for joining the group; it was the musical possibilities that had attracted him, especially the writing of cellist Fred Katz. After a year and a half, however, Katz decided to move on. "After Fred left Chico's group, the band changed, and it was no longer meaningful to me. It just wasn't happening, and by the spring of 1958 it was time to move on."

Paul left Hamilton--to be replaced by Eric Dolphy--and settled into the next phase of his career. It was time for him to fulfill his dream to "… travel to Hollywood and do studio work." It was a hectic and rewarding period, as Horn recalls in the notes to *A Special Edition:*

> During the 14 years I was in Los Angeles I had the opportunity to work with, among others: Oliver Nelson, Mongo Santamaria, Shelley Manne, Buddy Rich, Gil Evans, Duke Ellington, Joe Morello, Gary Burton, Lalo Schifrin, Nelson Riddle, Howard Roberts, Victor Feldman, Quincy Jones, Cal Tjader, Willie Bobo, Vince Guaraldi, Billy May, George Shearing, Ken Nordine, Red Norvo, Barney Kessel, Peggy Lee, Red Mitchell, Jim Hall, Miles Davis, Joni Mitchell, Nat King Cole and Nancy Wilson. All in all they were very full years.

Apart from his extensive studio work--which extended to on-screen appearances in *The Sweet Smell of Success* and *The Rat Race*--Horn also formed his own quintet and continued the series of recordings under his own name that began while he was still with Chico Hamilton. There were eleven albums altogether, culminating in 1965s *Jazz Suite on the Mass Texts,* with arrangements by Lalo Schifrin, which earned two Grammy awards. Paul's work was recognized in the *Down Beat, Playboy,* and *Metronome* jazz polls, and he was the subject of David Wolper's TV documentary *The Story of a Jazz Musician.*

Writing in *Down Beat*, John Tynan summed up the qualities of musicianship that enabled Horn to succeed on this level. His schooling, Tynan reported, had made Horn:

> ... a thoroughly educated musician who can hold down a woodwind chair in any top symphony orchestra and, with equal aplomb, speak eloquently and authoritatively in a jazz voice considered by many to be one of the more significant developing. His competency cannot better be illustrated than by the fact that Duke Ellington recently chose Horn to fill Johnny Hodges' saxophone chair during the recording of *Suite Thursday.* Hodges was ill with an ulcer and hospitalized in New York City at the time of the Hollywood session.

There have been many talented jazz musicians who have disappeared into the more secure life of studio session work, and Paul was doing as well as any of them, while maintaining a high-profile career in jazz at the same time. Yet a series of events conspired to turn his life and his career in a different direction. The first was of these was seemingly negative. In spite of the money and the glamor of his lifestyle, Paul's personal life began to fall apart; his marriage was failing, and the studio work was becoming a stressful grind. In essence, he was feeling profoundly dissatisfied. He writes that this was "a time in my life when confusion, frustration and chaos reigned supreme. I wasn't enjoying what I was doing and I guess I had been hiding from myself for a good many years." Seeking some deeper meaning in life, Paul began to investigate various spiritual teachings, which, in mid 1960s Southern California, were in plentiful supply. Then some friends introduced him to Transcendental Meditation and, later, to its founder, Maharishi Mahesh Yogi. This was the final catalyst that convinced Paul to make a change in his life; in December 1966, he packed his bags and headed to India where he spent four months with Maharishi, learning to become a teacher of TM, one of the first in the United States.

When he returned from India, Paul resumed some studio work in Los Angeles, but his heart was no longer in it. "It was as if time had stood still. The guys in the studios were still saying the same things, same jokes, same old gripes, and the same old conversations about the stock market, property, investments and new swimming pools. I could see how really different my thinking had become." In 1968 Paul went on the road with the pop singer Donovan whom he had met in India. He remarried. Then a visit to Victoria, British Columbia to play a concert convinced him that he should move to Canada. He left Los Angeles for good.

Victoria offered a new life for Paul and his new family, although it was not at all clear where his career should go. Then fate interceded again. On a second trip to India, while visiting the Taj Mahal, he found that he was able to get inside the famous building late at night. He made a recording of his flute improvisations reverberating around the great marble mausoleum with its twenty-eight second delay. Although it was never intended as a commercial enterprise, Epic Records purchased the tapes and released them on an album entitled *Inside.* It was a huge success, selling over three quarters of a million copies--without a doubt one of the most popular recordings ever made by a jazz flutist.

Inside was followed by a series of albums: *Inside II; Inside The Great Pyramid; Inside The Great Cathedral; Inside Russia; China*; and *Traveler,* which earned another Grammy nomination in 1988. With the success of these and other recordings came the freedom to pursue many further projects: an eighteen week series of TV shows; extensive goodwill tours of Russia, and China; interactions with musicians from many diverse cultures and traditions; the formation of Paul's own record label *Golden Flute Records.*

Like his career, our conversation was very wide-ranging. We began by recalling his days with Chico Hamilton.

I notice that in some of the writings about the early Chico Hamilton Quintet, they always seem to refer to you or Charles [Lloyd] or Buddy [Collette] as the group's flutist, ignoring everything else that you did, as if the flute stood out for them from the other instruments.

Back in those days, that was when the flute was first beginning really step into recognition in the jazz field. And Chico's was one of the groups that was a catalyst for that. Before that--well you're the historian, so you know Herbie Mann and Sam Most were really some of the first who went out on their own. But I think that the reviewers and critics and so forth began to take note of the flute as it was a feature of the Chico Hamilton Quintet. You had to be a multi-instrumentalist. And Fred Katz wrote very hard music; you had to be a flute player, a clarinet player, and a saxophone player. He had no mercy; he just wrote like you were supposed to be the quintessential player on each of those instruments.

Well, I read that you actually majored in both those instruments?

I majored in clarinet. That was my main instrument throughout the Conservatory, and I was a very good clarinet player.

But you were taking flute at the same time, as I recall from your book. That's very unusual. Wasn't that at the Manhattan School of Music?

Yeah. I doubled in the orchestra. I remember that happening. I was first clarinet there. I got a scholarship to be first clarinet in that orchestra. And then... they called it a Fellowship in those days, which is the same thing except you taught as well as got the money.

So you're saying when you went Manhattan School of Music you were studying with Simeon Bellerson and Fred Wilkins at the same time.

Yes, while flute was still my minor. That was at Oberlin. I didn't learn flute 'til I was nineteen years old. My second year in college was the first time I ever picked up a flute.

That's what I was going to ask you. You started on clarinet, and you also branched out into saxophone, so you were moving in the multi-instrumentalist area. But in these days, for people who are--what would you call them?--orchestral players, or students in that area, doubling is not something that they did normally.

Well, they even considered piccolo and flute a double in the strict sense of that word, because if you're a piccolo player in the orchestra you just play piccolo. Times have changed, and while you're still in classical music they don't have doubling. I don't know, oboe and English horn, and maybe flute and alto flute, but you don't switch around to different instruments like that.

There are embouchure problems though, aren't there?

Well, sure. The first band I was in was the Sauter-Finnegan Band and that band, they give you three beats to switch from sax to clarinet. You didn't have a chance to put your clarinet down and pick up the sax, so what you had to do is throw the clarinet in your lap and reach over and play the saxophone in the stand. That's how quickly they wanted you to make changes.

But doubling back and forth between flute and a reed instrument is something people can have problems with.

Oh, sure. So what you have to do is spend time on your weakest instrument. In this case it was the flute for me, because clarinet and sax was a double; that was automatic. If you wanted to play in a big band, like in the thirties and the forties, all sax players played clarinet. That was it, and I don't even think it was considered a double, that was just it if you were into pop music. Flute, no. Not necessarily. But you take your weakest instrument which is, in this case, the flute for me, and you have to spend more time with that to bring it up to the level of your other instruments. And then … yeah, then you go back and forth and back and forth. Then you should be able to move from one to the other without any problem. That makes sense. But I'll tell you, the hardest double for me with Chico Hamilton was between the tenor and the alto sax. Not the others, not the clarinet or the flute or the piccolo.

That's not a common double actually. Apart from Sonny Stitt, James Moody... Buddy Collette did it, but that was for Chico again.

Right. To me there was quite a big difference, not just in the embouchure but the feel of the whole instrument. For instance, Stan Getz, was a natural tenor player. A tenor was an extension of who he is. To me, the alto was. The tenor was not who I was.

No, I know exactly what you're saying. I'm an alto player, but I had to switch to tenor and soprano for a tour. The soprano was okay, but the tenor never felt right.

You know what I mean. It's what you identify with, and feel comfortable with. It's really an extension of yourself, emotionally and physically and everything else. The tenor never was for me.

I wonder if you think that the reason the flute was not very prominent in early jazz is simply because of the amplification problem, or whether there was something more to it.

That's interesting, but at least you had a microphone. It wasn't probably the greatest but if you played any kind of a gig, even in the old days, there was a microphone wasn't there?

Well, not so much until the mid 1940s. But the flute also needs a different approach--articulation and so forth--that early players struggled with a bit.

I don't know. You know, my mind works very differently from what you're describing. I never think like that. Either it's there or it's not there. I never thought about articulating differently on the flute--it would present itself, but this is what you have to do. I have a different instrument in my hand, I have the flute, not the saxophone, obviously it's a difference there. I identify with the flute and don't think that I'm a saxophone player playing the flute. I'm a flute player playing the flute.

Well, that's interesting. Some people have told me that their approach when they picked up the flute was to play it as though it were a saxophone. Other people have told me that was the worst possible thing you could do if you wanted it to be its own voice.

Well, I agree with the latter.

But you are identified with the flute more than anything else. Is that fair to say?

Well, that presents itself to me more. I mean I came on in 1956 to join Chico's group. Now that was when the flute was getting a lot of attention, and being recognized because there were a few people-- Sam Most being one of the best by the way as far as I'm concerned--he's a hell of a clarinet player, too. So I think that it got a lot of attention because it was sort of coming into its own, through the Sauter-

Finnegan Band, Chico Hamilton's group, and through an individual--Frank Wess with Basie. I mean somehow we were saying: "Hey, this is strange, the flute being such a delicate airy-fairy instrument, ethereal, angelic and all those things, and always used that way in classical music, like Ravel, to express delicate and beautiful and sensitive thinking. How can you put a rhythm section behind that and do anything?" Somehow there was a paradox but it seemed to work.

Well, let me add to the paradox. If you go into the ancient music systems, the flute is regarded as a little bit disreputable compared with stringed instruments. Think about Saraswati and Krishna for example.

That's interesting as the flute is one of the basic instruments of mankind, probably the first wind instrument. It's the voice, it's breath.

But getting back to you, one of your bios says there were two Paul Horns--pre-1967 and post-1967. Is there anything to that?

Pre-meditation and after-meditation!

Did you change a lot in that period? I mean I know your story, walking away from a very successful life in music, in L.A. Things did change for you after that didn't they?

Well, maybe you've had the same experience. During your time with Maharishi, everything changes. You're the main instrument. Your other instruments are secondary. I am the main instrument. I have to constantly--well, I don't even try. You just open yourself to evolving and to growing, and as you do, you change. Anything else in your life changes along with that basic change in yourself. If I'm a musician I pick up the flute, that's an extension of who I am, or the saxophone, or the clarinet, or any instrument. What's going to come out is what I'm feeling. You have to let go of all that crap about trying to impress your critics or your fellow musicians or anybody. It's when you're finally to that point where you've passed that, then you can begin to let some real music come through you. Otherwise your ego blocks everything and you're not really making it. Pre-1967-- whatever they said--those were my ego years and I'm not denying that, it was part of it and it was beautiful. But that was my jazz musician persona. I acted a certain way, I dressed a certain way, I assumed a certain attitude on the bandstand. I had my idols that I wanted to play with and all of that stuff, and again it was great! But then I hit a point where that didn't mean anything.

You were very well known, and I assume you were making a good deal of money in the studios, and with recordings.

Yes, but when I came back from India, from Maharishi, I couldn't play in a jazz club. I couldn't get it... If you want me to play I'll play concerts; I can't play in a club anymore.

But did you have any difficulty with the idea of jazz itself? These days some artists don't want to be associated with the idea of jazz, period.

Stupid!

Well, in your book I read at one point, I think you're in Russia, and you say "Thank God for jazz musicians because they can improvise." It's a whole other way of thinking.

About jazz, it's so honest, that I don't care what you say or what you do, or how you look, what comes out of your horn is who you are. Now with Miles Davis--I knew Miles very well, and he wasn't anything like how he was portrayed, that was a part of him, like all that stuff. But how can you play a ballad like that and not know who Miles really is? He was sensitive, man, that's why he put on all that armor, because he was so sensitive. When you're that sensitive you get hurt real deep, real quick, and the drugs sort of mask that too; there are all kinds of psychological reasons for that. But a jazz player is naked all the time and that's who that person really is. And you can't get anymore truthful than that, so if you really know what jazz is, it's improvisation. It's who you are at that moment.

When I was in India, talking with holy men, when they asked me what kind of music I played, I felt uncomfortable saying the word jazz.

Well there's a misunderstanding of that word for the average person. They don't really know what you're saying.

But the origin of the word is kind of crude--it didn't seem appropriate in that context. On the other hand, when I was hosting all these musicians from India, I had them staying in my house for many months, and I had fun playing them lots of different kinds of music to see what they thought about it. And not having been exposed to it before, they related to jazz much more than to classical or orchestral music. Have you had that same experience?

No, but I can understand that, because the basis of Indian music is improvisation. They understand improvisation.

It's not only improvisation it's the feeling of the music. I played them some Coltrane, and **Kind of Blue.**—*they just swooned over that record.*

Yeah, that's the record of the century! You know, it still sells five thousand a week? That's what I was told.

Another thing is, talking to flute players, I don't know if it's just the instrument, but their interests seem to be very wide, I guess because the flute is found in every culture. But the whole category of jazz is just sort of left behind half the time, it's just a question of where you come from, what your training was, and whether you learned to improvise and interact with other musicians.

Well, that's why I have to be thankful, very thankful, for my early jazz years, because the basis of jazz is improvisation, and what I went on to do would still be as an improviser, maybe not in the traditional sense of the word, jazz with a rhythm section. It's different. But to me... you don't mention in your categories, New Age. I'm not ashamed of that word, I just think unfortunately it got all entangled in religious ideas. New Age simply was a name that they put on a type of music which up to then didn't have a category. It's more meditative. The original New Age music I guess started with, so they say, my *Inside the Taj Mahal* album.

But there's a lot of New Age music where nothing seems to happen. Keith Jarrett calls it "Lobotomy Music."

Nothing's supposed to happen. From a critical standpoint it's boring, and what are you going to write about except like, what the hell is happening. You can't find a theme, you can't find any development usually, but that's not the point. There's a point to that music. The point is to take you within and then you'll transcend. That's the point of it. It's not intellectual music. You know Lee Underwood, don't you,? He wrote my book. He's a former editor of *Down Beat*, and I think he of all people that I've come across, articulates very well what New Age music and what the essence of it is. He is the only writer I've come across that can really express, because he's a writer, express himself very well, and express the genre very well. And basically, what I just said, you can't use the same criteria for evaluating that, it won't work, as other types of music--intellectual.

Musicians don't think about that, it's critics that think about that, and writers and what have you. You don't think about whether you're playing jazz or not playing jazz when you're playing something, and so it's a non-issue as far as a creative artist is concerned.

Well yeah, that's when music starts to break down, when you get into all of that.

Defining a genre is a very difficult thing.

And most musicians don't like to be categorized.

And many feel that the origin of the word and the genre is very demeaning, which is probably true. You know what the word meant originally so we don't have to go into that. And I sympathize with that, but be that as it may, your approach to music is we could categorize it as not jazz not pop not new age, but simply... .

Music. That's why one of the albums was entitled, *Music*. Just Music. You can call it what you want. I'm playing music! And depending on where I am, and who I am, and the circumstances, and whatever, that's the music that's going to come out of me. If I'm going to be a soloist with a symphony orchestra, as I've done, that's who I am tonight. Playing the Bach B Minor Suite. Or playing a solo flute at the Taj Mahal. That's who I am. Or on a concert stage--solo flute. That's who I am tonight. Or a duo with Roger Kelloway--great, great, great, jazz pianist. That's who I am tonight. And on and on and on.

... or sit in with some Indian musicians,

I don't want to leave that out, that's when I played with Ravi Shankar.

... all these different experiences feed into what comes out when you improvise, do they not?

Yeah, and to extend that just a little bit, I think what happened with India, with me, because that's the first time I really went out of the United States and went to other countries and just saw the world a little bit.

Was it a culture shock to start with?

No, the shock was coming back to my own culture! I felt very comfortable in India.

I had the same experience when I arrived in India. I felt totally at home..

That's right. Me too. Home, home, home. Well, past lives...

Well, we won't get into that!

What I found out was my music grows as I have other experiences, and don't even think about music. Then I think of my horn, ooh that's different. Why is that different? Because I'm different. That was my great experience, or one of the great ones in going to India was to realize that. I never practiced-- I don't even say that any more because people think I'm crazy. How much do you practice? They ask. I don't practice. Sometimes I don't pick up my flute for a month. If I have a concert in three days, I'll pick it up and start playing just to see if my chops are still there, and play along with a Jamey Aebersold record for about an hour a day for two or three days, and I'm fine. I don't practice! How can I practice being me? How can I practice being free... I never practiced licks when I was a traditional jazz player. I don't go memorizing Coltrane licks if it came out sounding like Coltrane. Well, that's okay, because I listened to him, and I loved it, and that was part of it. And all that stuff.

If you have to perform a piece of literature, that's different.

That's different, but Miles used to say "I pay you guys to practice on the stand." You don't practice at home. You practice on the stand. That's jazz. So that's my attitude, which is I guess not very common, because I've talked to other people, "Oh, how bad's your lip, and how about that." I never think about that, man. I put in so many hours and years of practice, and if I don't know my horn by now,

I never will. I never think about that, I always feel comfortable on the stage--it's a lot of fun. But I just don't think in those terms any more, and you know what--it's freedom. I feel so good because I don't care, I'm not out to please anyone, the audience, or critics, or anyone, or even myself. It's just who I am, and I'm playing music tonight. That's what I do.

That's what D. T. Suzuki--do your remember the Zen teacher--he said that for a great artist, performance becomes an artless art, growing directly out of the unconscious.

Suzuki said that?

Yeah. But everything that comes out of the unconscious is based on what you've put there in the years leading up to that moment.

I like that.

Not just your life experiences, but also all the music you've heard, all the music you've played, everything you've practiced.

Well, it's interesting, I have a thing sitting right on my desk here I'm going to read it to you, by Suzuki. This is Shinichi Suzuki, the music educator, not D.T. Suzuki the Zen teacher. He says: "Teaching music is not my main purpose, I want to make good citizens. If a child hears fine music from the day of his birth, and learns to play it himself, he develops sensitivity, discipline, and endurance. It's a beautiful heart." And that's tacked up on my wall, and that's coming from one of the great innovative teachers. It doesn't say anything about the music, it makes you a better person. It gives you a beautiful heart. Boy, that's a great phrase.

Well, on the intellectual level, going back to D.T. Suzuki, when someone asked him, "What is consciousness," he said, "What is asking the question?" I've been thinking about these things for twenty or thirty years, and...

I know, I'm looking forward to your book. Who writes a book coming from the background that you have in music, as a writer and a musicologist, and player, and all of that. And yet you're talking about consciousness. You may or may not talk about that in your book, but even if you don't, that's where you're coming from.

Well, I'm working on another book apart from this one, about music as a cosmological image. In the ancient world, music was considered to be the knowledge about how the universe was structured. Of course we've lost that, but the idea can be found in every major culture--the Chinese, the Indians, Greek, Western culture, until the 17th Century--you've heard of the Harmony of the Spheres? This was a very powerful idea that because music was considered the basic discipline for all knowledge in the ancient world.

Yeah, well, are you considering Pythagoras the ancient world?

He's a transition from the ancient world into the modern, Western world.

See, to me, New Age music--and we use that because we have to categorize things--the way it was originally meant was music that was not intellectual, it was just coming straight from the heart, without bypassing the intellect--it's right brain totally. That's healing--and that's coming back. You see it's Pythagoras' knowledge, explicit knowledge of music and how it can heal the body physically. To me that's the essence of what New Age Music started to be. It just takes the person within and the person transcends and the healing takes place. Without being more specific than that, I guess other people will take it onto more specific stages. And there's physiotherapists and getting it to music therapy and things like that. That's the deeper value of music don't you think? That it touches your soul, and it heals you in whatever way. Jazz will heal you too, just straight jazz.

Yeah. Do you think the flute has a particular role in that?

I do, because it's a more sensitive instrument to begin with. Just by nature, by its own structure. It's already there. It might be a little harder to have a trumpet do that, or a tuba...

Yeah, you think differently when you play the flute. I mean I love the saxophone, but the saxophone is broader, wider, funkier...

It's grosser… that's not derogatory. There are times when you wanna be gross, at least I do.

Sure, there are some things that only work on the saxophone. But when you play the flute, there's a certain kind of focus that is more delicate.

Yeah, but that's I think what will surprise everyone--it is a delicate instrument, and yet you can get pretty funky with it! And no one really thought about that until someone tried to do it one and day, and said, "You know, you can play some funky blues on the flute." "Oh Yeah?" And you don't have to growl and do all those guttural sounds, and hum along with the flute either, which I hate, personally.

But for you the flute has been an instrument that speaks to that deep level of music, deep purpose, healing and so forth?

Yes. I think that the real value in music, if anything is going to save this planet--and we are in deep trouble now--it's going to be music. That was my experience over in Russia, and in China-- anyplace I play--all these communist countries. Everyone freaks out as soon as you mention anything to do with communism or socialism. It used to be a free country where you can express ideas. Now you gotta be very careful who you say what to. I love this country and what I've said about it is that the freedoms that we have had all this time I feel we're abusing them--it's frightening what's going on today. But anyway, music being the universal language, if that goes, we're all gone. That's the structure of the universe and certainly what we're made of.

I was doing an interview with Pandit Vyas who was head of the music department at Bombay University--I was teaching there for a little while, courses in Western music history. I said, "What do you think would happen if all of music was removed from the world for a day? I mean, all of the elevator music and everything." He said: "People would tear each other apart."

I think of that too. I don't think the planet could survive if you couldn't whistle, you couldn't hum, you couldn't even have a tune in your head,--nothing.

But that does raise a very interesting question. Why does everyone love music, Paul? As a musicologist I found that no one thinks to ask that question. Why does everyone love music? Can you find anyone who doesn't love music? I don't mean people who are concert goers or connoisseurs necessarily. At the very least people like to whistle "Happy Birthday to You," or other simple things. Is there any culture on the planet that doesn't t have music? Why is it that the only things that we have as human beings that are universal to every culture are speech and music?

Because they're both sound. We're made of sound. Everything is sound. Everything is vibration. So that's our basic component. Sound. Vibration. Music. That's what we're made of. That's our source. That's who we are. We're made of music.

Perhaps such insights are beyond the scope of a book on jazz, even if they are sentiments many other flutists have shared with me. Yet Paul Horn is uniquely qualified to represent this viewpoint. It is interesting to note that the Grammy nomination he received for his album *Traveler* was not for jazz but in the "New Age" category. Indeed, from the time of his *Inside* recording Paul Horn has been called the "Father of New Age Music," a category that is anathema to many jazz fans and artists--indeed, pianist Keith Jarrett has referred to it as "lobotomy music." Yet the kind of music that he produces, the majority of it on flute, is of a different order than most of what passes for New Age or world music today. His instrumental capabilities reflect his classical training; his explorations of foreign musical traditions arise from extensive visits to their countries and genuine interaction with their musicians. Above all, Paul has never turned his back on jazz. As he told Rosemary Phillips (*Paul Horn: Jazz Flutist and Grandfather of New Age Music* www. quillsquotesandnotes.com/wrpaulhorn.htm): "I do wear two very distinct hats. I wear my old jazz hat which has high energy music played with a group of musicians, and my other hat which is the quieter, meditative, solo type of playing. I love them both."

Charles Lloyd: Dream Weaver

"The thing about jazz is that it really has the ability to touch something deep inside. It's so full of wonder played by great creators that it articulates universal truth. It has enough subtlety and refinement and drive. It has such beauty and depth, the power is awesome. In music something happens where you make a better world, a world of light and eternity."

Charles Lloyd

If the sixties was a time of great development for jazz it was also a time of great challenge. While the music was expanding into new and often experimental horizons, the same was true of rock and other kinds of popular music. As groups like the Beatles, the Grateful Dead and a hundred others also began to explore the exotic and the experimental, to engage in lengthy improvisations, and to expand the popular song from the three minute single to the extended "concept" album, jazz musicians increasingly faced fierce competition, not only for the dollars of young record buyers, but even for the right to stake out what was cool and hip. There was, however, one jazz group that emerged in the mid-sixties to challenge Janis Joplin, Jefferson Airplane, Jimi Hendrix and the other psychedelic rock acts. Somehow, a jazz quartet led by **Charles Lloyd** managed to capture the imagination of the acid rock audience, riding a wave of support from young listeners, many of whom were either listening to jazz for the first time, or failed to realize that the group's music was in fact jazz. As Lloyd himself rose to rock star status, the group appeared at venues such as the Fillmore auditoria (East and West), and recorded the first jazz album to sell a million copies. And yet his work over the last four decades has shown that he is much more than a mere popularizer. Indeed, he has helped to move the music forward in a number of ways. Perhaps it was no accident that the leader of the group was a flutist--at least some of the time.

Charles Lloyd was born in Memphis, Tennessee in 1938, and it was the music of that city that provided him with his earliest musical roots. Even though it was the saxophone that he took up at the age of nine, and the great jazz pianist Phineas Newborn who gave him his earliest musical training, it was the blues bands of B. B. King, Howlin' Wolf, Johnny Ace, and Bobby "Blue" Bland that offered him his earliest employment. When it came time for college, Lloyd left Memphis for Los Angeles to take a music degree from the University of Southern California, studying composition with Halsey Stevens, a noted Bartók student. This exposure to the Western canon was fulfilling to Lloyd, but only partially so. As he told *Jazz Weekly*'s Fred Jung in the magazine's "Fireside Chat:"

They showed me three hundred years of Europe and that is beautiful. I love J.S. Bach, but I wanted to know about Africa and Asia. I wanted to know about the whole thing and all this rich tradition, Duke Ellington and Bird. They didn't know anything about that stuff and weren't interested in it. I had to go out into the community and find Ornette Coleman, Eric Dolphy, Don Cherry, Billy Higgins, Bobby Hutcherson, Scott LaFaro… There were a lot of great musicians out here at that time.

It was still too early to find jazz or ethnomusicology in the traditional college music curriculum. So just as Miles Davis abandoned Juilliard for New York's 52nd street, Lloyd migrated to L.A.'s Central Avenue to complete his education, working, among others, with the big band of Gerald Wilson. But it was with another bandleader, one who had already helped launch the career of several flutists, with whom Lloyd first rose to prominence.

Chico Hamilton did not wait for the sixties to arrive to begin experimenting with new instrumental combinations; he had been at it since 1955 when he got together with Fred Katz and Buddy Collette. When Collette left the group he was replaced by Paul Horn. Later, Eric Dolphy came in. When Dolphy finally left Hamilton in 1959, Chico turned to Charles Lloyd to play saxophone and flute with the quintet. "I raised Charles Lloyd, gave him his first job, took him on the road when he came out of USC," Hamilton recently reported in *Down Beat.* As Lloyd recalls it, "I was trying to go back to New York. My friends Ornette and Cherry had left and blew back East. Eric Dolphy left and was playing with Chico Hamilton, and he left him to play with Mingus, and Buddy Collette called me and said that now it was my turn."

It seemed a logical sequence, but Hamilton was no longer satisfied with the sound of his quintet. His group had been built around the cello-plus-multi-reed front line for over five years. Lloyd came in at the tail end of this format; he can be heard, along with cellist Nate Gershman, on *The Chico Hamilton Special,* recorded in November of 1960. But clearly it was no longer interesting to Hamilton."I felt I had played myself out," he told Ralph J. Gleason. For a change of direction he turned to Lloyd, whom Gleason described at the time as "an out-and-out devotee of the New Wave of jazz." Lloyd agreed with this assessment. "I joined Chico Hamilton when he was still working with the chamber jazz instrumentation--a reed player who doubled, a cello, guitar, bass, and drums." Lloyd said, "There was a lot of written music--too much discipline. I had been listening to Miles and Coltrane, Sonny Rollins, Monk, and Ornette Coleman. Music was moving into a new, freer phase, and I didn't have enough room to move around." "I was caught up in his way of thinking," Chico reported, "and I decided to go along with it. He is the one who got me into it and he's the musical director of the group now."

It was indeed a new direction for Hamilton. By 1962, with the appearance of *Drumfusion,* the quintet had an entirely new sound. Gershman's cello is replaced by the more robust sound of Garnett Brown's trombone, and the guitar chair was occupied by newcomer Gabor Szabo whom Hamilton had heard playing with the International Youth Band at the Newport festival. Szabo had developed a unique style that blended jazz with Eastern European and gypsy influences that he had brought with him as a refugee from his native Hungary.

Listening to *Drumfusion* reveals a lot about Lloyd's later work. The writing, in particular (though, curiously, not attributed on the recording), is clearly Lloyd's, and is very evocative of his later quartet. His tenor work, referred to by many critics as a "lighter-toned variant of John Coltrane" is more than that, reflecting an array of influences, not the least of which the fact that he had recently switched from alto. More importantly, it is clear that the saxophone is his first love and primary focus. Lloyd's statement at the opening of this chapter, which is from the notes to his 1992 album *Fish Out Of Water,* also includes the following: "And saxophone can testify to the condition of the planet better than any instrument I know." Later (*Down Beat*, April 1994), he told Tom Conrad: "I am blessed that for whatever reason I got the saxophone, because it is an extension of myself. It somehow makes me whole when I can hold on to it. Sometimes when ''m playing, I really don't have to hold on. It's like levitation is happening ... It's weightless ... It's effortless ... It's so unto itself." Such a statement speaks volumes about Lloyd's aesthetic and his inner experience of music making. On a more practical level, it is particularly revealing about his love for the saxophone. Over the course of his career, especially recently, he has made a good many recordings without any flute. He is never without his tenor. A *Down Beat* "Caught In The Act" review in 1965 was perceptive in this regard. "Equally deft on flute, he does not overuse the horn, as do so many others, but employs it merely to add scope. Tenor, he admits, is his horn."

Drumfusion sets the tone for this relationship. Of the seven tracks, only *A Rose For Booker,* a ballad-like tribute to his boyhood friend trumpeter Booker Little, features his flute. On the subsequent Hamilton recording *Passin' Thru*, Lloyd's tenor again predominates, although he does feature the flute on the lengthy and impressive *Lady Gabor. Man From Two Worlds*, Lloyd's final recording with Chico, features his flute on the tender *Love Song To A Baby.* This is not to say that Lloyd's flute work is an afterthought, far from it. In fact, in many ways his flute has more originality than his tenor. The anonymous author of the *Passin' Thru* liner notes has it about right when he claims that Lloyd's tenor playing " has not as yet reached the individuality of his writing." He goes on to describe Lloyd's flute sound. "On flute, he achieves a pure sound of almost archaic quality, reminding us that our flute is a direct descendant of the oldest instrument made by man." It's a lovely description and, I think, an accurate one. And perhaps this archaic quality is one factor that can explain the unprecedented mass appeal that Lloyd was to achieve, this along with another archetypal value that underlies all his playing, his earliest influence--the blues.

Lloyd's tenure with Chico Hamilton undoubtedly provided an excellent foundation for his career, both in the opportunity it gave him to develop his ideas and the exposure it offered him with the record-buying public. His next gig found him with an even more prominent group, however, as he replaced Yusef Lateef in the Cannonball Adderley sextet. With Adderley, Lloyd was definitely a sideman, with much less influence on the group's musical direction than he had with Hamilton. He contributed several compositions to the band's book, and muscular tenor and occasional flute work to their performances and recordings, which included a live recording in Los Angeles in early August of 1964, a jazz version of *Fiddler On The Roof* in October, and the 1965 *Radio Nights* album based on a live broadcast from New York's Half Note. Lloyd's work is interesting throughout this period, but he is clearly sublimating his musical vision to that of the Adderley brothers. "I created a number of procedures during my three years with Chico," Lloyd told *Down Beat*'s Burt Korall (June 16, 1966). "With Cannon, however, the methods were more firmly established. Though I wasn't restricted and the group played my things and encouraged me to create, I felt I was going in another direction. In order to grow, I had to be on my own, no matter what the risk." To make this transition Lloyd sought different outlets for his musical vision. His duties with Adderley left him time to explore the New York jazz scene, where he interacted with musicians such as John Coltrane, Thelonius Monk, Charles Mingus, Coleman Hawkins and Miles Davis, gigged at the Five Spot, Birdland, Half Note, Jazz Gallery, Slugs and the Village Vanguard, and worked regularly with the Nigerian percussionist Babatunde Olatunji. While still with Adderley, Lloyd signed a contract with CBS and began issuing recordings under his own name. *Discovery! The Charles Lloyd Quartet,* from 1964, featured a quartet with pianist Don Friedman, bassist Richard Davis and drummer J.C. Heard, while *Of Course, Of Course* and *Nirvana,* both released in 1965, found him intriguingly straddling the sound worlds of Chico Hamilton and Miles Davis, with guitarist Szabo on hand from Chico's group as well as Davis' rhythm section of Ron Carter and Tony Williams. All of these recordings show Lloyd developing his unique blend of melodic content, semi rock rhythms, folk influences, and avant-garde, chromatic abstraction. They were impressive enough to bring him *Down Beat* magazine's New Star award for 1965. It was with his next recording, however, and his new group, that he perfected the formula that was to bring him fame and fortune.

It was as he left Cannonball in 1965 that Lloyd put together the best known version of the Charles Lloyd quartet, with future superstars pianist Keith Jarrett and drummer Jack DeJohnette. Lloyd described his first meetings with Jarrett to *Jazz Weekly*'s Fred Jung:

> Oh, when I was with Cannonball, I heard Keith Jarrett up in Boston. He loved my playing and I loved his playing. He was playing upstairs behind a singer in the lounge upstairs. I was playing downstairs with Cannonball and so he would come on his breaks to hear me and I would go up on my breaks to hear him. We had a connection and he wanted to play with me. He was on the road with Art Blakey and he calls [sic] me and he wanted to play with me, and I was on the road with Gabor and I said when I get back to New York, we would get together. And so we got together and that band was history, Cecil McBee, Jack DeJohnette, we broke a lot of ground. We made a lot of beautiful music.

With just one personnel change--Cecil McBee was replaced by Ron McClure on bass--the quartet was together from 1965 to 1969, during which time they achieved a level of commercial success that was unprecedented for a jazz ensemble. Remarkably, however, they appeared to do it without a hint of artistic compromise. "The music of Charles Lloyd does not always make for easy listening," wrote George Avakian in the sleeve notes to *Discovery!*, "but nothing that is fresh and contemporary is ever totally accessible on one hearing." The sound that they developed was based on a unique combination of musical elements reflective of Lloyd's background--classical harmonies, exotic rhythms, avant-garde abstractions, the blues. He summed up his approach very simply: "People are many things; so is music." Added to these elements was the chemistry that existed between the group members, particularly Lloyd and Jarrett, a partnership rivaling Brubeck and Desmond, Mulligan and Baker, Davis and Coltrane. They also exhibited a flair for presentation that attracted hip young audiences. It was a formula that was too compelling to fail in the musical and cultural climate of the mid-sixties. But through it all there seems to be a lack of conscious manipulation; the group members appear to be following their true musical interests rather than merely seeking a commercial formula. From the perspective of today's music business this is quite remarkable.

The group's direction is beginning to become clear in their first recording, *Dream Weaver,* which appeared in 1966. These are hard-driving, extended improvisations, music that seems difficult at first blush and yet remains accessible because it is full of color, movement, and swirling excitement, modified by moments of tenderness. "I like to take people on nice little trips, using variety of color and dynamics" he told Burt Korall. "I want to involve people in my music, excite and bring them to me," he said. "Jazz must come to that--direct communication between one person and another, drawing them closer together."

It is notable here that Lloyd does not use the flute simply for ballad material, or just on Latin-based numbers as many saxophonists do. On *Dream Weaver* he picks up his flute to tackle an up-tempo

Autumn Leaves, and a funky original that was to become one of his trademark pieces, *Sombrero Sam.* This follows the pattern of Lloyd's earlier *Of Course, Of Course,* where his flute is heard on the up-tempo title song and on a hard swinging blues, *Third Floor Richard. Dream Weaver* also introduces an emerging tendency in Lloyd's writing by including two little dance-type suites, *Autumn Sequence* and *Dream Weaver.* It is also clear from these recordings that both Jarrett and DeJohnette are already wonderful players with enormous potential.

Lloyd's next album captures a key moment in the life of the quartet. It is a live recording of their appearance at the 1966 Monterey Jazz Festival. They were a sensation, the biggest hit of the festival, and the album, *Forest Flower,* was an instant hit, selling over a million copies--the first ever jazz album to do so. It was obvious that most of their new found fans either did not know this was jazz or simply didn't care. It was just music that struck a chord with the "Flower Children" of the mid sixties. Fueled by this support, the quartet took off, and the next three years was a whirl of concert tours, appearing before overflow crowds across the globe. They toured Europe, both east and west, six times. They went to the Far East. They were the first US jazz group to appear in the USSR outside of State Department tours. And in the US, they appeared at rock venues like the Fillmore Auditorium in San Francisco, as well as at the major jazz festivals. They issued a number of albums, both live and studio recordings. They appeared in a documentary film, *Charles Lloyd--Journey Within* that was screened at the New York film festival. They were the subject of scores of articles, and Lloyd appeared on the cover of *Down Beat* as "Jazzman Of The Year" for 1967.

Then, sometime in 1969, it was all over. The group broke up and went their separate ways. McClure went to work with Carla Bley, Joe Henderson, Cal Tjader and the Pointer Sisters. Jarrett and DeJohnette joined Miles Davis--who was profoundly influenced by Lloyd's recordings--and later went on to form their own groups. As for Lloyd, ironically, as the jazz-rock fusion movement he had helped to launch was gaining momentum, led by Jeremy Steig, Miles Davis and others, for all practical purposes, he dropped out.

He did not disappear completely; there were half a dozen recording sessions between 1970 and 1982. But he made few, if any, public appearances. He withdrew to Southern California, to a semi-reclusive lifestyle.

> I started out in Malibu and that was a little too close to the city for me and so I moved up the road to Big Sur and lived in a cave at first. Then I had some students and they told me that there was a castle down the road by the sea that some guy didn't live in and the next thing I knew, they placed me there and I lived on this cliff in this incredible glass and cement structure that some crazy architect had built on a piece of rock. So I lived there and worked and worked on my tone, worked on my character, meditated a lot. I didn't get in cars often. I became a vegetarian. I got down to about a hundred and thirty pounds.

There were many factors contributing to Lloyd's self-imposed hiatus. Ten years in the fast lane had taken their toll. There were issues. There were drugs. His whirlwind success was a two-edged sword. It brought everything to a head, to the point where he needed to escape. But it also provided him with the wherewithal to do so. "Back then, when I had my first quartet, I thought that my music could change the world. When I found out that I was wrong, I embarked upon a long journey of trying to change my character and transform myself." And so he stayed in Big Sur, grappled with his demons, healed his body, and played his saxophone and his flute--for himself.

He has been in California ever since, venturing out, until recently, only occasionally. After a five-year silence, his association with Transcendental Meditation brought him into contact with the Beach Boys, and he made some recordings in Brian Wilson's studio. Another three-year silence followed. Then he received a visit from Michel Petrucciani, the brilliant French pianist with a crippling disease but a wonderful talent and a great spirit. Lloyd was so impressed that he came out of retirement and reformed his quartet with Petrucciani, on piano. They made two recordings, in 1982 and '83, which helped establish the Frenchman's reputation. As Lloyd puts it, "I got him started and then I went back to Big Sur." Another six year silence followed. Then, Lloyd reports, he had a near-death experience, barely surviving some emergency surgery. More healing followed but eventually, having stepped back from the abyss, he decided it was time to get back into circulation, into active music making. "I dedicated myself to this indigenous, beautiful tradition that we have, and picked myself up and dusted off and rededicated myself to the tradition of service."

The new and most recent phase of Charles Lloyd's career was announced with the 1989 recording *Fish Out Of Water*, which also introduced a new and important partnership for him. The recording was on ECM records, whose founder Manfred Eicher, in his role as producer and guiding light, has created a unique environment within which his artists, jazz as well as classical, can achieve high levels of creativity. Eicher's motto is "The most beautiful sound next to silence," and the ECM environment in general, and Eicher in particular, appear to have nourished Lloyd's muse over the last 20+ years. He has turned out a dozen fine albums, working with Bobo Stenson, Palle Danielsson, Jon Christensen, Billy Hart, Billy Higgins, Geri Allen, John Abercrombie, Dave Holland, Brad Mehldau, Eric Harland, and, most recently, tabla maestro Zakir Hussain. He has also been touring steadily, while returning regularly to Big Sur to recharge his batteries.

It is perhaps foolish to try to characterize two decades of an artist's work in a few sentences, but in Charles Lloyd's case such an assessment is at least feasible. For there have been no distinct phases in his career, no early Lloyd, or late period Lloyd. His style has remained essentially unchanged since his earliest appearances with Chico Hamilton. Since then it has simply matured and deepened, along with his personal vision. His tenor work remains instantly recognizable, while demonstrating a clear debt to John Coltrane which is also apparent in his writing. Lloyd's music stays fresh through the subtly changing contexts in which it is presented, either the quartets with Bobo Stenson, Brad Meldau, or Geri Allen as his main partner, the duo improvisations with his close friend Billy Higgins, or his new trio that pits his woodwinds against the drums of Eric Harland and the tabla of Zakir Husain.

As for the flute, it comes and goes enigmatically. Several of Lloyd's ECM albums have had no flute tracks. Tenor predominates, while the flute has to compete with his new interests, the *tárogató* and the Chinese oboe. When it does appear, however, as on *All My Relations*, or *Lift Every Voice*, it is still a unique voice. I can't think of any flutist who has been directly influenced by Lloyd's flute work, in the same way that Kent Jordan owes a debt to Hubert Laws, or Günter Wehinger to James Newton. But Lloyd's flute has been influential in two ways. On the surface, his enormous popularity undoubtedly introduced the instrument to a wide audience, even as critics were still quarreling about whether the flute was a valid jazz instrument. His audience didn't care. They didn't know if what they were hearing was jazz or not, they just loved it. Furthermore, Lloyd's subtle absorption of non-Western influences, long before the term 'world music' came into vogue, along with a strong classical training and four decades of jazz performance, has again established the flute as a link between jazz and the music of other cultures. Above all, the depth of Lloyd's playing reaffirms the archetypal reference to the archaic inner voice that is at the center of the flute's ability to hold sway over our inner world. With all of this, Charles Lloyd has made a significant contribution to the flute in jazz.

Jeremy Steig: New York Satyr

"Believe it or not, I'm a jazz flute player who also draws."

Jeremy Steig

From the outset, **Jeremy Steig**'s career has been divided between two interests. Born in New York in September of 1942, Steig's father was New Yorker cartoonist and children's book author William Steig, and his mother Liza was the head of the Art Department at Lesley College. With this background, not to mention these genes, it is no surprise that he has had a lifelong involvement with the visual arts. At the same time, however, music has vied for Steig's attention since his school years, and he has had a career as a flutist over the last forty years that has seen many twists and turns, resulting in over forty albums featuring him as either leader or sideman.

Steig was very much a child of the sixties, and this is very much reflected in his playing, which has been influenced as much by 'progressive' rock as by the jazz players to whom he was exposed. The ones he cites are John Coltrane, Thelonius Monk and Bill Evans, but his approach to the flute clearly reflects the impact of Rahsaan Roland Kirk who burst on the scene at the 1962 Newport Jazz Festival, the year before Steig's first recording, *Flute Fever*, appeared. The style that has emerged from these influences has proven effective across the boundaries between jazz, rock, and funk, and Steig has played and recorded with musicians from all these genres, including Joe Henderson, Eddie Palmieri, Yoko Ono, Jimi Hendrix, Tim Hardin, Jim Hall, Big Joe Williams, Junior Wells, Eddie Gomez, David Amram, Art Blakey, Paul Bley, Joe Chambers, Jan Hammer, Johnny Winter, Tim Hardin, Richie Havens and Tommy Bolin. Asked about the late rock icon Bolin, and what the guitarist might have accomplished if he had lived longer, Steig made his feelings clear about the value of jazz compared to rock. "He [Bolin] would have done more for music in that role than just to be another jazz musician. Jimi Hendrix raised everyone's consciousness by introducing great improvising to a huge audience."

The other significant factor in Steig's career as a flutist has been a physical one. As a result of a serious motor-cycle accident in Bermuda when he was 19, he was left with half his face paralyzed. "I took a week to decide whether to be a musician again or not. It was a tortured week. After all, I could make a living and a satisfaction at art." He decided to try and play again, although it took surgery and six months of recuperation before he could do it. Even then he needed the help of a special device. "I didn't have the muscles in the left side of my mouth to hold the air in," Steig recalls, "so if I blew, my lips would just open up. I figured that if I put something under my lips it would divert the air through the middle." So he created a mouthpiece out of cardboard and tape. Eventually he was able to rebuild his embouchure, although he needed to use the device to record *Flute Fever* and his second album, *Jeremy & The Satyrs* in 1968.

In an on-line interview with Scott McIntosh of the Tommy Bolin Foundation, Steig provided some insights into his early development as an improvising musician:

I started playing recorder at age 6, in first grade. I was improvising almost immediately, picking out melodies by ear, and then making up new parts to go with them. When I was 8, I "retired," to do all the things that kids do, until I was 11. At that point, my mother wanted me to take up an instrument again, and they were teaching clarinet and flute in the school I went to. I had never heard any kid play the clarinet without sounding like s--t, so the choice of the flute was easy. Luckily, the young flute teacher I had was Paige Brook, who had just joined the New York Philharmonic. To this day, I have never heard anyone play as good as Paige did. (He just passed away a few months ago.)

Apart from giving Steig a technical foundation, Paige Brook encouraged him to explore jazz and rock. It was a direction he was already intuitively pursuing: "As soon as I started playing the flute, I was playing by ear and improvising, just like with the recorder. I didn't know what I was 'after' until I was almost 15. I bought a Clifford Brown/Max Roach record, and I realized that I had been playing jazz all along, without knowing the word." This tendency was reinforced at the High School of Music and Art in New York where he met the great bassist Eddie Gomez:

I went to high school with Eddie Gomez. It was a music high school and we used to go into a room full of basses in between periods and play jazz duo. When the teachers caught us, we were reprimanded for playing jazz and would get "N" on our report card, meaning not satisfactory. Eddie and I are still playing together. By the way, the same school now has a jazz program. (I consider jazz education the kiss of death to the music.)

While pursuing his formal training, Steig took full advantage of the opportunities provided by the New York music scene, in both jazz and rock.

Back in the 60's, I used to sit in with everybody. Back then, musicians weren't so protective of their territory, and they all let me sit in with them. I sat in with a wide variety of musicians, and with rock bands, too. I found I could keep my "soloing integrity" while playing over a funky beat. One week, I had my band backing up Tim Hardin. In the middle of the week, Tim disappeared and never came back (as he was prone to do). For the rest of the week, we played Tim's tunes without him, and we were able to stretch out a lot more. And that was the beginning of the Satyrs. The next gig, I added a blues singer named Adrian Guillery. We decided that we'd invented jazz-rock. Of course, there were about 50 other people who had come to the same conclusion.

It is hard to say exactly who invented jazz-rock, but Steig was certainly part of its first wave, to which he contributed his second album, *Jeremy and The Satyrs*. But he did not restrict himself to this genre.

Like I said, there was a lot of sitting in going on. I had the greatest sitting in situation for any horn player, ever, because I sat in with the Bill Evans Trio (their last set) every night, for about 10 years, whenever they played New York. In those days, New York was a very passionate place. It was unbelievable how many fabulous musicians there were. Sometimes we would find spaces where we could play music, like lofts and stuff. We'd carry huge amplifiers up, maybe, 5 flights of stairs--just so we could get the right sound.

As well as working with Bill Evans, he played at a club on Bleeker Street with Paul Bley and Gary Peacock. "When Gary couldn't make it, Steve Swallow played bass, and when Paul couldn't, Carla Bley played." The sessions with Bill Evans eventually led to a recording, *What's New,* issued in 1969.

After completing these early sessions, Steig formed his own group, Jeremy and The Satyrs. They landed a two and a half month residency at the Dom on St. Mark's Place playing six nights a week. Soon they headed west where they played opposite Cream at the Fillmore and Winterland. "Cream was recording Wheels Of Fire," he recalled. "Fillmore sat 3,000 and Winterland 5,000. It was just an amazing experience." It was around this period that Charles Lloyd was appearing at these same rock venues. Between them, Lloyd's quartet and Jeremy and The Satyrs broke new ground in the area of jazz/rock fusion.

Steig has issued around forty recordings since then, in which he has continued to explore a wide range of genres. There have been duo albums with Eddie Gomez, fusion sessions with Jan Hammer, straight-ahead recordings with Urbie Green and Art Farmer. He has also worked with pop/rock artists such as Tim Hardin, Richie Havens, Yoko Ono, and Tommy Bolin. Whatever the context, Steig's playing has drawn on a variety of extended techniques, particularly the speaking-humming-playing technique associated with a number of jazz players, several of whom he counts among his influences. According to Celeste Sunderland in an *allaboutjazz.com* article:

> Bobby Jaspar, Roland Kirk, James Moody, and Yusef Lateef who inspired him to start singing into the flute, are in Steig's opinion, some of the major contributors to the instrument. He remembers how he could never get a gig in the high school dance bands because they only wanted saxophone players who doubled on flute. "Back then flute wasn't getting it's due. But since then it's been in small groups, and in a small group, flute has just as much to say."

Steig has clearly contributed to this process, and has plenty to say, but very much on his own terms. Idiosyncratic in the extreme, Steig belongs to no particular school and cares little about genres. His career has been an on-again, off-again affair since these early recordings. It seems to be in an on-again phase currently, as he has recently returned to performing, mainly in New York City, with a quartet featuring Vic Juris, Cameron Brown and Anthony Pinciotti, the group featured on his recently issued CD. (And his place in popular culture is secure after his work was sampled on a 1994 Beastie Boys recording, and his flute appeared as the Pied Piper in the film S*hrek: Forever After*, based on the character created by his father.) Jeremy Steig's strong, even wild approach to the instrument continues to add a vital ingredient to the tradition of the flute in jazz.

Part Four

From Big Band To Mass Media

Writing For Flute

The growing acceptance of the flute in a jazz context required not just the emergence of soloists on the instrument, but also its greater use by arrangers writing for jazz big bands and other ensembles. This process was amplified, as so often happens, when practices from the world of jazz were taken up in the broader worlds of the mass media.

Throughout the big-band era of the 1930s and '40s, jazz was very much an integral part of popular music, although the flute had little or no role to play in these larger ensembles, which were dominated by brass instruments plus saxophones frequently doubling on clarinet. But with the changes the music underwent in the 1950s, as the flute replaced the clarinet in popularity, its voice began to be heard more widely. Frank Wess' flute solos with the Count Basie Orchestra not only introduced the sound of the instrument to a national audience via the group's radio broadcasts, but also interested arrangers such as Neil Hefti in finding effective ways to write for the instrument in this new context. The first results, within the Basie band, found Wess' flute voiced with Joe Newman's muted trumpet on such pieces as *Perdido, Flute Juice* and *Midgets*. With Eric Dixon replacing Wess as flute soloist when Frank left the band, the sound became a regular part of Basie's reed section.

It did not take long for the voicings that Hefti had popularized with Basie to be picked up by other arrangers, Henry Mancini and Ernie Wilkins, for example, and Stan Kenton's writing crew on the West coast. By 1959 when Gil Evans wrote the arrangements for Miles Davis' recording of *Porgy and Bess*, the flute family was but one of the range of sonorities available to him. He chose to exploit it on *Summertime,* voicing three flutes under Miles' muted horn. Later, on the *Individualism of Gil Evans*, he exploits the sound of both flute and bass flute on *Barbara's Song.* This process has followed a logical conclusion until the present time, when reed sections are responsible for a whole range of instrumental colors, with almost every player doubling on flute, but also on clarinet since that instrument's comeback in the 1980's. Modern arrangers from Toshiko Akiyoshi to Maria Schneider have not hesitated to exploit these resources to their fullest. At a recent Kennedy Center concert by Schneider's band, I counted at least eighteen or nineteen instruments in use by the woodwind section--or what used to be called the reed section--several of them flutes. A detailed documentation of the transition from sax section to woodwind section within the big band would make a fine doctoral dissertation project. I can only touch on the high points here.

It is worth noting, however, that the popularization of the flute sound in contemporary music was greatly aided by its growing use in the popular American mass media. Here, Dr. Kamalidiïn picks up the narrative:

> Throughout the '50s, '60s and '70s, popular film, TV, and recording studio arranger/ composers, many of them equally known and adept as jazz artists, did much to make the flute as ubiquitous as it is today in commercial music by using all the members of the flute family to great effect in their creative orchestrations. Here we can list Quincy Jones, Henry Mancini (himself a flutist), Pete Rugolo, Hugo Montenegro, John Barry, Nelson Riddle, Lawrence Welk, Neal Hefti, Isaac Hayes, Don Sebesky, Johnny Pate, Lalo Schifrin and many others. The search for freshness and flexibility among infrequently used instrumental sound sources caused many of the film and TV composer/arrangers of this period to exploit the heretofore relatively less

used flute for its multiplicity of timbres, technical agility, and its evocative sonorities in contemporary music contexts.

The copious use of flutes even becomes synonymous with certain film genres based upon its presence in high profile films by certain popular composers, for example, Henry Mancini's use of the flute in the early *Peter Gunn* and *Mr. Lucky* TV series, as well as his movie scores, made the flute's sound (for a while) a required musical mainstay in the detective drama genre. John Barry heightened the dramatic tension and expanded the sonic palette of the early James Bond motion picture soundtracks (*Dr.No*, *From Russia with Love*, *Goldfinger*, *Thunderball*, etc.) making the flute's sounds a required ingredient in expressing that genre's "quiet, confident, cool component" by using a vibrato-less flute section, as well as both the alto and bass flutes in prominent solo roles.

In the language of musical embellishment of imagery in motion pictures, film scorers have caused the flute's sound to become synonymous with virtuous (i.e., pure, true, chaste) love or happy, upbeat, light-hearted emotions in the same way that the sound of the ("sleazy, bleating, growling, wailing, whining") saxophone has in some cinematic contexts become the musical signaler of illicit, raunchy or lustful sexually based "love" or emotions. The flute, as is the case with all musical instruments used in artistic products, is used to help establish the emotional framework of the cinematic work; to magnify the emotional impact of the film's subject matter and/or to communicate the verbally and visually inexpressible.

Because the flute came to be accepted (and expected) in so many diverse American musical environs, it was only a matter of time before it became an inextricable part of America's major musical contribution to world culture, jazz, and not by simply filling its role as a musical novelty, but as the powerfully affecting, contributing voice to jazz music that it is. The importance of the increased inclusion of the flute in many forms of commercial American music and its interrelated importance in jazz cannot be overstated.

A Note on Ellington and Norris Turney

Duke Ellington always wanted a flute soloist. It is not clear what inspired this desire. It could have been internally motivated by hearing a flute among the voicings he must have carried constantly in his head. Or it could have been stimulated by hearing flutists with other bands, Frank Wess with Basie, perhaps, or Buddy Collette with Chico Hamilton. He actually called Buddy at one time in the early 1950s and asked him to joint the band. Tired of being on the road, and with a family to take care of in Los Angeles, Buddy turned him down. (As he told me: "The hardest 'No' I ever had to say!") Harry Carney played some flute--he is pictured holding one in a 1934 picture of the band--but never as a soloist. And Duke brought in Les Spann to play the flute parts for his score of *Paris Blues*. But he still did not have a permanent flute soloist in the band.

Duke finally got his way in 1969 when Norris Turney joined the band. Initially there to stand in for an ailing Johnny Hodges, Turney came for two weeks and stayed for four years. He was still primarily there to play alto sax--that's what the arrangements called for and, indeed, what was closest to Turney's heart. An admirer of Hodges his whole life, it was a dream come true for him to be sitting in the master's chair in Duke's sax section. With all that, Turney was a reluctant flutist at best. Nevertheless, Duke wrote a flute feature for him which appears on the album "Duke Ellington's 70th Birthday

Concert" from 1969. Listed on the record as *Fifi* it is actually introduced by Duke as *Fife.* The following year, Turney's flute appeared on the track *Bourbon Street Jingling Jollies* from Ellington's "New Orleans Suite." In the sleeve notes we find:

> *Bourbon Street Jingling Jolies* introduced Norris Turney's flute, an instrument heretofore unknown in Ellington's orchestral palette. At the premiere in New Orleans, Ellington announced, "We would like to have Norris Turney come up for a solo spot. He, ladies and gentlemen, would like to give a tonal parallel to the excruciating ecstasy one finds oneself suspended in when one is in the throes of the jingling jollies of Bourbon Street."

It was not a very extensive exposure--just a few minutes--but it had a dramatic effect on Turney's career, at least as a flutist, as he won the flute division for Talent Deserving of Wider Recognition, in the *Down Beat* Critics Polls for 1970 and 1971.

Turney's tenure with Ellington ended in 1973, somewhat acrimoniously according to some accounts, including this one from Duke's son Mercer Ellington:

> Although he had never allowed Jimmy Hamilton to play flute in the band, he finally decided to feature Norris Turney on the instrument. Unfortunately, we were into a period when Pop was very dissatisfied with the rhythm section. One night he was screaming at it during Norris's solo, and Norris protested about this in a way Pop felt was defying his authority. So he waited until the situation duplicated itself, and then he needled Norris so much between numbers that Norris became furious, packed up his instruments, and left the stage during a performance. As a result, Ellington lost a capable musician, one who was as well equipped to take Johnny Hodges's place as anyone then around.

Turney went on to work in the Broadway theatre for several years, later with George Wein's Newport All Stars. The 90s found him working and touring with the Lincoln Center Jazz Orchestra under the leadership of Wynton Marsalis, and, later, with Louie Bellson's band.

Turney passed away in 2001. As for Duke, he replaced Turney with Harold Minerve, but there are no recordings of Minerve playing flute with the band. Duke never hired another flute player.

A Note on Basie and Eric Dixon

Count Basie acquired a flute soloist by accident. He had hired Frank Wess to play tenor and only later learned that Wess played the flute. Once he was used to having a flute soloist, however, he wanted to continue with that. When Frank decided to leave the band, it was Eric Dixon who took over the flute chores. Dixon had been recruited by Wess, but again, primarily to play tenor. His flute chops are evident, however, in some recordings by the *Kansas City Seven* that finds him and Wess playing together.

Dixon proved a worthy replacement for Wess until he too left the Basie organization. What happened to him after that is something of a mystery. Even Frank Wess has little idea, except that Eric freelanced for some time, and then passed away prematurely. As for Basie, he never hired another flute player.

Smooth Jazz

It must be recognized that the form known as "smooth" jazz has played an important role in introducing the sound of the flute to jazz audiences, as the instrument is featured quite prominently in that sub-genre, one that is very much in popular consciousness via many radio stations. Dr. Kamalidiin writes:

> The music known today as "smooth" jazz has many highly skilled flute artists as practitioners. Smooth jazz is a form of jazz that is heavily influenced by rhythm & blues idioms. It is primarily derived from vocally-oriented melodies and inflections, funk bass and drum patterns and relatively simple song-form chord changes or vamps.
>
> Some of the best smooth jazz flutists currently performing are: Alexander Zonjic, Najee, Ragan Whiteside, Althea Rene, Nelson Rangell, Jose Valentino, Horace Young III, Shana Kaye, Shani Andrews, Gerald Albright, Delandria Mills, Bradley Leighton, Dave Camp, Dwanye Kerr, Bryan Savage, Gerald Albright, Zig Noda, Phillip Bent and Eric Leeds. This musical style was pioneered by flutists Barbara (Bobbi) Humphrey (the first female jazz flutist to record on a major international label--Blue Note--under her own name), Sherry Winston, Tim Weisburg, Lennie Druss, Art Webb, and, on some of their recordings, Hubert Laws and Herbie Mann.

Space considerations do not allow further discussion of these artists here especially given that, as Dr. Kamalidiin points out, the smooth jazz genre tends to hover somewhere between jazz and popular forms, rather than exploring the jazz mainstream. This is seen particularly with regard to recording techniques, where mainstream jazz artists prefer the live interaction between musicians that is essential for creative improvisation, rather than the studio overdubbing techniques, characteristic of popular music, that is more often favored by smooth jazz artists.

Nevertheless, no one should underestimate the contribution of these artists to the growth of the flute in jazz.

Joel Dorn: Heavy Flute

"One of the things that people forget is that jazz used to be music to dance to. And it used to be music you went out to, to have fun. It's not all serious and complex and abstract."

Joel Dorn

Joel Dorn played a major role in the development of the flute in jazz, yet he was not a flutist, not a performing musician. Dorn, who passed away unexpectedly in 2007, was one of the most prominent record producers in the history of jazz. In the opinion of Chris Slawecki, in an *All About Jazz* column, "If you're a serious jazz fan, even if you're any kind of jazz fan at all, there's an excellent chance that in your collection you've got at least one piece of music that was produced by Joel Dorn." Dorn has not restricted himself to jazz, however. In fact, disregarding boundaries has been his stock-in-trade. Best known for his work with Atlantic Records, he produced records by Bette Midler and the Allman Brothers Band as well as by Charles Mingus and Cannonball Adderley. He produced hits by Roberta Flack, as well as sessions by Keith Jarrett, Gary Burton, Lou Rawls, the Neville Brothers and Leon Redbone. He received four Grammys and two "Record of the Year" awards. Edgar Bronfman, Jr., CEO of Warner Music Group--Atlantic's parent company--paid tribute to the producer at the time of his passing: "Dorn," he stated, "bridged the worlds of jazz and pop with enormous skill and grace, never compromising the integrity of his artists and their music."

Joel Dorn began his career in 1961 as a disc jockey with a Philadelphia jazz station WHAT-FM. But his desire to be a producer led him eventually to a meeting with Nesuhi Ertegun of Atlantic Records. Ertegun was sufficiently impressed with Dorn to offer him a modest trial project with the label, a small budget to produce one album, by an artist of his choice, for the company's jazz division. Joel's choice was to have an enormous impact on the history of jazz flute. Hearing Hubert Laws playing with Mongo Santamaria convinced Dorn that this was the artist he was looking for. He brought Laws into his studio and produced the flutist's first album, 1964's *The Laws of Jazz*. It was such a success that Dorn was elevated to the position of Ertegun's assistant at Atlantic. While Hubert went on to inspire a whole generation of jazz flutists, Dorn went on, between 1967 and 1974, to produce albums by Les McCann, Eddie Harris, Rahsaan Roland Kirk, Max Roach, Freddie Hubbard, Herbie Mann, Keith Jarrett, Yusef Lateef, Jimmy Scott, David "Fathead" Newman, Hank Crawford, Ray Bryant, Oscar Brown Jr., Mongo Santamaria, and Gary Burton.

This list includes several major flutists. Indeed, Dorn showed a particular affinity for the flute. This was to manifest itself in a compilation album, *Heavy Flute,* that included tracks by Herbie Mann, David "Fathead" Newman, Yusef Lateef, Hubert Laws, Rahsaan Roland Kirk, Leo Wright and Charles Lloyd. It proved to be one of the best-selling jazz albums in the Atlantic catalog, and it was the initial focus of my conversation with Joel, which was carried out over the phone while he soaked in his tub! His first comment was how much he loved the *Heavy Flute* album.

I mentioned that to Herbie [Mann] and he said you liked funk. Is that fair?

It's very fair. When you make records, if you start out in a certain thing, you're kind of typed like that. I started out making jazz records, a lot of funky jazz records, and then did some R&B and R&B-like jazz things where you couldn't tell where one started and the other stopped. So for the years I was at Atlantic, I did things by Roberta Flack and Bette Midler, and Donny Hathaway, a lot of funky things, you know. I was kind of typed as that, because it's one of the musics I really love. I love many kinds of music. But I love jazz, I love R&B, I love Wagner, I love country music, I love the blues, I love bluegrass, I love all different kinds of pop music, I love swing... I mean I don't love funk anymore than I love doo-wop or real country, but I've been involved in it, so I guess that's why somebody would say that. And I do like it, you know. And I've always loved jazz flute.

What would you say to the writer who claims that the flute is a marginal jazz instrument?

He's a f---ing idiot!

Well, okay. That takes care of that!

It's far from the case, and I'll tell you why. I'm 61. I came over in an era where the main instruments of jazz were the saxophone, the trumpet, and the piano. You know, you had piano players, trumpeters and saxophone players. And once in a while a drummer or a bass player would have a group, or a trombone player--you know what I mean? They were the main instruments of jazz. And through the fifties there were a couple of people who played jazz flute.

Right. Herbie Mann, Bud Shank, Sam Most, Moe Koffman in Canada...

So there were a few guys who were flutists. But they always were looked at as like... not oddities in that they were weirdos, but it's not a conventional jazz instrument.

Well, it was still a "miscellaneous" instrument.

Well, that was the point I was getting to--a miscellaneous instrument. You would always see a clarinetist, an accordionist, and ultimately at a certain point, flutes started coming up. Now Herbie, who was not the best of the flute players, but the guy who really did the most to introduce jazz flute to the broadest audience, was responsible I think, initially.

Although the guy that got mentioned in earliest polls was Frank Wess.

Right. Frank Wess was, and is, a terrific jazz player. But Dave Brubeck had *Take Five*, Ahmad Jamal could have *Poinciana*, Randy Lewis could have *The In Crowd*, Jack McDuff *Rock Candy*... There was a whole era of jazz things that crossed over into R&B and then into pop music. Frank Wess would never have a record that would do that, because he is a great conventional jazz musician. So you know, I don't count Frank in the flute-player category. I mean, he's a saxophone player who also plays flute, and plays it well. Same as James Moody--they're sax players.

Frank did take time off on the G.I. Bill and studied flute exclusively.

That's why he plays good stuff, I guess, he actually studied the instrument. But what was happening was when Coltrane had the *Favorite Things* album, he played soprano, and also he was emerging as the major force in jazz of his time. A result of Coltrane's ascendency was that now everybody starts playing like him. Every saxophone player I knew, whether he was an alto player or a tenor player--with the exception of the real honkers, you know--were now playing soprano saxophone. And many of them were also playing flute.

Soprano [saxophone] was also a miscellaneous instrument. And it was hard to get hold of good soprano saxes to begin with.

But the flute is legit, having its own voice. Listen, when 'Miscellaneous Instruments' was really a category of the day, I saw nearly a dozen guys that were playing jazz flute. I think jazz flute had a bigger problem with critics and writers than it did with anybody, because they decided that it wasn't a legitimate instrument.

Not just that, they decide what jazz is and what it isn't.

I still get in trouble with those people because I think it's a crock of s--t. I started out as a jazz disc jockey in Philadelphia. I was on the air from '61 through '67, and I was playing jazz flute [on the radio] when it was being looked down upon by the critical community. It was pushed off in the corner as "… maybe this year you'll end up in the miscellaneous category."

Right. I forget what year they actually started their flute category. I want to say 1960.

I'm sure it was in the first half of the sixties, because by then you really couldn't deny the instrument's existence. I think if you look at the long history of jazz you'll see that there was a period from the late fifties through the late seventies where the major jazz flutists emerged and set the ground rules. And when they were gone, or when that time was over, so too was the evolution of jazz flute. I started producing records incidentally probably around '63 or '64 when I was still on the air. But of all the flute players I've ever recorded, I think Hubert was the most accomplished, strictly as a flute player in the traditional sense.

Okay, but there are some younger players doing interesting things.

I'm never saying that there aren't. But what I am saying is, when you have the originators all blossoming at the same time that's different than the ensuing times. You know all the guys we were talking about if you go with Sam Most, and Herbie Mann, and Rahsaan, and Yusef, and Hubert Laws and anybody else you want to include.

*Well, several of them are on the **Heavy Flute** record. How did that all come about?*

I like to make combo compilations. And I've had a lot of success with compilations.

Orin Keepnews told me compilations are never successful--a waste of time, he called them.

Okay, but I've had a series that sold in excess of a million. I have an odd sense of timing, such as the fact that I was doing flute when it was sneered upon. I'm not going to say I have odd taste, but there are things that appeal to me that I record. Later, generally, they become validated, but not always at the time of the recording. Flute was one of them. By the time we got done ten years of recording flute it was a legit category, and every sax player who was working a club had a flute number. And now nobody looks at it as odd, there's so many flute players.

It's expected these days, both in the studios and in the schools.

Exactly. It's here now. The other thing is, talking about Orin's opinion about compilations, generally compilations in jazz did not sell. And I always maintain the reason was that they were throwaways. Nobody ever made them seriously. When I was a disc jockey I had to program an hour's worth of music every hour, and that's approximately the length of a compilation. And if you have a theme, a title, and deliver upon the promise of the title, and if there's a beginning, a middle, and an end, and if it flows like an hour of music should, compilations are viable. We had a series called *Jazz For...* about six or seven years ago: *Jazz For a Rainy Afternoon*, jazz for this, jazz for that: We sold in excess of a million of the five or six titles because it did the things you're supposed to do.

There's one thing you said a few minutes ago that I wanted to pick up on. You said that you wanted to work with various artists to help them get a little bit broader. This is where jazz critics will jump all over you and say it's not pure. But what does the artist think about it?

It depends. You don't do it *to* an artist, you do it *with* an artist. If you have a person who is a real artist, you're not putting them in a situation where they're compromising the integrity of what they do. The guys that appeal to me, I always thought of doing what they do and having them crossover, though it didn't always happen. It happened with Eddie Harris, it happened with Les McCann, both separately and together. It happened to a degree with Yusef and Rahsaan and Fathead. They didn't get smash hit records out of it, but they sold well, and they started selling in areas that they hadn't sold before. Jazz records were inexpensive to make, so if you could sell five, ten, fifteen thousand back in those days, that was good--that was really solid sales. Herbie had records that have sold hundreds of thousands, *Live at the Village Gate, Memphis Underground.* And you know, we had the flutists at Atlantic, because at one time we had Herbie, Fathead, Yusef, Rahsaan, Hubert, Charles Lloyd--I think all of those guys were on the label at one time.

Was it your doing that all those artists were on there?

All of them except for Charles Lloyd; he came in through George Avikian. Fathead was already there, then he left, but I brought him back. I brought Hubert. I brought Yusef. I brought Rahsaan. Leo Wright was already there and gone--he had moved to Germany by the time I got there. With Yusef and Rahsaan I saw what they did with the flute in clubs, and the response they got, aside from my own gut reaction on who I wanted to work with, based on the records of theirs that I had heard, or the response that I got to their records at the station. The other thing was going down and seeing them work. So I'd go to the clubs almost every night. I thought *Heavy Flute* was going to be the first in a series of heavy CDs. *Heavy Flute, Heavy Sax, Heavy Piano*, heavy this, heavy that. We did very well with that album, but unfortunately we lost our funding for the label, because people who were funding us were taken over by people who couldn't care less about records. So it died. But that album sold probably ten thousand CDs, which is gigantic for a compilation. And it backs up my thought that the flute, which is a fairly neglected instrument, basically appeals...

I love that record. I thought it was a nice cross section of Atlantic's representation of flute players, broad enough so that it didn't have a label sound. And you know, I'm glad it did well, because I keep thinking that people really react to flute.

I was telling you, I used to go into clubs, right? And anytime Yusef or Rahsaan, or Hubert with Mongo, or Fathead, or any of the guys got on the flute … or Herbie--Herbie had real hit records in the sixties. He wasn't messing around. He would fill the club when he came to town. By the time he got to *Coming Home Baby*, or *This Little Girl of Mine*, or something like that, the joint was jumping. And he always had bands. He used to find terrific personnel and put bands around them. He got people who could lay down what he wanted to lay down for him.

Anyway, I started talking about what the guys did in their responses--especially Yusef and Rahsaan--when they got in the club, with all those innovative uses of the flute, whether it was circular breathing, whether it was the triple tonguing and all that cute stuff, whether it was talking or singing through the flute--a lot of stuff--people really responded to them in the club. Now remember, these were generally real showpiece numbers. Rahsaan, Yusef, they would do like one a set--two a set sometimes--where they really stretched out on the flute, and did all the things that were, you know, their own thing. But if it goes well in the club, then we have to get that on record. So when I signed them, we did a lot of flute stuff in the album. They had recorded on flute well before they were recording with me. We did albums that were more thematic, you know? They weren't just jazz records. It wasn't just a quartet record or a quintet record, or sextet--you know what I mean? These were produced albums. I was trying to compete with the jazz artists who would cross over into R&B, and then, hopefully, ultimately, pop. So you know there were background singers and overdubs here and overdubs there, and all the stuff in the day that was used generally in pop and R&B production, and guys like myself were sliding it into jazz production.

And the artists were behind that? Is it the critics more than the artists who don't like this?

F--k the critics. The only critic that could say that is the guy who was in the room, who could have a recording, or a picture, of me saying to Yusef: "You do what I tell you or you're out of here." You know! I was in awe of these people. These are strong-willed, very focused guys.

Now I'm sure that there are artists who cashed the check and did what they were told. And maybe it worked and maybe it didn't. I don't know. But I've always tried to build upon who and what the artists were. If I did anything, it was to try and make a more accessible recording of what it was they did. But I started with them. I never told anybody to play like this, or do that. I would say, "Listen, I'd like to make an album with this rhythm section." And if they did, we did; if they didn't, we didn't.

I'll give you an example. The way we used to make albums--I would come up with a concept, and he would come back with a finished album, his version of the concept I'd laid on him. We did one project, the *Blue Yusef Lateef*, it was his interpretation of blues. All kinds of blues. It wasn't just a blues album. It was a broadly based, you know, blues experience. Yusef grew up in Detroit and at that time Motown was happening, and there was a great tradition of jazz players that came out of Detroit, you know, an exceptional group of people. So I said, "I'd love your impressions of Detroit." Then, when we went to record I said, "I would like to use a more commercial rhythm section this time." It was one of the R&B rhythm sections that we had in Atlantic that can play with the jazz guys. But he wanted to use his own group. I said, "Well I don't know if your group can really get the point across to take me to the place I wanna go." So he said, "Okay, but use both rhythm sections." So both rhythm sections are playing on that record, and the result was one of the earliest of the true fusion records, without sounding like it was what became fusion. I mean it was a fusion of two real rhythmic concepts, behind a guy who really knew what he was doing. And the album is a terrific album, and very cohesive. It's called *Yusef Lateef's Detroit.*

There is an example of me saying to somebody, "I'd like you to do this. I won't insist on it, but maybe we should go down to Muscle Shoals, or Memphis, or something, and cut it with one of those sections. I'd love to see you do something with horns." He didn't want to record with them, but he came in and played the Hammond B3 and wrote for six or seven horns. It was the only one album he ever made where it was all his writing, and him on the organ for the first and only time. I gave him an idea, and he came back with what he wanted to do. So as long as the guy wants to do it, I'm down. You know, I never work with people I can force to do anything.

What about Yusef Lateef? You have some more thoughts about his approach to the flute?

Yusef has a Ph.D either in music education or in improvisational music, I forget which. He got it from U. Mass, I think. He was going to college the whole time we were working together. In fact we named one of the albums *The Doctor Is In and Out*, in honor of his getting his doctorate. And he did it the long, hard way. But he was a guy who really learned how to play the flute. He wasn't a jazz guy who picked it up--you know, I wanna double on flute, I gotta a couple of licks down. He really played the flute. So did Rahsaan. And Fathead was a guy who was a saxophone player but came up with his own style and sound on flute. You know the Texas guys are so definitive as tenor players. To me Fathead was the only one of the Texas guys who became as good a flute player, or certainly as accomplished a flute player as he did.

He made a couple of records with Herbie

Yeah. I put him with Herbie. It was my move. David has got that magnificent sound and that whole Texas thing, and he came out of Ray Charles. So I thought he had the great combination of a real solid player who also had tremendous crowd appeal. I was trying to force David on him. I was trying to make the label a little more--you know, "let's get together and do stuff together." I thought Fathead was a perfect fit for Herbie. At first Herbie was a little reluctant then he fell in love with him.

Reluctant to work with another flutist?

No, just that Herbie had picked his own players out all by himself, without anybody's help, for years--and done a brilliant job of it. So that's why the Chick Coreas and the Roy Ayers, and the Sonny Sharrocks, and all those people, came through his band. Even with the lesser known guys he always had great players. And he always had interesting players, like percussionist Armen Halburian, not the regular jazz guys. So I said, "Make a record with him." But not so much as a flute player--the two flute thing never was the reason. I just thought Fathead's alto playing would be a great add on to what Herbie had going. So when they did get together it really worked, they had the old Atlantic studio thing, you know.

Herbie told me he didn't mind doing those kinds of commercial recordings, he just thought he did too much of it. He said it got old for him.

It did, you know, because what happened was... well here's the way it went. When Herbie had a hit with *Coming Home Baby,* that album was one of the biggest Atlantic albums of the year, and then he followed it with something else that did pretty good. He ended up making hit records. He had a disco hit called *Hijack*, and then he had the Memphis record, and the Muscle Shoals record, and stuff in between that did well, so he was a solid jazz seller. He was up there with the best of people selling jazz albums. So every time he got an idea, he had the freedom to go in because he was generating so many sales and making so much money for the label that he could record as much as he wanted. So he did over-record. But in the process of over-recording he came up with some really successful stuff. And once you get a taste of hits you want more hits. That goes with the territory.

But he said he made one or two records along the way that he wasn't too proud of.

Everybody does. And you know, in the last five or so years Herbie became a different guy. He sometimes was difficult to get along with. But boy when he became a good guy he was one of the nicest guys I ever met in my life. We spoke about a week before he died. So, Herbie's good twin took over. And let me tell you something: more than anybody, Herbie was responsible for the popularity of the flute. No matter what guys say about who's a better flutist, who's not--all of that s--t--Herbie was the guy that busted it through, and *Coming Home Baby* was the record that did it.

And then he won the polls year in and year out, until Hubert suddenly took over in the seventies. So what do you think about Hubert's records over there at CTI and all that?

I have ones that I like better or more or less. I could say I like his Atlantic stuff, although I'm emotionally tied to it. More than the CTI stuff. The CTI stuff was very well done, it was just a kind of commercial jazz. Some of us who made jazz records were interested in making jazz records that became commercial, not always putting jazz players into commercial situations. Creed Taylor came up with a combination that worked for a good while. But after a while that becomes the same thing. The trick is, if you're an artist you've got to stay fresh. If you're a producer, you know, a producer's like an NFL running back--you get your three or four years when you're just out of college and you're tearing the league apart. Then you gotta, you know, come up with something new. Maybe after that you don't play every play. You're a third down guy. Maybe after that you become a coach. But you're still in football. Same thing with producing. I've had to reinvent myself fourteen times since I started!

Joel Dorn was still reinventing himself until the day he passed. He worked with Columbia Records, Rhino Records and GRP Records to reissue classic jazz recordings. And he formed his own labels, the most recent being Hyena Records, where he was working on a five-disc tribute to his mentor Nesuhi Ertugen, *Homage A Nesuhi*. Dorn's was a distinguished career, and talking with him brought home to me how important record producers have been to the creation and preservation of music. Why is there no category for Record Producer in the *Down Beat* polls? Probably not many critics and virtually no readers would know their names! I was glad to meet Joel Dorn, however, and to learn about the contribution he made to the flute in jazz.

The Flute in Rock

While this book centers on jazz, jazz and rock have been in a symbiotic relationship now for over half a century. There are those who would lay the demise of jazz at the feet of rock music, and it is certainly true that rock music has dominated popular consciousness since the emergence of Elvis and the Beatles, largely usurping jazz' position at the center of American culture. But, by the same token, a degree of jazz sensibility gained broader acceptance through its appearance in the jazz-rock genre: the electric Miles Davis, George Duke, Jeremy and the Satyres and Gil Evans' treatment of Jimi Hendrix come to mind, among other examples.

In the case of rock itself, there have been enough flutists in that genre to warrant a Ph.D. dissertation at a British university. It was the work of Rebecca Guy, who was gracious enough to supply this overview:

It is, perhaps, surprising to discover that the flute has had quite a significant role to play in some areas of rock music. The instrument's entry into the genre, aided--as it was in jazz--by the possibilities of electronic amplification, is closely related to the advent of psychedelic and progressive rock of the mid-to late-1960s, and the expansion of the rock and roll sound-world that these eclectic styles embodied.

In particular, the flute has become an important part of the progressive rock sonic toolkit, with several musical routes into the genre. It contributes to the art-music influenced textures of progressive band such as the Moody Blues (played by Ray Thomas), King Crimson (Ian McDonald, Mel Collins), Camel (Andy Latimer), Van der Graaf Generator (David Jackson), Genesis (Peter Gabriel) and Focus (Thijs van Leer). As a well established instrument in jazz, it can also contribute toward jazz derived elements in the music of these groups, (particularly King Crimson and Focus), and appears in various fusion bands including Caravan (Jimmy Hastings, Geoff Richardson) and Gon (Didier Malherbe). The instrument's ubiquity in folk musics around the world enables it to contribute to "folk" and "world" aspects of progressive and other rock styles, and it features in the psychedelic soundscapes of Traffic (Chris Wood), Jade Warrior (Jon Field), Quintessence (Raja Ram) and Ozric Tentacles (John Egan), to name but a few.

The flute provenance in such diverse musical repertoires has implications for the listener too, as the instrument becomes a powerful vehicle for other-musical associations within a rock context. This raises an interesting question: can the flute ever totally shake off such associations of art, jazz, folk or world music? Can there be such a thing as a true rock flute?

The player that has come closest to developing a distinct "rock flute" style must surely be Ian Anderson of Jethro Tull. Anderson has engaged with a number of pre-existing flute traditions during his career, including Celtic-derived references and (in later albums) various world flute repertories. However, he is probably most well-known for his extensive use of a forceful, distorted playing style , based upon extended flute techniques also prominent in jazz-flute playing and avant-garde repertoire, and seeming at times to emulate and compete with the electric guitar. In his hands the flute's potential as a rock instrument has been firmly established; Jethro Tull has become a benchmark with which all flute using rock--both of the original progressive rock era and since--is almost inevitably compared.

There are other flutists in the rock world--Matt Eakle comes to mind for his work with David Grisman. But Dr. Guy is certainly accurate in identifying Ian Anderson as the prime figure in the world of rock music who is associated with the flute. He was kind enough to grant me an interview and I am happy to include him.

Ian Anderson: First Flutist of Rock

"Ian Anderson of Jethro Tull loved Rahsaan. He recorded one of the songs that Rahsaan actually made some money off of. Ian Anderson is a wonderful guy, well-spoken, intelligent, and I think he really loved Rahsaan."

John Kruth

There is probably no better example of a jazz-based instrumental technique leaking into popular music than the sounds initially associated with Rahsaan Roland Kirk's flute passing into rock through the work of **Ian Anderson** and his band **Jethro Tull**. Whimsically named after the eighteenth-century British agriculturalist, Jethro Tull has been a force in British rock music since 1967, having sold more than 60 million albums worldwide.

When I had the opportunity to interview Mr. Anderson it was clear that he had no hesitation in recognizing this important influence. He is a charming and very personable gentleman, whose stage persona tends to mask a considerable musical intelligence. I was struck, at the outset, by a connection we both had with Indian music. When I mentioned that I had studied with north Indian *maestro* Hariprasad Chaurasia he revealed that he had been in India playing with *Hariji* a few weeks earlier:

How was that? Was it fun?

Yes, it was interesting. He's very much in the sort of jazz approach to things, although of course there's no harmonic structure really in Indian music, it's all melody against open fifth drones, so it's kind of a different prospect.

He's a class act though, isn't he? He's a fabulous musician and one of the nicest men you will ever meet.

Yes. He's venerable, and a world talent. I guess he's state of the art. It's interesting playing alongside him, with both the Indian bamboo flute and most of the time I was playing the concert flute. It's kind of interesting because of the similarities and yet the differences that exist too. What we found obviously quite--I wouldn't say a drawback, but it does tend to immediately stand in the way of more joyful flights of fancy--is the limited harmonic vocabulary of such music. Everything in Indian music is usually in C sharp and F sharp and so Hariprasad tends to play most things in E major and related keys, but with the odd sort of minor scale as well. He plays a flute which is specially made for him which is a semitone lower than most folks have played in the past.

Well, the lower the flute the more seriously it's regarded in India.

Well it's harder to play, yeah. Especially for guys like me with skinny little fingers.

Yes, I have the same problem. How did this come about? Did you contact him?

No, his son contacted me about three or four years ago, and it's been an on and off project for a long time. It finally came together with three concerts just a few weeks ago. It's been a long time in the making; his schedule and my schedule were always at odds with each other. But this was a fitting thing to do in the context of our playing in India. We hadn't been to India in ten years, and Indian authorities don't like Western rock music, so the only way we could get in was to play with someone who gave it cultural credentials.

They do have a jazz festival every year in Bombay now.

Ah, but that's different. Jazz is considered culture. In fact it's a known reality that in a lot of countries around the world jazz is allowed to be played, whereas most rock or pop acts are not allowed in--simply not accepted in a lot of different venues. Jethro Tull actually gets away with playing at surprising places because I suppose in some people's minds we are not straight-ahead rock music, and we do just about manage to fly in the face of the rigid bans on certain music. So we do slip into a few prestigious concert halls and historical amphitheaters in different parts of the world that are not open to rock music as a whole. We seem to get away with it. But generally speaking, jazz has that cultural acceptability and thereby it's perceived with the same artistic values as classical music or ballet, which indeed is right and proper.

So jazz is culture, huh. That must be why no one can make a living at it! But funnily enough, at the British Library they've just sacked the jazz curator and subsumed jazz under popular music. I guess that's just a budget thing, but I said to them, "It's a shame jazz isn't popular if you're going to call it that!"

Well, it is. It's also worrying that jazz has now become fodder for the record companies in the guise of so called smooth jazz or contemporary pop jazz, or whatever titles are pasted to it. But you know the Nora Jones phenomenon is something that is a bit of a mixed blessing, I would have thought. It does allow certain jazz musicians to actually get a bit [of work--as] a backing group. But it's not quite what I and possibly more traditional fans and musicians would really call jazz, at least not what I've heard, for example. And Jamie Cullen, the new kid on the block, who plays youthful jazzy standards, is the hot act in the UK right now. What I've heard of him is okay. It's bringing some traditions of jazz to a different audience, but I'm not quite sure if it will stick.

One thing there is that everything is layered in the studio; they don't interact in real time with each other, and that's kind of a key thing for improvising musicians. There are several flutists who work in that genre and I'm not sure if I want to include them.

I actually don't know too many. I've never really been a big fan of jazz in any depth. Blues, yes, but once it gets a bit more harmonically diversified then it loses me. I don't have that experience of endless practicing of scales, and just as in Indian music or rock music, there are certain conventions, certain familiar patterns of harmonic movement in terms of the musical structures. I guess to a jazz player it's, "Ah yes well we know this one, it's this followed by that followed by that." And they kind of know where to go. That's something I guess they learn and they're able to do, but for me it's a mystery. I've never fathomed those relationships and arrangements and never played any jazz standards, so I'm not really in that world. My improvising comes more from blues and folk and classical influences rather than jazz ones.

Yes, well I've picked up on that. Actually I was quite surprised when I started listening to you again, because the last time I heard you was before I left England, in 1972, and I think the band has changed a good deal since then.

There are different members of the group, sure, but most of them with a fair history of musical work behind them and, so yes, all of us are probably familiar with different kinds of music right across the board.

*Yes, there's more of that in the band now than I remembered, but then that's a long time ago, so that may be a false impression. But I was struck with the material that you sent me and was very happy that we could put you in the book. I enjoyed the **DVD** and the **Divinities** record.*

Yes. This was music written for amplified flute and orchestra. Some of that stuff I have actually played with symphony orchestras in Europe, with this approach to improvisation. Basically, when working in the studio, the interesting thing is that for a lot of it you're just kind of winging it, but then you find something that you really like, after hearing it. Because I'm working in the process right through to the production mastering, and very often because what I put down is very early on in the recording process, particularly if I'm doing solo albums. I tend to get my flute down very early, you know, vocals and flute and guitars or whatever I'm playing, they go on right at the beginning. So I'm kind of running with flute solos that have been improvised with countless repeat listenings during the recording process--the mixing and then the production masterings. So by the time it actually gets to a finished record these things have stopped being in my head, they're no longer improvisation, they're just quick writing, very quick written music in the sense they've now become formalized--a series of tunes in their own right. So very often, when I play those things on stage, I try and stick--not rigidly but substantially--to the form of the improvised solo that I like so much on the record. Because it's not just one take, usually it's a mixture.

Sometimes there are bits from one take and then you play another bit and you compile something you drop in, and fix something, or change the flow of it half way through. So quite often it's something that's been quite carefully arrived at in the same way as a painter working on a canvas. You know, we'll have an overall idea of where things are going, but you can always--well, not in the world of watercolor, but in the world of oil painting-- you can go back over and paint over something that you don't like. So you can in the recording process as well. It wasn't so easy for Charlie Parker back then because we didn't have such sophisticated copy, cut, and paste mechanisms as we enjoy in the digital age. Nonetheless, you could still compile a tape from a number of out-takes or a number of different takes, just as they do in the world of classical music. There are a lot of razor blades slashing a lot of bits of tapes in classical recordings.

But you have had an influence in jazz, I think, and for the flute generally. I heard from a friend of mine--she's a flutist in New York--who tells me that whenever you have a new recording out, she gets swamped with calls for lessons. Suddenly kids want to learn to play the flute. Are you aware of that?

Well, I'm aware to some extent, because when I'm out and about I see a lot of young children, sort of the eight, ten, twelve-year-olds particularly, and sometimes going on into high school years--pre-teens. I think parents will produce their small children, usually girls, who are taking flute at school and those parents profess the child to have a great liking for Jethro Tull music or my music. Sometimes I believe them and sometimes I think they're just trying to worm their way into my heart, to get a meet and greet after a show. But usually it's perfectly nice, and certainly a lot of kids do it probably because their parents are saying, "Hey, listen to this and check that out." I think even amongst the music teachers these days there is an acceptance, however begrudging, that the flute does not just languish in the sixth row of the symphony orchestra--it's something that happens in a number of musical formats.

I suppose with rock music there's not too many people to choose from when it comes to internationally known flute players. There are a few other people who've brought the flute into the context of rock music, but I don't think perhaps with the same persistence maybe as me, or with the same global recognition, because I suppose there are some people who might be well known in Japan, but nowhere else.

Well apparently there are a few out there. There is a young lady in England doing a Ph.D. dissertation about the flute in rock.

Well, that would be pretty short! Because although there are lots of folks... you know there are a few notable pieces where the flute made a strong selling in a few bits of music. It tends to become a one-off thing. You know, there was (singing) *Men at Work*, an Australian group, and there is a flute solo in the middle of that which is very memorable. There's a dodgy flute solo in the middle of--I should say dodgy because the poor chap's just left--in the Moody Blues, *Knights in White Satin*, a memorable flute line. And these were things where flute has made a showing in a very memorable way. But they tend to be one-offs--they tend to be one hit wonders.

I'm aware of that because, when I was doing studio work in London, I did a lot of that--putting some flute, or sax, lines into rock albums for groups who didn't have a reed player.

Right. The flute appears in those different pieces of music, but I suppose it's only maintained a presence as a lead instrument in one band over three and half decades in the case of me. So I do feel like I'm not the only act in town. But, you know, it's kind of difficult to find anybody else. That's why I took the thing up in the first place. I was a guitar player and became aware of Eric Clapton when I was about seventeen or eighteen years old. At that point, after listening to Eric in his early days with John Mayall's Blues Breakers, I decided even turning the record to half speed wasn't going to help me learn those solos, so I cast around for something else to play, and it was very much with the idea of not having to compete directly with Eric Clapton, Jimi Hendrix, Jeff Beck, and all those other guys. I was looking for something where I could kind of be out there more or less on my own.

At this point, I asked Anderson about how he acquired his first flute. In keeping with the tradition established by several jazz players of picking up the flute by accident, Anderson recounts a similar story of acquiring a flute almost as an afterthought in an elaborate music store trade involving guitars and microphones. As he recalls on the Jethro Tull website:

> Around this time, I coveted the Shure microphones used by some of the professional bands around the Blackpool area. Trading in the Fender, I acquired the services of a Shure Unidyne Three and, to pad out the part exchange, a shiny Selmer Gold Seal flute, in neat carry case with no playing instructions; not even in Japanese.

This story about you getting the flute initially in this trade with the guitar and the microphone, is that apocryphal?

No, that's absolutely true. And so were the finances involved because it [the Fender] was a guitar which belonged to Lemmie--Ian "Lemmie" Willis of Reverend Black and the Rocking Vicars, of course known to the world later as Lemmie of Motorhead, in the days when he was a rhythm guitarist before he was a bass player. I either bought it from Lemmie or bought it from the shop where Lemmie would have had to have sold it to raise some money to pay for food. Things were that bad for musicians in Blackpool. Anyway, I part-exchanged it for a flute and a Shaw Unidine 3 microphone.The total value was somewhere around sixty pounds, I would think. And of course it was a guitar that today would probably be worth between fifteen and twenty thousand dollars. But there you go!

Once you got hold of the flute, maybe it was an accident to start with, but then you were telling me that you focused on it to go in a different direction. How long was it before you started to seriously realize what you could do with it?

Well when I first started to play I was trying to play guitar lines. I did tin whistle, and I also had a go on a saxophone, and of course, from my guitar playing two to three years prior to that, I was aware of a lot of people in the world of blues, and to some extent in jazz. You know I used to do this kind of scat singing thing with the guitar. I used to sing while I was playing, and I'd sort of done that a little bit with the saxophone as well--you could kind of sing into that while you're playing the note, and you could even do it to a limited extent with a tin whistle. So we could have a noise that was quite foul, quite animal, but I rather liked that. So when I started to play the flute it was just very simple things, witty things, you know, just kind of bluesy roots of the first two or three months of Jethro Tull's existence, sort of pre-Jethro Tull, just in the two or three months before we became known as Jethro Tull, which was February 1968. And somewhere along the way, a friend of mine who was at art school, who came to see us playing at the Marquee Club, or some blues club somewhere, turned me on to the guy who plays the flute and does that thing. And so I listened to it, and it was of course Roland Kirk with an album, I think, *I talked to the Spirits,* or something like that--it was Roland Kirk's flutey album. From that I learnt the song *Serenade to a Cuckoo,* after I'd actually given the album back. It was such a simple little memorable tune, I kind of just remembered the little ditty you know, the elements of the melody. So we didn't attempt to imitate it too carefully in terms of working out a chordal backdrop for it--it was just the tune. We kind of went with it and did our own thing with it. But that was actually probably the first flute piece that I played, other than that I'd only played in a supporting role, playing little riffy things and tootling the beginnings of some solos. That was the first actual flute instrumental set piece, you know, party piece.

I heard you in those days in the Marquee Club, so I know exactly what you're talking about, and then I had a copy of **Stand Up** *and by that time The* **Bourée** *was on there, right?*

That's right. And also there were other things that were coming into the music that. Back in the days before we called these things 'world music' I was listening to music from different places--I was also fascinated by the music from other countries and other cultures with other instruments. There were mandolins and balalaikas and the claghorn, an invented instrument with a saxophone mouthpiece and a toy trumpet sort of thing. Or was it a bamboo flute? I can't remember. It was something fastened together with parcel tape, and was a compilation of three different instruments I think! Completely out of tune of course, but it was just there to make a raucous noise! Anyway, that sort of eclecticism was where I was headed in the summer of 1968. But our guitar player Mick Abrahams was a dyed-in-the-wool blues kind of guy--he didn't connect with these other thoughts that I was having, so we ran against a bit of a brick wall with the stuff I was writing--he just couldn't fathom it, couldn't pick it up. If it wasn't twelve bar blues he just didn't get it, you know, and that was the problem. And so by the end of the year we'd parted company.

Yeah, most of the stuff that the people were playing at the Marquee was pretty blues based.

Yes, it was referred to as the "blues boom," and our contemporaries at the Marquee Club were the early Fleetwood Mac, and the Aynsley Dunbar Retaliation, The Boy Brown Chicken Shack, Gallagher … you know, a bunch of folks who were part of that--what middle class white kids did when they discovered blues.

Alexis Korner of course, in there?

Well, Alexis was kind of an avuncular sort of godfather in the background, he was a strange but potent influence on the early development of blues in the UK. I think his great role was as a catalyst to get people half of his age involved in the music.

I was very interested in what you said in this article about how you absorbed those kinds of influences because you said there that it's really boring if it just becomes an academic thing. But if it goes in, it becomes part of your subconscious and then gets under your hand, so to speak. Do you remember talking about that?

Oh, I've always thought that improvisation, whether it was at the hands of Bach or Ornette Coleman--to take something fairly polarized as another example--is just about composition and going a bit faster than other people. I think that's the great thing about doing the improvisation stuff--it is composing, but a couple of hundred milliseconds … probably, I would guess, something like the time it takes for the brain to say, "I think I wanna go here next," and the fingers actually connecting. With the mechanism of your instrument, you know, it probably takes maybe three hundred milliseconds to go to the next note, and so you're constantly making that adjustment in the same way that a racing driver is sliding a car around a grand prix circuit, just almost instinctively moving his hands on the steering wheel so instinctively and quickly that it is about reaction times in that order.

A tennis player on center court at Wimbledon is kind of reading what the other player is doing, and in a sense improvisation is a similar thing, which is why I think you'll find tennis players who want to be rock guitar players, and you know a few racing drivers who also want to be rock drummers or guitar players. There's a fascination really, mutually between these sports, because I think, subconsciously, we do recognize our spiritual brothers behind the wheels of racing cars, and you know, in that gladiatorial arena of Wimbledon, and they too recognize us as somehow peer group equals of some fascination and envy. Just as John MacEnroe wants to whack an electric guitar and Eddie Jordan wants to play blues rock on his drum kit, there are, I suppose, a few rock players who fancy themselves on the tennis court or behind the wheel of a racing car too! Obviously not in any of these cases with very much success, but I do think that there's a fascination ... there aren't so many people who get hooked on translating their improvisational musical skills into playing golf, or fishing, that doesn't seem to work that way. But I'm convinced that it has to do with the speed, the lightening reaction thing. It's the exhilaration that comes with the brilliant improvisation which is what sports like tennis and race driving are really about--that's why I think the analogy does hold good there.

So, as you say, it's much better to soak up the ambience of different kinds of music, the feeling of it, and if it comes through in your music, fine. If it doesn't, something else will.

Well, for me, because I'm lucky enough to travel around, I am constantly being given CDs by well-meaning people, and sent records by people who either want to be a support act for Jethro Tull or open for one of my shows, or want me to play on their record, or maybe just listen to it and write them a couple of lines of support. So I'm listening to a lot of people from a lot of different countries, not necessarily as a matter of choice but a matter of obligation, because people send me records and I always feel obliged, however crap they turn out to be, that somewhere else on the planet some aspiring musician has sent me their record, and I feel that kinship with musicians generally, that I owe them to at least listen. Nine out of ten are absolutely, perfectly horrible, but you know, once in a while, I hear something that excites me, and some of these folks really do get to be the opening act for Jethro Tull, or I really do play on their record. Once in a while it works out and it's a lot of fun when you find somebody who's got something musical to offer that you can just kind of share in the experience a little, and have the opportunity to maybe broaden your own--for me to broaden my own musical abilities and standards and appreciation a little bit through working with other people. I still maintain that I'm not a jazz flautist or any kind of jazz musician, but last year I played a few times with Al de Meola and [saxophonist] Bill Evans, and I've been on the same records as the Brecker Brothers and Anthony Jackson--the folks who seriously have jazz credentials.

Are there any jazz flute players that have struck you over the years?

I don't really know any. I came across ... the name Philip Bent comes to mind, a black flute player who I thought it was quite interesting because he had a fairly broad kind of approach. He wasn't just a jazz player, clearly he had some classical abilities as well.

Herbie Mann?

Yeah. Herbie Mann, Ian Anderson and James Galway, were the object of fantasy for some American promoter who, in the wake of the three tenors, decided that this would be like a really money-spinning concert to do the three flute players. I actually spoke to Herbie Mann and to James Galway about it. I was a bit ambivalent--I just thought it was somewhat cashing in on something else. I wasn't really feeling too good about it, but when you're in a position like that, and someone's trying to bring this together, you don't want to be the party pooper because you may offend the other guys.

So I thought the best thing is to call these fellows and say, "What do you think about this?" James Galway felt pretty much as I did, that it was all a bit suspect, and we found it difficult to see what we could play together on stage. Whilst we could do our separate things it would be quite difficult to find some common ground where things would work together. Herbie Mann, on the other hand, was completely for the idea--thought it was a great thing. Rather happily it sort of fizzled anyway, so it never came to the point where anyone was going to get to ruffle others' feathers by saying, "No, I don't wanna do this," or "Yes I do but I want more money than the other two guys!" It didn't come to anything which is probably just as well.

Subsequently I got a call from Herbie Mann once when I was playing in Albuquerque few years ago and, he was going to come to the show, and I was looking forward to seeing him. Then suddenly around sound-check time I got a call from his wife saying that Herbie won't be coming tonight, he's just come back from the hospital and he's got prostate cancer.

Yes, he passed away last June.

I liked the guy when I spoke to him on the phone, he just sounded such an open and genuine fellow, so keen to do things, and it's always an infectious thing when someone sounds energized and enthusiastic about a project. I was really looking forward to meeting him and sadly I didn't, and now I won't.

It is indeed sad that Ian Anderson never met Herbie Mann; they probably would have liked each other. They actually had a lot in common, with similar musical approaches within their respective genres. Both have taken--and, of course, Anderson continues to take--diverse elements and crafted them into an original form of expression. With Herbie there was a succession of such influences--Afro/Cuban, Brazilian, Middle Eastern, Soul, Reggae, Eastern European. For Anderson the process has built more slowly and steadily, and the sources have been blues, rock, Rahsaan, Celtic music, and a host of other subliminal inputs gained during years of traveling and listening. The result is something that, to me, is far more interesting than a lot of rock music--it has certainly proved a lot more enduring. For both

Anderson and Mann the common denominator is, of course, the flute and the deep attraction that it seems to engender. But if the flute has done a lot for them, both have done a lot for the flute.

Part Five

Flute Specialists in Jazz

Hubert Laws: Setting The Bar

"Exquisite execution, instant composition, beautiful sound and soul make him the Pied Piper the world would follow anywhere."

Victor Feldman

In 1965 **Hubert Laws'** first album, *The Laws of Jazz*, appeared and the history of the flute in jazz entered a new phase. A decade had passed since Count Basie began featuring Frank Wess' flute, and almost as long since Bud Shank's early *Flute And Oboe* recordings, Buddy Collette's work with the original Chico Hamilton Quintet, and Sam Most's duet flute recordings with Herbie Mann. All of these artists helped to put the flute on the jazz map, but Laws went a step further. While players like Wess, Most, Collette and Shank encouraged saxophonists to pick up the flute, Laws was the prototype jazz musician who came to concentrate exclusively on the instrument, setting the stage for a whole generation of dedicated, exclusive, jazz flutists--several of them his students. True, Laws can still be heard playing tenor saxophone on a Quincy Jones session as late as 1978, but while even Herbie Mann, who was totally identified with the flute, continued to turn to the saxophone from time to time throughout his career, Hubert reached a point where he abandoned all reed instruments to concentrate on the flute and the piccolo, bringing a level of technical accomplishment to instruments rarely if ever seen in jazz previously. Thirty-eight years after issuing that first recording, in August 2003, Hubert Laws was presented with a Lifetime Achievement Award at the annual convention of The National Flute Association in Las Vegas, Nevada.

This kind of recognition could be seen as unusual for a jazz artist if Laws regarded himself as one. But he does not, at least not exclusively. Indeed, he has tried to avoid categorization. As a typical example, he appeared not too long ago with pianist Billy Childs at a jazz festival in San Mateo, then, a few days later, he was the soloist with the California Philharmonic in Pasadena. In short, Laws' career has been about excellence in both jazz and classical performance. This is not completely unusual; there are several artists who excel in both of these areas–trumpeter Wynton Marsalis, his brother, saxophonist Branford Marsalis, and pianists Keith Jarrett and Fred Hersch come to mind, among others. But along with his accomplishments in this area, Hubert Laws has also acted as flag-bearer for a whole generation of jazz flutists. If Frank Wess was the first *Down Beat* poll winner from 1959 to 1964, followed by Herbie Mann for several years, it was Laws who took over the number one spot during most of the seventies, prompting the headline "Laws Dumps Mann" from the 1971 Readers Poll issue of the magazine. For a substantial period of time, therefore, Hubert Laws was *the* voice of the flute in jazz. Today, having returned to performing after a lengthy absence, he has achieved the status of an icon for jazz flutists.

Like virtually all our pioneers, Laws seemed destined at an early age for a career in music, although not necessarily as a flutist. His musical education began early and was broad from the outset. He was born into a musical family: his grandfather played the harmonica and worked as a one-man band, his mother was a gospel pianist, and several of his siblings, most notably his brother, saxophonist Ronnie Laws, have enjoyed professional careers in music. Hubert himself learned piano at an early age, and was soon playing gospel music in church, and rhythm and blues at neighborhood dances, including visits across the street to "Miss Mary's Place," described as an "honest-to-godness honky-tonk," which is still functioning in Houston's Studewood section.

Hubert quickly moved on to mellophone and then to alto sax. As he told me, "I started on piano, from piano to mellophone, and from mellophone to saxophone, clarinet, and the flute was really the next to the last instrument I tried to play, guitar being the last one." It was during his last semester at Phillis Wheatley High School in Houston that he was exposed both to jazz and to the flute. The latter entered the picture when he volunteered to fill in at short notice as flute soloist with the school orchestra, leading to his quickly mastering the fundamentals of the instrument with the help of the orchestra teacher. At about the same time, Hubert was exposed to jazz by his band director Sammy Harris. He was attracted to the freedom of jazz, and found that he had a talent for improvisation. Soon he was playing regularly with a Houston group known as the Swingsters. This became the Modern Jazz Sextet, then the Night Hawks, the Jazz Crusaders, and, eventually, the Crusaders.

After high school, as Hubert moved on to college, he added another dimension to his musical development, enrolling in the Music Department at Texas Southern University. Here he began to master the classical literature, although not immediately as a flutist. As he recalls:

When I entered Texas Southern University, I was forced to major on the clarinet because there was no flute instructor. So I actually went out on my own to find a flute instructor. It just so happened that one night I was going to a concert by the Houston Symphony Orchestra when I ran into the two flute players, David Kolvig and Clement Barone. I approached them, and just asked them outright if they would give me flute lessons. David Kolvig turned to Clement Barone and said, "Hey, you take him." That was the beginning of a wonderful relationship that exists to this day; he was responsible for a lot of what I've learned about the technique and the operational qualities of the flute. [Note: Clement Barone passed away since this interview took place.]

You started by studying classical technique on the flute. Was it your intention to apply this to jazz, or were you not thinking about that at the time?

Well, I don't think I had that specific purpose. It was just like chance. It was just like serendipity, you know, because what I ended up doing was just trying... I love classical music as well, and the only persons who could teach me flute were the ones who were playing classical music. I just applied that to what I knew from what I was already playing, in jazz.

But you were still playing the saxophone at that time, were you not?

Yeah, as a matter of fact I played with Mongo Santamaria, and recorded with him. I also recorded and played with *The Crusaders*. In fact I was one of the original members. And of course we still continue our relationship. As a matter of fact I just played with Joe Sample in Houston, Texas, about two months ago, at the new music center down there, and I speak to Stix Hooper who is the original drummer, and founder of the group. So we still have a good relationship. I played the saxophone--alto saxophone--with them along with the flute, and Wilton Felder was the other wind player there. At the same time I picked up the flute, he picked up the bassoon, and we had a very special kind of sound when we played those two instruments with that group.

It was with the Crusaders that Hubert left Houston after two years at Texas Southern. They headed for Los Angeles, but this proved to be a temporary move. In 1960, the year Frank Wess won the first Down Beat Critics Poll for the flute, its future winner, Hubert Laws, won a scholarship to the Juilliard

School of Music in New York. He set off in a 1950 Plymouth Sedan with $600 in his pocket. The scholarship covered his tuition, but not his living expenses. As he recalls, "It was the fall of 1960. I was down to my last fifty bucks and wondering what to do when the phone rang and it was a call offering me my first job at Sugar Ray's Lounge in Harlem. Times were tough then, but, I haven't looked back since."

Hubert has not looked back because he has been in constant demand. The market may be limited for a jazz flutist but Hubert was already much more than that, being fluent in several genres, from bebop and R&B, to Latin and classical music. Thus he was able to find employment in such varied contexts as Mongo Santamaria's group, the Lloyd Price Big Band, John Lewis' Orchestra USA, and the Berkshire Festival Orchestra at Tanglewood, the summer home of the Boston Symphony Orchestra. Meanwhile, at Juilliard, his flute studies were going on at the highest level.

Did you not study with Julius Baker also at one point?

Well, I did after I entered the Juilliard School in 1960--he was my instructor. And we also have an ongoing relationship. He's been around for quite a while. He's had positive influences on so many people. [Since this interview was conducted, Julius Baker passed away, aged 87.]

I just noticed he's on some Coleman Hawkins recordings.

I wasn't aware of that. He used to joke and kid with me when I was taking lessons that he could play jazz, but never was really able to improvise--he simply read things. He did play in that environment, but he never really improvised.

And so by the time you graduated from Juilliard, you were equipped to go in a number of different musical directions. What kind of work did you gravitate towards?

Well, when I left Juilliard I had already become a member of Mongo Santamaria's Ensemble, and I played with them for about three years, in New York. I spent most of my life in New York. I actually started playing with the New York Philharmonic with Bernstein and Pierre Boulez, who conducted there, and I was also at the Metropolitan Opera Orchestra for about four years, with James Levine and Herbert Von Karajan--a whole bunch of conductors who went through there.

Did that totally absorb your time or were you able to play some jazz also?

Oh, I was doing it all. I was playing during the day, I was recording here and there and doing TV commercials, and then at night with rehearsals--at times I was playing with the Philharmonic or the Metropolitan Opera Orchestra.

Laws' involvement with Western European Art Music has been extensive, reflecting his Juilliard training and his work with Clement Barone and Julius Baker. Apart from his time with the New York Philharmonic and Metropolitan Opera Orchestras, he has appeared as a soloist with the New York Philharmonic under Zubin Mehta, with the orchestras of Los Angeles, Dallas, Chicago, Detroit, Cleveland, Amsterdam and Japan, and with the Stanford String Quartet. He has given annual performances at Carnegie Hall, and has performed sold out performances in the Hollywood Bowl with fellow flutist Jean-Pierre Rampal. Yet this was not accomplished at the expense of his work in jazz and popular idioms. He has appeared at the Montreux, Playboy, and Kool Jazz festivals, and with the Modern Jazz Quartet at the Hollywood Bowl. He has recorded with Miles Davis, Herbie Hancock, Chick Corea, Ella Fitzgerald, Sarah Vaughn, Freddie Hubbard, Quincy Jones, Paul McCartney, Paul Simon, Aretha Franklin, Lena Horne, James Moody, Sergio Mendes, Bob James, Carly Simon, George Benson, Clark Terry, Ron Carter, Victor Feldman, McCoy Tyner and J. J. Johnson. His work on movie scores includes *The Wiz, The Color Purple, A Hero Ain't Nothing but a Sandwich,* and *Spot Marks the X,* collaborations with Claude Bolling for Neil Simon's comedy *California Suite,* and with Earl Klugh and Pat Williams on the music for *How to Beat the High Cost of Living.* His first recording under his own name was firmly in the jazz vein, and involved the finest jazz players:

And then you began making some of your own recordings, starting with The Laws of Jazz.
Yeah, that was the first one, on Atlantic. I was recording before I played with The Met and the Philharmonic. That was back in 1965 or '64 somewhere. It was while I was traveling here and there and playing Latin music.
Wasn't Chick Corea on the original recording?
Chick was on the original, yeah. Actually he was on several of the original recordings.
At what point did you abandon the saxophone and just focus on the flute?
It was not consciously done, it just sort of tapered off by itself through circumstances. The last time I played it was with Quincy. I was doing this movie, *The Color Purple,* and when I got a call from the service that contracts musicians. I'd been playing first flute on all the dates for all the two or three weeks they'd been recording, and then on the last day the contractor says, "Bring a tenor saxophone." I said, "What? I haven't played tenor saxophone in five or six years!" And he said, "No, longer than that!" But Quincy remembered it because I played it on his record *Walking in Space* on one track, and he remembered. He's got a memory like an elephant. He can remember everything. So sure enough I brought it and I ended up playing in the saxophone section with Benny Golson and Jerome Richardson, and some other saxophone players that were playing in that section for that movie.

Nevertheless, it is as a flutist that Hubert built his reputation. He was selected the No. 1 flutist in *Down Beat* readers poll ten years in a row, and was the critic's choice for seven consecutive years. And his own recordings feature his flute playing exclusively, except for his work on piccolo, an interest inherited from Clement Barone. However, if he has ended his involvement with other instruments, he has not settled exclusively on one genre. As he emphasized to me, "I never did say I was a jazz flutist, I never embraced the term. That's what people say but I play Latin, I play gospel, I play classical, I play so-called jazz as well. It's the industry or the business world that chooses to pigeonhole us." I mentioned that I didn't particularly care about having the word jazz in the title of this book, but after years in the music business, Hubert was very aware of the practical importance of pigeonholes. "You have to use a language people understand," he told me, "I understand that. I mean, it's a marketing tool. That's what it's all about." On the other hand, he agreed with me on the need to avoid pigeonholes when training musicians. And he has had several students himself, two of whom, Dave Valentin and Kent Jordan, have become top quality performers.

What's your advice to any flute players starting out who maybe haven't gotten into jazz yet? Would you agree with me that the way that musicians are educated is one-sided?
Oh, absolutely! There was no curriculum for anybody who wanted to improvise, at least not until recently. As a matter of fact, at the Juilliard School there was no outlet for jazz. I have talked to Wynton Marsalis and we had similar experiences when we were at Juilliard. I mean the only outlet that I had was when Chick Corea would form these jam sessions in the practice room. We'd get together and we would start playing. But I just heard a rumor that they have had a jazz program over at Juilliard now for the last

couple of years, and Mr. Polizzi, who's the President, has invited me to become part of the faculty there. I don't know that I'd be able to do it, but he certainly has made those innuendos. They are also building a jazz hall, specifically for jazz, over at that school.

That's great! But doesn't it work both ways? People that are in jazz programs don't get exposed enough to the other side of the coin. Isn't that the case in your experience?

Well, absolutely. They had access because that's all that was available. I mean when I wanted to study, I never did want to study jazz, because I was always playing it. I didn't make a conscientious effort to get involved in a discipline of jazz; I was simply always doing it. It's like somebody learning how to breathe when they've been breathing all their lives! But, when I thought of education, the only thing available for me for education in terms of music was classical repertoire.

So you would encourage people to get a fundamental education, to understand the classics, but also to learn what jazz is about, to learn how to improvise. At the university level, I've always been saying, let's just train the students to be all-round musicians, to read, to improvise, rather than making these distinct programs--jazz on the one side, classical on the other side.

I agree with you. I've always said that. I've always said that I'd like to clear away all those boundaries.

Do you think that's too much for the educators to cram into a four-year program?

Absolutely not!

Well, you are certainly an example of how this can work. You have really had to break boundaries the way you've developed the flute in jazz. As I have mentioned to several of the flutists I have spoken with, there are still people--one writer in particular--who say the flute is a marginal instrument in jazz. I'm sure you don't agree with that?

Well, I don't know what he means by marginal. But I know that traditionally, people in general are creatures of habit. So once they know the instruments we introduced forty or fifty years ago as traditional jazz instruments, like the piano, guitar, drums, you know, they appear not to accept anything that's fresh or new in the same manner. That's why some people don't graduate to the use of computers in business--they stay with the paper and pen. That doesn't mean it invalidates the computer, it simply means that the people haven't moved on. They haven't progressed to the point of accepting new technology. And in the musical sense there are some writers, and other people, who cleave and cling to their own forms, their own traditions, their own thoughts. The flute just happens to be another voice, another voice to use in order to express oneself in the form of music that's called jazz.

If you go back to the fifties you can find a statement by Jerome Richardson that he didn't think that people had really quite figured out how to make the flute work in jazz. That was something he was working on. You did a great deal to actually solve that problem in terms of technique and articulation, and exactly how to make the instrument work.

Yeah. Well that may be so. Perhaps it is because I learned to play the instrument and operate in a similar manner to classically trained flutists. For that reason it might have made persons accept it more because it did sound more like the flute, in the classical idiom. So it's for only bad reasons, perhaps. You know, I had a conversation with Herbie Mann recently--he called me actually. He was very sick with prostate cancer. He told me, "Hubert, you know, I want to tell you that I feel that you are the epitome of what a flute player should be." I said, "Man! That is a great tribute coming from you who's popularized the instrument." I mean, I feel he did that more than anybody, throughout his career. Anyway it was a very sentimental and emotional exchange between us because I knew what his condition was. But anyway, as I told him, it was quite a tribute for him to say that to me. [Note: Herbie Mann passed away on July 1st, 2003.]

Indeed. I think Herbie would have loved to have had the training you did. Do you think that in general the classical training made the difference? It contributes so much to the sound of the instrument the way you project it.

I think so. Here again, a person has probably heard the flute in the classical idiom, through the airways and through the symphony orchestra, so if that same kind of sound is projected within the jazz idiom, it perhaps would make it much more acceptable. I think first of all the musicians were more accepting and as a result it might have spawned an overall interest. I think that's what has happened because I get more comments and more praise and accolades from musicians than from anybody else. Or even educated people, I'm talking about doctors and lawyers. You know, those people used to gravitate more towards the esoteric forms of music, but this is something that's on a more popular level, you know.

I think a lot of early jazz flutists were great jazz players, but not necessarily great flutists.

Yes, that's true, but only because many of them were doublers, you know, so I guess they didn't concentrate on the sound and the classical approach to the instrument itself. So they came off with a sound that was not compact, or even fully usable, I mean, with the voice, the full extensions and the use of the flutistic parts of the instrument. They may have approached it basically like the saxophone so that the things that they did were probably not even flutistic. You know, like spreading of octaves, and jumping octaves, and being able to [play flurries of] your notes with them. All those things become flutistic--when you see the composers and the orchestra you can realize that quality and that characteristic in the flute. So they utilized that, but I studied the classical repertoire in the orchestra and all, and I began to use those techniques within the jazz idiom. So that might have contributed to something a little bit different that had not happened before.

Laws has continued to perform and record in both the classical and jazz idioms. On the classical side, he is particularly proud of an album he made as a tribute to Jean-Pierre Rampal, with whom he performed several live concerts during the 1980s. It featured all French composers: Fauré, Debussy, Gaubert, Ravel. When I asked him what he is currently working on, he mentioned that he has recently signed a joint contract with the Savoy and Denon labels, Savoy to handle his jazz releases, and Denon to issue his classical recordings:

I'm putting together some material... It is yet to be determined which ones we'll use. This is for the new CD. I've just completed recording all of the six Bach sonatas, and that's going to be presented to Denon for release, and the other material's going to be the jazz--those are yet to be determined.

Will you do the Bach with piano or with harpsichord?
Harpsichord.

Keith Jarrett and Michala Petri have recorded all six of them, as well as the Handel sonatas.
Is she a flutist?

She plays the recorder. They are beautiful recordings, and it made a bit of a shockwave amongst some classical musicians because Keith is saying, "I can do what you do, can you do what I do?"

Oh absolutely! We've been doing that for years!! Chick Corea can do the same thing. Chick and my piano player right now can do that, David Budley who played with me on that Rampal recording. He played with the Pittsburgh Symphony for years, and he's an excellent jazz improviser.

What Laws has done, on many of his own recordings, however, is to see how jazz and classical forms can be combined, with jazz adaptations of works by Bach and Stravinsky, on albums such as *Afro Classic* and *The Rite of Spring.* At the time of our interview he was re-mixing a work he had recorded, something called *New Earth Sonata* for a new CD to be called *Amazing Grace.* As he describes it, "This is a piece that merges classical, Latin, and jazz altogether in one piece. In three movements. And Chick Corea is playing the improvised piano solo on these three movements. This was done in 1986-87; I'm using some of the out-takes and I'm recording my flute over again on the same tracks." He also issued a tribute to Nat King Cole in 1998, and followed this with a purely Latin jazz album, *Baila Cinderella*, in 2002.

One thing I've found amongst a lot of jazz flutists is an interest in various kinds of non-Western music, because the flute is so universal. Have you branched out at all in that area? I mean, it's enough that you're doing classical work and jazz work so proficiently, but you have also been attracted by Latin jazz.

That's why I mentioned to you my first experience with that band, Mongo Santamaria--that was extensive experience in Latin music. I've always loved Latin music. On my last CD that I produced, called *Baila Cinderella,* most of the compositions were those I wrote for his band, but now I recorded them myself. So, Latin music has been a strong influence on my writing and playing.

I can see that you like to avoid being pigeonholed, however. This does make it difficult for the music business to handle you though. Where do we look for your records? For example, when you do the Bach, I bet you find people putting it in jazz bins because, in spite of all the classical work you have done, you are still thought of as a jazz artist.

Probably so. I'm sure, that's what will happen! But that's why I feel the Internet is such a fascinating marketing tool. By going through the Internet you can see you're not pigeonholed. If you go to my site you're going to see a variety of things there. It eliminates that one-bin mentality.

It is not just the retail side of the business for whom Hubert Laws presents a problem. Jazz critics have been ambivalent about some of his experiments. It is not a question of his performance abilities; Laws' technical proficiency is unquestionable, and anyone who has heard him tear up the changes on *Moment's Notice,* or *Airegin* can have no doubt that he is one of the finest practitioners of the art of jazz improvisation. But this goes to the root of the problem; jazz lovers want to hear more of it, simple and straightforward, rather than in the highly produced contexts of his CTI recordings, for example. This is not to say that these are bad recordings--he has, after all, won three Grammy nominations. Scott Yanow, of the All Music Guide, sums it up when he writes, "Hubert Laws has the ability to play anything well, but he does not always seem to have the desire to perform creative jazz." I put my version of this view to Hubert. His response did not really address the issue directly, although he did have some interesting recollections:

Can I confess a prejudice from my side--that the recordings of yours that I really like the best, at least on the jazz side, were the ones you made as a sideman. Some of the things you've done with Ron Carter, or McCoy Tyner, or Victor Feldman. Do you remember that stuff?

Absolutely! Oh yeah. I loved Victor. Victor Feldman and I were very good friends. I was around when his wife died, and then he died. I mean it was really... this man, he did a lot of things which he did not get credit for. I mean many people think that Miles Davis wrote *Seven Steps to Heaven,* but it was all Victor--Victor Feldman. I did my first direct to disc recording with Victor Feldman. Yeah, I think Harvey Mason was on that. This is a new technique back in... must have been somewhere in '81 or '82, between '81 and '85, where they would start the disc rolling and we went direct to disc. And we had to record about twenty minutes of music without stopping. So it was a really interesting technique. I've never done it since, but it was the first technique. It was supposed to be really clean, and was supposed to be somewhat innovative, and that's when he did some of his [Victor's] original compositions. I can't remember the titles of them right now, but I do remember the music right away, once I hear it.

He was a great player, Victor Feldman. I was sorry to hear about his passing.

Oh, he was a great player and a great musician and a great person. I remember I would go out to his place out in the Valley and rehearse at his home, and then we went to the studio and did that stuff.

There's a session with Ron Carter I'm very fond of too. The front line is Art Farmer, J. J. Johnson and yourself. You don't remember that?

I vaguely recall a recording with them, although I do remember recording with J. J. Johnson when he was writing movie scores out here. Listen, I've done so many recordings in my lifetime, I may not recall.

For the purpose of our readers, which of your albums do you want me to draw their attention towards? I need to recommend three or four albums that are available in your section.

I don't know if you've ever heard of *Storm Then The Calm*--you probably haven't.

Sure! I have it right here!

Also I did an album called *Family*. Actually I did everything--I arranged, did all the orchestration, I did most of the original compositions, That is one of my favorites. Also, *Morning Star. Morning Star* was recorded for CTI Records years ago. And it features Ron Carter along with Bob James and Freddy Waites and Jack DeJohnette. Those are some of the really good recordings that I know are not available right now because I was on the phone with Creed Taylor about two weeks ago, and we were talking about how CBS had really sequestered those recordings and made them their own. I don't even know if they distributed all of them, but they own the masters right now.

*It's **Storm Then The Calm** that you have transcriptions of, available through your website?*

I think so. You mean the flute solos? Yeah. I think they are. I think the recordings from way back, some available, some not. I have to check that website again and see what is available. There have been a number of transcriptions done, some people actually sent me transcriptions, like *Pensativa* and *Moments Notice.*

There are actually several transcriptions available from Laws' website, and flute students will find all of them worthy of study. They are brilliant statements by any measure. And Laws' Grammy nominations, as well as his showing in the *Down Beat* polls, demonstrate the esteem in which he was held, at least until the late 1970s. At that point, however, Hubert dropped out of sight for a while, deciding that he should devote his full attention to raising his children. Now that he is back he has resumed his recording career and has founded his own publishing companies, *Hulaws Music* and *Golden Flute Music*, to produce his own albums and those of promising new artists. But if Laws never makes another recording, and however his extant recordings may be judged, he has already made as significant a contribution to jazz flute playing as anyone can ask. By absorbing everything he could learn from Clement Barone and Julius Baker and applying it to jazz improvisation, he has demonstrated that the flute can project as powerfully as the trumpet or the saxophone. And by so doing he has paved the way for a whole generation of artists who perform exclusively on the flute in a jazz context.

An Appreciation from James Newton

In 2005, Hubert Laws was presented with the Duke Ellington Masters of Jazz Award by the Jazz Studies Department at UCLA. Presenting the award, fellow poll-winning flutist James Newton made the following comments:

In the mid 1960s Hubert Laws released his first recording, *The Laws of Jazz*. This release marked an entirely new direction for the flute's role in jazz. Prior to this recording Buddy Collette, Eric Dolphy, Paul Horn, Yusef Lateef, James Moody, Sam Most, Jerome Richardson and Frank Wess, among many others, made important contributions to the flute's position in jazz. What distinguished Hubert's performance was a new level of virtuosity on the instrument derived from a combination of extensive classical training and a visionary approach to jazz performance. This approach blended the influences of John Coltrane's *Giant Steps* period with Hubert's own flute gumbo, which incorporated gospel, rhythm and blues, classical, and Latin flavors.

I view Hubert as the Jackie Robinson of the flute. In the 1960s he was performing with both the New York Philharmonic and the Metropolitan Opera orchestras, conducted by such music luminaries as Leonard Bernstein, Pierre Boulez, Herbert Von Karajan, Zubin Mehta, and James Levine. To my knowledge, he is the first African American flutist to have played in these major orchestras. At the same time, he performed with the top names in the jazz and Latin fields: Mongo Santamaria, the Crusaders, Herbie Hancock, Chick Corea, Ron Carter and many others. This achievement paved the way for others coming behind him, such as Wynton Marsalis.

Aside from being one of the most important flutists of any genre, Hubert's contributions to the piccolo are unequaled. The clarity of his articulation and tone leave others standing in the rain waiting on the change!

Among the highlights of the 1970s are Hubert's groundbreaking CTI recordings; these were wildly popular and demonstrated great artistry. Any flutist who ever stepped into a church had to perform *Amazing Grace* after Hubert's stellar, soulful performance was released. His adaptations of Coltrane, Bach, Stravinsky, Fauré and others created opportunities to blend classical and jazz audiences. As we moved through the 1980s and 1990s and into the 21st century, his approach of blending musical genres has climbed to even higher plateaus. A number of artists have built major careers using Hubert's blueprint for successfully giving classical music jazz sensibilities.

After five decades at the top of his profession, and still performing at the highest level, Hubert is one of the greatest contributors to modern music. As great as his contribution is to the flute and the piccolo, like Charles Parker and other innovators, he has influenced players of other instruments and vocalists as well. Having won three Grammy awards along with many other accolades, Hubert Laws has already claimed his place in music history.

A New Landscape

With the emergence of Hubert Laws in the mid 1960s, the landscape changed for flutists in jazz. Hubert established new standards of performance for the instrument, demonstrating that a "legitimate" training could be combined with a jazz sensibility to finally turn the flute into a true jazz voice. This trend had already been set in motion by many of the early jazz pioneers. As we have seen, Frank Wess, Buddy Collette, Paul Horn and Bud Shank built upon training from "legit" teachers, Wess receiving a degree at the Modern School of Music in Washington DC, Horn attending the Oberlin Conservatory and the Manhattan School of Music, Collette and Shank working with private teachers. But Hubert Laws took this to its logical conclusion, studying at Juilliard with the legendary flutist Julius Baker, abandoning the saxophone to develop the fullest, richest possible flute sound, and working with Rudy Van Gelder to capture it on record.

It had an enormous impact. Saïs Kamalidiin remembers when he first heard Hubert, and the effect it had on his development as a flutist. "It was clear to me immediately that here was a new direction." It was not entirely new. There has been an on-again, off-again love affair going on between jazz and Western European art music since Paul Whiteman declared his infamous desire to "make a lady out of jazz." To a large extent, this was a sociological aspiration for jazz as much as a musical one. Born in the red light district of New Orleans, and coming of age in the speakeasies of Chicago and New York, jazz had grown up as the poor relative of concert music. Whiteman's efforts to bring the wayward youngster into the fold of respectability--which included presenting George Gershwin and his *Rhapsody in Blue* at Carnegie Hall in 1924--were only marginally successful, but formed a model for subsequent jazz artists to follow in attempting to merge classical and jazz forms.

This is a very broad topic, and well beyond the scope of this book. Suffice to say that there have been experiments along these lines in each generation. Artie Shaw utilized a string quartet in his 1936 band, and developed a clarinet concerto for himself. Not to be outdone, Benny Goodman commissioned works from Aaron Copeland and Morton Gould, while Woody Herman turned to Igor Stravinsky to write the *Ebony Concerto* and Duke Ellington began to write tone poems and suites—including eventually an adaptation of Tchaikovsky's *Nutcracker Suite*, as well as his ventures into sacred forms.

Following further efforts of a similar nature by Stan Kenton, Dave Brubeck and perhaps most famously by Miles Davis and Gil Evans in their famous *Sketches of Spain album*, the blending of jazz and Western European art music finally became a genre of its own, dubbed *Third Stream Music* by composer Gunther Schuller and the Modern Jazz Quartet's John Lewis, who, along with William Russo, J.J. Johnson, Jimmy Giuffre, Gerry Mulligan and others, produced a spate of compositions for a variety of instrumental combinations.

Many of these works were, perhaps, of dubious value, but the trend has continued and the quality has improved. Eddie Sauter's writing for Stan Getz and a string section resulted in a classic recording--*Focus*. Roger Kellaway's arrangements for his Cello Quartet and for Eddie Daniels' *Memos From Paradise,* and, more recently, Jim Snidero's writing for his own *Strings* album, and work by flutists Anne Drummond and the Canadian François Richard, are examples of how this music can work. And if it does work it is indicative of another trend. Since the launching of the first program at North Texas State University in 1955, jazz has been making steady inroads into university music departments, with a resulting improvement in the formal training of musicians in the jazz and commercial fields, while the earlier cradles of emerging jazz musicians--the big band and the jam session--were disappearing. Today there are dozens of such programs and, until its recent demise, an International Association of Jazz Educators to set standards for them.

All of this was too late for Miles Davis, of course, who abandoned Juilliard to seek his education on 52nd Street, and Juilliard had not changed much by the time Hubert Laws arrived there in 1960. Like many schools, even those dominated by African-Americans such as Howard University, or Texas Southern University where Hubert did his undergraduate studies, jazz was not merely unrepresented, it was frowned upon--another sociological phenomenon that deserves deeper consideration. But Hubert was not at Texas Southern or Juilliard to learn about jazz; he had already paid his dues in that area at Miss Mary's honky-tonk, with the Crusaders, and, while attending Juilliard, with Mongo Santamaria's band. No, Hubert went to school to learn the fundamentals of his instrument from the best possible teachers. Then he applied his beautiful tone and fleet technique to jazz improvisation. And it was this, much more than his own symphonic jazz experiments fifty years after Paul Whiteman's that has constituted Hubert's greatest contribution, to jazz in general and jazz flute in particular. The fact that he can perform at a high level in a symphonic context adds enormously to his jazz playing. And, significantly, it was a flutist who was among the first to blaze this particular trail.

Again, this has become a trend. Jazz is now routinely studied in conservatories and presented in concert halls. "Crossover" recordings have become commonplace from artists such as Wynton and Branford Marsalis, Dave Brubeck, Keith Jarrett, James Newton, Jan Garbarek, Fred Hersch, Victor Feldman, Ron Carter and others, all of them primarily jazz players. There is even a Classical Jazz Quartet, led by Kenny Barron. A number of "classical" artists have attempted quasi-jazz recordings, among them Itzhak Perlman, Yo-Yo Ma and flutists Jim Walker, James Galway, Jean-Pierre Rampal, Paula Robison, Robert Dick and Emmanuel Pahud, although with the exception of Jim Walker, and possibly Dick, they had their parts written out for them. Perhaps the only exception is pianist/conductor André Previn, who has made several fine albums as a jazz pianist. But one only has to listen to Yehudi Menuhin's duets with Stephan Grapelli to realize that jazz feeling often does not come easily or naturally to even the finest classically trained musicians. By contrast, a jazz artist, Richard Davis, could be both John Coltrane's and Igor Stravinsky's favorite bass player.

It is in this context that a whole generation of flutists has emerged in jazz, and the musical world they have entered is very different from that of the earliest jazz flute pioneers thirty years earlier. Indeed, in a sense, the flute is a very different instrument, not in its physical construction, but in its revealed possibilities. Interviewed shortly before his death by National Public Radio, Artie Shaw reported that the clarinet felt like a completely different instrument to him after he had undertaken some "legitimate" training in preparation to perform the works he had commissioned for his 1936 orchestra. Similarly, the instrument that has been inherited by Jamie Baum and Anne Drummond has been greatly enhanced by the work Eric Dolphy did in working with Charles Mingus and Edgar Varèse, the time Hubert Laws spent with Julius Baker, or James Newton's mastery of contemporary flute performance techniques. Against this background of accomplishment, a group of flutists felt confident to enter the jazz world concentrating entirely on their chosen instrument. The music they have produced has done a great deal to move the genre forward.

Time and space so not allow me to represent all of these players within these pages. I am chagrined to omit such artists as Kent Jordan, Gerald Beckett, Bill McBernie, Jill Allen, Jan Leder, Kenny Stahl, Dottie Anita Taylor, Damjan Krajacic and Nica Rejto, not to mention Richard from Canada, Cicilia

Kemezys in Australia, Eddie Parker, Gareth Lockrane, Rowland Sutherland, Andy Penai amd Keith Waithe in the UK, Chris Hinze and Mark Alban Lotz in Holland, Italy's Stefano Benini, Gunther Wehinger in Switzerland, Magic Malik in France and Jorgé Pardo in Spain. All of them, and more, will be featured on our website. The artists that are featured here form a cross-section of flute specialists in jazz, all of whom have interesting stories, and a very personal approach to the instrument.

James Newton: Flutist, Composer, Conductor

"I've always believed that the whole of the earth is a huge palette, and the cultures of the world are like colors. Most musicians use only a few colors. I like to use many different colors in many different ways."

James Newton

The early 1970s saw another major transition in the development of the flute in jazz. Hubert Laws, its standard-bearer for a decade, withdrew from active participation in music in order to raise his family. Just as he was dropping out of sight, a new figure was emerging, taking over as *Down Beat* poll winner in both the reader's and critic's categories, and remaining in the top two or three until quite recently. The new standard-bearer was **James Newton,** but he has taken the instrument in a very different direction, into territory that ultimately transcends the genre. As he puts it, "Only a certain percentage of the music that I do can fit within the definition or the boundaries of what people consider jazz."

If James' music is distinctly different from Hubert's, his background has many similarities. Both were immersed in black music culture in their early years, Hubert at Miss Mary's honky-tonk in Houston, James in the Baptist churches of Los Angeles, where he was born in 1953. While Los Angeles is not strictly the South, James feels that he had a southern upbringing. His father was a great blues enthusiast from Texas, while his mother, who was from rural Arkansas, loved gospel music. It was his parents, along with his grandmother and his aunt, who introduced James to the Baptist church, and these early experiences have left him with vivid memories of gospel music and performers such as Clara Ward, Cassetta George, Sam Cooke and the Soul Stirrers, the Dixie Hummingbirds, and the Five Blind Boys of Alabama.

Like Hubert, James took up music at an early age, and he also experimented with other instruments before deciding to specialize in the flute. In high school he took to rock and rhythm and blues on his first instrument, the electric bass. But he was soon drawn to the woodwinds, taking up the alto sax and bass clarinet. He was also becoming more aware of jazz. This combination inevitably drew him to the playing of Eric Dolphy which itself had another component--the flute. Attracted by its register, close to the female voice he so loved from gospel music, James picked up this instrument during his last year in high school. He quickly found himself following in Dolphy's footsteps. Seeking a teacher who was well respected in both jazz and classical studies brought him to the door of Buddy Collette, who had been Dolphy's teacher ten years earlier. Later he would study with Patricia Garside at California State University, Los Angeles, and with James Walker, then principal flutist with the L.A. Philharmonic. Proficiency on flute also opened new horizons. While still listening to jazz artists such as Charles Mingus, Duke Ellington and Miles Davis, James also performed in classical ensembles while studying for a music degree at California State College. His main jazz performance experience at this time was with Arthur Blythe, Bobby Bradford and David Murray, in Stanley Crouch's Black Music Infinity, and with clarinetist and composer John Carter.

With all of this, James was moving along a track similar to the one followed by Hubert Laws a decade and a half earlier. He was absorbing both the jazz and the classical traditions, and integrating these with his first influences from church and popular genres. In 1977 James moved to New York, but rather than to attend Juilliard, it was to seek more performance opportunities and interactions with creative musicians. He began to draw on the diversity of his musical background to strike out in a number of directions, and it was not long before he started to make recordings, both under his own name and as a sideman with artists such as Anthony Davis and Arthur Blythe. Since that time, his output both as performer and a composer has been remarkable both for its quality and its breadth. He has recorded tributes to Duke Ellington (*African Flower*) and Charles Mingus *(Romance and Revolution)*, and other highly personal statements within the jazz idiom. At the same time, he has composed works which have been performed by ensembles such as the Moscow Virtuosi, the San Francisco Contemporary Chamber Players and the Los Angeles Philharmonic New Music Group. His ballet *Gumbo Ya-Ya* has been performed by the San Francisco Ballet, and his opera *The Songs of Freedom* by the Virginia Opera. He continues to receive commissions for his compositions, and numerous awards and fellowships for his performances in multiple genres. He also finds time for teaching, giving frequent master classes and holding a professorship in music, first at the University of California at Irvine, then at California State University at Los Angeles, and mor recently at U.C.L.A.

While continuing his involvement with classical music, James Newton has also applied his creativity to advancing the role of the flute in jazz performance. He has pioneered the development of special sound production techniques on the flute, to compensate for the relatively small dynamic and expressive range that has limited the instrument's use in jazz for many years. To do this, he draws on two distinct traditions. On the one hand he draws upon the vocalization techniques associated with Rahsaan Roland Kirk and Yusef Lateef such as humming along with, and in counterpoint with, the flute, which, along with the bending of notes, have come into jazz from Africa via the blues. On the other hand, he has made an intensive study of multiphonics, alternative fingerings and other techniques from the repertoire of twentieth century art music.

It is in this area that James Newton's music differs most dramatically from that of Hubert Laws', however similar their backgrounds may seem. In his classical studies, and in his fusion of jazz and classical forms, Hubert has tended to focus on what is termed the "common practice" period of Western music, a repertoire centered on Baroque, Classical and Romantic composers such as J.S. Bach, Mozart and Tchaikovsky, with some forays into impressionism with Claude Debussy and early modernism with Igor Stravinsky. Similarly, his jazz playing has a "classical" feel, if you will, centered on the mainstream of the genre, the language of bebop, expressed in such classics as *Airegin* and *Moment's Notice.*

Newton has also merged classical and jazz forms, but in a quite different manner. His interests in European art music are very much centered on the contemporary era, with regard to both composition and flute performance practices. The jazz language that he applies to his improvisations is a unique blend of all his influences from Ellington and Mingus, through the entire history of jazz flute, with which he is thoroughly familiar, to a comprehensive vision of world music, be it European, African, or Asian. In almost every case, it is a music created from whole cloth; James rarely, if ever, plays jazz standards or show tunes. Virtually everything he presents, even when in the context of a tribute to another performer, is in the form of original compositions, either of his, or of other members of the ensemble with which he is working. Such a distinction points up the definition of two informal schools of jazz flute performance, two approaches to overcoming the instrument's inherent limitations. Laws, following Frank Wess, Bud Shank, James Moody, et. al., focuses on clarity of line, harmonic sophistication, unflagging rhythmic interest and a full, rich tone, with impeccable intonation. Newton, following Sahib Shihab, Yusef Lateef, Rahsaan et. al., adds other dimensions of sound and thus of expression to the instrument.

When I sat down with James at his home outside Los Angeles, he revealed himself as highly articulate and thoughtful, a teacher as much as a performer. His comments on some of the major contributors to the jazz flute tradition were most revealing and of great interest to our study. We began our conversation, however, by going straight to the heart of the matter--the unique genre that has emerged from the combined interests of jazz flutists:

During these interviews with jazz flutists I have been struck by the breadth and variety of subjects we have covered--flute players have such a broad intelligence. Why do you think that is?

We've had to. Flutists have had to forge their own place and identity within the context of jazz, playing an instrument that many people would consider to be on the periphery of jazz. But at the same time you have this dichotomy, because it's an instrument that's so essential to many different cultures of the world. So how do we deal with this dichotomy? I guess part of the way that we deal with it is that we have taken a lot of time to look at flute traditions that exist in other cultures and bring aspects of them into the jazz tradition when we're playing in that context. And one other point that I'd like to add is that, because we've looked at these other cultures, our music also moves outside of the realm of what could be defined as being jazz. I think only a certain percentage of the music that I do can fit within the definition or the boundaries of what people consider jazz.

Of what other people consider jazz.

Yeah. But not for myself... I don't see boundaries.

Tell me about the particular areas that you like to extend your awareness into, in your own music.

Well, let's talk about that right now. This is a scandalous statement to make, but I'm not very interested in playing changes that have been around for a long set of time. For me it's something that I might practice in the confines of my home, but it's not something that I want to get out and do. I mean, what I'm interested in now is breaking barriers with the instrument and getting to new areas of expression and techniques. And many varied things have influenced me to go in that direction, or to pursue that path.

Number one, harmony should be reflective of what's occurring in society at the time that it's being created and produced. So I can't think about harmonic structures that existed in bebop being on the cutting edge of an art form at this point in time. We're at the twenty-first century, you know, so that means that I'm going to look at models that occur from the past, but I want to create new harmonic platforms. I want to liberate harmony from following on the one and the three if we're dealing with swing. For me, one of the things that has been so stifling to music moving forward is the rhythmical liberation of harmony, particularly when you look at the music of Thelonius Monk. He was one of the people who really laid a platform for harmonic rhythm to go in another place. And also I'm interested in harmonic progressions that don't have to do with tonality, or if they do, it's obscured, maybe to the point where it's not even that relevant. And all of that factors in the way that I approach playing the instrument. Harmonic vocabulary can make a huge difference in the registers that I'm able to play with my instrument, number one. You know, if your harmony is set up in a certain kind of way, it can liberate the middle register of the piano to where, all of a sudden, the lower register of the flute becomes audible to the public. So there are just so many factors that I'm thinking about, micro-tonality being another, because I am a child of Duke Ellington, and when I heard *Daybreak Express*, all the micro-tonality that existed there, I was strongly affected by it. When I heard Johnny Hodges and Billie Holliday using micro-tonality, a lot of those things affected me, as I could I say with, chromatic traditions, Carnatic [south Indian] traditions, the *bansuri* [north Indian flute] tradition and so forth. So we can go on and on and we can look at the *deesa* traditions that exist, just the micro-tonality used there. All of those things become available to us. So if we're talking about the jazz context, there are certain things that we can take from those traditions and put in a jazz context to expand it. But certain things just fall outside of the realm of what people call jazz.

But there are certain jazz flutists that touched your heart, presumably?

Oh, many, many. You know?

Who comes to mind? It's a cliché, but you have to ask, what are your influences?

No, that's always a good question. I think, first and foremost I always talk about Eric Dolphy, because of the sense of exploration that existed in his music. And there was a cultural pluralism in his music that laid the groundwork for many of the innovations that came later on. His technique on the instrument was phenomenal, and I often tell the story of when I was going up to college and learned the Ibert Concerto for my senior recital. And people were talking about how tough that piece was. But it wasn't tough, anywhere as near as tough, as Andrew White's transcriptions of Dolphy songs, which I also learned. They demanded technically so much more than the Ibert. And I loved his sound. You know, this dubious quality that you talked about that exists in different flute traditions. Dolphy, to me, really had that. There was a certain playful aspect about his personality that came out--particularly in his rhythm--that really appealed to me. The other thing I loved about him is the fact that he was able to transfer--because he was such a great alto saxophonist also--some of the language of Charles Parker to the flute in a way that other flutists hadn't done.

Was he a good flutist, qua flutist, though?

He was a great flutist. I love his sound. And I think *You Don't Know What Love Is* is one of the great flute performances in recorded history. From *Last Date*. And I also love his solo on *Left Alone*. I could just go on and on and on, there's so many.

There's one track, **Glad To Be Unhappy,** *from his first album,* **Outward Bound.** *That made a huge impression on me. There was a review of that record by Benny Green, a critic in the UK. He said something like "Dolphy is being compared to Ornette Coleman. Well, you can compare a warped toothpick to the leaning tower of Pisa; they're both out of true."*

Oh, my goodness!

I don't know why that has stayed with me all these years... But he was criticizing his actual flute technique. As he saw it, bad breathing, thin tone--things of that nature.

Miss me with that! That's something we say in L.A. if we don't agree with something. Miss me with that! I couldn't disagree more. I know that people talked about the fact that he played out of tune, but Dolphy was very much into micro-tonality. I heard—well, different musicians have told me--that he had worked out all these quarter-tone fingerings and eighth-tone fingerings for the instrument. And the other thing that really struck me is the fact that of all his instruments he used the extreme registers, and that really appealed to me. And also the way that he used octave displacement, because for me, he was coming out of the Pygmies, and the second Viennese school at the same time. And Thelonius Monk. It was like, all of them. You know, if you look at a Monk melody, a lot of times a Monk melody can go two and a half octaves, and maybe somebody else did that also whom Dolphy worked with, and both of them were influenced by Monk. And then the other aspect of his playing is the fact that he was also well acquainted with contemporary European flute literature. When I visited Hale Smith for the first time he showed me the music that Dolphy had left in his house that he was going to pick up in '64, and it was really interesting, the choice of materials that he had there. I remember seeing Villa-Lobos, *Bachianas Brasileiras* No. 5. I remember seeing the Ibert *Flute Concerto*. And Berio's *Sequenza*, which had just been written a few years before, I believe that was in the collection.

So he wasn't necessarily considering performing this music, this is a question of him feeding material into his own unconscious to come out in his own inventions, which I think is a very big deal in jazz education.

It is. Although another point I want to make before we expound upon that is that Dolphy performed *Density 21.5* in public before--Varèse's piece. And Hale Smith had told me that he introduced Dolphy to Varèse, and Dolphy went to Varèse's house to work on the piece, and Varèse later told Hale Smith that Dolphy's performance was really excellent. That's a piece of unpublished information right there! There was a dialogue between them. And for me, there's one other important piece in there. I think Messiaen's *Le Merle Noir* might have been in that collection too.

But anyway, the way he used birdsong, he was into a lot of flutter tonguing, and I mean, just on all of his instruments, his technique was just incredibly impeccable... and he had a real sense of imagination. When people talk about what swings, what doesn't swing, I always thought that Dolphy really swung. And that there was a vibrancy in his rhythmical approach that was something incredibly special. And a lot of musicians that worked with him, would tell me that his tone was so huge, sometimes they'd have to put him behind curtains--for the alto saxophone. When he was touring with Mingus, Mingus would sometimes complain and have him play behind a curtain at a particular point because his tone was just so huge. So if you're putting that much air into a bass clarinet or an alto saxophone, by the time you get to the flute it's going to be a whole other kind of instrument compared with the degree of air that, let's say, a player in a symphony orchestra is putting into it.

I could talk about Dolphy forever--one other point that I want to add, Dolphy extended a lot of ideas that he learned from Thelonius Monk, and not only developed that into his compositional technique, but also his improvisational technique, on all of his instruments. So that gave him a whole other sensitivity to timbre and to range--the co-ordination of all of those different elements together for musical expression. I want to make sure that his thought is crystal enough... Let me give you another example. In the late forties, Messiaen came up with the idea of the total serialization of music--all elements-- dynamics, pitch, rhythm, and so on, I guess to get a certain control of music, but to also to explore what kind of music would be created by that. When I look at Dolphy, and the things that he was doing with pitch, timbre, color, rhythm, expression, the use of silence coming out of Monk, he took all of those elements, and he put them together. You have a very sophisticated, highly literate, explorer of musical terrain.

I talked to Chico Hamilton and he said Eric was the best flute player he ever had. And he has had a few over the years.

Oh yeah. He's hired the cats.

Eric, Charles Lloyd, Buddy Collette, Paul Horn... and some of the younger players, Eric Person, Erik Lawrence, Karolina Strassmeyer...

Quite a cadre of artists! But we have to talk about Buddy because that's who I studied with. Buddy had a gigantic influence on me also, in just the things that he taught me about sound, about being flexible and fitting in all these different environments. And I remember with such great fondness his recording of *Meditations on Integration* that he did with Mingus in '65, and a lot of things from the fifties that he did.

Buddy was like a second father to me, really. He's a great man. He made my life change totally when I started to work with him. He's not only a great man but a great teacher, and I mean a really great musician. We did an album in the eighties together called *Flute Talk* that was one of my favorites. Just the memory of it--we did a tour of Europe, I think it was about '87, '88, somewhere around there. We had such fun! Now Charles Lloyd is somebody that I heard oftentimes when I went to the barbershop in San Pedro. A lot of times they would play *Forest Flower* and *Dream Weaver*, they were some of the really big things. I also got to hear Charles play live when I was very young and it really left an impression on me. Devonshire Downs had a pop festival, and Charles Lloyd was up!

With Keith Jarrett?

Yes, I think Keith Jarret was with the band then. I went there to hear Jimi Hendrix. But I've always loved Charles' playing too--I listened to Charles through the years, you know.

You were talking earlier about saxophone players who transferred the saxophone to the flute. Do you see that as a major part of the jazz flute odyssey?

Absolutely. Now we can go to jazz flutists that I tried to learn something from, that really gripped me, that were probably saxophone players Yusef Lateef--I remember I took the time to learn a lot of his flute solos, *Take the A Train,* that he did in the fifties. I thought that was one of the great solos on the instrument. But many of his recordings touched me very deeply. And I always loved his tone, his sense of exploration, his using modes and scales from music other than Western music and incorporating them in his work.

He wrote a book about that as I recall, The **Repository of Scales and Melodic Patterns.**

Yeah. That book... I lived in it, as I did *Flute Book of the Blues*. Those are great... I have all of my serious students get those two books, for me they are bread and butter. The melodic scales and patterns--it had great influence on me. There are a lot of modes and scales, like the Egyptian minor, that I ended up using in a lot of my compositions that came later on. And he had a sense of also looking at world music, looking at African traditions, looking at Eastern flute traditions and musical traditions from all parts of Asia. This sense of exploration, for me, was something that was another model and another pattern. Plus the fact that if you want to talk about bebop, Yusef Lateef was one of the great bebop and blues players there is.

Especially on tenor. If Mingus and Cannonball Adderley hire you, you would probably have to be pretty decent in that department!

That's right. You have to be able to know how to play some blues also. And the other thing is that you have to have some church in your playing. Plus to me, the beauty of his tone is reflected in the beauty of the human being. I always felt that Yusef was one of the finest people I ever met in my life--a very inspiring human being.

Then Wayman Carver, with Chick Webb, is somebody I listened to a lot. There was a swing station that was about a quarter of a mile from my house and I just started listening to it, and they played a lot of Chick Webb and Ella Fitzgerald, and that's when I got to hear Wayman's playing for the first time, and I really appreciated it. I liked his tone a lot, I liked his swing, and I liked his playing in the third register. It was important to me to hear a great improvising flutist in pre-bop, because that gives you a whole lot of feeling. The flute is probably one of the least prominent instruments in the swing era, you know, and he is one of the few exceptions of flutists that were operating during that era. And then when we get to the bop period, and post-bop, we have all these flutists that enter the picture--I love Frank Wess.

You are putting him in the bop era?

Yeah, even though he got going in swing. You know, he's associated with the Basie recordings in the Fifties, and so on. To me he's one of those people like Hawk [Coleman Hawkins], to where he goes through different traditions. To me he is an exquisite player, and he takes on certain elements of each innovation and incorporates it in his playing. So, I associate him with bop. I know that there are things that are earlier, and there are things that have been done post. And then the New York Jazz Quartet in the seventies was one of my favorite bands of all--Frank Wess, Roland Hanna, Ron Carter, Ben Riley. I had all their recordings and I got to hear that band play live about three or four times.

What percentage of the time did he play flute with that group?

I would say something like thirty. And his sense of swing, the beauty of his tone--to me he is just a real solid flute player.

He was the first winner of the **Down Beat** *poll when they finally gave themselves a flute category.*
Wow! I didn't know that. That's great.

And he's still up there today. He actually won earlier in their "Miscellaneous Instruments" category. It was back in fifty something. Then they actually gave it a category, in 1960.

That's awful late! That's why we're still fighting--we're still not in the house yet!

Okay. Let's continue the list. James Moody. My goodness! Great, great player. His solos... I love the way that he sang and played on the instrument too, as did Yusef, and Roland Kirk. Plus James is another person, like Frank Wess, who's the most phenomenal bopper, maybe one of the greatest to ever play the flute. And you'd hear Moody playing *The Force*, you know, which is little bit more of the modern tune coming out of post-bop, and then you would hear a lot of really sophisticated chord substitutions that Coltrane and other people were using that Moody adopted also. I'm sure that so many players heard things Moody played. To me he's a very gigantic force on the instrument. *Wave* was one of his great solos that a lot of people looked at, and so many other pieces. But I love James Moody. And rhythmically, for me, he was one of the most exacting, precise, musicians in relationship to swing. You know, again we are talking about another human being that's a great man. A great human being. Then there's Rahsaan--Roman Kirk.

One thing about Rahsaan is that he did such amazing things, but occasionally when he just got one instrument in his hands for a while, it was astounding what he could do. He could have just played tenor for example and made a real impact. I mean, he was up there with Sonny Rollins...

Yeah, I know, I know.

And as far as his flute playing was concerned, that was, mmmmm, idiosyncratic!

(Laughing) I don't know. Maybe I look at things a little bit differently! I just think about the beauty of *I Talk with the Spirits.* I mean, for me, I love that, and so many things that he did were so very important to me. I think the way he played the blues... there was an awful lot of church in Rahsaan's playing. That's one of the things, coming up in a black Baptist tradition, that I could really relate to. And I know that, like so many other people, I was affected by the way he sang and played the flute at the same time. And there is something about... I don't care how many notes you play, but what are you making me feel? That's something I care about a lot more than how many notes you're playing--I love

238 The Flute In Jazz

the way that his music makes me feel when I listen to it. For me, that's much more important than someone's technical facility, or, someone else's interpretation of tone that might be a little bit narrower than mine. I mean, if somebody has a little bit of air in their sound it doesn't bother me that much. It's like, what are they saying? You know, so that's why I feel like I can learn and appreciate a lot of flutists. What are we going to come up with? That's the thing that I'm curious about.

I mentioned to you earlier that Jerome Richardson had said he was working on trying to make the flute a real jazz instrument, that he didn't feel that it had been up to that time. He said he was particularly trying to find ways of articulation on the flute that made it swing.

Yeah, that's the biggest challenge because you have to take an adaptation. I shouldn't say you have to... but the success, the little bit of success I've had in that way had to do with me taking adaptations of articulations that existed in trumpet playing and saxophone playing. And the person that I went to the most when I was coming up was Dizzy Gillespie. Probably no one will hear it in my playing, but in my mind the connection is there, because the range that he was using with the trumpet fit very well with the flute range. And when I listened to Bird and Dizzy together, coming up, Bird would just scare me to death. Dizzy's technical facility was astounding also, but there was something about Bird that was just, totally... You know, when you are learning an instrument and you hear somebody at that level, everything sounds impossible.

And Dizzy employed a lot of flute players.

Dizzy? Absolutely. [James] Moody, and Leo Wright, who I had the pleasure of meeting in Vienna-- a great man and a very nice person. He wrote out some things for me, different patterns and different things, and we talked a lot about articulation as a matter of fact. You have to make adaptations because, if you listen, a lot of phrasing in jazz is based on bebop, then you have to look at what happened before bebop, and what spurred bebop to develop in the way that it did.

When you listen to Armstrong's Hot Five and Hot Seven recordings and a lot of [Sidney] Bechet's playing, and Earl Hines' playing, you can just take that group of people and you can see how things that they played had a great influence on be-bop later on. So, if you're going to swing, there has to be sort of a connection. And one of the ways that I tried to work on swing is that I spent a lot time playing bebop heads with the recordings. Over and over and over, whether it be something like *Hot House* just to get my diaphragm to coordinate with my tongue to where there's enough punch coming from the diaphragm to where you get the feeling of having more of a jazz articulation. And so that's the way that I tried to transfer the articulation, from what I heard in the way that horn players played bebop phrases, coming from the compositions. So what that led me to do is to create a series of articulations that were almost like scat singing. Beyond that, this gave me the possibility of trying to approach some things on a swing level. And then Frank Wess taught me some articulations. He also told me that if you use articulations used in classical music, they just don't swing. I remember Bobby Bradford told me, he says, "I never heard double tonguing swing."

Hubert [Laws] tries it!

Well, Hubert does so many things successfully. I don't know--it's just the guy's an amazing flute player. Maybe the articulation that he uses is a little bit more classically based. But Frank Wess told me that Moody used diddle, diddle, diddle, diddle, diddle. So what I started to try to do was to come up with some phrases that sounded a little bit like my own, to combine things I learned from Frank, Dolphy, Diz and Bird and a number of other of people, people out here that I've played with like Bobbie Bradford, and Arthur Blythe when I was younger, coming up. I just kind of mixed them together. Then I figured out that really the articulation has to be active enough with the rhythm and with your fingers, to where there's enough variance, because the tone color of the flute isn't as wide as the tone color of the trumpet or the saxophone, right? So, it's like for me, it ended be like scat singing. (Sings)

But then you are double tonguing certain things within the phrase to make the whole thing hang together. Hubert tends to take 64 measures and double tongue the whole thing and then come back to a different articulation. I was just listening to him in the car coming up here.

Well, I think one thing is... he went to Juilliard, you know. That's not a criticism, just a statement of fact--that he subbed for Julius Baker with the New York Philharmonic, so he's a strong part of that tradition, not so much the mid-to-late 20th century aspect of the European flute tradition, but more the 19th century, maybe from Baroque to the early twentieth century. I don't hear *Density,* Berio's *Sequenza*, or any of the Darmstadt school in Hubert's playing, or any contemporary flute music that's existed since then. That's not a part of his language. It's more like the Romantic literature.

Then he finishes up doing Ravel and Coltrane on the same album.

Yeah, I can see that. Both of them were very much into harmony, exquisite harmony at that, and I've always been a big Ravel fan anyway.

It's one thing to play Ravel. It's a different thing to have Ravel absorbed into your being so that it's part of what comes out when you improvise. We were talking about being a sponge. You put so many things in and they don't have to come out through the same channels. That's an essential part of how to train musicians, I believe.

I understand what you are saying. Well, it's our gumbo. And it's like all of those ingredients that come together, and they are put together to create something really fascinating. You know, when I cook food I like a lot a different combinations of flavor. My wife told me once, "You really like complexity, don't you?" And I said "Yeah, I do." I mean that's really what I feel. I understand what you're saying, but...

That may change when you are eighty years old or something…

Yes, it might.

... when you try to distill things down to their essence. But you've never really felt that complexity, that interest, push you to experiment with other instruments, other colors in that sense? I know you played a lot of things before you finally settled on the flute--bass as I remember.

Yeah, bass. And I played a little bit of sax. But it wasn't me. I just didn't feel it. So then I said, "Well, if Rampal can make a living playing the flute, why can't I?" Not that I'm comparing myself to him, but within his tradition, why can't I make a living being a flutist in my tradition?

No one can say that he didn't succeed!

Exactly! And Hubert had done it before me. Even though our aesthetics are very different, there was Hubert, and Herbie Mann, even though Herbie doubled a lot when he was younger. But those were two flutists who made a living, and had been able to record a lot just playing the flute well.

Yes, I was astonished to see the extent of Herbie Mann's discography. But then there were all these different settings he put himself in.

Yeah, it's true. I remember, I mean there are a lot of things of his that I don't know, but didn't he do a project with Moroccan musicians or something?

Yes, and then with Japanese musicians, and Cuban of course, and Brazilian, and so forth. But as we were saying yesterday, the flute was so central to so many of these traditions that it seems to be the specialty of jazz flutists that they are drawn to these kinds of things. Like Bud Shank playing with Ravi Shankar, in the early days on Pacific Jazz, for example.

Right. Also with the *koto* player Kimio Eto.

And then the bossa nova things, of course. But now he [Bud Shank] doesn't touch his flute anymore. It's not him anymore. You have to respect that.

Of course we do. That's being honest. You know. But I think, maybe in a way we're also liberated by the fact that we don't have as much tradition on our instrument as a lot of instruments do. And there's a lot of freedom in the fact that not as many things have been defined.

Well, that's a very positive attitude. This particular approach seems to have really blossomed in this current generation.

Right. But we need to cover Sam Most. He is somebody else we talked about earlier who I very much like. And the thing that you were saying, as so many people say about Sam, is that his lines are phenomenal; he has a very interesting choice of pitches. You can tell that he's somebody that's really distilled bebop with a rhythmical language in a very powerful manner.

He made a very fine album with Joe Farrell.

Oh yeah, I remember that one. That's another player. Boy, that guy could play the flute. I mean, probably one of his most famous solos was *Spain*--that's just a really great solo. He was a very, very gifted artist.

I have to tell you that one of my favorite Dolphy solos was Olé Coltrane.

Oh yeah. He was George Lane on that date!

Going back to Ellington, why you chose to make an album of Ellington music also raises another question. I know the flute is central to Asian traditions, but I'm just ignorant myself about how it gets into African forms.

Oh, well here is something so beautiful. The Fulani flute tradition is something that I feel incredibly close to. I was on this odyssey that occurred over a period of time. It started at the Black Arts Festival in Atlanta. It was '91-'92 I think, when I was there. A woman ran up to me with a beautiful baby--I could tell she was African, and she said "You look like the people from my village and from my area." I said "Really?" And she said "When you picked up the flute I couldn't believe it!" I said "Well, why?" And she said: "Because it's the main instrument of our tradition." She was telling me that a lot of the Fulani are shepherds, but they are also flutists. They have a very powerful tradition, and one of things about their playing is that they not only play the flute but they sing a lot into the flute at the same time. A lot of the same rhythms are played--at times really pastoral and lyrical--long lines, and there are other times where it is very rhythmical, like a drum.

Where do you find the Fulani?

Well they're nomadic so they move quite a bit, maybe going through five, six, West African countries. But you can find them in parts of Niger and also they exist in Senegal, and I believe also in Mali.

What is that instrument like?

I'll show you. (Produces African flute and blows into the instrument). They play it to the side.

Like a ney?

But he lays his fingers flat like on the *bansuri*.

Are they fairly standard?

That's the flute they use in Niger.

It's made of bamboo bound with leather.

So, to continue the story:, she was struck by my flute playing because she said, "You sing in the flute just like they do," you know? And then all of a sudden I went, and I got some recordings and I said, "Man, some of that stuff sounds like Rahsaan. [Roland Kirk]" You can see a parallel in Gambia. When you hear the music of Gambia, a lot of times people call that the home of the blues. And so it's like one of these [genres] that came from West Africa that was brought to our country that resonated.

With both my parents being from the South, I think there are certain aspects about root music that existed in me very strongly, even though my music is modern. And so, it happened that the French organizers for *Banya Bleu*--I think that's it, the jazz festival in Paris--they wanted to put a great Fulani flutist and myself together, and we were going to do a workshop for about ten, eleven, days, with all these flutists from different parts of France. Well we did it, and we had a concert, and it went so well. I remember that I walked in the room and he was playing. He had his eyes closed, and I took my flute out and we played for twenty, thirty minutes together. His name was Yacouba Moumoni. And we played and he looked at me, and he hugged me and he says "C'est la même chose," you know. It was almost frightening when we played together, because so many things just fit to a T. And the promoters thought that it was so successful that they arranged another, really big, project, to where the *Cité de la Music* sponsored the whole project. They flew me from L.A. to Meami, Niger, and I stayed there and was able to rehearse with the band every day for about nine days. And then we did a concert in Meami, and I got to see the region, you know, outside of the city, and get somewhat of a feeling of the culture, which was an amazing experience to me. I was so excited, I could hardly sleep. It was just so moving. And the things that I learned really stayed with me. It made me change my music altogether.

When I came back home, one of the things I noticed was they used mainly pentatonic scales. But they were affected by American blues, and so you had elements of that in the music, and then modes that came out of the melismatic Arabic vocal traditions that influenced so much of West Africa through the traders. So it's a combination of all those elements in their music. I was writing all this complex music before I went there, and then I came back, and I just pared my music down, and I've been rebuilding it from the root up because of that experience.

And then the next year I came back, I think it was 2000 when I was in Africa, and in 2001 I went to Brazil. I went with my quartet and we played in Rio and Sao Paulo for the Jazz Festivals there. That put a whole other thing on my music. And then this year in March I went to Cuba and played in Cuba, and that added a whole other thing.

Danilo [Lozano] was telling me that the flute is the lead instrumental voice in Cuban music. Not quite the same in Brazil, although he flute really fits with what they're doing--you can always play flute along with that music and it fits so perfectly.

Oh yes, to a T. Brazil is really the completely package because the rhythmical concepts are so phenomenal.

Imported from Africa?

African, but also the language of the indigenous people of the region rhythmically is in the music also, as are the European influences. So all of those things together... It's like fesuada might be the most successful combination between gumbo and bouillabaise, and, you know, there's just something about the combination of all of those things.

One of the things in Cuban music that I long for a little bit more, the Cuban rhythm is much more sophisticated than what's being done in Brazil, but the harmony and the melodies of the music that exist in Brazil are so strong--very subtle and lush and very poetic also. I think a lot of it has to do with the fact you have such a beautiful sounding language with so many rounded consonants. All of that has an effect upon what occurs, as the lyric qualities of the language are transferred to melodic characteristics that end up in the music. And when you describe something like that, there's an aspect of the flute that's tailor made for that, you know?

So there are all these things--looking at the African diaspora, you have all of these people spread out in different parts of the world, that are putting all of these influences back together again. It's almost like a re-hybridization that's occurring, on a whole other level. And you see the great thing that Africa gave the world or one of the great things that Africa gave the world, is the significance of rhythm, and music itself talking.

And this was taken out of Western music by the church fathers because they wanted their worship to be different from everything else that was going on around the Mediterranean at that time, including North Africa.

I was just reading Kierkegard the other day and he was touching on that very point. So we've made this big circle, you know, talking about the Fulani which is just one of very many different African flute traditions. We have all these variations that exist in Fulani traditions and cultures themselves as they move to different areas. And for me, the most significant and the most influential African music that's touched me, is in music of the Pygmy. A lot of vocal music of the Pygmy--the hocketting--is something that I've tried to transfer to the flute. But every time I got into it and started to learn some things, I realized that I wasn't the first person there. Dolphy had gotten there already because the thing about the flute...Okay you have a B foot, you can go down to B. The highest note known to be played on the instrument is an F sharp, but I think I've figured out a fingering for a G that I can get every once in a while. So, one of the things Pygmy music made me think about doing is using the whole range of the instrument, because Pygmies would fluctuate between their head voice and their chest voice with such a fluidity and flexibility, and I wanted to try and achieve something similar on the flute. And then the other thing is, rhythmically, that's some of the most complex and sophisticated music ever created. This is a musical tradition that's probably thousands of years old, you know, and it's just been carried along, and innovations occur. There are a lot of aspects about Pygmy culture that I really found fascinating also, and it had a play into even the way that I set up my groups.

Oh, really?

Well one of the things that you'll find in later years in particular, if you listen to the *Suite for Freda Kahlo* for example, a number of things that I've done are a bit less solo-oriented than they are group-oriented--a group improvisation. That's one thing that I sort of wanted to change. I mean a lot of my earlier things were more solo-geared and driven, mainly because of the influence of Ellington. But also the Pygmies being nomadic, they have to really depend upon one another, and there's a certain strength in their numbers together. And they said when crimes are committed, which are rare, the punishment oftentimes involves the person moving out of their communal society and living alone, some distance from them. And that this is so unbearable to them that the desire to commit a crime against the community is diminished by that feeling, you know. And so, people can solo, but I'm really interested in the group concept a lot more instead of just being somebody in front of a group. That's much more appealing to me, and I think that's reflected in the recordings from really the early '90s on.

On the other hand, there are the solo flute recordings.

The solo flute recordings started in the '70s. I did some solo recordings in '77 that ended up being on an album called *Flutes* on Circle Music, a German label. And Sam Rivers was on it. He is somebody else I forgot to talk about--another great musician and somebody that influenced me, a real explorer, a person with a fascinating combination of pitches, you know his pitch selection, and the rhythmical choices are really interesting to me. So, *Flutes* came out in '78. Then I did a solo album in 1979 called *From Inside.* And then in '81 I recorded *Axum* which ended up on the ECM label and came out in '82. Then I think it was like '84 I did *Echo Canyon* for Celestial Harmonies, and in '87 I did *In Venice.*

And that stream runs alongside the group playing.

Yes. It's a very personal side. Musicians didn't always understand some of the recordings. They said, "What are you doing trying to make, new age music?" But it wasn't new age music.

No. Keith Jarrett referred to New Age music as lobotomy music, which certainly can't be applied to those recordings. But there's also a flute quartet recording, **Flutistry.**

Right. We did a recording called *Flute Force Four,* with Lloyd McNeal, Henry Threadgill, Frank Wess and myself, and boy, talk about a fun band. We had so much fun, and we played music by each of the four of us, and we played some clubs and a couple of concerts.

No rhythm section? Just the four flutes?

Just the four flutes.

There was another quartet recording with a different lineup.

That was with Henry Threadgill, Pedro Eustache, and Melessio Magdeluo, who is a wonderful flutist from the Bay Area, San Francisco, and he plays saxes and flutes, a really wonderful player. And what happened is Lloyd McNeal couldn't make the recording, so Malessio subbed for him. We did that in 1990.

So this group approach to improvisation is still your focus?

It's more where my heart is, though I tell you, I've really been thinking that this year I might, since it's been so long, do another solo flute CD. The last thing I did solo flute was when I did the classical CD *Sound of Many Waters.* It has chamber music on it and some solo flute pieces that I think are, I feel some of the best things I've ever recorded.

Oh good--but is it jazz? (Laughs)

Well, the piece *Mahalia Jackson,* has some elements of gospel and jazz. But with at least two things that I did for the New World CD I kept thinking about this quote of Franz Liszt's where he said he wanted to hurl the spear as far as he could into the future. And this was the way I was feeling about the recordings because they were based on Revelations and the Bible.

So we're not likely to hear a CD of you with piano, bass drums, playing standards anytime soon?

No. Blue Note ended up paying me x amount of dollars to not make another record because I refused to do an album of standards.

You did **African Flower** ***with them and what else?***

Romance and Revolution. But then they paid me five figures to not record the next CD because I refused to record standards. And my thing about standards--oh boy, here we go. A lot of those songs were forced on the people in the early days because the record companies owned the publishing rights and they wanted to turn around and pay themselves back. And I think, if you don't want to do something that you've written yourself, there have been so many great composers in the jazz tradition to where one shouldn't even have to touch Tin Pan Alley. But Tin Pan Alley being stuffed down the throats of... I think it stifled the development of the music, particularly from the perspective of composers and improvisation. You know, I think it's been a real detriment to the music rather than something that's enhanced it. Even though, I mean I'd die if I had to go without Miles playing *My Funny Valentine*.

It really wasn't Tin Pan Alley though, when he played it.

Right, but I really feel that way about a lot of standards. People say, in contrast to that, "Well, you know, look what Louis Armstrong did to *Stardust*." How can you argue with that? Because to me it's one of the most beautiful things I know, in all of music. But I would rather listen to Louis Armstrong play pieces that he wrote, or something of his contemporaries, you know. For the most part, I think that the music is a lot more interesting that way.

Well I'm struck by this idea of cycles coming around. I've heard recordings by the Kronos Quartet alternating pieces they had written for them by contemporary composers and transcriptions of music from the twelfth century Notre Dame school. And they sound incredibly similar. So I wonder if some of those kinds of things are beginning to happen, because growth always occurs in two stages. One cell becomes many cells, so you have differentiation. Then many cells become one organism--reorganization, integration. In nature it all happens together, whereas in human activity there are these delays. So I am wondering if we are in this stage of exploration and expansion, or of re-integration.

Really, most people say we're at reorganization, but I say we're at expansion. And for me when I think about picking up my instrument I'm thinking first and foremost about my dedication and faith to the Lord, and I'm thinking about the connection of all of nature. Not just the nature that exists on this planet, but I'm thinking, sometimes, solar systems. I'm thinking of a lot different aspects of the galaxy that this little mind can comprehend.

But that's not expansion in the sense of fragmentation. That's the wholeness value.

Well you can think about it in that way. I'm trying to think of connecting to all of those things also. At the same time, I think there are a lot of musical forms that I'm trying to deal with right now that, at least for me, are very real. And I look at the things that I've done in the last recordings and it's like I've really said, "I really don't care what you think about the way that I play the instrument, I really don't care about what you think about the musical language that I'm using. I'm not concerned. I'm just going after this vision." This thing that I have in my heart, in my spirit, in my soul, in the way that I want to glorify that. People want me to play like I was in a club environment and I don't feel that right now. I don't feel (sigh), traditional forms. That's as a flutist. Right now I want to work towards creating new forms. I just wanna toss out the safety net. I want the instrument to speak in new ways.

But you're still focused on the flute, not on... some people have felt they have to go beyond instruments to find new forms. But you are still centered on the instrument.

Well, I do composition as you know. It's a big part of what I am. But the other thing is, no matter if I'm composing, or if I'm playing the flute, or--well I can't say when I'm conducting, maybe that's the most conservative side about me--but I know that I'm composing and playing the flute I'm really interested in finding some new things.

James Newton has been finding new things for thirty years, with a focus on conducting, composing and teaching, as well as performance. Recently, however, he has taken a change of direction. After several years as conductor of the Luckman Jazz Orchestra and professor at Cal. State, Newton resigned both of these posts and left Los Angeles, moving to the outskirts of Albuquerque, New Mexico to refocus his energies in the area of flute performance. Subsequently, however, he was lured back to L.A. when he was hired as professor of ethnomusicology at U.C.L.A. There is a side to James that cannot be denied, one that cherishes, and wishes to preserve, the musical traditions upon which he has drawn so freely in his own music. At the same time, his creative vision continues to drive him forward into areas well beyond those normally associated with jazz, or even world music artists, explorations that exploit his skill as an improviser as much as his ongoing engagement with composition. It is no accident that the following statement from the liner notes to his 2000 recording *As The Sound of Many Waters*, (written by Stefan Zenni, translated by Pete Kercher) appear prominently on James website:

> As in the seventeenth century, perhaps the composer and the improviser of the twenty-first century will coincide in the same person, now with a more complete awareness of his or her role in a global culture. If all our diverse history and memory are welcomed to live in such a present, the horizon of peaceful co-existence between people becomes possible. This generosity of vision on the path to a world music is Newton's way.

When I spoke with James recently it was summer break and he was headed back to New Mexico to focus on his flute for a while. At the same time he had recently been to Italy for a performance of his new Latin Mass. He will probably find himself balancing these interests for a long time. The breadth of his work can only compliment its depth. But even if James Newton is far more than just a jazz musician, the results of his work in every area can only be an enormous gain for the flute in jazz.

246

Jamie Baum

"Baum demonstrates again and again (that) the jazz flute can be powerfully expressive in the right hands."

The Washington Post

As we have seen, more and more jazz flutists are benefitting from a classical training. But that background is not a single mold turning out identical artists. It may be for instrumentalists who are training to interpret classical literature, either as soloists or orchestral players. But jazz is different; jazz artists cannot simply be instrumentalists, they have to be involved with composition, if not written then in the form of improvisation. Several of the artists we have examined, beginning with Hubert Laws and continuing with Holly Hofmann, Ali Ryerson and others, have taken advantage of the conservatory to gain complete control of the flute in order to apply its resources to the creation of classic bebop. Others, such as James Newton, have looked more to the late twentieth century for contemporary compositional and instrumental resources. Both approaches, in their different ways, have advanced the flute in jazz.

Jamie Baum has taken something from each of these approaches to forge her own path, both as a flutist and as a composer. Originally from Connecticut, Baum's interest in music began at an early age, inspired by her mother who was a great music lover. Jamie began on piano, later switching to flute, and went on to attend the New England Conservatory, an institution that is no stranger to jazz, numbering pianist Cecil Taylor among its graduates. Jamie initially entered the "Third Stream" program which had been started at the Conservatory by Gunther Schuller, as a marriage between jazz and western European art music. Later she moved to the jazz program, and eventually graduated with a B.M. degree in both flute and composition. She then moved to New York where she would later earn a masters degree in jazz composition from the Manhattan School of Music while she studied flute privately with Ransom Wilson, Robert Stallman, Hubert Laws, Michel Debost, and Keith Underwood, jazz improvisation with Richie Bierach, Dave Liebman, Jaki Bayrd and Charlie Banacos, and composition with Richard DeRosa, W. T. McKinnley and Ludmilla Ulehla.

During these years of study, both in Boston and in Manhattan, Jamie took full advantage of the musical opportunities that these cities have to offer, building a solid reputation as a flutist, working in a variety of genres with a diverse group of musicians including George Russell, Randy Brecker, Paul Motion, John Abercrombie, Mick Goodrick, Kenny Werner, Fred Hersch, Kenny Barron, Tom Harrell, Charles Tolliver, Dave Douglas, Billy Hart, Mickey Roker, and Harold Danko. She has also been a member of the all-female group Sharp Five--appearing on their 1999 CD *Intersect*, which also features Roberta Piket and Virginia Mayhew–and the Baum-Wessel-Harris group along with guitarist Kenny Wessel, bass guitarist Jerome Harris and Jamie's husband, drummer Jeff Hirshfield. There have also been opportunities for performances overseas, with tours of South America, South and East Asia and the Middle East under the auspices of the Kennedy Center/U.S. State Department Jazz Ambassador Touring Program,

It is as a bandleader, however, that Baum has been able to develop her abilities as a composer, alongside those of flutist. With four recordings under her own name, Jamie has had the chance to write extensively for her own ensemble. One writer has suggested that she is a flutist first and a composer second. Another has made the exact opposite suggestion. Suffice to say that both of these aspects support each other, as the majority of her writing skill has so far been devoted to creating vehicles for her flute work within a small group context. The result is music that is always engaging, and it has caught the attention of the arts establishment. She has been the recipient of three National Endowment for the Arts awards, a Meet The Composer grant, and a Massachusetts Artists Program fellowship. She was named the recipient of the 1999 International Jazz Composers Alliance/Julius Hemphill Composition Award in the Small Group category. As a flutist, Jamie has had endorsements with both the Haynes Flute Company and Altus, has appeared several times in the *Down Beat* Critics Poll for Talent Deserving Wider Recognition, and was named one of the Top Ten Jazz Flutists in the 2000 *Down Beat* Readers' Poll.

The stream of influences coming into jazz music in the '60s and '70s, and the resulting cross-currents of influences has inevitably had a profound effect on musicians learning their craft since that time. Many of these artists are creating some of the most interesting contemporary music. Jamie Baum's unique solution to the problem of creating a viable jazz style on the flute is the product of her equally unique education, the broad variety of cultures and genres she has been exposed to--when I first spoke with her she had recently returned from a tour of South Asia--and the many different projects she is involved in. I suggested that the variety of musical contexts in which Jamie works resulted in her taking a direction that is quite different from that of "straight-ahead" players such as Wess, Ryerson, or Hofmann:

What I have found is that, the flute being common to all cultures, flutists like to venture into many interesting areas. In your case, you have been involved with quite a few different things, including your writing.

I think I'm like a lot of people these days in that I am involved in a lot of projects. I do my own thing with my own compositions, but then I also enjoy straight ahead music--like the group I toured India with--we were doing Louis Armstrong tunes, Monk tunes, things like that.

Well, that repertoire will be all new to people in India. I was teaching courses in Western music history at Bombay University, but they enjoyed calling it ethnomusicology. Had you been exposed to Indian music before you went there?

Yes, I had been exposed to a lot of different kinds of music through the people I work with. For example, Jerome Harris has worked with Samir Chaterjee, and with Ned Rothenberg. Kenny Wessel is in a group with Badal Roy. So I've heard a lot of things and I've worked in different contexts.

This puts you in a different category from straight-ahead players such as Ali Ryerson, Holly Hofmann, etc.

Well this is the *Down Beat* guide talking. And this is a real frustration for me. When I send my music to a straight-ahead label they say it is too "out" but when I send it to a more "out" label they hear too much melody and they say it is too straight-ahead. In a world music context it is too much like jazz... I do have a straight-ahead background. And I do play in situations like that. But, even though I have great respect for the tradition I don't like to limit myself to that.

A lot of your stuff is more abstract...

Yes, but there is the *Sharp Five* record, the quartet I toured with, etc. I would call the way I play a more "modern jazz" style.

Tell me more about your background.

I actually started playing piano very young--about three. My mom had gone to Juilliard Prep and wanted to go on to Juilliard. But, in those days...she got married and that was that. She was going for piano and trombone, and she also sang.

Did she work professionally?

No. She gave lessons, but no. In those days, unless you were really single-minded, or you were a child prodigy and you were really encouraged as a woman, it took a really unique person to make it as a performer--it was not the norm.

Even in classical music?

Well if you looked at orchestras in the 40s and 50s there were not many women. There were just a few exceptions. But, in any case, I started playing piano. My parents were really into art and music so I was very fortunate that they took me to hear lots of music. And when I was really young... my mother used to love to play big band records, like Frank Sinatra, Count Basie...

She was your first teacher?

Just by being around it, and getting to see Louis, Duke, Ella etc.

What literature did you like on piano?

Well I wasn't that serious about it, although I used to improvise when no one was around. I had no idea what I was doing. But when I was about 11 or 12 I decided I wanted to learn jazz piano. I'm not sure I knew what that meant at the time, but there was a gentleman named John Mehegan who was one of the first jazz educators; he was one of the first people to write an actual jazz book. My mother took me to have lessons with him. His whole theory was based on chord symbols--numbers not letters. I learned so much by ear--I didn't read well, or understand any theory, so it didn't work out. Then later in high school I took up flute and saxophone. I was into some jazz and blues--Edgar Winter--my elder brother had some Ellington and Miles and Coltrane records. It was still just fun--not so serious.

But still absorbing a lot by osmosis?

Right, but then my parents said I had to do one or the other. They were renting these instruments. And they really pushed me towards the flute--although I am pretty strong willed. But I also liked classical music and I didn't feel there was much repertoire for saxophone. Then, when I went to the New England Conservatory, I got in there as a Third Stream major.

Gunther Schuller's program?

Yes, and it suited me perfectly at the time because I liked classical music and I didn't want to limit myself to jazz. Actually, I started getting serious so late that, once I knew I wanted to go into music, I knew I wasn't good enough to get into anywhere good. So I took a year and a half in France where there were really good flute teachers. I took some lessons from Michel Debost--he was first chair with Orchestre de Paris at that time, but he was very busy so he hooked me up with the second chair, Georges Alirol, a younger guy who had more time. And I took some classes at the music school there.

So this helped you to get the sound quality that you have on flute?

Yes.

Many early jazz flutists were great jazz players but did not have a complete technical foundation as flutists. So it does help to have this kind of training doesn't it?

I think so. When I was starting to play my role model was probably Hubert Laws, because even though I really dug Eric Dolphy and Roland Kirk and Frank Wess and James Moody, Hubert really had that sound. In those days it was funny to me because there was an acceptable sound--if people heard a jazz flute and it was kind of raspy and wispy and breathy it was actually kind of cool you know. It was the desirable jazzy sound, whereas you would never find a sax player who would go out and play that way. But I think there are a lot of doublers now who really have a great sound. I think what it comes down to is the investment of time. You can get to the point where you can really understand what it takes to do it, but it's the time you spend with the instrument in terms of developing your own voice in order to create something.

Would you agree that making the flute work for jazz is largely a matter of articulation?
I would agree with that.

What kind of opportunites did you see for a jazz flute player at that time?
It's funny because... well, at the time that I really became serious about it, things were very different in the jazz scene.

When was this? You graduated in the mid eighties?
Right. But also, the first year I was at New England, I came to Manhattan and I had some lessons from Hubert Laws. He was really the only one who wasn't doubling at the time and he was working all the time, making all these records, for CTI for example, and film scores and jingles. And there were so many clubs--it was such a vibrant scene here. And I was totally naive anyway--I grew up in the suburbs, and I didn't know anyone who was into jazz there, not like Ali [Ryerson] for example whose dad was a musician. And also I went to the New England Conservatory. Had I decided to go to Berkeley I am sure they would not have let me only major in flute, I am sure they would have made me double. They would have said you can't make a living playing only jazz flute.

And it was hard enough for a woman in those days anyway.
Oh yes, I was the only woman in the jazz department, at first. A couple more women came in the following year. So I started out in Third Stream but after a year and a half I switched to the jazz department.

Did that take you out of Gunther Schuller's area of influence?
He left after my first year so he was no longer involved, except, of course, that he created the program.

What was Third Stream like?
In print it was an incredible idea, and really could be a wonderful program as say a masters, or other post-graduate program. But the problem is that the concept of Third Stream is of taking two or more kinds of music and synthesizing them to create your own voice. So if you were really into Coltrane and really into Greek music you would study them and somehow make something out of them both.

I did not realize that. I thought it meant jazz and classical... whatever term we use.
Well it was originally that but it became more. It was around Ran Blake at the time. So it was a really cool concept because...well I mentioned Paris because compared to here, at that time, there were so many immigrants there, from Africa and other places. There was African music, Brazilian music, and Arabic--from Tunisia and Morocco... I was so turned on to many different musics and different people. So this just sort of piqued my interest. I had a classical background and I was not good enough in jazz to get into a jazz department, but then this program, Third Stream, sounded right up my alley. So I got in. But after a year I realized that before you can develop your own style you have to have the basics.

Get grounded in something.
Yes. You have to master your craft. Like with Indian music, as you were saying, you can't go there for six months and claim to be an expert. You have to live that music.

It's a little bit circular though isn't it, when you are building your own voice. You have to decide which techniques you want to master in order to see which direction you want to pursue. But I imagine, from what you are saying, that this is too much for an undergraduate program.

Yes - it really would be better as an advanced program because what I saw from the other students... well I barely knew how to play a blues, or to read changes, so how am I going to be synthesizing Coltrane and Stravinsky?

Does the program still exist?

No. It was merged with the jazz department.

You know I dealt with that when I was advising on curricula. One school was experimenting with a world music program, but then they suddenly got cold feet and reverted to the old conservative approach. But how many people can find work with that kind of training? I told them they needed to train all-round musicians. I still believe that improvisation has a place in training any all-round musician, classical or whatever.

Oh, I totally agree.

Paper music is all well and good, but the jazz players know much more about theory than the pure paper-music people.

Oh, yes. I agree. I teach a workshop on The Fear-Free Approach to Improvisation for classical musicians. I started teaching this about ten years ago and I teach a lot of classical flute players. And it's mind blowing to me that, whether they pursue jazz or not, they always come back to me and tell me how much it helps their classical playing.

Of course! And how much theory do those people know?

Oh, they don't know anything. It's really unbelievable. It's my pet peeve.

And mine. It's like pulling teeth to get them into history classes. They just want to go and practice. In a way that's fine. But they lose so much, not just for their own playing but in preserving theory. We have lost so much since ancient times, in India and Europe.

The other thing, too, that I realized, is that music, which is an aural thing, is taught visually.

That's right. My Ph.D. final exams were all totally from notation, nothing aural at all. There's something very back-to-front about that.

Absolutely!

So you are not in any category. You are an American, improvising musician with a background in classical music, with so many different forms that feed into your sensibilities and come out through your solos and your compositions.

But I should say that I really am a jazz musician. Once I switched into the jazz program, then I went through probably a ten-year period of complete myopathy...what's the word?

Total focus.

Right. I didn't want to listen to anything but jazz.

Okay. But what is jazz? I have to say what it is at some point!

I don't know. But for me it was a question of getting rooted for a few years. I studied with various people. I studied with Jaki Byard for a while. He was one of my teachers at New England.

He was a broad individual.

Yes, very. And then I studied with a guru called Charlie Benacos. People were on a waiting list for two years to study with him--people who went through Boston.

He was a theory teacher?

Improvisation, and piano. And particularly for me at that time, being one of an extreme minority, being a woman...it was difficult at that time, because a lot of what you learn comes from hanging out with guys, you know, doing sessions, living in the same house, maybe. So while I may have preferred to have learned more organically, you know, by hanging with the cats and playing all night and so on, that wasn't really available for me. Maybe I wasn't that kind of person or something. But whatever, I had to turn more toward teachers at that point, like Jaki Byard and Charlie Benacos. I learned Coltrane solos, Rollins solos, Miles Davis, Lee Morgan, Freddie Hubbard. You name it.

And all on flute?

Yes.

Well, just to throw a wrench in the works, how do you adapt these forms to the flute? Some people have told me that it doesn't work to put saxophone phrasing through a flute. Although Herbie Mann did say he listened to trumpet players when he was developing his style.

Well here's my take on that. I think you can find melodic ideas from anywhere--and the intent of the ideas. I think that being able to achieve the same intent and articulation is where it gets different. In certain ways, I think that flute articulation is more closely related to the trumpet. So in that way I agree and I don't really know why they always put flute and saxophone together as a double. I always found that, when I tried to play along with a solo, or learn it, that I could really match more with Freddie Hubbard than with Sonny Rollins in terms of articulation.

Because the tongue is hitting the teeth rather than a mouthpiece inside the mouth.

Perhaps, but I think the articulation is closer. Not to mention the register. And the sound is closer as well. That's not to say, that if I really dig a phrase, that Rollins does a certain phrase, like on *Sunnymoon for Two*--some bluesy phrase--that I'm not going to try to learn that.

Of course, eventually this is all unconscious. You absorb all this stuff then it comes out when you play. Like, you can find bits of Stravinsky and Shostakovitch in Paul Desmond's playing. Then if you listen to Indian music, that influences your line, inflections and so forth.

Maybe for the next couple of concerts. It's an interesting thing, the flute. I look around and I hear Ali and Holly and James Newton and I hear some other people, and everybody has a different take on it. You hear some things and you say, "I really like that." But I approach it in a different way. It's something I have been struggling with this whole time, to find a way to make the instrument swing, yet to get different colors out of it, and different articulations. It's really hard to do. On the one hand, you learn to get really good technique on the instrument from studying classical music, but the thing about classical flute playing is uniformity of sound, and you have to approach the instrument that way to get a great sound. You spend a lot of time getting a beautiful sound through all the different registers, and articulation and everything. And to be able to have flexibility and articulation that's not stiff. And to have certain notes projected and others ghosted, and different things going on, and then at really fast tempo with jazz articulation, is really hard to do. I've been trying to get it to not sound flutey for 20 years!

Okay! So, what about Roland Kirk and that "dirty" flute sound?

Are you kidding? I love that. I love Roland Kirk. I'm not saying that I want to have this classical sound because I dig Roland Kirk--*Rip Rag And Panic*. I transcribed one of the tunes--a blues. And I'm just saying that for me trying to find a way to swing and to have a great sound, in a variety of articulations, and a variety of sounds, is really challenging.

I can see that. But you have another dimension with your writing. Did that just come along with everything else?

Yes, but just one thing I do want to say, because of this idea of being in a box--I spent probably more time playing and learning standards, and doing standards on gigs than any time I spent doing my own music. When my records come out, it's my music, and very modern. So I think people have the impression that my focus...Well, I've been thinking about that and, when I went to the New England Conservatory, I guess the people you fall in with in your formative years--who knows if it's the chicken or the egg in terms of that?--but at New England, being Third Stream or jazz, there was a lot of emphasis on developing your own style, finding your own voice and adding something to the music.

And that was in terms of repertoire as well as your own sound.

Yes, the complete package as a musician. The value was definitely placed on learning the roots and becoming a good jazz musician, but it was also placed on carrying the tradition forward. They felt that people like Coltrane, or Monk or Bird they didn't spend all their life perfecting what came before them. They did to some extent, but they devoted themselves to developing their own thing and moving the music forward. So that was the emphasis there. So everyone I knew who came out of there like Marty Ehrlich and Fred Hersch, at the same time as they worked on their craft they were working on writing their own music.

Fred Hersch has made some great recordings based on French and Russian Romantic music. Have you ever done any of that kind of thing?

No. Not really. But, actually, a lot of the gigs I do are straight-ahead jazz gigs. So I kind of had this weird feeling, you know... recordings, when I was coming up, were such a big thing, that to just do a record of standards didn't seem to be worth it. I felt that if I was going to do a record, I needed to put something out that had something...

... kind of serious?

Well, the older cats play standards better than I ever could. So I'm not making a judgement about anything--this was where I came from.

Are you getting more opportunities to record now?

I am, but it is also a funny time in the business for recording. Jazz is having a rough time.

At one time, when I was booking my quartet in Washington, the one thing club owners would say is "one thing we don't want is straight-ahead."But maybe when you have more chances to do recordings you might go in and be loose and have some fun with some standards?

I've been thinking about that.

James Newton told me he never wanted to play a standard ever again and that the need to play standards is the major inhibition on new players' creative development. Blue Note paid him money not to make a third album because he wouldn't do standards.

Well look at Blue Note. They just signed Norah Jones. Nothing against her, but they are not too interested in creative music these days.

So, what else feeds into your situation? What about your writing? How did that come into the picture?

I actually got my masters in jazz composition from the Manhattan School of Music. And my undergrad degree was double--flute and jazz composition.

So are you thinking about the flute, the best context for it, when you are writing?

No.

It's just another voice?

Hmmm. Well, from very early on I was always thinking about writing along with playing. It never seemed separate to me. I'm sure what I wrote then I wouldn't want to play for anyone now, but it just always seemed--I would hear melodies in my head and just write something. Writing, in a certain way, almost came more easily to me than playing. I always felt that was just another part of my expression. So I used to write tunes. Then when I got more into it there were certain things--the contexts I heard the flute in weren't too interesting. When I was trying to be serious about the flute, people were not taking the flute seriously.

So people were not writing things that worked for the flute?

I think what happened was that flute was either being used as a double, for a change of color for people who were using it, for a bossa nova or some kind of tune, as a double in big bands.

There were some people who were exploring different sonorities in big band charts, Gil Evans, Henry Mancini. But in terms of a quintet or sextet...

Right. I was coming from a point of view where as a flute player, I wanted to be taken seriously enough to lead a whole gig, not to be hired to play flute on a couple of tunes. And a lot of the flute stuff that I heard was either in a Latin context, or a ballad, or commercial fluff. I really wanted to find a way to have it be the meat. Not the icing.

There are a few recordings where the flute is an integral part of the front line. I'm thinking of Hubert Laws with Ron Carter or McCoy Tyner. But there aren't many.

The septet has flute, trumpet, alto [saxophone doubling] bass clarinet. I wanted to write things that made the flute sound like it needed to be there, and had the same weight and influence as the other instruments.

Now, with flute and saxophone, like in **Sharp** **Five**, *does the flute become a surrogate trumpet when you are writing for it?*

Well, you could look at it that way. But, it's not something I put together. It's a co-operative group. Everyone contributes to the writing.

I see. But for the septet?

Well my quintet came first, *Sight Unheard.* That's the one with Kenny Werner and Dave Douglas, That was the first group I started writing extended compositions for. And the septet came out of some writing I did while I was getting my masters. I was studying arranging and some courses in 20th century composition with Ludmilla Ulehla, who was a fantastic composer, and another guy named Nils Vigiland who was teaching a course on Stravinsky, Bartok, Debussy. So one of the pieces that I got very excited about, one summer while I was taking some theory to try and prepare myself to go to New England, was the *Rite of Spring.* This totally blew my mind. And when I went back to it again later, when I was studying composition, at Manhattan, it totally blew my mind again. And you know, when you are playing standards in a club, you play the head for like three minutes, then you take twenty choruses, and then the next person and the next person, and then you come back and play the head for two seconds. I just felt like I wanted to find some way to have more material to relate to and to use, to give more interest.

One thing that impressed me in that regard was Booker Little's writing, with little interludes and other things. Or some of Wayne Shorter's things with alternating modal and chordal passages that give you more to work with during a solo. Do you write backgrounds for soloists, for example?

Yes. I try to expand things, different settings for a soloist, not only to make it interesting for the listener but to grow as a musician.

People don't realize how important it is for an improviser what is going on around him or her. Backgrounds--the other players...

Sure. That's absolutely true.

Have you ever done any free playing?

Yes. I am involved with a group--I went to Germany in September for the *Documenta* Festival in Kassel, and Ursel Schlicht put a group together, Ursel on piano, myself on flute and alto flute, a cellist, an Indian tabla player who also played some drums, and another person we joined over there who plays an oud-type instrument from Afghanistan [probably a *rubab*]. And then there was Hakim Ludin who plays a lot of percussion, and a vocalist from Germany. They brought us there for ten days and we played every night. And half the performances were compositions that we each contributed and rehearsed in the afternoons, and the rest of the performances were free. We did trios, duos--sometimes the whole group.

There's a lot that goes into free playing, although it can create a box of its own, then it's not free any more.

I agree.

So are you doing all your writing for your own group or do you write some things for other people?

I have not but I would like to. I've written some classical type pieces, for flute and piano, more contemporary things. I've given them to other flute players.

So, generally, where do you go from here?

Well I made a CD in '96, *Sight Unheard*, and it got great reviews. But I had outstanding credits so I went back to finish my masters. Which was great, but it interrupted my playing career. Now, since 1999, I have been trying to get back into that. The last few years have been great. I have been doing things I dreamed of doing, like recording, touring to places like India--giving some performances in Delhi and Kathmandu--and having the opportunity to be a sideperson, because there are not many opportunities for a flute player. I have been doing more and more of that because you learn a lot that you don't when you are doing your own thing, when you pick the people and the tunes and the tempos and everything. But you also learn a lot when somebody says we are doing this tune at this tempo--you get put on the spot in a lot of different situations.

How does that work? Do you find people have a gig and think they need a flute player? Or are they thinking of you as a person more than the instrument.

Well, thinking of the gigs I have been hired to do, I think that it's a combination.

What kind of ensembles are we talking about?

Well, I did a couple of gigs with two different groups--one quite modern, the other more standards, a quartet with guitar bass and drums, and this German woman doing the more free things, and some things with a woman composer from Argentina, a 14 piece group with all kinds of different instruments, including some improvisation in it. So it's really been the whole realm. But we are coming full circle. I love playing jazz and I really think of my self as a jazz musician, but I totally get stimulated by playing other kinds of music and having interesting playing experiences. Then I make some money playing chamber music. So I love playing my own music and incorporating things that interest me.

Would you play in a salsa band if you got a call?

I played in a Latin group for a year! And a Brazilian group. I love Brazilian music. There's one part of me that's still learning to play jazz--it's such a challenging music to me. I will spend a lot of time trying to learn something modern, like an Ornette tune, or Coltrane, or go back and learn a Sonny Rollins solo. There are so many things that I want to learn to become a better jazz musician. I'm hoping that at some point I can go study Indian music, because that just totally knocks me out. When I was in India, when I got a chance to play a concert with V.M. Bhatt [North Indian classical performer who plays an adapted guitar], I was just totally blown away. I want to do it all!

But the flute gives you access to all these things more than the piano or the trumpet or something--it is so ubiquitous.

That's right!

Which is kind of the theme of this book. Thank you so much!

Not long after this conversation, I caught Jamie playing in another context, with the New York Jazz Flute Quartet, with Andrea Brachfield and two other flutists, at the memorial evening for Herbie Mann at the Blue Note in New York. Later, she brought a quintet into *Blues Alley* in Washington DC to perform some of the material from *Moving Forward, Standing Still*. And then I caught Jamie's septet in New York presenting the premier of *Ives Suite: The Time Traveller*, a work commissioned through Chamber Music America and the Doris Duke Foundation, and a quartet into DC's *Twins Jazz*, performing some standards mixed in with Jamie's compositions. More recently I was fortunate to work with her in the National Flute Association's Jazz Flute Big Band under the direction of Ali Ryerson.

Time will tell if Jamie will, like James Newton, feel pulled more and more into composition, but it is clear that she is currently continuing to seek out, or create, challenging contexts that bring out different dimensions in her own playing, and for the flute itself. It is perhaps because she is a flutist that her background has developed in such a unique way. And as she grows and develops in this effort, she is exploiting every dimension of this background, even as she expands it, thus making a major contribution to the development of the flute in jazz.

Ali Ryerson

"...easily the most important jazz flutist to have emerged thus far this decade."

The San Francisco Express, 1986

Those who play jazz on the flute exclusively are an elite group; several of them were on hand at an impromptu, mini jazz flute convention in New York City when *Flutology* came to Birdland. Two of them, Ali Ryerson and Holly Hofmann, were on stage alongside Frank Wess. Several others were in the audience. All of them have finally put paid to the idea of the flute as a "marginal jazz instrument."

Ali Ryerson is a prime example of what can be accomplished musically by combining a thorough classically-based training with a profound jazz sensibility. Having integrated these two ingredients of fine jazz flute performance, Ryerson has emerged as a leading voice on her instrument while maturing as an artist and clinician. Born into a musical family--her father, Art Ryerson, was a widely sought-after guitarist of the Big Band era and New York studio scene from the 1940s to the 1970s--her home was full of music as she was growing up. "The advantage she had growing up," reports her brother, "is that a lot of people learn jazz by playing along with records. She got to absorb it right there." All three of her brothers are, in fact, musicians. Indeed, Ali got an early start as a professional in their jazz-rock band while she was still in college--another great advantage for a developing musician, especially a jazz musician. "The essential element in jazz is using your ears," says Ryerson. "You're put in the middle with other musicians and you learn to play--it's the way you develop the true jazz feeling." Since then she has worked extensively in both jazz and classical contexts, working with such artists as Dr. Billy Taylor, Kenny Barron, Stephane Grappelli, Red Rodney, Laurindo Almeida, Art Farmer, Maxine Sullivan, Roy Haynes, Julius Baker, and (as principal flutist with the Monterey Bay Symphony) Luciano Pavarotti. And she has produced some of the finest jazz flute recordings of the past 20 years, although she remains less well-known than she deserves to be. In addition, as jazz chair for the National Flute Association, she has been very active in bringing awareness of jazz to NFA members, which includes conceiving and developing the Jazz Flute Big Band--the ultimate jazz flute choir, with rhythm section-- that performs alternate years at the association's annual convention.

As a clinician Ryerson has a lot to say about how to approach the instrument, as I have discovered as her student for the last three years and, in particular, during our interview for this book:

We were talking a little bit about your journey as a jazz flute player, and you mentioned that, to some extent, that's an odd thing to be. And I must mention there's a great quote I found that's going right at the beginning of the first chapter, some CD reviewer from England or something, which refers to the flute as "a marginal jazz instrument at best." Now, why in the world would that be? Why would the flute, which is an absolutely ubiquitous instrument in every single kind of music in every culture throughout history, not work in jazz?

Well, you'd have to look at the jazz idiom historically to understand why a comment like that is made. It's unfortunate that it's still being made today. With the big bands of the 30's and 40's you could not hear a solo flute because of the amplification capabilities. Anytime there was a full rhythm section, volume was a problem. The flute is a much softer instrument than the trumpet, trombone or saxophone, so without amplification it was not used often as a jazz instrument.

But the environment that I grew up in made it very natural for me to become a jazz flute player. I studied classical music, but I grew up in a jazz family. My father was Art Ryerson, a jazz guitarist who played with Paul Whiteman and Raymond Scott. He's on so many recordings, including the Charlie Parker with strings album. He was a part of the music scene in New York. While I was growing up many great musicians would come to the house and play, guitarists Barry Galbraith, George Barnes, Allen Hanlon and pianist Lou Stein. We had a bass sitting around so occasionally Milt Hinton would come by

You didn't think to take up guitar?

I played some guitar when I was a kid, very little. Actually I learned piano; I started piano when I was five, and I was a pretty good classical player. I have three older brothers and every one is a musician, everyone of us studied classical music and had a simultaneous education in jazz. Growing up, the albums my brothers played were by Bill Evans, Miles Davis, Chet Baker, Art Farmer. As I grew up, that's what I heard. I remember improvising on the flute--improvising came naturally to me. I would practice my *Anderson Etudes* on flute, and during study hall in school I would find a practice room and just improvise with my friend who played piano, sometimes just in duo, or with a drummer.

Did you ever embellish those études with some improvisation?

No. It's two different things to me. I've arranged classical pieces. I have a beautiful jazz arrangement of [Claude Debussy's] *Syrinx* and the Pachalbel *Canon* [in D]. I did have difficulty when I was playing in the school band not to add things, my own embellishments, because I'd get bored very easily.

Where did the flute first come in?

I was eight. My brothers and I all started on the piano, and then we all chose a second instrument. I first wanted to play the trumpet because two of my brothers played trumpet But my mother wouldn't let me because she... (laughing) wanted me to "save my lips for something else."

I'm not going to ask what that was! So it was about teeth, or embouchure issues?

Yes, it was. Trumpet players can get a red embouchure mark. She just didn't want that for me. My mother--bless that woman, bless her soul--was nearly forty two years old when I was born, so there was a big generational difference. To her, the trumpet was not an instrument for an eight year old girl. So that was that. Anyway, I chose the flute. I don't remember the day that I chose the flute, it's not etched in my memory or anything, but I remember that I just took to it right away. I practiced every day.

This is so essential to my story--I grew up in a household where practicing was simply what we did... I never felt it was being forced on us. We were musicians, and it was a priority in our lives. There was a set time: at five o'clock I sat down at the piano and I practiced, and the flute after that. When I hear kids today say, "I have so much homework, and I have sports, and I have this and I have that... " Well I had those things too.

But they watch 87 hours of TV a week or something, too...

Right! We were allowed to watch maybe a half hour, an hour on weekends, and that was it. It was a totally different thing. Music was a priority. I grew up practicing. I went to two conservatories-- one in Mount Kisco, New York, and the Westchester Conservatory--while I was attending junior high and high school. And also, while in high school, I studied privately with Harold Bennett, then principal flutist with the Metropolitan Opera Orchestra.

I think I was fifteen when I got my first paying gig, and it was because my brothers had gigs, and they would occasionally include me. My brother Rich, a great player, was very supportive and kind and gentle. In a nutshell, the way he taught me was, "Listen and learn the head." I learned the heads of all these tunes on the stand. I learned how to do it very quickly and easily. I would not take the first solo. I would listen and get the tune, listen for the changes in whatever way I was doing it at fifteen or sixteen years old, and then play. Rich would say "Ali, play when you feel comfortable." Of course I played on every tune, and so it was an education on the stand, using my ears.

When I was seventeen, I graduated from Byram Hills High School in Armonk, NY and attended Western Connecticut State College (now Western Connecticut State Univ.), majored in music, and was already playing some gigs. My brothers Art and Rich and I, put together a sextet and we were working five or six nights a week when I was in school, so I eventually quit school. Working until two in the morning and trying to make an eight o'clock class doesn't work.

No, I can vouch for that! What kind of music were you playing?

This was a jazz-rock band. It was a great band. Art's a piano player--he's also a trombone player--but he was the piano player/singer in the band, and Rich was playing trumpet then. This was in '71. And we had been doing it for maybe a year when our steady gig ended. Then the singer/impressionist Billy Fellows hired me--this was in 1973. He had a show band which eventually joined up with Sandler and Young, the singing team. So I went on the road for four and a half years, working six nights a week.

In that kind of band, isn't there pressure on you to double, to play some saxophone or clarinet?

No, not at all. I was a flute player and that's what I've always been hired as. I did play some keyboard and sang background vocals. I was with the band for 4 ½ years. I was traveling all over the country until 1977. We worked Vegas a lot, often with Sandler and Young. In Vegas you worked seven nights a week. Becoming a jazz flute player is not an easy thing to set out to do.

So it wasn't like--let's become a jazz flute player!

Oh yes! That was a totally conscious decision! I knew exactly what I wanted to do when I was eleven years old. The reality is that until a jazz career really takes hold, it's important to seize any opportunity to practice your craft, even if it's not specifically a jazz gig--it's still playing music. Early in my career I didn't have the luxury of taking only jazz gigs. Now I can because I'm more established. When students ask for advice on how to replicate my career I don't have an answer; I had unique opportunities. Today, who works six nights a week, five sets a night, for years? Those gigs aren't out there anymore.

I see. The opportunities for apprenticeships aren't there anymore.

Right. These gigs were great opportunities for me--not jazz gigs, although most of the players in the band were jazz players. And we always played a couple of jazz sets. The shows featured Billy's impressions of jazz singers, like Sarah Vaughan or Nat King Cole. It was all very hip material. Eventually I went back to school. I quit the road because I had eyes to become an orchestral player.

That's what I was thinking, because the first time I heard of you was when you were in the Bay Area, in the Symphony.

Yes. Well, I decided to go to the Hartt School of Music in Hartford, Connecticut, it's part of the University of Hartford. John Wummer was teaching there. He had published compilations of the flute orchestral excerpts. This seemed a good choice for a teacher if what I want to do is become an orchestral player. Previous to my quitting my road gig and going back to school, I had attended a Julius Baker master class. This changed my life; when I heard Julie play, all of a sudden, I heard my goal sound. He is my mentor on the flute.

Where was he teaching at that time?

He was teaching in Brewster, New York. I was working in Latham, New York, which is right outside of Albany. I was commuting daily, driving five hours a day for five straight days to attend his master class, then driving back to Latham to play my gig. I'm sure everyone knows who Julie Baker is?

Some of our jazz readers may not, although we already heard that Hubert Laws studied with him at Juilliard.

He was principal flute with the New York Philharmonic. I only took one private lesson with Julie, attended many of his master classes, sometimes as a performer. I was once hired to perform a Brandenburg concerto with him at the Williamsburg Festival. We became good friends over the years. His daughter even asked me to play her wedding! His playing had a profound influence on me.

For sound, technique and so forth?

He's the best flute player, period. My primary focus as a flute player, jazz or classical, is the sound. Whether you're a jazz player or a Celtic flute player, it has to do with sound.. and intonation, phrasing and musicality. Julie was the master. I learned by listening to him.

Baker did do some jazz sessions, didn't he?

Yes, he's on *Body and Soul* believe it or not. With Coleman Hawkins. He was just telling me about that. Anyway, in 1977 I began my studies at the Hartt School of Music. Sadly, the summer before I started, John Wummer was killed in a car accident. I never even met him. Fortunately, John Wion, then the principal flutist of the New York City Opera, was hired to replace Wummer. John became my teacher for my two years at Hartt. I was twenty five years old, and I practiced my tail off--I was just so focused. Returning to school was the greatest thing I could have ever done. It's not like first going to college when you're out of the house for the first time and just want to party. It was terrific. I played first chair in the school orchestra, as I'd already been in the profession for five years.

Is Hartt a conservatory?

It's a music school, part of the University of Hartford. Jackie McLean taught there. He started one of the first and earliest jazz programs in the country. [McLean's son René still teaches there.] But I was not there for jazz. I was there to become an orchestral player. I absolutely loved my school experience there. When I first started studying with Wion I had, for the previous five years, been playing into a microphone. So I had developed a technique for playing the flute amplified. John did something which was very disconcerting at the time, but I'm convinced now was the very thing that put me on the right road. I think I was a decent player pre-Hartt, but John helped me to understand about breathing, tone production, vibrato, everything from scratch. I started from scratch in a very big way, completely changing the way that I projected my airstream. For the first six months I felt like I couldn't play!

Have you read Yehudi Menuhin's autobiography? He did the exact same thing. In his case it was self-motivated. At some point in his life he suddenly felt that he had this great gift, but he really didn't know what he was doing. So he started examining every aspect of his playing, to understand it and to improve it. He called it a "circle from intuition through intellectual analysis to restored spontaneity." That must be a scary process.

Well, for example, I wasn't allowed to go to my lesson with a turtle-neck on, anything that covered my throat, because he wanted to see if I was tightening my throat or not. The whole concept of "open" playing, playing with an open channel, is essential. It is now essential to my teaching, to my playing, to my whole concept of flute playing.

This is what struck me when I first heard you play. That sound, especially down in the lower register... it's so much fuller and richer. There is always this problem, even playing with a mic, because the lower register is not just quieter, it also has this softer, broader sound. But in a jazz context, you tend to be pushed up into these higher registers in order to cut through a bit better and you don't use the whole instrument, you miss that soft, broad sound.

Right. And it's interesting you say that, because I started working a lot while I was at Hartt, while I was still in school. In the school office at the school, Grace Long fielded community calls looking for music students to hire. Grace kept me working. She was giving me gigs left and right. I had a little baroque trio, flute, violin and cello, which worked all the time. I got a gig at a local restaurant, the Signature Restaurant at the Civic Center in Hartford, and this turned into a gig that I had for over a year--five nights a week, solo flute, for two and a half hours a night. It was fantastic!

Solo flute? Literature? Improvisation?

Whatever I wanted, so I did both.

So you've played Syrinx a few hundred times!

Yes! I played a million things. I can easily pick up the flute and improvise on absolutely anything, or nothing. I had a blast. I would play Tchaikovsky--excerpts from the *Nutcracker*--and Bach sonatas and Handel sonatas and French repertoire; whatever sounded good for solo flute.

Were you getting people's attention, or was it background?

Yes and no. It was an elegant restaurant, not terribly noisy, and they actually wanted a flute player. So, it was a year of two and half hours of playing, five nights a week for me.

So you were being paid to practice essentially. The universe most definitely decided that you should be a flute player!

Yes! I also started doing some jazz gigs. I put together a quintet with my brother Rich again, and started working a lot. I was already out of school. Don Harris, the composition professor at school, came to hear me once and told me he really liked my playing. But he said "Why do you just stay in the mid-range of the flute? You've got more than three full octaves, why don't you use the full range?" I never forgot that. This just reminded me of something you were saying earlier. The upper range is another reason why I think that jazz flute is not the most popular instrument in the jazz world, because the upper register of the flute is not pleasing to the whole world.

So what I've done--you've followed my recording career--is to look for other musical formulas, where I can explore the lower register. This is one of the reasons I've gotten into alto flute. The alto flute is a great instrument for jazz, it's a softer instrument. But if it's amplified, even amplified well, any flute has difficulty competing with a tenor sax. This is the reality.

There are some groups with flute and another horn in the front line. Like Sharp Five with flute and tenor. They make it work. And Hubert has worked with trumpet and trombone in Ron Carter's group.

If you have a set group and the arrangements are tailored to that combination of instruments, that's one thing. But if you have a jam session with five horns, and you're the flute player, you're going to be the odd man out, or you're going to be playing in the upper register.

That's the only way it can carry through. Look at band parts--even for kids. The flutes are always voiced way up with the trumpets. They never exploit the low register. It's the opposite in India. The lower the sound, the more serious it's taken to be. So you find yourself using these bigger and bigger instruments.

That's interesting!

I've always been drawn to that low flute sound. There's something about it... I don't know what it is.

I find it's very sensual, and that's one of the aspects I like about the flute, to be honest. Anyway, back at Hartt, I was playing first chair with the orchestra. I won a couple of concerto competitions; I had many great opportunities to perform. I started taking some orchestral auditions, and that was a whole other world. Actually it kind of depressed me. I didn't enjoy the intense competition. I was used to the camaraderie of the jazz world.

I remember what John Cage said, "The reason I like music is that nobody wins!" I wish that were true. Would you have liked to have been an orchestral player for a block of time? And really focused on that?

Actually no, not anymore. I've done some freelance orchestral work and have performed with small chamber groups and played for a short time with the Monterey Bay Symphony as principal flute. That's when I worked with Pavarotti. But no, what I've realized is that there's such a huge difference in the freedom I have as a jazz player--freedom of expression. Many orchestral players become artistically frustrated. Jazz players can more easily shape their musical lives and stretch their musical boundaries.

It seems to me, that even if your goal is to be a jazz player, the more different kinds of music you expose yourself to, the better. They say listen to everything, but what about playing everything? Because those forms, those feelings, they will come into your improvisation.

Right, exactly.

And I think I can hear that in your work also to some extent. Not explicitly, perhaps. If you look at, say, transcriptions of Paul Desmond's solos, you can find chunks of Stravinsky and all kinds of stuff if you look for it. Not necessarily explicitly, I just mean in the forms, the shape of the phrases. All that gets more sophisticated according to what goes into your awareness and then comes out.

It also has to do with background. I had both. I had classical and jazz in my background. So, it's a natural thing for me to care about classical repertoire and to understand improvisation.

So then you spent some time in Europe. How long were you there?

On and off I lived there about three years, in Brussels.

It's a different setting. European jazz is a different genre almost.

Well, back in '85, I was freelancing in New York. I was playing at the *West End Café* and Peter Carr, a British agent, heard me and subsequently booked me for my first tour in the UK. Peter produced my first solo recording during the tour, in London. Six months later he re-booked me. The second tour was in the UK and Spain. The following year--in '86--I was booked on a tour with the drummer Oliver Jackson by agent Jordi Sunol from Barcelona, This tour included dates in Spain, France and Belgium. That's how my European connections began. I started working with some of the Belgian musicians, so I decided to move over there as there seemed to be a lot of opportunity for me. I started working with Charles Loos, a well known piano player and composer from Brussels. He has a background in classical and jazz which coincided with my background.

Do you find that to be more common amongst European musicians?

Not necessarily. Charles and I ended up recording three albums together, all his compositions. Europe opened my mind to performing original music written by my colleagues. Up to that point I was playing mostly jazz standards. While working in Europe, the importance of performing original work got into my blood. I don't think of myself as a composer. I have written some things, but my strength is playing. As a jazz player my creative needs are satisfied.

So then the task is to...

... find the right material. I began to get a handle on my musical taste, my particular voice. Working with composers like Charles Loos and Dutch pianist Diederich Wissels helped me to realize my musical direction in terms of choice of material. The lyrical side to my playing was emerging thanks to this experience. I try to avoid performing or recording a tune unless it's a tune that I really feel.

And since you got back from Europe that trend has continued?

Absolutely. I've recorded many compositions written by longtime colleagues, guitarist Joe Beck and Brazilian pianist/composer Weber Iago [formerly Weber Drummond].

So now, at some point, you started to make recordings with some really top flight American jazz players. I don't know of anything you've done that hasn't been with really excellent players. What was the first CD you put out?

The first four were recorded in Europe. While living abroad, I had been touring periodically with Stephane Grappelli. In the early '90s I played Carnegie Hall with Stephane and Bucky Pizzarelli. The legendary producer Bob Thiele was at the rehearsal. He had a new record label, *Red Baron.* He was at the rehearsal to ask Grappelli to record for him. It didn't work with Stephane's schedule. While talking with Stephane, he asked, "By the way, who's the flute player?" Bob had contracted many New York recording dates, and had often hired my father. He phoned my father that night to locate me. When we finally spoke, he signed me to his new label. That was my first recording contract in this country. For the first album Bob had complete control.

So he selected the musicians?

He selected them for *Blue Flute*: Kenny Baron, Roy Haynes, Red Rodney and Santi DiBriano. For the second recording date, *I'll Be Back*, I chose the musicians.

But on the first one he just told you who you would be recording with?

Well, we talked about it. He loved those guys and he thought they'd be great with me. I was thrilled. I'm so glad I had the chance to play with Red. Kenny is a dream. So is Roy Haynes. When we did the second CD, Thiele asked me who I wanted on the date. I asked for Kenny again, but this time a rhythm section I had worked with. Thanks to these recordings, I finally started getting reviewed in *Down Beat*.

My next label was Concord, and that connection was thanks to Ken Peplowski, the clarinet/sax player, who had been on Concord for years. Ken had mentioned me to Carl Jefferson, the head of Concord. I got a call one Sunday morning.. "Hello, this is Carl Jefferson." At first I thought Ken was playing a trick on me. What record label is going call you on a Sunday morning? It's got to be a joke! Anyway, Jefferson and I had a meeting and I signed a contract for three albums. I was totally in charge-- whatever I wanted to do. So the first and the second were straight ahead quartet albums. First I called Kenny Werner, one of my favorite piano players.

This is Portraits in Silver. *And the other one was?*

In Her Own Sweet Way, which I recorded with my working band: Harold Danko, Jeff Fuller and Terry Clarke. The third CD was a bigger project, a collaboration with two Brazilian musicians I had worked with in California. We worked together for a ten month period before going into the studio. Most of my recording dates take two days. The preparation for the Brazil album was closer to a year.

As we said earlier, there are a lot of flute players who get drawn into these different non-Western cultures, to exploit their instrument in that setting, to get away from the problems in playing straight-ahead jazz. To a large extent you've solved that problem. But you still felt drawn to the Brazilian thing because the flute plays so beautifully in that setting.

To me, it's not like being drawn to another genre. It's certainly a different rhythmic world, but yet so closely allied with jazz.

I see your point. Now tell me about your work with Joe Beck.

The way that happened, Joe was working at a local Connecticut club with a friend of mine, pianist Pete Levin. I sat in. Joe called me the next morning and said "We should be working together."At that time I had a quintet tour booked in Florida. Pianist Harold Danko was booked, but had to cancel at the last minute. I called Joe to sub for Harold. The first concert was a duo concert. We hadn't played in duo before. When I first played my alto flute, it all just clicked. This prompted Joe to have his alto guitar built, an instrument he had conceived of years before. It's tuned down a fifth, with the middle two strings displaced up an octave and the bottom two strings from a Fender bass. It enables closer, pianistic voicings, along with a distinct bass line. The alto flute with the alto guitar is a great match. At the time, Joe owned a recording studio in New York City. We went in daily, arranged and recorded for months, and created the duo. [Note: Joe Beck passed away in 2008.]

So, today, if someone were to call you and say, "Okay, I've got a gig for you. Money's no object, bring who you want," would you still bring the duo, or would you prefer a full rhythm section?

Oh, I don't know. I now work with several groups. *Flutology* is a big thing in my musical life now.

Tell me about Flutology.

Sure. Holly Hofmann and I have been friends for a number of years and had been toying with the idea of doing something together. We booked a couple of things with a double duo, with Joe Beck and Holly's duo partner, pianist Bill Cunliffe. Then, in the spring of 2002, she was working with Ray Brown at Birdland in New York, and she invited me to come down and bring my flutes to sit in. After we played together, Ray told Holly, "You guys should do something together." Frank Wess was in that night. On the break, we went to say hello. We talked about doing something together, with the three flutes. Mike Wofford wrote us some charts, as did Bill Cunliffe and Frank. We tried them out on two or three gigs, including the jazz festival in upstate New York that I booked as musical director for several years. Tom Burns of Capri Records then produced our first recording in January of 2003 with Peter Washington and Ben Riley, Mike and the three flutes. So that group is a reality. We've played several festivals and tours. This band is happening, and the arrangements are very strong. What's fun for me, for all of us, is being able to play in a flute section with cats who can really play.

You have other projects?

Well, for the NFA [National Flute Association] convention I made the proposal to have a jazz flute big band using a local rhythm section--I'm newly appointed jazz chair for the NFA. I'm already amassing a book of arrangements for this instrumentation, thanks to my annual jazz flute master class in California. I commission arrangements for my student jazz flute big band each summer. I do hope to at some point do an album with a pro jazz flute big band. Another exciting aspect of my career is jazz flute and orchestra. I've been working periodically with several different orchestras as jazz soloist. And another recording that's coming out this year... I did a trio recording with Steve Rudolph, a wonderful piano player based in Harrisburg, and Steve Varner on bass.

You have more freedom that way, with the trio?

When I'm playing with *Flutology*, it's really high energy and I love the flute section idea. With the trio, because there are no drums, the subtleties of the alto and C flutes are more evident.

Juggling all of these projects, along with work as a clinician, Ryerson continues to perform at a very high level. Currently, however, apart from her work with *Flutology*, she is unrepresented by a major record label. As I wrote in a recent review of *Soul Quest*, her recent trio recording with Steve Rudolph, "It is indicative of the current state of the music business when artists of this caliber are to be found distributing their work via the Internet on small, independent labels rather than through the jazz bins at Tower Records and Barnes & Noble. Perhaps it is a reflection on the commercial power of cyberspace, but I fear it is more illustrative of the sorry state of the mainstream recording industry which continues to concentrate on commercial pap, hip hop obscenity, and 'jazz light.' It is a damn shame when artists such as this have to labor in relative obscurity while Oprah swoons over Chris Botti! But so it has always been and so it will continue."

In Ryerson's case there are a couple of strikes against her: she does not write her own material, and she does not inhabit the fashionably edgy territory that gets you noticed by jazz critics or indulge in over-produced, 'smooth jazz' recordings. Rather, she works the musical and emotional area that jazz has now staked out as its classic mainstream, drawing material from the Great American Songbook, and the work of the finest jazz--and Brazilian--composers. With this material, and in the various settings she has developed, she continues to produce improvisations of great elegance and sophistication, always with an unfailing sense of swing. There has always been a place in jazz for beauty of tone and refinement of expression, and it is the essence of what the flute, in the hands of a performer such as Ali Ryerson, has to offer this music.

Unperterbed, Ryerson has pursued a slightly different career course. As chairperson of the Jazz Committee of the National Flute Association, she spent her five year term promoting jazz among her peers in the flute world. She founded the Jazz Flute Big Band (30 top performers chosen by audition, plus rhythm section, performing arrangements by such artists as Bill Cunliffe and Mike Wofford) which performs at NFA conventions every other year, alternating with jazz reading sessions where convention participants are given the opportunity to try performing the band's arrangements. These programs, along with an annual jazz flute master class, overseen by Holly Hofmann, have proved enormously popular. (For the sake of disclosure, I should reveal that I am also a member of the NFA Jazz Committee and, in 2009 and 2011, of the Jazz Flute Big Band.)

These contrinutions to the flute in jazz have carried their own reward. Ali has been asked by a major flute manufacturer to develop a line of flutes under her own name. They are also underwriting a new recording featuring Ali with some other truly distinguished jazz artists. So we have not heard the last from Ali Ryerson.

Holly Hofmann

"You know when you go to see her that you are seeing the real deal... the summation of the history of the jazz flute."

Bill Cunliffe

"Along with Hubert Laws, Holly is frankly the best jazz flute player today."

Phil Woods

However useful it has been in tracking the history of the flute in jazz, the annual *Down Beat* Critics Poll also demonstrates the shortcomings of jazz criticism. A case in point is that **Holly Hofmann** has only recently been recognized in its flute category. She also appears in the "Rising Star" category, around the middle of the list--after more than twenty five years of performance and 11 high-quality albums. Another ten years and she might become an overnight success!

Hofmann has consistently refused to follow fashionable trends, or to produce the kind of music that is often necessary to garner critical attention. Rather, she has faithfully followed her own muse which has led her down the dead center of the jazz esthetic, its hard-swinging, bebop-based, mainstream, avoiding both the excessive roughness of the avant-garde and the excessive smoothness of what is commercially acceptable on much jazz radio. As an additional strike against her, Hofmann has established her base of operation in San Diego, which is not a center for many musicians building a national reputation. And, of course, the biggest hurdles of all, she is a woman--and a flutist.

In spite of all this, Hofmann has worked steadily ever since 1984 when she arrived in San Diego from her native Cleveland, equipped with a BA in performance from the Cleveland Institute of Music and an M.M. from the University of Northern Colorado. Initially, she reports, she was not sure whether to build a career in jazz or in classical music. "They were my only two options, since that was all I was allowed to listen to at home. I realized that, anyway, my classical studies were going to be invaluable even if I finished up as a jazz musician."

It was soon clear that jazz was going to win out, and she did not need much help from critics to get established; her talent was quickly recognized by other musicians. An early mentor was another flutist, James Moody, and she also studied with Frank Wess and Slide Hampton. With their help, and the opportunity to perform regularly with fine players such as pianists Kenny Barron, Mike Wofford and Bill Cunliffe, guitarist Mundell Lowe, bassist Bob Magnusson and drummer Victor Lewis, she has applied the technique acquired through her classical training to the development of a jazz style which has been described, unusually for a flutist, as "hard-hitting." Notes Bill Kohlhaase in the *Los Angeles Times*, Hofmann: "one of the most accomplished flutists around, has single-handedly destroyed the stereotype of the delicate female flutist, thanks to her muscular attack and improvisational abandon."

Every artist needs a break and in Holly's case her career received perhaps its biggest boost from her association with legendary bassist Ray Brown. Having already demonstrated his acceptance of the flute by hiring Jerome Richardson for an early record date, Brown recognized Holly's talent and featured her in his group for the last two years of his life, giving her valuable exposure at New York venues such as the Village Vanguard. After the bassist's passing, Holly continued to get calls from the prestigious club. "That was quite a coup," she recalls, "I'm the first flutist in the club's history to be hired as a leader!"

With this and similar appearances, and a couple of fine recordings for Capri Records, Holly did begin to get some critical attention. Leonard Feather, writing the notes for her second recording, noted that what had struck him when he first heard Hofmann performing with Slide Hampton, was "... the extent to which her classical training had enabled her to achieve such admirable control, along with a confident sound and fresh, challenging ideas." His conclusion: "Holly Hofmann's quartet deserves to work together as long and as often as it can, and an artist of her unquestionable talent deserves to be heard on a much larger scale. Today, San Diego; tomorrow, let us hope, the concert stages, jazz parties and festivals of the World."

To a large degree, Feather's hopes have been borne out, as Holly has continued to develop her capabilities and to produce high-quality recordings, not the least of which has been the debut CD of *Flutology*, where her style blends and contrasts with the other two flutists, Frank Wess' no-nonsense, technically nimble improvisations and Ali Ryerson's elegant, slightly more mellow approach. Indeed, Hofmann's partnership with Ryerson underscores the parallels in their respective backgrounds. Not only did they both grow up in musical families, but, in fact, both their fathers were jazz guitarists. I asked Holly about this when we sat down for a conversation in her New York hotel, between *Flutology* recording sessions:

So, your father was a professional jazz guitarist. That brought you to jazz; what brought you to the flute?

It was a musical family. My sister was eight years older than I was and when she got to junior high, my father asked her to bring home an instrument that a tiny person could play. As you can see from my hands, that's an issue. I can reach a seventh on the piano. I was really tiny at five. But I wanted to play an instrument so she brought me home a flute, which was not only something I could carry, but something I could hold. I couldn't really reach low C or anything, but I didn't need to at that point. And I was already playing a plastic flutophone when I was five.

Is that similar to a recorder?

It was played like a recorder, but it was plastic and they called it a flutophone. And so I was already playing with my Dad. We were learning tunes that I could play that didn't have a lot of notes in them, by ear. This was before formal lessons began. One of the first tunes I ever played was *Springtime Beautiful Springtime*, which is not a terribly heavily moving line. By the time I started my classical lessons in Cleveland, at seven, I could play about ten jazz standards, just melodies, and we started improvising a bit. The way I learned to improvise was, I would learn the melodies really well and then my father would sing a jazz phrase and I would play it back to him until I had it. And then he'd say: "when you come to this part of this tune play that phrase."

Well, that's a very common approach in many Eastern cultures. It's a tried and true method. So you were learning by ear mostly?

Well, if you don't learn by ear there's a certain feel for jazz that you miss. I mean there are so many schools who teach young jazz players primarily from the standpoint of chord changes and scales. And when you're teaching this way and not doing ear training at the same time--jazz ear training--then you may be able to play all the chord changes correctly and all the scales, but you'd be missing some of the finer elements of jazz, which are jazz rhythms, jazz phrasing, blues and so on.

How is jazz ear training different from the traditional, standard approach?

Well, it's learning jazz phrasing in an immediate, distinctive way rather than the kind of ear training that you find in traditional Western music programs. I had *solfegio,* and singing intervals properly but not really anything to do with jazz. It was good just the same. Any ear training is good, but jazz ear training is unique. You can learn a lot from just listening to great jazz recordings also.

Once you started lessons, these were with a classical teacher?

Yes, at seven. My father and I played every night after dinner. So, as I was starting the classical lessons, I started dividing my time. And it was very natural for me and very easy. The flute came so easily that I couldn't believe that anybody thought it was difficult, because I was playing without the lessons. Someone told me it was like blowing across a soda bottle. And when I used to start beginners, that's precisely how I taught them. And then we switched from the bottle to the head joint. It was incredible for me--I think I was playing and learning jazz from the womb. My mother said at two, when Dad would play, I was bouncing on two and four on her lap!

Your folks encouraged you to play the flute. Was there never any pressure to double?

I did try the saxophone, because I was told from the time that I began school programs that I would never have a career in jazz if I didn't double on saxophone.

You were a music major?

Yes, undergrad at the Cleveland Institute of Music Conservatory and graduate school at the University of Northern Colorado in Greely Colorado. It was in Colorado that I was told many times I had to double because the eighteen-piece big band configuration was where woodwind players had to start in jazz careers. One instructor insisted that I try the saxophone.

How long did that last?

It lasted until my next orchestra rehearsal when the conductor said, "Madam, assistant principal flute, I don't know what you're doing with your sound, but stop it!" I stopped it.

So the saxophone didn't last too long. But when you started trying to work, were they right or wrong?

I have been incredibly fortunate to be always able to make my living playing jazz, and some classical along with it.

That's wonderful, given the obstacles women still have to face in jazz, not to mention women flutists! But when did you start working professionally?

Well, I first started working when I was in Colorado in graduate school. I would drive into Denver to work gigs occasionally, and I was asked to sit in with a lot of people there who were very good to me.

When did you get to California?

After graduate school I moved to California. And that's been fifteen years. I started working with my now husband, Mike Wofford.

Did it help being married to Mike?

Well, Mike and I are relative newlyweds. He played piano for me for all the years that I've been in San Diego, but we were married more recently. I really landed with a wonderful rhythm section. On the first two discs it would be Mike Wofford, bassist Bob Magnusson and drummer Sherman Ferguson. That was my first band in San Diego and the first group that I recorded with.

All straight-ahead sessions with flute plus rhythm?

That's correct.

There are critics who've written that the flute has no place in jazz. You've come across that?

Oh, many times!

Did you find, early on, that you had any problems getting accepted by audiences? Being asked when you are going to play some saxophone?

Well, if they see me come to the gig and they don't know what they're coming to hear they assume that I'm a singer. But no, they don't ask about saxophone. I've had, early in my career, a hundred or more people who have said, "I came to this concert disliking jazz flute, and knowing that I probably wouldn't enjoy the concert, but now I kind of like it." It is very interesting because the preconception about how the flute is going to sound in jazz is very, very stereotyped.

Did they elaborate and tell you why they had developed that line of thinking?

Well, they only mentioned Herbie because it's the only person that people can name as their reference point. Herbie Mann is the only voice they can call on when they're trying to be knowledgeable, as all audiences want to be.

Okay. But what did they say they didn't like about it?

Well the interesting comment, that musicians and audiences alike have told me, is that they like my approach because it isn't above their heads. In other words it's not what some would call *avant-garde.* You must have heard non-jazz people, who listen to very little jazz or who are very limited in their scope, they often say, "I don't understand. They play a melody and it's fine but then they go off and just do stuff and you can't follow it and you don't know where they are." I've heard that hundreds of times. So I try to incorporate snippets of melody, snippets of really basic harmonies even if I'm taking something out, so to speak. I think it's more accessible for them. And maybe that's what they're talking about.

How does **Flutology** *fit into this?*

Well, the first few performances with this band have been incredible. We've done three gigs. And they were all extremely successful and people went crazy. The interesting thing about this band is that I've been calling to book it for the festival season, and I often get, "You know, I don't have room for a jazz group, I have horns, I don't want flute..." I get a lot of that. But as soon as I throw out what this group is, they say: "when can I book it?"

What do you tell them? Do you tell them who's involved, or...

Well, I think it's who's involved, but I think it's got commercial appeal because they think--three flutes with a rhythm section doing tunes like *Bebop* and *Giant Steps*, and it's an immediate grabber.

They don't ask for **Swingin' Shepherd Blues?**

No, no. Thank God! Everybody asks for that tune!

You know... getting back to the early jazz flutists, there were comments from some, Jerome Richardson in particular, that it was not altogether obvious right away how to make the flute work in jazz. Were you aware of that when you started?

I didn't know, because I never listened to flute players as a young person. My father had big band records, Oscar Peterson, Coltrane--no flute players. I didn't know what other flute players sounded like until somebody gave me a Paul Horn record when I was thirteen. I didn't know that flute wasn't just another jazz horn. I simply assumed that my father's collection just didn't have jazz flute players in it. So, I learned how to improvise from sax players and trumpet players and listening to big bands. Also, piano players like Oscar. In fact, one of the great delights in my life has been because the first record I purchased with my allowance money at ten, was a record called *We Get Requests*, with Oscar Peterson, Ray Brown, and Ed Thigpen, and I learned every solo off the record, totally by ear because I couldn't write at ten. Then, thirty years later, I was touring with Ray Brown's trio. You don't get many of those experiences in life!

But then you must have studied some flute players?

Well, as I said, at thirteen I'd heard Paul Horn. Paul Horn was nothing like anything I was doing, because really, in those years, he was doing things like *Here's That Rainy Day,* with lots of reverb and effects. But I had no interest in that. I didn't know anything about that. I didn't even know how the sounds were created. So, then I got a Yusef [Lateef] record and I got an Eric Dolphy, and that seemed closer to what I wanted to do. I remember that seemed closer to what I wanted to do, but Eric Dolphy was harder for me to understand in my early teens.

I can remember how Dolphy was received by the critics in the UK. They said he didn't know how to play the flute, poor intonation, bad breathing...

Breathing can't be wrong. It can only be your own breathing.

Still, Dolphy came at you out of left field!

But I liked it. It wasn't where I was headed, but I liked it. And Yusef's playing seemed closer to what I was striving for. Then dad got some new big band records with Frank Wess playing flute solos, and then I really got excited. And actually my early ballad style completely came from Johnny Hodges. Some people can pick it out. In fact, knowledgeable reviewers will comment on it, especially in Europe if they've really listened to a lot of Duke. At some early age, like eight or nine or ten--right in there--my dad remembers me saying: "Daddy, I want my slow playing to sound like that saxophone player." And it was always Johnny Hodges.

I suppose that means that you're looking for breadth rather than speed, on ballads.

Hodges, always sounded so smooth and fluid to me, and I loved the way he phrased. I wanted to know how he did that, and my dad described that to me as: "He doesn't come in on one, he holds back."

Are there other flute players that you came across? Bud Shank...

Yes. In fact I did a gig with Bud a couple of years ago and he very kindly announced that he was "passing the flute torch" to me. It was shortly after he quit playing the flute.

That's a real compliment, coming from him. It's a shame he quit because I loved the way he played flute. But anyway, there are other technical issues that come and go. You have to do something about amplification, and getting a balance at recording sessions. Did you have any problems in that area? Because a jazz group is out of balance even with a saxophone player, never mind with flute.

I think that's valid.

You still work with microphones? Have you tried any pickups?

Yes, I play with microphones. Companies send me pickups all the time and ask me to endorse them. But I've never found one. And quite frankly, I play some halls without any amplification. I have a large sound in terms of being able to fill a hall, because I studied with a teacher who sat in the last row of Severance Hall in Cleveland where the Cleveland Orchestra played, and I stood alone on the stage and played things, and I got: "I can't hear you, I can't hear you. Where is the air velocity, where is the air direction? You have to reach me..."

There's still the problem that, with a rhythm section, it's hard to make yourself heard in the lower register. You get pushed up high in order to cut through.

That's true. Part of the key to that is having the right rhythm section. Drummers, often times, cannot play energy without volume. Ben Riley on the *Flutology* recording is a good example of one who can.

He plays with incredible energy, and no volume. He also knows that when you're with a flute player you must use dry cymbals so that the sound doesn't wash over the middle range timbre of the flute.

Pianists also have something to do with that.

Yeah. Well, the pianist has to understand what octave to play in. But I mean, as far as drummers, drummers will be the thing that will cover you the most in terms of the wash of sound. So I don't play with those drummers anymore. And if I'm on a festival where I'm thrown in with a bunch of other people, of course there is amplification there.

Have you had any interest in world music? Any other traditions outside of jazz and classical music?

I listen to many music genres and I've done some interesting recordings in San Diego and L.A. for other people. But I find jazz, writing, and all the other things in my career are demanding enough. I do some classical recitals, and I work on my Quartet with Strings book. I have two orchestra books for strings or up to full orchestra that have been written for me. One is a tribute to Antonio Carlos Jobim. It is for piano, bass, guitar, drums and percussion with string orchestra. The other is a tribute to Duke Ellington and Billy Strayhorn with similar instrumentation.

How often do you get requests for classical recitals?

Well, not often, but I did give one in November. It took me a lot of preparation and I found that I'd lost a command of ornaments, just remembering exactly how things were done for the period. It took me quite a long time to polish up. I played Poulenc and the Prokofiev sonatas.

Well the ornaments are not so complex in that literature.

No, it's just a question of trying to make things articulate properly, and was this the period when the note was this length or this length...

At least you weren't trying Baroque things?

Oh yes, we did C.P.E. Bach. We also did a contemporary Argentinian piece.

Yes, now that does get more specific. My dissertation advisor, Prof. Eugene Helm, was involved in producing the C.P.E. Bach edition. Thirty years writing back and forth to other editors in Germany discussing whether in measure 370 the F was a sixteenth note or a grace note... I kept telling him that I didn't think Carl Phillip Emmanel wanted it so rigid--he improvised too!

That's interesting.

But it raises a question, one I have raised with several people. Do you think a classically trained flutist can learn to play jazz, can learn to improvise?

It depends on what level that person is interested in obtaining. I don't think it's possible for a classical musician to start out, and then suddenly, after a certain amount of time, have a jazz career. Because the feel of jazz isn't ingrained enough--depending on what age that person is. I mean, I work with tons of classical flutists who say they have the technique to play, the Aebersold scale method for instance. They say, "I can play all of these scales. I can run my triads. I can spell all these chords. But I can't make jazz out of them." Well, that has to go back to ear training, and the so-called methods that are out there do not offer anything for the young flute player. And not just young, but also highly trained graduate students in flute who don't know how to put the elements together into making jazz out of it. So yes, it would be hard.

Perhaps that's because, at the conservatory, it's like pulling teeth to get the students to do any theory.

Well, because of my travel schedule I only have seven adult students, but I teach from the standpoint that they learn by ear and they use theory as a back-up. And all they're required to do is to be able to spell the major and minor triads. And four or five of them can go to the jam sessions in San Diego and do fine. And they started as either classically trained, with no ability in jazz, or starting from scratch. And now they can all go and play five or six tunes at a session.

Do you think it should be a goal for students to be become equally fluent in jazz and classical genres, the way Hubert Laws and Wynton Marsalis and some others have done?

Well, you can count them on one hand. I feel that jazz educators don't know how to teach by ear. And it would require them to teach by ear in order to make that mix between jazz and classical, because the ear can be used for both genres. There are hundreds of clinicians out there who teach that Aebersold method. But the student still comes back and says, "I can do all those things, how do I make jazz out of it?" No, it can't be done with that method only.

Can you be more specific about your teaching methods?

Well, for instance, I work on a standard. (I don't work with children any more so I'm talking adults now, college level and up.) I take a standard that they know, like *Summertime*. We learn it properly, in the Aebersold method book for instance. They can play it with a rhythm section CD. Then we close the book, and we work from embellishing the melody, which is, of course, how jazz started anyway. We begin trying to embellish the melody slightly. Once we get a nice, loose, nicely phrased melody, we start playing together on the melody, and we learn not to come in on one, as my dad said, we learn to hold off, we learn to anticipate in our phrasing. We learn to lean on this note or that note. It's all ear training. Then, when they get to a certain point with the improv, we go back to the Aebersold book. They learn major and minor triads. And, as the CD is playing, they can run their triads up and down, up and down. Then we go back to the ear.

Do you see any correlation between running those and what they finish up playing? I know that I played by ear for years, but then I wanted to go back and understand what I was playing, in terms of theory. It came out of years of listening to the genre.

Well, you don't have to analyze. I have a listening list that my students must listen to. And one thing we do, we take a ballad or something, from one of records and they learn by playing with me. We do a lot of trading of fours, and trading of eights. Perhaps osmosis is not the right word, but there's a peripheral kind of learning that goes on. You get it, but it may come a year later. You may have heard Hubert play something that affected you in some way, and when you've arrived at that exact moment in your own music you call it forth. But you don't know why and you don't have to know why.

Everything you hear goes in and may come out later. I used to analyze Paul Desmond solos, and you'd be amazed how many snippets of Stravinsky and Prokofiev are in there.

Oh yes, for sure. That's not surprising.

To follow up on your comments about ear training and elaborating on melodies, when I was studying in India the teacher, Pandit Hariprasad Chaurasia, gave us a sixteen beat cycle on Raga Yaman to syudy. It had a a fixed composition through beat eleven and then he had us improvise for the five beats leading back into the composition. We had to make 100 versions of this.

That's wonderful!

Well, it shows your methods are based on very traditional ideas.

I'll just finish with this one thought. Very often I have rooms full of very well trained flute majors at a university who are coming to a jazz clinic for the first time. Absolutely no one will get up and play.

They are terrified. Classical musicians, most often, are terrified about playing the wrong note. And I say to them, "If I can give you all the right notes on this blackboard to come and play this blues with my rhythm section and me, would you do it?" They say: "Well yes, but you could never do it." And I say, "No, if I could do that, would you come up?" "Yes, we'd come up." So I write out the blues scale in F and I say, "You can play these two notes, the first and the third notes, all of them up, all of them down, patterns of four over every single note. These were the right notes, you can play just these notes in any order in any permutation, any arrangement. And you'd be playing right notes for the blues." And then everybody gets up. Because they have the right notes and they can read them.

Well, have we missed anything do you think?

The only thing I say to every interviewer when they say, "What do you want people to remember about you in a history book, after you're passed?" And my whole thing that I want to do is make the flute just another jazz horn. So that people don't have to write about the flute as a separate thing, just a jazz horn, just like saxophone or trumpet. And that's it.

It may be some time before the flute becomes accepted as "just a jazz horn, just like saxophone or trumpet," but it's getting there. Once that acceptance is achieved, no one will have played a greater role than Holly Hofmann.

Nicole Mitchell

"I have a spiritual purpose for creating music. It is to create positive visionary art that inspires hope, empathy towards the human experience, and positive transformation for the individual. I also have a deep love for black people and strive to contribute to the great legacy of African-American creativity that continues to impact the world."

Nicole Mitchell

Nicole Mitchell is yet another example of an artist whose vision has grown out of a disparate set of influences and experiences, of the kind that seem uniquely available to flutists. In her case, she has integrated what might seem to be mutually exclusive opposites--classical, European art music training and African sensibilities. She has a Master's degree in classical flute performance, but includes among her influences, Duke Ellington, Sun Ra, Charles Mingus, Pharoah Sanders, Ornette Coleman and Donald Byrd. "The result," according to a Chicago Tribune review, "is a wholly original music that seduces listeners with the fundamentals of indigenous African music-making, the harmonic sophistication of Western art music, and the spontaneity and deep swing rhythms of African-American jazz."

Growing up in Syracuse, New York, Nicole reports that she was "influenced by the natural music of the woodlands near her home and the creative spirit of the Black Folk Art Gallery of Syracuse, of which her mother was a member." Her father, however, moved the family to southern California, to pursue his career as an engineer. Encountering racial prejudice at the all-white schools in conservative Anaheim, the ten years she spent there was an unhappy time for Nicole. The one positive experience for her was her growing interest in music, which led her to pick up the flute at age fourteen.

At the outset, Nicole concentrated on fundamentals with a classical teacher, but her college years opened her up to new horizons. First she worked in the jazz program at UC San Diego with trombonist Jimmy Cheatham.who introduced her to the flute playing of Eric Dolphy and James Newton. Transferring to Ohio's Oberlin College exposed her to another top-quality jazz program which brought her in contact with Donald Byrd. But Mitchell only remained in this program for one year, feeling compelled to move to Chicago's south side to explore her recently deceased mother's roots.

This turned out to be a very good move for Nicole. It wasn't easy to begin with; she started out playing music in the streets. But soon she came into contact with members of the AACM--the Association for the Advancement of Creative Musicians. The AACM is one of the most successful of the musician's cooperatives that emerged in the 1960s, and it is still active in Chicago and New York. Consisting of predominately African-American musicians who wished to retain control of their own work, the loose conglomeration of performers tended to emphasize free improvisation leavened with African and other folk elements. Many of the ensembles, such as the The Art Ensemble of Chicago, have introduced elements of theater and other media into their performances.

This seems to have been the perfect setting for Nicole's vision and talents, and she flourished as part of this circle. She found herself performing with a highly diverse group of musicians and composers, including Ed Wilkerson, Leroy Jenkins, Roscoe Mitchell, David Boykin, Ernest Dawkins, Malachi Favors, Fred Anderson, Hamid Drake, Joseph Jarman, Chad Taylor, Maia, George Lewis, and others.

She was co-founder of the AACM's first all-women ensemble *Samana,* before forming her own group *Black Earth Ensemble*, which has provided a forum for Mitchell to develop her compositional skills, and with whom she has made several interesting recordings.

Above all however, Mitchell's primary focus is on developing her own music. Interviewed by *Cadence* magazine, she was asked about her choice of instrument:

> I chose flute before I chose jazz. The sound drew me in and I identified with it spiritually. It never occurred to me that it was unusual or unpopular as an instrument though I realize that is why I was not exposed to playing jazz earlier (because others around me didn't consider flute to be a "jazz" instrument). It was music that I loved first, just music, and later I grew to find my identity as a creative musician.

She was asked: who were the most influential artists in her approach to the flute? She responded:

> The first most influential flutist as an improvisor was Eric Dolphy and then James Newton. I think Hubert Laws is an awesome flutist. James Newton played it like I never knew was possible. Growing up I focused more on saxophonists because I wanted to find my own voice. I listened a lot to Coltrane, Ornette [Coleman], Cannonball Adderley, and Dolphy. The first flute I ever listened to as a child over and again was Rampal, and later James Galway. They had a big influence on my sound.

It is hard to imagine a more diverse background than Jean-Pierre Rampal and Ornette Coleman. It was this diversity that provided a point of focus for my initial discussion with Michelle. I began by asking her about the boundaries between jazz and other genres:

I have been talking to many flute players, and so many of them are interested in things outside of what might be considered to be jazz--although no-one knows what jazz is, right?

Or everyone has a different idea about it...

Some people won't even talk to you if you mention the word jazz.

They feel offended. I have some historical question marks in terms of the original meaning of what that word was. I have just recently read some words by Louis Armstrong, and he said that back in his day, they spelled it JASS which really kind of gave reinforcement to the idea of big insults that they tried to use for the name and for the music.

What is jazz, what isn't jazz? If there was another word or another title I could use for what we are trying to write about, I would use it in a heartbeat. But the marketing of things requires instant labels. You know how that is.

Even though some people have tried to step out of that definition and call it creative music, and I'm sure probably a whole lot of other things. But then you can't really get away from it, it has that historical connection.

Tell me about how, and where, you came to be doing this kind of music. How did you start on flute for example?

I started on flute at the end of eighth grade. My desire to play started in fourth grade when I heard the instrument live, and it took that long to convince my parents to allow me to get one and to take lessons. I was lucky that they had instrumental programs in my school. I was born in Syracuse New York, but I moved to California at the age of eight, to Orange country—Anaheim,which didn't turn out to be a very positive experience for me.

But you were in the school system?

Yes. They had a band at my junior high school and in my high school. I started music doodling around on my mother's piano when I was about five. And part of the reason why they didn't want to give me a flute in fourth grade is because I had already started the viola and they didn't think I was going to be responsible.

Do you remember what it actually was you heard on flute?

Not in terms of what the music was. All I really heard was the sound of it. It touched me in a way that I knew that was my instrument. After that, I would tape classical flute off of the radio and then I when I was in bed at night I would play those tapes and pretend that I was playing. I went along like that until, in eighth grade, I finally got one. Then I started from the beginning with lessons. I started out with classical flute, and actually really didn't know much about jazz. My parents played Art Blakey, and they had some jazz records that I would listen to. But being introduced to that instrument I wasn't introduced to jazz with that instrument, so I didn't really make the connection ..

There weren't really many jazz flutists at the time.

I hadn't heard any! I had heard a little Herbie Mann.

So you had a classical teacher, and therefore a good technical foundation.

Right, and then I wasn't turned onto jazz until I went to college. I started out at U.C. San Diego in 1985.

So what was going on in the eighties that you were exposed to, or was it some classic things that you heard?

Well, the first experience that I had, and probably the most powerful for its impact, was with Jimmy Cheatham, the jazz trombone player. He taught at U.C. San Diego. And he still does. He had a jazz improv class. Also I had met some drummers who played on campus and I started improvising a little bit.

Do you remember what kind of thing was taught in that class? Was it harmony or was it more open things?

One thing was, we spent a whole semester playing the blues, and he had this idea that he called the "permutation," which was his own way of expressing improvisation dealing with chord tones. This is just allowing the students to realize how many different combinations that you could have, just with the chord tones alone. This isn't even dealing with scales yet, just with permutations of chord tones.

Was he just dealing with triads, or did he put the seventh on there?

He dealt with sevenths.

So using the seventh chord in and of itself was enough for a whole semester?

And he made all the students learn certain tunes on the piano. But the other thing that really impacted me was two things that he did. He sent me to the library with a little slip of paper with the words "Eric Dolphy" on it--that was my first real experience with hearing Eric Dolphy. His flute playing had a big impact on me. The other thing that he [Cheatham] did was he brought James Newton into our class and he played for us live, and spoke with us. That was probably one of the most impactful experiences in my development.

Did he play solo or did he bring some people?

He played solo. He played *Amazing Grace* with his singing along with playing which I had never heard before. And years later I ended studying with James for a while. The way it came about was that improv class really had a deep effect on me. I really looked up to him as a mentor. I was also soul searching. I should tell you the story of how, for all those years, I didn't see him, and then I met him here in Chicago not too many years ago. And I'm like, "He probably won't remember me." But he did, because when I was taking lessons with him I was playing on the street, mostly--I was also welding believe it or not-- but when I went to my lesson I would pay him in change!

You mean a big bag of nickels and dimes?

Right! That was kind of every time.

Well, you say you were drawn to the flute and you knew that you wanted that instrument, but did you also know that you wanted to be a musician?

For life? I think so. At the time I was also focused on classical music. While I was at UC San Diego I was in the Youth Symphony in San Diego, and I also played in the La Jolla orchestra over there, so I was doing a lot with the classical aspect. At that time I hadn't been playing that long and I still hadn't developed a foundation, but even then UCSD was more focused on twentieth century music--I actually was very fond of Shostakovitch and Prokofiev.

So you like that very rich, harmonically complex genre...

Right. And they have John Fonville. He had some ground breaking work with microtones on the flute.

Is he a flute teacher?

Yes. He was actually the grad teacher, but I was blessed to be able to study with him. And also Ann Laberge and John Sebastian Winston. So I had three flute teachers. Ann does a lot of work with flute and electronics.

So there were different genres evolving in your mind, as it were, at that time.

But the other aspect is... I don't think you can really separate people's personal experiences from their attraction to different types of expressions in music. I had had a really difficult time from the time that I moved to California because when I was living in Syracuse I went to an all-black school. When I moved to Anaheim I was going to an all-white school.

That's really the burbs, isn't it? No sidewalks. They encourage cars but not people!

Well it was kind of like that. If I walked in front of someone's house they would come out and tell me to move, because I was downgrading the value of their property by standing in front of it. It was a very racist area. I was really ready to get out of there as soon as I could.

And your family was having similar difficulties?

Yes. And my mother died when I was sixteen. It was awfully difficult.

What does your dad do?

My father was an engineer. He's still there! He likes it!

So then you went to Oberlin?

Yes. From there I wanted to be around more musicians, more people that were really thinking about learning music. I had started playing on the street as soon as I'd started learning about jazz. That's when I really started playing on the street, in San Diego and when I went to Oberlin.

By yourself? People gave you money?

They gave me money.

So you went out there and practiced, basically.

I would create... I didn't play tunes. I would make up everything that I played.

Improvisation is a big obstacle for a lot of people, but you...

I just kind of jumped in.

I'm hoping that quite a few classical players will read this book. What would you say to them about how they would get their feet wet with improvisation?

I would say there's nothing to it but to do it. I actually had a flute teacher when I finished my undergrad work, and after I finished with her, a few years later, she came to me and asked for lessons in improv. She had been asked to play at a funeral. They wanted her to play *Amazing Grace*, and she didn't want to just play the melody, she wanted to be able to improvise and really give something.

And this was a classically trained player?

Yes, she has a classical quintet, and she also plays with the opera here in Chicago.

So what did you tell her, or how did you move her in that direction? Do you remember?

We first dealt with melody, of course, memorization of the melody and hearing different ways of expressing emotion. I didn't necessarily deal with, "Okay, this scale is for this part of it, or this scale for that part of it." But what I really wanted her to come from was the emotional inflection, like dealing with bending notes, and dealing with tempos, because she would be doing a solo. She didn't have to play it perfectly in time, just add just a little bit, not go way far away from the melody, just use different expressions, inflections.

You would think that a classically trained player would have been exposed at least some improvisation in Baroque music. Listening to Michala Petri or someone like that.

Well, she wanted it to be hip! It was a black funeral and she didn't want it to sound clever...

To get back to you! Yyou were at Oberlin. Did you transfer there to finish up your degre?

I transferred to Oberlin. I went for one year and Donald Byrd was filling in for Wendell Logan when Wendell was on sabbatical.

And did he offer a class on improvisation also?

No. But he was very open to students who were passionate about learning, so he spent a lot of time with a few of us. And I think his talking about the music and about his life was just as important as when he was trying to share some music with us.

And after that? At this point are you gigging?

No. I didn't really start gigging until I moved to Chicago. I didn't end up finishing at Oberlin. When I went the first time they didn't even have a jazz major. I had been recommended to go there just because of the environment. It was very inspiring--I learned a lot there. When I went back the next time Wendle Logan was there and he had just started the jazz major. I was the only female in the program.

And how did you do in the jazz major?

Well, I actually wasn't happy with it because I just wasn't being encouraged, except for Wendle who was always encouraging. I had a private teacher, but he was not a flute player, he was a saxophonist. He didn't see much value in jazz flute--he would basically tell me in my lesson, "You'll never get anywhere playing jazz flute."

That's pretty typical. Teachers were--perhaps still are--are conscious that there issn't much of a market for jazz flute players. Band leaders don't often think: "I need a flute player, who can I call?"

Exactly. But that's the exact thing that made me be a leader--because you've got to create your own projects.

Was there not some gigging in between, where other people called you?

Actually, I guess I forgot a little. I have to go back to California. I did play with some West African highlife bands, and I played music for plays, so that was the first gigging that I did. It was with a band called *Une Igede*--they weren't necessarily that well known.

I can see how these different influences started to create the approach you have now.

And my parents had a lot of Indian music, and I was very attracted to that.

Did you hear any bansuri?

Yes. My parents took me to a different church every week, and one church that we did go to a lot was the Self Realization Fellowship--they are very open and respectful and honoring of all traditions. It was founded by Paramahansa Yogananda. Musically it was very Indian. And it would also lead to an influence with Sun Ra.

Yes, I was going to say that what I hear in your albums is an African thing, but there's also a Chicago/Sun Ra/AACM sort of thing going on. Is that fair?

Yeah it is.

And did you ever see Sun Ra?

I did. I met Sun Ra when I was in LA at a concert. It was a funny experience because I went to the concert, and I guess from the way I was dressed they thought I was in the band! I went to pay for my ticket and they said, "Oh, the band is in the back, go ahead." I went backstage and got to sit there with them for an hour or so before the show. I met everyone, and talked to them. I always had this dream that when I was ready I was going to show up at his doorstep. All these things happened when I moved to Chicago.

So you inhabited the heliocentric world for some period of time.

Right!

And what about the AACM folks?

I met Leroy Jenkins at Oberlin. He'd come to visit. And there were some AACMs that performed at Oberlin, the Ed Wilkerson Shadow Vignettes. So when I left Oberlin I came to Chicago, and the first thing I did... I had gotten a research grant to study the aesthetics of house music [a dance form that originated in Chicago] for the summer. I had a mentor here in Chicago, and that's how I ended up coming here. My mother was born and raised in Chicago, and I spent all my summers and Christmases here. So I always had this desire to live here, not being very happy in California. I was always wishing I was in Chicago, so coming here later made sense. It was in 1990.

When you got to Chicago, how soon did you form your own ensemble?

Pretty quickly. When I first moved here I started playing on the street right away. And playing on the street I met everyone that I needed to meet in terms of the music! And the first person that I really connected with was Maia. She's a vibraphonist/flutist/cellist/vocalist/composer, and very grounded in African cultural expression, I would say. She's like a multi dimensional artist. She was going to the Art Institute at the time--she does visual art and music.

So you were a flute player, and you'd also made the mistake of being a woman. So if you wanted to play music you had to create your own environment.

Right. And meeting Maia... we instantly wanted to start a group together. She had a group with her family Phil Cohran--Kelan is his new title. Even though there's not a lot written about him, he's a major player in the development of Chicago music He is very much a community centered person, and she was his wife. But because they were so busy playing she wasn't originally interested in making a band with me. But then three months later they broke up when she left Kelan, and that's when we started the group *Samana*. *Samana* would become the first all women group of the AACM.

How many people were in that?

Originally it was a trio, myself, Maia and Shanta Nurullah. She's a bassist, but she also plays some sitar; she studied in India.

And where did the material come from?

We made it up.

Did you write compositions down? Or was it free improvisation?

Yes, we wrote our compositions down.

And what training did you have that helped you in composition? Did you pick up some techniques at Oberlin and UC San Diego as a music major?

Right. But I didn't take any composition classes.

Well, do you think you would've benefitted from that? Or would it have got in the way?

I ended up taking composition for a year at the University of Chicago, later.

And did that help?

Yes, it did. I studied with John Eaton. He's mostly known for his composition for opera.

He was fantastic. We connected very well because he had spent years in Europe hanging out with Eric Dolphy and playing jazz. So *Samana* was the first group. And for a long time I focused most of my musical energy on that group. And we all contributed to the compositions. We have one recording. And the group eventually expanded to a five piece which was me, Shanta, Maia, and then Coco Elysses--she played congas--and Aquilla Sadalla who played clarinet, bass clarinet, and violin and sang. Shanta put it out on her label. I have my own label so I'm talking to them to put it out on that.

Did you work much with that group?

With *Samana*? Yes, we played for the Chicago Jazz Festival. We did a lot of really nice gigs in Chicago and played in a lot of arts centers throughout the Midwest. And we played for Hilary Clinton's birthday one year--it was a park that was being opened. That was nice. I can tell you a little bit about the music, though, because you can see by the instruments, by having sitar, and the mix of instruments that we had, we wouldn't necessarily call it straight-ahead jazz. So there was a lot of modal music, and a lot of vocal music, because all of us sang. You could almost call it folk music, but it was with an African emphasis.

There's a good deal of African music that has nothing much to do with flute, isn't there?

When we say with African focus, it's more the rhythmical concept.

So how does the flute work in that context? In your picture here on **Vision Quest** *you're playing an alto [flute].*

I had gotten that a little bit later. And I did a little bit with the saxophone too, on tenor, and then I moved from tenor to alto. But I don't really consider myself a saxophone player. It was more of a curiosity, and also a rebellion, with people saying "If you play [the saxophone] it's going to ruin your tone." I'm a closet saxophone player! I think it helps me to play better jazz flute.

Some players simply take what they play on the saxophone and push it through the flute.

I don't agree with that!

Yes, well others think that's the worst thing you can do.

It's a different way of breathing.

You are playing on bass flute and alto flute. Are you drawn towards those lower sonorities, rather than the real high, piercing quality the instrument can have?

I think I do like the lower sounds. I'm waiting for Jupiter--they are supposed to be having a bass flute come out in the real low price range in the next few months.

So Black Earth emerged out of this approach--from the work you were doing?

Well, from playing in *Samana* I have to say the next big experience... well from there I did also play in a collective, *Kuntu Drama,* and I started doing work for children's shows, African- American story telling and music. And that allowed me to do acting and singing as well as playing flute. And Hami Drake and I started a group with Glenda Baker, called *Soundscapes*. And this was the first place that I really had the freedom to just play whatever I wanted to play, and have the space to really stretch out. Because *Samana* had a philosophy--the philosophy of only playing music that is uplifting and joyful. For me there were a lot of other emotions I wanted to express--a lot more that I wanted to do musically that may have been outside of what *Samana's* philosophy was. So when I started playing in *Soundscapes* that gave me another outlet, and then from there I met David Boyken in 1997, the tenor saxophone player, and this was really,... See in *Samana*, Maia and Shanta were like fifteen years older than me, so for all that time I felt isolated in terms of being the age that I was, and not really being close to anyone else that was really serious and passionate about the music. So really, even though when Coco came into the group in *Samana* she was about my age, but she was also an actress and does a lot of other things. But when I met David Boyken, he was the first person that I met who was kind of in the same place I was; he had kind of raised himself through the music. Because, as you see, I haven't really had a lot of teaching in terms of "this is jazz flute, this is how you approach it," and so on. When I studied with James Newton we mostly focused on tone, not simply improvisation. I wasn't really that happy with what I did at Oberlin, so I really kind of had to figure stuff out on my own. And so I started playing in David Boykin's group, *David Boykin's Outet*. He's a tenor saxophone player and composer. And then shortly after that I started *Black Earth Ensemble* because I had at this point a whole pile of compositions that weren't being played.

So now you feel like you've found your focus?

Yeah.

And the Black Earth Ensemble changes in size, doesn't it?

It changes all the time, from performance to performance.

Like a jazz workshop kind of thing?

Yeah. It's a different project all the time. I guess what it's been so far is two to fifteen. I started with a bass player, Darius Savage, and we worked up to me, and Sam Williams, who now only wants to be referred to as Savoir Faire.

Is it jazz?

Yeah. I consider it to be jazz. My concept is that I'm coming out of a tradition, and I connect myself with that continuum, you know, and there's no other way around it in terms of that music. Even though when I was in *Samana*--that was when I joined the AACM, and I'm still a member. But a lot of people in the AACM only want to be defined as "creative musicians." I consider myself a composer, and so it's always limitless in terms of each piece is a world in itself, so I don't really see myself as in one vein. I'm kind of going back to the sound I had with *Vision Quest*. I'm working with strings in one setting where we're playing acoustically, which means I took the drumset out. There's just percussion, because that acoustic sound is really where it's at. I call that *Black Earth Strings.*

Now the other album, **Afrika Rising,** *is that also Black Earth Ensemble?*

Yeah. There are about seventeen people. There's a pretty big development between the two CD's, I think.

A lot of writing? Or open improvisation?

Yeah. The last piece on *Afrika Rising* is guided improvisation, meaning that I'm guiding it in certain directions conceptually, but it's mostly improvisation. We tend to do that in our live performances. I just don't necessarily use that for the recordings because I might have a specific goal with the recording. I might put out a live recording and then I would probably use that.

Do you have rehearsals, and talk a lot about what goes into that kind of improvisation? With the Spontaneous Music Ensemble we used to talk endlessly about creating the soundspace and trying to make a whole that was greater than the sum of its parts. When that is really working it can make your hair stand on end!

Yes, I know! Well, what's important to me is the people that I choose to play with. I think chemistry is essential. I know that was important to Sun Ra as well.

Didn't you have to live in his house in order to be in his band?

Yes. They still live together even though he's passed. They still perform his music. They still call themselves the Sun Ra Arkestra. Marshall Allen is leading it--the alto player. [They are] in Philadelphia. He moved there a long time ago. But he planted the seeds of what would become the AACM while he was in Chicago, because many of the founders of AACM had played with him. He really practiced all of that--about African music pointing the way to the future, incorporating African instruments into jazz, and all of that.

But it must be great that your ensemble takes different shapes and grows with you.

Yes, and I think the people work with that pretty well.

Going back to the flute though, you still find no limitation in the instrument as the medium of expression that you're looking for?

The flute? The thing is that, coming up, when I started listening to jazz I didn't listen to a lot of flute players.

Do you now? You must've heard quite a few.

I have, but I'm always disappointed, not because of people's playing but because of the tendency for flutists to be too soft and flowery, and to me, to romanticize the instrument in that way, even though I like to play that way... I just want more meat. And the expression, especially when you have someone who plays the flute as a secondary instrument, then I think the flute really gets put in a box in terms of stereotype that it's supposed to be this kind of song. Eric Dolphy is probably still my favorite, and Rahsaan. I spent a lot of time listening to saxophone playing, o I listened to all the saxophonists but I played the flute.

Any players in particular?

It's kind of like I came to jazz through the back door and really listened to the avant-Garde before I listened to bebop. I was really turned on by Ornette Coleman, Abert Ayler and Archie Shepp, and of course John Coltrane and Eric Dolphy. Not to say that was the only thing that I listened to, because I'm definitely not anti bebop, that's a part of what the music is. If you play "creative music" or the idea of free jazz, I don't really agree with that title because I don't think the music is free--it has structure and concept.

Of course, because a structure always emerges. But then a lot of people profess to be playing totally free...

But they all sound the same! We even made jokes the other day, we recorded washing dishes, and we said, we'll stick this on our next CD!!

So if anyone called you and said, "We've got a gig we're going to be playing down here with piano, bass, drums, out of the **Real Book***," would you do it?*

Oh yeah! I did some of that here, you know, I had lead a jam session a year ago for a little while, and I have no problem with playing tunes. For my masters I did classical and jazz.

The thing about the flute is it doesn't lend itself to too many "noise" elements. That's the one thing that differentiates it from the saxophone.

I do play a little flutaphone--I take the head joint off [the flute] and I play it with a soprano saxophone mouthpiece. I do have fun with that. The scale is completely incoherent in that it doesn't follow a chromatic scale, it's something else.

That's because it's throwing all the overtones off all the way down the tube. You do know what you get with each finger position after a while, so you can work with it?

You can work with it.

So what's the future, Nicole? What do you think? More of the same unfolding, all the possibilities from Black Earth Ensemble, more traveling, more influences from other parts of the world... what kind of things?

Yeah, in a way I think I've just begun.

And you are still involved with education?

I didn't tell you that I graduated from Chicago State--that's an Illinois state college. Then I went on and got my masters at Northern Illinois University. Now I'm teaching flute at Chicago State. I'm teaching beginning music theory and flute.

You're happy with the flute for the future?

Yeah, I feel that it's part of me. It's just come along with me on my journey.

And Nicole's journey has been continuing in the months since this interview. She continues to write for and perform with her own ensemble, in venues as far afield as Italy, France, Canada, and Finland. A recent high spot of her career was a performance to mark the 40th anniversary of the AACM, of which she is now a vice president. This performance was especially rewarding for Nicole as she played alongside her early mentor James Newton who was a guest artist with the *Black Earth Ensemble*. Later came the news that Nicole had come first in the Rising Star Flute category of the *Down Beat* Critics Poll. Meanwhile her music has drawn some impressive reviews from critics. "Mitchell's flute... produces some of the most haunting and disarming tones in instrumental jazz," wrote Howard Reich in the *Chicago Tribune*, while Phillip McNally, in *Cadence*, has hailed her arrival on the scene as "... the most exciting debut on the flute since [James] Newton came to light over 20 years ago." This kind of recognition is indicative of the strength of her work and the unique contribution she will make to the flute in jazz.

Anne Drummond

"Anne is an incredible musician with a rich sound. She knows how to navigate the chord changes so well--her sound really speaks to me."

Kenny Barron

"Anne has the most beautiful sound I have ever heard on flute. She is so soulful; you can't help but fall in love."

Avishai Cohen

Among the so-called "Rising Stars" on flute in recent *Down Beat* polls, in contrast to the mature performers receiving belated recognition, is one truly new arrival to the world of jazz. **Anne Drummond** is only a few years out of college, but already she has been gaining attention for her original and engaging flute playing, while working and recording with some leading contemporary artists. This could be a career to watch.

Anne first garnered critical attention while still at high school in her native Seattle, winning several competitions on flute, piano and trombone, including a six-year winning run at the prestigious Lionel Hampton Festival. She went on to gain national attention with her performance at the *Essentially Ellington Competition* sponsored by Jazz at Lincoln Center, where the judges--including such musicians as Wynton and Branford Marsalis and Slide Hampton--gave her a top solo award.

Following these early successes, in 1999, Drummond moved to New York City and entered The Manhattan School of Music. Here she found herself studying piano with the legendary Kenny Barron. "I was always able to express myself most easily on flute," she says, "but for whatever reason I ended up as a piano major. Fortuitous, given that I met Kenny that way." Barron was not aware of Anne's abilities as a flutist until, during one of their practice sessions, Drummond brought along a flute she had just purchased. Seeing her with it, Barron asked her to play. Immediately impressed, he gave her the opportunity to make her professional debut with his ensemble--as a flutist. This group was called *Canta Brasil* and included the top-notch Brazilian group Trio da Paz, featuring guitarist Romero Lubambo, bassist Nilson Matta and drummer Duduka da Fonseca. "I was happy to be introduced to the scene in the company of wonderful musicians," Drummond says. "I learned fast with them on the bandstand." Indeed, Drummond learned fast enough to appear on Barron's 2002 CD, *Canta Brasil*, leading her to be named a Rising Star in Down Beat's 2003 Critics Poll, and on his 2004 CD *Images*, which includes a commissioned suite written by the pianist featuring Anne.

Upon Barron's recommendation, Anne was also hired by composer/vibist Stefon Harris for the recording of his jazz suite *The Grand Unification Theory* on Blue Note Records, which received a Grammy nomination for Best Jazz Album. "Anne Drummond is a consummate professional," says Harris. "She has a warm, beautifully lush tone, and a great set of ears to boot." Anne has subsequently recorded a follow up CD with Harris, *Evolution*, and an album with bassist Avishai Cohen, while also touring with Barron and Harris, performing regularly in Manhattan with her own groups, and continuing to collaborate with other performers, which, until now have included, most notably, the Lionel Hampton Orchestra, Wynton Marsalis and the Lincoln Center Jazz Orchestra, Gary Dial, Dick Oatts, and Ingrid

Jensen, among others. She was a featured artist at Alice Tully Hall as part of the Jazz at Lincoln Center Gala, and has already begun to make her mark as an educator, teaching theory and piano courses at jazz workshops in Salzburg, Austria and teaching with pianist Gary Dial at jazz workshops. The flutist is currently composing her first score for an independent short film, *Revolving Door* from the award winning director Aimee Dixon. With this kind of exposure, Anne Drummond, "a remarkable young musician" according to *The New York Times*, while still only in her twenties, is moving her career into high gear.

Our first conversation took place a few days before she departed for a tour of Europe with Kenny Barron's group. I asked her if she needed anyone to carry her bags! "Not really," she responded, "my flute fits in my purse!"

First of all, you play just flute, correct? You're not a doubler?
I also play piano.
But you're not a reed player; you don't double on saxophone?
No I don't.
The fact that you play piano is a separate issue.
Yes, that's completely separate. The thought of playing reeds never entered my mind.
So where did you go to school?
I went to the Manhattan School of Music, actually to major in jazz piano. Kenny Barron ended up being my piano teacher and that's how we met.
I see. So you didn't encounter the whole thing of trying to be a flute major in a jazz setting, and being pressured to double and all that stuff?
No.
But you understand how that goes?
Of course. There's really not a place for it. I mean it's very difficult, just because it's not traditionally a jazz instrument. But it was great to study piano, and really it helps so much with my writing, and understanding theory and all of that. I've always studied classically on flute.
Who were your teachers?
Linda Chesis. She's a protégé of Rampal and head of the woodwind department at the Manhattan School of Music.
And so you didn't take flute as a minor at Manhattan, or take any formal instruction there?
No.
You just focused on piano and you've been pursuing the flute that separately.
Exactly. Although at Manhattan they realized that. They gave me a lot of opportunities to perform with the flute, a lot of features.
I have a quote of Bud Shank right at the beginning of chapter one: "I think the flute is a stupid instrument to be playing jazz music on." He admits that he was being a little intemperate when he made that statement, but it was around the time that he decided to …
…quit.
Right--to quit playing the flute. As you know he did that, what, fifteen years ago or something.
Sure.

But there are other people who say that the flute is really "a marginal instrument at best for jazz." So what's your feeling on that?

I think that it's a delicate situation. Because often times in jazz the textures of the sound, like sonically coming from the rhythm section, overpowers anything that the flute can do. A lot of times flute players will play, like, I will feel kind of forced to play the high register ..

Oh yeah. Tell me all about it! I know all about that.

Yeah--so that I can be heard. And that's really frustrating. It's not a flashy instrument either, because it's not physical looking, you know? And once you're dancing around with it...

Unless you're Ian Anderson! See, my thing is that, if you define jazz in terms of what most people are doing, that's fine. But if you take the flute and adjust the environment to suit it and continue to play in that genre, why is that not still jazz?

It absolutely is.

So, you know, it just seems like narrow thinking to me. There are a lot of jazz players who like to play with guitar and bass for example, or in duos with guitar. How does it work with you with Kenny Barron?

It's a challenge for me because I feel that my strengths are in my musicality and my nuance. I think that Kenny understands this. And so every gig we do we usually do a duo piece that just features me. You can hear my every breath, my every ornament. The challenge is when the rest of the band steps in, when you take away those qualities about my playing, I need to shine in other ways.

Even when you're amplified, those are still hard to project?

Still hard. Sometimes I wanna take my flute and bash it over someone's head. I feel so much energy, I get so inspired by the energy coming from the rhythm section and I want to just dig in. Sometimes I wanna dig in in the low range, but I know I won't be heard.

Yeah. I understand exactly. I got tired of playing flute in those settings, and drummers particularly can be insensitive.

Yeah. So it taught me how to play more rhythmically, you know, which is a way of communicating with them.

Does it have to have that energy level for it still to be jazz? If you're outside of Kenny's group, if you just want to feature yourself with other musicians so it captures the strengths of your playing, what kind of context do you create?

Oh! Textures! Guitars. A lot of times you're going to want that melody reinforced by another sound, because there's something that can be a little bit unsatisfying about just the flute alone. Sometimes with my music I'd want something doubling, whether it be guitar or vibraphone, you know, they complement the flute beautifully. I've asked cellists to join me, and I could keep it kind of obscure like that, as far as the horns go. I never ask trumpet, saxophone, any of those, you know, traditional jazz instruments to join me.

Unlike Jamie [Baum] who tends to play with a trumpet player and sort of go toe to toe with him.
Uh huh.

I have a quote here from Ali Ryerson. "The flute is a beautiful instrument as opposed to a strong instrument. You have to add the percussive side yourself. You have to develop an articulation that will bring the flute closer to the jazz idiom and you have to pick your material very carefully because not everything fits the flute." You agree with all that?

I do. I do. And I do feel that the thing I try to capture... First of all, there's nothing I feel closer to than the human voice and the vocalists. When I listen to music I'm usually listening to vocalists. And any way that I can figure out how to speak through this object, you know, cry through it, or whatever, and touch people in the way that a singer would, that's my mission.

And in this ideal group do you have a drummer, or a percussionist?

Well, gosh, I've had so many projects. The one I'm putting together now will have a percussionist.

Of course, one way that people compensate for the small flute sound is to develop various special techniques, the whole humming thing and all those additional sonorities. Do you indulge in any of that, or do you try to keep the flute tone pure?

I will at some point. At this point I'm trying so hard to develop a real tone, a tone with depth, that is beautiful and without the garbage. Once I accomplish that I will add some garbage and experiment. (Laughs.)

Okay. So backtrack a little bit. What got you started in all this?

My mother plays the flute. My father studied with Nadia Boulanger. He plays classical guitar.

Aha. And did you start with flute or with piano?

I started with flute.

Okay. And your mother, does she play standard literature?

Yes.

And so jazz wasn't the thing that motivated you initially?

Initially... oh gosh, I was five years old. But then I did discover jazz on my own, it's nothing that my parents introduced to me. They introduced music to me, you know the instrument itself, and of course I grew up with classical music.

What kind of literature do you like in the classical side?

I love French music.

Romantic? Impressionist?

Yes, because that's basically jazz, right?

That's right. I've done some of that with Fauré, for example. It totally lends itself to a jazz treatment.

Absolutely, absolutely. And, of course, Bach.

Do you remember what you first heard in the way of jazz that got your attention?

Duke Ellington, and Miles Davis, and Bill Evans. Oh yeah. I had some LPs that I just burned holes through as an eight year old. It was kind of unusual. But I think the best thing is to transcribe other instruments. To be honest, I don't listen to other flute players.

But you must have heard some that made an impression at some point.

Yes. Rahsaan Roland Kirk, because I felt like he was able to really kind of speak through it, even if he wasn't technically a great player. It was almost like... I can't really describe it. But I haven't been listening to flute players, I guess I want to not really be influenced.

Tell me how you got the sessions you have done so far. This was because of your relationship with Kenny Barron, as his piano student, right?

Yes, that's right.

Then he became aware of your flute work and asked you to appear on his recording as a flutist?

That's the way it worked.

I guess he didn't need a pianist! And from there you made contact with Stefon Harris and Avishai Cohen. These do seem great musical environments for your style of playing. Did you feel the same way?

I think so. I'm kind of a chameleon, though. I can kind of jump in to any environment and adapt to it. That's one of my strong points.

Will your own writing be in a similar genre?

No. It probably won't be at all. I am still deciding exactly how I want to go next. I am working in several different styles but I need to pick one road and take it. That's what I am working on right now.

So is there a project in the works? A CD of your very own?

Yes, well, that's an interesting question. I just recorded another Brazilian record, this one with [Trio Da Paz bass player] Nielson Matta. I am on three or four of the tracks. Claudio Roditi plays trumpet, Hellio Alves is on piano, Vick Juris on guitar, Paulo Braga on drums, Harry Allen is on saxophone.

I asked Herbie Mann, if he had to choose one genre out of all the ones he explored, which would it be? What do you think he said?

Brazilian?

That's right. It has all those dimensions to it.

Absolutely. But now, for my own recording, I want to explore some new ground. Whatever I finally do I don't want to rush anything. I've had opportunities to record already that I turned down because they just didn't feel right. I've been asked to do a record a number of times by these Japanese labels. You know, some straight-ahead things--just to pump out some tunes. But that didn't appeal to me. I think I will have something more special to present when I'm ready.

I get to see a lot of artist's first efforts, but I find it takes most people two or three recordings to really find their voice.

I hope it doesn't take that.

Will you be playing piano on any of your recordings?

Possibly--piano is something I may do on live performances.

But do you think of yourself primarily as a flutist.

I do!

Anne has every right to think of herself primarily as a flutist; she has just come in at the top of the *Down Beat,* Rising Star poll for jazz flute performance, along with artists who have been at it years longer than she has. She works and records with top-quality artists and appears to be on the verge of an excellent career. Of course, time will tell. She is still facing the potential problems inherent in a career that gets an early boost but needs to mature and be sustained over decades. But if she can negotiate these pitfalls, Anne Drummond has the potential to make a significant contribution to the flute in jazz.

Steve Kujala

"Steve Kujala is one of the most phenomenal musicians to walk this round planet."

Peter Sprague

"... to produce jazz on the flute at the level I want to hear it... the guy who is the closest is Steve Kujala."

Bud Shank

It was a great pleasure for me when I finally met **Steve Kujala** in Pasadena California, not just because he is a superb flutist--I knew of Steve from his recordings with Chick Corea in the early 1980s--and a thoughtful musician--we had already had an several absorbing telephone conversations--but because of an intriguing connection with my past that suddenly came to light. Many years ago, in Birmingham, England, when I purchased my first flute--an Armstrong Model 90--it came with a set of educational pamphlets. One of them--*The Flute-Position and Balance*--had a picture of a flutist demonstrating the correct way to hold the instrument. Half-way through one of our conversations we realized that this was Steve's dad--Walfrid Kujala, formerly the principal piccoloist with the Chicago Symphony Orchestra. It was immediately clear that, with this background, Steve's taking up the flute was no accident. What I wanted to know was where he had been over the last twenty years, because after recording with Corea, he had, for all intents and purposes, disappeared.

Kujala's career--at least as a jazz performer--has been one of fits and starts, although he has worked steadily in a variety of genres since coming out of the Eastman School of Music in 1976. Initially he was part of a jazz-rock type fusion band called *Auracle,* until he replaced Joe Farrell with Corea's *Tap Step* group. The recordings he made with Corea represent something of a landmark in their exploration of the territory between jazz and contemporary European art music, particularly in the relationship between notation and improvisation. By 1983, however, after several tours with Corea, Kujala found himself with a young family, and with opportunities opening up in the L.A. studios he discontinued his touring schedule and devoted himself to the life of a session musician, with all that implies in terms of versatility and professionalism, but also of relative obscurity as far as the public is concerned.

There were jazz gigs during this period, and there were some recordings under Kujala's own name, but few of them were really jazz recordings, and his name has not been found in any polls. This is a pity, because he is a truly excellent flutist with an approach to jazz improvisation that is both interesting and unique. Recently, one or two more jazz-oriented recordings that have featured Kujala confirm that his is a voice worthy of some attention.

Our first conversation began with a discussion of his first sessions with Chick Corea:

I understand these were recorded in Johannesburg, South Africa. How did that come about?
Yeah. We did that record in a studio that was part of the South African Broadcasting Corporation, in probably 1983 or 1982. They had this beautiful multi-million dollar studio that nobody ever used. And we happened to be on tour and they said, "Would you guys like to make use of our studio!" So we

literally just went in and spent an afternoon, or maybe it was a whole day, and just recorded everything that we were doing on tour, just one take on each tune. It was not with the idea of ever putting out a record, we just wanted to have kind of a reference tape of what we were doing at that point of time. Then the folks at the Elektra Musician label asked Chick, "Do you have anything current?" And he laid the tape on them and they said, "This sounds great, we'd like to put it out!"

This is definitely a jazz recording, but are you a jazz flutist? Can we call you that?

That is certainly one of the hats that I wear, although I don't wear it as frequently now as I did back in the Chick Corea era--the 1980s. But that was certainly part of my upbringing and part of my education. But it's hard to know how to classify me because I indulge in so many different kinds of music under so many different kinds of conditions.

That seems to be something flute players are prone to.

Yeah, and I have some theories about that.

Good! We'll get to that. But for the moment, back up and tell me about your getting started.

Yeah. My Father was a flutist with the Chicago Symphony since 1954; he just retired a couple of years ago. So I was kind of born into the flute world. The first musical notes that I heard after I was born was the sound of the flute, because my father practiced for hours every day.

So you were a music major?

Yes, a music major in college. And by the time I got to college, which was the Eastman School of Music, I had been playing flute in various community youth symphonies, and civic orchestras, and of course the high school orchestras. And I'd also been playing tenor sax in the jazz ensemble, and electric guitar in rock bands. So I had classical flute, jazz saxophone, and rock-and-roll guitar for a good three or four year period. All those three things overlapped--those three elements. By the time I got to college I gave up rock-and-roll and pursued flute as a major instrument. My idea was to follow in the footsteps of my father and become an orchestral flutist, but the jazz program at Eastman was so strong at that point...

It was run by a guy named Rayburn Wright. He'd taken it over from Chuck Mangione a few years before I got to school in 1973. I remember hearing stories about how, just a few years prior to my arrival, jazz was kind of a four letter word there.

And after Eastman?

After Eastman, in 1976, I moved to California with the group that we had formed at Eastman called Auracle, which was a jazz-rock fusion group. That was kind of the heyday of all the fusion groups, so we were pegged as a second-generation fusion band along with the likes of Seawind, Caldera, Spyro Gyra, Matrix and so forth. We moved to Los Angeles looking for a record deal. Two of us in the band--myself and Rick Braun the trumpeter--we had not finished our degrees at Eastman; we left after our junior year and took an official leave of absence to try our luck in the L.A. area. We wanted to see what would happen within a year, and if nothing happened we were going to go back and finish our degrees, and do whatever we were going to do.

This is quite a lot of amplification in that kind of group. Playing flute can be problematical in that setting.

Exactly! That's why I held onto the tenor sax because at least I could be heard!

Did you play anything in the lower register at all for a couple of years? On the flute, I mean.

Yeah--some.

Or any alto flute? When I was on the road I loved to play the flute over the P.A. to an empty theater after the roadies had set up the equipment and gone off to the pub. Doing the gig was another thing! But I know what you're talking about. Are there any recordings of this group?

Yes, we did two. None of them are in print anymore but I see them occasionally on E-bay. We did two records for Chrysalis which was Jethro Tull's label. The first one was called *Glider,* and that came out in '78 I believe, and then the second record was called *City Slickers.* That first record was a real gem. It was a very good representation of the six people in the group; we all had so many different influences, from Bartok, to Miles, to Chick Corea, to all over the map. We were just a young, fresh out of college kind of group, and we were out there to play some s–t!

Who did the writing?

We all did. But on that particular record most of the writing was done by the piano player, John Serry Jr., who is now in New York. He is a brilliant, brilliant writer, and he was kind of the *de facto* leader of the group, although it was technically a democratically run organization. He was really the most outspoken and the most musically aggressive fellow in the band, and he went on to do two solo records of his own for the same label. One was called *Exhibition* and the other was called *Jazziz,* as in the magazine *Jazziz.* In fact they named that magazine after his record. We toured Europe and ended up in the Montreaux Jazz Festival in 1978. We had a lot of critical acclaim, and then the band broke up quickly, and that's when I hooked up with Chick Corea. That was 1980.

Okay. So then you were working with Chick, and by '82 you were in South Africa ...

Right. That would've been our second or third tour together. The first record that I did with Chick was a record called *Touchstone.* I think I only played on a couple of cuts on that record, it has a lot of different groups on it. There's one with *Paco de Lucia,* there's one with Lee Konitz, there's one with various members of *Return to Forever*--Lenny White, and then the current band at that time, which was touring, which involved myself and Al Vizutti, the trumpet player. That's one of my favorite records actually. It's got a lot of cool things on it. Chick tends to be very eclectic in the idioms that he explores and in his sense of programming. I think it got reissued on CD.

Now Chick had worked with Hubert [Laws], so he had an ear for a flute player.

Right, he loved flute players and he also loved people that played tenor sax and flute. That was evident by his use of Joe Farrell for all those recordings, those great *Return to Forever* recordings, and that one called *Friends*--that came out later. Joe was one of my early influences. I had a whole bunch of his records in high school and when I got to Eastman he was a fellow that they brought out to do a clinic with us.

Did you know him that much?

I knew him briefly. I'd met him of course at Eastman as a student, and then when I came on with Chick's band I was actually replacing Joe--he was leaving and I was coming in. So we had a three or four day period when we were both playing together with Chick, just for me to learn the music, and for Joe to kind of hand off the baton so to speak. So I got to know him a little. He was kind of a dark figure, not easy to get to know--always wore dark sunglasses. He was always kind of a mysterious fellow.

So this time with Chick Corea, is this like the high point of your jazz activity?

Yeah, I would say that the whole decade of the eighties. Because of course I'd been playing a lot with *Auracle* before they broke up, and then I joined up with Chick Corea. I was playing with a couple of big bands in town, the Les Hooper Big Band, whom we did a recording with. I also played with a

Brazilian fellow named Moarcir Santos. I don't know if you've heard his name, but a lot of his students are famous Brazilian musicians, such as Sergio Mendes. So I played in his band for several years.

Then I hooked up with a guitarist named Peter Sprague who's one of San Diego's local heroes. He and I have an ongoing musical relationship--we played a lot of clubs back in those days. and nowadays we're both so busy that we play maybe three or four times a year at a club in San Diego called Dizzy's. We have a trio with myself, Peter Sprague and Bob Magnusson, the bass player, or John Leftwich. It's actually a great setting for a jazz flute to play in, because you're not competing with a lot of the heavy artillery, like in a drum set and so forth. We bring in a percussionist, but just a hand-held percussion like Tommy Arros or Ron Wagner. Ron was the drummer in *Auracle,* my group that came out from Eastman--he's an amazing tabla player. We did a thing that I wrote in 13/8 which made use of his tabla. I also do a lot of percussion on my flute--I do flutter-tongue through the flute but I don't make a tone, I just make an air sound so it kind of sounds like a snare drum. So when Peter is playing a guitar solo I will kind play the role of a second percussionist. We did a recording called *Heads Hands and Hearts*, for a label called *Sonic Atmospheres.*

So, after you were with Chick, you got pulled into the studios more and more?

Yeah, you know that kind of happened accidentally. The fellow that produced us was a guy named Jim DiPasquale who used to be a student of my father's at Northwestern University. So Jimmy became our producer for that first record, the *Glider* record, and he was also forging his own name in the business as a film composer. He would hire us for his sessions, and then, of course, being on his sessions we would be in the view of other players and other contractors, and just a couple of us ended getting busy, getting outside work in the studios. It took a long time but, and I'm jumping ahead here, by 1983 or '84. By that time I was off the road with Chick Corea--we weren't touring as much--and I was starting to get a lot more calls for TV and film work, and that was really paying the bills.

Well, they say that a Republican is really just a Democrat with a mortgage. I guess a studio musician is just a jazz musician with a mortgage!

Well, exactly. And there are an awful lot of them out here. It just became increasingly more difficult to live with a family and having to lay down roots and so forth. It was much less practical for me to be taking off and doing tours when there was a good living to be made in town, and I could also do my jazz on the side, in the clubs, just locally or down in San Diego. But of course now, in the 21st Century, there is very little studio music left. We are down to maybe a few hundred musicians from the several thousand that were doing it when I first came into town. Because there's no more T.V. work, it's all done by people with small studios in their bedrooms. There are no more record dates because it's all machines. There are no more jingles, and half of our film work has gone overseas--to London, Australia, Germany, Toronto--it's very global now. A lot of people have had to leave the profession altogether, and do other things not even related to music. Some people have managed to find teaching jobs in universities. It's pretty amazing.

What year did that start to really go down?

I would say by the early 90's. We started to see the erosion then. And this had already happened in New York, so a lot of people in New York were moving to L.A. to find work. We had a whole influx of people in the eighties; people were coming here by the droves.

So you were doing your jazz work in the early eighties, and then studio in the late eighties. Then you had a four or five year window in there, and then what did you do?

Well, then I started doing my own projects, and by projects I mean I'm also a composer. I had a lot of different interests, a lot of different areas that I wanted to explore. So I wrote a piece for piccolo and piano that my father did at one of the NFA (National Flute Association) conventions. He finally published that actually several years ago. That's a piece called *Eurhythmionics.* Then I wrote a string quartet called *Mambomaniacs* which was a cross between Bartók and Cuban music. And I started getting into song writing--this would've been the mid to late eighties. During this period I was also doing my own records, I've already mentioned *Heads, Hands and Hearts*, and then you said that you found one called *The Arms of Love*, on E-Bay, and then I did another one called *Pipe Dreams*. Those three records were all done in the late eighties. A label called *Sonic Atmospheres*. And before that I did my solo album, *Fresh Flute*, for CBS, and that was supposed to have been the beginning of my solo career where I'd go out and tour on my own and so forth. But between having my family and getting busy in the studios that never really materialized. They were only recording projects; they weren't big touring projects.

During your more active jazz era you were playing flute and tenor throughout, right?

Yeah. Although the interesting thing was that, with Chick I started to develop my voice on the flute much more rapidly than on the tenor. With the tenor sax I always felt I was emulating or even imitating the strong tenor voices that were out at the time, which for me began with Joe Farrell and then ended with Michael Brecker... and also Jan Garbareck. Those were my main three influences. And, of course, Coltrane, through Brecker, because Brecker was a proponent of Coltrane--you could hear a lot of Coltrane in his playing. But he took it to another level technically, and theoretically and harmonically. Chick loved those players. He loved Joe, and of course he played a lot with Michael Brecker in his younger, and in Michael's younger years.

And Joe Henderson also ...

And Joe Henderson. So he loved the tenor and he loved my tenor playing, but I never found my own voice on the tenor. That was somebody else's voice. But I was emerging as a flute stylist at that point, because I had developed a technique which I called the "fretless flute technique," and I was the only one in the world that could bend notes on the flute like that.

Yeah, I noticed that in just listening to that little bit from that first track. How do you do that?

Well it's hard to describe. I'm actually writing a book on that right now. It's going to be video/CD ROM type book where I make a video of this technique from all different angles.

But does it come from the embouchure, or from the fingering, or both?

It basically involves the lifting of the fingers. You have to have an open holed flute, that's the only equipment requirement, and then what you do is starting with the left hand, the A and the G key you have to lift those fingers off those two tone-holes simultaneously, while leaving the keys down, so you're only lifting the fingers off the holes. That's the first half of the technique. Then after you've uncovered the holes, you allow the keys to come up very slowly. If you put that together and do it more quickly, then you play a *portamento* between G and the B flat if you're using the thumb key, B natural if you don't. That's how you start. That's how I teach it. And then what you do is you gradually add some of the fingers in the right hand starting with the F sharp and then the F natural, and then the E and then the E flat, and you can eventually get it all the way up to a sixth between D and B.

But you can't do a smooth gliss past each note presumably?

Well, let me tell you about Robert Dick. I first met Robert in the mid-eighties--we'd done a tour together called *The Flute Caravan Tour*, which was with Carol Wincenc. I don't know if you know her, she's the classical flute professor at Juilliard right now. But she had the idea of putting together a tour of musicians from all over the world to play different styles of music and different types of flutes. So she called me to do the jazz segment, she called Robert Dick to do what they called "future flute," they had G.S. Sachdev do the Indian classical flute, they had Carlos Nikai doing the American Indian flute, they had Tim Liu do the Chinese flute--he lives in New York-- and then they had a couple of guys from Peru playing pan pipes. And Carol did the classical flute. We used to do a ten minute segment in this thing. We did a college tour, I think maybe twelve or thirteen concerts, and that was when I first met up with Robert. We had heard of each other by reputation, but we'd never actually heard each other. I'd heard him warming up in the practice room there and he was doing a portamento from the low B all the way up to the high C. But it was very, very, very slow. And then he heard me doing my fretless flute technique, where I could play very very rapidly between these intervals, and we gravitated to each and were comparing techniques, and we realized that we were accomplishing basically the same thing, via a completely opposite technique. He actually slides his fingers off of the keys, whereas my fingers are lifted off of the key just as I described to you, and then I can play very rapidly. So we were captivated with each other's techniques. And the reason I brought him up is that he has, you may have heard, that he has experimented with different types of flutes--custom made flutes, that have been made especially for him. He has a head joint with some extra attachments on it, and he has something he calls a whammy-bar, officially called a glissando head joint [available from Brannon Bros] so that he can basically play it like a slide whistle. I haven't actually seen it, but it's been described to me. It's operated by the right thumb which is normally used to balance the flute. It doesn't serve any other function besides that, but by putting the thumb into this ring, the ring is then attached to a slide inside the head joint, so it really does become like a slide whistle. So from any note on the flute you can slide to any other note on the flute. I never was interested in that because I thought, for me, it would be cheating!

Hard to say which of all this is cheating and which not cheating! But you can hear these techniques on your recordings.

Yes, indeed.

Well, we'll post the various websites and people can make up their own minds about these things. But now, bringing us up to the present, you are still involved in all these different kinds of projects?

Oh yeah, I've always had projects going, it's the only thing that keeps me sane because playing on other people's sound tracks and records and so forth, that's their projects, I'm just kind of a sideline musician on their projects, and I need to express my own ideas and creativity, so one of the projects is this flute book which will be done over the next two or three years. I've upgraded my studio so I'm now a digital video editor and so forth, and it'll be done in that kind of a format. Then I have another project that I'm doing with a friend of mine named Bill Purse, who's the one that produced my first flute record. I have a website under construction about this project. It's called "Tuttiflutti.com."

Through all these years, Steve with studio work and so forth, what percentage of the music you were playing did you find interesting or satisfying, and which was just automatic?

Well, I always try to find something that is satisfying in everything that I do whether it's a motion picture soundtrack, or whether it's another person's record. I derive a great deal of enjoyment out of kind of mastering the different aspects of these things. In other words, there's a whole different discipline to playing in a studio orchestra than there is playing, for instance, in the symphony. A couple of months ago I had the opportunity to play piccolo with the Los Angeles Philharmonic doing the

Shostakovitch 4th Symphony. It's a whole different set of muscles! And then going down to Dizzy's in San Diego to play two sets with Peter Sprague and Bob Magnusson. That's another set of muscles!

Now what percentage of all this is flute work, Steve? Are you exclusively playing flute on these sessions or are you still having to double?

Well on the studio stuff, and on Peter's stuff, that's all flute, one hundred percent flute. But where I start to double a little bit, for instance, I'm doing a show called *The Producers*, and my book is half flute and the rest of the book is divided between clarinet, which I hate, bass clarinet which I absolutely love--I think it's a very fun instrument to play--and alto sax. Of course, I used to play a lot of saxophone in the Chick Corea years, but after I'd left that situation, I didn't play so much saxophone anymore. There's a whole thing that happened here in town where doublers, you know, the people that were dedicated doublers, did all that work, and the rest of us did what we call the legit work, and it was very seldom that you'd find anybody crossing that line into the other world. But some people, some contractors, in town, still thought of me as a doubler, or at least somebody that could play sax, because they remember me from that time. So with this show that we're doing now, called *The Producers*, I'm playing basically in a big band.

Yeah. But if you go to do your own music, to play for pure enjoyment, does it occur to you to play anything but flute? Do you consider playing a reed instrument?

No. Not ever. It's all flute. I mean I am a flutist. That is my voice and that is how I represent myself. Anything I might do doubling-wise is just something to make a living, and I don't ever advertise it, and I don't ever promote myself as doing that.

I did want to ask you about the educational thing because I have a bee in my bonnet about the separations between different genres that clutter up our curriculum. When you were at Eastman, you say that there was a jazz program, but presumably you were not exclusively consigned to the jazz department, were you?

No, in fact when I got to Eastman I'd actually decided that I was going to not pursue jazz at all. In fact I left my tenor saxophone at home; I brought only my flute. I was there to become a dedicated orchestral flutist but the jazz program was so strong at that point, there was so much strength, and such a great reputation in that school that it was hard for me to resist. And somebody had heard that I played some great jazz flute and they wanted me to play in this group which as I said became *Auracle*. But once I started playing in that group and then Ray Wright found out about me and said, "Hey, I hear you play tenor sax, we could use somebody in the B band." When I said that my tenor was back in Chicago he said "why don't you send for it?" So, to tell you the truth, I started to be wooed back into jazz and I found that intermixing these disciplines, pursuing the theoretical knowledge of jazz and the technical discipline of the classical music that I was studying, I found that very stimulating at that point.

I was talking to Hubert Laws yesterday, and I was asking whether he though that the, as you put it, the discipline of classical training was what made the flute work as a jazz instrument.

Possibly, but that's a half truth because there are a lot of classical players that would love to learn how to play jazz, and some of them make it and most of them don't. And it has mostly to do with rhythm, and feel, and groove.

Absolutely. If Hubert hadn't had a feeling for it there's no amount of classical training that would've made a difference. At the same time, I think you'll agree that there were a lot of good jazz players playing flute in the early days but they were not necessarily great flute players.

They weren't trained on the instrument. They approached it more as a doubler would approach it, and that's really kind of the history of jazz flute, that's how it came to be in the first place. I mean, you go back to Sam Most of course, and Herbie Mann, and Moe Kaufman, Bud Shank, all these guys, they were primarily saxophone players.

Bud made some interesting recordings with Laurindo Almeida of classical literature, which worked quite well I thought. But why was flute not...

Well here's my theory. The flute, like the violin, is not dynamically powerful enough to hold its own in a rhythm section, as is the saxophone or the trumpet, or any of the brass instruments. There's kind of an edge that you can get, a certain kind of dynamic range, that those instruments have that the flute and the violin do not have. They're almost considered too pretty, I think. But acoustically, there are things that you could do phrasing-wise, dynamic-wise, and multiphonically on a saxophone--I mean just to keep it in the woodwind realm--that you cannot possibly do on the flute. That is almost true on the clarinet, although the clarinet kind of bridges the two worlds. The clarinet was such a prominent instrument in the big band era; it's a reed instrument, but it's a sweet reed instrument. You know, I use the sushi bar analogy. If you go to the *edo* style sushi bars they have a list of the fish going from the least fishiest to the most fishiest; you eat them in that order. If you used the same analogy for instruments in jazz, you can certainly argue that flute would be at the top of the scale in terms of sweetness, and then a small handful of jazz oboe players, that would probably be next, then the clarinet, then the saxophone, and bassoon is in there somewhere--there's only a couple of jazz bassoon players. The saxophone definitely has the edge. It really is a very dynamically powerful instrument and it is possessed of many, many different colors. I don't know if you've ever played saxophone...

Oh yeah, I started out on saxophone.

So you know about that then. In fact, during the Chick Corea years, whenever I had a flute solo--talk about a pet peeve--very often we would change the book from the original saxophone solo, to "Why don't you play flute solo?" I said, "Fine, I'll play flute, that'd be great, I'd love to." And I'd start out playing flute, and the rhythm section would be down there with me dynamically, they'd be right down there in my range supporting me. As soon as I made one dynamic leap, say from a piano or mezzo to a forte, just a spike, and then come back down, the rhythm section would come up with me and they would stay there. They wouldn't come back down. So I kept making these plateaus, these dynamic plateaus, and painting myself into a corner because I could never get back down to where I started from.

Yeah, but this assumes that there is a central core to jazz, a tradition that we're trying to replicate. It doesn't assume that we want to create a new sonic environment in which the flute suddenly becomes more relevant. Like Chico Hamilton did for example.

Well my solution to all this stuff, well, in a fusion environment, what invariably happened there is that I would simply put the flute down and pick up the tenor and finish the solo on the tenor, because it was the only way that I could compete with them! In later years, that's when I started playing with Peter Sprague and we started just losing the drummer all together. He said, "Let's just play with a trio, with just a percussionist." That turned out to be the correct environment in which to present the flute.

And then Herbie Mann told me that he suddenly felt what worked for him was the rhythmic change into the Afro Cuban feel.

Exactly. And that influenced people like Dave Valentin.

Yeah. And the flute does feel more comfortable. I mean if I'm playing in a trio just playing flute I play more bossa nova. If I want to play **Harlem Nocturne** *or something I want to play alto saxophone. The flute's not sexy!*

The right tool for the right job.

Exactly. But it's interesting that with Chico's group, when the writers talked about the people that he had--Charles Lloyd, Eric Dolphy, Buddy Collette--they tended to refer to them as his flutists, ignoring the fact that they were playing saxophone and clarinet.

And you know, there are other things that we could do on the flute that can make it more indigenous to jazz, and this is something that I get whenever I'm teaching classical musicians how to improvise, or how to get into jazz. I always have to kind of bridge the two worlds, and I have to take them out of what I call 'recital mode' when their elbows are up, and they're making a nice pretty sound, and the vibrato's just right, and the tone color's there. I have to kind of de-program them from what they've been used to learning, and teach them how to make a note dirty instead of so clean. Teach them how to tongue a low B and honk it out. And not be afraid to crack the note. Because cracking the note can actually sound really cool!

Can I give you an analogy that works for me? I'm British, and whenever I go back to London I start to speak English instead of American. There is a total difference in the two languages. There is a muscular relaxation in the mouth and the jaw to speak American that I notice very forcibly when I go back to London. When I start speaking English properly it takes more effort, and the elbows are as you say, and you're wearing a necktie, and you drink tea out of a little cup, and then you come to America you loosen your tie and you drink coffee out of a mug... Do you understand what I'm talking about?

I do. That's what I'd do with the students. I'd put a pair of sunglasses on them, I'd reposition their bodies, I'd drop their elbows, I'd make them slouch over, and I'd actually paint the picture for them. I'd say, "here you are in a smoky jazz club somewhere, and the cash register's going and people are talking, and people are drinking, and they're not really listening to you, and you're playing the blues man, and you're just down and out." You're actually drawing them into this different kind of musical environment.

The interesting thing, I think, is what has happened to jazz over the last forty years is with the advent of proper jazz education. I mean we have now degree programs--when I started the masters program in jazz at Eastman, I think they already had that in Indiana, and Texas State, and maybe a couple of the other jazz schools. But you know prior to 1960, there was no jazz education, you learned it from your fellow players, you learned it in the street. And then they had all these jazz camps, you know the Stan Kenton camps, and the Jamie Aebersold camps, and all the Aebersold records and books and all of that.

Okay, but this is a pet peeve of mine. How do we re-inject this back into the educational system so that we have musicians who can function on both genres, reading and interpreting classical literature, understanding jazz, how to improvise, how to swing. Is this too much to ask? Hubert does it. You do it.

I used to go up to British Columbia, I did a festival up there for five years, teaching master classes and playing concertos. One of the years--it must've been '87 or '88--I played the Griffes poem with the orchestra there, the Victoria Symphony, and in the middle of the little flute cadenza that's written, I motioned the conductor to stop, but I kept going. I played a three or four minute cadenza that I improvised, much to the astonishment and horror of the critics in the audience who were very Victorian, very kind of proper--this is a mini retirement community. They want their music very traditional and very properly played, and I took a chance, I went out on a limb, I used my powers of creativity and imagination, and I said, I'm going to do like they did in the old days, I'm going to invent my own cadenza.

But the critics didn't go for it?
Not at all.

Steve's experience perfectly illustrates the enigmatic hinterland between jazz and "legitimate" music, and says a lot about his career. Critics, distributors and consumers like clearly defined genres, while many artists love to work in the boundary lines between them. Kujala's work has been criticized, not as poor performance, but simply as "not jazz." This is fair enough regarding the more pop-oriented recordings that he has made, but not so much in the work he has done, and continues to do with Chick Corea--he concertized with Corea again quite recently--and not with reference to recordings with Peter Sprague and his own trio. Kujala does not play bebop, but jazz is much more than bebop. His work is not exactly avant-garde either. But it branches out into areas that enrich the jazz tradition and makes a strong contribution to the flute's role in it. Bud Shank's statement quoted above places quite a burden on Steve Kujala's shoulders. I for one will be encouraging him to fulfill it.

Part Six

Doubling

To double or not to double...

... that is the question. This is certainly a controversial topic among woodwind players, and one that is beyond the scope of this study. However, it is important to acknowledge that the vast majority of jazz flutists are doublers, most of them saxophonists. It is reasonable for us to focus on the specialists, but of all the pioneers we have discussed, none were specialists. Indeed, until we come to Jeremy Steig, there are no players in our story who have played the flute exclusively. Even Herbie Mann played tenor sax from time to time until late in his career. And the So we cannot exclude doublers from our discussion.

The idea of exclusive devotion to one instrument is a relatively recent one. Mozart was playing the viola in a string quartet with Joseph Haydn between public appearances as a pianist. Thousands of Baroque sonatas are marked "For flute or violin." And would a modern school of music tell J.S. Bach "Sorry. It's organ or harpsichord. One or the other. Make up your mind!) But as music changed, the demands on the performer intensified. It was the conservatories of the nineteenth century that started to demand a single choice of instrument in response to the virtuosic demands of Romantic composers.

But jazz and commercial music have different demands. Why would a record producer in New York or Los Angeles call three or four players to handle the various woodwind instruments when one person--a Romeo Penque or a Paul Horn--could cover all of them? The super-doubler phenomenon is still alive and well--among flutists we can point to Pedro Eustache and Vinny Golia. But we must also point to hundreds of saxophonists who are playing the flute, often very well. Flute specialists claim that they can always spot a doubler playing the flute--there is something lacking in the sound, they say. This may be true but no one can deny the quality of Joe Farrell's flute playing, even as he was gigging on tenor saxophone and learning the oboe to increase his studio calls. No one can deny the power of Sonny Fortune's flute work, standing alongside Ravi Coltrane in the Elvin Jones Rhythm Machine, or the quality of Carol Sudhalter's flute, fronting the Astoria Big Band. And where would Toshiko Akiyoshi or Maria Schneider be without multiple woodwinds in their sax sections?

It is undoubtedly a challenge to play two or three different instruments; Bud Shank famously decided that it was too much for him. Lew Tabackin, on the other hand, has persisted with both saxophone and flute, at the cost of becoming a musical schizophrenic. (See below.) But the quality of doubling performers is growing. Chris Vadala, who runs the jazz program at the University of Maryland, College Park, tells me that students are no longer allowed to think of secondary or tertiary instruments; they are expected to perform at an equal level on all of them. So Chris has published a book of exercises for doublers, moving back and forth between saxophone, clarinet and flute. So quality is increasing dramatically. (The only person left out in the cold in this process--the poor flute specialist trying to make his/her way through a jazz program!)

This is an extensive discussion, and it will continue at *www.fluteinjazz.com*. Meanwhile, here we will profile two exceptional experts in the art of instrumental doubling, Lew Tabackin and Jane Bunnett.

Lew Tabackin: Musical Schizophrenic

"I don't really consider myself a jazz flute player. I just have this little world, an idealistic world. I listen to flute players, usually classical flute players, and I hear things sound wise, tonally, that excite me, and I try to find a way to create some kind of musical idea or attitude based on sound."

Lew Tabackin

Lew Tabackin is a musical schizophrenic, and he freely admits it. As a tenor saxophonist, he carries forward one of jazz' richest traditions, one that begins with Coleman Hawkins and extends to the present through John Coltrane and Sonny Rollins. Tabackin has managed to blend these influences into a highly personal voice, characterized by a huge sound, unfailing melodic inventiveness, and a passionate delivery. As Lew's own website describes it, "His distinctive tenor sax style includes the use of wide intervals, abrupt changes of mood and tempo, and purposeful fervor, all in the service of showing the full range of possibilities of his instrument." Fair enough--Lew would be a significant jazz player just as a tenor saxophonist. But as if this was not enough, he has also developed one of the most influential jazz flute styles, one that seemingly owes little or nothing to his other stream of influences.

In point of fact, Tabackin began as a flutist largely by accident, when he was in sixth grade. He took up the tenor later, while he was in high school, driven by his interest in jazz. Philadelphia in the 1950s had an active jazz scene, one with many opportunities for up and coming musicians to perform, mainly in jam sessions. Lew served his apprenticeship in this environment, mainly developing his skills as a tenor player. Enrolling at the Philadelphia Conservatory of Music, however, Lew found the curriculum oriented toward classical music, and so the flute was his major until he graduated in 1962. (He also undertook private studies in composition with Vincent Persichetti.) And so, during these years, both lines of influence--jazz saxophone, classical flute--were being laid down, simultaneously but separately.

A spell in the army followed graduation, but when that was over Tabackin headed first for New Jersey and then for New York, where his apprenticeship matured into professionalism as he worked with Tal Farlow, Don Friedman, Joe Henderson, and Chuck Israels, as well as in the big bands led by Cab Calloway, Les and Larry Elgart, Maynard Ferguson, Thad Jones and Mel Lewis, Clark Terry, and Duke Pearson. There was also work with smaller groups during this time. Tabackin's own trio held a long-term residency at the La Boheme club in Philadelphia during the late sixties, while he also worked as a sideman with Donald Byrd, Roland Hanna, Elvin Jones, and Attila Zoller. And steady work came with Doc Severinsen's band on the *Dick Cavett* and *Tonight* shows. He also spent some time in Europe as a guest soloist with the Danish Radio Orchestra and the Hamburg Jazz Workshop.

1968 was a turning point for Tabackin, as he met, and then married, the Japanese-American composer and bandleader Toshiko Akiyoshi, beginning a musical relationship that was to have a profound effect upon his work. The big band that Akiyoshi and Tabackin went on to form created a showcase for Tabackin's skills as a soloist and brought his work to the attention of a national audience, while constantly stimulating those skills through Toshiko's writing ability. At the same time, Toshiko's work, and their travels in the Far East, opened Tabackin to an Asian influence that added another dimension to his already idiosyncratic flute style. Their association also prompted a move from New York to Los Angeles for a number of years. While on the west coast, as the big band was beginning to establish itself, Tabackin also reconfigured his trio, working at various times with Billy Higgins, John Heard, and Charlie Haden, later with drummer Joey Baron and bassist Michael Moore. Tabackin also developed a musical relationship with drummer Shelley Manne that resulted in a number of recordings.

By 1982 New York beckoned once again and Lew and Toshiko headed back to Manhattan, where the big band, and Tabackin's trio, re-emerged, with different personnel but the same ethos. Recognition for their work, and a series of high-quality recordings followed. Tabackin started to show up in *Down Beat* polls for flute, in both the critic's and reader's listings. This has been possible through the exposure that has come from his continuing role as major soloist with the Akiyoshi-Tabackin orchestra, and his appearances with a number of all-star bands, including George Wein's Newport All-Star Band, the New York Jazz Giants, and the Carnegie Hall Jazz Band.

Through all of this, Lew has continued to develop his flute and tenor work side by side. Unlike Bud Shank, who decided he could not keep up the flute and the saxophone, Tabackin continues to bear the cross of musical schizophrenia. From time to time he escapes to concentrate on one or other of his instruments, such as the 1978, all-flute recording *Rites of Pan* and his 1996, all-tenor CD *Tenority.* But schizophrenic he remains, and he is the first to recognize this. He warmed to this theme when we met in his Manhattan apartment:

Last time we talked you told me you were a schizophrenic...
Something like that, yeah.
That's what I was feeling, but I'm glad you said it yourself! But everyone has their own story on why they took up the instrument in the first place. You mentioned to me that you got the flute because there wasn't anything else available at that time?
Yeah, there was a public school situation and I thought it'd be nice to play something. Actually, for some strange reason--don't ask me why--I wanted to play clarinet. But they didn't have a clarinet. The only thing they had was a flute which I didn't know anything about--I mean I hardly knew what it looked like. This was probably junior high, or the end of elementary school--around sixth grade. They had a few people who were interested in an instrument, and the criterion was who could get a sound out of the head joint. One girl couldn't get any sound but one guy got a pretty big sound right away--he had actually more ability in that direction from being able to get a tone out of blowing into a bottle. I got a little something. Basically, it's a very interesting concept for choosing a potential student, but anyway, I got it by default.

I took it and it was better than nothing. I thought it would be interesting. Problem was, I had a horrible teacher. They provided you with a teacher at no cost. They would hire music teachers to come to the school. And obviously the guy who was teaching me was not a flute player. I developed all these horrible ways of playing--if you can imagine playing with the flute on your shoulder. Basically I was learning by trial and error and it took me years to get rid of all those bad habits. So anyway, I wasn't very serious at this time. I had a school instrument, and played in a little orchestra, such as it was, with a public school education, and I tried to take some lessons from some different people, trying to correct some of these bad habits which took years to correct.

But you were interested in jazz, so didn't you want to drop the flute in order to get a tenor?
There were guys playing flute. Actually Herbie Mann had a hit record, a Charlie Parker tune, *Little Suede Shoes.* I could play that, and I would go to the high school and the guys were playing jam sessions and stuff after school, and I brought my flute and I actually played that tune. It felt good. I didn't know

what I was doing, but it felt good. I was really horrible but I started fooling around with that. I was thinking of getting a tenor saxophone. Actually I did play a little clarinet before, I had a horrible clarinet and was fooling with that.

You mentioned that it wasn't too cool to be seen walking across south Philadelphia with a flute.

First of all, no one knew what it was. Nobody was into classical music. And flute was non existent in that environment, except for some forms of Latin music that weren't part of my social environment. So nobody knew what a flute was, and it wasn't exactly a macho instrument.

Was it thought of as a girl's instrument?

I guess if they thought it was anything, although there weren't many girls playing it at that time. It was just like, you played the trumpet or maybe saxophone or trombone and you were cool. I mean, I'm talking about the 1950s. So it wasn't something that was really socially advantageous to be involved with.

The reason I bring that up is because it's a commonly held idea that the flute didn't catch on for the first fifty years of jazz or whatever just because of the acoustic problems. But there are these social issues also, gender issues.

Well, I mention this quite often because my daughter was playing the flute, so I bought her a couple of Marcel Moyse's books. And there are a couple of his essays translated, and one of the first things he says is, "The flute is a minor instrument." In a classical music sense, piano and violin are major instruments, repertoire wise. I think this has a lot to do with dynamics. I think his point was basically that the flute has also limitations, and you have to spend a lot of energy and effort to try to overcome some of these acoustical, dynamic limitations. And in jazz it's even worse, so it's really a minor instrument in jazz. I try to utilize it in a way that doesn't show up the limitations, you know, so basically I don't really consider myself a jazz flute player. I mean, I just created my own little world that I deal in, and that's the schizophrenia aspect, you know, which you mentioned. I just have this little world, an idealistic world. I listen to music, I listen to flute players, usually classical flute players, and I hear things soundwise, tonally, that excite me, and I try to find a way to create some kind of musical idea or attitude based on sound. It doesn't necessarily lend itself to bebop playing.

Well, do you consider yourself a jazz saxophone player?

That's it exactly.

So when you're playing the flute it's just a whole different thing. But when you started, who else was there to listen to, apart from Herbie?

Well, there were guys to listen to. I think Frank Wess was a quintessential jazz flute player. With all due respect to other people, he played jazz music on the flute with a lot of elegance and control of the instrument. It wasn't gimmicky, you know it wasn't just, "ah yes this is a different kind of sound." To this day he has a lot of integrity in how he plays. James Moody plays the flute, not from a flute point of view, but from a bebop point of view, and from an articulation point of view, executing saxophone music on the flute in a special way.

There's a lot of continuity between their saxophone playing and their flute playing.

Both of them; it translates well. In terms of people I listened to... there were not a lot of people. Sam Most was a very interesting player. But I always felt that, I don't know, there's something missing, because I'm sound oriented. So I want to hear the beauty of the note, and I want the note to tell me how to play. I want the sound to influence the line and it doesn't necessary lend itself to a "bebop" kind of playing.

There are a lot of players who can put bebop lines very beautifully through the flute but who don't necessary have a great sound on the instrument. They are not necessarily great flute players.

That's the whole point.

And that wasn't attractive to you?

No, that wasn't attractive to me. I mean I fooled around, and the better I got at playing the flute, the worse it was to play the stylistic jazz flute at the time. So I decided that I was just going to find my own way of playing. I moved to New York and I started practicing really hard. My last teacher was Murray Panitz, the first flute player at the Philadelphia orchestra; he died not too long ago. Before him I didn't really care about the flute. I was playing saxophone and I was trying to play jazz and trying to find my voice, or trying to find some kind of direction. Flute wasn't really important to me. But when I started spending time with him he showed me basic fundamentals, things dealing with the overtone series, really very simple fundamental things, and I really made a lot of progress. I was able to take his concept and work on it on my own. And to this day I listen to recordings like... jazz players listen to recordings to get inspiration and steal a few licks or whatever from their heroes or people they like. Well I would listen to flute records, classical flute records. I listened to Julius Baker, and I loved William Kinkaid--he was in Philadelphia at the time--and Rampal. So I started listening to those people and trying to form some concept, a tonal concept, and I kept on working on it. When I came to New York I was practicing quite a bit and there was a bass player who started an ensemble, his name was Chuck Israels, he was kind of a composer/bass player.

He was [pianist] Bill Evans' bass player for a spell?

Yeah, same guy. Anyway he used Bill Evans' music as a springboard for some of his compositions, and he started to write things that were almost more contemporary classical music. He knew how I played the flute and so he wrote stuff for me to play, and I tried to develop almost a French... I mean I listened to French impressionistic flute music, and tried to develop improvisations along those lines.

I hear that. I mean last night when you started playing I immediately wrote down "Debussy meets Thelonius Monk." That was the first thing that came to my head. But did you also work out those same kinds of methods yourself?

Well, I tried to. I did a certain amount of it. There's so much to go through I never had enough time to develop that--there were so many other things. I could never really do what virtuoso classical flute players do, but I believe in fundamentals, so I constantly work on the tonal aspects.

But what comes out depends on what goes in, not just in terms of listening but also what you actually practice, what you put through the instrument when you're working.

Yes, to a certain extent, and it might sound funny, but I don't practice a lot of what I play. I mean sometimes I leave myself pretty naked and I don't know what I'm going to do, because if I try to plan something I usually fail.

I understand that process, but it sounds to me from listening to you that you are exposing yourself to that kind of literature. And then it comes out unconsciously.

Yeah, I'm sure it does. So anyway, that's how I started to develop an approach. Then later on Toshiko started the band, and she would draw on Japanese traditional things. So I said I wanted to investigate a little bit of that, because when she leaves me an open space, I wanted to play something that I could relate to what I wanted to do, especially in programmatic music and narrative pieces. I like to know the story; I like to play the story. Like another form of Lester Young, I mean there's gotta be a story. So I started to listen to some Shakuhachi music, and I really was attracted to the idea of the one note concept. I could play one note a hundred different ways.

Yeah, Eastern music is different from Western in many respects, but one aspect is a lot of the music goes on within the tone rather than just building structures out of tones.

Exactly. Exactly. Well I picked up on that and I said "Wow!" And then you kind of mesmerize yourself. Sometimes I can do it in public. Say, if I play a low E, display it, play it again, play it a little differently, change the pitch a little bit, and then eventually I'm like in some kind of a trance--I go into another world of not thinking.

This is so intriguing because what I've found since starting this project is how much flutists are drawn into these very interesting areas beyond jazz.

The flute is a first instrument. Even before the voice, even before the drum. It is really the natural... it exists in nature, even without anybody playing it--just the wind blowing through a reed. It is a universal instrument. You can pick up a flute and play it in any situation and people can relate to it. Pick up the saxophone and you start playing some bebop or something like "jazz music," and in some situations it doesn't quite relate.

I noticed with Indian music that the flute was perhaps the easiest instrument for Western audiences to relate to as an introduction to the music. But now, I am sure you are familiar with James Newton and the techniques he has brought to jazz from contemporary serious music. (I hate these terms!) In your case, you have incorporated some things from traditional Japanese music?

I noticed when I first heard Toru Takemitsu, when I heard his *November Steps,* he has a full symphony orchestra, which is very contemporary, Western style, and then he has Japanese traditional instruments, the *shakuhachi* and the *b'iwa,* playing the way they play. And they sound totally avant-garde. When the *shakuhachi* comes in it sounds so out, but it's very traditional. So it's the setting that determines what the effect is. All of a sudden you hear this very traditional *shakuhachi* and it sounds totally like it's from another planet.

There's also a CD by the Kronos Quartet where they alternate very contemporary pieces with twelfth-century Notre Dame organa and other ancient pieces, and it's extraordinary how they fit together--it's the same phenomenon.

Yes, it points out a lot of things. For example, about the concept of fashion in art. Whatever kind of approach you choose, if it's artistic, that has nothing to do with fashion. Fashion is fleeting, so with music. If the standard is really high and the music is sincere, it's always contemporary. And all these relationships, like what you were talking about, enter into the picture. So I try not to be concerned with what is fashionable, what is in, what is not in, just continue on a road and deal with it the best I can. Anyway, the whole thing that attracted me to that is not so much the Shakuhachi and Koto stuff but it's a real Zen kind of thing, and I try to use that feeling when I play, especially when I play unaccompanied. I also try to relate that feeling in a jazz context when I'm playing with my little group. I'll get out and I'm playing my saxophone, and whatever, and I try to establish that oneness with the environment and the audience, which is a similar feeling to playing that one note on the flute and just drawing the energy in. So I don't think--I try to get out of the thinking realm.

Are you claiming that this occurs more when you play the flute than when you play the saxophone?

It occurs differently, mainly because the material that I set myself up when I play the flute lends itself to that. Saxophone stuff is out of the tradition. Musically it's different, but I do try to as much as I can to get into the same kind of non-thinking, Zen kind of thing. I would like to have it happen when I'm playing the saxophone. It's a little more difficult because the music is a little bit more technically complicated, and there's a lot more happening around it.

Have you ever seen a book by Hazrat Inayat Kahn, from the Sufi tradition? He talks there about how different kinds of music engage different levels of the personality.... the body, the intellect, the heart. And the highest achievement of all is when we can hear the music of the spheres. That was his terminology.

Well, you can't argue with that. I mean that's the ultimate goal and it's the most difficult. Sometimes you can get close to it, it keeps you going. I almost played it but I don't know where it came from...

Maybe it's tough in jazz because the rhythm aspect keeps the body involved and makes it hard to transcend to those deeper levels...

I don't know, I'll have to check out that book...

You must've handled the shakuhachi?

I have one. I bought one in Kyoto. The problem was that I tried to play it and I couldn't find the holes! So I said, "I just can't deal with it." I just put it away.

But you applied those things to your flute playing?

Yeah, I figured I'd better just forget about being a *shakuhachi* player.

I had the same problem with the bansuri, because my hands are too small. Are you playing any alto flute?

Yeah, I like to play the alto. The alto flute is very funny. When I play the alto flute I feel more like a bebop kind of thing

Oh really? You'd think it would go the other way.

Because when I play it, I approach it more like a saxophone. It has that kind of register and resistance factor. I've done some recording work where I've played kind of like bebop style alto flute.

Which ones are they?

I'm trying to remember... I recorded with an orchestra. We did *Speak Low* with alto flute, and I know I've done some other things.

There's something about the saxophone... the flute is so much tighter somehow.

The alto flute is looser.

I've always felt the difference is like between speaking British and speaking American--'cause I do both. One is just tighter than the other. Do you understand what I mean? When you speak British, the muscles are tighter here (indicating the throat and jaw), you're more controlled, it's more articulated. If you just relax and let it go, you're speaking American--like stepping out of church and loosening your tie!

Yes. I understand that. It's an interesting analogy. I like that. You're right--it is just looser to me. It's maybe like the difference between flugelhorn and trumpet, that's one analogy. And when I pick it up it's kind of like...there's room for the articulation that I want. I can feel more comfortable playing bebop because I don't have the same kind of intensity. It's not as rigid.

I've also thought about the fact that, when you hear musicians, particularly jazz musicians, from different countries, the way they play is different probably because their language is different. So the nuances will be different, or should be different.

So that jazz in Europe very often is a different genre. It has another dimension to it.

Yeah, it's not jazz, basically. I may be a bit narrow, but I think a certain element should exist to be called jazz. Like what we were talking about. Some of the stuff that I do, or some other people do, might be valid musically, might be good or better, whatever, or different, but it's not necessarily jazz. Just because it's improvisation--and there's improvisation in all kinds of music obviously--but with jazz music... Well, let's put it this way, I like to hear a little bebop sensibility, a little blues sensibility. Even if the person is a great improviser, and fluid, and all the harmonies are great, and everything is happening, the jazz element can be totally gone. So I don't have any problems saying that it's not jazz. Everything is jazz. It's becoming like the 1920s when if it wasn't classical music it was jazz, and it's becoming like that now. All instrumental music is jazz.

Yes, well I get sent some things to review, and some of the things that fall under "smooth" jazz... I can't figure out why exactly, but I don't want to listen to it.

But the point is, as far as the categories are concerned, they call it jazz; everything's jazz. I would really like to have something, my own personal review of it and feel comfortable saying, "I really like that, it may not be jazz but I really like it." Or "I don't like it because it doesn't have jazz elements." You mentioned Wynton earlier. He's a bit reactionary. I don't want to be reactionary, I don't think I'm a reactionary, but I like to hear certain elements in the music.

But what's intriguing to me is how people react to the music. I had a fellow who was helping me with some work in my house, an African-American guy, and I had some music playing, something straight-ahead, Phil Woods or something, and he says to me, "... that sounds like restaurant music."

The sad thing about it, you know, when I was a kid it seemed like jazz was really part of Black culture and people listened to it all the time--they understood the music. You played a club and the audience would be predominantly black, and they understood what you were playing. And if you played better the night before, or if you were playing bad, you know. they could feel they were really part of the music. Then, for some reason, that whole thing changed. Now--it's unfortunate--now audiences are predominantly white. You know, we play at Birdland every Monday night, we've been playing there for five years, and the audiences are mainly white, or tourists--Japanese tourists, European tourists.

It's the same way in Washington, at places like Blues Alley and the Kennedy Canter... It's like going to the Redskin's game, you go to see and be seen and all that. You played at the Kennedy Center a few months ago? It was the same thing, was it?

Yes, I guess so. I think it's sad. I think the main problem is they spend a lot of money and effort on "jazz education," which is a joke. It's more a jazz educational industry, to produce adequate players who will never be able to work, who become teachers and teach more kids... something that doesn't quite make sense. The point I'm trying to make is, with all the effort they expend trying to make people into musicians they should put into music in all school systems, especially in the minority school system where the young black kids need to be inspired, and talk about the great legacy and the great tradition and all the great black heroes. I've never gone into a school and asked if anybody ever heard of Duke Ellington or Charles Parker or Louis Armstrong. They've heard of Michael Jackson.

When I came over here as an English guy, in undergraduate school in California, I found out I knew more about jazz than any of the music majors. What does that tell you? I was shocked.

Everyone's shocked when they come to America.

Is that just California, or would it be different in New York?

It's maybe a little better here. The people are more exposed to jazz music--there's more of it.

There's one thing, though, that differentiates jazz from the smooth jazz thing that to me is almost like a bright line. It's live in the studio rather than laying down tracks and soloing over them. Have you every tried to do that?

I've had to do it. I've had to do like overdubs and it's really uncomfortable.

But not for your own music?

Oh no, no, no. I would never do that. But I've had... like the day before yesterday I had a call to go in, and some guy was making a record, a big band, and he wanted me to play two solos. So he put me in a booth. It was live, but still, I'm in a booth! And I felt like--it was almost the same as an overdub. It feels like the same as if you're not playing with them. You've got a headset on, there's no contact with any of the musicians. If it's commercial music it's okay, but if you're trying to play jazz music it's like... (Shrugs)

I know what you mean. I've done my share of that.

Yeah. It's like product music.

Exactly. How does the [Toshiko] big band do now? Does it have to depend on grants?

No. We never depended on anything. In fact, you know, the band has retired, at the end of the year. We produced a concert at Carnegie Hall October 17, like a thirtieth anniversary, farewell concert. And now we're finishing up. We're going to Japan in about a week to do a couple of things for Blue Note and a couple of other gigs, and finish up in Berlin, and that's it.

And then what?

And then Toshiko will concentrate on playing the piano. It won't be much of a change for me because I've been doing my own little things--except it changes people's perception of you.

Do you like the stuff that you've done with the orchestra?

Oh yeah. I mean, our music is special. So much of our music is not just tunes, it's true compositions and real narrative stuff, something you can sink your teeth into. As a soloist I can get into it, beyond just what goes with what chord. I can get into it from a point of view of continuing the story, or adding to a story.

And she has written some flute features. Which ones should I list? Do you have a discography?

Not for the big band.

How about other albums? Rites of Pan, *for example?*

That was my first flute album. Then the album called *Lew Tabackin* was my first trio album. That was the beginning. With the big band, there were certain seminal pieces like the third one, *Kogun.*

Like many of Toshiko's pieces, *Kogun* is programmatic, an extended work with both Western art music and oriental influences. It is in just such contexts that Tabackin has developed his unique approach to the flute, described by his website as: "at once virtuosic, primordial, cross-cultural, and passionate." It is telling, however, that Tabackin thinks of himself as a jazz artist while playing tenor, but does not consider himself a jazz flutist. It is through the flute, not the saxophone, that he has been able to explore these influences, to create a unique, highly personal world, while drawing on soundscapes unique to that instrument, from a variety of cultural settings. In so doing, Tabackin has created a body of work that must be counted among the finest examples of the flute in contemporary music, whether or not it is jazz!

Jane Bunnett: Canada, Cuba, and Points In Between

"Jane's individuality and imagination reveal that she is both an important and underappreciated artist"   *Don Heckman, L.A. Times*

When I began working on this volume I had a plan, some neat and tidy categories to put flutists in: pure flutists, doublers; straight-ahead players, Latin players and so forth. Then I ran into **Jane Bunnett** and all this went out the window. Jane will not fit into any of these, or rather, she fits into more than one of them. To begin with, she is an accomplished doubler; she is winning polls, in *Down Beat* magazine, for example, both for her flute work and her soprano sax playing. She also works freely in a variety of genres, including, but not limited to: Latin music--specifically music from Cuba, with which she has had a deep involvement since 1982; free jazz, which she has recorded with Paul Bley and Don Pullen; contemporary post-bop with her own group, which has included such players as Stanley Cowell and Dewey Redman. A recent CD features her adaptations of folk music from all over the world. It is perfect for the flute but, being Jane, she plays them on soprano! Overall, even though she is from Toronto, Canada, she is probably best known for her work with Cuban musicians. We began our conversation talking about a unique project from 1997.

Tell me about Havana Flute Summit.
It's on *Naxos Jazz*, it was done in Cuba, and it's got Richard Egues--he's not the inventor of cha-cha-cha but he's one of the most famous exponents of it. It's a good record in that it's got Richard on it, being the oldest at 82, and then the youngest which is Maraca Valle. He's pretty much considered the hottest Cuban flute player on the scene, from Havana. I mean people feel that he can really outplay even Dave Valentin. But this record has four flutes. In *Latin Beat* Magazine it was the record of the year a few years ago.

So the four flutists are yourself and the three Cubans.
Yeah. Maraca Vallé, Richard Egues and Céline, she's married to Maraca. She's French but lives in Cuba.

Are these the major flute players in Cuba, or are there many?
There's a lot. Flute is one of the most typical classic instruments in the groups. Even in the *salsa* groups it's one of the strongest soloing instruments.

I understand from Danilo Lozano that in charanga *it is the lead instrument.*
Yeah, exactly. So much of the popular Cuban music stems from those traditional styles.

More so than other Latin music?
I think so. Trumpet, congas, flute, violins, are very traditional instruments. For example, when I do my school project every year--I raise money every year and take instruments to Cuba--one of the instruments that is needed more than anything are the flutes, because all of a sudden you'll have fourteen or fifteen students sharing one flute--pretty gloomy. It's a very popular instrument.

Do they prefer to use the wooden head joint?
They're not seen so much anymore. There are people who still play them, but I would say it's a bit of a dying art form partly because they're hard to get.

Have you tried them? Nestor [Torres] uses a regular flute with a wooden head joint.

Yeah, I have a couple of wooden head joints.

The lip plate is thicker, isn't it?

Yeah, there's no embouchure plate on it, so you've really got to have strong chops. I find for playing with a lot of percussion that I can't really cut through. I can't play as forcibly on the wooden head joints as I can on a standard flute [where] I can bully it a little bit more.

It gives the flute a unique quality. For example on **Havana Flute Summit** *were they using that type of instrument?*

No, everybody was playing silver.

Nestor feels that the sound can get irritating for that kind of music if you don't mellow it out a little bit with the wooden head joint. But anyway, how did you get involved with Cuba in the first place? You're from Canada, right?

Well, it was really a pretty flukey thing. In 1982 Larry [Jane's husband and musical partnerLarry Cramer] and I went on vacation to Cuba. I had gone to Mexico two or three times and had gotten ill every time I'd gone. And somebody told me that the water was okay in Cuba. So I gave it a shot. It was a very low-priced trip advertised in the paper and I just felt there was nothing to lose.

You just wanted to soak up some sun?

Yeah! And of course we always take our instruments with us. I took my saxophone and my flute. And from the moment we got there... there was a band playing in the airport, another band that lead us onto the bus, and when we got off the bus there was another typical sort of *comparsa* group as they're called playing, and then that night there was an eighteen piece *son montuno* which is like a big band playing mambo. It was just unbelievable!

We went into the city a couple of days later, and there were just music stores and records-- there seemed to be an abundance of music everywhere, one of the few things that there was an abundance of in Cuba, because there was nothing else! But there were LPs, and so I started buying LPs and brought them back to Canada and started listening to them, and so many of them were just stupendous, I was blown away by the music.

I was playing a little bit in a salsa band in Toronto. Often, as you know, with jazz players, you can get hired because you're able to solo, and with a lot of these *salsa* bands there are sections where you have these repeated vamps, and being able to solo, and being able to read charts from Chile, Columbia, Peru, Equador, etc., when you got to these improvising sections they'd often fill out the band with some *gringos* that were doing the soloing and playing the charts, whereas the group may be made up of different people from Latin America. I hadn't been exposed to this. I don't think there was any Cubans at all in Toronto at that point, but I was playing something that was sort of what I heard in Cuba. But when I got to Cuba it was the real deal, 100 percent Cuban music. It was just really powerful.

Before you started to get exposed to even those experiences, you were a jazz saxophone player?

I was playing jazz. I had started out playing classical piano, and then later on I started having some problems with my hand. I went to San Francisco and I'd heard jazz before, but I'd never been out on my own traveling and exposed to hearing it night after night, which I did at Keystone Corner.

What was your initial training?

My training was a bit of school band, and early class piano lessons at the public school I went to. A little bit later, when I turned eleven or twelve, I started some private lessons which I absolutely hated, but I continued to play because there was a piano at the house that my parents bought.

What kind of literature did you like?

It was always the Latin American Composers. I got quite serious about the piano after quitting a couple of times, and then eventually actually quitting school early too. I decided I just wanted to play piano. I was really trying to find myself in some way, and I started to work very hard at the piano. I was playing a lot, but then this was when I started to have some injury in my hand. I was playing [Alberto] Ginastera, and Villa Lobos, and Aaron Copeland, and things that sort of had a bit of Latin flavor to them.

So you were obviously born in Canada by some kind of karmic mistake!

It's funny! It's just something... I liked the swing, and I just was drawn towards rhythmic music; that was the thing that opened the door. On weekends I would get together with friends, and I think in my last year of high school I picked up the flute. I needed to get out of school and I took a pretty lame last year of high school, so I could just get my grades and get out. So I took the flute, which I always wanted to play, because later in public school I was playing the clarinet. The flute was really my first choice but I didn't get it. So, later on, I started on the flute and I picked it up very quickly. And even though I was studying classical piano, on the weekends I was getting together and playing with friends--there were bongos and guitars and basically just folky jam type things. I seemed to improvise pretty well, by ear. I didn't really put two and two together--sometimes I would play in A minor and then in D7. It was one thing to be reading music and another to abandon paper and just play by ear. But then it was really after this trip to San Francisco that I decided that I wanted to play jazz full-time. I finished up my piano studies, I did my grade 10 that year, and then decided that I really wanted to play jazz. And I had a pretty eclectic jazz collection. I have an older brother, and I'd go into his room and grab stuff, and he would have some Herbie Mann and Bill Evans and Yusef Lateef and [Thelonius] Monk...

So you had heard some jazz flute then?

Oh yeah, and saxophone and piano. I had a couple of Monk records that I got from him. I also had Joni Mitchell and Bob Dylan, the *Youngbloods*, and *The Band*--all over the map really. After this trip it was like "this is what I wanna do," and it really hit me. And from there, I was walking home one day and I saw this house that said "School of Music." So I just walked in the door and this guy had some university students that were in a jazz program at New York University. It was summertime, and they were outside of this house teaching some jazz workshops, and guitar, and there were a few people in there teaching jazz. So I just sort of jumped right into that and started hanging out with other people there that were going out to hear music. I'd go into the record stores and ask people to play stuff for me. And that's how it all happened. So when I got to Cuba in '82 I had probably been playing pretty seriously for about five or six years, and gigging. Flute and saxophone. I played alto, but it was the soprano that I really liked after hearing Steve Lacy play.

That's a difficult double, soprano and flute.

I have a tenor and it's a little bit easier on the chops. I have to work at it and I think that's one of the reasons why I decided to focus on soprano and on flute. And not look at myself as a real doubler because it is such a jump.

What percentage of your time these days are you devoting to each instrument? Is it 50/50?

It really depends what is coming up in front of me. I did an engagement last month where we arranged a number of folk songs for a recording I'm going to be doing from music from all over the world, a couple of Cuban pieces, a Brazilian piece, and a piece Jim Pepper wrote--I think it's a Navajo song--and some other traditional things, like *Black is the Color of My True Love's Hair*, and things like that. And I did it with a string quartet with drums and acoustic bass and piano. It's somewhat jazzy--

there's a lot of blowing on it. But on that record it was only soprano, and during that time the flute took a back burner for a while. And there's cases where I've had a lot of flute stuff that's come up, and I've just sort of focused on the flute. Generally they're half and half. I find it easier sometimes to do a couple of flute things and then do a soprano thing and then a couple more flute things. It takes a lot of concentration and automatic focusing on muscle groups and stuff.

So now, you've discovered Cuba, and that started to dominate...

We have about thirteen/fourteen records out, and I've always tried to alternate, with doing a Cuban release to doing something in between that. After I did *Alma de Santiago*, I did a record with Dewey Redman and Stanley Cowell which was more traditional straight--ahead jazz. Then we did *Cuban Odyssey*. I still really see myself primarily as a jazz artist working in the two idioms.

You seem to always have a unique approach.

Well, on *The Water is Wide* we did probably more traditional things, like Michelle Le Grande's *You Must Believe in Spring* and I did a Monk thing, and...

But each project has a unique structure to it.

I think it's really important to try and give it a bit of a point of view. I've never been a person who just played all standards, but I've never been a person to do all originals either. For me personally, I like to try and keep a balance between the repertoires. It's an ongoing thing to continue to study Charlie Parker, and Monk, and Bud Powell, and at the same time to be learning standards, because some of the standards are just the most beautiful pieces to improvise on ever. But then I feel it's important to try and write, to try and come up with something of your own, if you ever feel the impulse to do that. If it doesn't come it doesn't come, but if you don't practice it a little bit it won't really come. It's like anything else--it takes practice to write a good composition. Some people do it much better than others. I've got earlier things that I've written and they're stinky!

So for your next project, is it back to Cuba?

There is a new CD it's called *Cuban Odyssey*. The next one will probably be... well I'm preparing for a live recording with the working group that we're on tour with. That's going to be with special guests. It's going be an unusual record because I'm going to be bringing a lot of surprise people over the course of three nights to Toronto to record, in live performance. But I have a feeling maybe this folk song record will get done before that. All soprano. There are other things like *Rittmo and Soul*, there's a lot of flute on that. That's on Bluc Note/EMI, too.

Tell me a little bit about how the Paul Bley session came about.

Well, he actually called me in Montreal to do it. He's Canadian also. We'd just walk in the room and start playing. It was very demanding and scary at the same time. But it was really fun, and it just felt great to play with him. He just has monstrous ears and hears so much, and is an incredibly supportive partner on that record.

There may be many readers, flutists maybe, who don't know much about jazz, but the concept of completely free improvisation must be even scarier than taking a solo on a song.

I felt like after I did that session I really grew as a musician--like I just got over a huge heap. I was nervous about it because I kept calling him saying "What are we going to play?" At the time I had recently been back from Paris where I'd just been playing pretty much Monk's music with Steve Lacy. And I was kind of excited about maybe doing some Monk. But Paul said to me, "That's great, do it on your next record!" I still didn't know what the material was going to be, and I called him and got his wife and she said "Well, you know, Paul doesn't do repertoire." And I was like, "Okay!"

We met for breakfast--the session was at 12--and I just asked about stuff and what pieces we could maybe do, and he kept changing the subject. So when we were on the way to the studio, still no repertoire had been picked, and when I got there he said, "Okay, play whatever you want," and then later, "Okay, let's do this soprano," and later, "Okay, let's do this flute." It was definitely one of the most memorable and unusual recording experiences. But I really cherish it because it was great.

I'm sure the Cuban music is more tightly structured. When you work with Cuban musicians are they traditional compositions?

It really depends. All the records I've done have been different situations. Sometimes we've done very traditional things. You know the folklore chants which date back hundreds of years, we've taken those and added a harmonic bent to them and arranged them. Sometimes some of the stuff that I've done has been original music, like on *Ritmo and Soul.* There's a lot of original music on that, but it's written within the context of using really traditional rhythms, Afro-Cuban rhythms. There's kind of like a funky rap thing that's on there which is a very traditional chant used in their religion, but we did it in a funky fashion. Because I used the traditional *bata*, the religious drums, those are the three headed drums, sort of hourglass shaped drums, and three different people play them at once--those things have been based on very traditional rhythmic cycles. And the music's all written. I've worked with tapes, working with those rhythms and writing my material to fit in with that.

A rhythmic cycle?

Yeah, a rhythmic pattern. In the Afro-Cuban religion many of the rhythmic patterns are hooked up to the particular vibrations of the saints, because the Afro-Cuban religion is kind of a mixture, in a sense, of the Catholic and the African. They use the Catholic deities, but take the African gods and superimpose them on these Catholic saints because they were ruled by the Spaniards in Cuba.

So anyway, these particular drum patterns are still used for religious purposes, but they've totally filtrated into popular Cuban music too. But I go back and use these on our recordings, because I work with many musicians that are still very much into the religion there. The sole purpose originally for those rhythms was to connect with the outer spirit, through the dancers.

So, does it fit into a certain number of measures?

Well, they do, but it's like the African drum patterns, they're kind of hard to nail down. Most of the time it's compound and simple time. Timewise it's pretty measured but still the tempos speed up.

Could you see yourself taking a vacation in Bulgaria or China or somewhere, and going in a whole different direction again? Or do you think you're pretty locked in on Cuba now?

Well, strangely enough I have been working with an Indian *ghazal* [light classical music from north India] singer, Kirin Aluwalia, in Toronto. I'm very interested in Indian music. I know it's a huge one to take on. But, who knows?

Who knows, indeed? Perhaps Jane Bunnett will delve into Indian music for inspiration, or perhaps she will go more deeply into the Cuban tradition, or other world music traditions, alternating, as she has in the past, with work derived more directly from jazz. The only thing her recorded output tells us is that she is totally unpredictable. But this is what makes her work so interesting. And, in spite of Don Heckman's statement at the beginning of the piece, she has been steadily gaining in critical acclaim in recent years.

Jane has been recognized as the number one "Rising Star" on flute by Down Beat magazine in 2004, and has also received numerous Juno awards and two Grammy nominations for her recordings--

Best Latin Jazz Recording, 2002 for *Alma de Santiago* and 2003 for *Cuban Odyssey*. Beyond that, again in 2004, she was the appointed an Officer of the Order of Canada, the highest civilian honour given to Canadian citizens "for outstanding achievement and service to the country or to humanity at large," and she also holds an honorary doctorate from Queen's University in Ontario. She continues to tour internationally, and her most recent album, *Embracing Voices,* does just that, featuring guest vocalists performing songs in English, Spanish and Creole.

And yet, as she expands her range of influence, Jane Bunnett is clearly no dilettante; whatever she has gone into she has embraced wholeheartedly and in a highly professional spirit. Whatever she has produced is of the highest quality. And whatever she explores in the future will undoubtedly advance the flute in jazz.

Part Seven

The Flute in Latin Jazz

The First Fusion

Some time ago I was talking with the great Cuban clarinetist/saxophonist **Paquito D'Rivera** about a concert he had just given at the Duke Ellington Jazz Festival in Washington DC. The concert was exceptional in that it featured musicians from several Latin-American countries--Mexico, Cuba, Brazil, Peru--as well as jazz players from the U.S. When I congratulated Paquito on his success in blending together these diverse elements, he said to me, "What enabled me to do this was a common language-- the language of bebop."

The compatibility between jazz and Latin music, their common language, has been evident for many years. Jazz histories tend to focus on this relationship in one of its more brilliant manifestations, the encounter between Dizzy Gillespie and the *congista* Chano Pozo in 1947 that led Dizzy to experiment with Afro-Cuban rhythms with his big band. First known as Cubop, then Afro-Cuban Jazz, this genre gained acceptance through such compositions as George Russell's *Cubano Be, Cubano Bop*, commissioned by Dizzy for his band--featuring Pozo--and is seen as the source of a trend that runs through the mainstream of jazz to this day. Along the way, what is now known most typically as Latin jazz has received major contributions from Gillespie, Charlie Parker, Alberto Socarras, Ernesto Lecuona, Mario Bauza, Machito and his Afro-Cubans, Juan Tizol, Noro Morales, Tito Puente, Chano Pozo, Stan Kenton, Chico O'Farrill and many others.

Gillespie is to be given great credit for bringing these colors into his bands, both big and small. It is a mistake, however, to attribute exclusive attention to these events as the source of Latin jazz. Dizzy himself was responding to a socio-cultural revolution in the 1930s and 40's, particularly in New York City, that transcended racial lines between black, white and Latino musicians. And yet it is quite clear that there has been a connection, indeed a cross-pollination, between such musicians, and their respective genres, since at least the 1880's. These connections are explored in John Storm Roberts' book *Latin Jazz: The First of the Fusions, 1880's to Today*. He writes: "If Latin music, and specifically, Brazilian, Cuban, Argentinian, and Mexican music have been enormously influential in the U.S. in general... they have been particularly significant in jazz."

Roberts' narrative describes such interactions extending, as his title suggests, for well over a century. He describes, for example, the strong commercial links between New Orleans and Havana during the formative years of ragtime and jazz, leading to equally strong cultural links. The historical record is, at best, sketchy, from this period, Roberts reports. "Still," he writes, "it seems plain that nineteenth-century New Orleans--and therefore early New Orleans Jazz--was in more of a position to be influenced by Latin music than anywhere else in the US." Jelly Roll Morton was a major source for this information, explaining to Alan Lomax in the latter's biography of Morton, *Mister Jelly Roll:* "We had Spanish [read "Latin"], we had colored, we had white, we had Frenchmen, we had Americans, we had them from all parts of the world."

It should hardly be surprising that influences should flow back and forth between different parts of the African diaspora, but this was just part of the New Orleans melting pot. Even the distinctly European-sounding quadrilles, schottisches and mazurkas that made their way into the repertoire of early jazz ensembles such as the Buddy Bolden band may well have come via Jamaica and Mexico. The *habanera* that provided an essential rhythmic framework for ragtime, for Jelly Roll's "Spanish Tinge," came from Cuba, the *maxixe* that found its way into Eubie Blake's left hand was from Brazil. If it is hard to estimate the extent of these influences, it may be equally hard to over-estimate them.

This cross-pollination has gone on ever since. The *tango* was a national mania in 1913, not in Buenos Aires but in New York, bringing with it musicians from Cuba and Puerto Rico with their *rhumbas* and *danzones*. After *tango* mania came the *rhumba* craze of the 1930s, then the *mambo* hit the ballrooms in the 1940s. It was in this context that Dizzy Gillespie dropped Chano Pozo into the mix like a catalyst into a super-saturated solution. If Latin jazz was born at that moment, it had been gestating for 50 years.

The process has not slowed; indeed it is still accelerating. The opening of Brazil to American jazz musicians in the 1960s had an enormous impact on the music of both cultures. But the *bossa nova* (new trend) of Jobim, Gilberto and Bonfa which arose in Brazil was aided and abetted by Stan Getz and Herbie Mann. This was followed by the *tango nuevo* of Piazzolla in Argentina, with the active participation of Gerry Mulligan and Gary Burton. Now we no longer talk in terms of influences and fusions. Not only is Latin jazz an established category throughout the music business, with its own sub-categories--Brazilian, Cuban, Afro-Rican--but 'Latin' has become simply a common instruction on jazz charts, and a whole slew of artists such as Gato Barbieri, Eliane Elias, Michel Camillo, and Paquito himself can no longer be categorized as Latin artists--they are jazz musicians whose music exudes the language of Gillespie and Parker as much as the rhythms and colors of their native countries.

It should come as no surprise that the flute has a significant role to play in Latin jazz. As we have seen in Chapter One, it plays a prominent role in most of the traditions which contribute to that genre, particularly the *charanga* ensemble of Cuba, but also in ensembles in Brazil, Peru, Bolivia and elsewhere. So it was that the very first jazz flute solo on record was the work of a Cuban immigrant, Alberto Socarras, who spent the majority of his time working in Cuban, rather than jazz, ensembles. Similarly, another trailblazer in jazz flute, Latin and otherwise, arrived from Panama. His name was Mauricio Smith.

Still remembered fondly since his passing in 2002, Smith arrived in New York in 1961, already, at the age of 30, a highly accomplished performer on both flute and saxophone. He had begun his studies with his father, himself an orchestral flutist, and continued his studies at the Panamanian National Conservatory. His arrival in New York coincided with a revival in the *pachanga* dance craze, so there was no shortage of work. He found himself playing with leading Latin artists such as Tito Rodriguez, Eddie Palmieri, Mario Bauza, Willie Colon, Cesar Concepcion, Candido, Frank 'Machito' Grillo, Machito, Dom Um Romão, Victor Paz, Chico O'Farrill, Andy Gonzalez, Milton Cardona, Willie Colón and Mongo Santamaria, appearing on the latter's seminal *Watermelon Man* album in 1963. It was his mastery of a variety of genres, including Cuban *descarga*, West Indian *zouk, calypso*, French Antillean music, bebop and more that kept him in constant demand.

By the 1970s, Mauricio was working with Dizzy Gillespie on some of his Afro-Cuban recordings, but his skills were also recognized beyond the realm of Latin music when he became a founding member of the NBC Saturday Night Live Band in 1975. He was also active as an arranger, for such artists as Harry Belafonte, Mighty Explainer, King Obstinate, and the Mighty Arrow. He composed film music for Crossover Dreams (1985) and Dionysos (1984).

It is hard to over-estimate Mauricio Smith's influence on Latin jazz musicians in general, and flutists in particular. As well as blazing the trail that others such as Dave Valentin have followed, he has been instrumental in the careers of Nestor Torres and Andrea Brachfeld. These artists, Andrea the American, David and Nestor from Puerto Rico, and Danilo Lozano, whose roots are Cuban, are the artists in our section on the flute in Latin jazz. There are, of course, many more who will be profiled at ***www.fluteinjazz.com.***

Dave Valentin

"If you're tired, stay home; if you can't walk, sit down; if you can't drive, don't; but if you are going to play, PLAY!"

Tito Puente

If this provocative statement from the great bandleader Tito Puente applies to any jazz flutist, it would be the one who, for several years, acted as his musical director--**Dave Valentin**. For the last thirty years, of the handful of performers who have defined the role of the flute in Latin jazz, Dave Valentin has been in the forefront. A virtuoso flutist from New York, but with family roots in Puerto Rico, Valentin has combined a variety of influences that run the gamut of Latin jazz styles, plus elements of pop, funk, R&B, and world music. These influences have been with him since his earliest years growing up in the Bronx. He recalls that, walking down the hallway of his apartment building, "You could smell lasagna, chicken soup, and rice and beans being prepared all at the same time." But from all of this he has managed to arrive at a synthesis, to create a style that is uniquely his own. That it qualifies as jazz is born out by his recognition in polls from *Down Beat* and *Jazziz* magazines. That it is an accessible style is born out by Grammy nominations and awards in R&B and Latin Jazz categories. But none of this success has been the result of any kind of compromise; Dave plays the music he loves and, like his mentor Tito Puente, projects a sense of joy while doing so. This is, perhaps, the essence of Latin music and in Valentin's hands the flute is the perfect vehicle for expressing it.

David Valentin was surrounded with music from an early age: "When I was five, my parents were playing Latin music in the house, including Tito Rodriguez, Tito Puente, Machito and others. I became a percussionist for years and attended the High School of Music and Art. But in college I wanted to meet a girl who happened to play the flute. I asked her to show me something on the flute so I would get to talk to her. She showed me a C major scale and I was able to borrow a flute. A month later I came back and played for her but she never talked to me again! She got jealous, so I lost the girl. But I kept the flute!"

Once devoted to the flute, David set out to master the instrument. Largely self-taught, he did take some lessons, from classical players Hal Bennett and Hal Jones. But probably his greatest influence was the great Hubert Laws whose recordings, Valentin reports, were "a revelation." But he was not satisfied with studying solos from a record. David looked up Laws' number in the New York Musicians Union Directory, called him, and asked for lessons. Laws took David under his wing for the next several months, persuading him to give up playing the saxophone to focus exclusively on the flute. "He told me that if I wanted a great tone that I should concentrate on the flute and not play sax."

Once David had made this commitment, Hubert helped him to develop the full, rich sound which is a central component of David's playing. On this basis, he developed the tonal projection, fleet articulation, and unique percussive phrasing that came from many years of working with Latin bands of every kind. He was profoundly impressed by Latin flute masters Richard Egues and Rolando Lozano, and Cuban dance bands such as Orquesta Aragon, but also worked with mainstream jazz artists such as McCoy Tyner and Billy Taylor and listened to jazz flutists including Lew Tabackin, Frank Wess, James Moody, and Joe Farrell. Eventually, he was to become music director for Tito Puente, and to record with Ricardo Marrero and Noel Pointer. Then, in 1979, it all paid off. He came to the attention of Dave

Grusin and Larry Rosen just as they were launching GRP Records. Although Latin music did not have an established market at that time, they went ahead and signed him as their first artist.

It was a smart decision. The market was beginning to grow world wide, and over the course of eighteen albums for GRP, and several for Concord, Valentin developed the synthesis of *salsa, merengue* and other Latin-tinged forms that was uniquely suited to it. His popularity grew, spilling over into the pop and jazz categories, and by 1985 Valentin received a Grammy nomination as best R&B instrumentalist. Another eighteen years of recording and performing followed, playing for audiences at venues around the world, from Carnegie Hall to Europe, the Far East, Australia and Indonesia, and providing the incidental music for a season of the *Cosby* show. Then in 2003 David revisited the Grammys, this time winning the award in the Latin jazz category for *The Gathering,* with the Carribean Jazz Project.

Dave Valentin is now established as a leading influence in Latin music. At the same time, he has maintained his jazz roots—one recording of his is part of a tribute to Rahsaan Roland Kirk on an album by trombonist Steve Turré. And he relishes all of it. "One of the highlights for me has been being the musical director for Tito Puente, an idol of mine who I grew up listening to," he says. "I mean, Tito Puente slept in my house! Also, playing with McCoy Tyner was like being in heaven. And I remember the 70th birthday party at Wolf Trap for Dizzy Gillespie; that was a great moment for me. I have also been a guest with Machito, Ray Barretto, Celia Cruz, Michel Camilo, and many others."

When I sat down with David I found his attitude alternately--almost simultaneously--serious and light-hearted. I started our interview by asking if he found the Latin jazz label too restricting.

What do you think about this Latin jazz thing?
Well, music is music, you know.
But is the label a problem for you? Do you get tired of always being called a Latin jazz player?
Not really, because it is Latin jazz.
Except when you play Equinox *on the bass flute. What makes that Latin?*
Well, we did it in 6/8. That's Afro-Cuban.
Okay, but last time we talked you started to tell me a little bit about where this Latin jazz idea came from.
Latin jazz, this combination of Afro-Cuban rhythms with jazz, goes back to Peruchin [Cuban Pedro "Peruchin" Justiz who made his name in Havana's *descarga* (jam session) craze of the 1950s] on piano. Or you can go back really to Machito when he did those albums with Doc Cheatham and Cannonball Adderley. And Dizzie Gillespie. There was really no marketing for Latin jazz at that time, but those are great records.
So how do you characterize the difference. When you spoke on NPR it was simply the rhythmic emphasis that was different.
It's a combination of Afro-Cuban rhythms, with jazz. And that's basically it!
What about the harmonic structure? Do you have to simplify that at all?
Not at all. You keep all the harmonic structure from the jazz tune. If you're going to play *Milestones,* you know, (singing) with Afro-Cuban rhythm, you keep the same harmonics. In fact you even put substitutions on it. If you're going to do *Giant Steps* you can do it, you keep the same harmonics. You just put in a little bit of rice and beans!

It's very demanding technically, I mean when I tried playing along with you here at home, I was floundering!

Floundering?

I mean you have a great technical facility. It's so clean and precise. I love that.

Thank you very much. I appreciate that.

And I love the directness of it. But when you play a ballad--you also play some ballads--there is no Latin rhythm, you are just playing a ballad.

Well, when I'm playing a ballad I listen to every one whoever sang it, because before you can play that instrumentally you have to know the phrasing of Ella Fitzgerald, or Billie Holliday or Alberta Hunter before you can play a ballad like *I Loves You Porgy, We'll Be Together Again*, or *Prelude to a Kiss*. But you really have to listen to everybody's phrasing, and then you inject your own phrasing into it. That way you got some old timers who are going to listen to that ballad, and say, "Okay, that's good."

There's nothing complicated about that. But apart from that, all those influences have come in from different places, the Cuban thing, for example. I had a nice clinic from Danilo Lozano when I was out in L.A.

Oh yeah? His father was one of the greatest of all time.

Right. And he sent me his thesis on Charanga, so I'm getting up to speed on that. But I do know that Latin means a lot of different things. It's not just one thing.

Actually, what the Puerto Ricans did is that we adopted the Cuban music. That's what it is.

Okay. So your folks are Puerto Rican?

We're Puerto Rican. Right. In Puerto Rico we have *la dansa*. But in Cuba you have *el danson*. And also we have *la plena* and *la rhumba*. That's Puerto Rican. But what we did is that we adopted the Afro-Cuban rhythms of Cuba. And then eventually somebody had an idea for marketing, they called it "*salsa*."

Which means?

Well Tito Puente used to say, "That's a condiment!"

Well, it goes with the rice and beans!

Yeah! But *salsa* was just a marketing term to make it generic, you know, across the board where everybody goes, "Yeah, this is *salsa*." They didn't know whether it was a *mambo*, or a *cha-cha*, some *montuno*. You know what I mean?

Yeah. But then there is the other way. If musicians from Puerto Rico are playing--not jazz musicians, purely Puerto Rican music--is there less improvisation?

No, it's the same. If you're playing *bomba* or *plena*, or *dansa*, there's an equal amount of improvisation, and exploring the possibility of the music from within the tunes.

So it is jazz then? Kind of.

It's improvisation.

So when I take Danilo's stuff I can put it under jazz flute and not have to worry about it?

If you say Latin jazz you should include maybe Hilton Ruiz. Or if you're talking about flute players, Jerry Gonzales, Paquito D'Rivera, Danilo Perez.

Paquito plays flute?

Not with me. He refuses to bring his flute when I play with him. But he plays great flute! He's a closet flute player. And he's a great guy too.

But is flute a very popular instrument in all these different genres in Puerto Rico? I know that it's very important in Cuba.

Yeah, especially in the *charanga*, or *pachanga*, the flute is the mainstay, you know, Richard Egues.

And this is what influenced you to take up the flute originally?

No, it was a girl.

Oh, right. I've read the story. You wanted to sit next to a girl in the flute section in school.

Right. It was a girl. Don't know what happened to her. But you know, then I started to listen to all these great, great players.

Did you play saxophone anytime?

Yeah, I did. I played alto sax.

Just for a bit, and then someone said you should concentrate on the flute?

Hubert. Hubert Laws.

Oh, right, to get the real big sound?

Yeah, he said because... well my teeth were crooked on the bottom, so every time I bite down and have to play these *montunas* for ten thousand bars, I would bleed! So I stopped playing!

You know, in Europe we don't use that embouchure of biting down on the top. We don't touch the top of the mouthpiece with the teeth.

I found about that later. But I bought a Czechoslovakian alto sax from a pawn shop!

Yeah? Well, my saxophone came out of a pawn shop. It just happens to be a Selmer, but I just lucked out on that one.

Hubert said your embouchure changes from sax to flute, so if you want to get a good sound, just don't play the sax.

Well you know, there are different opinions about that. I just talked to Paul Horn about it, for example, and he doesn't hold with that at all.

Yeah. Well, another one is Joe Farrell who had a great sound on the flute. But if Hubert Laws tells you something, well, it's true. But of course I didn't have a different way to bite down on the embouchure. I didn't have that technique at all.

Yeah. It says you're largely self-taught in these biographies.

Yeah, I'm a street guy, man.

Just a few lessons here and there to get you started, from Hubert and...

Hal Bennet, also.

So you didn't go to college?

No, I just took a few lessons, classical lessons. Hal Bennet was one, Hal Jones was another one, then Hubert and that was it, basically.

When you do most of your recordings, are you doing everything in real time or are you...

Real time!

There are no studio, layered things?

No. What you see is what you get.

That's almost a definition of jazz for me--everything in real time, responding to each other.

No. It needs a conversation, and the only thing you can do about it is just to play.

I've done studio work where you go in last and all the other tracks were down and I'd stand there all by myself...

Then you've got to try and make believe you're playing live with them, you know.

Yeah. It's like making love to someone who's asleep.

Exactly. That's right.

Well, I'm so glad to hear that. Are there some other Latin jazz artists who are more commercial in your view? I noticed that when you talk about one of your recordings you say "We took a more commercial approach." Do you remember that?

It may be on *Sun Shower.* I did my own experiment to see what...

But what does that mean, more commercial?

Well, I hate to say this, but to try to cater to what stations are playing, but not to degrade the music. But after that I said "f--k!"

But did it sell any more than any of the others?

Actually, no!

There you are! But did you think it was any less musical?

No. I don't think it was less musical. Not at all.

My least favorite album of yours for some reason is the one with Herbie [Mann]. I don't know why.

Were you happy with that record?

That was a different engineer.

Did you have a good feeling about it while you were doing it?

It was difficult with Herbie. I didn't know it at the time but he was pretty sick by then.

I see. It didn't seem quite as flowing, or as effortless sounding.

Exactly.

But I love **Live at the Blue Note.** *That live recording. I liked that Beatles thing you do--* **Blackbird.** *That's the one I like to play along with.*

Yeah. We did *Footprints* there too. That's a classic example of Latin jazz--the Wayne Shorter tune. He did it in 6, we did it in 4, and it's still *Footprints.* It's still a C minor blues, but we went ahead and just kicked it.

If you don't have the extra percussionists can you still get the Latin jazz feeling? I mean if you just have a regular rhythm section--piano, bass, drums--you can still play the, er...

Yes, because the drummers are used to it. They have cowbells, and they can do all those parts. That would be Robbie Ameen, or Dafne Sprieto, or Robbie Gonzales,. They all have their cowbells and they can do all those parts.

But they have to understand the genre...

They have to understand the genre. I wouldn't use them otherwise.

Do you ever do any gigs with musicians who are not schooled in Latin music, just straight jazz?

Yeah, Hilton Ruiz. We did a gig in Detroit with no mics! And no drummer, man, just bass, piano and flute. It was straight ahead, and it was great!

So, you don't believe that Latin jazz is anything complicated or difficult to understand?

All I can say is complication is simplicity, and simplicity is complication. It's how you look at it.

How about Brazilian influences? The Brazilian feeling is a little bit different from some of those other traditions, don't you think?

Of course it's different. But in a way, you know, everything happens in analogy. Everything's connected one way or the other, there's a line across all the music. All those things influence us.

And then there's tango, did you ever... ?

Oh yes, of course--Carlos Gardel, are you kidding me? (Singing.) He was one of the greatest tango singers of all time. In fact when he died in a plane crash, the country shut down. That's how famous he was.

So, which are your favorite recordings?

Live at the Blue Note, *Kalahari*, *Line Time* and my first album, *Legends*. Oh yeah, and *Musical Portraits.* That's a lot of original stuff. My whole family is on the cover--all the baby pictures of all the guys in the band. I was looking at my family album at the family portraits, and I just got an idea, *Musical Portraits,* and I got all the baby pictures of all the guys--family portraits.

And that was your first recording on bass flute, on Primitive Passions?

Yeah, *Equinox*.

That's another nice record. You know, as you list your favorites, it strikes me how consistent your recordings are. When I was looking for a clip for my movie, I found I could use almost any track.

Well, thank you.

Do you spend a lot of time traveling in Puerto Rico and Brazil and these places where your influences come from?

I do Puerto Rico about twice a year. It's the greatest tourist place in the world, man. You can go to a hotel . . there's one, San Juan hotel, that's like a city. You don't even have to leave the hotel! And everybody speaks English, and they speak Spanish.

What else should people know about the flute in these various areas?

They should know that when they listen to *charanga* that is a six-hole, five-key, wooden flute. And that's a French antique--on all that old Cuban stuff. I have one, 1875.

Danilo [Lozano] was telling me about that instrument.

Yeah. It's a whole different thing--left is right, right is left. But when you listen to that, try to play that on the metal flute, what they do on that wooden flute, you'll be amazed. You can't even do it.

I tried a baroque flute once--same thing.

Right. It's like the Irish, they have the same flute, where they play that ethnic genre. That flute. But what you think is an A is not! You have to learn a whole new fingering.

And not just that, but you have to adjust on every note to make a balanced sound.

That's correct. And your fingers are the pads so you've gotta be careful.

I spent some time in India trying to play the bansuri which was very difficult--the holes are huge.

Yeah, I tried to play the *shakuhachi* man, and I almost died!!

Yeah. There's a guy in New York who plays jazz on the shakuhachi, Ned Rothenberg. And another in California, Art Maxwell.

Yeah, that's familiar. Amazing sound.

The strange thing is when you play avant-garde jazz on that instrument it sounds very close to Japanese classical music. These things all bend round and come together.

Yeah. Then the other is *la kena* from Bolivia and Peru.

So do you have any advice for flute players who are maybe classically trained and would like to branch out a little bit?

I would suggest that they listen to everything that they can get their hands on.

Who in particular? Which jazz players have really impressed you on flute?

Lew Tabackin, Frank Wess, Paul Horn, Hubert Laws, Herbie Mann...

Have you heard this group with Ali and Holly and Frank Wess? It's a three flute group.

Great! Great! The more the better, that's what I say. The more the better because the flute "Well, that's not a jazz instrument!"

I was about to say, I've just read that recently---that the flute is a marginal jazz instrument at best. I'm ashamed to say it's a Brit that wrote that!

I hope he doesn't come to the Bronx 'cos he will disappear!

Well, he just has a very narrow idea of what jazz is.

Well, it's unfortunate that people take that kind of comment as law. At least you are making an effort to find out, and you're just getting everybody's point of view.

Yeah. Well, I don't want my ego in this too much.

Right. We all have egos, but at least you're finding a point of view of everyone. As opposed to just somebody writing some s--t that they don't even know what they're talking about.

You know what, I just say, "Go for your heart, and look inside." There's a tone poem. There's something inside of you that you need to bring out. It's in there. All you gotta do is find it. When you find it you'll be flying. It'll be great. But you have to work for it. It doesn't come by magic.

It comes by magic--eventually. Then you can be an overnight success after thirty years.

Right. It's like you don't even have to breathe anymore. You just go out there and you play! That's it! It's a wonderful feeling!

That's exactly what Paul [Horn] was telling me. He doesn't practice anymore, except for a little warm-up for a day or two before a gig.

No! We don't!

People don't realize that. But then you've paid your dues for years, and now it's just there.

Yeah, and the minute you pick up the flute, boom! And then it's great to have musicians who understand the concept, because you don't even have to talk! If I'm doing 6/8, right? And I do a phrasing that seems to wanna go straight-ahead, 4/4, the guys are there in two bars. Boom! There we go.

You certainly can't do that with prerecorded rhythm tracks!

I'll tell you what jazz is--American concept. Jazz was born here.

There's a guy on the radio here in DC, Rob Bamberger, who does a show--Hot Jazz Saturday Night. He talks about all the places jazz came from, but, he says, "It's assembled in America."

Great! Assembled in America. Look at Louis Armstrong. Come on. Let's go to the root of it. This is where jazz was born.

Well, it's African, and Andrea was telling me how different slaves came to different parts of South America and the Caribbean, brought their music there to mix with what they had there. And that again goes through another stage and is transported into the U.S. to create Latin music, or Latin jazz.

Everything. There is so much strings all attached all over the place.

That's what world music is.

That's what it is. We all live in one world, and if people could just be nice, it would be a wonderful place. All we want to do is play good music, and we all want to have a good time. If life was based on that there would be no wars. Do nothing bad. Don't kill nobody. Be nice. Listen to some good music! And make love, and have babies or whatever you wanna do!

326 The Flute In Jazz

Having reached the top of his profession, Dave Valentin is heavily into giving back. This is not new—he taught Latin jazz to inner city youth for seven years in the 1970s before entering full-time into his career as a performer, developing a special anti-drug program for gang members. He still visits twenty to thirty schools a year, many of them in the Bronx where he still makes his home. Asked why he has never left, David is quick to respond, "Because I don't want to. I'm proud to live in the Bronx. We have a true community again."

He is very active in this community, participating in fund raisers with hospitals and schools. He has also been honored by the Puerto Rican Educator's Society for his contributions to his parents' hometown of Mayaguez, Puerto Rico. Wherever he goes, he loves to quote Tito Puente's credo that appears at the beginning of this chapter, and he tells students and kids: "As my father told me, 'It doesn't matter what you decide to do, do your best. If you want to wash dishes, be the best there is. If you want to repair cars, be the best mechanic there is.'"

I remember David's visit to Howard University in 2005 where he was the featured artist in Dr. Kamalidiin's annual *Flute Fête*. As the other guests--Frank Wess, Yusef Lateef, James Newton, James Spaulding, Nicole Mitchell and others--have done, David performed with a group of faculty and students. He has no need of this kind of gig at this stage in his career, but it is the kind of thing he loves to do, spending several hours rehearsing the group the day before, and then providing a clinic in both Latin (*Oye Como Va, Footprints*), and straight-ahead (*Equinox, Milestones*) jazz, playing for the students. Half-way through the set, between numbers, he suddenly pulled his Grammy from his bag and gestured towards the student flutists on stage with him. "If I can do it, you can do it!"

Later that evening, he invited me to his hotel and, after buying me dinner, he spent an hour giving me a flute lesson, gratis. He may think of himself as a street guy, but David Valentin is a class act. And he has done as much as anyone to establish and popularize the flute in jazz.

Nestor Torres: Nuevo Latino

"There is nobody else like him." Roger Ebert

Of all the flutists I have interviewed, **Nestor Torres** is the closest thing to a popular music superstar, at least in the Latin realm. Consider the following from his website bio. "Jazz flutist and Latin Grammy Award winner Nestor Torres has been captivating audiences with his sensual mix of Latin, jazz, and pop sounds for more than fifteen years." He is certainly the only jazz musician I know to have a fan club, definitely the only one whose PR materials emphasize their good looks:

> Blessed with handsome features, a warm smile and a charismatic demeanor, this remarkable virtuoso has earned a devoted following. By transforming the flute's role in the contemporary musical landscape, Torres has practically established a new genre of popular music.

Reading this one could easily peg Torres as superficial; my conversations with him have revealed quite the opposite. As for the significance of his work, he may not have single-handedly transformed the flute's role in modern music, but his recordings could be said to represent something of a new popular instrumental genre. He certainly plays beautifully articulated flute lines, and has an unfailing sense of swing that blends jazz and *charanga* sensibilities. To put all this together while snagging a Grammy is no mean feat!

Unlike Dave Valentin and several others, Torres did not take up the flute by accident. He began playing the instrument at age twelve in his home town of Mayaguez, Puerto Rico. He went on to pursue it formally at the Escuela Libre de Música, and Puerto Rico's Inter-American University. Moving to New York with his family at age eighteen, Nestor was exposed to Cuban *charanga* music, which was a major formative influence on his later flute style. "In *charanga*, the flutist improvises a great deal," he observes, "and the focus of his solos are to make people dance. Even when I play today, my approach is still very rhythmic and melodic."

Formal studies continued at New York's Mannes College of Music and the New England Conservatory, where he developed both instrumental technique and a knowledge of classical literature. A classical foundation and a love of jazz pointed him towards a particular role model. "I was very inspired by Hubert Laws," he says "who was the first one to bring classical flute music and improvisation together with such a high level of virtuosity. After all, the flute is a universal instrument, a fundamental primal voice in many cultures."

Returning to New York after his time in Boston, he worked in a variety of settings, including the legendary Tito Puente orchestra. He also released three recordings, with limited success. But warmer climes beckoned and in1981 he moved to Miami, where he continued to develop as a performer, eventually releasing a recording in 1989, *Morning Ride*, which did very well in the Contemporary Jazz charts. Torres' career seemed to be taking off, only for it to be interrupted by a horrendous boating accident that left him with some very severe injuries.

This was the low point of Torres' life; his problems were compounded when his record company dropped him and his wife left him. He was on the verge of losing his home, but friends and fans in the South Florida community rallied round with both moral and financial support, including a benefit concert organized by a local radio station. With a little help from his friends, Torres' situation began to turn around, a result he also attributes to his practice of Nichiren Buddhism which, for him, brings "an appreciation for life and a realization that we are all interconnected."

As he recovered his health, and his life re-emerged from crisis, Nestor released an album whose title reflected this process--*Dance of the Phoenix*. Three more releases followed, and enjoyed considerable success, until he was awarded a Grammy for his 2001 release, *This Side of Paradise*. Not surprisingly, since then, his career has been going from strength to strength. In view of this, when I reached him for an interview, I was not sure what to expect. What I found was a warm, humble, thoughtful individual, whose primary focus was his music. Our conversation began with the ever-present issue of genre:

Do you consider yourself a jazz player, or do Latin players not like to be lumped in with jazz as an overall description of what they do?

Yes and no. I hear you asking me if I prefer to be labeled as a jazz flutist or not. I don't mind it at all, perfectly fine with it.

Is it a problem if we have a section in the book devoted to Latin jazz?

No, because as such, so it is. Understanding as you just mentioned earlier that the labeling can be a little bit limiting. But you see, our tendency might be to take issue with the labeling--it's better not to be labeled, etc. But as we're speaking at this moment it occurs to me that rather than trying to resist the tendency of such a thing, I think it's just simply worth it to re-examine it and maybe readjust it a little. What I'd appreciate is that if you include me in that category, you qualify that. Although I'm okay with the Latin jazz genre, the fact is that when I get nominated for a Grammy, the Latin Grammy I won was in the category of pop instrumentalist. So I consider myself more of a pop instrumentalist than Latin jazz per se.

What would the difference be?

First that Latin jazz, as I mentioned earlier, has a very strong, Afro-Cuban, rhythmic foundation. It might go into Brazilian, or some other things. In fact it's broader, with a standard Brazilian, Incan, or other, strongly percussive, strongly Afro-Cuban influence. The second thing is that my approach to my work and my recordings is much more melodic, based on a song structure. I will write a song and interpret songs, and I do improvise, but the focus remains the song. Whereas in Latin jazz the song is usually an excuse to just improvise. Mind you, when I do that, I do that in live performances as well. But I really consider the songs as important as the improvisation aspect itself. And my music really reaches a very broad spectrum. There are many Nestor Torres fans who are not necessarily Latin jazz lovers. I will be the one to tell you, if you have not already heard about it. There may be some to say that Nestor Torres is not a Latin jazz musician because he does this other diluted stuff. To that I have no problem. I let my playing speak for itself. If you listen to *Alma Latina*, it's a very pop, commercial-oriented record, but my playing speaks for itself.

Well, the review in **Down Beat** *said that you transcended that environment.*

They wrote something about me in *Down Beat*? I was thinking about that. I need to stay in touch with this improvisation and see what's going on with that.

Jazz has come to take on different meanings for different people. But in a very broad sense it really reflects your education, your training. Were you trained in improvisation or just to read off the page? You had some classical training yourself, did you not?

Indeed. And I continue to go there. I do a bit of work as a soloist with symphony orchestras, within the pop symphony realm.

Are there any composers that you tend to favor?

I am a pretty traditional guy. I love Bach--I stick to Bach and Mozart. And because of the pops symphonic context I'll do usually the *Chaminade,* or the *Carmen Fantasy,* you know--show pieces. But I really enjoy playing Bach. I love the Pergolesi *Concerto in G,* as well as the Mozart concerti. But I don't get to do those as much, once again because the settings in which I get to play are like symphonic pops so to speak. But I do have my own arrangements of Latin American compositions. I have my own compositions, orchestrated for symphonic setting.

There some Latin American composers who are writing some interesting literature.

Well, you know, Paquito D'Rivera just wrote a concerto for Marina Piccinini. I heard her at the flute convention perform the concerto. So he's doing some of that. Hubert Laws, have you talked with him? He is so important to this instrument. There is a tradition for piano, guitar, trumpet, trombone, drums, bass. These instruments do have a tradition--even the violin--within the realm of jazz. The flute, specifically in the context of jazz, is a rather limited field. I mean it's still at the beginning of it.

It's getting much richer. The new generation of players, since Hubert I guess, have really figured out how to make it work in a pure jazz context.

Yes, I think that's true. In my case, I would consider myself as a pop music instrumentalist, because my approach is very melodic and specific. I can play jazz, and I continue to do it; my improvisation invariably has that kind of a jazz approach. But whereas in jazz you come from a very harmonic approach where you're exploring the harmonies and the melodies are very much based on harmony, the virtuosity of your ideas, my approach is very much melodic--it's always song oriented. I try to create a melody and a groove, and to get the groove. And that comes from my *charanga* background in which the goal for the flute player is to get the dancer to move. *Charanga* flute players play music for people to dance. If we go back to the origins of jazz it comes from danceable music.

That's the Latin influence, an African influence but a couple of steps removed. Right?

Yes, though the bottom line--rhythm is what really sets it apart. Jazz and Latin jazz, really the defining difference, what really sets them apart, is the rhythmic approach. When we think of Latin jazz, for example, just going back a little, for me personally when we speak of jazz, I think of the African-American musical improvisational tradition.

Blues based?

Blues based. What started in the delta, New Orleans, in those early days, all the way from Louis Armstrong, through Ellington, then to Charlie Parker, Dizzy Gillespie, Miles, through Coltrane.

And it's noticeable that there are no flute players in that line of development. In fact, if you watch the Ken Burns' shows on jazz I don't think he mentions any flute player once. I am not sure that it gives the public the right impression of what jazz is. That may be the main trunk of the thing, but there are a lot of branches going off in all kinds of interesting directions.

But it's not part of their reality. And that opens another Pandora's Box in terms of dialogue, because it brings us to art and culture and what it means, whether American or not. Interestingly, the exciting part of jazz flute, so to speak, in terms of the tradition, is what you stated: that the tradition of the flute in jazz or jazz flute, is--I don't know if I should say a shallow, but rather a very young, recent tradition, from right before Herbie Mann, Sam Most was playing flute like that, and this Puerto Rican player, Norma Morales' brother, Esi Morales. They started doing that, and in fact there's another--I don't know for the life of me why this gentleman never got his due--Alberto Socarras.

He's always mentioned in the histories of the thing because he did make at least one recording that we know of. But Frank Wess told me that he knew both him and Wayman Carver, and that they were both excellent flute players, probably with some classical training. They played flute for their enjoyment, but it didn't have much application to the professional stuff they were doing every night.

Socarras--I got to study with him, and I became familiar with some of his work. He did quite a few recordings, and he was very successful in a very tough time in the late 20s. The story with him is that he escaped--he left Cuba disgusted because of the racism so pervasive there at the time, and he said, "If I'm going to be prejudiced against, I might as well be so in a country other than my own." So he arrived in the U.S. at the height of the depression, and he started working on Broadway, I think with the Black Poets or something like that. And he was working quite a bit. He had one of the first black orchestras to play at the Glen Island Casino, right alongside Duke Ellington--he may have been the first one.

The thing with Socarras is that he was actually using the flute as a solo voice, because he was a great doubler. He mastered the saxophone and clarinet with no problem. But the flute was really his forte, and in fact he was known because he had this style of playing where he would move the flute according to where he would be playing, he moved his position from the microphone, to wherever the flute sound was coming from, to get this interesting effect. Go figure! At that time! But I think his legacy has been rather unheralded or unrecognized.

So we fast forward from these guys, Morales and Most, and Herbie Mann of course was I guess like, what Rampal did for flute in classical music Herbie Mann did for flute in jazz. And no question about the fact that he was so fearless, and that he was doing his work at the time in which he was able to do Middle Eastern stuff, and Brazilian, and Afro-Cuban, and beatnik, and more pop of the times. He did some lovely work with string quartets, really remarkable things.. At the very least, his sense of experimentation and his feel are to be commended. At the same time, during the period that he did it, it was much more doable than today, which is frightening.

Of course there are artists that say he was just trying to make a buck, but that sounds like sour grapes to me.

Yes. I mean, and there's nothing wrong with him having a business sense.

No. It was interesting though that he took up flute by accident. He had to learn in a real hurry to get a gig he needed.

I remember when I first started playing the flute. My father's a musician, so the fact that I was playing the flute… Why the flute? Who makes a living playing the flute?

That was your first instrument, your only instrument?

Yes, I picked up the saxophone after that, while still a kid, simply because to get a job you really needed to be able to play the reeds. You have to play sax, but the flute was always a feeling to me, although I was never able to play in tune in the very high register. And it's funny because what you're telling me of Herbie's story reminds me of my thought at the time, which is, you know, listening to Coltrane and Michael Brecker, and so many others, I thought, "There are so many incredibly gifted tenor sax players, and there are not that many flute players out there, so I think I'm gonna stick to this."

I've had the same thought. In London, back in the sixties, I got work because I was the only jazz flute player they could find. So your dad is a pianist?

A pianist and a vibraphonist as well. He played organ too, Latin music. We're obviously both from Puerto Rico, and he would listen to the radio--Latin music,. He was very influenced by Machito, Tito Puento, Tito Rodriguez, Cal Tjader, George Shearing--these were strong influences for him. By proxy, that's how I ended up--those were my early influences as well.

I understand that the flute is very prominent in Charanga, but I'm not sure if you hear much flute in these other Latin genres.

You are correct about that. When it comes to Afro-Cuban music, we must be specific with that. It's such a fascinating subject and discussion, but I don't have a chance to speak with many people about it. When we think of Latin jazz, the reality is that it comes from the Afro-Cuban tradition that happened in the forties when Mario Bauza from the Machito orchestra started combining African American jazz with Cuban dance music.

This is before Dizzy Gillespie picked it up?

Exactly. That's where that was coming from. Dizzy was part of that movement, because Mario Bauza was the originator and then Dizzy was very hip to it, and then they did stuff together--that's where it comes from. That's where Latin jazz started, back in the forties. *Charanga* music is a totally different thing because the big band sound was the ground, the fertile ground for what is known today as Latin jazz. Then you have Machito, then Puente, and then Rodriguez did a little bit of that. Then of course Cal Tjader started picking up on it. So that's where that comes from.

I listen to the purely Latin radio station here in Washington from time to time. I don't hear any flute solos.

There are next to none. In the early sixties it did come up to the U.S. and people like Johnny Pacheco made it popular, and Jose Fajardo came here, and Charlie Palmieri was playing--there was a bit of a *charanga* or *pachanga* craze in the early sixties. I know it existed in New York City. I don't know how much of it spread nationally, if at all. It came back during the mid seventies. I was very lucky because I was able to get work as a *charanga* player. There were a few *charanga* bands but it did not survive. It faded because it's not a very pleasant sound--a very high-pitched, slightly out-of-tune flute with high-pitched, same-sounding out-of-tune violins. It's not very appealing. Are you familiar with *charanga* music?

Somewhat, but not as familiar as I am with tango. Who else is important as a flutist in Latin jazz?

Mauricio Smith, who just passed away recently, a Panamanian--excellent flute player. He was in New York for many years, and actually was a very hot young talent back in the early sixties. He became a fixture on the New York scene. He was an extraordinary flautist as well as sax--a complete musician.

Tell me more about your own background. You were u a music major at the Escuela Libre de Musica in Puerto Rico. This was at the undergraduate level, right?

Yes, I started there in junior high school, it's junior high through high school. That's where I studied.

What kind of angle are they taking at a music school in Puerto Rico?

At that time it was very basic: solfège, sight reading, some of the basic techniques of the instrument.

Do they expose the students to classical literature, or to Puerto Rican music? Are they trying to preserve their own tradition?

It was just the basics of that time: the Rubank Method, marching music, some of the *Symphony of the New World* for concert band, that kind of thing.

By the time you were 18 you lived in New York, and if you live in New York you are exposed to everything.

Indeed. At the time though, I was fortunate that I was able to get work. In fact it was Mauricio Smith who heard me playing with Tito Puente. My father had moved ahead of us to New York and took me and my cousins to hear Tito Puente and Machito at some club. I had the nerve, I have no idea how, to ask Puente if I could sit in. So I jammed with the band. I had no idea what I was doing, but Mauricio heard me, and he stayed in touch with my father. When I came to New York he called me to sub for him, so I got some jobs from him, and that's how I started. He was the one who opened the doors for me.

Would Puente have had a flute player in his outfit?

Oh yeah, they always had them. For some of the *cha-chas*, they had a little bit of a *charanga* feel.

Would they be doubling on saxophone?

Oh yes, that's what usually happens in these bands.

And then of course Dave [Valentin] was with him for three or four years.

But that was when Puente had the Latin Jazz ensemble.

Were you also being exposed to straight ahead jazz at this time in New York?

Yeah, even in Puerto Rico I was already familiar with Charlie Parker and Coltrane and so forth, so we were listening to jazz at that time. But it wasn't until I came to New York... Interestingly enough it was at the Mannes School of Music. They were a very hard core, classical institution, but they were just starting to have adult or night programs, some jazz classes by a man named Jack Reilly, a pianist. And I started to take a little bit of jazz there. Then I started playing with a group from New York called *Conjunto Libre*--the Gonzalez brothers, Andy and Jerry Gonzalez, Mannie Oquendo. They had already played with Dizzy and were heavy into jazz, and that was where I really learned a lot about Latin jazz and a lot more about jazz playing.

When did you make your first recording?

In 1978, and it was called *Colombia in Charanga*. There was this Colombian record producer that wanted Colombian songs in a *charanga* style. So I did that record with instrumental *charanga* music in '78. After that I did two *charanga* records in New York for independent producers. That's the one with the baby picture, *Canciones Primeras*. My first jazz record was *Morning Ride*.

Which is the one that won the Grammy?

This Side of Paradise. It's okay, in that it won the Grammy, but I would not include that as a must listen. *Alma Latina* is a must listen. *Dance of the Phoenix* is a must.

That's the one I like best. Some of your recordings have more of an edge than others. Is that your intention?

It's been a combination of factors. For example, *Talk to Me* has been the smoothest of them all. In fact, those around me, the closest people who love and care for me, have not very good things to say about *Talk to Me.* It's the most diluted one from the essence of who I am. Although I'm very proud of it for what it was, it certainly has a couple of weak points.

In the studio, do you do everything in real time or are you laying tracks down?

No, we lay down tracks. I do the overdub and I will construct a solo. Sometimes like in *Burning Whispers* for example, the solo I took on *Cafe con Leche* was a one-take. I'm a one take kind of a guy, so I will usually do one or two takes, three at most, and then either construct from those or just fix them. I don't mind that kind of a building or crafting a solo, at all.

Have you ever considered baring your soul a little more, and going in with a small-ish group and doing everything in real time?

Indeed I have, I'm tempted to do it. I really want to do it much more organic. But it's a struggle between the three aspects: one, how do I translate the energy of what I do live, which I really don't know what I'm gonna do until I perform live, so how to translate that to a record; two, how to make that viable, to a general audience; and three, dealing with the fundamental function of what a recording is to people's lives. You and I are music lovers, musicians, colleagues and this is what we do. And there is a select group of people who are very passionate about the music and it really takes a front seat or the foreground. But for most of the population it's not much more than the sound tracks of their daily lives, which I think is very important.

You're saying that all the ambient music is like the oil that makes the machine work smoothly.

Absolutely! The music and culture and the function of that.

On your live gigs, how many people do you bring for a performance?

I usually have a five piece band: [flute], bass, percussion, keyboards and guitar.

I wanted to ask you what was behind your move to Miami: just a personal thing, or was there a different music environment there?

No, it was relatively personal, although I choose to think that there was a deeper meaning that I did not understand at the time. Basically, New York was getting very cold and unfriendly, expensive, and rather hostile. I'm born and raised in Puerto Rico, not even in the capital, in Mayaguez. I thrive in New York and I love New York, but after a while, the relentless cold, the greyness of it, the hostility, a certain harshness about the city--it was very uncomfortable for me.

Has your playing changed since you left?

Most certainly. My entire career and my style and everything I am and do musically, I have no doubt that it would have been totally different had I stayed in New York.

The albums that have more of an edge, is that a New York influence?

No. *Dance of the Phoenix* was my second jazz record. And I was early recovering from a pretty nasty accident. The setting is that I was married at the time. My ex-wife at the time was my manager. That collapsed. My life was in turmoil, totally collapsed, so the record company was a saving grace in that I spent six weeks in L.A., woodshedding and working on the record with Ronnie Foster. It was very intense at that level, and very musically oriented. I was able to do many different things and there was that bit of intensity with it.

Each record was different. I guess that's what we were talking about earlier: was it my intention to do different things each year, or not? It was a matter of the circumstances. The first record, *Morning Ride*, almost like, "Do what you can with what you've got." *Dance of the Phoenix* was rising from the Phoenix, so there was that kind of a raw intensity to it. *Burning Whispers* was one of the finest productions. It has some faults technically, but I spent two years creating the music and I worked with two producers that are very well known today. So the craftsmanship of the songs in the concert was very much who I am. So that was that, whereas *Talk to Me* was something done once again in L.A., with Andre Fisher, who was a top producer.

It was a strange period with the label, a transition. My manager at the time was on the way out. This gentleman was almighty, so it was a little like looking up to him, a little intimidated. I did not have enough material, so he kind of took the lead. It was a very light kind of a thing. That's the lightest of all the records I've done, although many people to this day love the record. Then *Treasures of the Heart* begins a very difficult period. I had what I only recently discovered was focal dystonia so I could hardly play. There was very little control of the right middle finger, so that *Treasures* and *This Side of Paradise* I recorded virtually not being able to play.

Is it better now?

Yes, the condition is still there but I have made peace with it, and I just play around it. I'm practicing and working with it and I feel very good about it now.

But each record has been a reflection of the particular experiences in my life at the time, and of course having to contend with the reality of the recording industry. Many stations would not play my records; they dictated that the flute doesn't work in that format, never mind that my music is very well received.

It doesn't work in that format?

That's what they say.

They don't play your work on those stations?

They do. They will. They have some stations. But there is a consulting firm called Broadcast Architecture. They dictate what works and what doesn't on radio.

Well as all the radio stations are soon going to be taken over by one company we can kiss good-bye

to any freedom. That company will probably be in control of the whole thing.

It's already happening. Radio has nothing, absolutely NOTHING, to do with music. It's about formulas and about payola, about influence, purchasing power. Of course you always have to have a great song, but there's an awful lot of awful songs that get air play and become successful.

So what pressure does that put on you?

Well I'm coming to realize that it puts as much pressure on me as I allow it. But lately I'm taking a different approach, in that I'm not being rebellious about it. I'm being very methodical and open about it. I'm very focused as to making sure that whatever I do is going to be very honest and very much in accordance with what I want to accomplish, which is, in effect, empowering music. This is really what I do. I'm not doing anything different, but to really do it with a much stronger focus and a lot more commitment on my part. Because what has happened is that what the pressures of the expectations have done for me, has been, on the one hand, I feel the pressure that I have to be, play, do, something that I'm not. On the other hand, as a result of that, I'm rather discouraged and sometimes even fearful to really put something out that is very raw and over the edge, so to speak. So I've been walking that tightrope. And although I'm very proud of the work I've done so far in recordings, I yet feel that the best is yet to come. So I'm at a point in my life where I'm making peace with the fact that this is the reality of the environment for the arts and culture, and as a recording artist these are the expectations that are being set. At the same time, it's my challenge. How can I use the system, how well can I learn and master the rules of it so I can break them effectively? So it becomes that part of a journey. It's interesting.

Well it might be interesting to do something in between two other records that is simpler. I'll tell you my bias. When I listen to Hubert, for example, I like some of his recordings; many I find overproduced. But many that he made purely as a sideman with people like Chick Corea, Ron Carter, Victor Feldman, Terry Gibbs, Milt Jackson, where he just plays--they're breathtaking! And sometimes wish I could hear more of that from Hubert. But I understand how those pressures work.

Are you talking about the work he did back in the '70s, or some of his recent stuff?

Back in the '70s, but there has been some good stuff recently too.

Yeah, he did some brilliant work. Do you remember that record, it was a double album called *In the*

Beginning? That was pretty brilliant, where he did *Moment's Notice* and some interesting things. I mean Hubert Laws, the work he did at the time... It set a standard yet to be matched.

Let's talk about the instrument that you play. It's a regular flute with a different head joint?

Yes, I play a Pearl flute, 14 karat gold, with a Howell Roberts head joint. It gives me very dark wood, very warm and dark sound. In the low register it makes it richer and very sensuous; whereas in the very high register when I play very percussively for *charanga* style, it's not as piercing.

Danilo plays the full-fledged five key* charanga *flute I believe, does he not?

I believe he does--a very elaborate kind of expensive flute that he has.

That gives you a softer sound in the upper register?

... by virtue of the fact that it is a wooden instrument. But it's much harder to play, and much harder to keep in tune.

It does have a lip plate doesn't it?

Actually mine doesn't. It has a lip plate, but it's part of the wood.

So the shrillness you're trying to avoid is from the metal flute--that is what you get from the wooden head joint.

Right. And it comes from playing *charanga*. When I was a kid, just arrived in New York, the other musicians were telling me, you have to play a wooden flute. Fortunately, Mauricio Smith told me I didn't need to listen to them. But I was fascinated by that. And someone, a flute repair person who was designing head joints, told me that, after experimenting, it was proven that ultimately the sound quality of the flute is not determined by the instrument, but by the head joint. And that's what I've been using since. It's become a trade mark of mine.

Do you play any alto flute?

Occasionally I will, and I also play the piccolo, but I haven't played it in years. Piccolo is extremely demanding so you have to be committed to it

So Nestor, *how many years has it taken you to become an overnight success*?

(Laughs) I would say, since 1984. It took me five years to get to the beginning. Then I had to start over after the accident, so we're going on about twenty five years. But I'm very pleased with the fact that it's' been a very slow but very steady journey, which has allowed me to create a very solid foundation for myself as an individual, a human being, building the character as well as my credentials as a flutist.

Two of my early musical mentors in England, initially jazz musicians, went on to achieve some success in the pop charts. It is said that, before achieving this success, they would get together to talk about music, but after it, they would get together to talk about money. This does not seem to be the case with Nestor Torres. Music, and its effect, remains his primary focus. "Of course it was a great honor and privilege to win the Grammy," he reflects:

That being said, the fact that I was to receive it on 9/11 gave my work and my music a stronger sense of mission and purpose. Terrorism and violence come from ignorance, anger, arrogance and hopelessness. Music and culture inspire and empower; they soothe the human heart and enlighten the spirit. I have made it my prime point to create music and live my life as an artist and a human being in a way that does just that.

An entirely fitting goal for a flutist!

Danilo Lozano

"Expert modulations and tonal colors qualify Lozano as one of the finer talents we have heard."   *Flute Talk.*

It was fortunate that James Newton introduced me to **Danilo Lozano** because I was unaware of his work as a flutist, and of the position he holds in the world of Latin jazz. I quickly learned that he has also developed impressive credentials in contemporary music performance, as an educator and as a musicologist.

The son of one of Cuba's most respected musicians, flutist Rolando Lozano, Danilo followed his fathers footsteps, delving into the Cuban music tradition, but not until he had acquired solid performance and academic credentials. He holds a master's degree in ethnomusicology from UCLA, and a degree in flute performance from USC. A founding member of the Hollywood Bowl Orchestra, he has also appeared with the Los Angeles Opera Guild Orchestra, the El Paso Symphony Orchestra, the Mexican Arts Chamber Symphony, and the Pacific Symphony Orchestra. He was the performer for the world premiere recording of the Blas Galindo Concerto for flute and orchestra with the Mexican National Symphony Orchestra and was a featured soloist in Mexico City's 15th International Forum of New Music. He has also appeared in more commercial settings with the likes of Linda Ronstadt, Babatunde Olatunji, Michael Jackson, The Chieftains, Natalie Cole, Gregory Hines, Arturo Sandoval George Benson Garth Brooks, Dionne Warwick, Peter, Paul, and Mary, John Clayton, Luther Vandross, Carol Burnette, and Whitney Houston. "In consideration of his unique musical background and wide ranging interests," his official bio reports, "Antoinette Handy, National Endowment for the Arts official writing in Black Perspective in Music, found Lozano to be 'a fresh new voice of outstanding ability and rare musical sensitivity.'"

Lozano is currently tenured professor of ethnomusicology, Whittier College, Whittier, CA., having served as chairman of the department from 1997 to 2001. While the responsibilities of such a position keep him off the road as a performer, its stability enables him to devote himself to an eclectic range of musical interests. First and foremost however, it is his native Cuba whose music provides his research interests, and the flute that remains his primary means of expression. We met at the studios of *Voyager Productions* in Glendale, CA, where I was working on the development of some documentary material. Our conversation was remarkably wide-ranging, but it centered on his work as a flutist.

Are you a pure flutist, or are you a doubler?
I'm a flutist.
A jazz flutist?
I'm a flutist and I'm a musician. I'm a chameleon of sorts. It just depends on the style of music and the context, and I just do it.
Until we know what jazz is, it's hard to exclude anything! I think jazz is expanding to fill all possible spaces between American music and Indian music and Cuban music and all the rest of it.
(Laughs) Right!
But we have some very interesting people in here as a result. Think about someone like Jane

Bunnett for instance.

Jane is an interesting case because the Cuban style of music that she's interpreted comes from the eastern side of the island rather from the west side where the capital, Havana, is.

But in your case?

Well, I do a little bit of everything. In fact, what I try and do is experiment a little bit and mix and match with some of the ideas that come from the eastern half of Cuba and from the western half, just to see if they work.

Are there really two schools then?

There are just regional styles, and different approaches on how to interpret Cuban music.

The flute is a central player in this?

Yes. Absolutely. From the tradition I come from the flute is the principal instrument--in Cuba's popular music, which is the *danzon*, the *charanga* tradition. It's vocal music, but the flute is the principal voice. In other words when the improvisation takes place, it's the flutist who gets to elaborate and extemporize.

So a typical ensemble would have a vocalist and a flutist, a pianist or a guitarist.

It would have flute, strings, violin, bass, piano, It's like a chamber orchestra. And it has a rhythm section.

I'm not so familiar with Cuban music, but it does seem to be a very rich tradition.

It's a wealth of music. Just think of where it is located, geographically.

Ah, a crossroads at that point in the Carribean. Many influences. And, of course, a strong African influence.

Yes.

I don't come across a lot of flute playing in Africa. Again, I'm not an expert there.

There are flute playing traditions in Africa, but it's not as prominent as, say, in India, and the perception is that it's so much driven by percussion, with membranophones and ideophones. There are some chordophones also, but sometimes the flute playing gets slighted. But there is a very strong tradition of African flute playing. We just don't know much about it, still.

How did you get started on the flute?

Well I come from a prestigious family of Cuban musicians. My father is Rolando Lozano who is considered the foremost exponent of Cuban *charanga* flute playing in the United States. In fact, he was somewhat of a novelty in the 1950s because when Mongo Santamaria and Willie Bobo and Cal Tjader were doing all these things with Latin jazz, it was my father who was the principal flute player on all those recordings. He's now retired. Of course, he still plays at home. He's a very quiet man; everything he says is with his instrument. So I come from a family of prestigious Cuban flutists.

I was making music from the time I can remember. Then of course, by the time I was eight years old my father said, "You need to get serious about an instrument." And I said to him, "Well, I'll play the flute because that's what you play." He didn't teach me until years later. He didn't want to impose music on any of us brothers. He says, "You do what you do in music and if that's what you decide to do years later..." I have two brothers and they're both musicians, a bass player and a pianist/percussionist/producer.

Did you study music in college?

Oh yes! I have a very interesting story. I went to the University of Southern California, where I did my bachelor's, and the wonderful thing about it was that I studied classical flute there with Patricia

Garside, who happened to be James Newton's flute professor. So I became a classical flutist. Then it was at that point, when I finished my undergraduate degree, that my father said, "Okay, now that I know that you know music, you're allowed to go ahead and start improvising and doing these other things." He didn't let me actively partake in it, but I was around the music all the time.

I assume you weren't using the wooden Cuban flute for the classical studies?

I was using the regular one, the regular silver flute. And then I started working professionally. And then I went to UCLA to get an ethnomusicology degree because I soon found that Cuban music was incredibly rich, and I wanted to study it and know more of it, not just an education from what I learned at home, but one that was formulated on theory and methodology. I actually got a chance to work with some fabulous Cuban musicologists, ten years later, studying the music and traveling to New York and doing research and things like that. That's when I started playing the wood flute. That's the instrument that traditionally was used for playing *charanga*; it was a five-key wood flute.

And there are craftsmen in Cuba who make these?

They were made in France. These were baroque instruments, and the Cubans took them to express them in their popular Cuban music. And they were able to keep getting a supply until the 1950s. Now Cuban flutists are playing the style on a regular Cuban flute, or on a flute like mine, which is a modified instrument, a wood flute with a Boehm system.

How does it feel different from playing the silver flute? Is the response different?

It's extremely different. To begin with, because we play in the context of a lot of drummers, the instrument is always playing and improvising in the higher register. And we go beyond the normal range of a silver flute. And with the wood, of course, you have that really strong, pure, piercing quality that allows you to cut right through a band.

I would have thought a wooden flute would have a softer sound.

Not in the upper register. Just think. Through the thirties and forties they were using a five-key, wooden flute with a conical bore. It was like a piccolo only larger, real thick at the head joint and thinner at the foot joint. It could really only be used in that type of music because, with the conical bore, if the upper register is in tune the lower register is out, and if you tune the lower register then the top of the instrument is out of tune. So the only thing you could do is to tune the upper register and play those high notes.

How high does it go?

Oh, we play up to F and G, up above C4. The Cubans just sort of adapted it to play that way.

So, when did you first get to go to Cuba?

I was born in New York and I didn't go back until 40 years later, in 1997, to meet my grandfather who was my father's flute teacher. That was my first time ever on the island. I was there for two weeks. I met everybody I wanted to meet, and I got to play with them, and do all sorts of stuff, hang out with Richard Egues, Javier Zalba, Policarpo Tamayo, and all these great folks, and get to see all of my father's friends. You can imagine, just the fact that I was the son, and someone had returned after forty years of not coming back, it was quite emotional, and an incredible time. I learned a lot about my father of course, musically, and about why Cuban music is the way it is. It was wonderful being there, making music with them. I try to visit at least once a year.

Along the way you've done some jazz playing also?

Yeah, quartets with rhythm section, or quintet. Sometimes they ask me to do some recording for Brazilian music, and I get to do Luis Bonfa and all that kind of stuff. I consider myself a sponge. I've been around it so much and I just absorb it. And I've been fortunate that I've always had great people that have always pointed out the virtues of whatever music and style that they're playing.

How do Cubans approach music now? Are they very particular about preserving tradition, or do they like to be sponges also?

They are sponges as well.

So they must be changing and evolving constantly.

All the time. In fact, music in Cuba is ever changing. You'll hear something today and you'll say this is going to a fad or a fashion, and it'll be gone in two weeks. You have to continually reinvent yourself in order to stay on top of the game, because the listening public wants to hear new music all the time.

It used to be that way in Europe, even with what we think of as "art music." People were waiting in line to hear Handel's latest operas. Now getting people to go hear new music is like taking them to the dentist. Where did we go wrong?

Well, improvisation used to be part of that expression.

Well that's a discussion for another day. Tell me about these Cuba L.A. recordings.

They were made here in L.A. All the musicians are second generation Cuban musicians. And they live in L.A., which is why it's called Cuba L.A. This was during the time when the Buena Vista Social Club had hit big, and Narada was a New Age record label who wanted to do some Cuban music. So they asked me if I'd be willing to do it after they heard me performing and playing, and I said okay. And they said, "Can you go to Cuba and do it?" and I said "Sure." Of course there's legal problems with that. They wanted me to record in Toronto, but logistically it was going to be a nightmare getting all those Cuban musicians flying into Toronto. Then they asked "Are there Cuban musicians living in L.A.?" and I said "What are you talking about? This is a wellspring of Cuban musicians." The only problem is that, geographically, we're much closer to Mexico. We don't ever get to really see them all in one place, or playing Cuban music. They want to play many different kinds of music. So I said, "Sure, there's a whole second generation of Cuban musicians, like myself, work in the studios, with Madonna, with different people," So they gave me the opportunity to play our own music, the music of our cultural heritage, and that's what these Cuba L.A. recordings are.

It was interesting, you know how it is with instrumental music, we didn't have big budgets. So they said, "We want you to go into the studio and record the most popular tunes." Of course, the most popular tunes are 98 percent vocal, but we can interpret them instrumentally. And they said, "But we want you to do it like a jazz session. In other words, we don't want arrangements, we don't want any of that kind of stuff." And I said, "Boy, that's great! Because it's going to give us the opportunity to create and allow the music to take us into places that Cuban music normally doesn't go."

So these Cuba L.A. records are a little bit different, especially the very first one, *Cuba L.A.*, because they've been approached with a jazz sensitivity. That's a lot different than how a lot of Cuban music is produced, with the exception of people like Cachao for example. He's a legendary Cuban bassist and composer--his real name is Israel Lopez. He writes a *descarga*, like a riff, and people just improvise. [Note: Cachao passed away in 2008.] But still, even within this context, we're talking about people not just playing a riff, but getting started and then letting the interaction take place.

I imagine there is some good research done on Cuban music.

The Smithsonian Institute recently published a book (Chronicle Books, 2002) called *The Perfect Combination* that has been released in conjunction with their traveling exhibit which is called *Latin*

Jazz: The Perfect Combination. Now they are working on a boxed CD set in which you will hear many flutists, and among them my father.

Let's say I were to sit in with your group. I'm a decent jazz player--would I know just from a general sensitivity to music how to play a good solo in that context, or would I have to really immerse myself in the culture for a period of time?

What I would say is that the approach to playing in a Cuban context would vary just slightly. You would have to manage rhythm a little differently than you would if you were in jazz. There's so much syncopation in the music that usually, when jazz musicians come to try to play the music in a stylistic fashion, in Cuban music they usually have to sort of get used to managing the rhythm. But once they do that, they fly.

Harmonically, there's no big difference? So a jazz player can blend right in harmonically?

Yeah. You're talking about music, within the tradition you're talking about, with diatonic harmony. You're talking about tonic/dominant harmony. Some modal things, but basically it's just two and three chord structures. So then you say, "Well how do you develop a solo just off two or three chords in a rhythmic texture?" Well that's where the rhythm provides sort of a great deal of tension and release that's a lot different than what you would do if you were playing jazz.

I hope I can get a sense of it by playing along with these recordings. And will I find much Cuban music here in L.A.?

Oh, absolutely! I just did a concert here with the Jazz on the Latin Side All Stars. It's an eighteen-piece ensemble with all the top Latin players in Los Angeles. We did the Jazz Bakery, and we will be doing the big venues also. And we are getting ready to make a record.

In terms of teaching, are you teaching flute, qua flute, or...

What I teach at Whittier College, I teach flute, all styles. I'm a trained ethnomusicologist, I teach all the courses that I can, including Cuban music and, certainly, jazz history. I'm currently teaching at Cal. State Los Angeles, a class in Afro-Cuban arranging, so I sort of cover the gamut. I'm very fortunate, because at the institution that I'm at they value my professional development a great deal, so I have a great deal of flexibility to do work outside of the institution. Of course they like being mentioned, as my being one of their resident faculty!

Tell me about this other recording.

Do you know the composer Ed Bland? He was producer for Vanguard Records for many many years back in New York, and he's a fabulous jazz composer and arranger. He's now living in Los Angeles, and he's dedicated his entire life to composing classical works. He started experimenting with computers and music, and this idea, virtual world percussion, is sort of his maiden voyage into producing music with a computer. And once I heard it, I said, "Where's the flute part?" So he wrote the part, and what comes out is what is developed from that. It's a CD called *Dancing through the Walls.* It's very interesting because he wrote a flute part and he says "I don't want it to sound as though it was written, I want it to sound as though it was improvised and free."

Wow, it really works in that way. If you had improvised over the top of what he had produced, would it have come out very differently than the part he wrote?

Probably not much.

Sometimes I wonder about the effort that goes into notating things when a good improviser can do it off the top of his or her head. But it says here, in your notes, "How can I combine the three major influences, Cuban, classical, and jazz?"

Well, I'm always in the quest. That's me. Figuring out how I can express myself in a way that represents the musical influences and the experiences that I've had in each. So that's where I'm going. I still think that I'm a work in progress in many ways.

I don't know what world music is any more than I know what jazz is!

(Laughs.) Precisely. To me music is just music. But people do make stylistic distinctions, and differences. I believe that if a record that I produce defies classification, I'm making an artistic statement.

Absolutely. But then you have to figure out which bin to put it in at the record store.

Even the record companies, once they have material in their hand, they have difficulty figuring out how they're going to market it.

I understand. It's not about the music it is just about marketing! So, is this dance music?

Cubans listen to the music through their feet. Always. But in the U.S. it's turned into something entirely different, where people are interested in hearing it as concert music.

Does that seem strange?

No. Not at all. In fact, I welcome that.

They're still tapping their feet!

But they're sitting down listening and, in fact, appreciating what it takes to be able to pull it off.

Of course, musicians have played music, sometimes great music, for dancers for centuries without getting their full attention. I have a wonderful record at home: Great Dance Hits of 1600!

Yes, but we're just now getting there! Cuban musicians are more appreciated now than I can ever remember.

But it must be refreshing to get back into a club and get people dancing again.

It's all a question of context. The music comes out a little differently if I am playing for a concert or playing for dancers in a club.

You don't play piccolo at all?

I play piccolo, I play alto flute, I play bass flute--when I get the call. I got a call, for example, to do film music.

There are many good saxophone players and clarinetists in Cuba?

Oh, absolutely! There are fabulous saxophone players. If we start with our own Paquito D'Rivera and keep going on down the line, American jazz has had an incredible influence on Cuban musicians. Cuban jazz has always been part of the Cuban landscape.

Outside of Cuba, are there flute players that you particularly like?

Well, I love James Newton. He's my brother--definitely. I love Hubert. I love Jeremy Steig. Yusef Lateef--I'm crazy about him. I enjoy Herbie Mann quite a bit. I'm crazy about Orlando "Maraca" Valle, an incredible flutist from Cuba, also Jose Luis Cortez, another fabulous flutist from Cuba, Emmanuel Pahud, a fantastic classical flute player. I mean, it just depends what genre you're in, and there you have my favorites. They just sort of pop up--the old guys and the new guard.

Tell me about this other recording, that you have produced, **Oru: The Natural Order.**

Well that's my good friend Gary Stroutsos, who studied jazz flute, studied *charanga*, but it didn't take for him. So he started working with Native-American Indians playing Native American flute. The interesting thing is that he's interpreting melodies that are not Native American, and then he's improvising on them. I'm the producer. My involvement was actually dressing the flute, using the instruments, because it's a very soft transparent sound, and we're using boxes and thunder drums, and all kinds of gadgets to make sure that the music continues to evolve as it transpires.

There's one flute that Carlos Nikai plays. Is this the same instrument? It's like a fipple flute.
That's right.

It's not hard to actually get started on that instrument? Sound production is not difficult. But there area lot of inflections and things. That's the hard part, like Eastern music, the little subtle inflections. There's so much that goes in within the tone itself, rather than just stringing tones together.
That's correct!

Do you enjoy playing "paper" music?
There comes a certain gratification out of playing pieces that really have a very strong emotional thing to them, like for example, some of Bach's sonatas. I think about someone like Andres Jolivet, his pieces, especially those that are just straight solo flute; Toru Takemitsu's pieces. So there are some things that I definitely love to play, just fabulous pieces, stuff like *I Hear the Water Dreaming*, wonderful for flute. There's another piece that he wrote called *Air*. That's just fabulous.

There are these gems, but overall there is a lot of fragmentation in our culture and in our music. That's why I have been interested in some ancient traditions where all these things are more integrated.
Well, I know that different musicians do different things, but I'm not sure that they integrate it into their music. I know some musicians who say, "I'm into Yoga and I integrate and it will help my breathing," and all that. But when they sit down and play, it's like, wow, and all these things start to happen. I'm wondering what would happen if you integrated some of those ideas while you're making music. I know that my father, for example, when he used to practice, he used to listen to birds and then focus in on it. And then when he would hear the bird he would try to imitate that and communicate, so in our house there was always this bird music going on. Outside and inside. When he would start playing they would start responding.

Reminiscent of Eric Dolphy.
Right. But it's kind of crazy, because my father didn't talk much. Everything would come out in music. I knew what he meant when he was playing. When he talking to me, I'd say, "What are you talking about?" But when he was playing, I knew what he was talking about. So I think there's a connection there to nature in some way shape or form.

But, again, we only have to make these connections, to re-make these connections, because it has all become so fragmented in our environment.
In our times, the post-modern world, people are moving too fast to even want to consider that. And that's a problem. That's unnatural. The problem is, certainly as I see it in this country, that there is no value put on the importance of sound, and on those instruments that produce sound. So, for example, I compare the music education of Cuba to that here, and the fact that in Cuba people sing all the time, people dance all the time, people play all the time. It's just music, you know. You go to this one place and they'll have a rhumba session and they're playing on boxes. But you know, they got the kids right there! They don't exclude them from the music-making process. In the United States if you have drummers performing on the street, they call the police on you!

There is still this discontinuity between what the public wants and what musicians want to create.
That's right.

But I do like this piece. (Listening to **Dancing Through The Walls.***) Are the percussion parts notated also?*

No, it's a machine. He just pushed a button.

Of course! I can see that now. He could have had a machine play the flute part.

No. He said the human part to this whole thing is the flute player!

But, I don't see it getting much air play. Who would play it? Is it jazz?

Well, I didn't get into music because I wanted to sell a bunch of records. I got into it because I said, "God, there's a song in my heart and I'm going to put it out there!"

So the human part to the whole thing is the flute player! It is this statement that perhaps provides the key, or, at least one key, to understanding the strengths and limitations of contemporary music, indeed, of all music performance, ancient or modern. At some point, humanity--human consciousness--enters the picture. And there is no musician, flutist or otherwise, who exudes more humanity than Danilo Lozano. It takes a lot of that to perform a duet with a machine and make it work! It could well be the same value that attracted the people and drew them off the streets in Mexico City. It was not any melodic or harmonic structures, however elegantly designed, but the humanity that emanated from the performer! Interestingly, James Newton exhibits very similar qualities. Could the fact that both are flutists be a contributory factor?

At this writing, Danilo Lozano remains a highly respected musician in both Latin and contemporary performance circles, in Los Angeles, and certainly in Cuba. In the United States, on the national level, he is certainly less well known. He does not show up in any "Rising Star" polls and is unlikely to do so any time soon. This has nothing to do with the quality of his art, but to his unswerving dedication to the song in his heart. However he chooses to pursue that, he will be making a significant contribution to the flute in jazz.

344

Andrea Brachfeld

"With all due respect, she plays her 'buns' off; one of the first ladies to disprove the concept that only men can deal with the 'real deal.'"

Dave Valentin

"Her marvelous tone and technique are astonishing. Her adventurous writing equals and rivals her playing. She is definitely among those who deserve recognition not only among her peers, but the public in general."

Hubert Laws

Andrea Brachfeld belongs in the Latin jazz category largely by default. Andrea has worked in a number of genres, including straight-ahead, acoustic jazz, and when first I caught her in New York, she was performing with Jamie Baum, Michel Gentile, and Anders Boström in the New York Jazz Flute Quartet, an *a cappella* group featuring arrangements by Baum and others. As is evident from her comments to me, she is not too comfortable with any labels. But much of Andrea's background--and, I think it is fair to say, at least a good portion of Andrea's heart--is in Latin music. A list of her musical associates is a mini Who's Who of Latin jazz--Dave Valentin, Nestor Torres, Joe Quijano, Ruben Blades, Tito Puente, Ray Barretto. The recordings she has put out feature Latin music, and she shares her phone answering machine with *Latin Jazz Flute Explosion!*

In Andrea's case, however, as I have suggested, this Latin jazz orientation is not a one-sided affair. To begin with, she has had a solid, classical training as a flutist, receiving a degree from the Manhattan School of Music, studying with Andrew Loyla at Manhattan as well as with Samuel Barron and Harold Bennett. She also has a substantial grounding in jazz performance, studying with Hubert Laws, Joe Newman, Jimmy Heath, Yusef Lateef, and George Coleman privately, and through organizations such as *Jazzmobile.* She also led a jazz quartet from 1970 to 1980. Yet, as her career began to unfold, it was Latin music that beckoned. And as with Nestor Torres, Mauricio Smith had a hand in this. As she explains it:

> Latin music chose me. I was sitting in with a friend, Lloyd McNeil, at the Tin Palace, a club in the city, and Mauricio Smith was in the audience. He asked me if I was working enough, to which I responded I wasn't. So he put me in touch with Mike Perez who at the time had a *charanga* group called *Tipica New York.* Felix Wilkins, the Panamanian flutist, took me under his wing, so to speak, and taught me a lot about *charanga* music.

On the basis of this experience, Andrea began a series of associations with Latin bands, most prominently with *Charanga 76,* with which she recorded an album and won--twice--the Latin New York Music Award for her flute work, as well as a plaudit from *Down Beat*, which referred to her as "One of the finest jazz flutists around." Her career in the U.S. was interrupted, however, when an engagement to perform in Venezuela turned into a two-and-a-half year experience. Then, when she returned to the U.S., the arrival of a daughter turned into a fifteen year hiatus while Andrea focused on raising her child.

During this time she also returned to graduate work, this time in the field of education, receiving a Master's degree from Rutgers University.

Music never disappeared from Andrea's life, however; it moved to a back burner, but one that was still turned up pretty high for most of that time. Continuing to perform and to lead bands of various sorts in her local area, Andrea kept her skills honed until, around 1998, with the support and encouragement of Dave Valentin, she put out a CD of her own music. Another, *Son Charanga,* appeared in 2003. Further recordings followed, all of high quality, as did a variety of different projects showcasing Andrea's performance skills, as well as her musicological interests such as her workshops on "The Role of the Flute in Afro-Cuban Music."

Aware of Andrea's background, I was very interested in learning some more about Latin jazz. I was not disappointed, but her first comments centered on more universal values of music, specifically its spiritual importance. "Music to me is very important in my life because it's one of the only things that have been true to me," she told me. "It has never let me down, it is very consistent. It is almost as if, in a way, you can say that you've never let yourself down--because music is you, right?"

Your music is quite varied. That must mean your influences are also?

As far as influences are concerned--you know it's such a hard question, because so many people have influenced me and continue to influence me. Last night I went out and I jammed with some people, and they influenced me. Now I'm taking jazz harmony lessons with [pianist] Mike Longo, and he is influencing me an immense amount.

I understand. You change constantly, and what you put out into the world is a result of the experiences that come in, and how you process them. But the specifics are interesting. For example, is it a problem for you to be labeled as a Latin jazz player, first of all? Do you find that limiting?

Yeah. Well, you know nobody likes to be labeled unless they've decided that's how they want to be labeled, because then it stunts your growth. My mode of playing the flute is playing jazz, Latin jazz, and *charanga* music, and that's really where I'm at. And anything that would put me in a category where I can't do that, or somebody would say, "Oh, well you know she only does that," yeah, I wouldn't like that.

Your recordings get categorized as Latin jazz. Is that fair?

Well, yeah. But the problem, Peter, is that people have a lot of concepts of what Latin jazz is.

Well, help us out with that. Can you give us some background of what that means to you? Or what the pitfalls are of that term.

Well, when the average white American thinks about Latin music, nowadays, they think about somebody who's halfway hip, or they think about the the Buena Vista Social Club--which is not that hip but at least it's better than nothing.

But that's what made it onto the media radar screen.

Right. And you know, if they are truly interested in pursuing their knowledge of the music, perhaps they'll go into more Cuban sites and they'll check out *timba*. Now a lot of people wouldn't consider *timba* Latin jazz, they wouldn't consider *timba* any kind of jazz. They call it *timba, salsa.*

Right. It's not jazz at all. But there is a connection.

It can be Brazilian jazz. It can have the Brazilian influence, the Puerto Rican influence, the *bomba* and *plena.*

These labels are all very problematic, jazz included. The problem with that is that you have to

somehow circumscribe what you're covering--to be comprehensive about all these different genres would be impossible.

A better term for Latin jazz, for me, would be Afro-Caribbean influenced jazz, because that's really what it was. I mean if you look at the history, you have the Indians who are already in the Caribbean, all over South America, all over Central America, and then the Carib, which is the word Caribbean came from, Carib Indian, Ararak Indian. And then you have the Spanish, who came in and decided that they had found the Indies. They hadn't, but they called the area the West Indies. And then they decided, "Well there's all this gold here."

So they start robbing all the gold from everybody, and killing everybody. Then they discovered that everybody was dying from all these diseases that they had brought. All these Indians died--they weren't prepared for this kind of invasion from the outside world. Then there was pressure from the King and Queen of Spain for the settlers to make money. So they decided to plant sugar and other different crops. But since the Indians were dying off they started looking for a group of people who were stronger to run the plantations. Unfortunately, groups of West Africans who were fighting among themselves were willing to sell their captives to the Europeans as slaves. We all know what happened next. The result is that you have the influence of all these different kinds of people in that area.

This is similar to the mixing of cultural influences that took place in New Orleans at the turn of the century that led to jazz, or similar influences in Buenos Aires that led to tango. All these streams are feeding into one another and then throwing off other streams, and it's a constant ongoing process.

Yeah, except that the Africans who were enslaved by the Conquistadores were allowed to practice their drumming, and keep their language and retain their culture. They were supposedly converted to Christianity, and then they were put on this same level as the Christian missionaries, the people who converted them, which is why they were allowed a bit more freedom. This is why the music is very rich in those countries. And then you come over here, and eventually, when the slaves were freed in the late 1800s, they went over to New Orleans. There was a lot of mixing of different kinds of music, but the West Africans here weren't allowed to practice their religion, or be educated, so it turned into a different kind of music. So if you're going to talk about Afro-Caribbean influenced jazz, you have to talk about all the different Africans that came over, from the different parts of Africa, to Peru and Argentina, to Puerto Rico and to Chile, and all these different places that created all these different kinds of music. Now, if you listen to somebody like Danilo Perez, or David Sanchez, they take all of these types of music, and they put it into a record and they call that jazz. So then the typical person is going to call Latin jazz a Latin rhythm section--bongo rhythms--with jazz harmony, and jazz standards. But that's a very limited way of thinking of Latin jazz. So, you know, I think it gets worse when you try to understand it more in a way, because it opens yourself up to so many questions, and non-labels, or more labels. I don't know!

But you're not thinking about any of those things when you are writing for example, or creating the frameworks that you want for your recordings. You're not taking a little bit from here, or a little bit from there, because art comes from the unconscious and the unconscious is constantly being fed by your conscious experiences.

Well, okay. Let me give you an example. I'm finishing this album that I've just done. It was very focused on *charanga* music. The kind of music that originally came over--or a form of it came over--

from Europe, was called the *contra dance*, from France, the country dance from England. So what I decided to do, because I was known for *charanga* music before, I thought, let me try and elaborate on that. So I decided to make a *charanga* jazz record--I took traditional rhythms of *charanga* music with a lot more jazz harmony, and I think I created something a little different from what other people have done so far. But when I wrote the music it wasn't unconscious at all, it was very conscious--the focus of the kind of music was very conscious. But it's impossible to describe how you get ideas. It's just sounds that I put together that I really like.

What is the harmonic structure of the music you put together? On the recordings of yours that I've heard, the harmonic structures are fairly straightforward. Some of them are modal, some of them are just one or two chords. Has that changed in the new settings that you are putting together?

No, it hasn't, that hasn't changed. I guess it's just a matter of my harmonic growth which is something that I'm really trying to work on now. I'm trying to get more complex. Some of the harmonies are more complex, but I would say in general it's not anywhere near bebop.

Well, there's so much rhythmic motion that you can have too much harmonic motion in that context. You have to balance it, I guess.

You could say that.

Talk to me a little bit about the flute. The flute is found in all these different contexts. I know it's very important in **charanga**. *Is it also found in these other genres that you've been mentioning to me?*

I would say probably it is not. I think the flute has always been looked upon as a doubling instrument, and thank God we've got Herbie Mann, and Hubert Laws, and Eric Dolphy and you know, all the other people... Buddy Collette, who paved the way to make the flute a more acceptable instrument on its own. But I don't think it has achieved that status yet either.

Well, there are people who still write that flute is at best a marginal jazz instrument. What would be your response to that?

I would say that doesn't respect people's voices. Everybody has their way of wanting to communicate on the planet, and for anybody to limit that by saying that your voice is just playing one instrument is a shallow person.

It means perhaps a rather limited definition of what jazz is, a certain kind of sound, and outside of that isn't, and now we're back at these annoying categories.

Well, I mean, yeah. It's just people tend to have to have limitations in order to survive on the planet. If they say, well, flute is not a jazz instrument, then that eliminates the necessity for them to have to play the flute.

You mention Eric Dolphy. Was he the first jazz flutist that made an impression on you?

Well he was the first, that's for sure.

And then you were able to study with Hubert Laws?

I studied with Hubert for a little bit--not too long. But we've maintained a wonderful friendship since I've studied with him. I've studied with a lot of different people. I studied with Eddie Daniels-- Eddie Daniels is a great flute player. I studied a lot of classical music. When I got out of high school I won this award, called the "Louis Armstrong Award for Outstanding Jazz Student" from Jazz Interactions. That was run by Joe Newman. There were two different workshops that were going on when I was growing up. One was Jazz Interactions, run by Joe and his wife, and then Jazzmobile, and I went to both of them. Jazzmobile was five dollars a year--it was up in Harlem on Saturday mornings, and they had all kinds of ensembles, and we did some concerts. I studied with Jimmy Heath up there. I don't know how much recording he's done on flute, but he was the flute professor there. That was Saturdays. And then, I think it was Thursday afternoon when Joe had his thing, and Yusef Lateef actually used to be one of my teachers. Barry Harris was there also. I remember those two people there.

What was Yusef Lateef's focus in teaching?

It was more just thinking about music.

He has a rather unique viewpoint!

Yeah. Well, thank God! You know. We've got all these different people with different ways of thinking, it makes life interesting. But you know, I guess the most I've studied was when I went to The Manhattan School of Music. Everything else was more or less informal. I did go to Jazzmobile consistently, and Jimmy would teach me stuff, but I really didn't understand what he was teaching. But I figured I'd just go there every week and one of these days I'd understand what he was teaching. And now I understand it!

You absorbed it by osmosis and then finally figured out what he was talking about.

Yeah. I mean you just do it. You just keep on going. Eventually something turns up. I was actually employed by Jazzmobile. They had this C.E.T.A. grant--Comprehensive Employment Training Act or something like that. But they had a grant to hire a jazz big band and then an Afro-Cuban band. Actually, it's a funny story. I must have been 22, 23 or something. I'd graduated from Manhattan, but I was working at Sam Goody's, as a cashier, and Billy Taylor was on my line, buying some records. He recognized me, and said, "Andrea, what are you doing?" And I said, "Well, I have to earn a living." And he said, "Well, you shouldn't be doing it this way, you should be playing music. There's a new program that Jazzmobile just got a grant for, and you would be perfect for it, so you should go and audition for it." And that's how I got that. I ended up being the leader for this band, and I did that for a year.

So it was right in New York, and the grant gave you time to rehearse and to perform also?

That's right. That's what the grant was, performing in community based places. They would be free concerts essentially, but we were on a salary. We had about six guys. We rehearsed at the Phoenix house.

Was this Latin music?

It was. It was kind of Latin jazz. Anyway, a couple of months after that gig ended, because it was only for a year, I got this phone call from this millionaire, and he was looking for a woman flute player to lead this band. He was from Venezuela. And his name was Renato Capriles. He owned a couple of bands that were very popular. He had a business. He performed all over Venezuela and he wanted to create a new band with a woman flute player as the featured person.

Why that particularly?

God knows! I couldn't communicate in Spanish that well at that point, so I couldn't ask him!

I really didn't want the gig. I had a jazz group at that point with really great players, and I was starting to work in the City. So I told him I'd go for a month, but I ended up going there for two and a half years.

And you didn't regret it?

No, not at all. That's when I actually started writing for the Latin jazz thing.

So this really reinforced the whole Latin side of things for you?

No, I don't think so. I think it reinforced actually the jazz part, because I ended up being in this band for a year, then meanwhile when I was off I would go to these jazz clubs and sit in with people, and I got this gig playing jazz for eight months in Caracas.

Is there a lot of jazz going on there?

They had a couple of clubs. And it was kind of cool, because whenever anybody came through Caracas, or whoever it was, they always came to this one jazz club after their gig. And so I got to meet a lot of people.

And there were some local players also?

Yeah, there were some local players, and so I formed my Latin jazz band. As a matter of fact, just before I left, I opened for Chick Corea in a venue called *El Poliedro*, which was really a stadium sized venue. It was wonderful. Chick came up to me and said he really liked my music. At that point I think I was five or six months pregnant, so it was kind of funny.

So then you came back, but New York wasn't quite as easy to break back into after two and a half years?

Well, you know, when I came back I was almost ready to give birth, and my focus was different, although I did have a jazz quartet when I came back. There were some really great players in the band. We did a lot of nice gigs. And after the baby was born we did a lot of nice gigs, but then I realized that, you know, I couldn't do both and really be a good mother, so I kind of put music on the back burner for a while. I stopped going into New York. I just did a lot of local gigs. I did a lot of trios. I was playing with *Charanga 76* for a while, but then I moved down to where I live now, actually.

So this is why they can say in this article, "Andrea's back!" So when you came back that's when you put together that particular recording. Is that correct?   Are we back to 1990 something?

No, when I came back it was the eighties. About a year after Shaina was born I decided to go back to school and pick up my masters, and I continued to go to school for thirteen years after that.

Where was that?

I went to Rutgers, and I went to Kean University.

And your masters degree is in what?

Elementary education. Then I kept on going back to school, and I ended up getting six certifications in different areas. One thing kind of went into another, and went into another.

When did you feel you were ready to make a recording then?

Well, I kind of gave up in '98. I had written a lot of music, and thought, "Oh, I'll never make it." But I called Dave Valentin, and I hadn't spoken to him for about twenty years, and I said, "You know what, I was wondering if you were doing any recording, if you might need some music." And he said, "Well, you know what? Come to my house and I'll check it out." I went to his house, and he said, "I don't think I need any of this, but why don't you record it?" And I said, "I don't think I'm good enough any more, you know." But he really encouraged me to play again. If it wasn't for Dave I don't think I'd be playing now. And every time I wanted him to play something, he said, "No, you do it!" So he was very supportive that way, and he's always been supportive.

Dave is just an all-round classy guy! You were happy with the record when it came out?

Yeah, for the most part. It's hard, you know, because, for me, every time I do something I'm growing at the same time. So by the time the record was done, I had other ideas of things I wanted to do, you know.

Do you do everything in real time in the studio? Or is it layered?

I like to do it as live as possible. I like the basic tracks to be live. And I actually got a lot of flak for doing it that way.

Now that's interesting to me. Tell me why that is. Who would give you flak?

From people who don't realize that's how music is supposed to be played!

Yeah, you did it live so that you were playing at the same time as your rhythm section, rather than laying down tracks and going in? I mean, that's almost the definition of jazz in my mind. The music should be live--reacting to each other.

Yeah, so that you can get that energy thing happening. I think layering is a pretty superficial way of playing, but I think a lot of people think the music is cleaner that way. To me it's artificial.

Yeah, I agree with you one hundred percent. I've done a good deal of that and I don't care for it. So if you play with the rhythm tracks and so forth, is there something laid in afterwards on that?

Oh yeah, there's always something overdubbed. There's also that issue since I'm in the Latin field a lot, there's a lot of machoism in the field, you know. I find that, for the most part, I don't have problems with men, I think I have a lot of respect from the men. But there are some times when my suggestions are, to put it politely, beaten down.

On your own recordings?

Yeah, well, I always listen to everybody's suggestions, but there are a couple of times when I had to get a little forceful and say, "Look, this is the way I'm going to do it. I appreciate your input, but you're not doing it the way you want--this is my record." But I'm pretty happy with the CD. I do have, other, you know, other ideas to do other stuff. But ...

When you were playing with the quartet, was that also a Latin context?

No, that was a jazz quartet.

With piano bass and drums or guitar?

With piano, bass and drums.

And what kind of material would you have been doing?

Well, you know, I wrote a lot of the music. We did standards and we did a lot of original stuff.

And can you play Latin jazz with that line up, or do you need extra percussion really to make it work?

I don't think you need extra percussion. It depends on the players. And it depends on what your concept of Latin jazz is. There has to be an underlying agreement of vocabulary, of what the music is. And then as you're playing it changes anyway, you know, if you're into just improvisation, it could go anywhere. But there's a structure, it can go out of the structure also, you know.

Andrea's second CD was called *Back With Sweet Passion*. It's a lovely title, because Andrea is definitely back--indeed, she has been back for some time--and her music is infused with sweet passion. It is a passion that fuels a number of performance projects and all of them are informed by a range of experiences, both musical and personal, that have deepened her approach to music. She has already received a Lifetime Achievement Award from *Latin USA*. Yet at this point in time, her career is poised to benefit from all this experience, and yet with ample time for her to fulfill her potential. And she is expanding her interests. At this time, she is studying north Indian classical music with the American *bansuri* master Steve Gorn, a genre that she is incorporating into solo performances with what she terms "meditation music and story telling." Andrea Brachfeld will clearly make a significant contribution to contemporary flute performance--Latin, jazz, or otherwise!

Hermeto Pascoal: Tudo É Som--All Is Sound

"I do not play Brazilian music. I am Brazilian and very proud of it, but the only label I will ever accept for my music is *Universal*."

"Music holds the world together, as long as we live."

"All is Sound, and all Sound is Music."

Hermeto Pascoal

To conclude the section on Latin jazz, we turn to one of the most remarkable artists in any genre. In fact, Latin jazz is much too confining a category for the great Brazilian genius Hermeto Pascoal. He has certainly performed with great distinction within the brilliant and subtle musical world of his native Brazil. But, like his countryman Airto Moreira, he has demonstrated a great facility within the world of jazz, and has also been a member of Miles Davis' group,. Sometimes compared to Rahsaan Roland Kirk, Pascoal is one of those rare artists who seem somehow plugged into the music of Nature in an entirely innocent way, and who seem to transcend the limitations of any particular instrument, although the flute has always been an important part of Pascoal's music. We are fortunate to have this tribute to Hermeto by his close friend, and colleague, Jovino Santos Neto, himself a fine flutist, pianist and arranger, and sometime music director of Pascoal's ensemble.

In the rich and diverse universe of music in Brazil, the presence of Hermeto Pascoal shines like a comet, crossing several eras and musical circles, leaving a strong influence on generations of musicians, and building a name that represents unbridled creativity and inspiration. Better known as a genial multi-instrumentalist, he is capable of extracting music out of the most unexpected objects, while exhibiting his virtuosity on piano, flute, saxophones, strings, percussion and many other conventional (and otherwise) instruments.

Hermeto Pascoal was born in 1936 in Lagoa da Canoa, a small village in the interior of Alagoas state, in the heart of the fertile tobacco-planting interior of north-eastern Brazil. The son of a peasant shopkeeper who moonlighted as an accordionist at weekend parties, he was soon enveloped in the sounds and traditions of the rich culture of his birthplace. As an albino child, he could not stand the fierce tropical sun, and spent his hours sitting in the shade of a tree listening to the birds while carving small makeshift flutes and whistles out of leaf stems, with which he would engage the birds and frogs in musical conversations.

His grandfather was a blacksmith whose backyard shop was a constant source of wonder for the young Hermeto, who used to search for sonorous scraps of iron in the junk pile at the back. A restless and inquisitive child, he soon found the place where his father kept his *oito baixos* (8-button diatonic accordion), and his first attempts on the instrument were aimed at emulating the bell-like sounds of the scraps of iron he found in the yard. Within a few months, Hermeto and his brother José Neto, who was also albino, were accompanying their father in local parties and festivities, taking turns on the *oito baixos*, triangle and *pandeiro.*

At the age of 14, Hermeto left Alagoas for Recife, the busy capital of Pernambuco state. His goal was to land a job as an accordionist at the prestigious Jornal do Comércio radio station. In the 50s, a lot of music in Brazil happened in live radio broadcasts. Famous singers would tour the country, performing with local groups, known as *regionais*. The musicians in these ensembles had to be extremely versatile, learning new songs by ear and creating new arrangements and key changes on the spot. The music director in Recife, however, turned Hermeto down. He could not believe that this albino teenager, with his poor eyesight, could be ready for the task. Hermeto went instead to the inland town of Caruaru, where he was immediately hired for the job at the Difusora radio station. During his years there, he became a favorite of the older musicians, who loved his curiosity and affinity for music. Caruaru was also the center of the *agreste* region, and its local street market attracted crowds of farmers, artisans and the *cantadores*, vocal improvisers who created music on the spot in exchange for coins. In a few years, Hermeto was summoned to Recife, as word got out about the young new accordion master making an impression through the airwaves.

From the mid-fifties on, Hermeto's musical development accelerated, as he came into contact with musical influences from many different places, such as jazz, Italian, French and Gypsy songs. He soon started to play piano, and his harmonic and melodic concepts expanded to add a modern twist to his growing knowledge of music.

In the late 50s Hermeto moved to Brazil's political and cultural capital, Rio de Janeiro. He arrived there as musicians like Antonio Carlos Jobim, Luiz Bonfá, and João Gilberto were combining modern chord changes with a sophisticated samba beat to create what became known worldwide as *bossa nova*. Hermeto was there, playing at the same clubs, but he was careful not to associate his name to any kind of musical "movement." His music needed more room to expand, and he found himself in São Paulo, where a vibrant music scene was being created. He took up the flute (as always, entirely self-taught), and soon created a unique sound that made him a favorite of recording studios, while playing at up to three different clubs every night. He was quickly developing his talent as an arranger, and worked with many popular artists of the time, as well as in commercial jingle production. During the famous song festivals of the late '60s, where MPB (Brazilian Popular Music) was forged by composers such as Chico Buarque de Holanda, Milton Nascimento, Edu Lobo, Caetano Veloso, and many others, Hermeto was a constant presence. His brilliant flute playing in Edu Lobo's *Ponteio*, the winner of the 1968 festival, brought him national acclaim through TV broadcasting.

At this time a new musical group was formed: the *Quarteto Novo*. With Hermeto on flute and piano, Airto Moreira on percussion, Heraldo do Monte on guitars, and Theo de Barros on bass, this was an ensemble devoted to creating instrumental music with a definite Brazilian flavor, blending serious artistry with an earthy devotion to the country's rhythmic treasures, a deep mixture of African, European, native and Eastern historical and cultural influences. Up until then, the music from the interior of Brazil was considered rude, uncultured and almost relegated to a secondary plane in comparison with *bossa nova* and foreign styles. It was *caipira*, or hillbilly, music. The *Quarteto Novo* challenged that assumption, steering clear of jazzy phrasing (even though all of the members were excellent jazzmen) and introducing new ways to produce sound, such as a donkey's jaw and the ancient *viola caipira*, a 10-string guitar that descended from the Moors who once colonized Portugal.

Soon after, Airto Moreira relocated from São Paulo to New York City, a move that led to an invitation for him to join Miles Davis' group. Miles loved the different sounds and the way Airto created rhythms and effects. When Airto told him about the "crazy albino" living down in Brazil, an invitation was quickly sent to Hermeto to come up, which he accepted. This visit led to Miles' recording of two of Hermeto's compositions, *Nem Um Talvez* and *Little Church*, for the *Live Evil* album. Even with the language barrier (neither spoke the other's tongue), a deep musical affinity was created between Miles and Hermeto. Around that time Hermeto also recorded his first album as a leader, originally titled *Hermeto*, and featuring some of the finest jazzmen in New York: Ron Carter, Joe Farrell, Hubert Laws, Thad Jones, and several others, creating a full big band plus strings, all written and arranged by Hermeto. These recording sessions became legendary, and musicians such as Herbie Hancock, John MacLaughlin, Gil Evans, and others came to pay their respect to Hermeto's genius.

An invitation followed for Hermeto to stay in the United States and join Miles's new electric group, but he declined and returned to Brazil. He intended to create his own group in São Paulo, along with some young players he had met there. And that he did, starting a collective of musicians for which he wrote and arranged a wide variety of music, ranging from delicate woodwind ensemble work to all-out free explorations. His 1973 release *A Música Livre de Hermeto Pascoal* (The Free Music of Hermeto Pascoal) represents this period. Meanwhile, he did return occasionally to the US, collaborating with Airto and his wife, singer Flora Purim, in a number of recordings that continued to establish his reputation as a musician's musician. He picked up the soprano, and later the tenor saxophone and again developed a strong personal style on the reed instruments.

Back in Brazil, Hermeto's group went through several personnel changes, culminating with his move back to Rio de Janeiro in 1976, the same year he recorded *Slaves Mass* in Los Angeles, with Airto, Flora, and a host of great musicians, and featuring the sound of live pigs grunting and squealing musically on the title track. In 1977, Hermeto invited me to join his group as a pianist, and this marked a turning point in my life as a musician. In the following years a nucleus of young instrumentalists formed around him, as we started to develop a routine of daily rehearsals. Eventually, in the early '80s, the *Grupo* took its most constant form, with Itiberê Zwarg on bass and tuba, Carlos Malta on flute and saxophones, Marcio Bahia on drums, Pernambuco on percussion, and myself on piano and flute. Hermeto's son Fabio Pascoal joined the group, also on percussion, in 1988. We all ended up living as neighbors in the West Zone suburb of Jabour, an hour's drive from downtown Rio, as the *Grupo* became a literal full time activity for us.

This was an extremely fertile phase for Hermeto. He composed literally thousands of themes, exploring all aspects of the musicians' talents, encouraging us to expand the boundaries of what we could do. He would often write extremely elaborate arrangements, while urging us to play as intuitively and creatively as possible. His strong presence as a leader inspired and coaxed us to practice and rehearse more and more, while the *Grupo* went on several tours of Europe and recorded a number of albums for the *Som da Gente* label. Hermeto's own restless spirit led him to write music for jazz big bands, symphony orchestras, string quartets, and many more line-ups, while his own playing as an improviser reached new levels, supported by our tight ensemble work. He started to play the flugelhorn and wrote his own technical exercises in the form of brand new music.

In 1992 the *Grupo* went through its first personnel change since 1981, as both Carlos Malta and I left the band to pursue our individual careers in music. I moved with my family to Seattle, and started to organize a musical archive that I had been maintaining since the beginning of my tenure with Hermeto. This included a mountain of manuscripts, loose parts and some music kept mostly in the players' memories. This is an ongoing effort, and hopefully the book you now hold in your hands will be followed by others, focusing on the varied facets of the life of a true musical genius, the likes of which our planet only rarely sees.

Today, Hermeto continues to be a major force in the music of the world. The *Grupo* still plays in Brazil and abroad to large audiences, and Hermeto has been composing almost during all of his waking hours. In 1996 he celebrated his 60th birthday by writing one piece a day for a full year, resulting in a publication issued in Brazil, *O Calendário do Som* (The Calendar of Sound), with 366 themes ('96 was a leap year) arranged by date, so that, according to him, everyone, regardless of date of birth, can have his or her own song. Recent collaborations have led him to England for a big band concert of brand new music, and he recorded a solo CD, *Eu e Eles* (Me and Them), where he plays over 60 different instruments. He continually stretches the boundaries of music in all its aspects: rhythmic, melodic and harmonic. He has developed a concept of harmony that offers new ways to create and improvise, giving musicians new options that go beyond the merely linear use of scales and modes. His profound knowledge of the hundreds of rhythms from Brazil is reflected in his music, which ranges from sublime and lyrical to intense and fierce. He also created a new concept, *O Som da Aura* (The Sound of the Aura), by which human speech is set to music and treated as a melody, a refined technique that requires a sharp musical sense of hearing, something Hermeto started to develop from birth.

One of the most remarkable proofs of Hermeto's total and complete dedication to music happened just a few weeks before I wrote this tribute, when Dona Ilza Pascoal, Hermeto's wife of 48 years, passed away in Rio after a battle with pancreatic cancer. The news came to Hermeto as he was about to play a concert in Copenhagen, Denmark, with the *Grupo*. He went on to play the entire concert with all his energy, and ended by dedicating a beautiful piano solo to the love of his life. Only then the audience found out what had happened, and as they applauded him in tears, the musicians returned to the stage for a 30-minute encore that expressed through music the entire range of human emotions.

I came to know Hermeto and his music in the '70s, and for 15 years of my life I worked on a daily basis with one of the most amazing persons I have ever met. I continue to be inspired by his beautiful and challenging compositions, and he remains as an example of true dedication and commitment to music. "All is Sound, and all Sound is Music."

Part Eight

Looking Ahead

The Flute in Jazz: Looking Ahead

"... the only label I will ever accept for my music is *Universal*"
Hermeto Pascoal

"There is beautiful music in every country--in Spain, in Hungary, every country.
But the only music that travels to every part of the world is black American music."
Ahmet Ertugen

It is said of software projects that they rapidly reach a point where they are 90 percent complete and stay that way for ever! It turns out that a similar fate can befall a book of this nature. This became very evident when my publication deadline approached and there were still flutists who had not been discussed or included. And yet this failure is partly due to the instrument's very success. From a handful of performers in the 1950s we have seen an explosion in the use of the flute in jazz and all its various related genres, both esoteric and commercial, both in the US and abroad. The result is that there are far more flutists active in jazz than I ever anticipated. The flute may not have replaced the trumpet or the saxophone as the wind instrument of choice in the post bop jazz mainstream--although a number of flute players have arisen who are quite capable of swimming strongly in that stream, holding their own with the other horns. But a major role for the flute has been in the smaller streams that flow into and feed the mainstream from various cultural highlands, whether it be the world of Latin music that brought us Hermeto Pascoal, the *avant-garde* that has brought us the Sam Rivers and Henry Threadgill, or the classical crossover that has brought us the stylings of Jimmy Walker, Jean-Pierre Rampal or Sir James Galway.

At this point we may realize that we have never actually defined what jazz is, even after such a lengthy discussion of jazz artists and their work. Is jazz one of those things we cannot define, but only recognize when we see it--or in this case hear it? "Until we know what jazz is," I said, in my conversation with Danilo Lozano, "it's hard to exclude anything! I think jazz is expanding to fill all possible spaces between American music and Indian music and Cuban music and all the rest of it."

There are those who would agree with Quincy Jones when he said, "People have called me a jazz musician, but that's ludicrous. I have yet to figure out what a jazz musician is." This is not a recent problem. In the 1940s, as the the Swing Era was fading out under the challenge of bebop, the editors of *Down Beat* magazine found themselves faced with growing confusion about the definition of jazz. As recounted on the magazine's own website (*About Down Beat: A History As Rich As Jazz Itself www.downbeat.com*):

So in July 1949 Down Beat took it upon itself to announce a contest for the best word to replace "jazz."The magazine offered to pay $1,000 in cash to the person "…who coins a new word to describe the music from dixieland through bop," the headline said. Second and third prizes included the services of Charlie Barnet's orchestra and the Nat Cole Trio for one night in one's home. Even Norman Granz, whose Jazz at the Philharmonic tours were keeping a mass market interested in jazz, contributed $400 worth of prizes. In November

came the word that the panel of judges deemed preferable to jazz: crewcut. Other
alternatives included jarb, freestyle, mesmerrhythm, bix-e-bop, blip, schmoosic, and other
equally contrived specimens.

It goes without saying that none of these alternatives caught on, and 60 years later we are still no
closer to really pinning down what jazz is or is not. For the purpose of our discussion throughout these
pages, I have been using a working definition of this elusive genre supplied by Chick Corea as "...what
the person who said the word meant when he said jazz."

And yet it is this elusiveness of definition that may well prove to be jazz' main strength going
forward, because whatever it has been in the past it can no longer continue to be. "Jazz was born in a
cradle of many cultures," said the Philadelphia Inquirer in 2005 "and the music's future is likely to be
full of cultural excursions to new realms." Its future certainly seems uncertain on one level. We have
reached a point where college jazz programs are producing hundreds, perhaps thousands, of highly
trained jazz players just as the market for jazz seems to be retreating--three of the major jazz clubs in my
area have closed their doors in the last couple of years, and it is getting harder and harder just to find
somewhere to play, at least, on the local level. Even as established an artist as Holly Hofmann is finding
that she cannot often find work for much more than a duo these days. Jazz festivals and cruises are
popular, but are often filled with artists from the periphery of the music, as well as some who have
nothing to do with jazz at all.

But while the jury is still out on the commercial viability of jazz and its various sub-genres, I believe
that it does retain a very important role as one strand of an emerging world music. And the flute has a
vital role to play in this.

Such a view is expressed by Mark Weinstein. Weinstein began his career as a trombonist,
developing a role for the trombone in Latin music while working with Herbie Mann, among others.
Giving up music--or more accurately the music business--to pursue a career as a professor of philosophy,
Dr. Weinstein eventually got back into performance, but for his second chapter he picked up the flute
instead of the trombone. Since then he has produced a series of highly interesting recordings that explore
a range of cultural settings--Brazilian, Cuban, African and Jewish as well as straight-ahead American
jazz. He has a very definite opinion about the future role of the flute in these genres:

It is no surprise that flute remains on the periphery of jazz; even with the aid of microphones,
the flute has little of the power of saxophone, particularly in the low register, and its high
register pales in comparison to the energy that screaming trumpets add to a solo or ensemble.
Moreover, both sax and trumpet have comparable fluency, and much of the language of jazz
improvisation has been developed on those instruments. Nevertheless, the prevalence of the
flute in world music and the richness of its expressive capabilities as evidenced by the classical
repertoire, give hopes to flutists who want to use the instrument to make a contribution to jazz.
For me, Herbie Mann and Paul Horn showed the way.

The future for flute is to draw broadly from world genres, especially Latin American,
African and Indian music, a direction increasingly evident among jazz musicians as world
music--based jazz proves both a way to move beyond the epochal contributions of the '50s and
'60s, and path toward new sonic terrain. The acoustic context of much world music is flute-
friendly, unlike the traditional bebop rhythm section, which is geared to sax and trumpet. Flute

is without equal in its ability to blend with the string and percussion instruments used in much world music. The flute also permits the basis of world music to remain true to its sound and texture, even when it is used to extend basic forms with the harmonic, melodic and rhythmic elements of jazz. This is true of all of the flutes, concert, alto and bass.

Weinstein is hinting at a future music that is already forming in the work of a number of visionary artists. In many cases they are labeled as jazz musicians, although not all of them would accept this classification. Saxophonist (and occasional flutist) Jan Garbarek would fall into that group. "I suppose what I'm doing is not really jazz because I have a very strict and somewhat limited definition of jazz," he told *Jazziz* magazine's Fernando Gonzalez. "I'd say jazz started with Louis Armstrong and went into the '60s up until mid-Coltrane and mid-Miles. And then, the way I see it, it's no longer jazz. It's something else. And I might love some of it, but to me, what comes after *Bitches Brew* or *Ascension* is not really jazz."

However, Garbarek realizes that, whether or not his music can be said to be jazz, it is dependant upon a jazz sensibility. As he told Gonzalez, "I usually put it this way: Whatever I do, it wouldn't be possible unless I had a knowledge of jazz. I have a background of jazz, and it's not just the improvisation aspect or certain harmonic ideas or rhythmic developments that come with that. It's the whole package, and these are the tools that I use." He cited trumpeter Don Cherry as an example of this approach. Garbareck came to see Cherry as a sort of prototype: a global man, "... walking proof of the possibilities of [cultural] mixes. He had an African-American and Native-American background, lived in Scandinavia, wore African clothes, played Turkish music, and read Indian philosophy." Equally at home collaborating with such Indian artists as Hariprasad Chaurasia, Zakir Hussein, Trilok Gurtu, L. Shankar and Ustad Fateh Ali Khan, Brazilian Egberto Gismonti, the Stuttgart Chamber Orchestra, and Early Music specialists the Hilliard Ensemble, Garbarek himself has demonstrated the effectiveness of Cherry's mentorship.

It is from such examples that we see a jazz-based sensibility providing a vital strand in those genres that will emerge from the world music melting pot. In this context, one thing has always seemed significant. If we look at all the artists who excel in both jazz and classical music, artists who have made high-quality recordings in both genres, we find that, almost without exception, they are jazz artists. And again, the artists who have been able to interact most effectively with musicians from Cuba, Brazil, India and elsewhere are, for the most part, from the jazz world. What this suggests is that there is some essential musical value that jazz artists, in order to be successful, must cultivate in the course of their training. It could be the universality of the "language of bebop," as characterized by Paquito D'Rivera, the spirit of invention and flexibility called for by the needs of improvisation, as found by Bud Shank and Paul Horn in working with Japanese or Russian musicians, or simply the porous nature of the genre, so open to foreign influences but so good at assimilating them.

Some recent research has shone some light on these qualities of jazz by studying musician's brains during various kinds of performance:

A pair of ...scientists [Drs. Charles J. Limb and Allen R. Braun] have discovered that when jazz musicians improvise, their brains turn off areas linked to self-censoring and inhibition, and turn on those that let self-expression flow. The joint research, using functional magnetic resonance imaging, or fMRI, and musician volunteers from the Johns Hopkins University's

Peabody Institute, sheds light on the creative improvisation that artists and non-artists use in everyday life, the investigators say.

The research, described by Dr. Limb on *youtube* ("Your Brain on Jazz"), shows that the part of the brain known as the dorsolateral prefrontal cortex, associated with planned actions and self-censoring, slows down during improvisation, whereas more activity is observed in the medial prefrontal cortex, which sits in the center of the brain's frontal lobe. "This area," writes Dr. Limb, "has been linked with self-expression and activities that convey individuality, such as telling a story about yourself." He continues:

> Jazz is often described as being an extremely individualistic art form. You can figure out which jazz musician is playing because one person's improvisation sounds only like him or her. What we think is happening is when you're telling your own musical story, you're shutting down impulses that might impede the flow of novel ideas. This type of brain activity may also be present during other types of improvisational behavior that are integral parts of life for artists and non-artists alike. For example, people are continually improvising words in conversations and improvising solutions to problems on the spot. Without this type of creativity, humans wouldn't have advanced as a species. It's an integral part of who we are.

Presenting this research at a recent National Flute Association convention, I went a step further and suggested that this style of brain function, which appears to be essential for successful jazz performance, may also be behind that special quality, that effortless expressive flow, that the most successful classical artists exhibit, that quality all music teachers recognize but few know how to impart. As musicologist (and P.D.Q. Bach) Peter Schickele puts it: "It don't mean a thing if it ain't got that certain *je ne sais quoi*!"

Whatever this quality is, it seems clear that it will be an essential aspect of performance for those who wish to see world genres draw closer to each other, Eastern and Western, improvisatory and compositional. And flutists will be an essential part of this process as thay have in the past. We only have to think of Frank Wess and Hubert Laws at the forefront of bridging the gap between jazz and classical training, of Paul Horn virtually inventing new age music, the influence of Herbie Mann in popularizing Afro-Cuban and Brazilian forms, the work of James Newton of bringing together African and contemporary Western performance techniques.

And so much more. Some of the best progress in writing for strings in a jazz context has come from flutists: Anne Drummond in the US, François Richard in Canada, Günther Wehinger in Switzerland. We see a flutist from Croatia, Damjan Krajacic, living in Los Angeles and developing Latin jazz under the guidance of Danilo Lozano. We see exponents of the *shakuhachi* applying it to jazz improvisation: Ned Rothenberg in New York, Art Maxwell in California, John Kaizan Neptune in Japan. We see exponents of the north Indian *bansuri* creating another kind of blend, as in the work of Hariprasad Chaurasia with John McLaughlin, New York's Steve Gorn with Jack DeJohnette and others, Ronu Mujamdar's experiments with artists from the Water Lily Acoustics label, and John Wubbenhorst's *Facing East* ensemble with its mix of jazz and Hindustani flute forms. Reversing the trend, we find US-based Deepak Ram, after issuing several recordings of traditional Hindustani *ragas*, recording a CD of jazz standards such as *Giant Steps* and *All Blues*, performed on *bansuri* with a jazz rhythm section.

There is every reason to expect these trends to continue, and for flutists to be deeply involved with them. As we have seen, our instrument gives us a special insight into world music cultures; jazz gives us the common language needed to bind them together.

We can express this vision in the words of Brazilian flutist Hermeto Pascoal, writing of his musical heir and friend, Jovino Santos Neto;

> Music has a special role in the bridging of the gaps that still exist between the cultures of our planet. It will take uniquely talented individuals, grounded in the traditional heritage of their homeland and at the same time ready to speak at a universal level... to bring about the evolution of music as an art form, and as a tool to make our world a better place to live.

We can be sure that there will be flutists at the forefront of this evolution, so the story of *The Flute in Jazz* is really just beginning.

Appendix: The Poll Winners

The polls conducted by *Down Beat* magazine have been mentioned on several occasions in the course of our narrative. I have been careful to downplay their significance: "These are by no means a perfect guide to jazz history," I wrote in the introduction, "but they can be a useful barometer." With that caveat in mind, the winners of the *Down Beat* Critics and Readers Poll winners for flute are reproduced below, beginning in 1956 when the instrument was first included in the Readers Poll, and in 1959 when the flute first appeared as a "Miscellaneous Instrument" for the critics.

While there are many interesting names in each year's complete list, only ten flutists have been outright winners of the *Down Beat* Critics or Readers Poll.

Critics Poll:
1959: (Miscellaneous Instrument – flute) Frank Wess
1960-1964: Frank Wess
1965-1966: Roland Kirk
1967-1974: James Moody
1975-1978: Hubert Laws
1979: Sam Rivers
1980-1981: Lew Tabackin
1982-2004 James Newton
2005: Frank Wess
2006-2007: James Moody
2008: James Newton
2009: James Moody
2010-11: Nicole Mitchell

Readers Poll:
1956: Bud Shank
1957-1970: Herbie Mann
1971-1980: Hubert Laws
1981-1982: Lew Tabackin
1983-2000: James Newton
2001: James Moody
2002-2003: James Newton
2004-2006: James Moody
2007: Hubert Laws
2008: James Moody
2009-10: Hubert Laws
2011: Nicole Mitchell

Index of Names

CPSIA information can be obtained at www.ICGtesting.com
Printed in the USA
BVOW07s0048200615

405283BV00005B/33/P

9 780615 310879